# ART PURPOSES

Object Lessons for the Liberal Arts

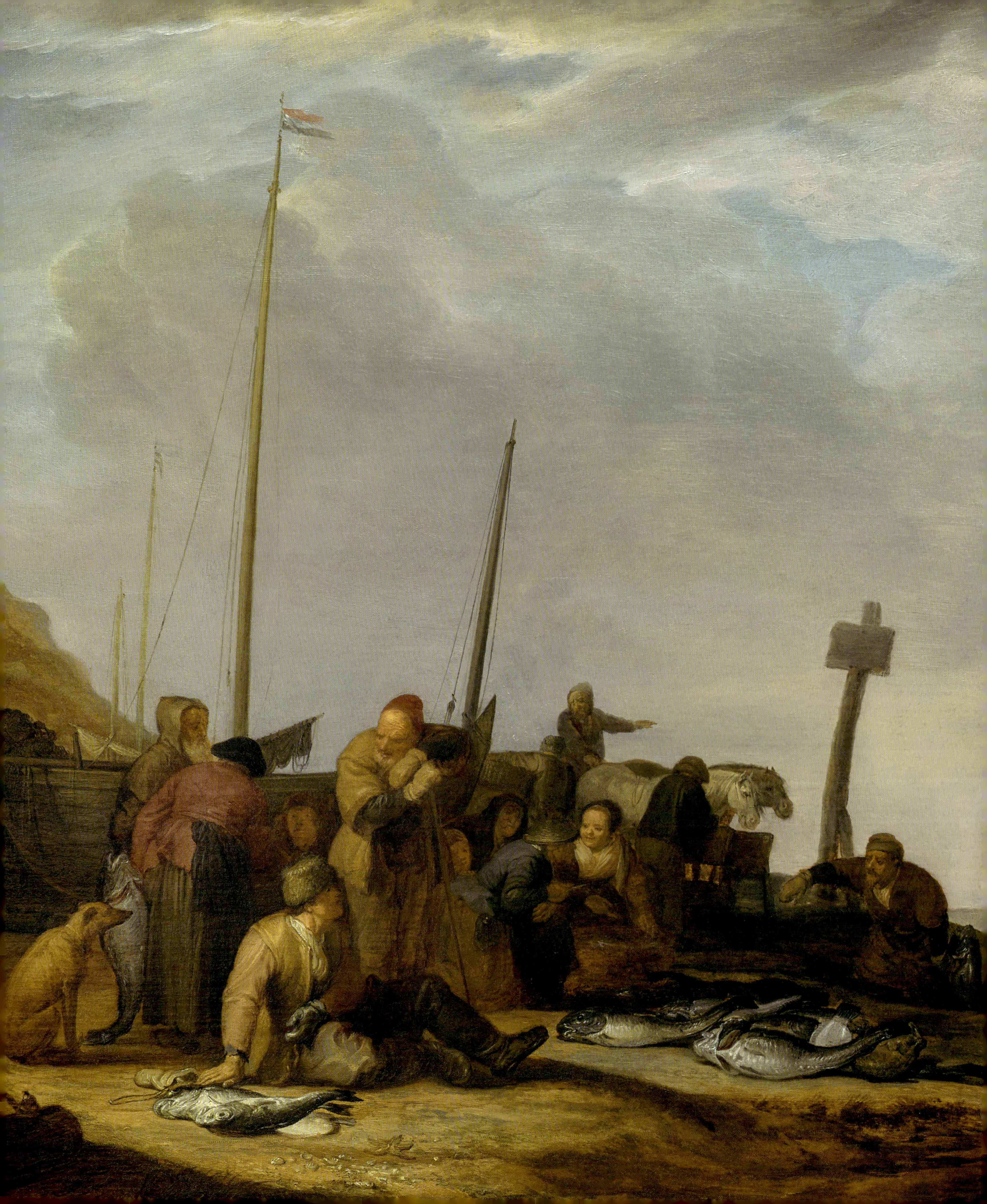

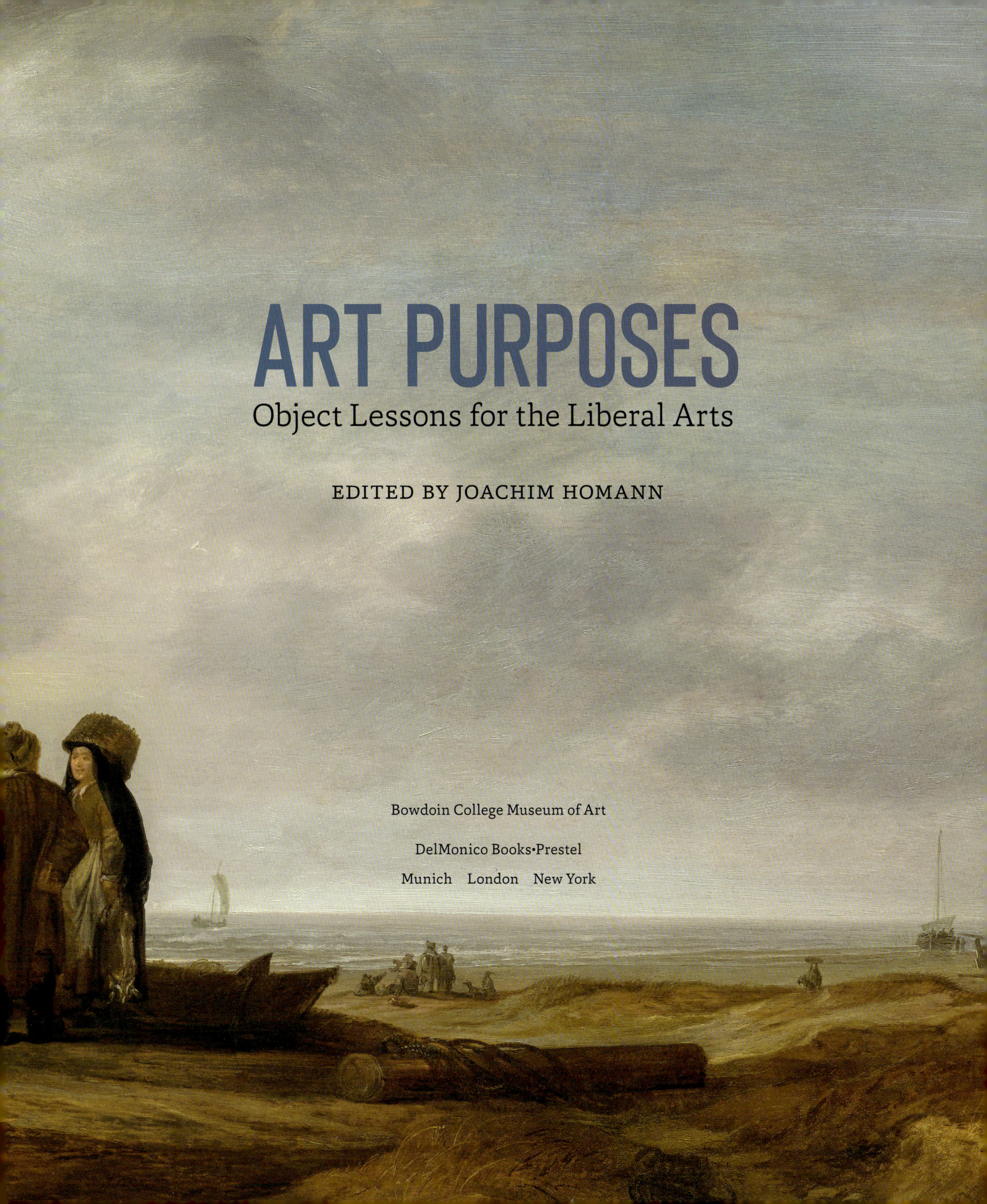

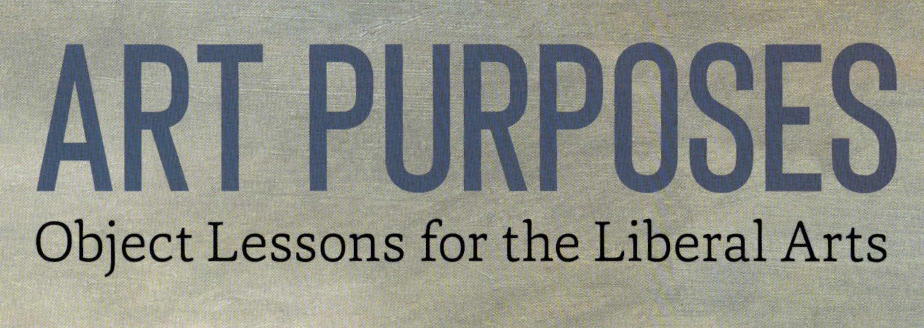

# ART PURPOSES

## Object Lessons for the Liberal Arts

EDITED BY JOACHIM HOMANN

Bowdoin College Museum of Art

DelMonico Books•Prestel

Munich   London   New York

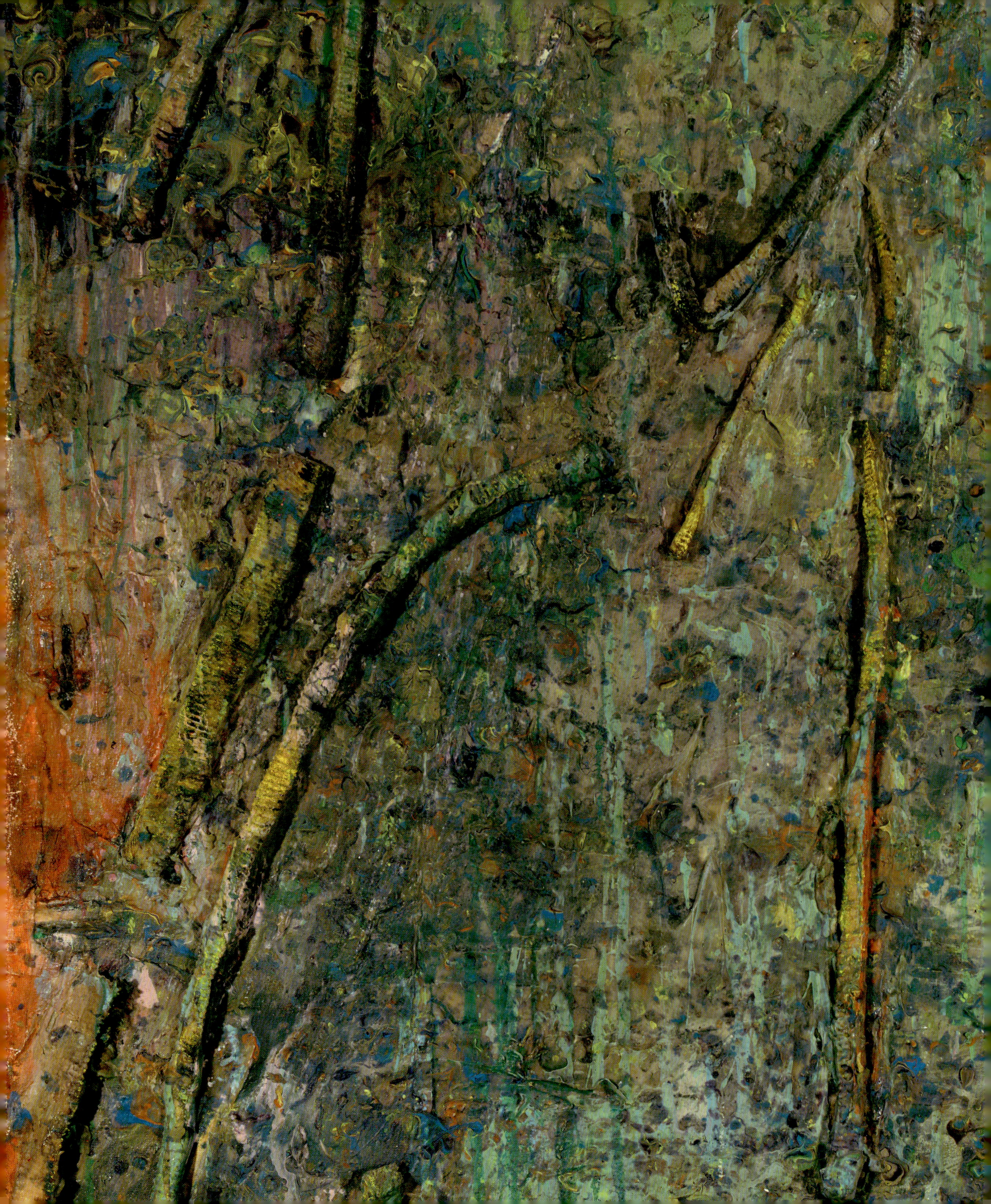

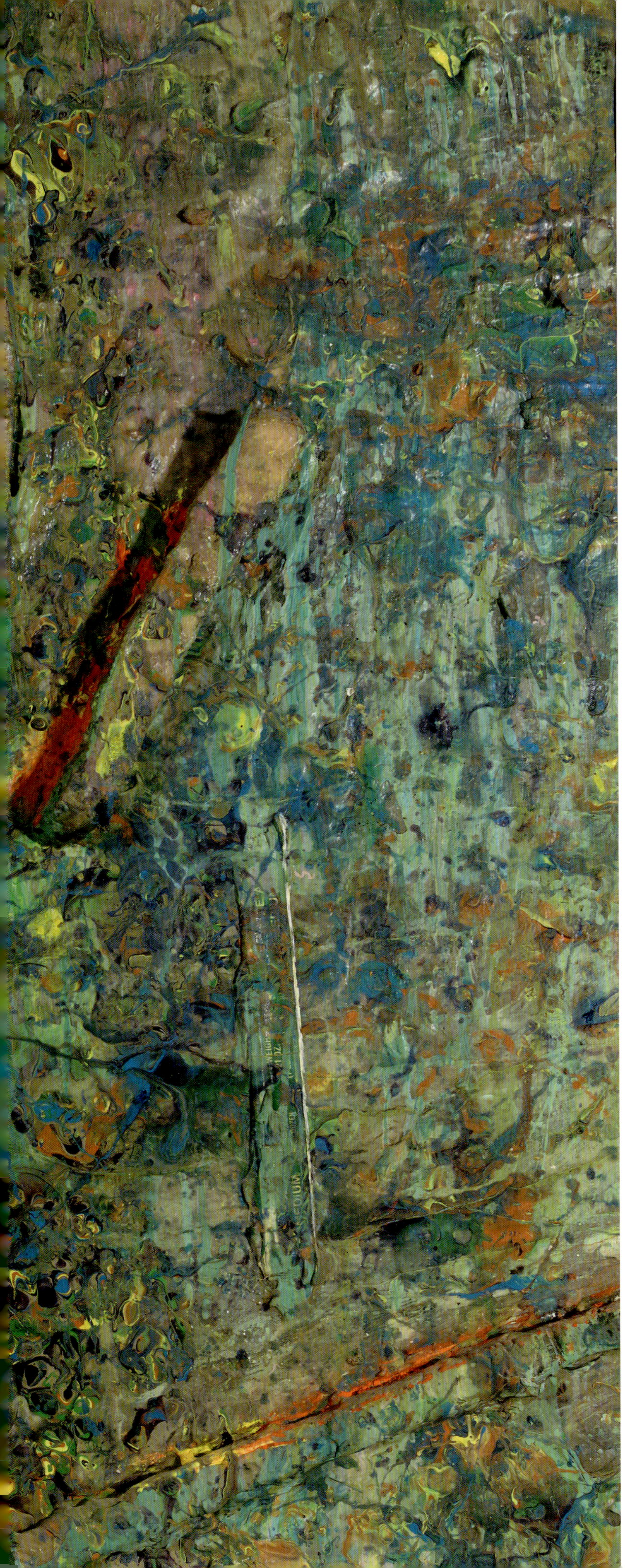

# CONTENTS



FRONTISPIECE: Detail, Simon de Vlieger, *A Coastal Scene near Zandvoort* (see p. 81)

OPPOSITE: Detail, Frank Bowling, *Skowhegan Green II* (see p. 183)

# A NOTE FROM THE PRESIDENT

Works from the collection of the Bowdoin College Museum of Art serve as powerful catalysts for current debates in the academy and beyond. In the following pages, Bowdoin faculty, students, and staff and international scholars and curators share thoughts on art objects from around the globe and across time, reflecting on art's capacity to unsettle conventions, foster learning, and inspire creativity. Bowdoin College has long embraced the value of studying original artworks for the education of our students. This publication invites readers to join the conversations that regularly occur in the Museum's study room and during class visits to the galleries.

The Museum's collection is a unique and an essential resource for Bowdoin's academic community, as well as for scholars and visitors. The bequest of European paintings and drawings in 1811 by James Bowdoin III, the first benefactor of the College, laid the foundation for the collection. Since then, each generation has contributed in support of the College's educational goals. Spanning 3,000 years and encompassing works from the Americas, Europe, Asia, and Africa, selections featured here include iconic American works such as Gilbert Stuart's portraits of Thomas Jefferson and James Madison, as well as historic and contemporary international art of exceptional significance, such as the recently donated painting *Going Home (Suzhou)* by the celebrated twentieth-century Chinese artist Chen Yifei.

In 2019, Bowdoin celebrates the 125th anniversary of the opening of the Charles McKim–designed Walker Art Building. The "Offer of the College," written in 1906 by Bowdoin's seventh president William DeWitt Hyde, invites students "to count art an intimate friend." This book makes good on that promise and encourages engagement with the objects in our collection. Works of art, old and new, inform our understanding of the world and ourselves. By studying works of art, we strengthen the skills of observation, the synthesis and classification of information, and the representation of complexity. Works of art express identities and exemplify diverse cultural traditions—they are points of crystallization for conversations about difference and shared experience. Original works of art stand for values of authenticity, creativity, and innovation that are deeply ingrained in artistic production and at the same time lie at the core of a liberal arts education.

Clayton Rose
President of Bowdoin College

# DIRECTORS' FOREWORD

Collections are at the heart of the Bowdoin College Museum of Art. They are invaluable educational resources that serve faculty, students, and visitors from near and far. They are the basis of research, tools for teaching, and sources of inspiration.

Collections are not static, but are always evolving. The objects stewarded by any museum are part and parcel of its identity, and we are proud of the BCMA's heritage as a leading academic art museum with encyclopedic holdings. Over the last two centuries, the BCMA has built a collection of almost 25,000 works ranging from Assyrian reliefs to contemporary installations. Given the global reach of the College's curriculum, we are dedicated to nurturing a collection that includes outstanding examples by artists from throughout the United States and around the world.

Museums are also collections of people. Following the example of James Bowdoin III, whose 1811 bequest laid the foundation for a collection of fine art at the College, supporters have stepped forward to build its holdings. Individuals and families from every generation since the early nineteenth century—and more recently foundations—have generously contributed important works. These and others have also provided the financial resources to support the BCMA's strategic collecting goals. The roster of our major donors over the last 200 years is too long to list here, though you will encounter many of their names in the following pages.

Since the opening of the Walker Art Building in 1894, the BCMA has had many thoughtful and energetic directors, curators, and professional staff members. These people have cared for the institution, nurtured relationships with artists and supporters, and guided the process of adding new works to the collection. Faculty and College administrators have likewise given much to support the BCMA as a vital educational resource.

As we mark the 125th anniversary of the Walker Art Building and the 225th anniversary of Bowdoin College, we pause to celebrate the history of collecting at the BCMA with this new collections catalogue. We also want to use this occasion to consider afresh the purposes to which collections of art serve a liberal arts education.

The contributors to this catalogue deserve recognition and thanks. We are exceedingly grateful to the authors for sharing their insights, to the publication teams at Bowdoin and Prestel for a seamless collaboration, and to the generous funders of this book and accompanying exhibition. We wish to acknowledge Eric S. '85 and Svetlana G. Silverman P'19, The Devonwood Foundation, Robert A. and Elisabeth Freson, anonymous donors, halley k harrisburg '90 and Michael Rosenfeld, Selina F. Little, Steven P. Marrow '83 and Dianne A. Pappas P'21, Mary K. and John F. McGuigan Jr., Peter J. Grua '76 and Mary G. O'Connell '76, Katharine J. Watson, Lindsay R. '95 and Peter Stavros.

On behalf of the BCMA, we thank everyone who has had a hand in the creation and growth of this outstanding academic art museum.

Anne Collins Goodyear
Frank H. Goodyear III
Co-Directors, Bowdoin College Museum of Art

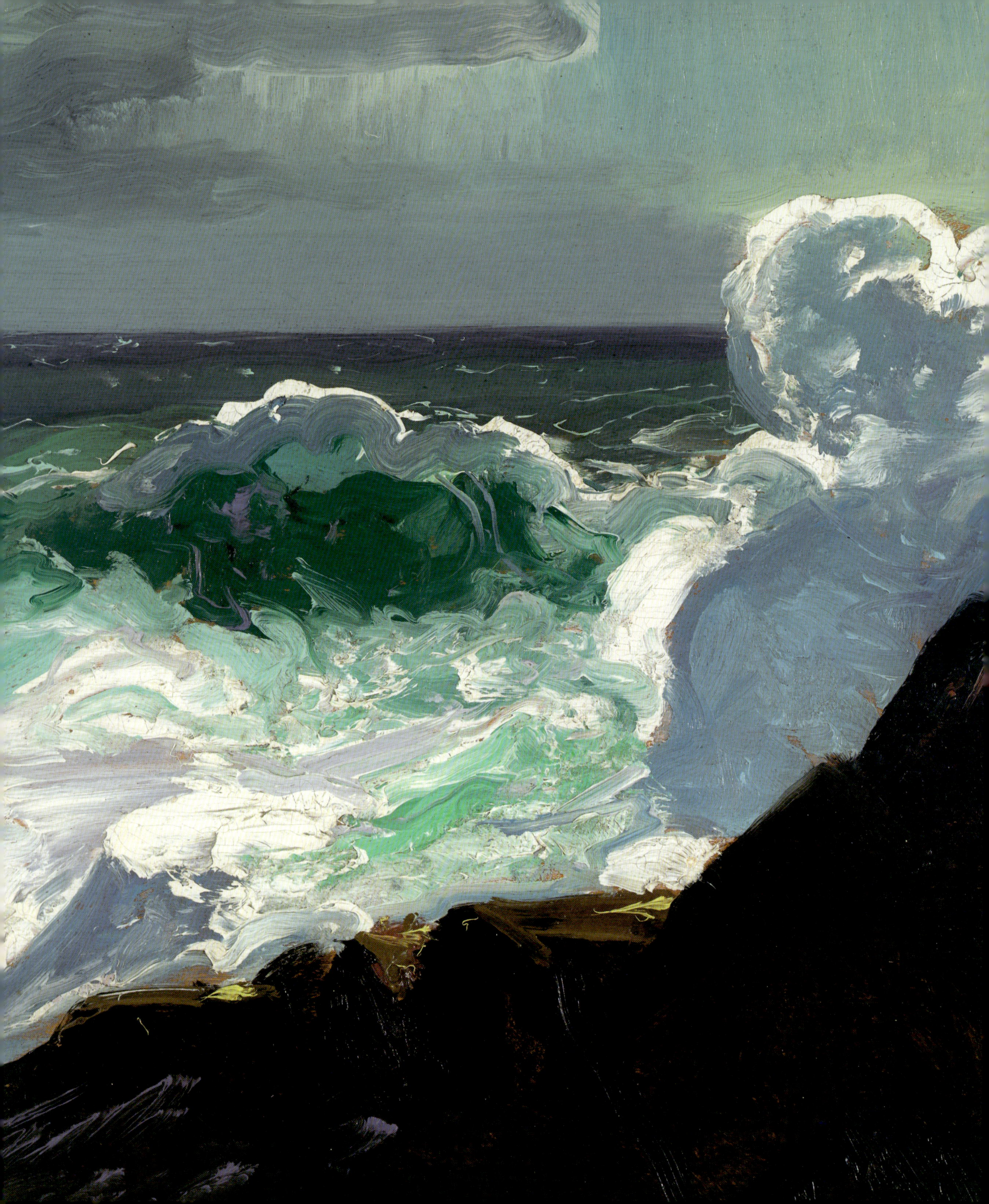

# ART PURPOSES  Joachim Homann

### MAKING

Students enrolled in Professor James Mullen's class "Landscape Painting" might find inspiration on the bucolic, tree-studded campus of Bowdoin College in Brunswick, Maine, or they might explore the nearby coastline for a close-up view of granite rocks and crashing surf, or visit other sites in the region that lend themselves to painting. But it is rarely the experience of being outdoors that motivates someone to first pick up the brush. "In my experience, most people today don't look at nature and think: 'Wow, I need to paint this!'" Mullen recently explained in conversation in his studio. "When you see a beautiful painting of a landscape, that's when you think: 'I need to try this myself.'" Consequently, Mullen and his colleagues in Visual Arts not only encourage students to take a fresh look at the world around them, they also spend time with them each semester immersed in the Museum collection, examining and discussing works of art as points of departure for their own creativity. As they mine the collection, artists model a fruitful response to historic objects, and one day their own art might become part of institutional collections as well, completing the circle. They set an example for all who observe, research, interpret, innovate, and communicate—that is, anyone learning about and practicing the Liberal Arts.

This book is indeed the result of a long-standing commitment at Bowdoin College to use art objects as catalysts for the academic curriculum that generate opportunities for interdisciplinary learning. In case studies ranging from Assyrian reliefs to contemporary art, this volume introduces exceptional works of art as avenues of inquiry—not only in regard to art and art history, but to thoughts, perceptions, vocabularies, and conversations that will inform the reader's own. The following illustrations and brief interpretations offer an unprecedented introduction to the Museum of Art's holdings, which have grown significantly since the last publication of a collection catalogue in 1981. In fact, since the

reopening of the Museum in 2007 after extensive renovation and expansion, more than 10,000 works of art came into the Bowdoin collection, which now encompasses about 25,000 objects. A fraction of them—old and new, longtime favorites, acquisitions, discoveries, and even some promised gifts—are presented here to exemplify the many reasons the study of art is central to the educational mission of Bowdoin College.

It has been no easy task to select works for publication that demonstrate the quality and breadth of materials kept under the roof of the Museum, illustrate the major phases of collecting over more than two centuries, and, most importantly, highlight the collection's academic uses (and usefulness) at the same time. The traditional format of a catalogue of collection highlights, often presented with authoritative explanations in an anonymized institutional "voice," seemed inadequate at a time when grand narratives of all kinds are suspect, the established canon of art history appears severely compromised because of its embedded prejudice and inherent bias, and new media and modes of communication challenge habits of seeing and personal expression. Instead, we let artists and interpreters take the lead, as we looked for objects in the collection that continue to raise questions and for writers eager to consider works about which they are passionate and curious.

What is at stake in such explorations can be gleaned from three paintings that have recently entered the

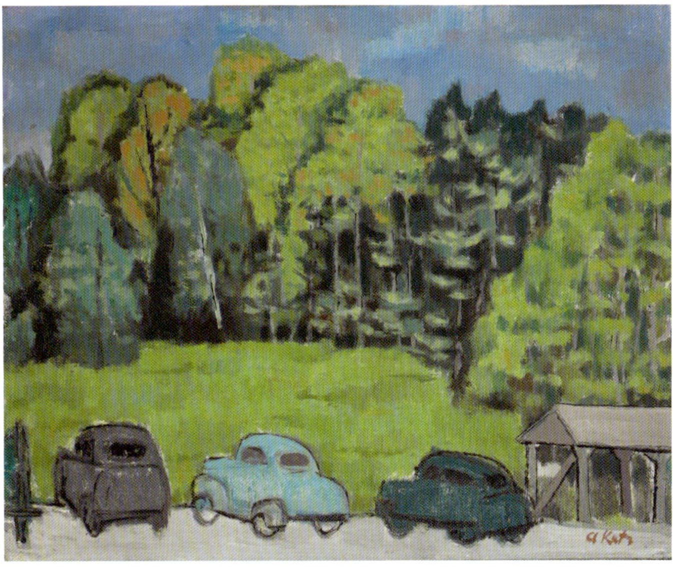



OPPOSITE: Detail, George Wesley Bellows, *Green Breaker* (see p. 129)

FIG. 1. Alex Katz (American, b. 1927), *Untitled (Landscape with Cars)*, c. 1954. Oil on fiberboard, 16 × 20 in. (40.6 × 50.8 cm). Bowdoin College Museum of Art, Gift of the Alex Katz Foundation, 2010.25.2

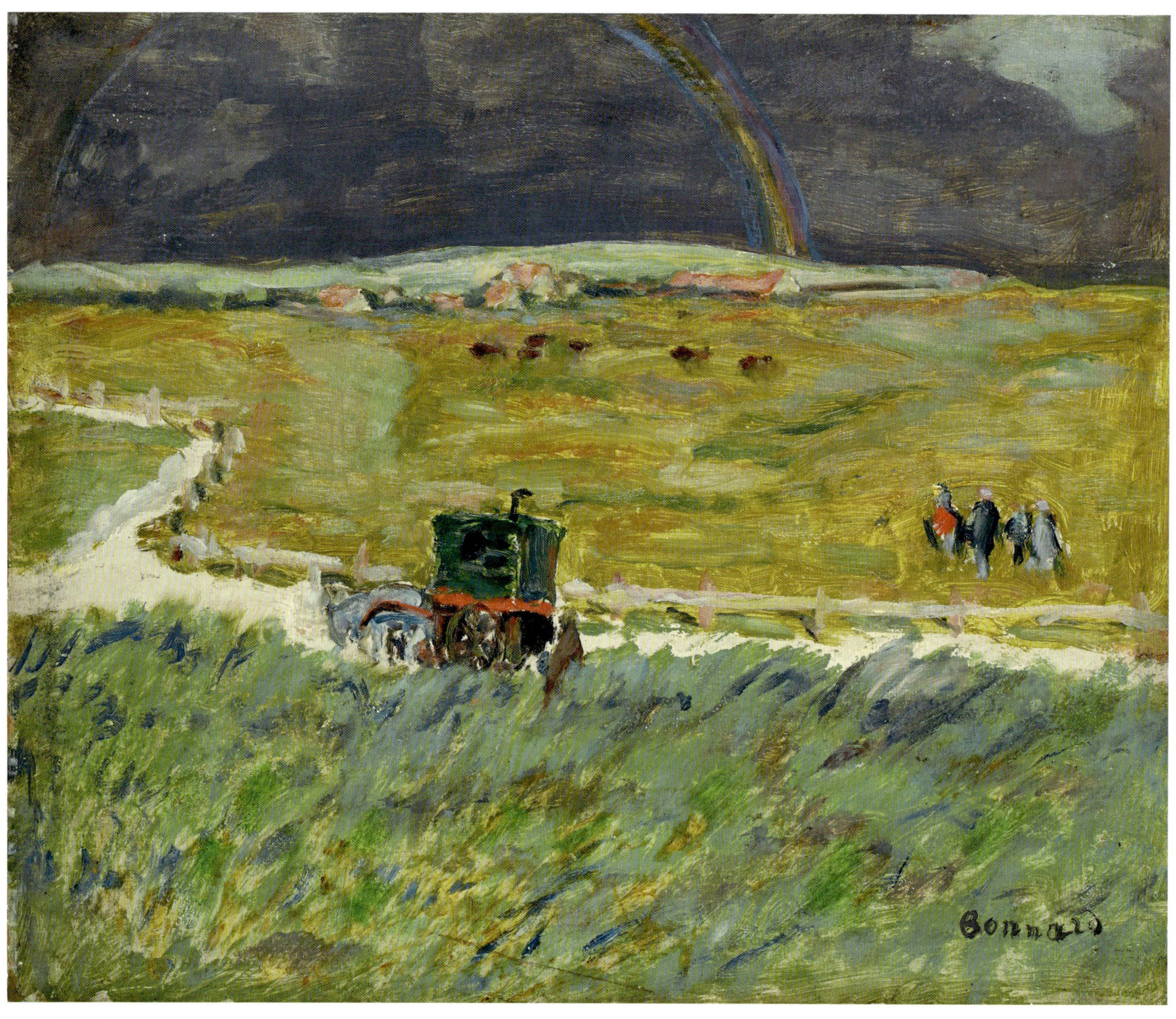

FIG. 2. Pierre Bonnard (French, 1867–1947), *L'arc-en-ciel, La roulotte*, 1909. Oil on board laid down on cradled panel, 15 × 19 in. (38 × 48 cm). Bowdoin College Museum of Art, Promised Gift of Alex Katz

collection, all by artists close to the Bowdoin community. Alex Katz, the doyen of contemporary American painting, sent an early landscape (fig. 1) based on an unspecified location in Maine. The lush greens, from the high-keyed grass to the rhythmically accentuated darker edge of a mixed-growth forest, are contrasted with a row of parked cars and modest open shelter in the foreground. Balancing between the abstract appeal of a flattened picture plane and the richly satisfying representation of a summer day, the work is not just the result of observation. It is an homage to the art of the French Post-Impressionist Pierre Bonnard, whose work, across continents and generations, offered the young American painter guidance and encouragement. A work by Bonnard from Katz's own collection, a promised gift to Bowdoin, invites comparison (fig. 2). "With Bonnard," Katz wrote, the painting "becomes a field of light over figures and landscapes, still lifes and interiors. That power influenced a lot of painters in the early 1950s." For Katz, whose own work still reflects the "expanding light" he first encountered in Bonnard, museums are not jewel boxes, they provide tools and contexts to the painter's benefit.[1]

When Elise Ansel visited the Museum to discuss a small exhibition of her paintings, she caught sight of an elegant and compellingly descriptive painting of the Annunciation by Denys Calvaert from the late sixteenth century (p. 77). She was intrigued by the oil's brilliant colors and dynamic composition, but immediately recognized, too, in the encounter between Mary and the angel, a template for the restrictive behavioral codes to which young women were subjected in the early modern period. Claiming, as a female painter and feminist, the legacy of Western painting, Ansel set out to improvise in paint on the composition of the earlier masterpiece, ultimately filling a whole gallery with increasingly abstract renderings of Calvaert's work that liberate colors, gesture, and minds (fig. 3).[2]

The ambiguity and multivalence inherent in fluidly applied paint on canvas has been Katherine Bradford's love affair for many years. The Brunswick painter, who spends winters in Brooklyn, lives down the road from the Museum and once explained that as a young mother she liked to stop there when running errands in town, would admire canvases by Marsden Hartley, Andrew Wyeth, and others, and then carry bursts of inspiration to the aisles of the local supermarket. In a painting from 2001, Bradford delivers a bravura painterly performance on a stage of her own making that puts her energy, imagination, and irreverence on full display. The community she envisioned when arranging, in her work, the auditorium's empty seats has indeed at last been convened, as the artist finds enthusiastic audiences here in Maine, in New York, nationally, and internationally (fig. 4).[3] Like Alex Katz and Elise Ansel, Bradford does not create in a vacuum, but inserts herself in a dialogue with works of art by historic and contemporary practitioners. Art's purpose might very well be its ability to engage in such conversations and enable viewers to define their perspectives and make contributions of their own.

## EXHIBITING

The Museum's architecture, decoration, and inscriptions do not make immediately apparent that it serves as a space for inquiry and experimentation with implications beyond the building's well-defined perimeter. "To Be Used Solely for Art Purposes," the admonition from which the title of this book derives, is set in brass lettering into the floor of the Walker Art Building's former entrance Rotunda. It is dated 1893 and signed by donors Mary Sophia Walker and Harriet

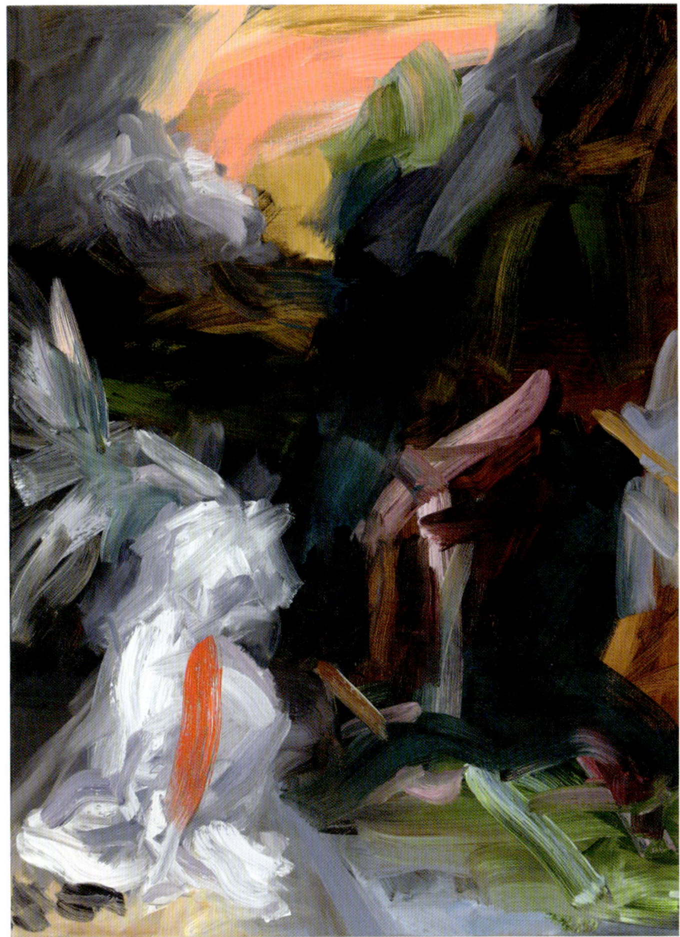

FIG. 3. Elise Ansel (American, b. 1961), *Revelations IV (after Denys Calvaert)*, 2015. Oil on linen, 40 × 30 in. (101.6 × 76.2 cm). Bowdoin College Museum of Art, Museum Purchase, Jane H. and Charles E. Parker, Jr. Fund, 2016.23

Sarah Walker. The sisters used parts of the inheritance from their uncle Theophilus Wheeler Walker to establish Bowdoin's first freestanding building for the visual arts.[4] Previously, the historic art collections, bequeathed by the College's first benefactor, James Bowdoin III, and further enriched by donations from the Bowdoin family and others, had been on display in gallery spaces attached to the chapel (in part financed by Theophilus Walker), and before that works of art had been housed in provisional quarters in Massachusetts Hall, the first College building to be completed. The Walker sisters had every reason to be jubilant about their accomplishment—to provide a dedicated space on the Bowdoin campus in which the visual arts could thrive—and they might have felt protective about it, too. With their dedication plaque, they effectively established a threshold between the everyday world outside the Museum's walls, and the uplifting experience that awaited visitors inside the galleries.

Each year—weather permitting—Bowdoin's Commencement ceremony is held on the steps of the Walker Art Building. Unfolding on the stagelike, granite-framed platform that elevates the Museum above the Quad, the pageant uses the structure's ornate facade as backdrop. For students and their families, the momentous event marks the transition between years of study filled with intellectual, athletic, and artistic endeavors, in the company of like-minded peers, and the yet unknown challenges posed by "real life" that await each graduate. Anxiously, or confidently, graduates anticipate putting the knowledge and skills gained at Bowdoin to the test, not quite sure whether and how the insights of their sharpened minds will translate into valuable qualifications in the next phase of their lives. The event is a threshold moment in the participants' lives, and its *mise en scène* on the architecturally articulated threshold of the Museum is entirely appropriate. However, the high-minded ideals expressed in the building's facade seem to demonstrate little concern for the graduates' lives ahead.

The iconographic program of the Walker Art Building articulates the donors' view that artistic pursuits or "purposes" are separate from and transcend the profane reality of daily lives. Commissioned by the Walker sisters, Charles McKim designed a structure that heralds the arrival of unprecedented opportunities for the arts.[5] His Walker Art Building must have seemed as novel and out of place to the Mainers of the 1890s as the star-architect-designed museums today that resemble extraterrestrial spaceships. Indeed, McKim's historicizing architectural design asserts visually (and experientially) the threshold that the Walker sisters established conceptually. His elegantly balanced facade amounts to a display of cultural ambition, enticing viewers to pay attention to the sculptural references to Greek antiquity, and to study names of ancient and historic European artists and architects evoked in imposing lists—not surprisingly, an all-male, all-white cast. An elegant flight of stairs sweeps visitors into an Italianate loggia and through the entrance to the grandiose Rotunda (p. 122), where they are invited to raise their eyes (and sights) to the magnificent allegories of four cradles of Western civilization: Rome (originally titled *The Art Idea*, painted by Elihu Vedder), Athens (John La Farge), Venice (Kenyon Cox), and Florence (Abbott Thayer). Each city is personified by a female figure in a varying state of dress and undress, making this interior space quite literally the site of a revelation. On behalf of the Walker sisters, the female personifications appeal to viewers to leave behind their everyday frame of mind (in which classical nudes would register as inappropriately naked) and enter an enlightened perceptive and cognitive state in which beauty and truth are one.

Today's visitors are routed differently through the galleries. Since the renovation and extension of the Museum building by the architectural firm Machado Silvetti in 2004–7, the historic facade and Rotunda have lost their original function and are themselves put on display (fig. 5). While deemed cultural accomplishments worthy of preservation, they no longer reflect today's goals for the institution. These are embodied in an architectural reinterpretation that guides visitors through a new access route from a side entrance to the lower gallery level and from the back into the former main level, flipping conventional patterns and forcing users to come to terms with the building in new ways. This spatial re-formation implicitly questions the Museum's ideological foundations as well. Manifest in the architecture of the rejuvenated building is the emphasis on student and faculty engagement through a study room, flexible exhibition spaces, and increased access to the behind-the-scenes workings of a cultural repository. The Museum now serves as a focal point for many forms of interdisciplinary inquiry. Through research, programs, and exhibitions, faculty, students, and curators constantly generate conversations around objects from the collection. Collaboratively, they expand knowledge by exploring new perspectives, by tracing forgotten histories, and sharing ideas. Rather than reiterating the authoritative narratives of the past and presenting conclusive answers, current efforts invite intellectual engagement not only with the exhibitions in the galleries, but with the curatorial process as well.

The retooling of the Museum as a space for participation and exchange will not be lost on the Bowdoin seniors who graduate on the Museum steps. They carry with them memories of class visits, gallery talks, concerts, and festivities. Some will have seen their own object labels on the wall or even have curated an exhibition themselves. Rather than being intimidated or constrained by the cultural assumptions inscribed in its facade, they might appreciate the unique opportunities for learning and enjoyment the Museum provides. This book is dedicated to those students who take the initiative to learn from Bowdoin's collection and invites them—and indeed anyone—to consider exceptional objects for the intellectual insights they make possible.

## COLLECTING

Throughout their four years at the College, students encounter in the galleries a staggering range of objects that represent an entirely improbable variety of media, themes, cultures, and periods of human creativity. Some will ask, what makes this assembly of disparate things a "collection"? It is true that without the institutional threshold demarcated by the Walker sister's dedication plaque, "To Be Used Solely for Art Purposes," it is difficult to conceive of anything these objects have in common. The conceptual framework, and the distinction "art" that was granted regardless of the makers' original intentions and without their approval, inserts the *tertium comparationis*. At the dawn of the twentieth century, the Walkers and their generation of art aficionados claimed for art an autonomy that applied to artists, interpreters, and collections—anyone and anything purposefully engaged with or associated with art. The philosophical foundations of museology have been critiqued ever since for being

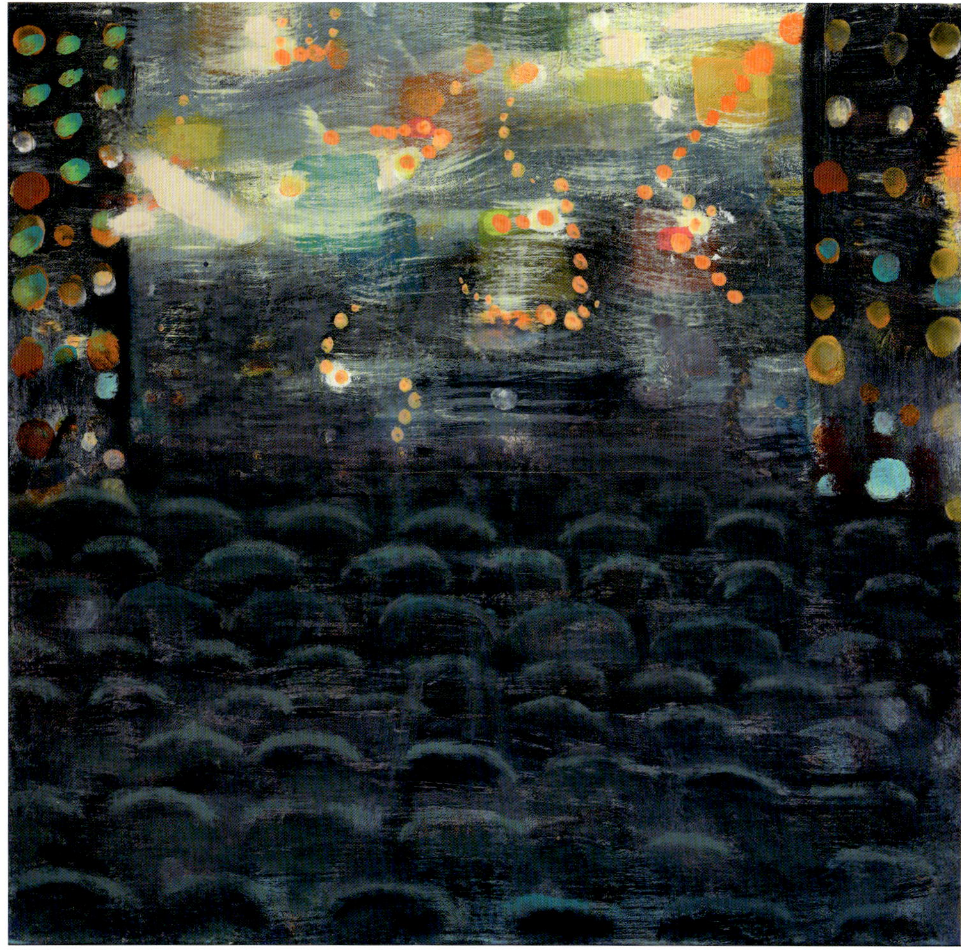

FIG. 4. Katherine Bradford (American, b. 1942). *Theater (Watson)*, 2001. Oil on canvas, 19 × 20 in. (48.3 × 50.8 cm). Bowdoin College Museum of Art, Gift of Katharine J. Watson in Celebration of the Artist

oblivious to the limits of "art" as an epistemological device. But the model of institutional collecting for public benefit, the desire to explore art as a tool for learning, are proudly upheld. The idea injected in 1894 into the academic discourse of the College, while historically inconclusive and culturally insensitive, established a legacy that has not yet been surpassed.

"Art" proposes a concept for objects deliberately shaped by human intervention, subjected to aesthetic contemplation, and, once they enter a museum, exempted from general circulation. This "Art Idea" immediately outpaced the classical iconography first used to formulate it at Bowdoin and elsewhere, as artists and collectors raced to test the boundaries of "art." Already at the turn of the last century, the concept was applied to Japanese sword guards, a Winslow Homer watercolor, ritual masks from New Ireland, and colonial American furniture, to name but a few

items that entered the collection at the time. The Walker Art Building was erected at an exalted moment of American politics and culture, exemplified by the World Columbian Exposition in Chicago in 1893, which suggested that all the world's resources were available to the members of advanced Western societies. Exhibitions and newly founded museums, such as Bowdoin's, offered unprecedented opportunities for public education, the ferment of American democracy.

However, as lingering ideas of American exceptionalism draw the attention of today's critics, the colonialist roots of the nineteenth-century art museum, which are deeply intertwined with such national aspirations, are questioned as well. What are the ethics, what is the intellectual validity of institutions that remain committed to featuring collections of encyclopedic breadth in the twenty-first century? Who benefits when one applies the label "art" to an infinite

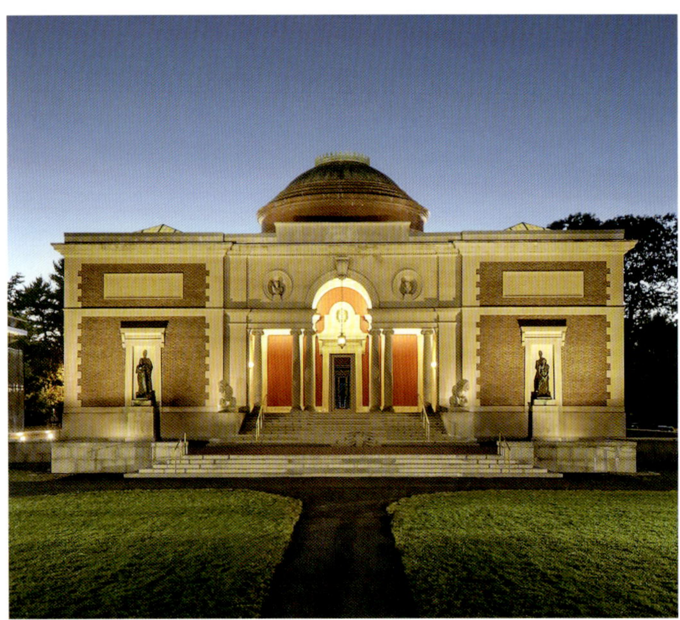

FIG. 5. Exterior of the Bowdoin College Museum of Art at dusk, 2007

number of things that were never intended by their makers to be placed on public exhibition? Does this packaging function as a cover-up for the many histories of disenfranchisement and destruction that are the precondition of the accumulation of wealth and goods in Western museum collections?

Examples from the following pages illustrate the difficulties faced when prioritizing "art purposes" over other concerns. And they exemplify ethical questions raised in courses such as professor of anthropology Susan Kaplan's class "Who Owns the Past?" Bowdoin's carvings from the Palace of Ashurnasirpal II were donated in 1860 by Henri Byron Haskell, a graduate of Bowdoin's medical school who traveled the Middle East as a missionary. As Ada Cohen explains in her essay, imposing fragments of the decorations of the palace in Nimrud can be found at the Louvre, the British Museum, and elsewhere. The original site in Iraq, however, has been further decimated by ISIS terrorists. How has the meaning of the Assyrian reliefs in Western collections changed since they were first acquired, when they were appreciated for offering archaeological validation to the literary record of the Hebrew Bible? Has their status changed with the recent destruction of the excavation site? Nineteenth-century travelers on the North American continent, too, acquired and successively donated objects that for indigenous communities carry meaning far beyond their artistic value. Figures from the personal possessions of

a Tlingit shaman that might have been used for healing are much more than the exotic curiosities previous generations of nonindigenous viewers might have seen in them (p. 105). Taken out of context in a museum exhibition, they deserve respect and appreciation for their spiritual significance as well as their formal qualities.

Modern and contemporary artists consciously touch on culturally and psychologically sensitive issues in the hopes of promoting awareness and healing. In her photographs of sites of the Holocaust, Judy Glickman Lauder finds visual equivalents for a humanitarian catastrophe too large to be grasped. Inviting viewers to ponder historic locations adds specificity to the crime of genocide and aids future generations in the remembrance of individuals lost (p. 195). Artists have long guided viewers through the circles of hell, much like Virgil chaperoned Dante. Being part of an artistic genealogy does not diminish the courage such an undertaking requires. Heather Dewey Hagborg takes viewers to the frontier of forensic DNA phenotyping and raises the prospect of biological surveillance (fig. 6). Reconstructing portraits of people based on DNA they accidentally left behind on cigarette butts, chewing gum, or hair, she makes apparent how much information is available to those who are capable of deciphering it, with consequences that make conventional notions of privacy seem ridiculously outdated.

Where is the space for art in the information age? And why does it matter?

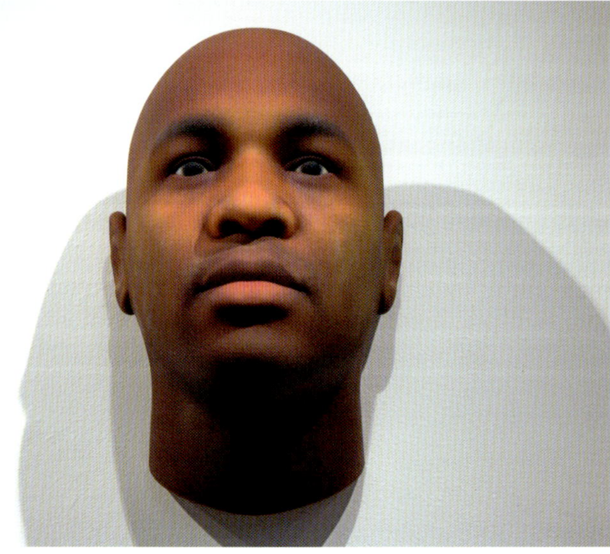

FIG. 6. Heather Dewey Hagborg (American, b. 1982), *Stranger Visions: Sample 7 NYC (Reconstruction of a Face Based on Found DNA, from the Series "Stranger Visions")*, 2012–13. Polymer, 12 × 7 × 4 in. (30.5 × 17.8 × 10.1 cm). Lent by a friend of the Museum

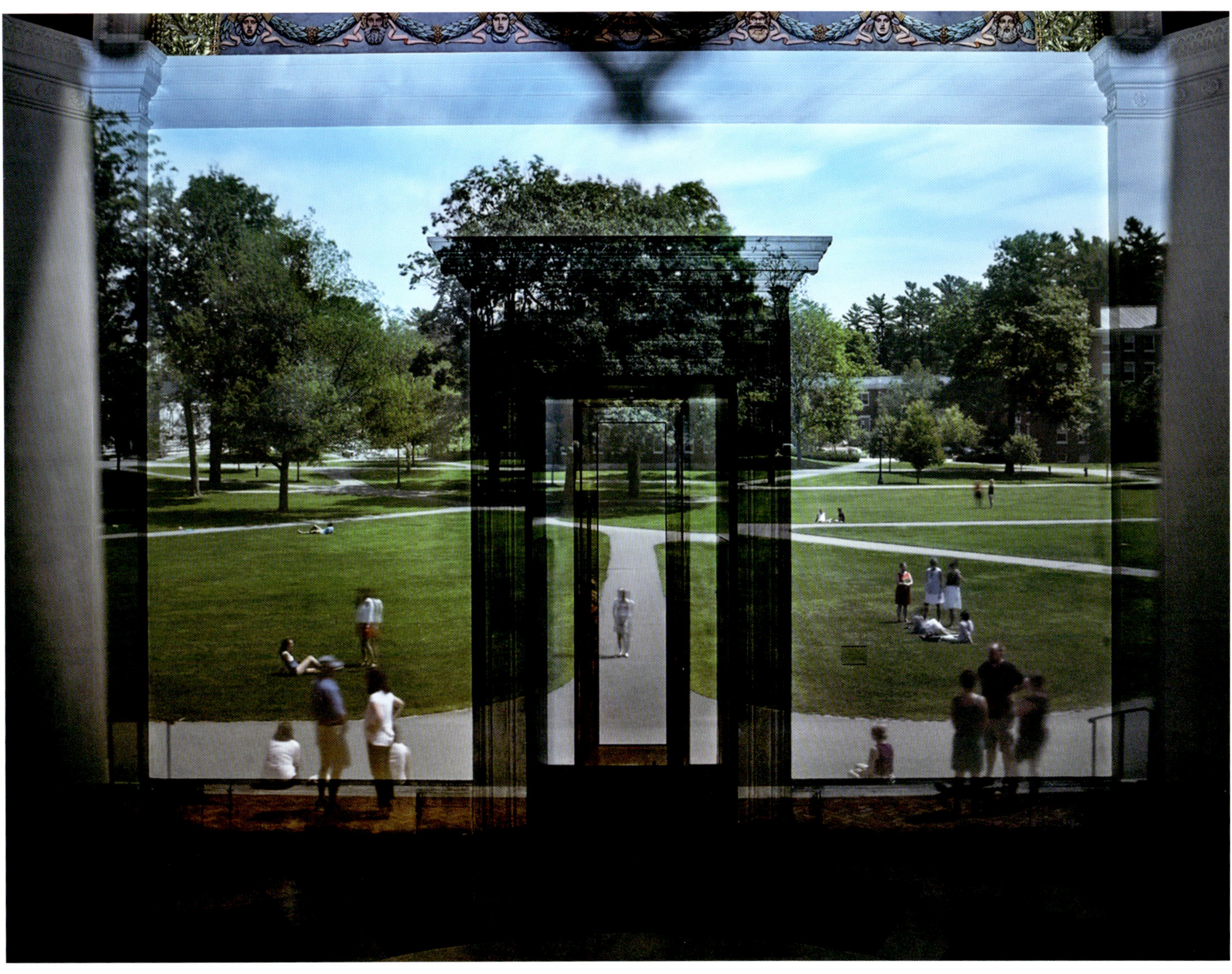

FIG. 7. Abelardo Morell (American, born Cuba, 1948), *Camera Obscura: The Campus Quad Inside the Bowdoin College Art Museum Rotunda Gallery, July 30th, 2015*, 2015. Archival inkjet print on paper, 28 × 35⅛ in. (71 × 89 cm). Bowdoin College Museum of Art, 2015.40

## REPRESENTING

When photographer Abelardo Morell, Bowdoin class of 1971, returns to his alma mater, he is reminded of the Museum's pivotal role in his education, as it opened to him the doors to the world of art. Countless hours of museum visits, art history lectures, and object photography behind the scenes were vividly on his mind when he recently transformed the Rotunda into a camera obscura. Using a prism stuck to the entrance door as photographic lens, he projected, on a bright summer day, the Bowdoin campus into the darkened Museum space. A digital photograph provides a record of this magical transformation as the outside world appears on a wall idealizing the "Art Idea" (fig. 7). The image is a vivid reminder of the Museum's unique potential as a viewing device where one can begin to see oneself within a much bigger picture.

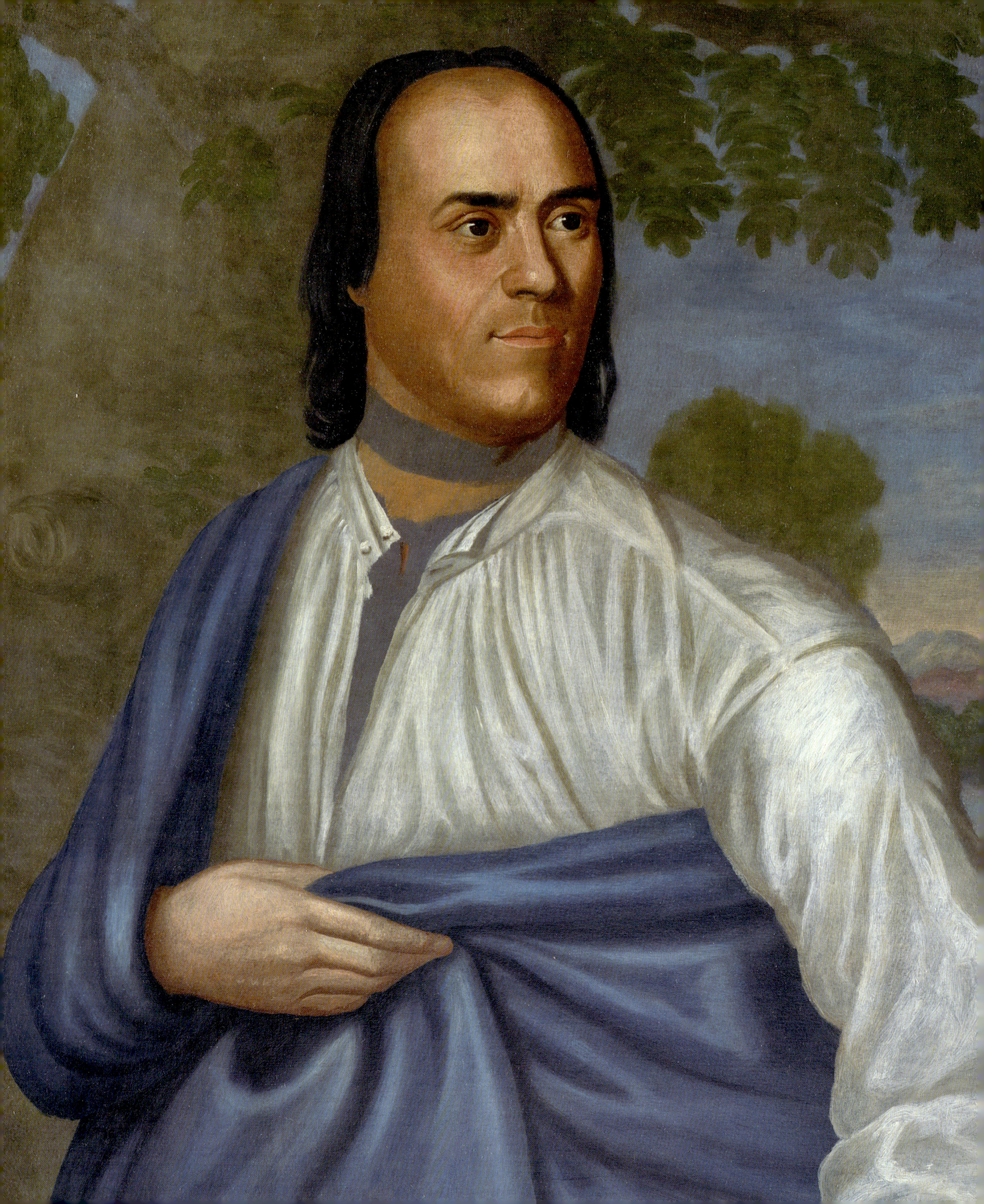

# TWO CENTURIES OF ART WITH A PURPOSE AT BOWDOIN[1]   Anne Collins Goodyear

"To make itself alive, a museum must do two things: It must teach and it must advertise."
—John Cotton Dana, 1917

"[T]he museum, which to many people seems to look only backward,
is in reality one of our chief means of looking forward."
—Walter Pach, 1948[2]

In 1917, determined to clear what he described as "The Gloom of the Museum," John Cotton Dana strongly asserted the need of the museum to serve as an educational tool, to enliven itself through the act of sharing—and being enriched by—new ideas. If his addition of the notion of "advertisement" seems somewhat surprising, Dana, himself a museum director, was among the first to recognize that "Museums of the future . . . will travel abroad through their photographs, their textbooks, and their periodicals."[3] He recognized that such "advertisement" would not only extend the reach of museum collections, but attract the public to experience works of art in person.

Intriguingly, Dana's comments were offered only a little over two decades after the Bowdoin College Museum of Art opened the doors of its current home—the Walker Art Building (p. 14, fig. 5)—the 125th anniversary of which we now mark. In constructing a purpose-built museum of art, Bowdoin College demonstrated its own commitment to supporting the important educational mission of the Museum, in theory and in practice. The College's recognition of the unique contribution to be made by the work of art to a liberal arts education has long roots, deeply relevant to its present-day recognition of the importance of cultivating students' "creative disposition," which promises to define important elements of its future.[4]

The intersection of history and potentiality was evident to the artist, curator, and art historian Walter Pach, who observed in 1948: "the museum, which to many people seems to look only backward, is in reality one of our chief means of looking forward." Deeply familiar with the Bowdoin campus, and with its Museum of Art, an association born of lecturing and teaching at the College in addition to being father to Raymond Pach of the class of 1936, Pach would commemorate his relationship to the institution not only in his study *The Art Museum in America*, but also through a series of sketches.[5] One in particular stands out: a view featuring a well-defined depiction of Massachusetts Hall (fig. 1), the College's oldest building and first home to its collection of fine art, opposite a less clearly defined Winthrop Hall, made from a vantage point just north of the Museum, now occupied by the Visual Arts Center, yet to be designed by Edward Larrabee Barnes. Pach's own viewpoint, embracing Bowdoin's history, seems to acknowledge the critical role played by art in a Bowdoin education, even when students may have least suspected it. It also anticipated, composed as it was from a position adjacent to the Museum's

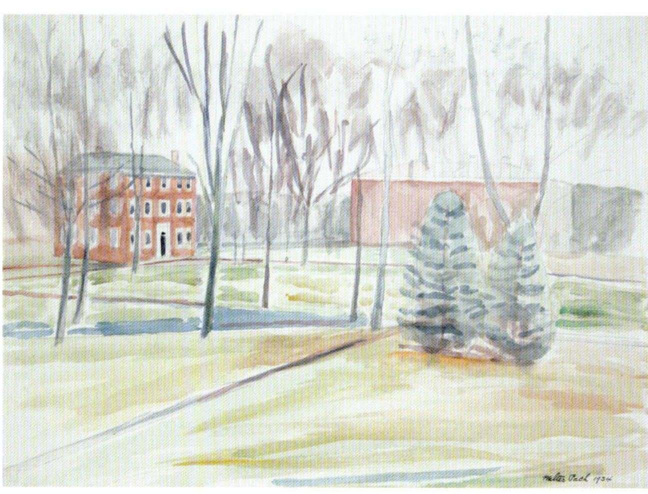

OPPOSITE: Attributed to Nathaniel Smibert (American, 1734–1756), *Portrait of Reverend Samson Occom*, ca. 1751–56. Oil on canvas, 30⅛ × 24¹⁵⁄₁₆ in. (76.5 × 63.3 cm). Bowdoin College Museum of Art, Bequest of the Honorable James Bowdoin III, 1813.4

FIG. 1. Walter Pach (American, 1883–1958), *Untitled (View of Massachusetts Hall, Bowdoin College)*, 1934. Watercolor and pencil on paper, 10⅜ × 14½ in. (26 × 37 cm). Bowdoin College Museum of Art, Museum Purchase, Jane H. and Charles E. Parker, Jr. Fund, 2016.15.1

landmark building, that the importance of collecting art for Bowdoin would take on ever-increasing visibility, becoming a defining feature of the Bowdoin experience.

Indeed, the Walker Art Building, home to the Museum's distinguished collection, now serves as the location for Bowdoin students' first official assembly and for their graduation, and is a rallying point for important impromptu student gatherings around sensitive and provocative issues. Today one of approximately 700 academic institutions hosting a museum of fine art or college gallery, Bowdoin College houses one of the earliest collections of fine art in the United States, including the nation's first public collection of drawings, bequeathed in 1811 by the College's founding benefactor, James Bowdoin III.[6]

As Bowdoin's own education reminds us, campus museums trace their intellectual origins to the Renaissance tradition of the *Wunderkammer*, or cabinet of wonders. A member of the Harvard Class of 1771, James Bowdoin III witnessed the conversion of the school's philosophy chamber into a picture gallery in 1768 by President Edward Holyoke. A child of privilege, who had grown up in a household boasting Boston's largest collection of art, Bowdoin could not have failed to have taken notice of a dramatic act of iconoclasm during which students attacked John Singleton Copley's portrait of the unpopular governor Francis Bernard.[7] Though Bowdoin did not participate in the event, he surely recognized the passionate response a work of art had stimulated among his peers. After leaving his alma mater early due to poor health, Bowdoin traveled to England, where he enrolled at Oxford, remaining until 1772. There the young aesthete had access to the Ashmolean, the first university museum (opened in 1683), as well as to the British Museum, which had recently opened in London as the world's first public museum. This early exposure to European culture would be expanded by an opportunity to make a Grand Tour of the continent and Great Britain with Ward Nicholas Boylston between 1773 and 1775.[8]

Recalled to Boston due to the impending war with England, Bowdoin and his father, James Bowdoin II, would take up the cause of the American patriots, offering political leadership in the early years of the new republic. As the son of the second governor of Massachusetts, a member of the Massachusetts state legislature, and a participant in the state's constitutional convention, Bowdoin may have become increasingly sensitive to the intertwined nature of political authority and cultural expression.[9] In 1780, James

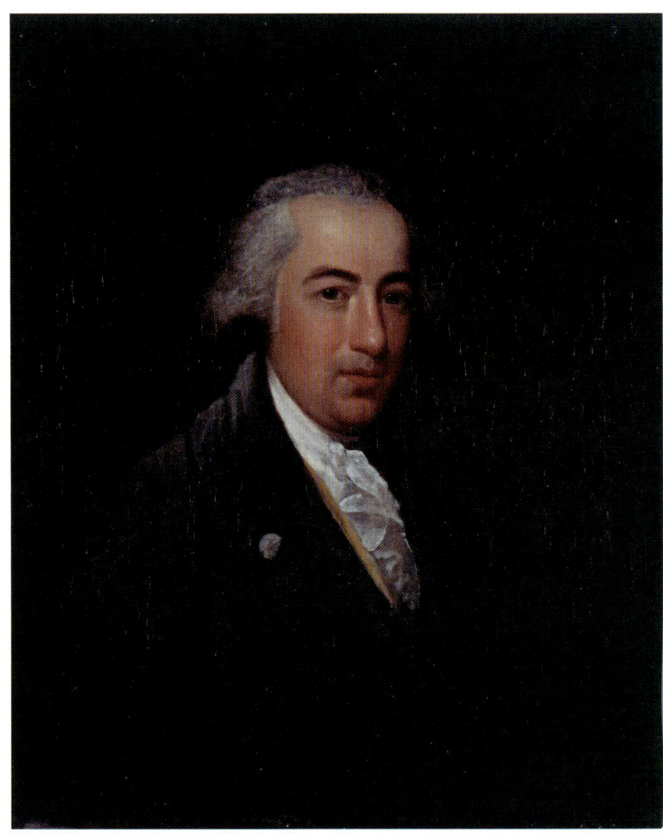

FIG. 2. Gilbert Stuart (American, 1758–1828), *James Bowdoin III*, c. 1806–12. Oil on canvas, 29⅛ × 24¾ in. (75.9 × 62.9 cm). Bowdoin College Museum of Art, Bequest of Mrs. Sarah Bowdoin Dearborn, 1870.6

Bowdoin II, in whose honor his son would name Bowdoin College in 1794, became a founder and the first president of the American Academy of Arts and Sciences, dedicated to cultivating advanced knowledge critical to nurturing the new democracy. James Bowdoin III would be inducted in 1786.

In 1804, a fellow Academician, President Thomas Jefferson, would appoint Bowdoin Minister Plenipotentiary to the Court of Spain. In honor of the occasion, Bowdoin commissioned Gilbert Stuart to create pendant portraits of Jefferson and Secretary of State James Madison for his diplomatic apartments in Spain (p. 117), perhaps anticipating that these likenesses would play an important role in immortalizing the nation's founders, much as Stuart's famous depictions of George Washington had helped to enshrine the likeness of its first president in the popular imagination of Americans.[10] (Indeed, Stuart would travel to Bowdoin College in 1821 to paint copies of these likenesses, transforming them into popular prints and establishing them as key pictorial documents in the

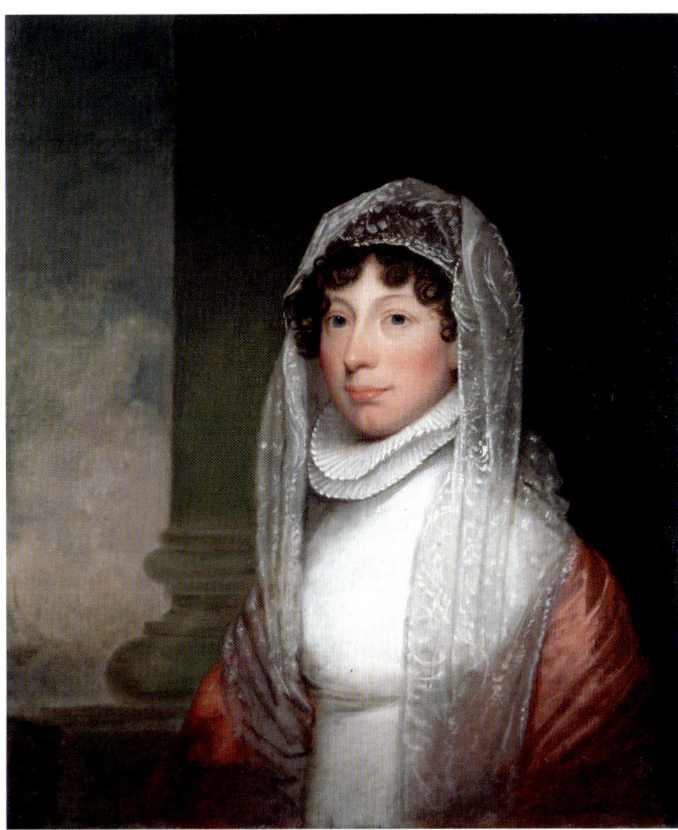

FIG. 3. Gilbert Stuart, *Mrs. James Bowdoin III (née Sarah Bowdoin)*, ca. 1806–12. Oil on canvas, 30⅛ × 25³⁄₁₆ in. (76.5 × 64 cm). Bowdoin College Museum of Art, Bequest of Mrs. Sarah Bowdoin Dearborn, 1870.7

early history of the American republic.[11]) Bowdoin would also use the occasion to hire Stuart to create smaller portraits of himself and his fashionable wife Sarah, who appears in a Spanish mantilla, alluding to his appointment (figs. 2, 3).[12]

Shortly before embarking on his diplomatic mission, Bowdoin sent the Commander-in-Chief a parting gift that testified to their mutual admiration for the arts and recognition of their important role in the republic. In a note that accompanied a small marble copy of a Hellenistic sculpture in the Vatican collections, then believed to represent the likeness of the historic ruler Cleopatra (now known to picture Ariadne), Bowdoin apprised Jefferson of his willingness to "tender . . . my services in procuring for you any Specimens of ye Arts, either in Sculpture or painting."[13] Jefferson replied the following month, possibly while making arrangements to sit for the portrait by Stuart, and expressed his appreciation for the gift, promising to house it with "the memorials of those worthies, whose

remembrance I feel a pride and comfort in consecrating there."[14] The sculpture remains at Monticello to this day.

Unable to work in Spain, as intended, due to a combination of political and personal circumstances, Bowdoin conducted his affairs as an American diplomat in Paris from late 1805 until the spring of 1808. There he continued to nurture a love of the arts, procuring art supplies requested by Gilbert Stuart, and visiting museums newly consecrated in the wake of the French Revolution, explicitly aligning access to culture with democracy and republican values.[15] In addition to an account of a visit to the Louvre by his wife Sarah, among the paintings Bowdoin bequeathed to the College upon his death was a copy of Rubens's *Saint Simeon Holding the Infant Christ* (fig. 4), made after the right wing of the artist's triptych for the Cathedral of Our Lady in Antwerp. The work was on view at the Louvre during Bowdoin's residence in Paris, having been brought by Napoleon in 1794 to the French capital, where it remained until 1815.[16] In addition to the Louvre, Bowdoin appears to have visited the Musée des Monuments Français, established in Paris in 1795, adding both its 1803 and 1806 catalogues to his library.[17] Indeed, as Susan Wegner has suggested, Bowdoin may have taken special notice of the preface to the 1803 edition, which opens: "Cultivation of the arts enlarges a people's commerce and prosperity, purifies its morals, makes it more gentle and ready to follow the laws by which it is governed."[18]

Like Bowdoin, Jefferson recognized the importance of exposure to the arts as part of the education of a capable citizen, and, in 1806, suggested founding a national university that would incorporate Charles Willson Peale's Philadelphia Museum. Although the president's initiative was unsuccessful, just five years after the proposal was made, Bowdoin College would accept a generous bequest from James Bowdoin III, making it one of the first institutions of higher education in the United States to boast a significant collection of fine art, and putting the school he had endowed on a footing comparable to that of his alma mater.[19] The donation included 141 drawings, 70 paintings, his library, scientific equipment, and his collection of minerals.[20]

Bowdoin's recognition of the edifying role to be played by the visual arts in an educational setting is clear from a passage marked in his 1788 copy of *Sketches of the History of Man* by Henry Home, Lord Kames: "Beauty was studied in objects of sight; and men of taste attached themselves to the fine arts, which multiplied their enjoyment and

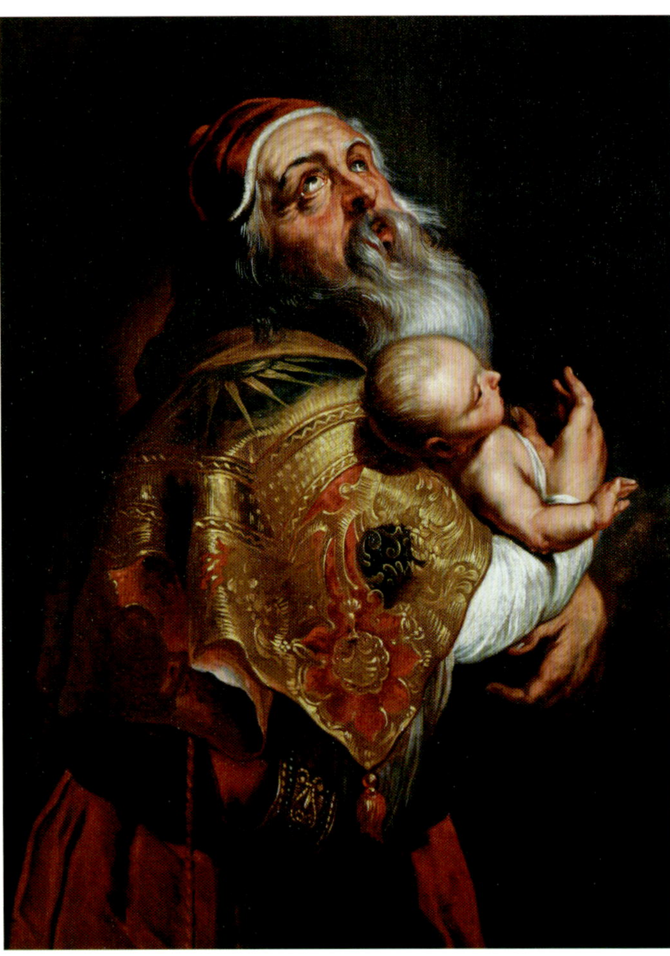

FIG. 4. After Peter Paul Rubens (Flemish, 1577–1640), *Saint Simeon Holding the Infant Christ*, n.d. Oil on canvas, 45 × 34 in. (114.3 × 86.3 cm). Bowdoin College Museum of Art, Bequest of the Honorable James Bowdoin III, 1813.11

improved their benevolence."[21] With just such conviction, paintings testifying to the value of personal honor, compassionate leadership, and patriotic loyalty, such as John Smibert's copy of Nicholas Poussin's *Continence of Scipio* (p. 113) and Frans Francken III's *Achilles at the Court of Lycomedes*—a work attributed by Gilbert Stuart to Rubens— were installed in Massachusetts Hall.[22] Indeed, the 1817 *Laws of Bowdoin College* prescribed that the College's "Executive Government" should require the students, as part of the course of their instruction, to spend time in the "chambers of the College," where these overseers should, in a passage marked for emphasis by a reader, "observe and superintend the deportment and morals of the students, assist them in their studies, and encourage them in the practice of virtue."[23] A local visitor to Massachusetts Hall

reported in 1820: "The philosophy chamber is capacious and handsome. It is dressed throughout with exquisite paintings, presented by Bowdoin. They are from the pencils of the first masters of Europe. The worthies, the patriarchs, and the martyrs of antiquity seem to have risen from the tomb."[24] Among the portraits donated by James Bowdoin III to the College was a likeness of Reverend Samson Occom—attributed to John Smibert's son, Nathaniel (see frontispiece). Echoing Bowdoin's own commitment to funding an institution of higher learning, the work pictures the Monhegan minister who, with the aim of increasing educational opportunities for other Native Americans, donated substantial proceeds, raised by delivering sermons during a tour of the United Kingdom, to the school that would become Dartmouth College.

If exposure to works of art was intended to inspire audiences, it must be acknowledged that the public these works served was circumscribed. Bowdoin students of this period were young men of European descent, and the entry of Maine as a "free" state into the Union in 1820 would be predicated upon the expansion of slavery into Missouri. The College, like the nation of which it is a part, would, of necessity, epitomize the thorny conundrum of negotiating privilege and access—a persistent struggle.[25]

While this challenge continues to resist reconciliation, James Bowdoin III, educated in the tradition of the European Enlightenment, in making available to Bowdoin College students not only a library, but also vaunted examples of European and American art, particularly those objects with ties to the artist John Smibert, emulated the efforts of Bishop Berkeley, who in 1728 had invited Smibert to travel with him to the New World from Great Britain in order to found an institution of higher learning, bringing books, drawings, and paintings for purposes of study. Although funding for the envisioned university did not materialize, prompting Berkeley to return to England, Smibert remained in New England. The artist ultimately settled in Boston, where the Bowdoin family became one of his most important patrons. Indeed, the collection of drawings bequeathed by Bowdoin to the College would be composed largely, if not exclusively, of works transported by Smibert himself to the colonies for educational purposes.[26] In addition to the works on paper, examples of Smibert's painted copies of works by revered European artists, such as *The Continence of Scipio* by Poussin and portraits by Van Eyck and Tintoretto, became part of the collection Bowdoin transmitted to the College.[27]

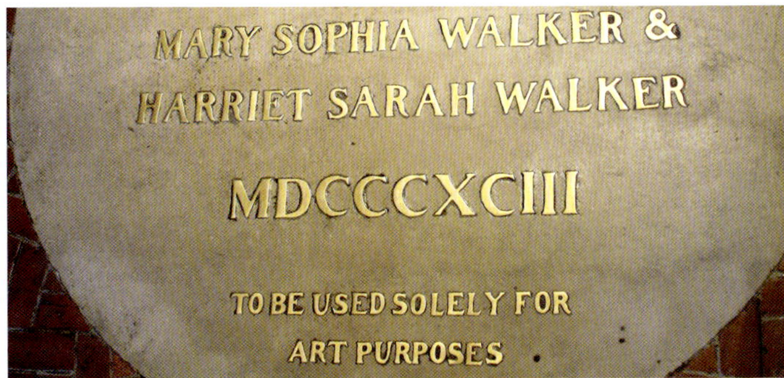

FIG. 5. Inscription in the Museum Rotunda



As the reputation of Bowdoin College's art holdings grew, together with sensitivity to the moral lessons it could impart, the College took steps to care for the collection, through cleaning, pruning, and better housing.[28] To this end, a gallery was established in a new chapel constructed on campus between 1844 and 1855 by Richard Upjohn, under the presidency of Leonard Woods. Further cementing the perceived relationship between artistic inspiration and moral fervor, Woods sought to emulate at the College what he had observed during a visit to Oxford, namely: "a magnificence of architecture, an assemblage of paintings, statues, gardens, and walks; above all a solemnity and grandeur of religious worship which does more to elevate the taste and purify the character than the whole encyclopedia of knowledge."[29]

The power of art to communicate humanistic ideals also influenced the distribution of an important group of Assyrian reliefs to American colleges in the mid-nineteenth century, discovered during the excavation of the Palace of King Ashurnasirpal II at Kalhu (constructed 883–859 BCE) by the British diplomat and archaeologist Austen Henry Layard in 1845 (pp. 24–27). Thanks to the efforts of the missionary Henri Byron Haskell, class of 1855 of the Medical School of Maine at Bowdoin College, five reliefs came to Bowdoin, where they were installed in a gallery adjacent to the new chapel. In the same period, a deeper understanding of the aesthetic power of art was beginning to take shape. Major museums opened in New York, Boston, Chicago, and elsewhere between the mid-1870s and the mid-1880s. They embraced the notion that "knowledge of art in its higher forms of beauty would tend directly to humanize, to educate and refine a practical and laborious people," as Joseph Hodges Choate, one of the founders of The Metropolitan Museum of Art, put it in 1880.[30]

In 1894, Bowdoin College would open the Walker Art Building, one of the first museums on a college campus dedicated exclusively to fine art, underwritten by Harriet Sarah Walker and her sister Mary Sophia Walker, nieces of Theophilus Wheeler Walker, a dedicated Bowdoin trustee. Through the bronze inscription they commissioned for the Museum's Rotunda, the sisters ensured that the building would be forever dedicated to "art purposes" (fig. 5). As Martin Brimmer, president of the Boston Museum of Fine Arts emphasized in his remarks at the time of its opening on June 7, 1894, the Museum had a critical educational mandate, one which emanated from the collections it housed:

> The place of the Museum on the College grounds forbids us to suppose that it was put here only that its contents might amuse the leisure of the visitor. It stands here to affirm, conspicuously and deliberately, that Art is a great instrument in man's education, that it rounds and completes a training which would be imperfect without it.[31]

Designed by Charles Follen McKim of McKim, Mead & White, one of the most prominent architects of his era, the Museum would emulate the architecture of the Villa Medici in Rome, the historic home of the French Academy, reinforcing the structure's larger pedagogical function.[32] The murals commissioned by McKim that occupy its distinctive Rotunda—by the American Renaissance artists Elihu Vedder, representing Rome (originally titled *The Art Idea*) (p. 123); Abbott Thayer, depicting Florence; Kenyon Cox, picturing Venice; and John La Farge, capturing Athens, clearly reflect the architect's commitment to the legacy of classical antiquity idealized in the West since the European Renaissance. Increasingly cognizant of the limitations— and even the embedded prejudices—of the mythic ideals embraced by the building's architectural style, the institution has consistently sought to share with the College through its collections, exhibitions, and programs myriad models of creative excellence. It now stewards works made from antiquity to the present day by artists from numerous cultures around the world. This has largely been made possible by the extraordinary support of remarkable donors and patrons, whose generosity is evident in the works highlighted in this catalogue, in addition to many others that could not be included in this publication, which represent inspirational aesthetic achievement.

The opening of Bowdoin's new galleries in 1894 was part of a spate of similar buildings established on distinguished campuses across the country between 1890 and 1895,

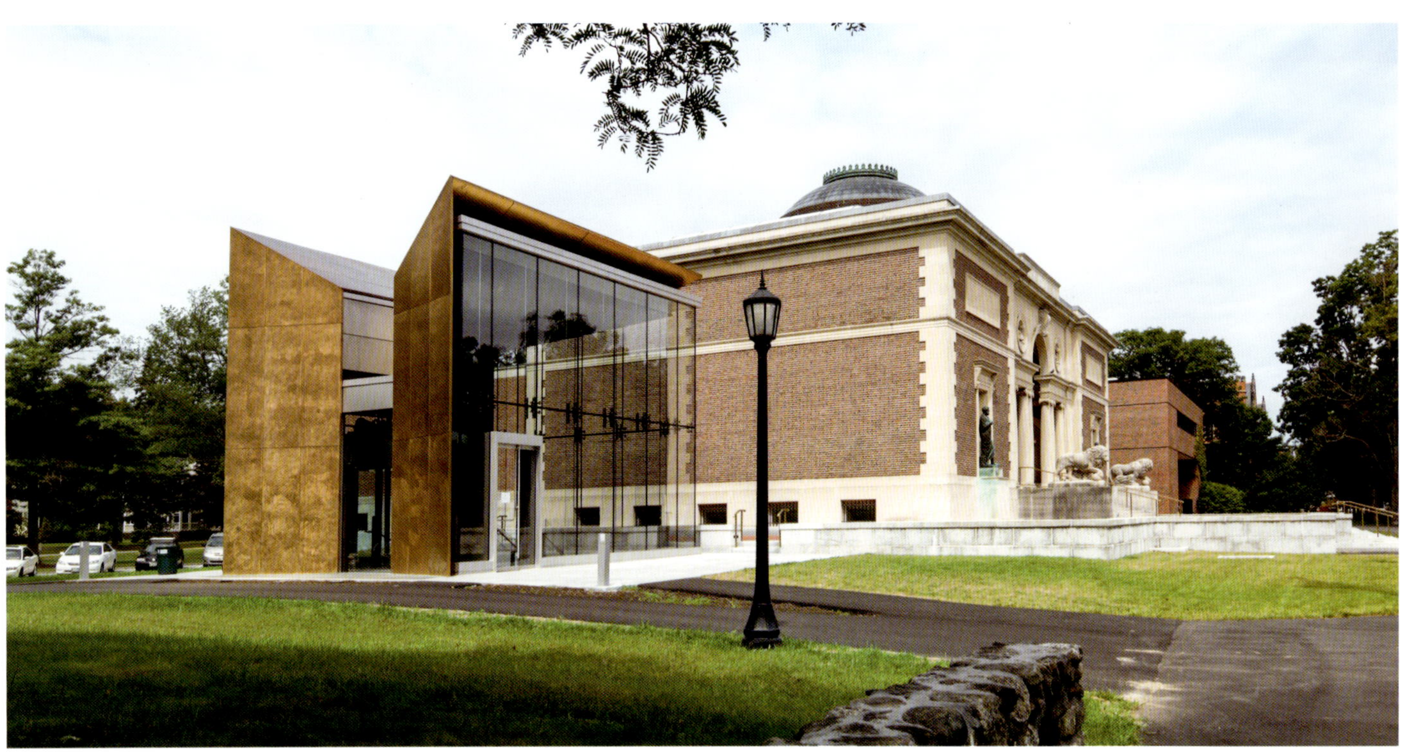

FIG. 6. Museum expansion by Machado Silvetti

including at Princeton, Stanford, and Harvard. Collectively, these museums would create new strategies for integrating the fine arts into higher education and into public life by training new professionals in the visual arts.[33]

In 2007, after a two-year closing, the Bowdoin College Museum of Art unveiled an expansion by the Boston-based architects Machado Silvetti, who preserved the character of Bowdoin's historic McKim building largely by excavating rather than expanding the building's footprint (fig. 6). They increased the Museum's gallery space, added a classroom and a space dedicated to student-curated exhibitions, and, just as importantly, symbolically opened the Museum to the world beyond Bowdoin. A new glass-curtain wall makes the galleries transparent to passersby. The glass pavilion that rises out of the ground next to the 1894 building provides two entryways, one to the campus and the other to the street bordering the Museum. Repositioning the Museum as an institution that enthusiastically welcomes not only the campus, but also the local, national, and international community reflects both a physical renovation and an intellectual restructuring: a posture of emphatic openness.

Such physical accessibility has been complemented by the addition of new staff tasked with reaching out to students and faculty across the campus to facilitate academic engagement with the collections.[34] Today faculty and students from departments as diverse as mathematics, oceanographic science, physics, dance, and classics work regularly with the Museum, and the number of class visits by professors and students from a broad range of disciplines continues to grow.[35] Students and faculty regularly curate exhibitions. Digital resources expand the reach of the collections beyond the physical parameters of the Museum, making them accessible for new approaches to teaching and resources, particularly with the growth of digital and computation studies at the College. Among the Museum's most important commitments today is to equity and inclusion, ensuring that our collections, programming, and academic outreach benefit the community as broadly as possible.

Recognizing that exposure to the arts through the Museum has the capacity not only to change individual lives, but also to benefit the field more broadly, the Bowdoin College Museum of Art is now working to develop strategies to incubate the professional development of future museum professionals from all backgrounds. The "art purposes" the Museum has long embraced thus promise to inform the world far beyond Bowdoin's campus, and even to demonstrate that such purposes have a significance for our community that ranges far beyond the broad scope of the arts.

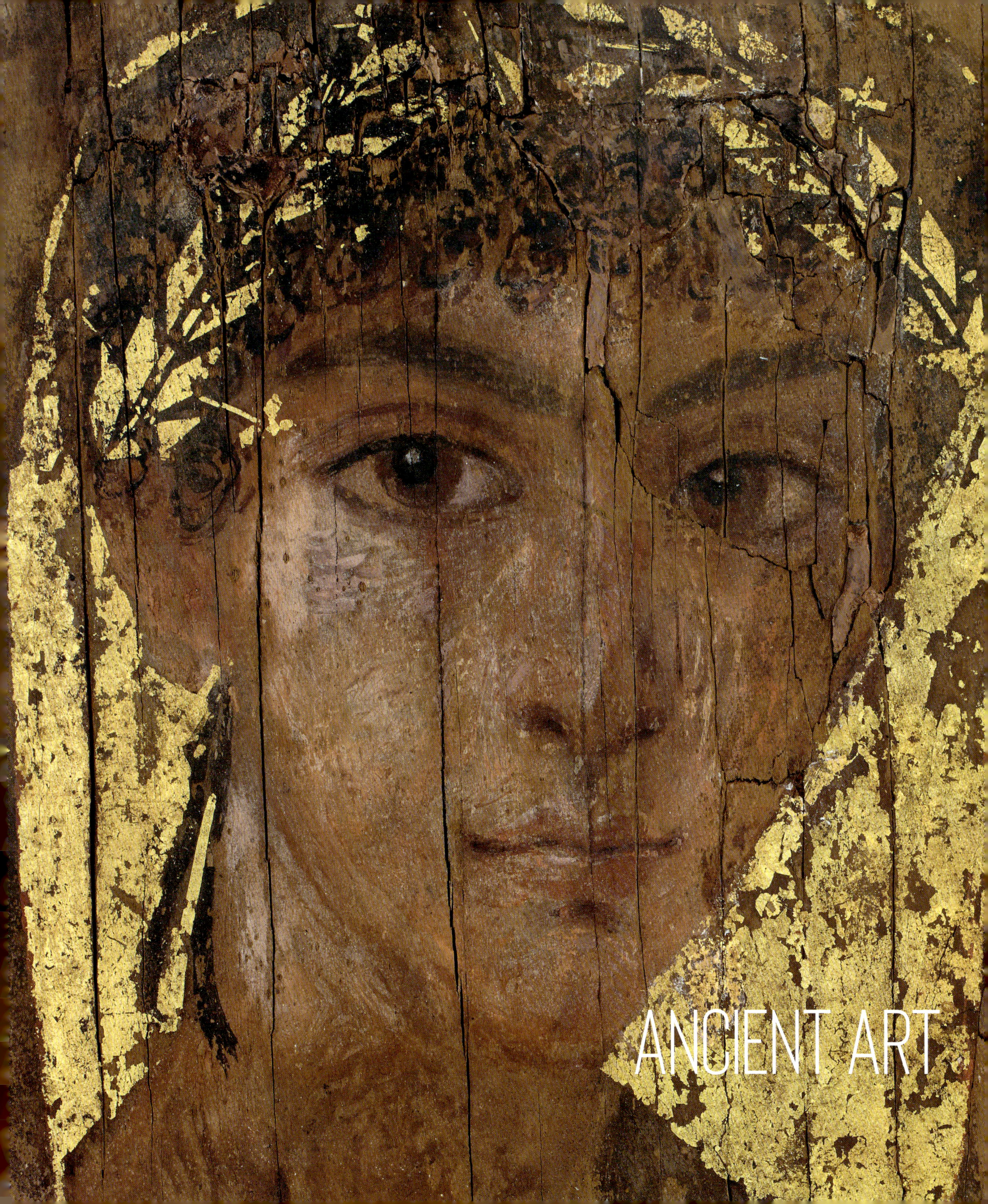

ANCIENT ART

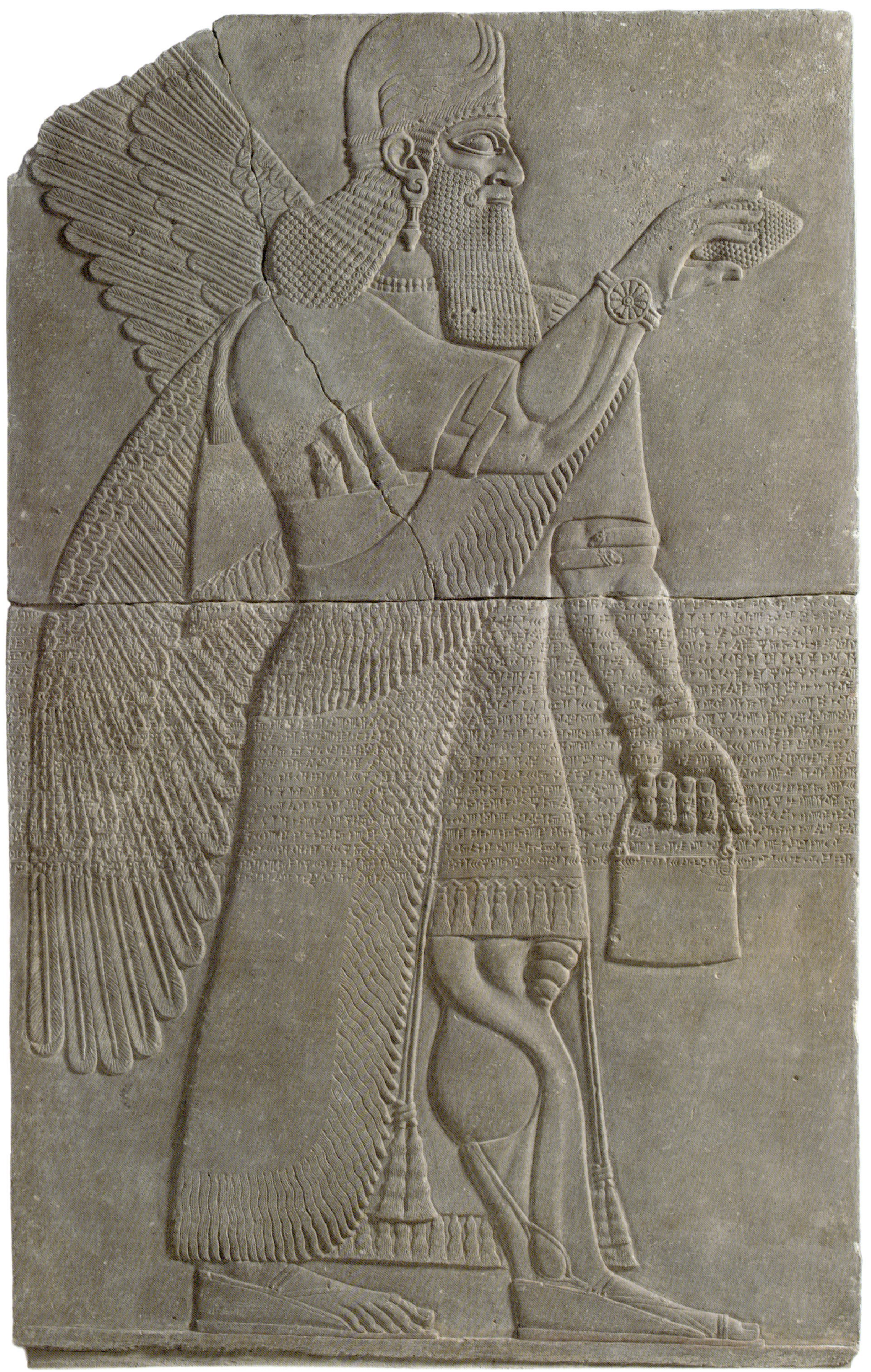

# Three Assyrian Reliefs from Kalhu (Nimrud), Iraq

c. 875–860 BCE

Gift of Dr. Henri Byron Haskell, Medical School Class of 1855  1860.2, .3
Gift of Edward Perry Warren, Esq., Honorary Degree, 1926  1906.4
Critical support for the Assyrian Collection at the Bowdoin College
Museum of Art is provided by the Yadgar Family Endowment

As visitors move between the glass-enclosed Assyrian Gallery and the adjacent Walker Gallery, they find themselves framed by two large and imposing human-headed winged genies (*apkallu*). The one facing them on the left (pl. 1) would have occupied an analogous position in the magnificent Northwest Palace of the Assyrian king Ashurnasirpal II (r. 883–859 BCE) at the site of Kalhu (modern Nimrud in Iraq), guarding a doorway and gesturing apotropaically toward the void.[1] The one on the right (1860.4), similar but not identical, directs his attention at a strikingly stylized tree, whose intricate branches end in palmettes. Only half of this tree (along with the edge of a second) is contained in the slab, but one can notionally complete it by looking at a smaller slab nearby (1860.1), which features two bird-headed genies symmetrically tending a full tree. Like their human-headed counterparts, each holds a pinecone-like object in his upraised right hand and a pail in his left. Some scholars animate these otherwise static scenes, imagining the figures dipping the cone in the pail and sprinkling its liquid content toward the tree in a fertilization ritual that may allude to real-life agricultural activities. But the gesture, as we saw, may also be directed toward a void, while yet another relief at Bowdoin shows a third variation, whereby the gesture is directed toward an equally imposing but wingless figure readily identifiable by his long gown and fez-like hat as the king (pl. 2).

The museum is fortunate to possess not one but three figures of the king. The second is shown accompanied by his courtiers in a small relief (1860.5). One of the courtiers protects Ashurnasirpal with a parasol and one with a fly whisk, as he prepares for a libation in the aftermath of a martial or hunt-related victory signified by his bow and sword. A third king (pl. 3) is both the most fragmentary and the most crisply preserved. Only the facial profile traveled out of Iraq. It has an irregular shape that hints at the variable circumstances under which Ashurnasirpal's reliefs were extracted in the second half of the nineteenth century from their architectural context, in this case his throne room. The fragment is striking not only because it draws our attention to the face but also because of the uncommon preservation of paint on the beard, hair, and frontally rendered eye. The white of the sclera is readily visible against the darker pupil, giving the figure rare focus and animation and providing a glimpse of the polychromy that once enlivened the reliefs on the walls of the palace and other buildings on the citadel of Ashurnasirpal's capital city.

The physiognomic similarity between mortal king and supernatural figures speaks to the special access to the divine that Ashurnasirpal enjoyed and that buttressed his authority. Let us look more closely at the stunningly carved and preserved genie (pl. 1), whose divine status is communicated by a horned headdress and textured wings. The elaborate curls and waves of his hair and beard, his pendant earring, necklace, armlets (one animal-headed), bracelet with rosette, and fringed and tasseled tunic point to a world of luxury and affluence. His stiffly upright pose, the massively muscled leg and arms, as well as the daggers tucked under his shoulder announce Assyria's power, a message also communicated by the so-called Standard Inscription laboriously carved in cuneiform on this and virtually all palace reliefs. The twisted perspective in which face and body are organized is a standard Near Eastern convention that gives optimal exposure to each part.

The more one lingers on the forms, the more details emerge; for example, faint incised decorations on portions of the figure's garment. Although not one of the most elaborately detailed garments on Assyrian reliefs, it is intriguing nonetheless. A distinction employed by philosophers of aesthetics and ornamentation—articulated by Kant in the eighteenth century and reworked by Derrida

PLATE 1. *Winged Spirit or Apkallu*, Northwest Palace, Room S, panel 17. Gypsum (Mosul alabaster), 90⅜ × 58¾ × 6⁷⁄₁₆ in. (230 × 149.3 × 16.4 cm) (1860.2)

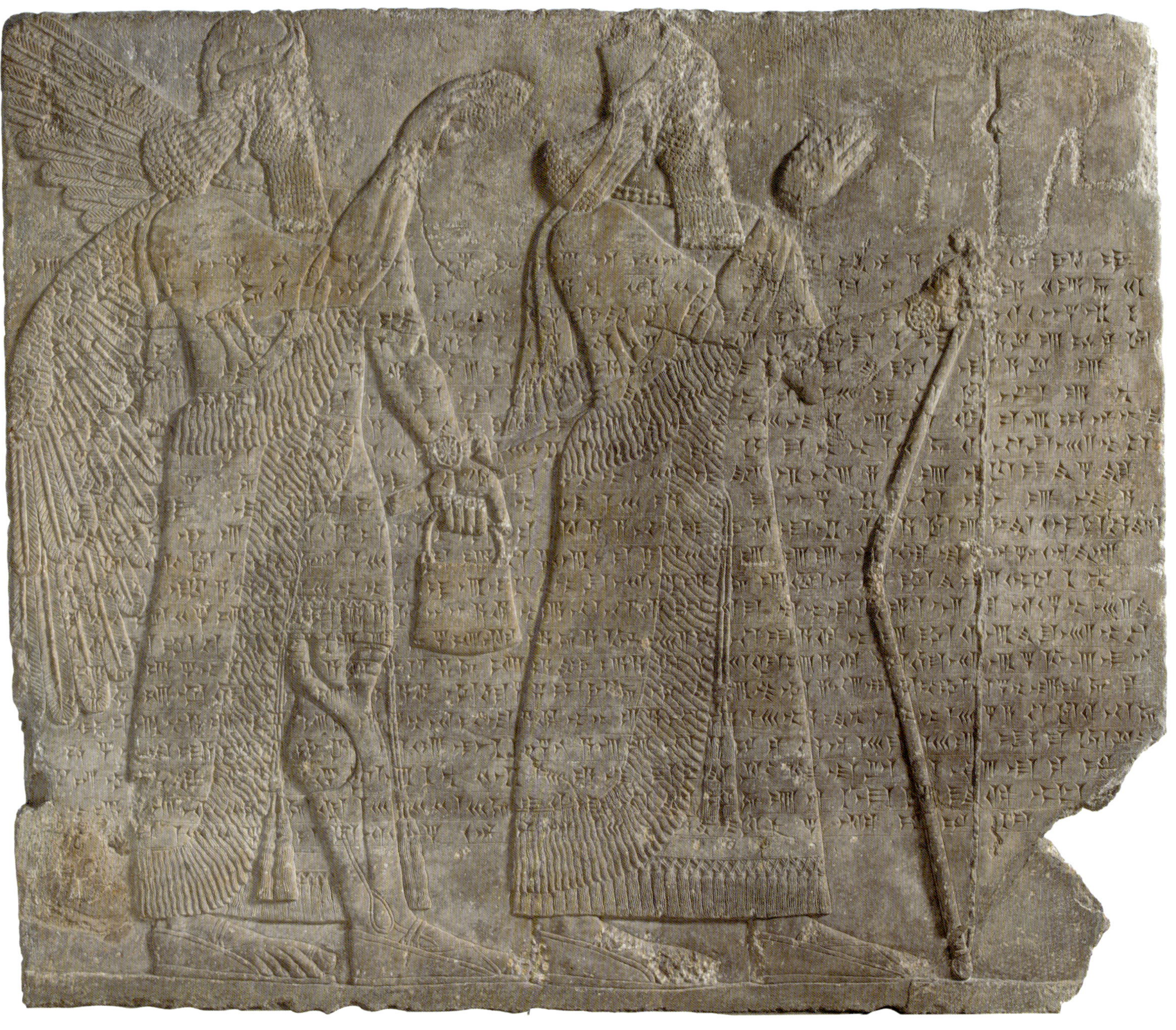

PLATE 2. *Winged Spirit or Apkallu Anointing Ashurnasirpal II*. Gypsum (Mosul alabaster), 65¹¹⁄₁₆ × 78⅛ × 6⅜ in. (166.8 × 198.5 × 16.2 cm) (1860.3)

in the twentieth—between *ergon* ("work") and *parergon* ("sidework")[2] sheds light on the variability in detailing Ashurnasirpal's garments and those of human and divine attendants on the palace reliefs. All "works" repetitively obey the basic parameters of the Assyrian body and its accoutrements; but some, and those differentially, are further exuberantly embellished with "sidework" that speaks to individual carvers' creativity, the reliefs' location,

and other parameters that elude us today but make each figure singular while simultaneously typical.

The Bowdoin relief that combines genie and king (pl. 2), which comes from a building other than the palace, brings another angle to the Kantian distinction. If the genie previously discussed is distinguished by superb aesthetic values, this relief, unusual both for its size and the details of its inscription, stands out for its historical value.

Extensive chisel marks mar its surface, the result of selective intentional defacement, most likely perpetrated by Babylonian, Median, and/or Elamite forces during Assyria's fall circa 612 BCE. Facial features, hands, and feet received the brunt of the enemy's iconoclastic wrath. Next to the battered figures appears a stunning *parergon*, a ghostly, disembodied head chiseled at a later time as if audaciously to challenge Ashurnasirpal's profile. Scholars identify it as the head of a now-ascendant enemy. Visual scrutiny reveals yet another *parergon*, a tiny profile lightly incised within this head, a sort of "cartoon" for the uncompleted addition.

The intent behind Ashurnasirpal's original artwork was preservation into the deep future, and warnings were issued against potential attackers. We know less about the eventual attackers because we only have the effects of their actions. An unusually contemplative statement comes from a later period when the Greco-Roman author Plutarch described the destruction wrought by Alexander the Great when he conquered Persepolis, the Persian capital, in the late fourth century BCE. There Alexander encountered a statue of the fifth-century king Xerxes, which "had been toppled from its pedestal and heedlessly left on the ground by a crowd of soldiers, as they forced their way into the palace, and Alexander stopped and spoke to it as though it were alive. 'Shall I pass by and leave you lying there because of the expedition you led against Greece, or shall I set you up again because of your magnanimity and your virtues in other respects?' For a long while he gazed at the statue and reflected in silence, and then went on his way."[3]

On their part, the Museum curators surely reflected on whether to repair and mask the damage on their relief, something readily accomplished by observing the details of the other Bowdoin fragments.[4] Its damaged state, however, is as telling about human affairs as was its original beauty. This version of iconoclasm[5] was not directed against images in general but against their referent, whether understood as Ashurnasirpal II or as an Assyrian king. By contrast, when Islamic State unleashed attention-seeking rage against Nimrud's antiquities in 2015, the stated target was imagery deemed idolatrous. Both versions of iconoclasm prove more complicated as we ponder their conscious or unconscious ideologies.

Ada Cohen
Professor of Art History and Israel Evans
Professor in Oratory and Belles Lettres,
Dartmouth College

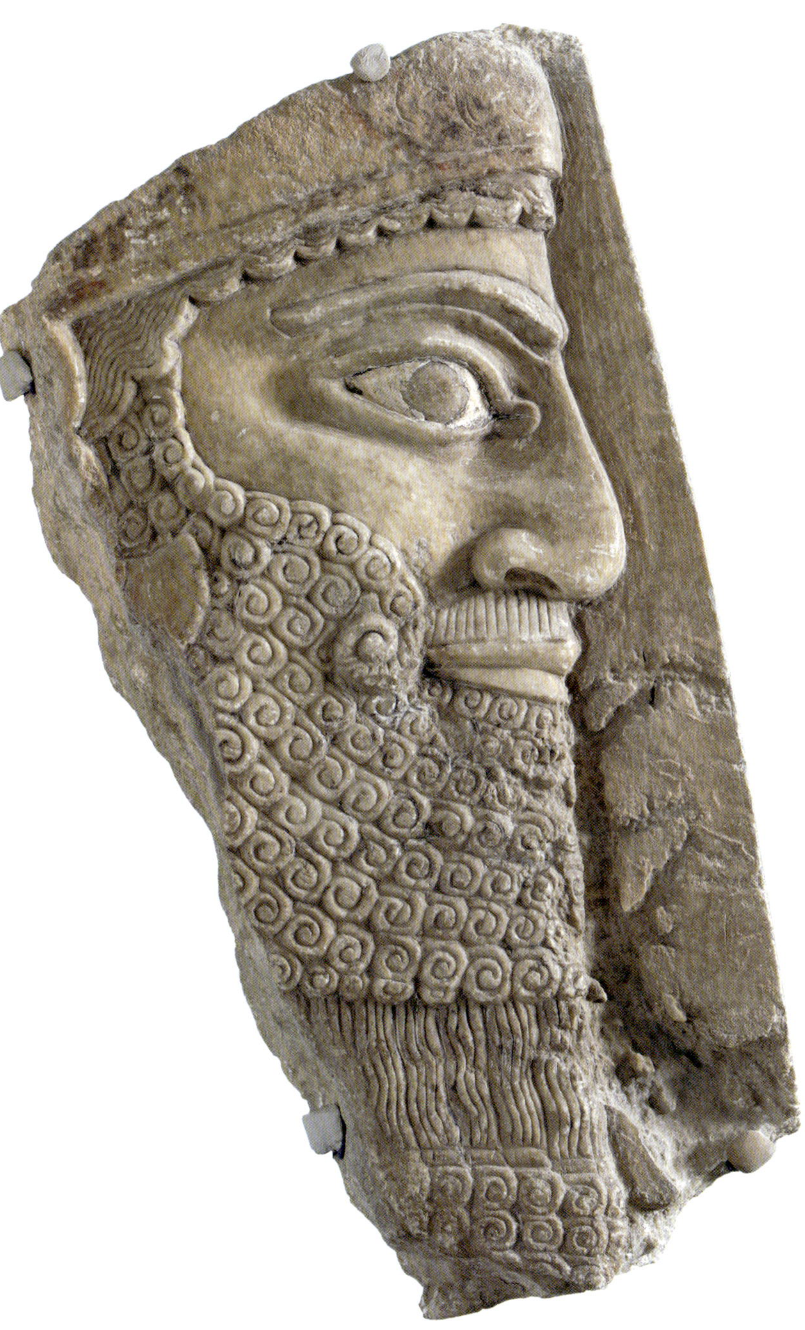

PLATE 3. *Head of Ashurnasirpal II.* Gypsum (Mosul alabaster) and traces of pigment, 13 9/16 × 7 1/16 in. (34.5 × 18 cm) (1906.4)

# Bail-handle Oinochoe or Olpe

Sappho Painter, c. 500–475 BCE
Greek (Attica)
Clay, 14⅝ × 5½ × 4½ in. (37.1 × 14 × 11.4 cm)
Museum Purchase, Adela Wood Smith Trust, in memory of Harry de Forest
Smith, Class of 1891  1984.23

Oinochoai are single-handled jugs used for pouring liquid such as wine (Greek: *oinos*). Bowdoin's oinochoe, with its ropelike handle, would not have permitted easy pouring. Rather, the vase, with its depiction of a funeral, was designed specifically to be placed with the deceased in a tomb as a burial offering. It is attributed to an artist known today as the Sappho Painter, who was active in Athens during the late sixth and early fifth centuries BCE as a vase painter using the black-figure technique. The Sappho Painter was fond of burial scenes and of adding nonsensical inscriptions to his compositions.

Here, the scene unfolds around the body of the vase. The elements suggest an interior, filled with figures young and old, female and male. At the center is the only known illustration of a body being placed in a coffin in preparation for the *ekphora*, or procession to the tomb. Upon death, the body would be laid out for viewing inside the home. For men, this laying out of the body, called the *prothesis*, would take place in the *andron*, a room reserved for male gatherings. The *prothesis* lasted for two days, and in the early hours of the third day, while still dark, the body would be conveyed to the cemetery for burial. The central image on the Bowdoin oinochoe includes details that recall this tradition: lamps suspended from the ceiling provide light for the assemblage, and the shield hanging above the deceased pinpoints the location as the *andron*.

The mourners gathered for this ritual, depicted in various activities that anticipate the procession, together provide a rare glimpse of the Greek family engaged in one of their most solemn tasks. An adult male lowers the head of the deceased into a coffin. Behind him, a woman reaches out toward the corpse; her central position suggests that she is either the wife or mother of the deceased. Two women, their hair disheveled from grief, assist with the feet of the dead man. Painted letters that resemble inscriptions fill the spaces between the figures but, aside from the text above the deceased, all defy translation. In the space above,

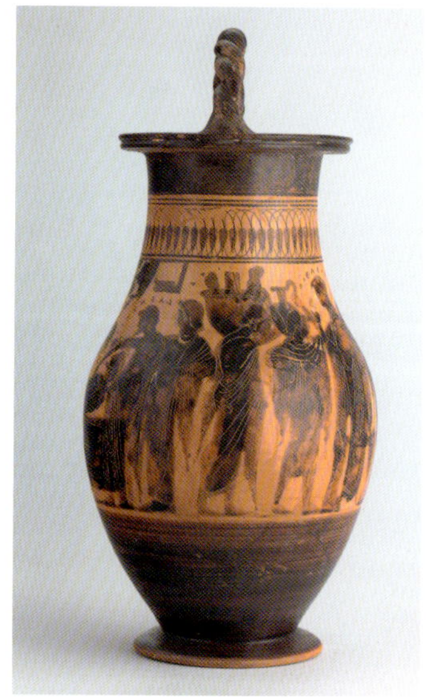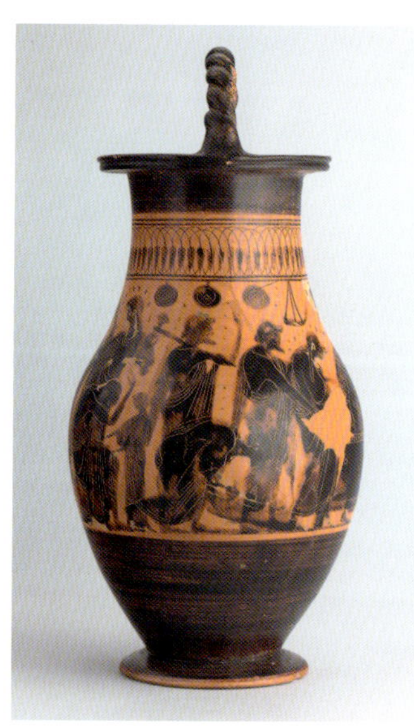

an inscription running right to left appears to read "lab[e] me lituta," or "hold me very gently."[1] Behind the women are two bearded men, one of whom holds an ax over his shoulder (possibly a carpenter). Their gestures suggest that they are bidding farewell to the dead man. Beside the man with the ax, a woman picks up a basket carrying cylindrical bottles called lekythoi. A lekythos is a container for oils or unguents and is often associated with burials. Seated on a stool, an old man mourns, consoled by a girl who reaches out to him with both arms. Behind, a woman cries and wipes her tears while another comforts her. The final group of two men and a woman appear to carry supplies for the burial feast to be held after the body is laid to rest. Though not specifically depicted, this oinochoe is clearly self-conscious of the use of vessels in the Greek funeral.

James Higginbotham
Associate Professor of Classics on the
Henry Johnson Professorship Fund
and Curator for the Ancient Collection,
Bowdoin College

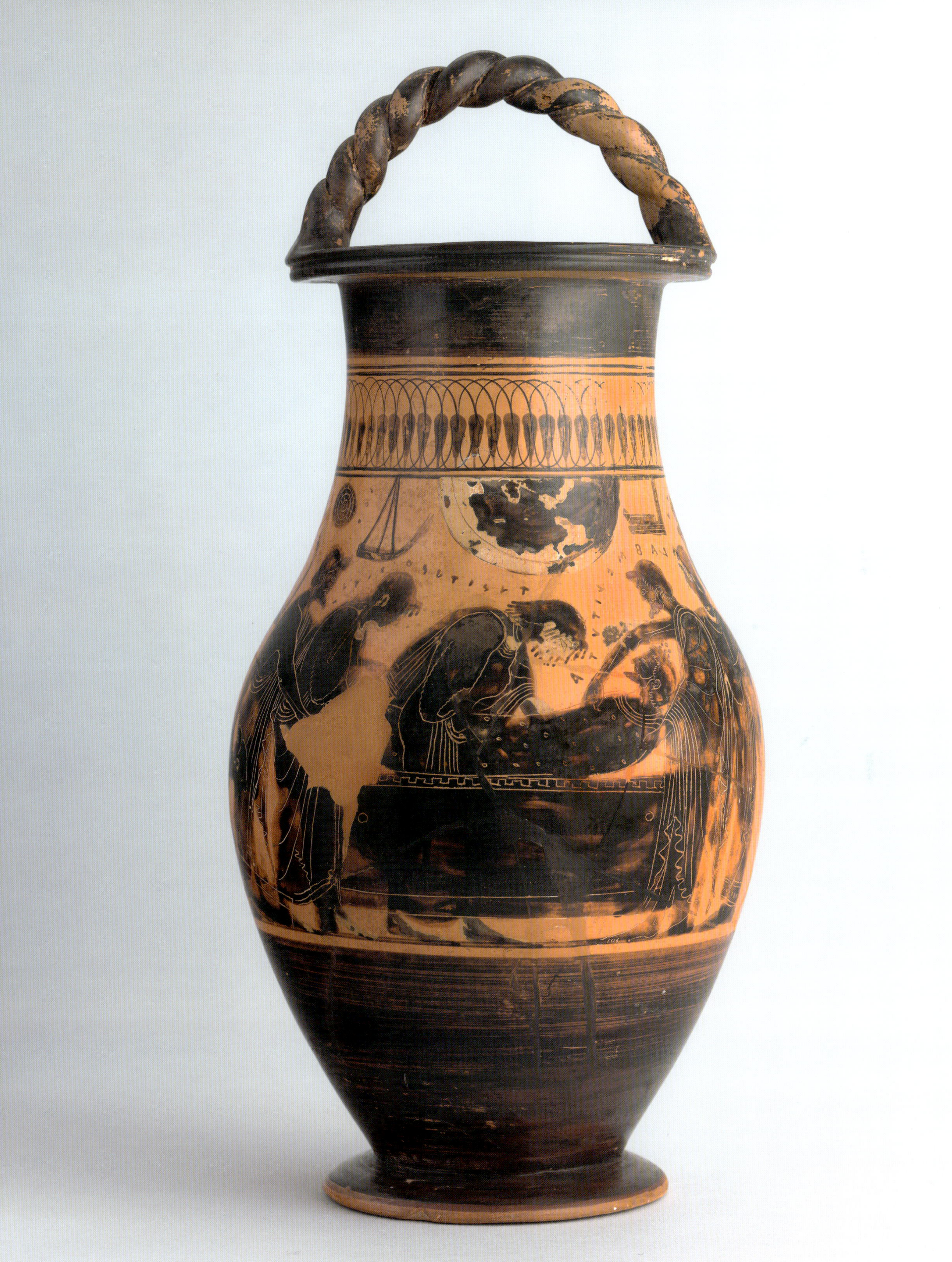

# Decadrachm of Syracuse

Original die created by Euainetos, c. 400 BCE
Greek (Sicily), minted in Syracuse under Dionysius I
Silver, diameter 1⁵⁄₁₆ in. (3.4 cm)
Gift of Edward Perry Warren, Esq., Honorary Degree, 1926  1914.6.1

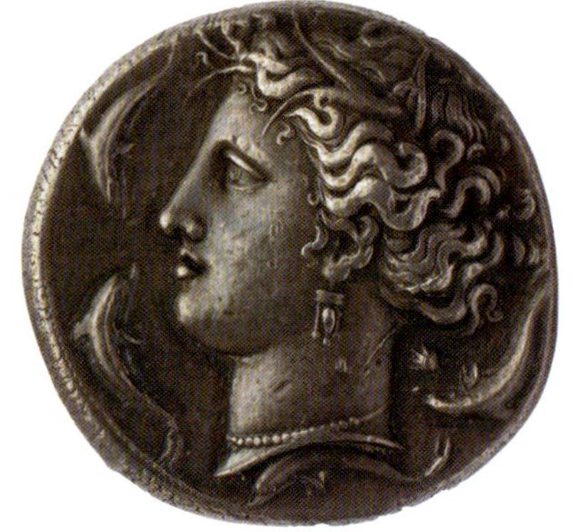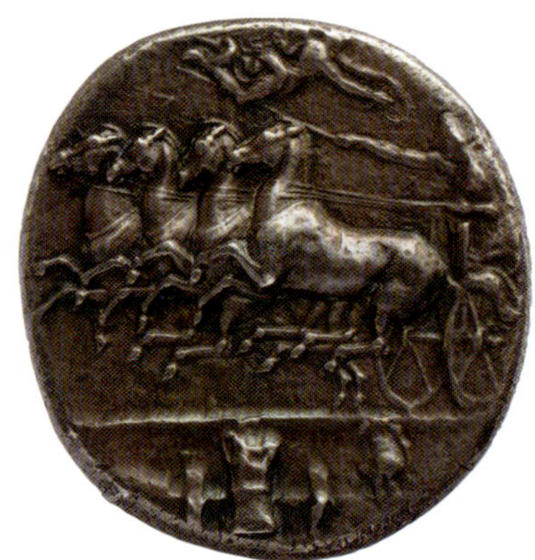

The decadrachm, one of the largest silver coins minted by the Greeks, was issued only on rare occasions and by just a few Greek cities. Prominent among these was the Sicilian city of Syracuse, located on the southwest coast of the island. Syracuse was established as a Greek colony during the eighth century BCE and prospered to become one of the most powerful city-states in the Mediterranean, a rival of Athens, Carthage, and Republican Rome. During the rule of the Syracusan tyrant Dionysius I (c. 405–367 BCE), an unusual series of large silver coins was minted in the city, many with dies prepared by the master Sicilian engravers Euainetos and Kimon, who incorporated signatures on many examples of their works. Though the Bowdoin coin is unsigned, the artist's distinct style permits a confident attribution to Euainetos's workshop.

This coin was struck using two carved dies: one, the obverse, was secured to an anvil-like work surface, and the other, the reverse, was placed in the end of a metal punch. A blank disk of silver, carefully weighed, was placed over the anvil die, then the punch was positioned on the other side of the blank. With a hard and precise hammer stroke to the punch, both sides of the coin were impressed at once. In Syracuse, unlike the standard elsewhere, the portrait head was, early on, part of the reverse design. This harkens back to the archaic coining tradition at Syracuse where a small image of Arethusa or Persephone was placed at the center of a quadripartite square on the coin's reverse. The portrait "grew" over time but remained on the reverse. Toward the end of the fourth century BCE, Syracuse finally conformed to the normal configuration and "flipped" the design.

In line with this tradition, the reverse of this large denomination presents the beautiful portrait in profile of the water nymph Arethusa surrounded by four dolphins. She wears a wreath of reeds, a pendant earring, and a necklace. A small scallop shell behind her neck may complement the aquatic scene or be a signature mark of the artist. According to legend, the Nereid Arethusa, pursued by the river god Alpheus, fled her home in Arcadia under the sea and emerged as a freshwater spring on the island of Ortygia in Syracuse. Arethusa's spring, still visible today, was believed to flow underground linking distant parts of the Mediterranean with Sicily, and thus she symbolized the divine origins of Syracuse and the city's connection to Greece.

On the obverse, a charioteer drives a quadriga, a four-horse chariot, with a winged Nike crowning the driver from above. Below the ground line appears a warrior's armor: a cuirass between two greaves, with a Phrygian helmet to the right. The chariot on Syracusan coins is emblematic of the culture and self-image of those minting coins in the city. The ruling class used coins to communicate their elevated status as wealthy men of leisure with expensive tastes, chariot-racing chief among them. The horse teams sponsored by prominent Syracusans, among them the tyrants Hieron I and Dionysius I, won victories at the Olympic Games.

Coins of this size were of little use in everyday exchange and may have served as pay for the soldiers and mercenaries in Dionysius's employ. Minted in small numbers, most of the issues circulated for a very short time and were subsequently melted down, accounting for their relative rarity today.

James Higginbotham

# Fish Plate

Perrone–Phrixos Group, c. 360–320 BCE
Apulian
Terracotta, 1¾ × 7⁹⁄₁₆ in. (4.5 × 19.2 cm)
Museum Purchase, Adela Wood Smith Trust  2018.1

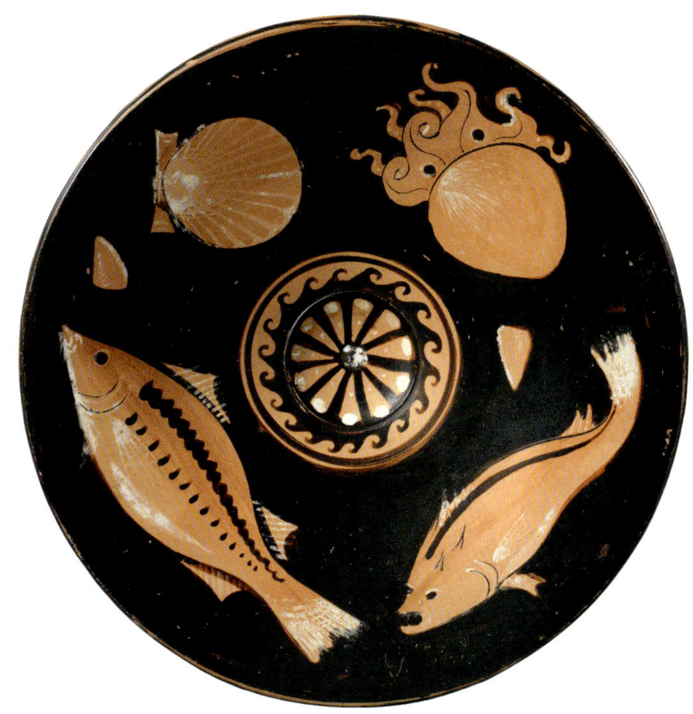

"Fish plates" take their modern name from the maritime themes illustrated on most decorated examples. Although the ancient name for this shape is uncertain, two possibilities are attested. The word *oxybaphon*, literally "vinegar saucer" in ancient Greek, was found inscribed on the bottom of a fish plate discovered at the Greek city of Olynthos. The more likely name, and closer to the modern label, is *pinakiskos ichthyeros*, or "fishy little painted boards or plates," which is attested in a comedy of Aristophanes first performed in 388 BCE.

While the fish plate may have had its beginnings as a design created in ancient Athenian workshops, the type was most popular among potters and painters in Sicily and southern Italy. This area, known in antiquity as Magna Graeca, was home to many of the most prosperous Greek colonies beginning in the eighth century BCE. As Athenian ceramic exports declined in the fourth century BCE, South Italian artists served the market with their own production of expressive red-figure ceramics. Workshops in the regions of Apulia, Campania, Lucania (Paestum), and the island of Sicily account for about 80 percent of the known fish plates.

Fish plates were designed with stout downturned rims, or edges, where the vessel could be grasped, and equipped with a small concave cup at the plate's center to hold sauces or juices. All figural examples are decorated using the red-figure technique. The body of the vessel is largely painted with a glaze (or slip) that turns black once fired in a kiln. The "figures" and other decorative elements are left reserved, or unglazed, so they turn red to orange during the firing process. Finally, dilute glazes and pigments were often applied to delineate shapes and accentuate details. In many South Italian examples, the palette of added color (*sovradipinto*) included white, deep red, pink, and yellow.

The Bowdoin fish plate is a complete (unrestored) example attributed to the Perrone-Phrixos Group. Arthur Dale Trendall, the eminent authority on ancient South Italian ceramics, considered this group to include the most accomplished of the ancient Greco-Apulian painters.[1] The

plate is set on a hollow foot that has a short stem and a ring base. The rim, painted with a laurel-leaf pattern, is turned down, and the central circular depression is decorated with an eleven-petaled rosette framed by a wave-pattern border. The gently sloping floor between the rim and the central depression provides the canvas for the detailed illustrations depicting "living" maritime species. As a final flourish, white and red pigment add detail and volume to the figures.

Though ancient artists are known to have taken liberties with taxonomic details, some of the species depicted here can be identified. They are arrayed as if swimming in the sea, moving right to left around the vase in a clockwise composition that includes an octopus, a telline or wedge shell, an anglerfish or monkfish, a drum fish (?), another telline, and a scallop shell. The inclusion of smaller sea creatures between larger ones is characteristic of Apulian fish plates, helping to fill the voids and creating a highly decorative effect. All species represented on this plate were part of the diet in the ancient Mediterranean but also could be observed in their native coastal shallows.

The fish plate is one of the more iconic forms associated with this region's artistic production, and while the ceramic shape is fairly common, just over 1,000 decorated examples exist in collections today. Fish plates have been found in various archaeological contexts that suggest uses connected to dining and meals associated with burial practice. The decoration on the most detailed plates, including this example, provide rare illustrations of Mediterranean sea life.

James Higginbotham

# Marble Relief of a Sleeping Heracles

Roman, 2nd or 1st century BCE
Marble, 36 × 30⅛ × 5½ in. (91.5 × 76.5 × 14 cm)
Gift of Edward Perry Warren, Esq., Honorary Degree, 1926  1906.2

This unusual marble relief—a large fragment with a rare subject from the Hellenistic period—features the large, sprawled nude body of a drunken Heracles along with four nude boys (wingless erotes). The bearded Heracles rests on his lion skin, while two of the boys struggle to lift his knotted club as if to steal it. Another boy is halfway into a wine cup held limply in the hero's left hand—a droll vignette of drinking the dregs. Beneath him, a boy carries off a small two-handled amphora. The mighty Heracles is shown as a vulnerable mortal being duped by impish boys. In this way, the artist has presented an amusing and engaging scene, a hallmark of Hellenistic art. The fragment may well be part of a representation of the myth of Heracles being sold as a slave to the Lydian queen Omphale. A Pompeian fresco, a century or two later than the Bowdoin relief, preserves a version of this scene—a clothed, beardless Heracles lays on the ground, drunk and harassed by five male toddlers (fig. 1). The enthroned queen looks down on him from the upper left corner of the painting.

Such imagery went well beyond humor. Hellenistic artists were creative in their retelling of popular myths, casting them as allegories in order to highlight their moral implications. In this case, the artist played on the theme of Heracles's submission to Eros, represented by his sexual liaison with the queen and by the mischievous erotes. This was an effective visual means to explore the human experience of powerlessness in the face of overwhelming desire. Even the mightiest of heroes and gods succumb to the power of Aphrodite, goddess of desire and mother of the erotes. In the same vein, ancient artists depicted Mars, the god of war, as being disarmed by a small army of erotes. A relief in the Museum of Fine Arts, Boston (Res.08.34d)—a gift of Edward Perry Warren, the same donor of the Bowdoin relief—demonstrates the hero's weakness in an erotic encounter that takes place outdoors near a rustic shrine. Heracles reclines on his lion skin beneath a woman, most likely Omphale. The ancients would have understood this to represent a feminization of the hero and his submission to a more powerful divine force, Love. Such reliefs may well have been hung on the walls of private bedrooms or stood on pillars in ancient gardens. In the Hellenistic period, popular epigrams played on the weakness of Heracles and the surprising power of Eros, who is sometimes envisioned holding the club of Heracles and wearing his lion skin.

The American classicist Edward Perry Warren (1860–1928), known as Ned, was a dealer and collector of antiquities as well as a writer and philosopher.[1] While it is unclear why Warren chose to be so generous to Bowdoin,[2] he was the source of the College's many interesting Greek and Roman antiquities. At the turn of the twentieth century, Warren and his close associates (especially John Marshall) became the pivotal tastemakers of their generation for the collecting of antiquities. Their insights and connoisseurship played a formative role in shaping the world-class collections of classical art at the Museum of Fine Arts in Boston and The Metropolitan Museum of Art in New York. Warren's circle was particularly drawn to works that revealed the Greek penchant for homoerotic subjects. In that respect, their collecting tastes were remarkably perspicacious, and today their selection of works of art offers unique insights into ancient life.

Christine Kondoleon
George D. and Margo Behrakis Senior
Curator, Greek and Roman Art, Museum of
Fine Arts, Boston

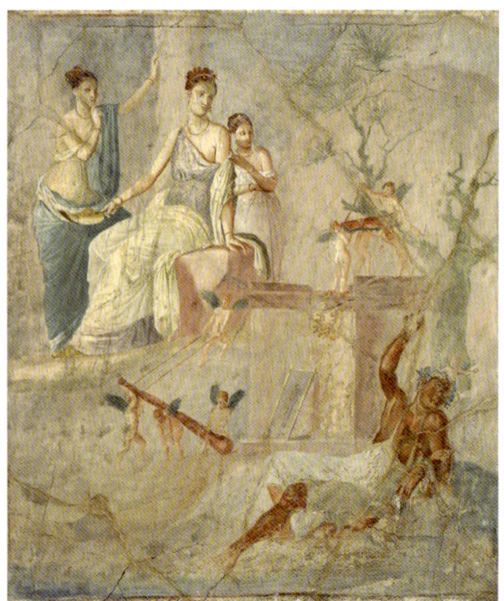

FIG. 1. *Drunken Heracles at the Feet of Omphale.* Fresco. Casa del Forno di Ferro, Pompeii, 1st century CE. Museo Archeologico Nazionale, Naples, 8624

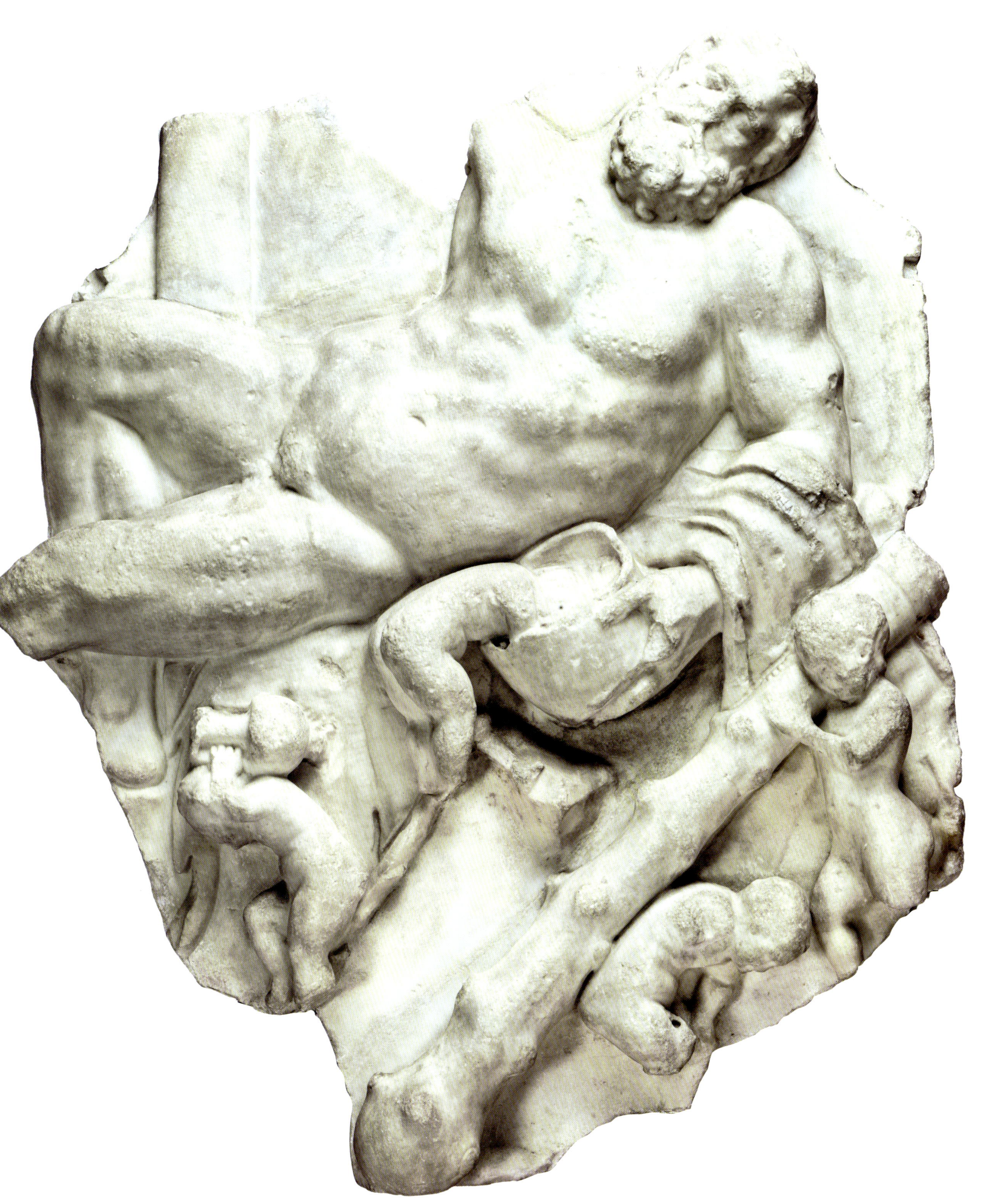

# *Portrait of a Youth Wearing a Gilded Wreath*

Roman Egypt (Fayum?), 100–200 CE
Wood (limewood, *tilia*), wax-based paint (encaustic), and gold leaf, 15½ × 8 × ⅟₁₆ in. (39.4 × 20.3 × 0.16 cm)
Museum Purchase, Adela Wood Smith Trust  2015.38

He lived more than 1,800 years ago, a member of a prosperous settlement founded close to the banks of the Nile River. Egyptians, Greeks, and Romans made up the core of diverse communities like his, and their art blended traditions spanning nearly 3,000 years. When the youth died, he was buried following the ancient Egyptian practice of mummification, which included a portrait so that the deceased could be recognized in the afterlife. While the use of mummy portraits extended back to pharaonic times, the Bowdoin work belongs to a tradition of Greek panel painting practiced in Roman Egypt and generically called Fayum portraits.

The earliest Fayum portraits date from the late first century BCE, and their production ended around the mid-third century CE. Fewer than a thousand examples survive from antiquity, and almost all of these come from Egypt, where burial practices and environmental conditions conspired to leave us this rare example of ancient painting.

The Bowdoin portrait depicts the head and upper torso of a young male, perhaps only fifteen or sixteen years of age. He wears a dark red tunic with a mantle over one shoulder. The youth is beardless and sports a tuft of hair, or "Horus lock," tied with ribbons that hang down over his right shoulder. The figure faces forward and looks toward the viewer from an angle that is slightly turned. The boy's face is illuminated from an imagined light source that shines from his right. The portrait was painted on a thin panel of wood in an encaustic technique using pigments blended in hot wax. After a base coat of whitewash (distemper or white lead), the wax-based colors, either molten or emulsified with egg or oil, were applied with a brush and could be shaped with a harder tool in a painstaking process highly prized in the Greco-Roman world. An ancient epigram conveys the prestige of the technique:

Blessed is he who painted you and blessed is this wax
that knew how to be vanquished by your beauty.
—*Anthologia Graeca* XII:90

It is uncertain whether this portrait represents the age when the youth died or looks back to an earlier moment in his life. Current research suggests that these portraits were painted well before death and meant for public or domestic display. Upon death, and after the lengthy process preparing the body for the afterlife, the portrait was trimmed and placed over the head of the mummy. The edges were then carefully secured in the wrapping with strips of linen, leaving the face of the portrait exposed. As a final touch, gold leaf was applied to frame the face and to create a wreath of leaves and flowers around the head. The gold preserves the line where the linen wrappings stopped.

Under Greco-Roman rule, Egypt was the site of several Greek settlements, mostly concentrated in Alexandria, but also in a few other cities, where Greek settlers lived alongside native Egyptians. The earliest inhabitants of the Egyptian Fayum were Greek soldier-veterans and elite military officials, or *cleruchs*, who were settled by the Ptolemaic kings on reclaimed lands. Native Egyptians also came to settle in Fayum from all over the country to undertake the labor involved in the land reclamation process, as attested by personal names, local cults, and recovered papyri. By the Roman period, much of the "Greek" population of Fayum was made up of either Hellenized Egyptians or people of mixed Egyptian-Greek origins. The Fayum mummy portrait is an important expression of the Greek presence in Egypt and the enduring Hellenic traditions in this part of Africa.

James Higginbotham

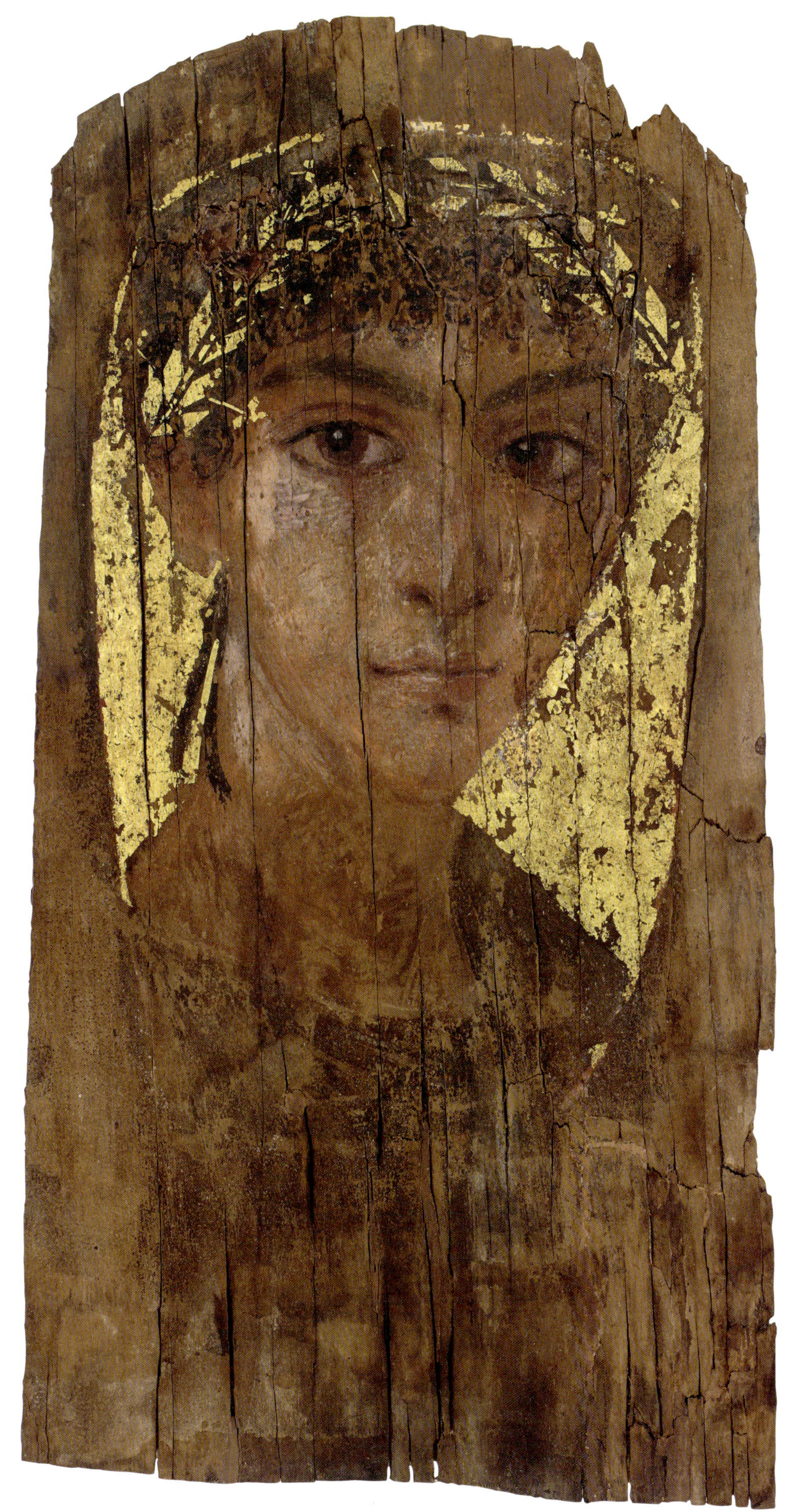

# Portrait Head of Emperor Antoninus Pius

Roman, c. 140–150 CE
Marble, 14¹⁵⁄₁₆ × 8³⁄₁₆ × 8¹¹⁄₁₆ in. (38 × 20.8 × 22 cm)
Gift of Edward Perry Warren, Esq., Honorary Degree, 1926  1906.1

In this tranquil and sympathetically carved countenance of the Roman emperor Antoninus Pius (r. 138–161 CE), we may detect echoes not only of the calm, composed demeanor of the emperor himself, but of the stability and peacefulness of his reign, a period during which Rome experienced no revolts or uprisings. Created within the first decade of his reign, the Bowdoin portrait shows the emperor with his head turned to the left, his eyes directed ahead and slightly upward. Originally part of a larger statue or portrait bust, the elegantly carved fragment takes full advantage of the Parian marble of which it is carved, a material highly prized in antiquity for its fine grain, even coloring, and translucent quality.

The image offers the impression of a mature ruler able to bear the cares of state with poise. Gentle furrows in the forehead and on either side of the nose allude subtly to Antoninus's age (he was then in his fifties). The brows, heavy and undercut, droop ever so slightly over the outsides of deep-set eyes. These are drilled at the ducts and feature scribed irises and half-moon pupils. Their distant gaze lends the emperor a careworn, resolute expression.

The hair is swept forward from the crown, falling over the brow in clusters of artfully arranged curls that sit heavily at the temples and cover the tops of the ears. Deep modeling and extensive use of the drill create dramatic shadows. Like the hair, the beard was the product of careful grooming. It appears fuller at the sides but trimmed close to the face at the chin and underneath, with a carefully clipped mustache and a tuft of hair under the lower lip. The emperor's curly locks and beard create an essential contrast with his smooth skin, an effect originally heightened by paint, red traces of which remain.

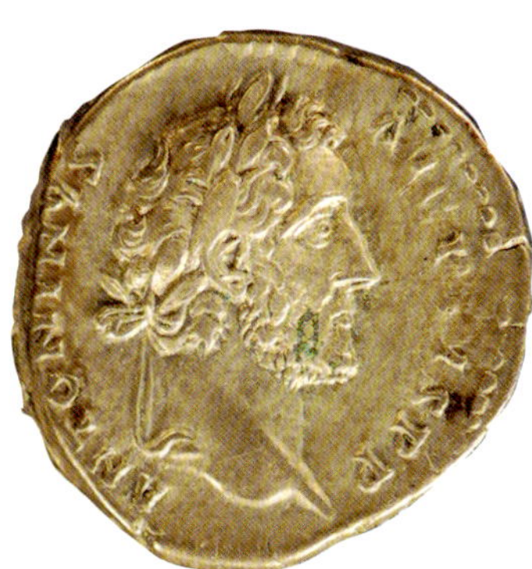

FIG. 1. Denarius of Antoninus Pius, 145–161 CE. Silver. Bowdoin College Museum of Art, Gift of Mr. and Mrs. Mark M. Salton, 1997.21.105

Despite his relatively long reign, only two portrait types of Antoninus Pius exist. The earlier and much more common is the "Formia" type, of which the Bowdoin portrait is an example. More than 100 copies of this type exist, all characterized by pincerlike locks of hair on the forehead, heavy curls at the temples, and a subtly furrowed brow. In this group, the Bowdoin portrait is one of roughly two dozen that take a freer approach to rendering the essential characteristics, especially the curls of the hair and beard, resulting in a more natural look. On more precisely composed examples, such as the one in the Munich Glyptothek (337), the hair is even more deeply modeled, and the beard is composed in places of individual ringlets.

Antoninus Pius left Rome only twice, and it was through his portraiture, scattered across the Roman world on coins (fig. 1), mosaics, public monuments, and bronze and marble busts and statues, that his image—and authority—were recognized. Such objects asserted the emperor's rule throughout an empire of over 50 million people covering nearly two million square miles. The propagandistic potential of portraiture was not lost on the imperial courts of Rome. Each carefully curated the image of the emperor, and the attention lavished on the hair and beards indicates that these were particular focal points for both distinguishing successive emperors and communicating dynastic continuity. Hadrian, who adopted Antoninus Pius as his heir, was the first emperor to sport a beard, and male fashion (and imperial portraits) followed suit for years after. Antoninus's close-cropped and carefully groomed beard hews closely to Hadrian's, while his prominent brows and heavy eyelids also evoke images of his predecessor. These shared features suggest that much attention was paid to signaling the legitimacy of Antoninus's succession as an adoptive son and thereby the stability of the imperial dynasty.

Sean Burrus
Andrew W. Mellon Postdoctoral Curatorial Fellow, Bowdoin College

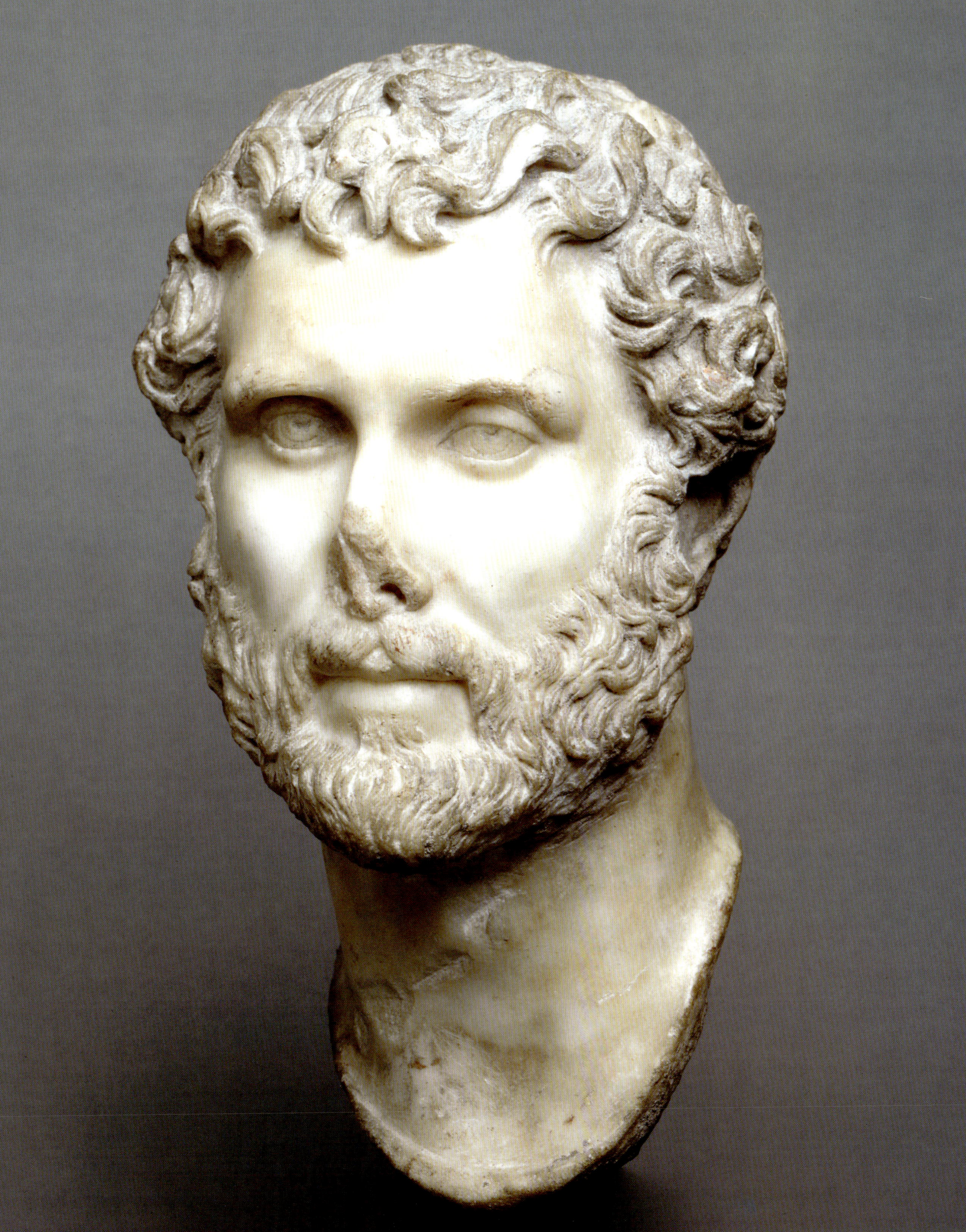

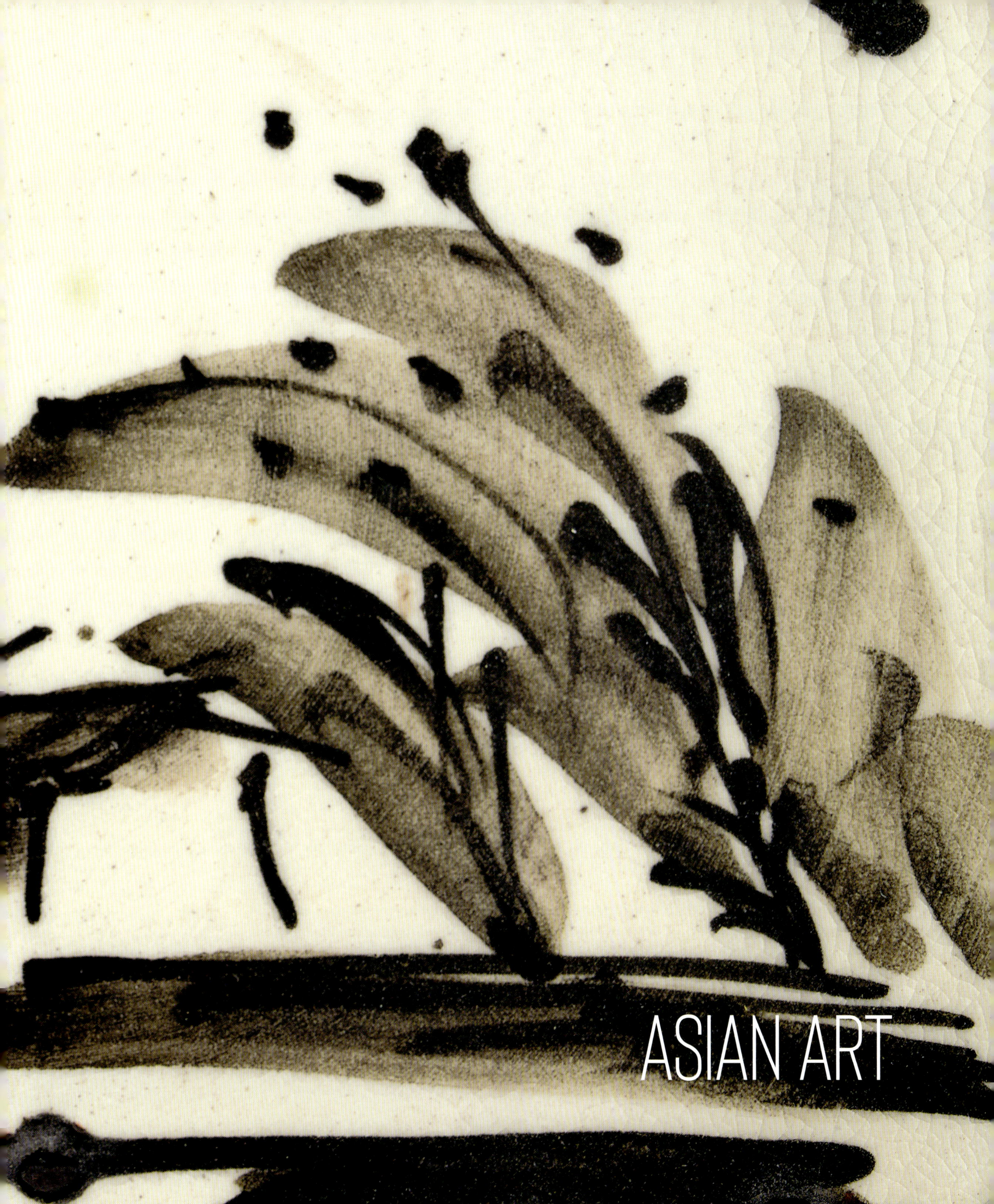
ASIAN ART

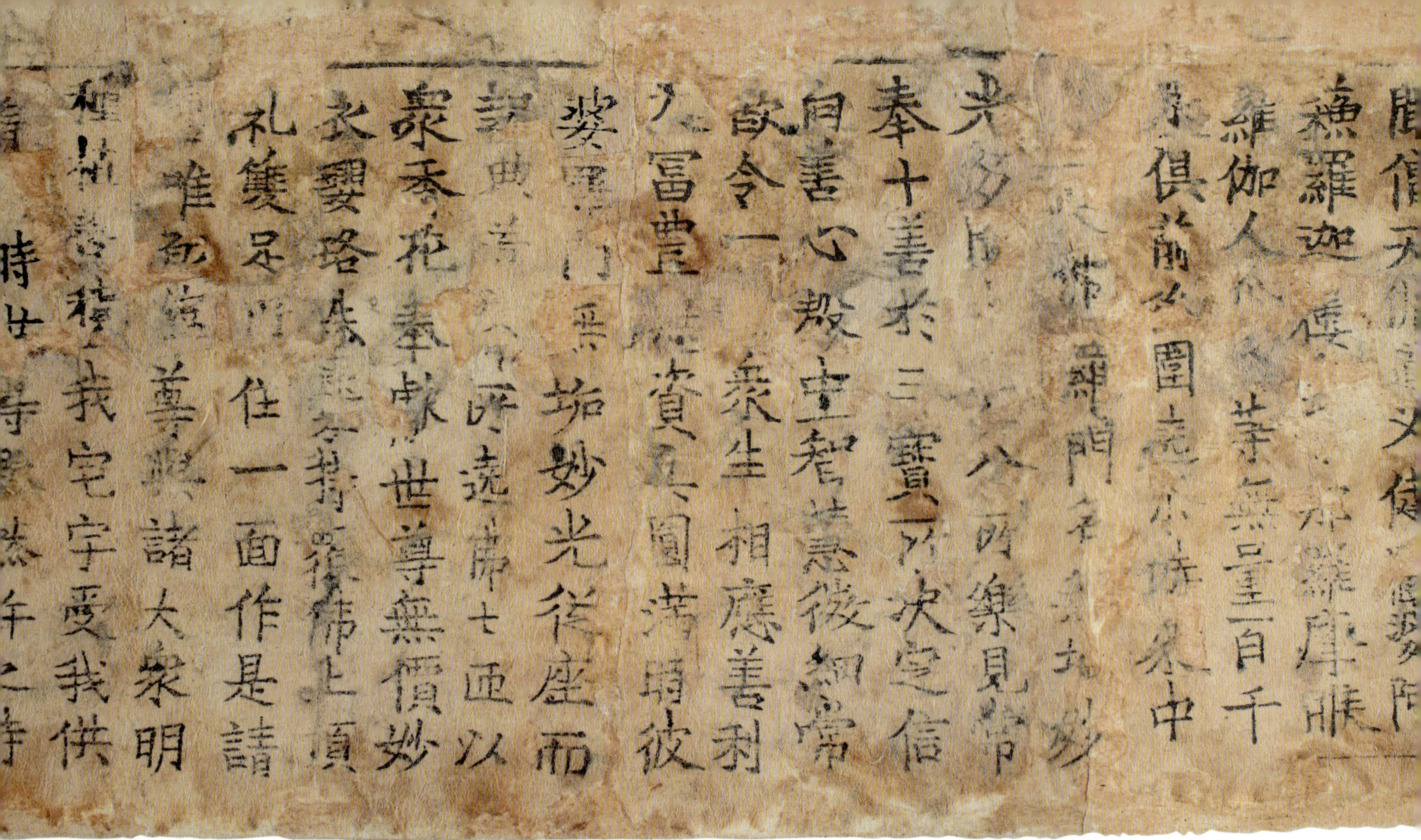

# Amitabha Dharani Sutra from Leifeng Pagoda

Chinese, 975
Ink on paper, 2⅞ × 81⅜ in. (7.3 × 206.7 cm)
Gift of Mr. Charles R. Bennett, Class of 1907  1957.55

Visitors entering the upper gallery of the Bowdoin College Museum of Art are greeted by six immense sculptures in bas-relief from the royal palace at Nimrud, a magnificent cultural treasure that includes among its distinctive features numerous lines of cuneiform text cut on the gypsum surface by Assyrian scribes. Mesopotamia, where these panels were produced in the ninth century BCE, is where writing as we know it emerged 2,000 years before that. The medium then was abundantly available on the ground of this rich alluvial plain between the Tigris and Euphrates rivers, pliable clay that could be moistened, shaped into tablets, incised with wedge-shaped characters by a sharpened reed, then baked solid in the searing sun or by a fireside—giving us what amounts to humanity's first books.

The introduction of paper to the world as an instrument of textual transmission, and the equally miraculous application of woodblock printing, were each a marvel of ingenuity so consequential that both are regarded by the Chinese who developed them in the early years of the common era as two of their outstanding inventions.

A single object in the Bowdoin art collections, the Buddhist scroll printed on handmade paper known as *Amitabha Dharani Sutra from Leifeng Pagoda*, illustrates these advancements—the kind of transitional milestones called "defining technologies" by some, "paradigm shifts" by others. Dating precisely to 975, it has a dedicatory inscription that gives the time of year, the eighth month, when it was deposited in the brick temple of the Western

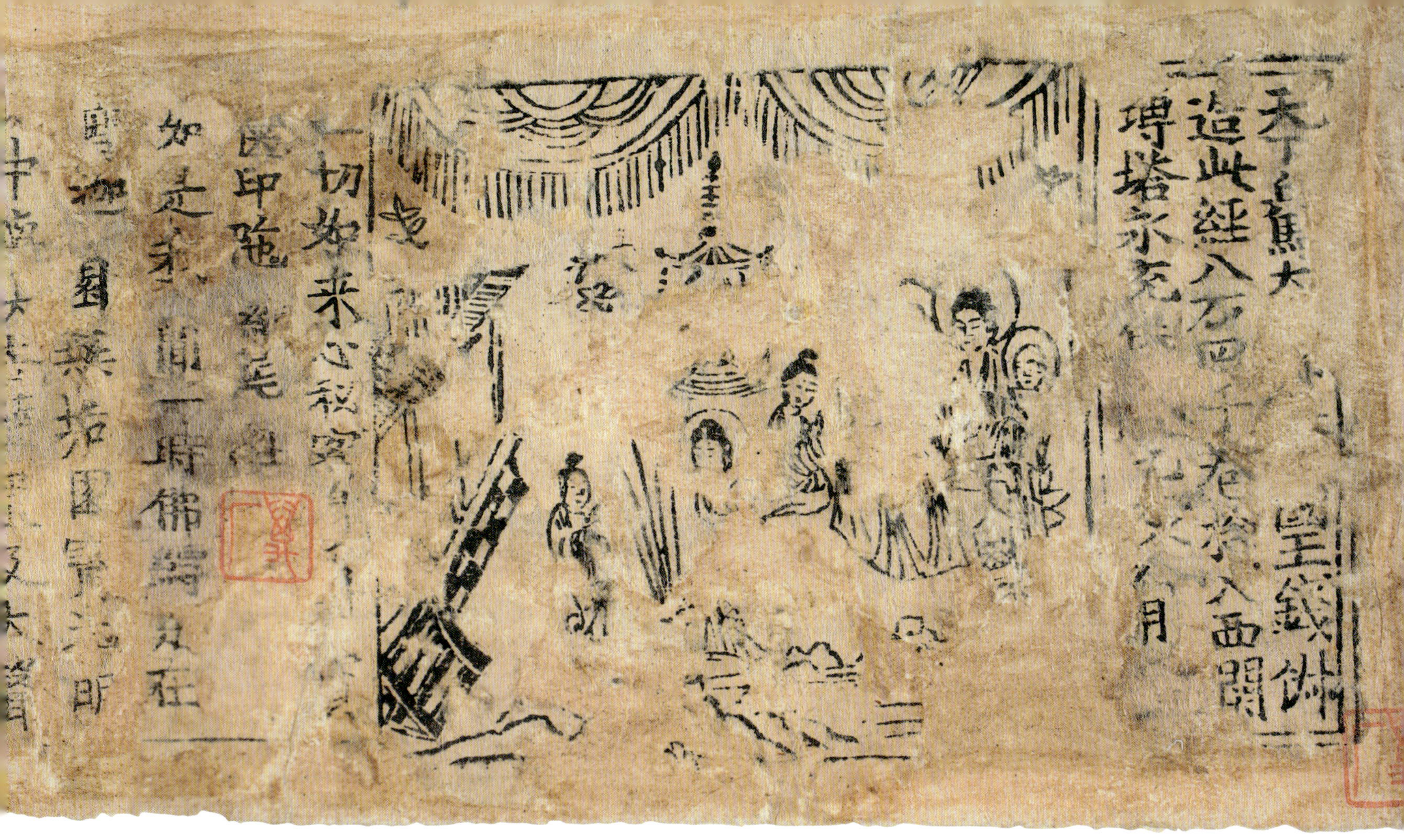

Gate, known as the Leifeng Pagoda. In conformance with a Buddhist tradition that mandates the widest possible distribution of sacred charms and sutras, the document also states that Qian Chu, the king of Wuyue (in present-day Hangzhou), had commissioned 84,000 copies. The only expeditious way to comply with such a formidable task was through a means of replication, in this instance woodblock printing.

To make a sheet of paper, according to the original Chinese formula, a slurry of beaten mulberry, hemp, and rag fragments is passed through a screen mold; the thin film left behind is then dried to produce what Sir Francis Bacon called "an absolutely singular substance." The process demands finesse, and has to be taught. Because virtually any vegetative source will work in papermaking, the formula is adaptable to regional resources, and thus highly mobile. By the late tenth century, when the scroll at Bowdoin was produced, the proprietary formula had already been brought to Korea and Japan by Buddhist monks, and was making its way in the other direction along the Silk Road. From Central Asia, it proceeded into the Middle East and North Africa, crossing from Morocco to southern Spain around 1150; a country by country migration continued through Europe over the next three centuries, England being among the last to come on line, in 1490.

Germany's first paper mill, meanwhile, had been established in Nuremberg in 1390; about sixty years later, in Mainz, Johannes Gutenberg developed an apparatus for printing that used movable metal type. Elizabeth Eisenstein titled a seminal book on the seismic ramifications of what followed *The Printing Press as an Agent of Change*. It is all part of a grand continuum, one that is enlivened for our edification by the availability of material artifacts such as the *Amithaba Dharani Sutra* that allow us to appreciate, and fully consider, the wonder of it all.

Nicholas A. Basbanes
Independent scholar and author

# Bowl

Persian, 1175–1225

Earthenware, 3⅝ × 8½ in. (9.2 × 21.6 cm)

Gift of Miss Elizabeth P. Martin  1968.33

This eye-catching bowl is a striking example of Persian Minai ware, executed in turquoise glaze with blue and black underglaze, and overglazed accents painted in characteristic white, red, and gold. The tondo, the medallion at the bottom of the bowl, bears the image of an Arabian camel lavishly outfitted with a rich red blanket patterned with stars and gilded tack. Minai wares such as this represented a technical advance for Persian ceramists. Where previous decoration had been restricted to underglazed motifs painted or incised in slips of limited colors, typically blues and black, Minai wares (from the Arabic word for glaze) are so-named for the introduction of overglaze painting, which allowed vase painters to use additional colors, such as the red, white, and gold accents featured here on the camel's saddle and halter. With a variety of colors at their disposal and a freer technique, the artists responsible for Minai wares were able to execute more complex and naturalistic scenes, drawing heavily on contemporary traditions of book illustration and illumination. As is typical for surviving examples of Minai ware, this piece features extensive modern restorations. (SPB)

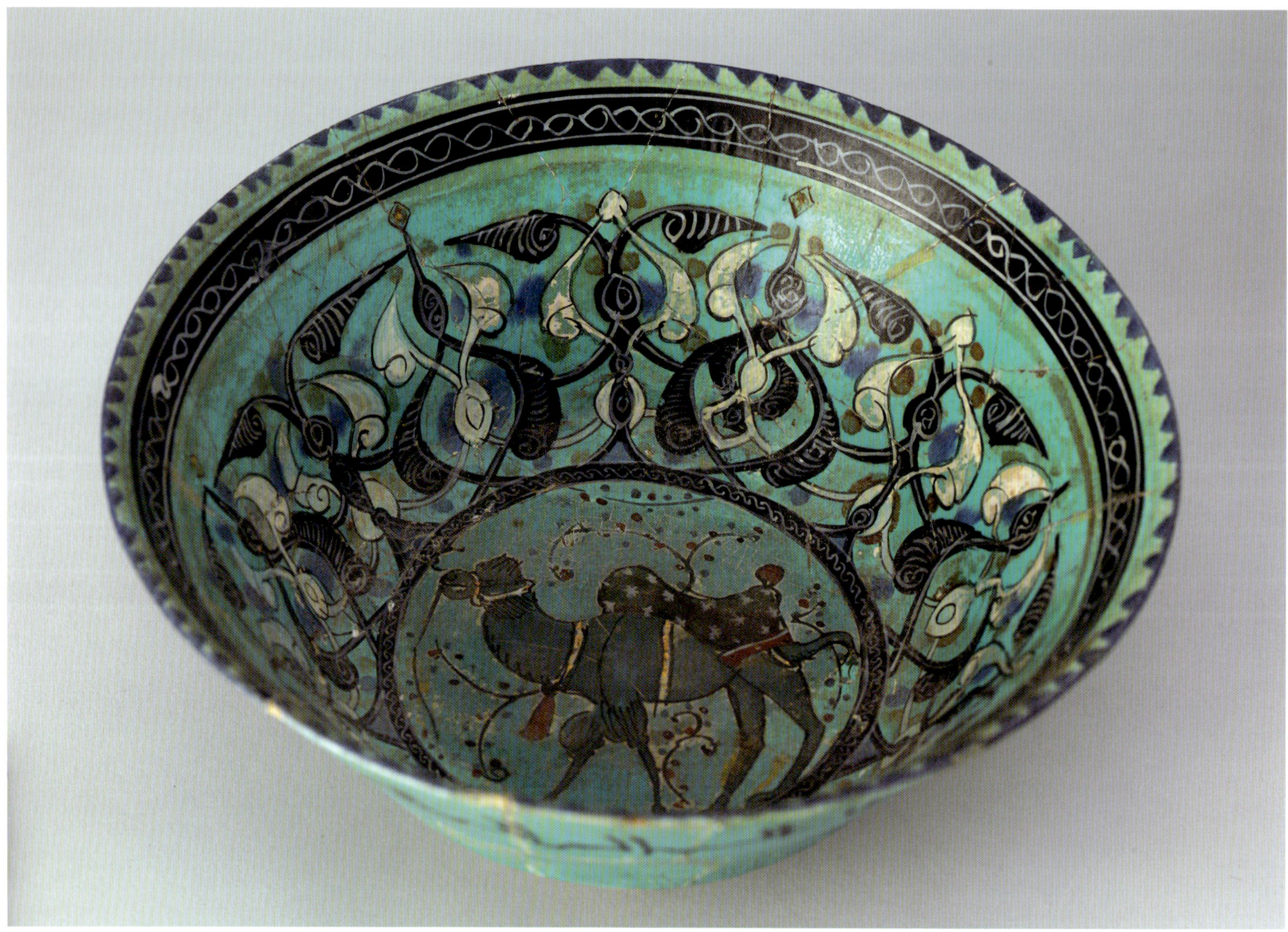

# Folio from the *Materia Medica* of Dioscorides

Probably Baghdad, probably 13th century
Ink and gouache on laid paper, 11¾ × 7¹⁵⁄₁₆ (29.8 × 20.1 cm)
Museum Purchase  1962.29

This thirteenth-century folio is a fragment from a much larger manuscript documenting the medicinal uses of plants, animals, and minerals. Originally written in Greek by physician Pedanius Dioscorides (c. 40–90 CE), *De Materia Medica*, or "The Materials of Medicine," identified more than 700 medicines, serving as the preeminent source on pharmacology for nearly 1,500 years. Dioscorides's descriptions of botanical specimens provided new knowledge of the natural world and new uses for natural resources. This particular folio depicts the Elder Tree, said to both expel water and be bad for the stomach. Pendulous clusters of dark berries branch off from the foliated stem, and fluffy white flowers emerge from the top. The flowers' white pigment has worn over the years, leaving ambiguous smudges clustered around the buds at the top of the stem.

Translated into Latin, Syriac, Arabic, and Persian, Dioscorides's text was widely recognized as a foundational study in the development of Eastern and Western pharmacology and botany. Its translation into Arabic and Syriac during the Islamic science period in the eighth century prompted the development of a new Arabic botanical classification system. As scholar Rifat Yildirim explains, because Dioscorides compiled his research from all over the world, translators were unable to identify equivalent botanical and medicinal names for all of the specimens. However, because it was such an important resource, they altered their taxonomy to better align with the new scientific data. (HW)

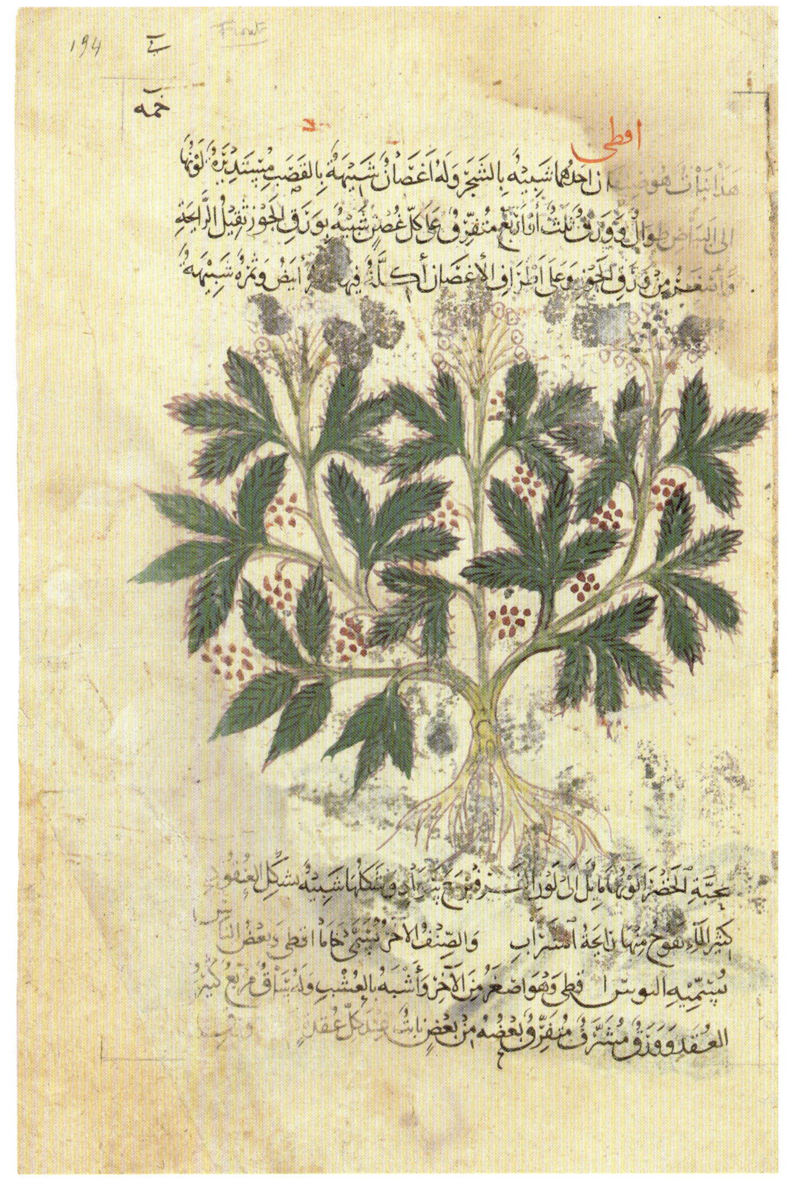

# Leaf from the *Book of the Seven Climes* by Abū al‑Qāsim al‑ʿIrāqī

Probably Egypt, 13th century
Tempera on laid paper, 11¾ × 7⅞ in. (29.9 × 20 cm)
Gift of Miss Elizabeth P. Martin  1968.82

This single leaf is likely all that survives of the earliest known copy of an Arabic alchemical work called the *Book of the Seven Climes with Allegorical Illustrations* (*Kitāb al-aqālīm al-ṣabʿa dhāt al-ṣuwar al-tashābīh*). Abū al-Qāsim Muḥammad ibn Aḥmad al-ʿIrāqī is best remembered as an alchemist who wrote books on various forms of magic, including *sīmīyā*, or "letter-magic," from which he earned his sobriquet al-Sīmāwī, "the Letter-Magician."[1] Although al-Sīmāwī's family origins were in Iraq, his own writings inform us that he worked in Mamluk Cairo in the latter half of the AH seventh/CE thirteenth century, where he conducted research among the collections of the royal library. The script, paintings, and paper of the leaf held by the Bowdoin Museum all suggest a production date in the late thirteenth century. The leaf thus takes on special significance, since it is the earliest known, albeit fragmentary, manuscript of the *Book of the Seven Climes*, and may well have been copied within al-Sīmāwī's lifetime.[2] It is, at any rate, a marvelous example of early Mamluk painting.

Al-Sīmāwī loved to use secret codes in his books to hide certain key magical or alchemical ingredients and procedures from unserious readers. Here, the Egyptian context is apparent in his choice of a code employing symbols reminiscent of pharaonic hieroglyphs.[3] These can be seen above and below the upper illustration on the recto side of the present leaf. Just as al-Sīmāwī's codes hide the magician-alchemist's secrets, so the allegorical illustrations code the ingredients and processes of alchemy in such a way as to be inscrutable to the uninitiated. In the *Book of the Seven Climes*, al-Sīmāwī compiles a great number of such illustrations from earlier Arabic alchemical books and accompanies them with a riddling text that is every bit as mysterious as the images it contains. The sources for his alchemical images that still survive attest to the accuracy with which he copied them. The majority of those sources, however, are now lost, making the *Book of the Seven Climes* an extremely important work for the little-known history and early development of allegorical alchemical visual arts in the Islamicate world.[4]

On the recto side of the present leaf, the upper image shows two royal figures with crowns on their heads, clothed in red and seated on yellow chairs in front of an urn held over a table or brazier on which there are red objects, perhaps charcoals. Each figure holds a flask, the one on the right containing a red substance. Five red and four white flasks are suspended above. In alchemical symbolism, red often refers to gold and the making of gold, while white often refers to silver and the making of silver. The note in the margin, which reads "an allusion to the nine irrigations which they mention in their books," may indicate the significance of the nine flasks. Below, a green bird pecks at the eye of a yellow serpent. The accompanying text explains that a substance is being submersed in vinegar and then solidified fourteen times, and the reader is invited to "regard the images and their description."

The illustrations on the verso side are indeed supplied with literal descriptions within the text. From these we can tell that, in the upper image, al-Sīmāwī intended the crowned man seated on a yellow chair to be clothed in white, not in red, and that the alchemical vessel which rests on top of the furnace and is being held and pointed to by the crowned man is meant to contain a compound that is "green at the bottom and red at the top." As the tree to the left of the furnace is not mentioned in the text, are we to imagine that this was an artistic embellishment of the illuminator and thus should not be interpreted as part of the allegory? In the lower image, a man in a green garment and seated on a yellow chair watches as a queen dressed in red is pecked in the nose by a raven. As the queen dies, she reveals a red disk. Such allegories were able to be read and appreciated on a number of different levels, while their gruesome and outlandish nature made them at once forbidding to the casual reader and memorable to adepts.

Bink Hallum
Arabic Scientific Manuscripts Curator,
British Library, and Wellcome Research
Fellow, University of Warwick

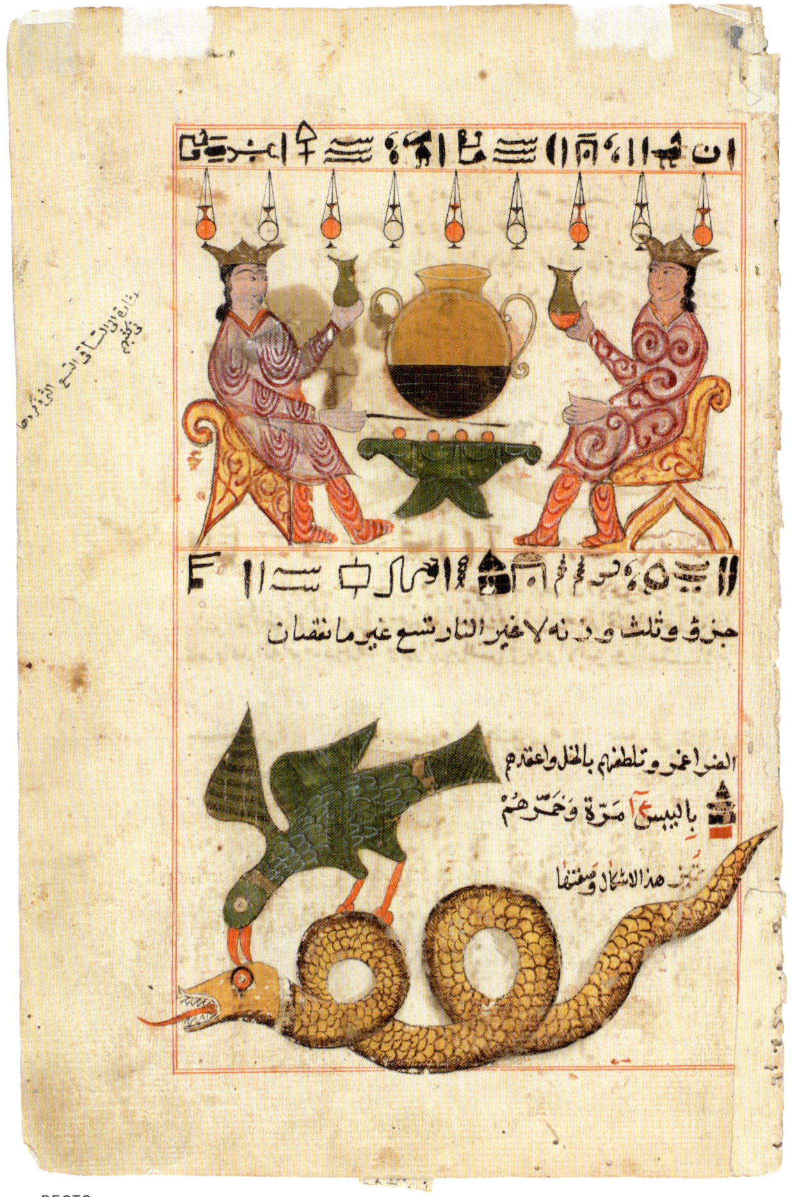

RECTO

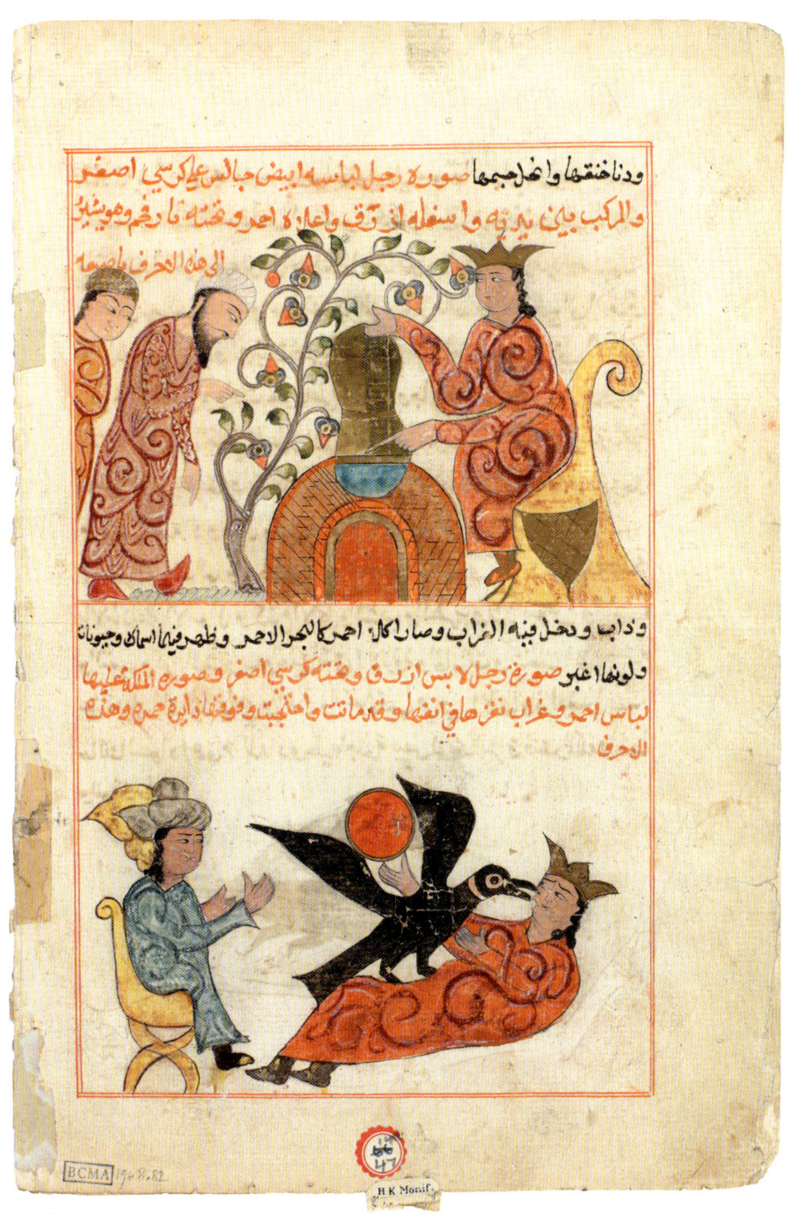

VERSO

# White Heron

Chinese, Ming dynasty (1368–1644), early 16th century
Ink and colors on silk, 48¾ × 16 in. (123.8 × 40.6 cm)
Gift of the Honorable Karl Lott Rankin, Honorary Degree, 1960, and
Pauline Jordan Rankin  1971.51

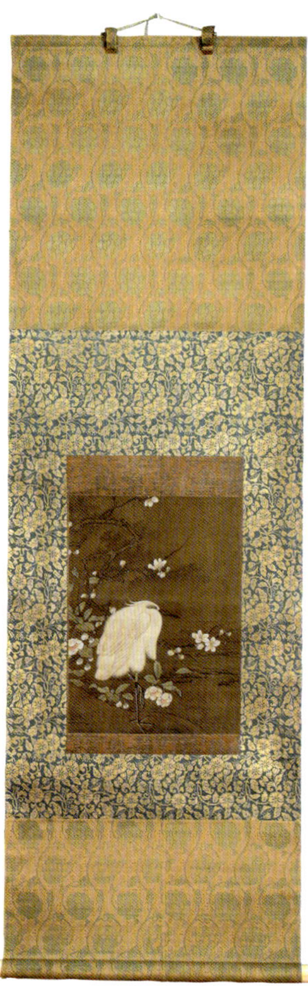

With his brilliant white plumage puffed up to ward off the cold and his long neck tucked into his torso, the solitary egret balances on one leg, asleep at the quiet riverbank. The delicate blossoms of winter plum and crabapple framing his elegant form suggest that spring has just arrived to awaken the chilled and silent landscape. The artist, whose name may never have been known, used a variety of tools to describe this moment of seasonal transformation. He built up finely applied strokes of white clam-shell pigment to suggest the billowy softness of egret feathers and applied carefully graded, translucent washes of pale pink to evoke the frail flowers and buds defying the lingering winter frost. The spare, monochrome ink treatment of the surrounding landscape contrasts with the sensitively wrought plumage and petals, thus heightening the elegance of the brilliant bird and his botanical companions.

The painting carries an old attribution to the Yuan-dynasty painter Wang Yuan (c. 1280–after 1369); however, its subject matter and style, as well as its treatment in multiple media, clearly mark it as a product of a sixteenth-century commercial workshop catering to the tastes of the Ming-dynasty educated elite and wealthy Japanese collectors of foreign luxury items. The extravagant silk mounting on this scroll points to a Japanese provenance, and although it is impossible to know exactly when and how the painting arrived in Japan, the artist may have created it expressly for the export market. Once in Japan, the small size and narrow format made the painting a perfect candidate for hanging in the *tokonoma* (alcove) of the tea room, where it would be admired as a rare antique treasure.

The egret had long served as a metaphor in Chinese poetry and painting, although its meaning was not fixed, thus allowing for greater expressive range.[1] Flocks of egrets, in their untainted white robes, evoked a gathering of distinguished courtiers; a single bird, alone in the wilderness, symbolized a reclusive gentleman of unsullied moral virtue indifferent to the tawdry affairs of the world. A stilly poised egret intently staring into the shallows for unwary fish sometimes represented the government censor surveying his territory for corrupt officials. Alternately, the aloof egret could stand for a man who despite his brilliant talent goes completely unnoticed, as in a portion of Liu Xu's (1426–1490) inscriptional poem for a painting of a white heron in a spring landscape: "A snowy-robed gentleman, stands on a fragrant isle. / Pure in thought his whole life, no one has truly recognized him, / Alone, facing the setting sun, the white-headed man sighs."[2]

A pair of egrets could appear in the embroidered insignia square on the chest of a Ming-dynasty official's robe, emblematic of the wearer's place as a sixth-rank officer. All of these metaphors equate the egret with a man of integrity upholding Confucian values.

In another common visual system, Chinese artists played with rebuses, in which homophonic phrases for the word "egret," or *lusi* in Chinese, together with the names of specific botanical motifs, rhymed with a well-known idiom. Common rebus combinations in the Ming visual lexicon included a single egret with a peony (a rhyme for *yilu fugui*, meaning "prosperity and honor throughout life") and a single egret with lotus pods (a rhyme for *yilu lianke*, "constant success on exams"). Although further research may uncover a rebus in this painting, its unusual combination of motifs has thus far resisted decoding.

Ankeney Weitz, Ellerton M. and Edith K.
Jette Professor of Art, Colby College

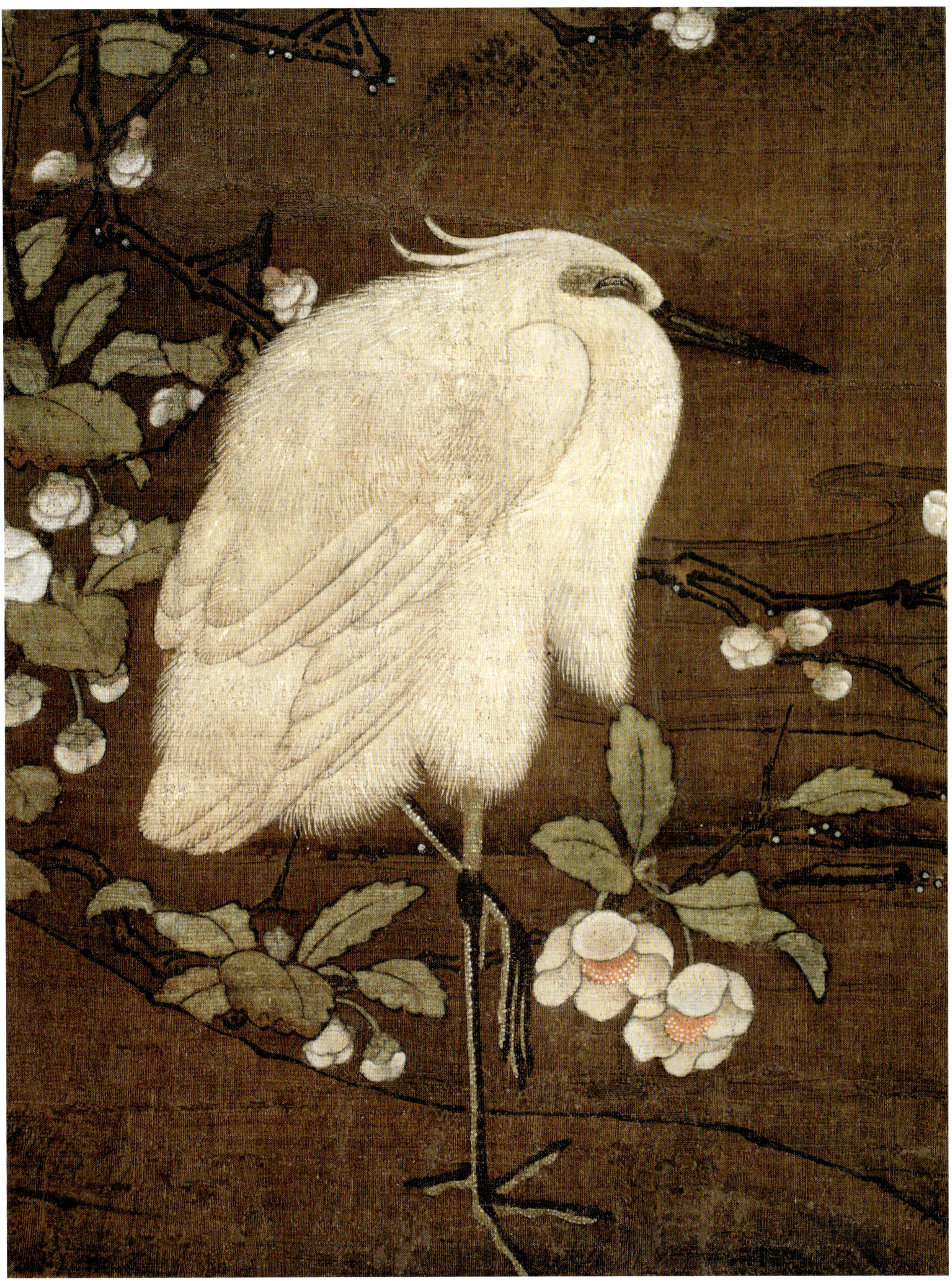

# Two Chinese Jades

18th–19th century

Gift of Mrs. Frederick Blackmore, in memory of Frederick Blackmore
1953.12, .17

Two Chinese jades, an auspicious emblem in the form of a long handle-like object with a large mushroom-shaped head, traditionally known as *ruyi* ("as you wish" 如意), the other a lotus-shaped bowl, entered the Bowdoin museum in 1953 as part of a gift from Mrs. Frederick Blackmore in memory of her husband. They were presented together with more than a hundred items of Chinese art. With her planned move from New York to Cundy's Harbor, Maine, Mrs. Blackmore probably wanted the collection close to her new home, to be enjoyed by her and other local residents.

Shaped from an evenly pale gray-green nephrite from the foothills of the Himalayan mountains that surround the Gobi Desert in Central Asia, these two jades tell interesting stories about the Qing-dynasty emperor Qianlong (乾隆 r. 1736–95) and the fate of art objects over time. They also illustrate the importance of close examination, a fundamental skill for all students, collectors, and lovers of art.

As the longest-reigning emperor of the Qing dynasty (1644–1911), Qianlong was known for his military prowess and literary accomplishments, and as an avid collector who amassed the vast collections that are now divided between the two Palace Museums in Beijing and Taipei. His passion for jades from all periods earned him the nickname "the Jade Idiot" (*Yuchi* 玉痴). His writings include many poems praising both antique and contemporary jades in his collection. One of these, composed in 1752, appears on Bowdoin's *ruyi* (pl. 1), the diminutive characters executed with exceptional refinement in clerical script leaving large blank spaces. The poem praises jade's superiority over other artistic materials, the *ruyi* shape's long history, and its power to bring blessings from the heavens on its owner. As an auspicious emblem, the shape was thought to have originated as a simple branch or stick used as a back scratcher by Buddhists and Daoists in earlier eras. The shape became standardized and widely popular both in imperial and elite social circles during the Qing dynasty.[1]

In spite of the imperial authorship of the poem on the *ruyi*, it was probably an apocryphal addition made after Qianlong's reign, in the nineteenth or early twentieth century. An imperial association would certainly have enhanced the object's importance and value. It also reinforced the widely accepted notion that Qianlong raised standards in jade-working throughout the land to its highest levels, so that a connection with the emperor would be synonymous with top-quality materials and workmanship.

The lotus-shaped bowl (pl. 2) well demonstrates these high standards. Its near-flawless, even color, generous size, thick walls, careful shaping, and decoration produce an object with such substance and *gravitas* that would be fitting for an emperor. A different motif occupies each of the eight overlapping petals that form the walls of the bowl, together constituting the Buddhist symbols for the Eight Auspicious Blessings (*Bajixiang* 八吉祥)—the wheel, conch, victory standard, parasol, lotus, vase, double fish, and infinite knot.[2] Qianlong was an ardent Buddhist, and the lotus is the preeminent symbol of enlightenment and purity in Buddhist teaching. Its imperial connection is further supported by a faded mark ("Made during Qianlong's reign" 乾隆年製) in clerical script on the outside bottom.

However, close examination reveals that the mark's unusual wear extends to its surrounding area, as if attempts had been made to remove it. Unlike the *ruyi*, it is as if the imperial association in this case was deemed undesirable. Changed historical circumstances might account for this apparent inconsistency. If this bowl was indeed originally made for the Qianlong emperor and used somewhere in his palace, the unsettled political conditions that came with the fall of the Qing dynasty in the early twentieth century might have precipitated its departure from the palace. Under these circumstances, erasing the mark might represent an attempt to remove the stigma associated with this departure.

Jenny F. So
Chinese art historian and Adjunct Professor, Department of Fine Arts, Chinese University of Hong Kong

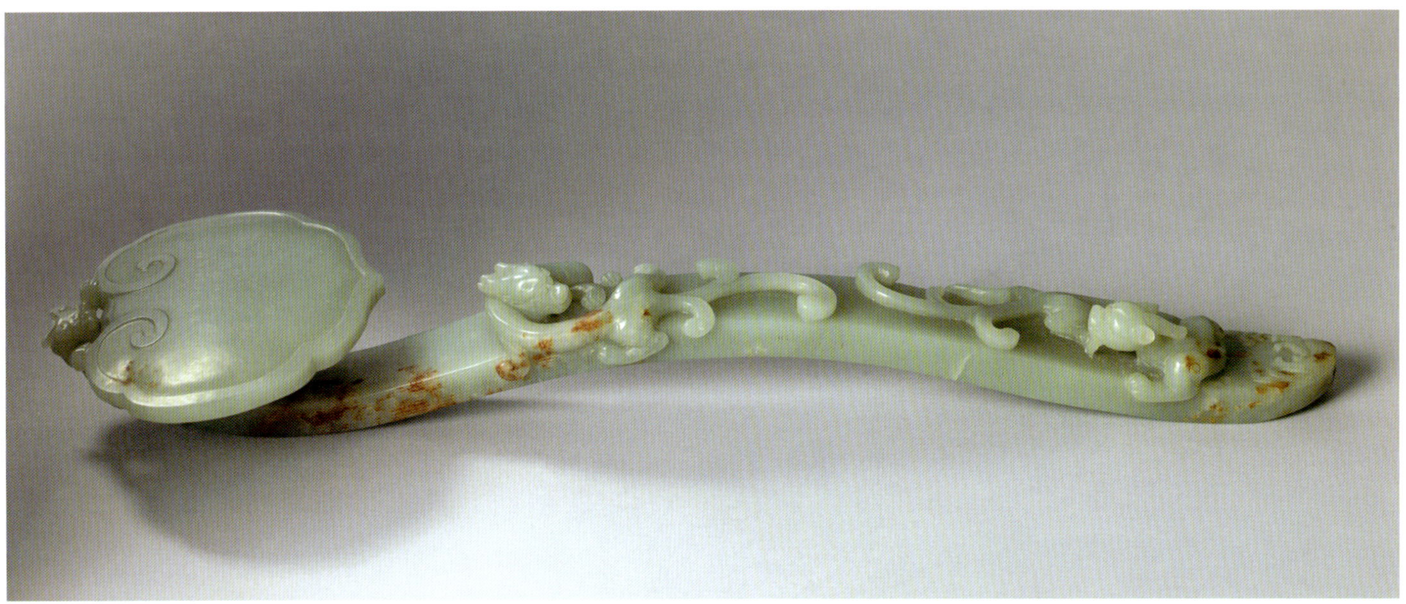

PLATE 1. *Ruyi* (Emblem), Qing dynasty (1644–1912), late 19th–early 20th century. Jade, 6¼ in. (41.3 cm) (1953.17)

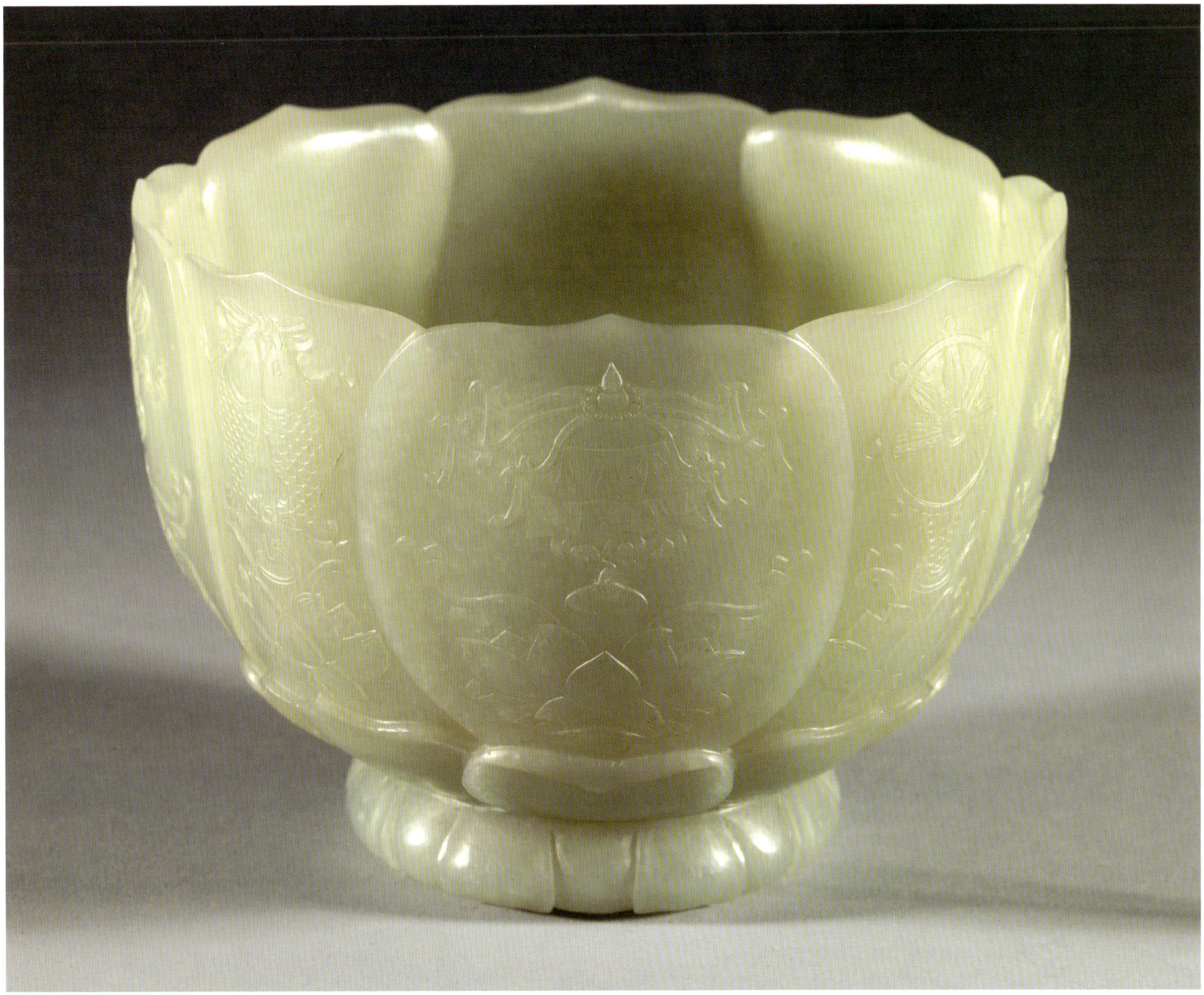

PLATE 2. Bowl, Qing dynasty, Qianlong period (1736–95). Jade, 3¹⁵⁄₁₆ × 5½ in. (10 × 14 cm) (1953.12)

# *Prunus Branch*

Dai Xi (Chinese, 1801–1860), 1836
Ink on silk, 73¾ × 13⅝ in. (187.3 × 34.6 cm)
Gift of William Bingham II from the Peterson Collection  1942.14

A single broken branch of blossoming plum floats diagonally across the silk, its sprightly blossoms energetically reaching toward the sky. Rendered in monochrome ink, Dai Xi's painted plum embodies both strength and fragility; the twisted, hoary line of the limb puts forth new life as delicate pale-ink blossoms. This juxtaposition of the bent and broken with the exuberant and beautiful encodes the symbolic meaning of the plum tree, for despite the bitter cold, it is the first to generate new blossoms, often when snow is still piled on the ground. This emblem of the Confucian scholar suggests his perseverance in the face of adversity, his steadfast moral integrity. These are the virtues held dear by the two men who made this scroll.

The inscriptions encroaching to the left and right of the branch recount the story of the painting's creation and express the fond familial and artistic relationship between Dai Xi and his younger brother Dai Xu. On the lower right, a short inscription written by the artist on the day he painted the plum modestly criticizes his work: "After sketching this, I looked at it with regret. I wonder if I can really give these flowers to someone after all. Painted by Hengshi [Dai Xi] on a winter's day in *bingjia* [1836]."

Dai Xu added the longer inscription, written in smaller characters but in a similar style, a little over a month later:

My older brother sketched four pillar [i.e., vertical] scrolls, but he was in too much haste and quickly finished them only to relieve himself of the duty. Who would have thought they would be taken for mounting and then brought back here with an order to add an inscription? Wanting to write a few words to record this, I set brush to paper, only increasing [our family's] embarrassment. Forty-three days after [this] was painted, on the tenth day of the twelfth month, [Dai Xi's] younger brother Dai Xu blew the chill off [of his hands] and recorded this.

The brothers were members of a venerable clan of landowners and government officials in the southern city of Hangzhou. At the time of this work, in 1836, they were thirty and thirty-five years old, and although Xi had already passed the highest level of the civil service examination and assumed a position in the Hanlin Academy of Worthies in Beijing, both brothers were at home in Hangzhou observing the three-year mourning period for their mother, who died in 1835. They resumed their careers in 1838, but their greatest achievements—Dai Xi's in public service[1] and Dai Xu's in mathematics[2]—lay ahead. The inscriptions suggest that Dai Xi had already claimed a name for himself as a painter whose works could be used as gracious gifts, and despite the self-deprecating inscription, the new owner cherished the paintings enough to have them mounted for display. When the owner returned seeking another inscription, Dai Xi must have been away on business, so Dai Xu stepped in on Xi's behalf. Xu's calligraphic style closely emulates his older brother, demonstrating respect for his sibling and asserting a familial aesthetic.

While this polite presentation piece records a decorous moment in the life of a scholarly family, the tenor of the times was anything but peaceful. Hostilities with foreign nations came to a head in the Opium Wars of 1839–42 and 1856–60; a civil war with the Taiping Heavenly Kingdom raged from 1850 to 1864. During the insurgents' attack on Hangzhou in 1860, Dai Xi, serving as an honorary Deputy Director of Defense, helped the imperial forces defend the city. When the rebels captured Hangzhou in March, he committed suicide by throwing himself in a pond. Dai Xu, in an act of loyalty to his brother, drowned himself on the same day.

Ankeney Weitz
Ellerton M. and Edith K. Jette Professor of
Art, Colby College

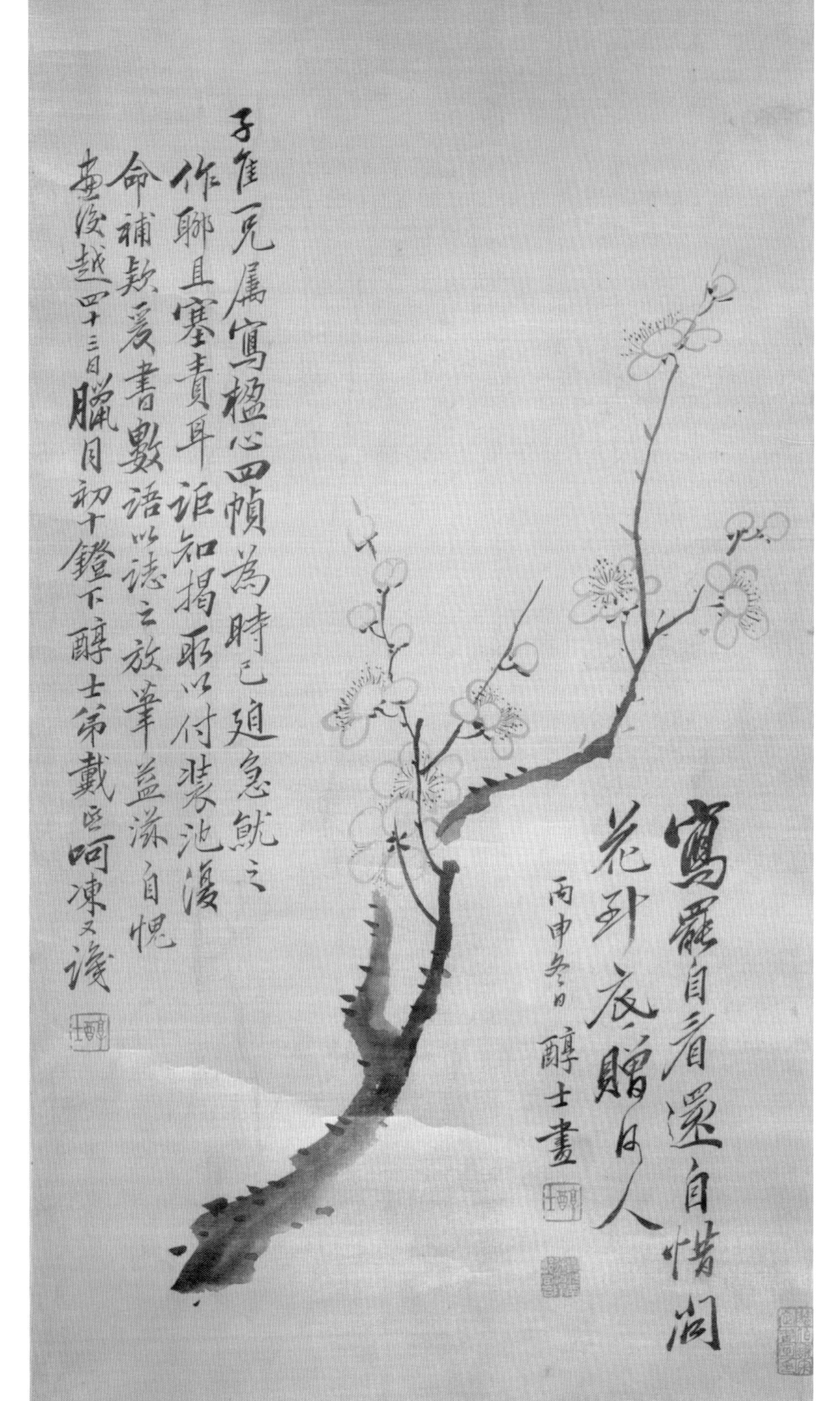

子雀兄屬寫樹心四幀為時已迫急就之
作聊且塞責耳詎知揭取以付裝池後
命補款爰書數語以誌之放筆益漾自愧
塗沒越四十三日臘月初十鐙下醇士弟戴熙呵凍又後
寫罷自看還自惜闊
花邨夜贈月人
丙申冬日　醇士畫

# Covered Box

Chinese, Ming dynasty, Wanli period (1573–1620)
Porcelain with underglaze blue decoration, Jingdezhen ware,
4½ × 8⅞ in. (11.4 × 22.5 cm)
Gift of Mr. William Tudor Gardiner, Honorary Degree, 1945, and Mrs.
Gardiner  1940.388.a & .b

The technical finesse of the lidded porcelain box is immediately apparent in the perfectly rounded shape, tightly closing lid, and flawless application of blue underglaze painting. Its decoration revels in humorous details, as it shows boys in a garden who read and play. One of the little boys rides a hobby-horse, another holds a kite. The idyllic scene of an elite education would have been a welcome gift at childbirth and other family occasions. The image is surrounded by bands of five-clawed flying dragons that chase flaming pearls, a symbol associated with imperial power. The box originated in Jingdezhen during the Ming dynasty, a time that many consider the high point of the long tradition of porcelain manufacturing in China. (ND/JHo)

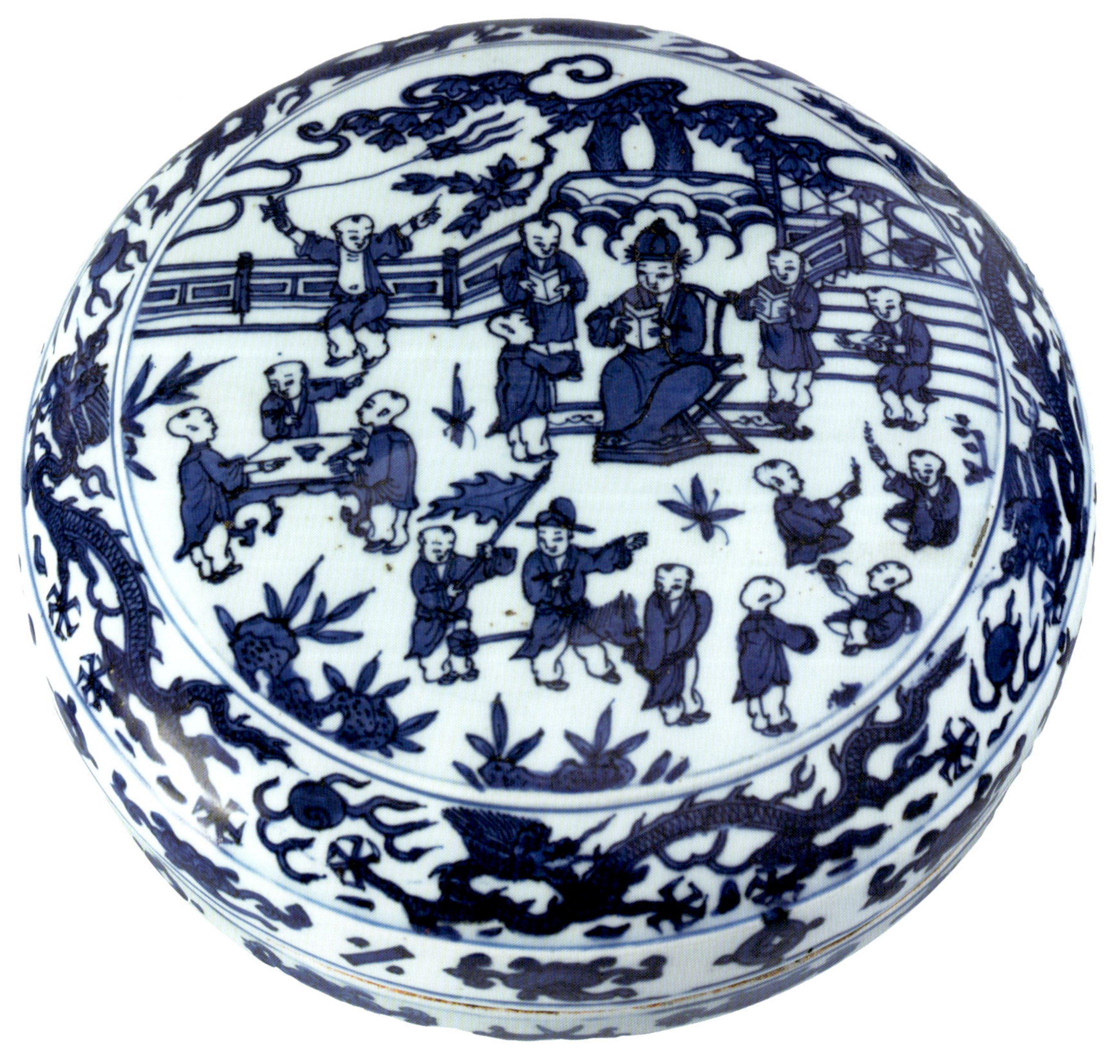

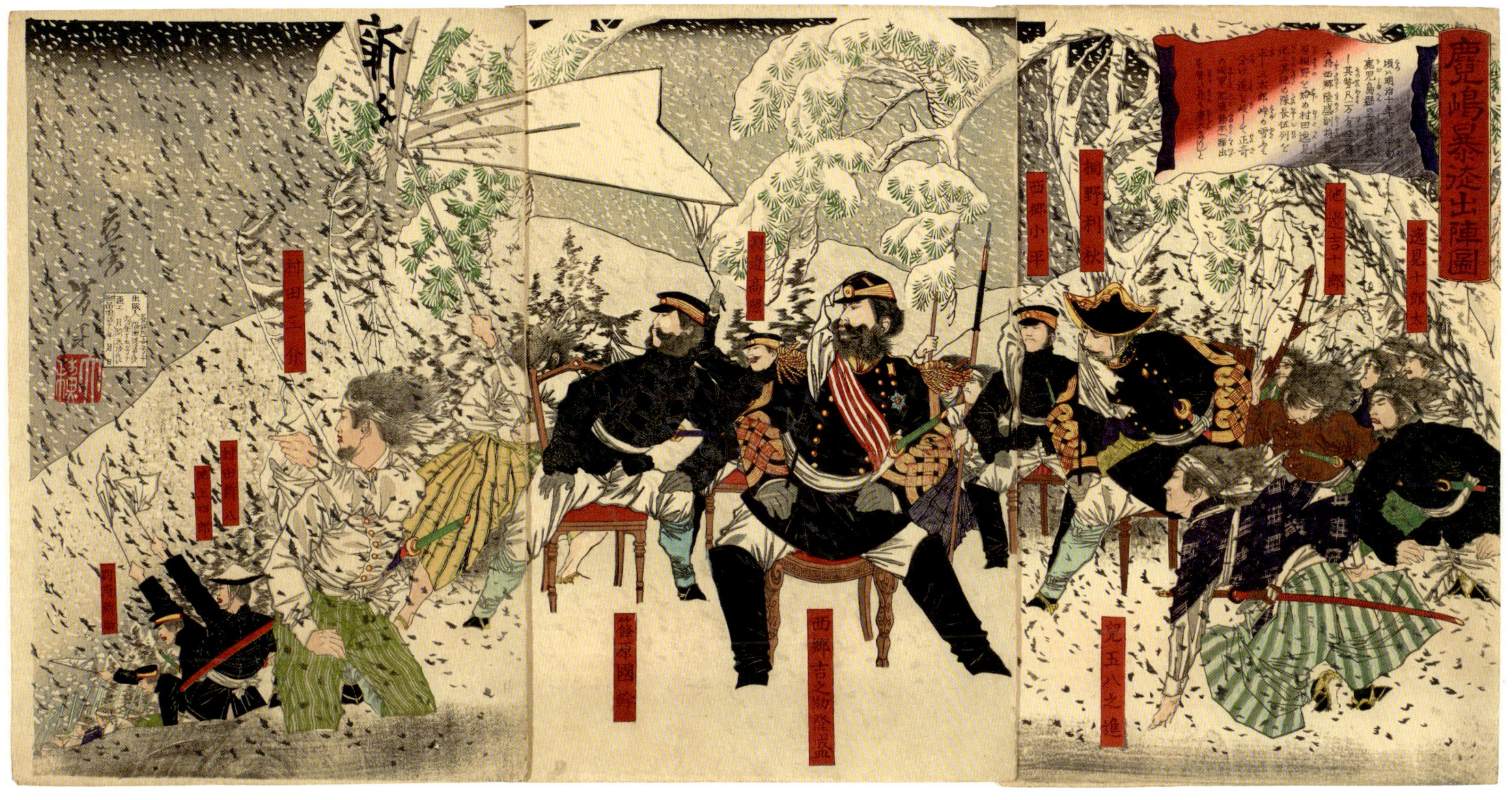

# *Japanese War in Kagoshima (Kagoshima boto syutuzinzu)*

Tsukioka Yoshitoshi (Japanese, 1839–1892), 1879
*Oban tate-e* triptych woodblock print on paper, 14¾ × 30⅛ in.
(37.5 × 76.5 cm)

Museum Purchase, Art Collections Purchase Fund  2017.28.a–.c

Tsukioka Yoshitoshi established his reputation as a disciple of Utagawa Kuniyoshi, following closely the manner of this master's work in warrior, kabuki, and comic subjects. Impacted by the insecurity and violence he experienced at the close of the Tokugawa period, Yoshitoshi's work began to include brutal, gruesome subjects differentiated from the work of his master by their stark presentation. After the government ban on the illustration of current affairs was lifted, Yoshitoshi became one of the first Japanese artists to document the Boshin War, which put an end to pro-Tokugawa forces, and also made numerous prints, as this one, of the Seinan War, or Satsuma Rebellion.

This signed and dated triptych illustrates the last stance of Saigō Takamori (1828–1877), the legendary "Last Samurai," a rebel leader against the imperial government during the rebellion. A retired imperial general who had helped to reinstitute the government he now perceived as a threat, Takamori in this image dons the uniform of the emperor's forces as he takes position against them in September 1877, surrounded by samurai who had flocked to his school. The confrontation represented here is recognizable by the densely falling snow during battle. While the early snow seemed auspicious to some, it did not stop the enemies from massacring each other, ending with the defeat of the samurai. Thanks to his heroism, Takamori posthumously assumed superhuman status in the eyes of many of his followers. This triptych dramatizes a pivotal moment in Japanese culture, in which history turns into legend. (Staff)

# Plate (Bamboo Grove on a Moonlit Night)

Tomimoto Kenkichi (Japanese, 1886–1963), 1948
Stoneware, 1¹⁵⁄₁₆ × 10⁵⁄₁₆ in. (4.9 × 26.2 cm)
Bequest of Mrs. Herbert S. Ingraham  1990.3.15

This unassuming plate, freely painted with a moonlit pastoral scene, evokes traditional Japanese ceramics yet is distinctly modern. Why it looks older than it is and how it ended up at Bowdoin, though, are stories specific to the twentieth century. Its potter, Tomimoto Kenkichi, was widely revered in Japan and among the first group of craftspeople designated Living National Treasures in 1955. Unlike traditional potters who served long apprenticeships, Tomimoto attended art school and studied in England, where he learned firsthand about the Arts and Crafts movement. With Bernard Leach, Hamada Shōji, and Yanagi Sōetsu, he founded *mingei*, a movement related to Arts and Crafts that sought to revive Japanese folk craft as an antidote to industrialization. The Bowdoin plate embodies *mingei* philosophy in being handmade and utilitarian, and in its direct reference to the natural world in both materials and imagery. Through the pottery and writings of Leach, *mingei* became foundational to the studio craft movement in the United Kingdom and North America in the post–World War II decades. Tomimoto broke with *mingei* in 1946, rejecting its revivalist aspect in favor of design and a focus on highly refined and luxuriously ornamented porcelain.

Also in 1946, Caroline Louise Daggett Ingraham (1906–1983) moved from Milo, Maine, to Tokyo with her family. Her husband, Herbert S. Ingraham (1898–1982), was a high school principal and Bowdoin alumnus who trained ROTC students at the University of Maine during World War II. Following the Japanese surrender, he was charged with leading the American School in Tokyo for children of Occupation forces. The Ingrahams lived in Japan from 1946 until 1948.[1]

Caroline Ingraham had studied ceramics at Alfred University in upstate New York and at the School of the Museum of Fine Arts in Boston.[2] While living in Tokyo, she continued her studies with Hajime Katō (1900–1968), a rising potter who would become a Living National Treasure in 1961. Ingraham traveled to his studio in Yokohama two or three times a week, a distance of about fifteen miles from her base at U.S. General Headquarters and surely an unusual trip for the wife of an Occupation officer. She encountered Tomimoto Kenkichi's work for the first time at the Okura Ga Gallery in Tokyo. She developed a broader interest in *mingei* ceramics with a visit to potter Hamada Shōji and her acquisition of historical folk pots, including an earthenware Bizen jar that she also gave to Bowdoin (fig. 1).[3]

Tomimoto's plate and Ingraham's interest in *mingei* can be situated within the broader context of postwar American cultural diplomacy. As art historian Meghen Jones has argued, folk pottery, both actual and inspired, helped to reframe Japan as a place of "comfortable naiveté" and as a nonthreatening and democratic ally to the United States.[4] Appreciation for folk pots added dimension to American understanding of Japanese culture, often casting it as "timeless" and "primitive" while softening the image of the Japanese as keepers of enduring traditions.[5] The plate's moonlit bamboo grove stands in stark contrast to the scenes of destruction Ingraham must have witnessed on her train rides to Yokohama.

Made just after World War II, Tomimoto's plate evokes a gentle, traditional Japan and embodies the idealisms of both the potter and collector. For museum viewers today, it can represent not only the twentieth-century revival of craft traditions, but also the complex trajectories of cultural diplomacy that inform how we see the world.

Sequoia Miller
Chief Curator, Gardiner Museum, Toronto

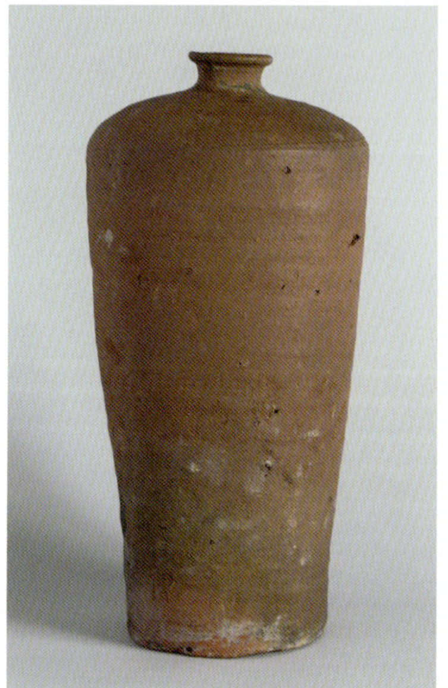

FIG. 1. Bizen ware vase, 1700–1800. Earthenware, height 11³⁄₁₆ in. (28.4 cm). Bowdoin College Museum of Art, Bequest of Mrs. Herbert S. Ingraham, 1990.3.8

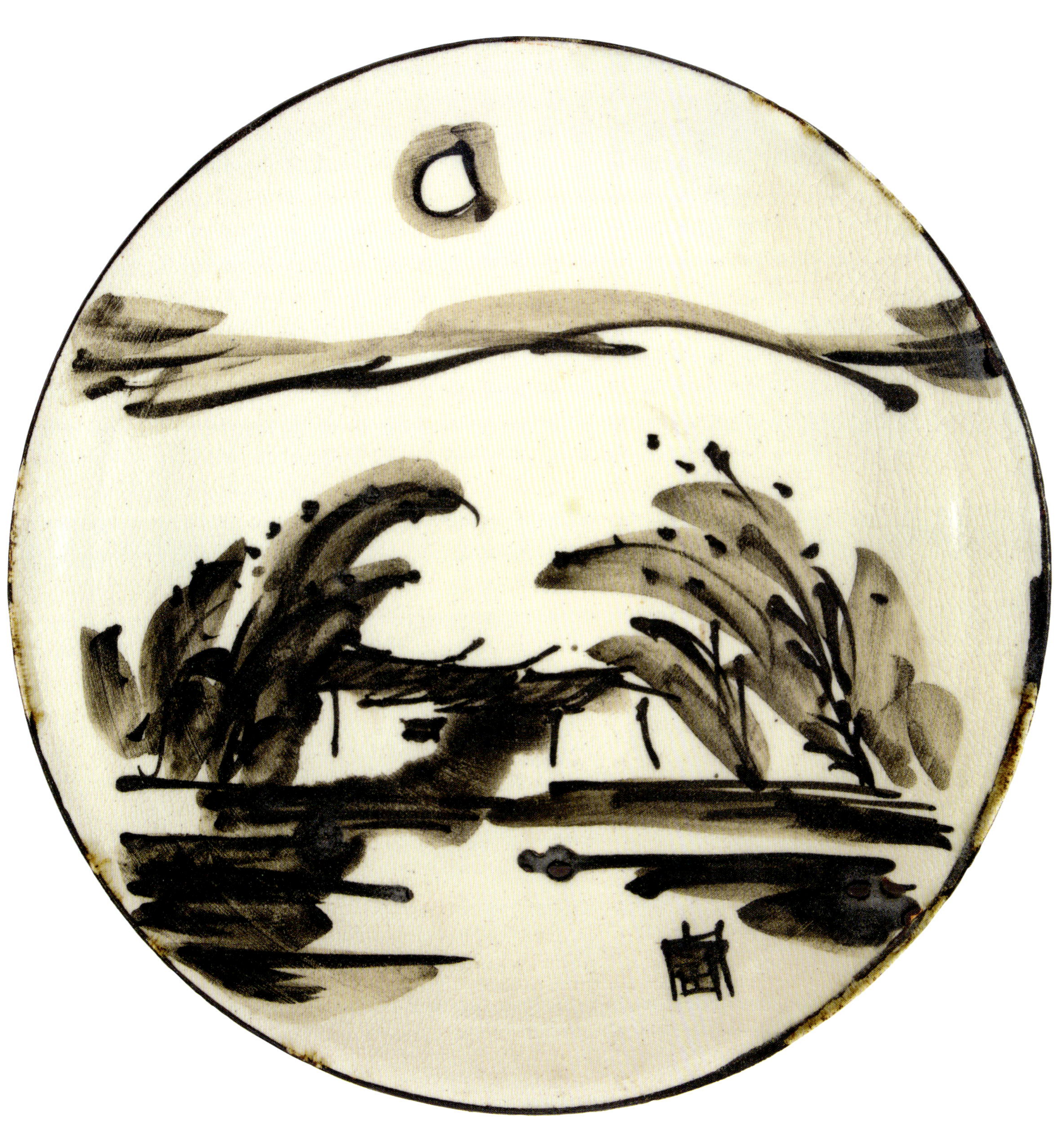

# *Going Home (Suzhou)*

Chen Yifei (Chinese, 1946–2005), 1986
Oil on canvas, 34 × 42 in. (86.4 × 106.8 cm)
Gift of Irving Isaacson in memory of Judith Magyar  2018.9

Chen Yifei's lyrical landscape takes viewers to Suzhou, the scenic city in southern China renowned for its footbridges and winding canals. A curve of buildings rises up from a languid stretch of water to fill the canvas with texture and light. In Chen's appeal to the picturesque and placid, one could easily mistake this painting for an Orientalized vision of the "East": a wistful view of an unchanging China comprised of ancient, rundown architecture dressed up in an air of romanticism. Chen's fascination with beauty in art might strike viewers as equally anachronistic. However, produced in the wake of the Great Proletarian Cultural Revolution (1966–76), this painting is not so much a nostalgic look back as a paean to new possibilities in art ahead.

Chen graduated from the Shanghai College of Art in 1965 and spent the following decade producing theatrical vistas that transmitted the grandeur of his country. Trained in Soviet Socialist Realism, he was particularly adept at creating heroic scenes of intrepid strength. Always with a clear narrative and identifiable protagonist, these paintings followed Mao Zedong's strict dictates for cultural production: to produce art in the service of the nation. With Mao's death in 1976, and the end of the Cultural Revolution, artists were faced with a pivotal moment of reckoning.

In 1979, Chen produced a remarkable self-portrait titled *Thinking of History from My Space*. Across the canvas, historical events appear in a dreamlike collage. Chen painted himself into the work ruminating on this sweeping panorama of collective memory. His painting is one of many by his generation of artists who, through their art, contemplated the recent past and their place within it. With the new ethos of Opening and Reform on the horizon, artists shifted from the chaos of past decades to new avenues for art in the future.

The painting in the Bowdoin Museum is an example of just such an experiment. Chen moved to the United States for further studies in 1980. He continued painting prolifically and exhibiting widely before returning to Shanghai in 1990. During his time abroad, he explored and incorporated what he considered to be the most critical aspects of art. His resulting work showcases the deliberate choices that he made, and should not simply be seen as an indiscriminate application of existing Western styles onto Chinese content.

In his embrace of the rustic and sentimental, Chen Yifei channels his facility for romanticism but empties it of overt revolutionary content. In subject matter, *Going Home* celebrates the solace of quietude. Indulging in the visual effects of form, he delivers a resounding commentary on art. Chen lavishes attention on the architectural exteriors present in the landscape. Daubs of bright wintergreens and pastel blushes dot the ramshackle rooftiles, while patches of ivory and pale yellow sit atop eroded coats of rusty browns. From the richness of weathered walls to luminous watery surfaces, he revels in the possibilities of form. Just a decade earlier, such an experiment with form would have been condemned as bourgeois and self-serving. This painting shows the artist championing beauty as a valid reason for making art.

Peggy Wang
Assistant Professor of Art History and
Asian Studies, Bowdoin College

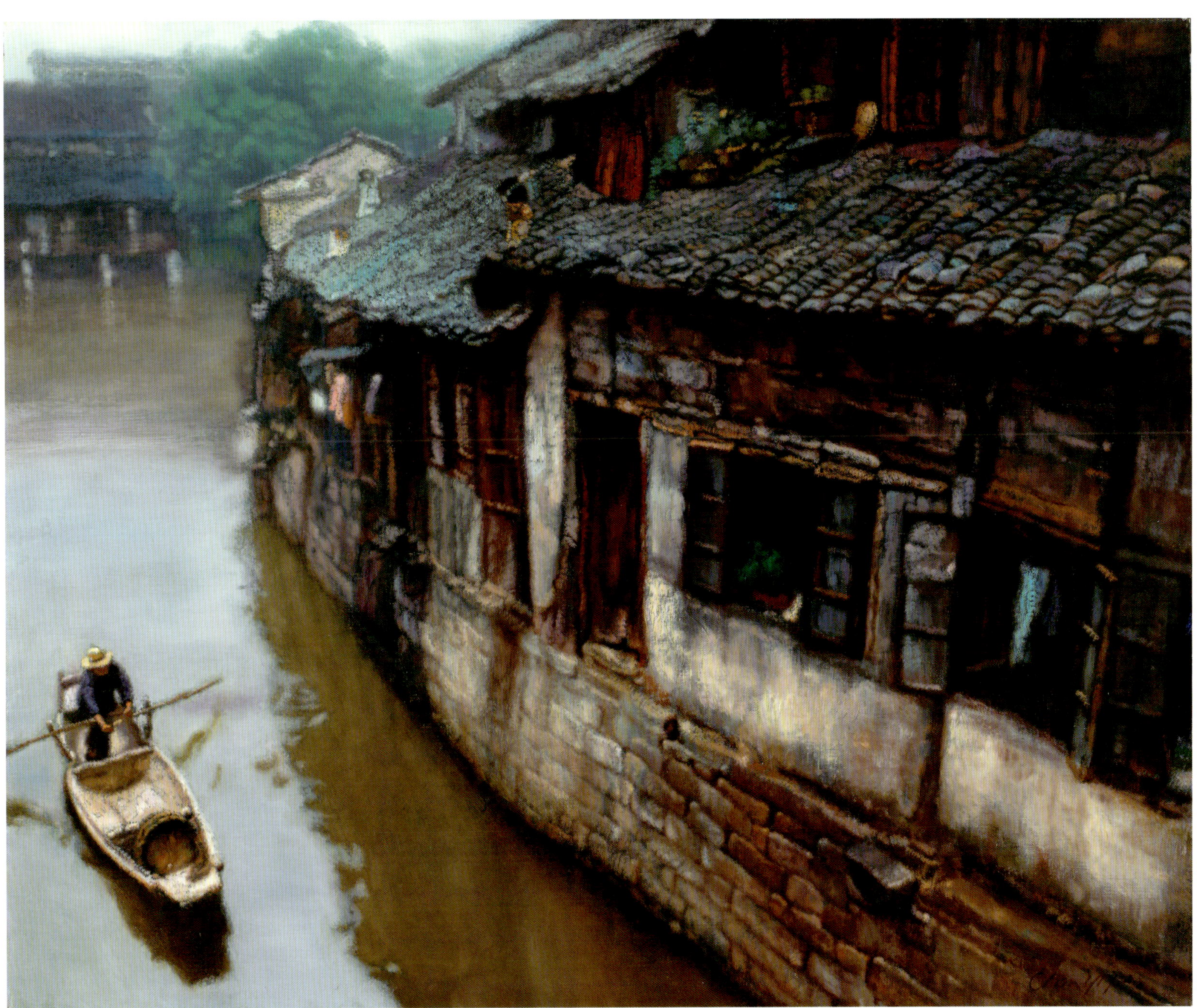

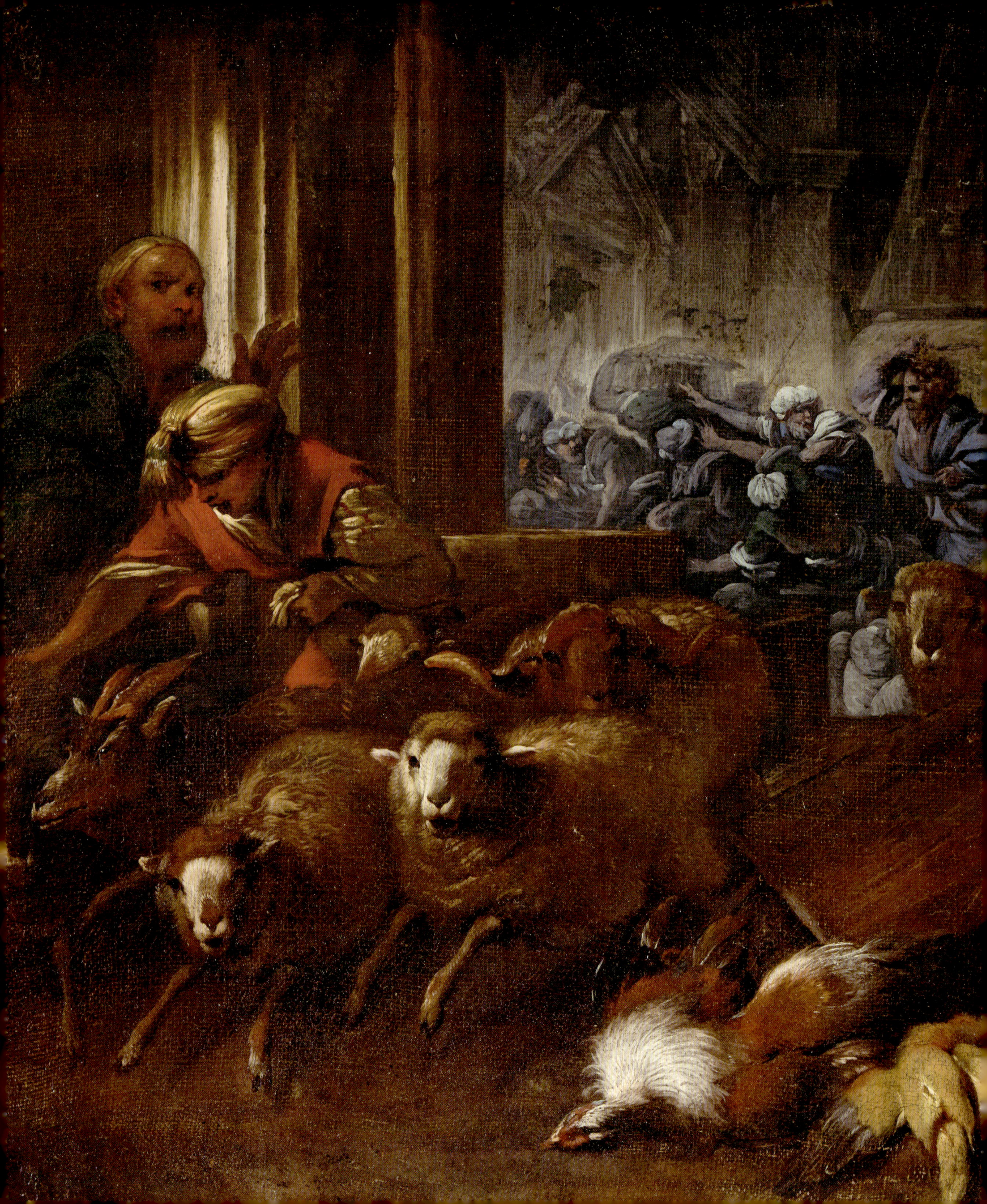

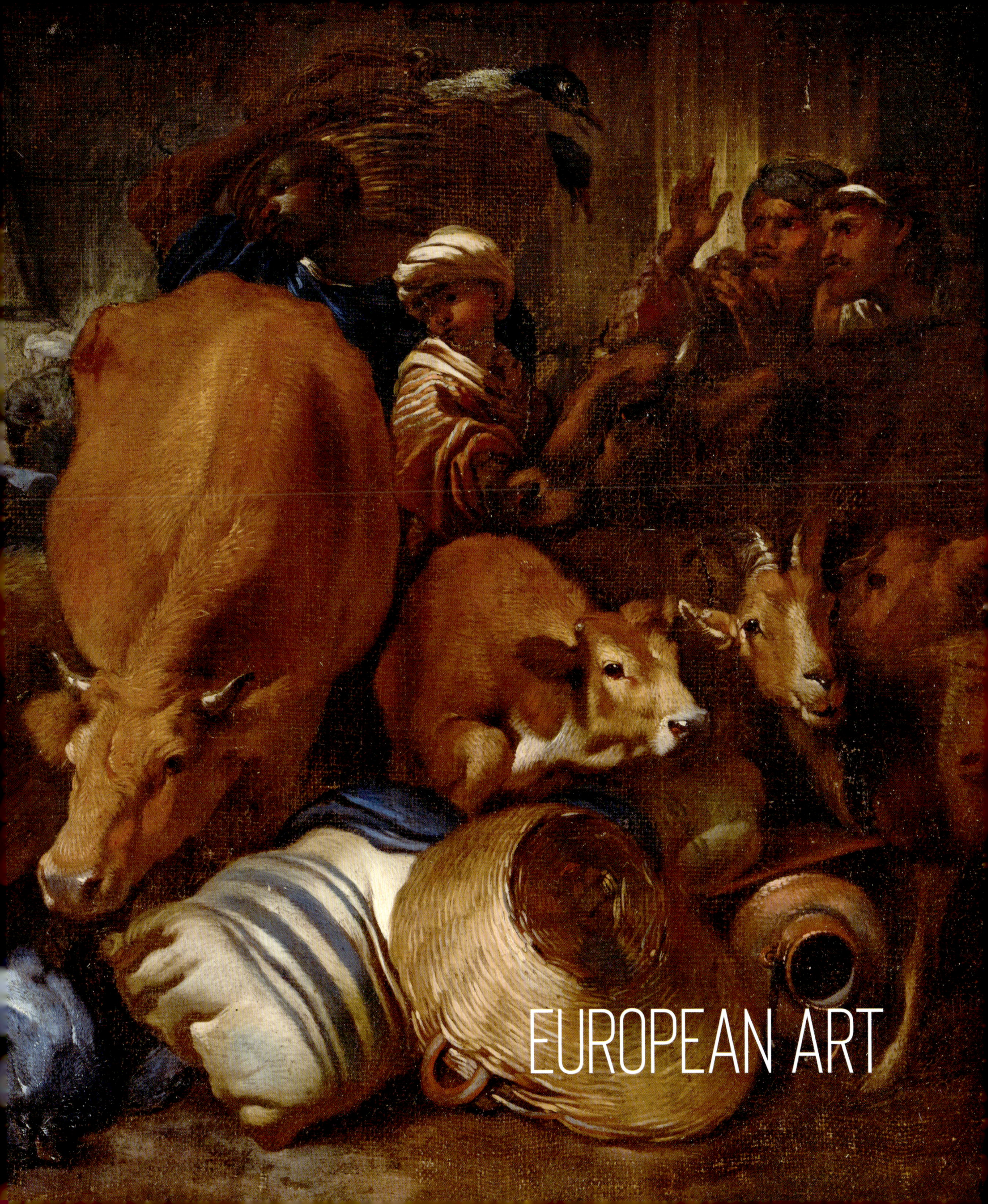
EUROPEAN ART

# Head of a King

France, Chartres (Eure-et-Loire), Chartres Cathedral, from
the destroyed choir screen, 1220–30
Lutetian limestone (Paris Basin), Conflans–Sainte–
Honorine quarry (?), and traces of color, 6⅛ × 5¹³⁄₁₆ × 5⅛ in.
(15.6 × 14.7 × 13 cm)
Gift of Edward Perry Warren, Esq., Honorary Degree, 1926  1915.100

In 1763, the great limestone choir screen of Chartres Cathedral was demolished as part of the renovations to make the celebration of the Eucharist more accessible to the laity. The original construction of the choir screen, a loggia spanning the nave at the east end, is undocumented. Because of a reference to wood choir stalls in 1221, the screen is thought to date between 1220 and 1230. The reliefs below the parapet facing the nave depicted eight episodes of the Childhood of Christ. Its general configuration is known from a 1697 engraving by Nicolas de Larmessin.[1] A dozen heads from the choir screen reliefs were removed so that the relief panels could be recycled as pavements in the choir area using their smooth flat backs. The Bowdoin head of a king, among the dispersed fragments, was linked to the cathedral in 1971.

Carved of a fine-grained limestone from the Paris Basin, the head is a rare work from one of the key monuments of medieval art. Severed from its original context, the youthful king's head might seem a mere curiosity, but the astonishing quality of carving and his physical presence immediately seize one's attention. Being a sculpture for the interior, there is no evidence of weathering, with damage only to the crown and nose. His finely chiseled face yields a certain expressive power and nobility. Traces of yellow ochre in the hair indicate that the entire head, and its larger context, was brilliantly colored.

The choir screen reliefs exhibit multiple styles, suggesting that they were either produced over a period of time or simply assigned to different sculptors. In 1971, Léon Pressouyre linked a cast of the Bowdoin king with a headless bust in the cathedral's storage.[2] Brooks Stoddard then noted that "although a wedge of stone about 2.5 cm . . . is missing on the right hand side, the fit along the break on the left side is almost perfect."[3] The original location of this bust is uncertain.

However, an alternative scenario suggests that the Bowdoin king comes from the choir screen's *Magi before Herod* relief. The fairly flat break joins at the neck of the two left figures on this relief are not unlike that of the Bowdoin head (fig. 1). One head, in a private collection, has been securely linked to the figure of Herod, the enthroned despot at the right.[4] Additionally, a head of the middle Magi has been proposed by Jean Mallion as one in a Parisian collection.[5] Characteristic of this sculptor is refinement and meticulous detailing. In many respects, the Bowdoin head technically and stylistically relates to *The Magi before Herod*: the Herod and Bowdoin heads are of similar size, portions of the crowns are unfinished, and both have bracket attachments. Thus, the Bowdoin head may be from the figure of the first or second Magi.

The head's *antiquissant* style, also most evident in *The Magi before Herod*, reflects a tendency around the year 1200 to echo classical modes.[6] Both his physical serenity and noble expression make the Bowdoin king a commanding work.

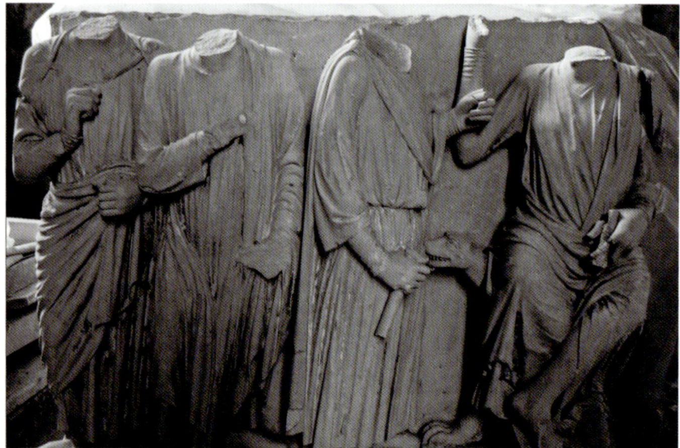

FIG. 1. *The Magi before Herod*, original in Chartres Cathedral storage, plaster cast in the Musée National des Monuments Français, Paris.

Charles T. Little
Curator Emeritus of Medieval Art and The
Cloisters, The Metropolitan Museum of Art

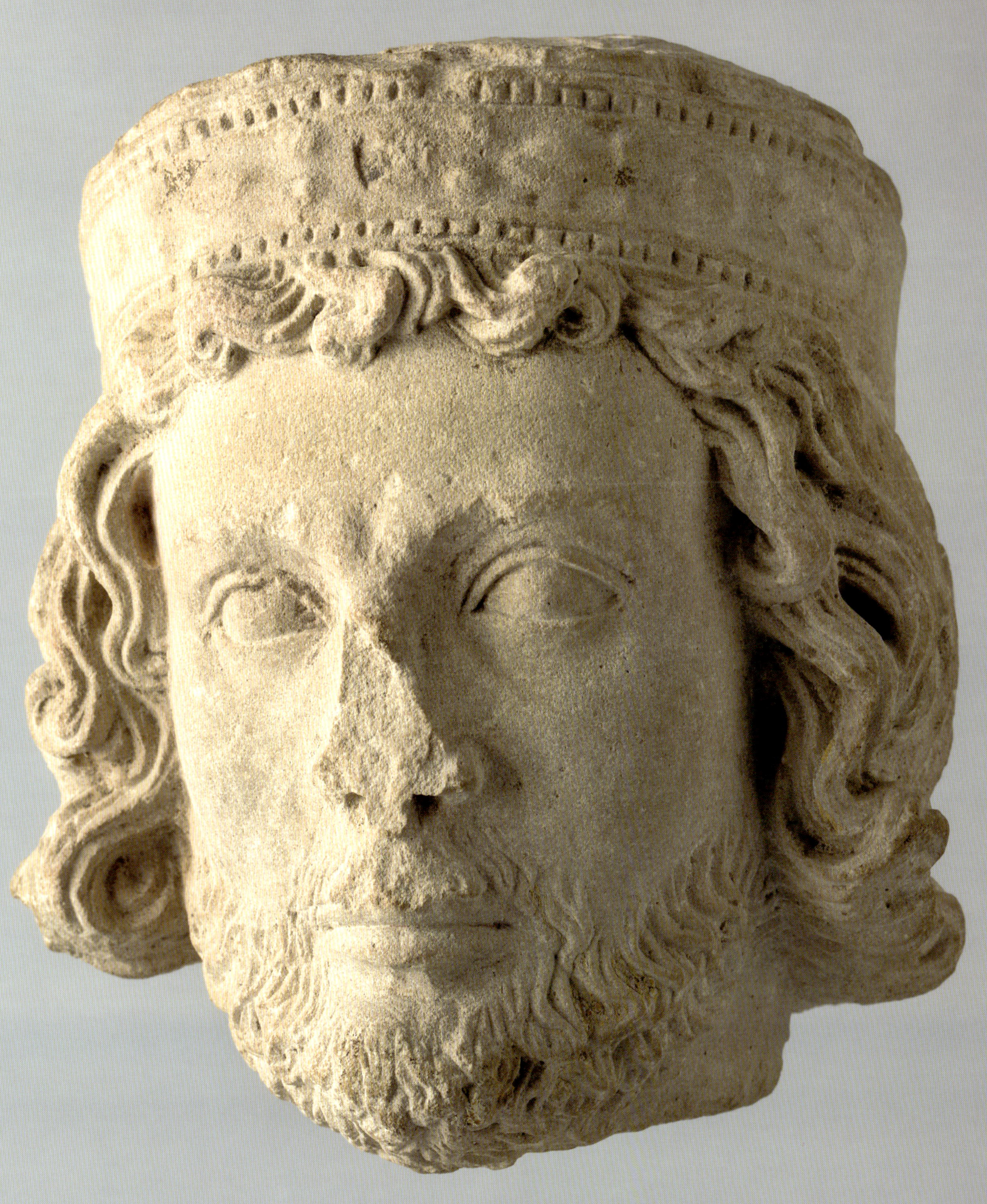

# Ivory Diptych

French, c. 1300–1325
Ivory with traces of paint, 3¾₆ × 4¹¹⁄₁₆ × ½ in. (8.1 × 11.9 × 1.3 cm)
Museum Purchase  2005.3

A diptych is comprised of two hinged panels that open like a book or fold shut for protection and portability. When opened, the diptych reveals a pair of scenes that, in this small, delicately carved example, perfectly embody the primary tenets of Christianity in late medieval Europe.

On the left, the Virgin Mary is flanked by a pair of angels holding candles who reverently face her, like a celestial honor guard. Mary tenderly cradles her infant son, Jesus, who squirms in her arms, while reaching toward a fruit held by his mother. Jesus's recognizably childlike behavior, his playful curiosity, and Mary's solicitous, maternal gaze underline a key tenet of the Christian faith: that in Jesus, God became fully human. The stress placed here on Mary's role as both a mother and a caregiver for Jesus, and (with the inclusion of a crown upon her head) as Queen of Heaven, echo the ways she was consistently presented in sermons, poetry, music, and art of the era. Pious late medieval Christians directed their prayers to Mary as a fellow human entrusted with a momentous divine role, requesting her sympathetic intervention with God on their behalf.

But this panel also hints at additional meanings. The fruit held by Mary could call to mind the fruit from the Tree of Knowledge. In Genesis, Eve falls prey to the serpent's beguiling exhortation to taste that forbidden fruit. In her perfectly virtuous nature, Mary is presented as redeeming the sin that misogynist strains of medieval theology had placed upon Eve and all her female progeny.[1] The price of that redemption appears on the facing panel: Jesus perishes, sacrificed upon the Cross, his body buckling under its own dead weight. To the left, Mary raises her hands in a gesture of shock and horror as she witnesses the death of her grown child, while at the right, Jesus's close friend and follower John the Evangelist bows his head and touches his cheek in grief.

This piece thus perfectly encapsulates many of the key devotional practices that held sway in late medieval Europe.[2] Its subtle carving, too, beautifully expresses the central trends of its era: the gentle sway of Mary's body and the bemused grin on her face, the painful and yet elegant calligraphy of Jesus's broken body, the ornamental range of pointed arches that crown both scenes—all are emblematic of the art produced during this late "Gothic" period.

But at the same time, this object points to much broader cultures and histories. These ivory panels were once part of the massive tusk of an African elephant, a material prized in the European and Mediterranean worlds since antiquity. For nearly a thousand years after the collapse of the Western Roman Empire, ivory had been in short supply in Europe. In the thirteenth century, however, ambitious merchants in Africa and the Mediterranean began to form extensive networks of long-distance trade. These networks linked together traders in a chain that brought costly materials—including ivory—from sub-Saharan Africa to the burgeoning market cities of northern Europe, Paris in particular.[3] Seen in this light, Bowdoin's diptych speaks not only of the religious impulses of European Christians, but also of shippers, merchants, and traders who connected with each other across a vast swathe of the globe in this premodern era.

Stephen Perkinson
Associate Professor of Art History, Chair of the Art History Division of the Department of Art, and Associate Dean for Academic Affairs, Bowdoin College

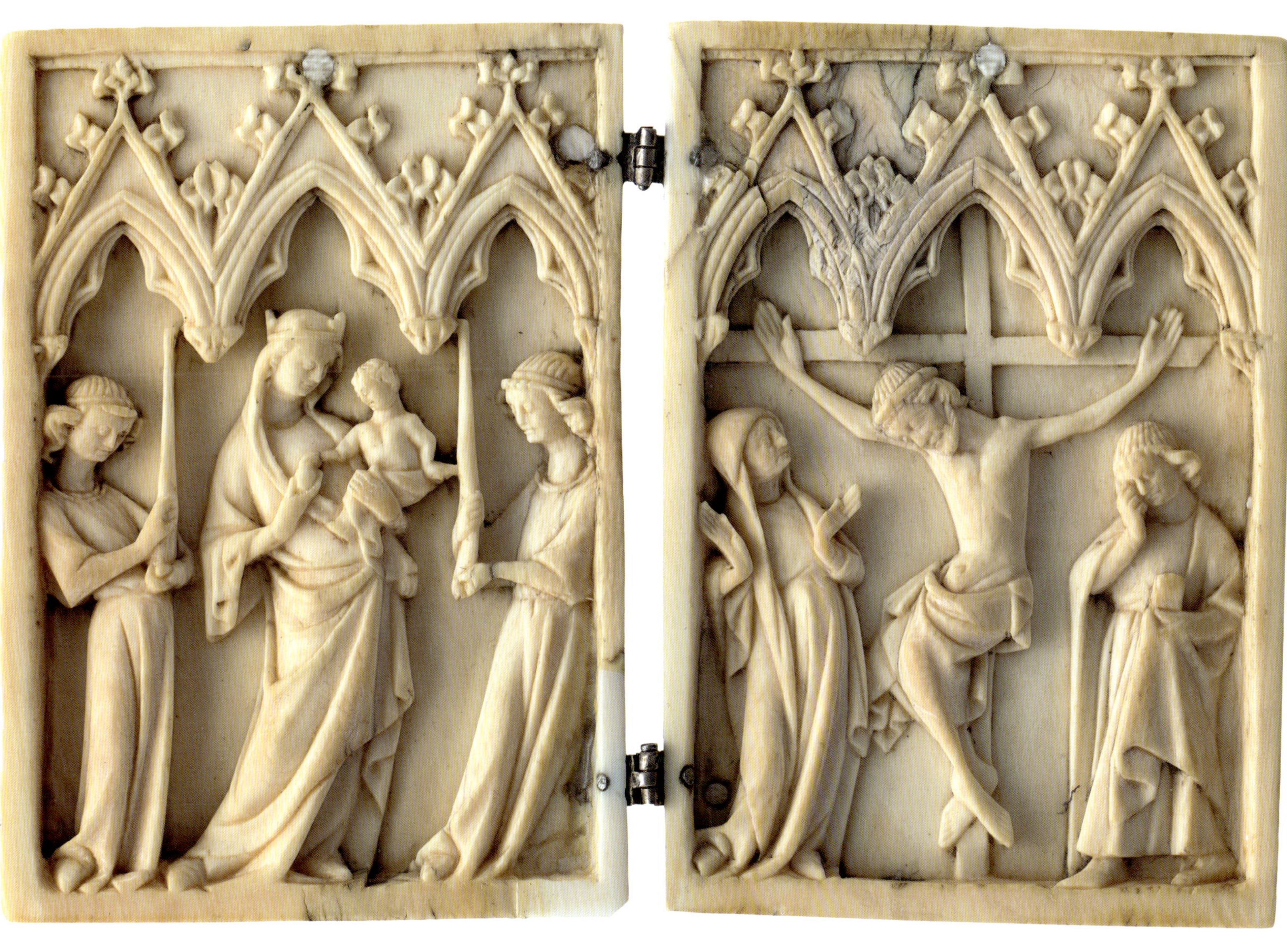

# St. Mary Magdalen between St. Peter Martyr and St. Catherine of Siena

Gherardo del Fora (Italian, 1445–1497), c. 1475
Tempera on panel, 16¾ × 11¼ in. (42.5 × 28.5 cm)
Gift of the Samuel H. Kress Foundation  1961.100.11

Gherardo di Giovanni di Miniato del Fora's biography is recounted in Giorgio Vasari's *Lives of the Artists*, and documents attest to his activities as illuminator, mosaicist, painter, stationer, and organist.[1] Born into a family of artists in Florence, he spent part of his life as a lay brother at San Marco, the Observant Dominican friary where Fra Angelico's frescoes enriched devotional practice.

In this rectangular panel, the *Noli Me Tangere*—Mary Magdalen's encounter with the risen Christ, when he says "touch me not" as she seeks to embrace him—is viewed within a window behind a haggard, hair-clad figure of the Magdalen, upon whom the Dominican saints Peter Martyr and Catherine of Siena fix their gaze. Structuring the composition in this way shows the Magdalen as both the first witness to the Resurrection and a penitent.

For whom was this painting made? It is undocumented, but the iconography may provide clues to its origins. Mary Magdalen, a patron of the Dominican order, and Catherine of Siena, the Dominicans' first female saint, commonly appear in art made for Observant Dominican women.[2] The inclusion of Peter Martyr, who is glorified with the triple crown of martyr, virgin, and doctor, suggests the panel could have been painted for San Pier Martire, an Observant Dominican nunnery in Florence.[3] Gherardo's own association with the order strengthens this hypothesis.

Too small to be an altarpiece, the painting may have been intended for a nun's cell in San Pier Martire, for which Fra Angelico's fresco of the *Noli Me Tangere* in a lay brother's cell in San Marco provides a precedent (fig. 1).[4] The depiction of the *Noli Me Tangere* in a verdant, walled garden akin to a cloister is similar in the two works; however, Gherardo reverses the position of the two figures. Placing the Magdalen on the right focuses attention on her reaction to Christ's appearance and thus celebrates her role in the Passion.[5]

The prominent foreground figure of the penitent Magdalen, a sinner lost in prayer, is laden with pathos. Her bony body and overgrown hair and toenails evince her renunciation of luxury and vanity. She is a spiritual athlete. This painting is a profound statement of the devotional aspirations of its original user.

Trinita Kennedy
Curator, Frist Art Museum, Nashville

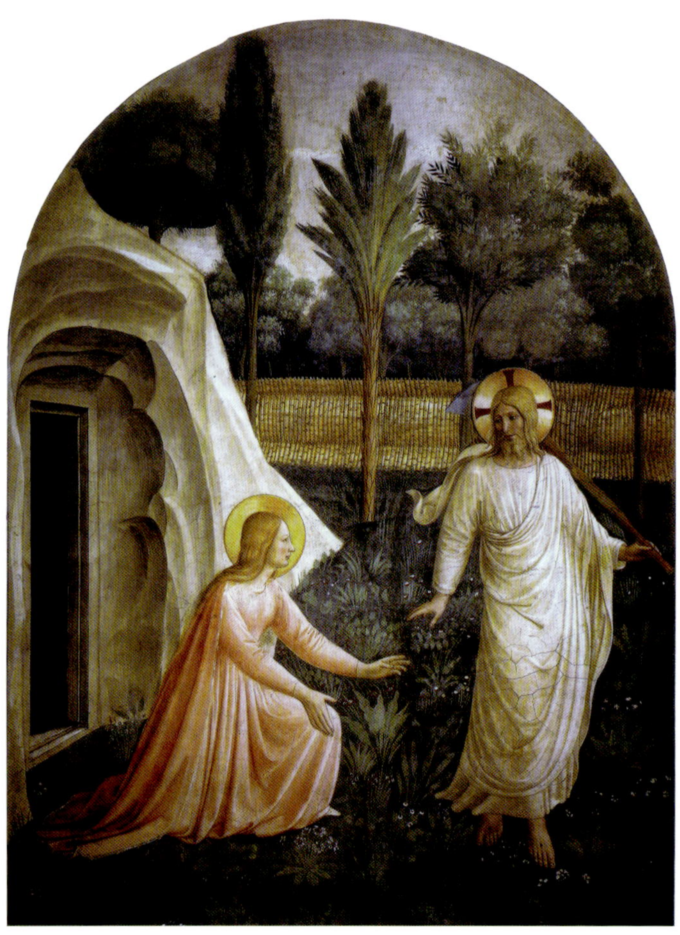

FIG. 1. Fra Angelico, *Noli Me Tangere*, 1440–41. Fresco. Convent of San Marco, Florence

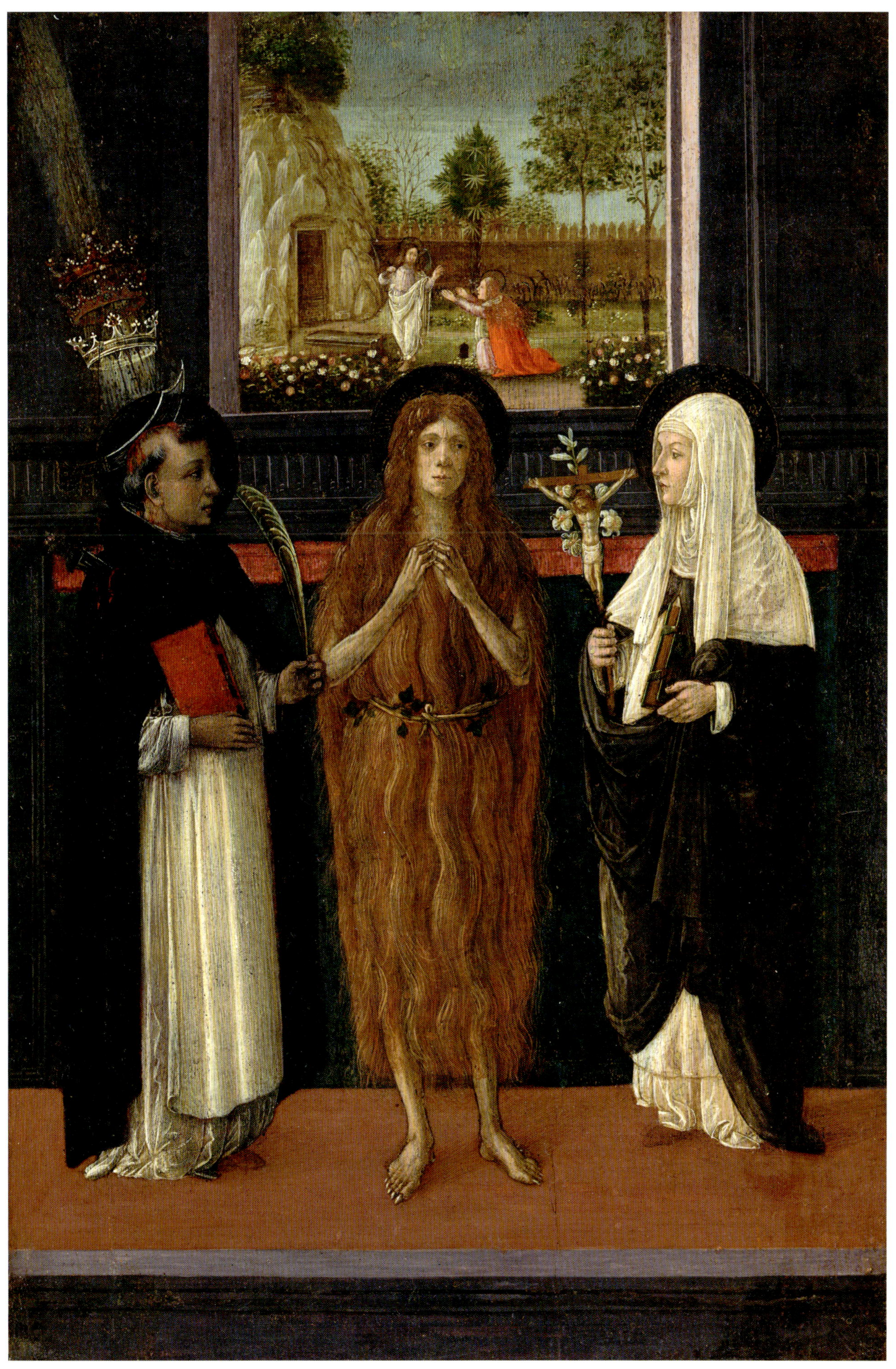

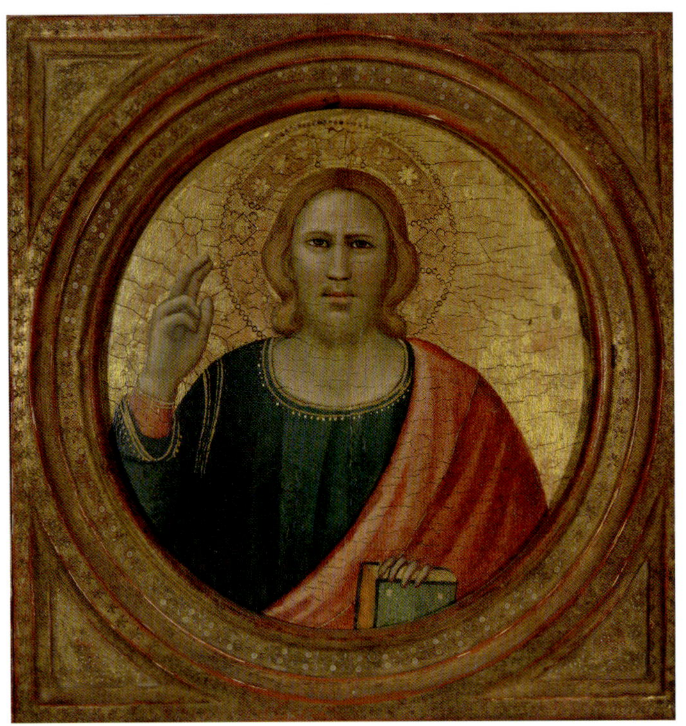

## Christ Blessing

Allegretto Nuzi (Italian, c. 1316/20–1373/74), c. 1360
Tempera on panel, 7⅜ × 7⅛ in. (18.7 × 18.1 cm)
Gift of the Samuel H. Kress Foundation  1961.100.4

This beautiful fragment of a triptych or polyptych (altarpieces with multiple panels) is in a very fine state of preservation. Originally, the tondo might have been part of the frame of a larger altarpiece, in which it would presumably have graced the gable of the central panel. Art historian Roberto Longhi identified the work's "simplicity and amplitude of shape" as telling signs of Allegretto Nuzi's training in Florence, around 1330–40, under the strong influence of Giotto. Despite the small scale of this painting, the half-figure of the haloed Christ in the act of blessing possesses monumental dignity. Nuzi's panel depicting Saint Anthony Abbot, a wing of a major altarpiece for his home town of Fabriano, is today in the National Gallery of Art, Washington, D.C., and like this work, a gift from the Samuel H. Kress Foundation. (JHo)

## Portrait Medal of John VIII Palaeologus

Pisanello (Antonio Di Puccio Pisano) (Italian, by 1395–c. 1455), c. 1438
Lead, 4⅛ in. (10.5 cm)
Gift of Amanda Marchesa Molinari  1966.103.a

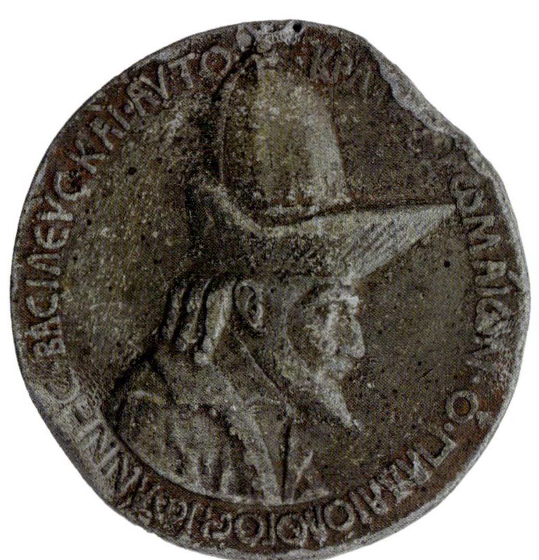

Pisanello, a trained painter, combined his interest in classical coins with portraiture to produce a medium that is durable, portable, and easily reproducible: the portrait medal. He cast the first modern portrait medal around 1438 to commemorate the participation of Byzantine emperor John VIII Palaeologus (r. 1425–48) in the Council of Ferrara (later moved to Florence to avoid the plague), which secured him political protection against the Ottoman empire through the gesture of uniting the Byzantine and Roman churches. Coincidentally, the presence of elite Greek scholars in John's entourage greatly encouraged the rise of Renaissance humanism in the West. Pisanello's highly influential work ignited a craze for portrait medals, and his masterful profile view of Palaeologus's face influenced future painters, sculptors, and medalists alike. This early uniface example is cast in lead. The malleability of the metal, which allows sharper impressions, is also responsible for the extensive surface damage visible today. (BW/AO)

# *Apollo and Daphne*

Jacopo da Pontormo (Italian, 1494–1557), 1513
Oil on canvas, 24⅜ × 19¼ in. (61.9 × 48.9 cm)
Gift of the Samuel H. Kress Foundation  1961.100.9

The charisma of Renaissance cities was most memorably expressed by the dozens of carnival, tournament, parade, and feast-day celebrations that punctuated local calendars. Florence was arguably without equal in this regard. Engaging all the senses, the city's festivities were intensely communal affairs, talked about for generations. Carnevale arrived forty days before Easter and amounted to a city-wide party before the sobrieties of Ash Wednesday and Lent. The Carnevale of 1513 carried special significance, as it marked the first such occasion since the return of the Medici after eighteen years in exile. The restoration of the city's *de facto* ruling family simultaneously spelled the end of civic republican rule. Pontormo's pair of small mythological scenes, preserved in the Bowdoin and Bucknell (fig. 1) collections, were jointly conceived for the elaborate ritual as part of a much larger program of painted and sculpted ephemera.[1] Together, the carefully choreographed decorations served to mark a particularly charged political as well as social event.[2] The turn in political fortunes, already signaled during Carnevale, was strongly reinforced just a month later, with the election of Giovanni de' Medici as Pope Leo X in Rome.

Only age eighteen at the time, Pontormo was entrusted with a project of great personal prestige.[3] The commission as a whole was extraordinarily ambitious: to decorate all three wooden cars celebrating the Compagnia del Diamante (Company of the Diamond), overseen by Giuliano de' Medici, duke of Nemours and younger brother to the new pope, as one of the three sons of the celebrated Lorenzo "il Magnifico" de' Medici.[4] Giuliano adopted the diamond as his *impresa*, or personal device.[5]

Pontormo's haunting renditions of the tragic legend of Apollo and Daphne take place in a spectral setting: neither bucolic Arcadia nor Thessaly, but a shadowy nowhere land. Not only are the chiaroscuro forms living sculptures of a sort, but those of Apollo in the Lewisburg canvas and

Daphne in its Brunswick partner are about to undergo irrevocable change. From the ancient poets Hesiod, Catullus, and Ovid to Petrarch and Poliziano, Cupid (or Eros) was shown to be an extremely powerful figure—and a terrible troublemaker. His bodily form may appear as smooth and perfect as marble, but he burns with fire. The Lewisburg canvas portrays the dialogue between Apollo and Cupid as described in Ovid's *Metamorphoses*, just prior to the moment when the slighted Cupid shoots his gold-tipped "love dart" at Apollo in retribution, causing him to fall in love with Daphne at first sight, his eyes "gleaming like stars."[6]

The Bowdoin canvas depicts the aftermath of Cupid's mischief, showing the love-struck Apollo chasing

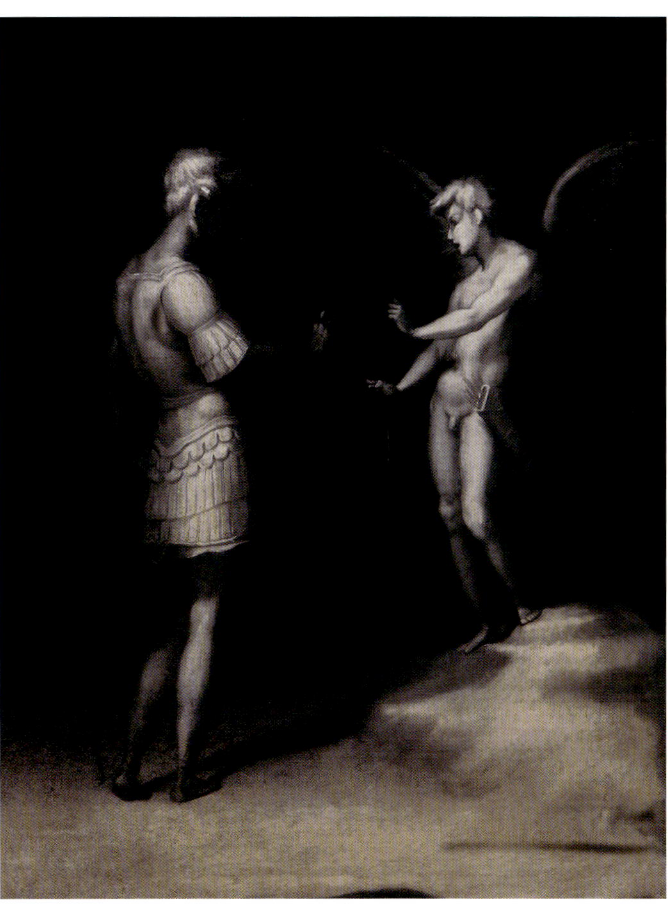

 Pontormo, *Cupid and Apollo*, 1513. Oil on canvas, 24 × 18⅝ in. (61 × 47.3 cm). Samek Art Museum, Bucknell University, Lewisburg, Pennsylvania, 1961.K.1618

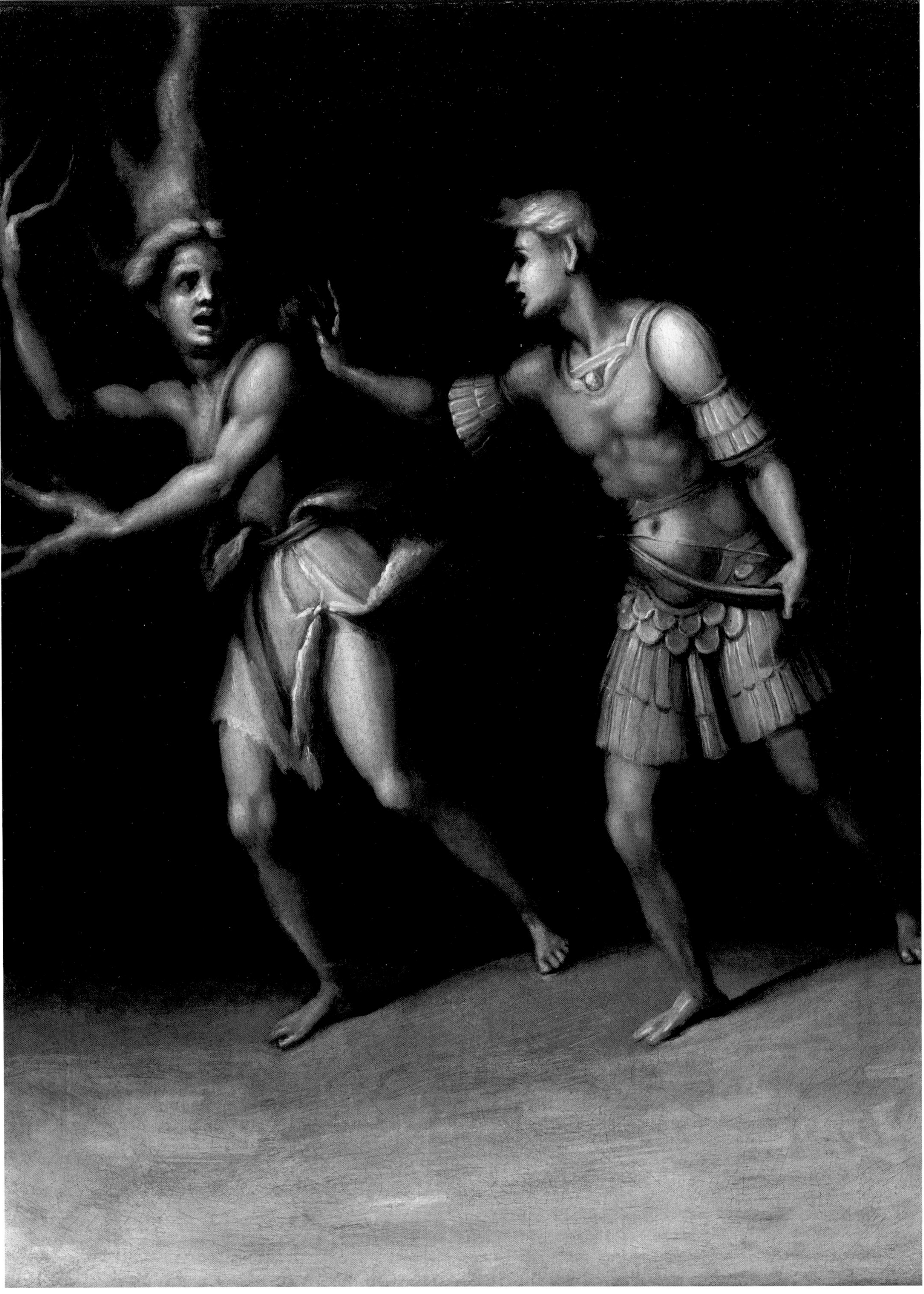

Daphne—shot with a blunt leaden shaft, inciting antipathy—and losing her forever.[7] Daphne was the most beautiful of the Naiads, the nymphs that inhabited rivers, springs, and waterfalls. Her peaceful pastoral existence is shattered upon her rejection of Apollo. Growing exhausted from his relentless pursuit, she implores her river god father—or, in other accounts, more appropriately her mother, the primal earth goddess Terra (Gaia, in Greek myth)—to save her. The chaste maiden's prayers are answered. Just as Apollo is about to overtake her, she is transformed into a laurel tree. In Pontormo's painting, we witness the initial instant of Daphne's transformation, branches springing upward from her arms, while the rest of her body still retains its human form. The grieving god of music and poetry adopted the laurel as his sacred plant in memory of his beloved, and the crown wreathed with its leaves came to be appropriated in celebration of poets and public triumphs since ancient times.

What would have been the larger significance of the evergreen laurel's symbolism in early sixteenth-century Florence? Its meaning and that of the diamond are, in fact, intimately aligned. A laurel branch sprouting new leaves appears in Pontormo's own *Portrait of Cosimo de' Medici, the Elder*, c. 1519 (Gallerie degli Uffizi, Florence), signifying the regeneration of the Medici family. If a branch is cut, a new one springs forth—or, if the Medici clan is exiled, it too shall always return! Signifying eternity itself, the diamond is a still clearer reminder of resilience and endurance.

The spectacle glorifying the Compagnia del Brancone (Company of the [Laurel] Branch), staged four days earlier on February 6, was overseen by Giuliano's nephew Lorenzo de' Medici, duke of Urbino.[8] All of the accompanying painted decorations were again entrusted to Pontormo, of which two canvases, now on deposit in Palazzo Montecitorio, Rome, also survive.[9] One might imagine the subject of the Bowdoin canvas to be still more appropriate to the Compagnia del Brancone's decorative cycle, in fact, as Daphne's fateful transformation into laurel (Piero de' Medici's *impresa*) echoes the popular moniker of Lauro for Piero's father Lorenzo—himself a poet worthy of Apollo's laurel wreath.

Sharing the keenly personal, experimental impulses of his early teachers, Leonardo da Vinci and Piero di Cosimo, Pontormo is a tantalizingly evasive artist. The subjective quality of his art extends from his often-veiled meanings, deflecting any one reading, to the originality of his stylistic solutions and ways of working. In his festival decorations, he cleverly chose to adopt the grisaille technique, simulating sculpted relief. Encountering these scenes today, evenly illuminated in their modern museum settings, one is left to imagine their bravura grisaille effects at nighttime, when the Carnevale procession appears to have taken place, by torchlight. The flickering lights and dramatic play of light and shadow would have animated the gesturing figures—accentuating their contradictory sense of stony *rilievo* (relief) and illusion of movement. A chant would have accompanied the moving masquerades, further stimulating the senses.

Intended for temporary use, both canvases are rapidly yet very attentively painted. A number of passages testify to the teenage master's already evident technical resourcefulness, although many of the finer touches no doubt would have evaded the audience's shifting gaze as the triumphal cars passed through the city streets. The positions of the legs of both pursuer and pursued virtually echo one another. Daphne's right hand, turning into craggy branches before one's eyes, is a virtuosic passage in its upward-reaching offshoots. A thin strand of her trailing hair is shown slipping through the outstretched second and third fingers of Apollo's right hand. Other engaging details include the little winged putto head (Cupid himself perhaps?) on the neckline of Apollo's cuirass, and the lower part of Daphne's ambiguously textured tunic: part fabric, part animal skin (note the frayed, uneven ends, and furlike underside), or even part bark.

As the late winter day wore on and the Medici-sponsored marvels of Carnevale passed through the streets and piazze, the people of Florence were encouraged to forget that just months before, their city was still a republic, free of single-family rule. For a moment, we in turn can almost hear the music, the singing, the rolling wheels of passing floats—and the excited whispers of the amazed onlookers crowding all around us.

Dennis V. Geronimus
Associate Professor of Art History,
Department Chair, New York University

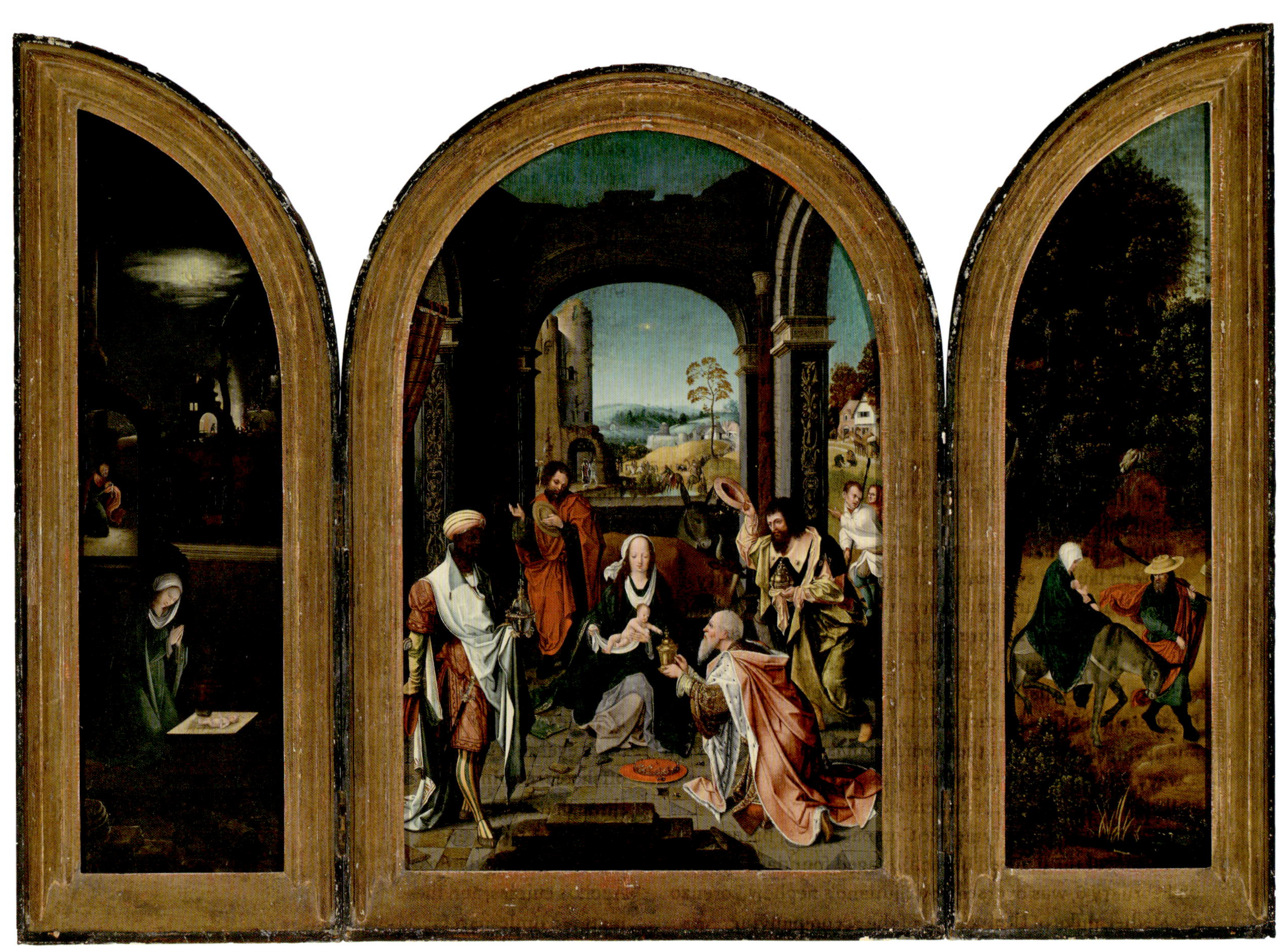

# Adoration Triptych

After Jan de Beer (Netherlandish, c. 1475–before 1528), c. 1518–19
Oil on panel in an engaged frame, central panel: 31¼ × 21¼ in.
(79.5 × 54 cm), wings: 32¼ × 9⅝ in. (82 × 24.5 cm)

Museum Purchase, Lloyd O. and Marjorie Strong Coulter Fund, Jane H. and
Charles E. Parker, Jr. Art Acquisition Fund and Laura T. and John H. Halford, Jr.
Art Acquisition Fund  2018.25

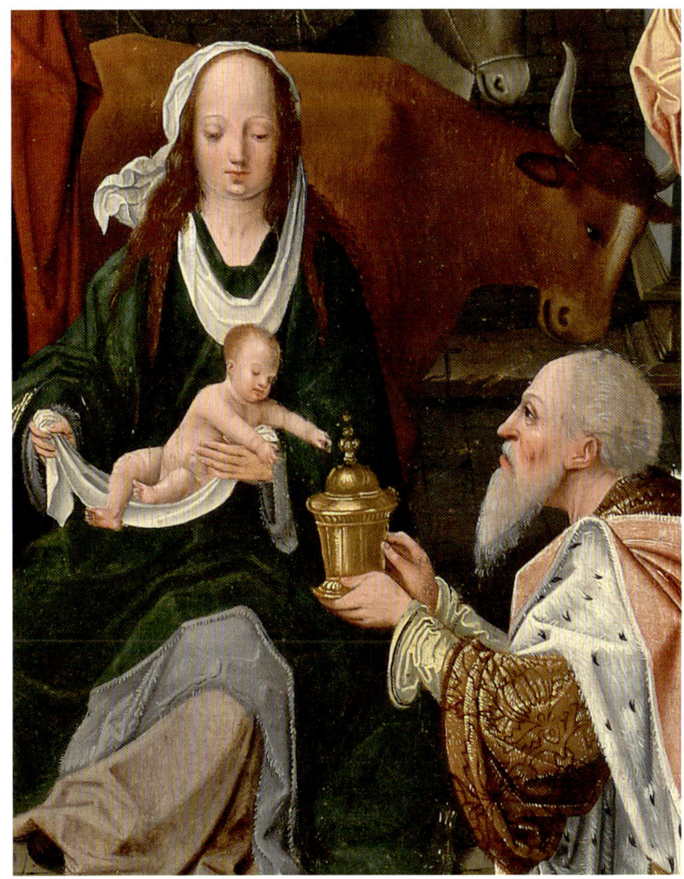

This recently acquired triptych embodies key aspects of
painting in early sixteenth-century Antwerp, then the
leading art center in northern Europe. It is one of two
exceptionally faithful copies of a lost Adoration triptych
by the Antwerp painter Jan de Beer. The other triptych, in
Munich, slightly smaller, is closely related in design, colors,
and details. Both match de Beer's stylistic repertoire and
visual finesse to a far greater degree than the other fifty-two
copies, an indication that each was likely produced in de
Beer's workshop by studio assistants.[1]

The left wing depicts Christ's midnight birth. In the rear,
shepherds gather round a bonfire as the Annunciation to
the Shepherds unfolds. The center shows the three Magi
presenting their gifts. The African Magus, Balthasar, is the
most theatrical, with his erect stance, colorful headpiece,
striped stockings, and almost balletic foot positions. Behind
Melchior, two shepherds run in from the fields to join the
celebration. The journey of the Magi with their caravan is
seen in the background. In the right wing, the Holy Family
flees Israel to Egypt, in response to Herod's decree to kill all
Bethlehem children under the age of two, in fear that the
Messiah was born.

The Adoration of the Magi was the predominant
religious theme in Antwerp painting, and one of the few
instances in which black Africans regularly appeared in
Renaissance art. The Magi—foreigners from distant lands,
transporting luxury goods—came to be an important part
of the city's identity, regarded as analogues to the numerous foreign merchants trading in Antwerp, Europe's largest
commercial market. Like the Magi's gifts of gold, frank-
incense, and myrrh, the city's economy was based upon
the luxury trade. Pepper and rare spices from India and
Africa, sugar from Madeira and the Canary Islands, silver
from Germany and Bohemia, and diamonds from India all
poured into Antwerp. Many Antwerp Adorations, like the

Bowdoin panel, make the Magi/merchant analogy explicit
by depicting the Magi's attendants as porters transporting
cargo. Here, in the right-center background, they unload
packs from the camels, set them on the ground, and open a
chest of valuables.[2]

The fifty-four copies of de Beer's prototype made it the
artistic "bestseller" in Antwerp. The city had become the
largest open market for art, and artists supplied it partly
through serial production—producing multiple copies and
variants from a prototype. Painted copies were normative
in the Renaissance. They ensured that the growing demand
from churches, wealthy merchants, nobles, and kings for
popular paintings would be satisfied by painted copies
rather than reproductive engravings, conveying the
colors, visual presence, and facture of the originals. Other
Antwerp artists were even more involved in serial copying.
Joos van Cleve's much larger workshop produced many
series, including twenty-nine replicas of Leonardo's lost
*Madonna of the Cherries*.[3]

Dan Ewing
Professor of Art History, Barry University

# *The Entombment*

Girolamo Francesco Maria Mazzola, known as Parmigianino
(Italian, 1503–1540), 1529–30
Etching, 11 × 8¼ in. (28 × 21 cm)
Gift of David P. Becker, Class of 1970, in honor of Katharine J.
Watson  1990.63

Parmigianino was a sixteenth-century Italian painter and a virtuoso draftsman, known for his elongated Mannerist figures executed in sinuous brush and line work. He was also the first Italian artist to exploit the potential of the recently developed application of etching (long used to decorate armor) as a printmaking technique in the second quarter of the 1500s.[1] Despite his small output of some seventeen different compositions created in a burst of experimentation around 1527–30, he is widely regarded as the first great painter-etcher before Rembrandt, and his prints and drawings had a profound influence on other artists.

Parmigianino's two etchings of the Entombment of Christ are considered the pinnacle of his printed oeuvre and masterworks of early etching. Both versions—the first, an impression of which is in Bowdoin's collection, the second, illustrated here by the example in the Philadelphia Museum of Art (fig. 1)—share the same basic composition: a tender scene in which Mary Magdalen gently leans over Christ, whose slouched, elongated body lays on a stone for final blessing, while his mother, the Virgin Mary, gazing in his direction, swoons in grief, and at right, Joseph of Arimathea (presumably) presides over the burial preparations; an additional seven figures are crowded within a shallow, vaguely defined space in the background. The second version (executed in reverse of the first) is slightly larger, more deeply etched, more resolved in certain details—such as Joseph's arm, which is now raised above Christ's head, holding aloft the crown of thorns that lies on the ground in the first version—and some have noted a generally bolder, more confident manner of execution.[2]

However, the first version, in its less finished, lightly etched, open-air qualities, offers a greater sense of immediacy that heightens the intimacy of the scene. Here, Parmigianino's affinity for the fluidity of the etching medium is revealed: delicate fine lines suggest without rigidly defining forms, contours and passages are left incomplete or blank to describe the fall of light on flesh, hair, and drapery, in a marvelous flowing shorthand carried over from his drawing practice. Joseph's outstretched arm dissolves into the shoulder of the Magdalen, leading the eye to the two Marys and Christ united by the circular formation defined by their tilted heads and Christ's raised knee. The slightly angled, ill-defined block of stone beneath Christ is nearly dissolved in light, and

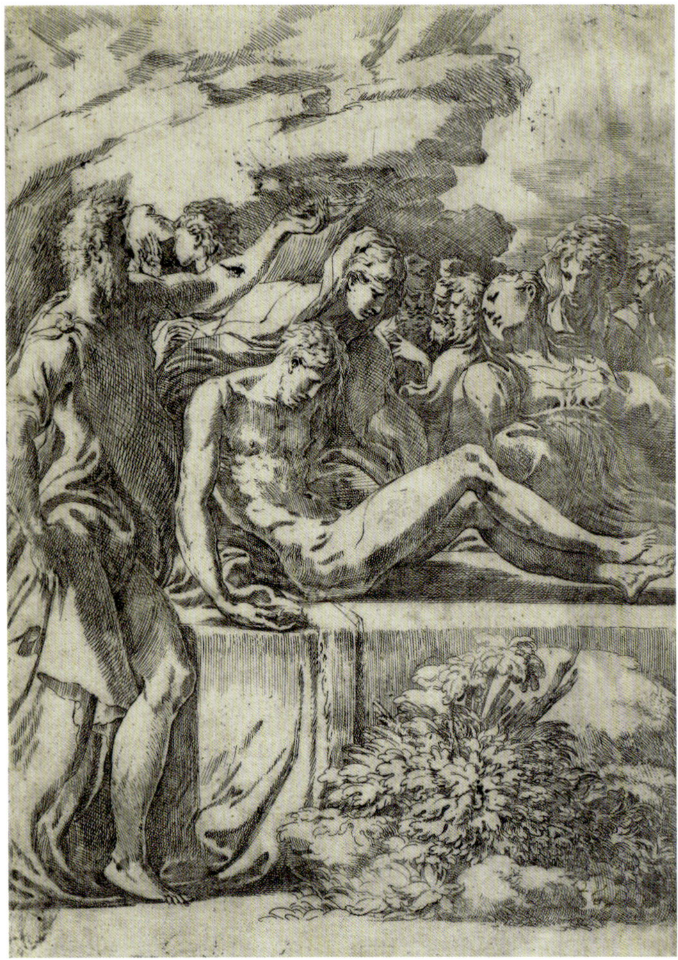

FIG. 1. Parmigianino, *The Entombment (Second Version)*, c. 1530. Etching and drypoint on paper, sheet: 12¹³⁄₁₆ × 9⁵⁄₁₆ in. (32.5 × 23.7 cm). Philadelphia Museum of Art, The Muriel and Philip Berman Gift, acquired from the John S. Phillips bequest of 1876 to the Pennsylvania Academy of the Fine Arts, 1985-52-1798

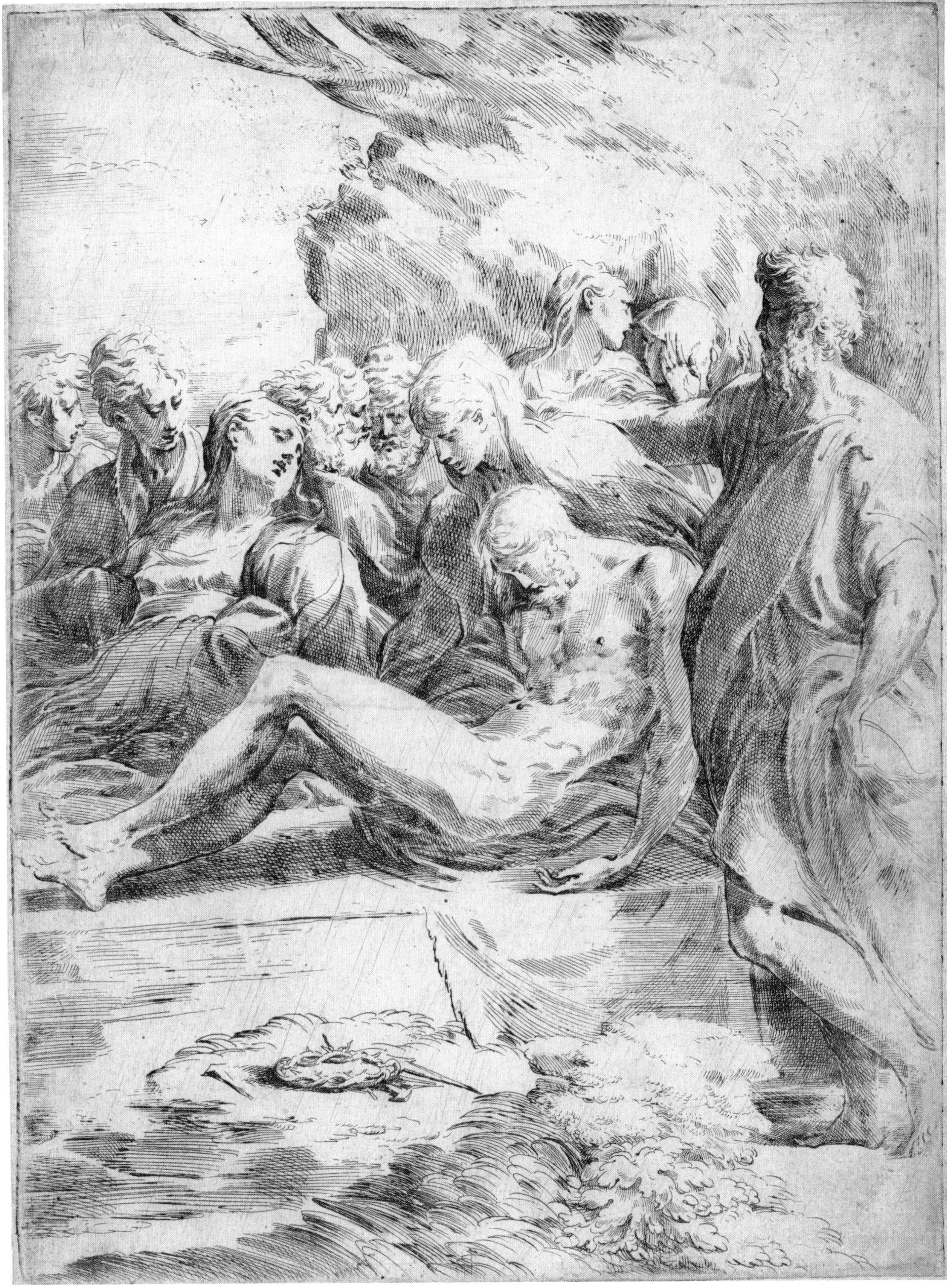

while lacking the more emphatic solidity of the horizontal slab in the second version, this effect enhances the ethereal, spiritual atmosphere of this rendering. The overall luminosity, harmonious grace, and delicacy of line invite comparison with Parmigianino's masterful Roman and Bolognese drawings.

This is the first print in which Parmigianino fully gave himself over to the purely etched line and the freedom allowed the hand by the pointed etching needle's ease of movement through the ground on the copper plate to inscribe the design in a manner akin to drawing on paper. The lines of exposed copper were then bitten into the plate when it was immersed in an acid bath, the rest of the ground was removed, and the plate could be inked and printed. Previously, the only available print media were engraving and woodcut, executed by trained printmakers skilled in the difficult art of incising directly into metal plates with a burin, or in carving wooden blocks. These printmakers would often work closely with painters and other artists to translate their imagery into print.[3] But etching opened the door for painters and other artists who lacked training to directly produce their own prints and explore original ideas as they worked. Rather than creating a specific drawing model for his Entombment etching, Parmigianino culled his ideas from existing studies he had made of the subject as well as other themes, to conceive a new composition.[4]

Bowdoin's *Entombment* was the magnificent gift of print collector, art historian, and connoisseur David Becker, Bowdoin graduate and Board of Trustees member. As a milestone in the history of Italian printmaking that offers insight into an artist's discovery of the expressive potential of a medium and the beauty of the etched line, the work would be a celebrated treasure for any collection.

Shelley R. Langdale
The Park Family Associate Curator
of Prints and Drawings, Philadelphia
Museum of Art, and President, Print
Council of America

## Hercules Slaying Cacus

Hendrick Goltzius (Dutch, 1558–1617), 1588 (printed c. 1615)
Color woodcut on paper, 16¼ × 13⅛ in. (41.3 × 33.3 cm)
Gift of Charles Pendexter  2009.16.316

This is the largest and most complex of Hendrick Goltzius's chiaroscuro woodcuts, a technique of layering prints from a line block and additional tone blocks to achieve a sensation of depth. The image is based on the tenth labor of Hercules, who in this scene violently kills Cacus, the fire-breathing son of Vulcan, for stealing cattle from him when he slept. Hercules himself had heisted the cattle from the monster Geryon. Hercules took revenge, freed the herd from the barricaded cave where Cacus had hidden them, and later sacrificed the animals to Hera, in an effort to redeem himself after murdering his wife and six sons in a rage. The rendering of the upper body of Cacus is quoted from Cornelis Cornelisz's *Companions of Cadmus Devoured by a Dragon*, which Goltzius engraved in the same year as he worked on *Hercules Slaying Cacus*. For viewers of Goltzius's time, many of the artist's prints took on political meaning. In the light of the ongoing Dutch War of Independence against the Spanish hegemony, the so-called Eighty Years' War (1568–1648), the representation of mythological struggles offered covert but poignant political commentary. (JHo)

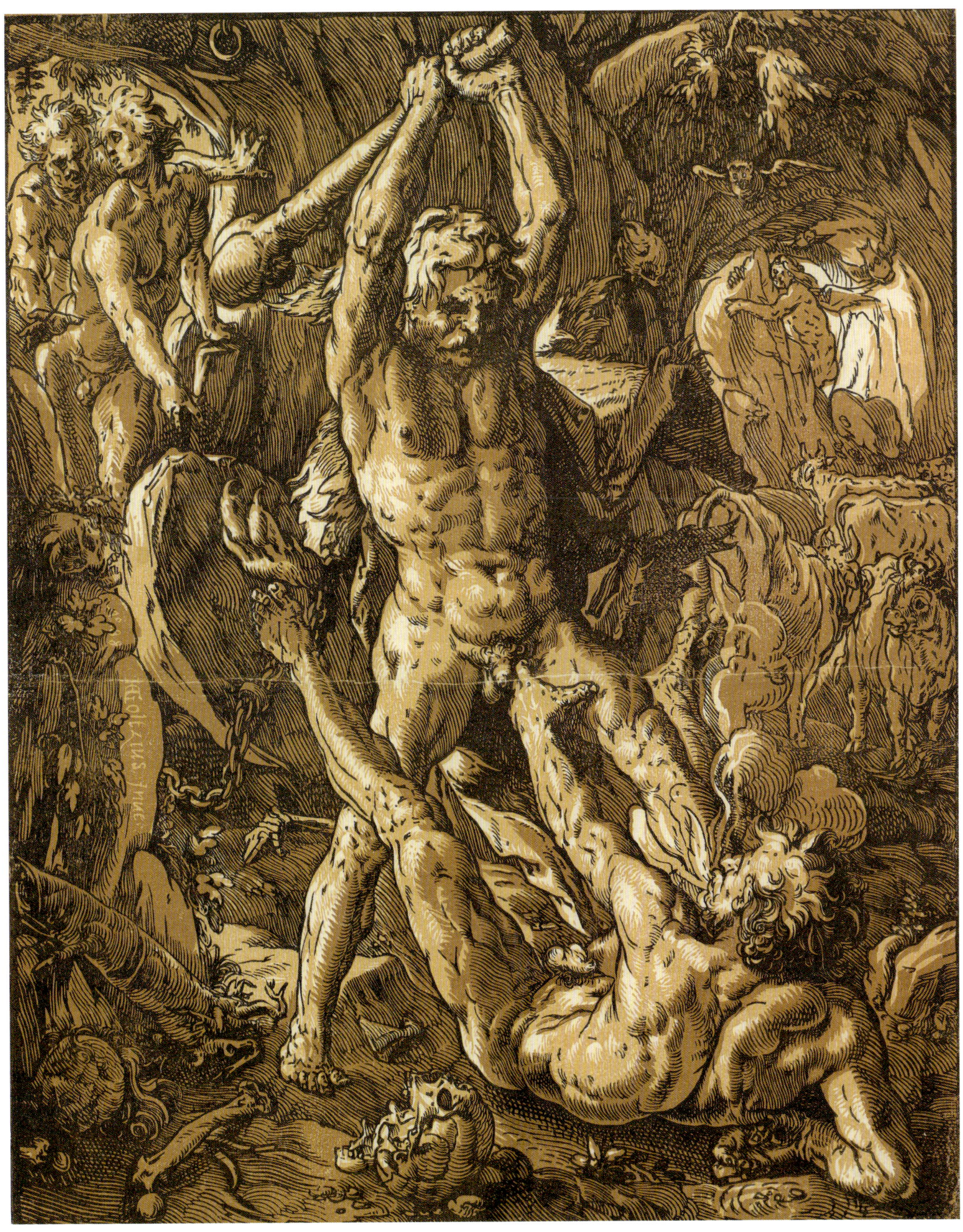

# *Annunciation*

Denys Calvaert (Flemish/Italian, c. 1540–1619), c. 1595
Oil on copper, 20¹³⁄₁₆ × 15⁷⁄₁₆ in. (52.9 × 39.2 cm)
Museum Purchase, Laura T. and John H. Halford, Jr. Art Acquisition Fund,
Lloyd O. and Marjorie Strong Coulter Fund and Jane H. and Charles E.
Parker, Jr. Art Acquisition Fund  2010.36

This painting of the Annunciation presents an opportunity to reflect on its moralizing significance for early modern viewers, as well as on its contextual use and value as an art object that circulated between multiple hands and spaces throughout its lifetime. The Annunciation is among the most frequently depicted religious themes across Renaissance Europe. It illustrates the dramatic moment when the angel Gabriel announces to Mary that she will become mother to Jesus. In Denys Calvaert's 1595 oil-on-copper rendition, it is easy to locate familiar tropes. A trio of bodies expressively enacts the incarnation; interior and exterior spaces set the stage for the narrative of redemption. Gabriel's instructive gesture appears before the backdrop of a garden, the *hortus conclusus* emblematic of the immaculate conception, which is symbolized in God's penetrating hand, parting the heavens and emitting light. Mary welcomes the divine presence with modesty within a contained domestic setting, flanked by lilies, a sign of purity. She interrupts her reading of an open book, shaped like the tablets of the commandments. This small painting, housed in a precious historical frame that retains its single hook to be hung on a nail, was likely commissioned and used in personal devotion. As a visual presence in a pious household, the work surely had a tangible impact on the lives of the residents. Counter-Reformation Europe experienced an upsurge in devotional art and literature, and new spiritual movements and meditative practices centered on the establishment of a closer, more personal relationship with God.

Depictions of the Annunciation provide insights into social, cultural, and religious aspects of early modern society, particularly the implementation of gendered codes of conduct. Catholic preachers and writers of numerous works on the life of the Virgin emphasized Mary's obedience and submissiveness as characteristics of model behavior for women.[1] Humanist treatises and conduct manuals, rapidly circulated throughout Europe since the advent of the printing press, argued for reformations within the church and larger society, encouraging audiences to emulate these prescribed models of gendered behavior. Guidebooks for husbands and wives, for example, were extremely common. Evoking the injunctions of these conduct manuals and humanist treatises, early modern visual culture frequently fashioned a Marian ideal as a way to reinforce and promote these types of gendered expectations. Calvaert's poignant rendition of Mary is emblematic of behavioral norms set for women and popularized by the Cult of Mary: modest appearance, downward gaze, protected posturing, reading material as evidence of her dedication to study.

Although it is certainly possible to emphasize the controlling and containing effects of this prescription for female behavior, Jennifer Haraguchi also makes the compelling argument that many early modern women (lay and religious) "embraced this type of religiosity since it involved a more realistic, relatable role model for them to emulate."[2] In this way, Annunciation paintings testify to a variety of vexed emotional and spiritual relationships, as both imitative model and resistive practice. At Bowdoin, Calvaert's interpretation will continue to fuel lively conversations about the visual representation of women, literary and visual modes of instruction, negotiation, self-presentation, and performance.

Margaret E. Boyle
Associate Professor of Romance Languages
and Literatures, Bowdoin College

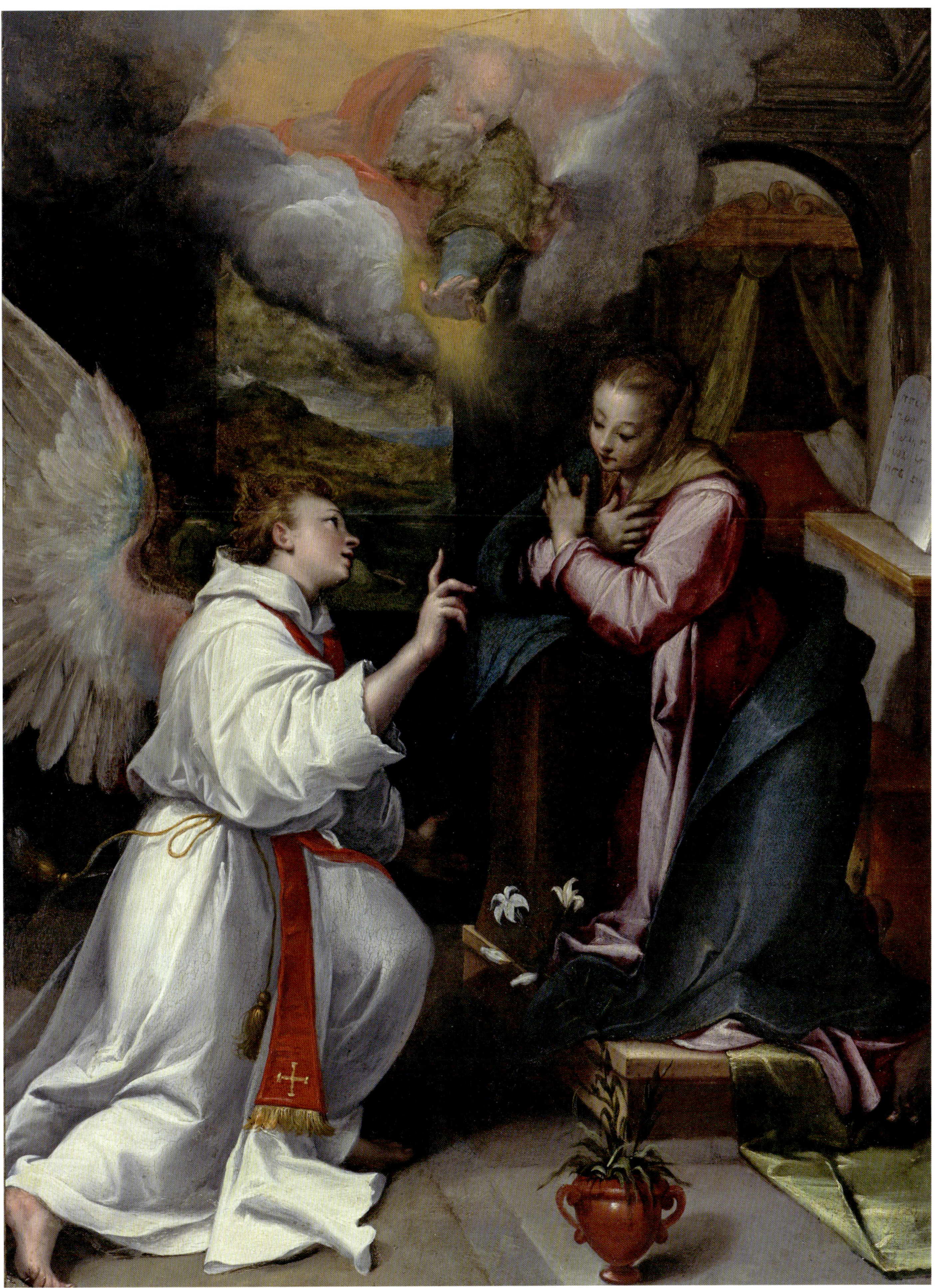

# *Study of an Archer*

Jacob Adriaensz. Backer (Dutch, 1608/9–1651), c. 1640
Black and white chalk on blue antique laid paper, 14⅛ × 8³⁄₁₆ in.
(35.9 × 20.8 cm)
Museum Purchase  1930.231

Why was this drawing of a curiously dressed man created? Finely rendered in black and white chalk with smooth, flowing lines and intricate areas of light and shade against the middle tone of its blue paper support, it depicts a figure in an unusual pose and costume, seen from behind. He steps carefully to the right, with lowered head and intently watchful eye, grasping a bow in his right hand and raising his long coat with his left. Other attributes include a quiver of arrows strapped to his back and a fancifully plumed hat with fur trim. Is he stalking prey? Did he come upon a surprising scene while out hunting, and is attempting to observe unseen? Is he a soldier about to attack an enemy?

Jacob Adriaensz. Backer was a portraitist and history painter active in Amsterdam in the second quarter of the seventeenth century. Then considered to be the highest form of painting, history subjects encompassed a range of depictions taken from respected written sources such as the Bible, ancient historical texts, poetry, and plays. Such scenes required artists to invent fresh and compelling—and often multifigural—compositions to best convey the story's narrative, climax, and didactic point. Before putting brush to canvas, however, most artists, including Backer, used drawing to test ideas for compositional strategies and, as is the case here, individual figures' poses and costumes. As was customary, artists drew from clothed models to render figures such as this.

But how do we know that Backer had a specific painting in mind when he drew this sheet? Could he not have simply drawn it as an exercise, to hone his skills at depicting both the human form and the fall of light across drapery? Theorists contemporary with Backer, including Crispijn van de Passe in his *'t Light der teken en schilderkonst* of 1643–44, advocated figural drawing as part of artistic training and practice.[1] In some instances, the painting for which a figural drawing was done survives, and we can see a close, if not exact, match between the drawn figure and the painted one. Many times, however, there is no clear painted counterpart to a drawn figure, which is the case here. Either the painting has not survived, or Backer drew it for more general purposes. Given the figure's unique costume and pose, a specific intent is more likely.

Considering Backer's known corpus of paintings, the Bowdoin drawing shows similarities to his pastoral subjects, including moments in shepherds' plays such as *Granida* (Pieter Corneliszoon Hooft, 1605) and *Il pastor fido* (Giovanni Battista Guarini, 1590), then popular among sophisticated, urban audiences.[2] Within this context, the figure's costume suggests he is a hunter, perhaps the character of Silvio from Guarini's famous tragicomedy, who accidentally shot his unwelcome admirer, the nymph Dorinda. Her near death at his hand turned Silvio's scorn into love, and, although he was fated to marry another, through twists in plot the couple ultimately wed.[3] This tantalizingly tentative identification proves no detraction, however, from this drawing's window into Amsterdam studio practice and artistic tastes during Holland's Golden Age.

Susan Anderson
Curator, Maida and George Abrams
Collection, and Curatorial Research
Associate, Harvard Art Museums

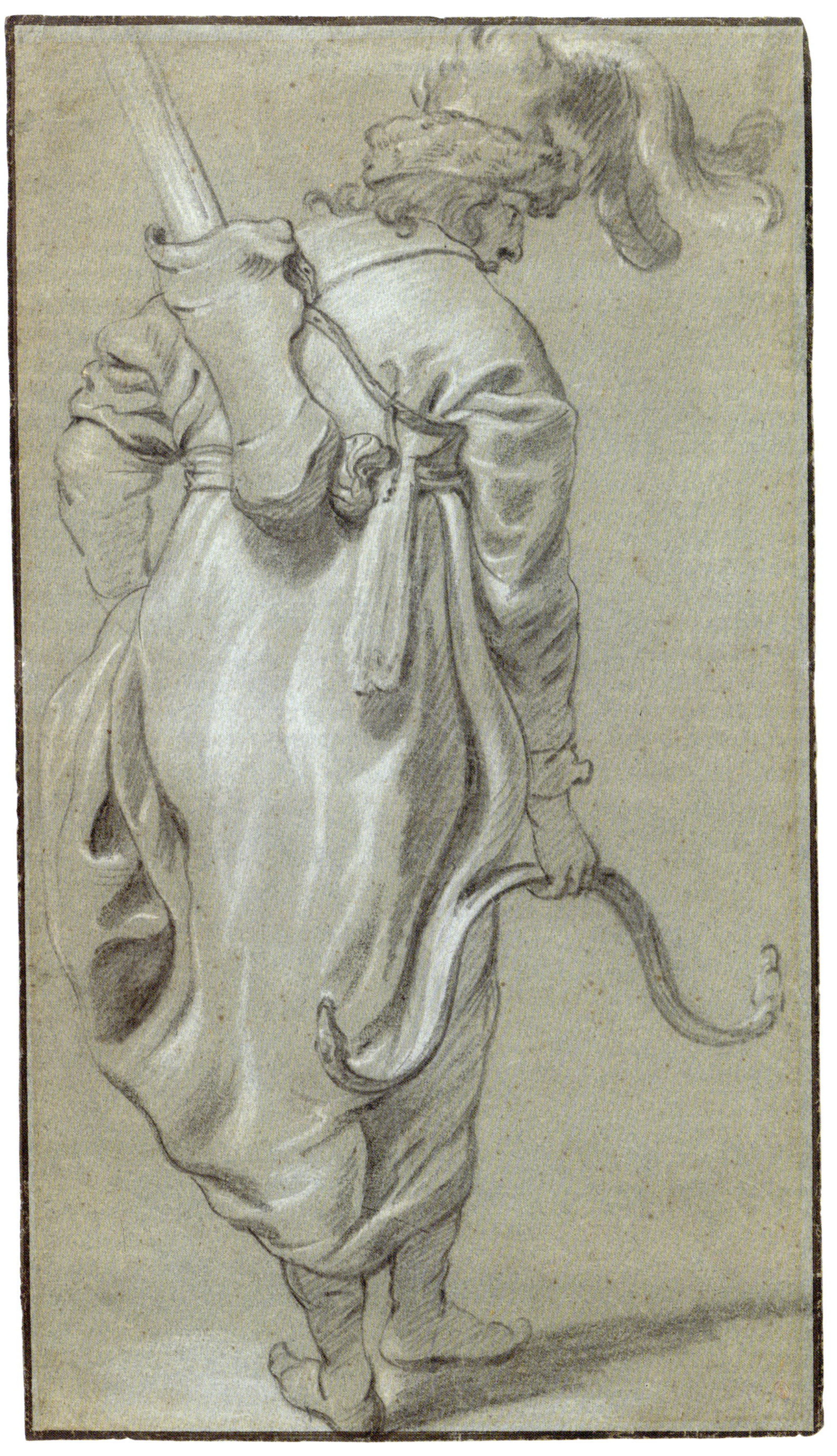

# A Coastal Scene near Zandvoort

Simon de Vlieger (Dutch, c. 1601–1653), c. 1640

Oil on panel, 22¼ × 34⅞ in. (56.5 × 88.6 cm)

Museum Purchase, Lloyd O. and Marjorie Strong Coulter Fund  2014.16

Simon de Vlieger was one of the pivotal marine painters of the Dutch "Golden Age." He was also one of the rare Dutch artists of the seventeenth century with wide-ranging interests outside of his field of specialization. He excelled as etcher, draftsman, and designer of stained-glass windows as well as in mathematical perspective. His subject matter included representations of architectural ruins, topographical views, wooded landscapes, genre scenes (mostly gatherings of fisherfolk on the beach), and depictions of trees and domesticated animals.

De Vlieger's contribution to marine painting remains underestimated. To a unique degree, he was responsible for the transition from the spirited beginnings of Dutch marine art to its most august and refined stage in the years around 1650. His great predecessor, Jan Porcellis (1580/84–1632), shifted Dutch marine art away from large-scale history subjects to focus instead on the unique, restless, and ever-changing atmospheric effects of the sea. De Vlieger brought these innovations to new levels of refinement. He realized this goal by envisaging the constant yet ever-changing rhythm of the sea under vaulting clouds that filter the sunlight playing across land and sea. In pictorial terms he harmonized all these variables into a seamless, fully orchestrated whole. His most notable maritime themes include ships in calm and stormy weather, often along forbidding rocky coasts; ships moored at jetties; fleets in calm weather awaiting important dignitaries (known as parade subjects); ships under sail; and beach scenes.

Essentially, de Vlieger's beach scenes fall into two distinct categories—views of the beach parallel to the coastline, often with identifiable buildings rising above the coastal dunes, or scenes viewed from the high dunes looking directly out to sea. In one uniquely audacious example, de Vlieger represents a view back to the beach from shallow water (ex-Ellesmere collection; current location unknown). In an early masterpiece now in the National Maritime Museum in Greenwich (fig. 1), de Vlieger includes all the components that would continue to define his absolute mastery of his subject. These encompass gentle waves lapping on the sand, sailing vessels drawn up onto the beach or often under sail further out to sea, and fisherfolk gathered in groups, all under vaulting, drifting clouds that magically filter the sunlight.

*A Coastal Scene near Zandvoort* probably dates approximately a decade later than *The Beach at Scheveningen* in Greenwich and belongs to the second type in which the distant sea is viewed from high coastal dunes. A gathering of fisherfolk peddling their catch dominates the foreground. The artist's

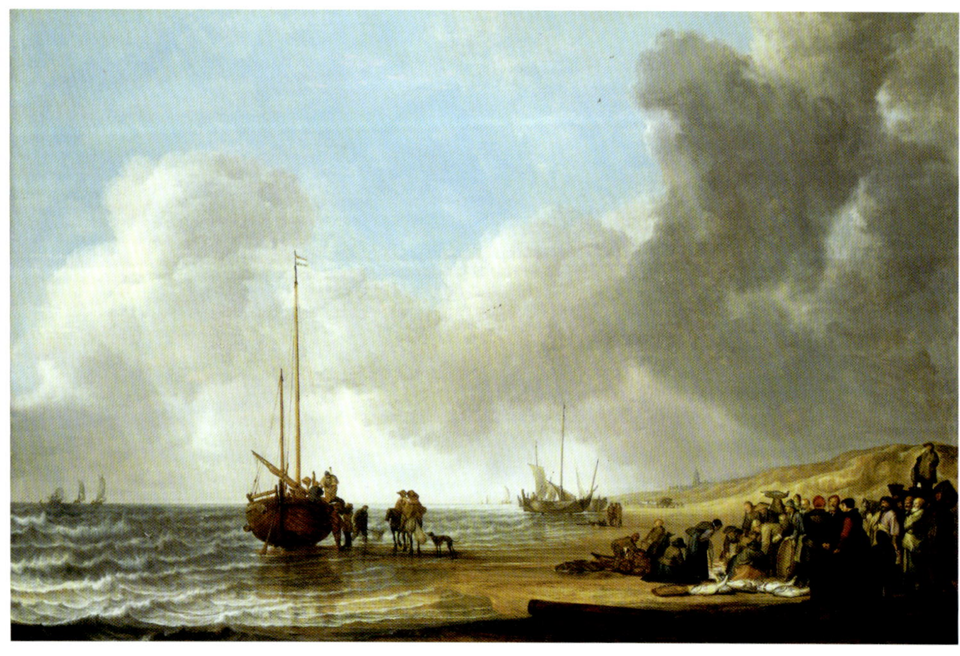

FIG. 1. Simon de Vlieger, *The Beach at Scheveningen*, 1633. Oil on panel, 27 × 42 in. (68.6 × 106.7 cm). National Maritime Museum, Greenwich, London, Palmer Collection. Acquired with the assistance of H.M. Treasury, the Caird Fund, the Art Fund, the Pilgrim Trust and the Society for Nautical Research Macpherson Fund

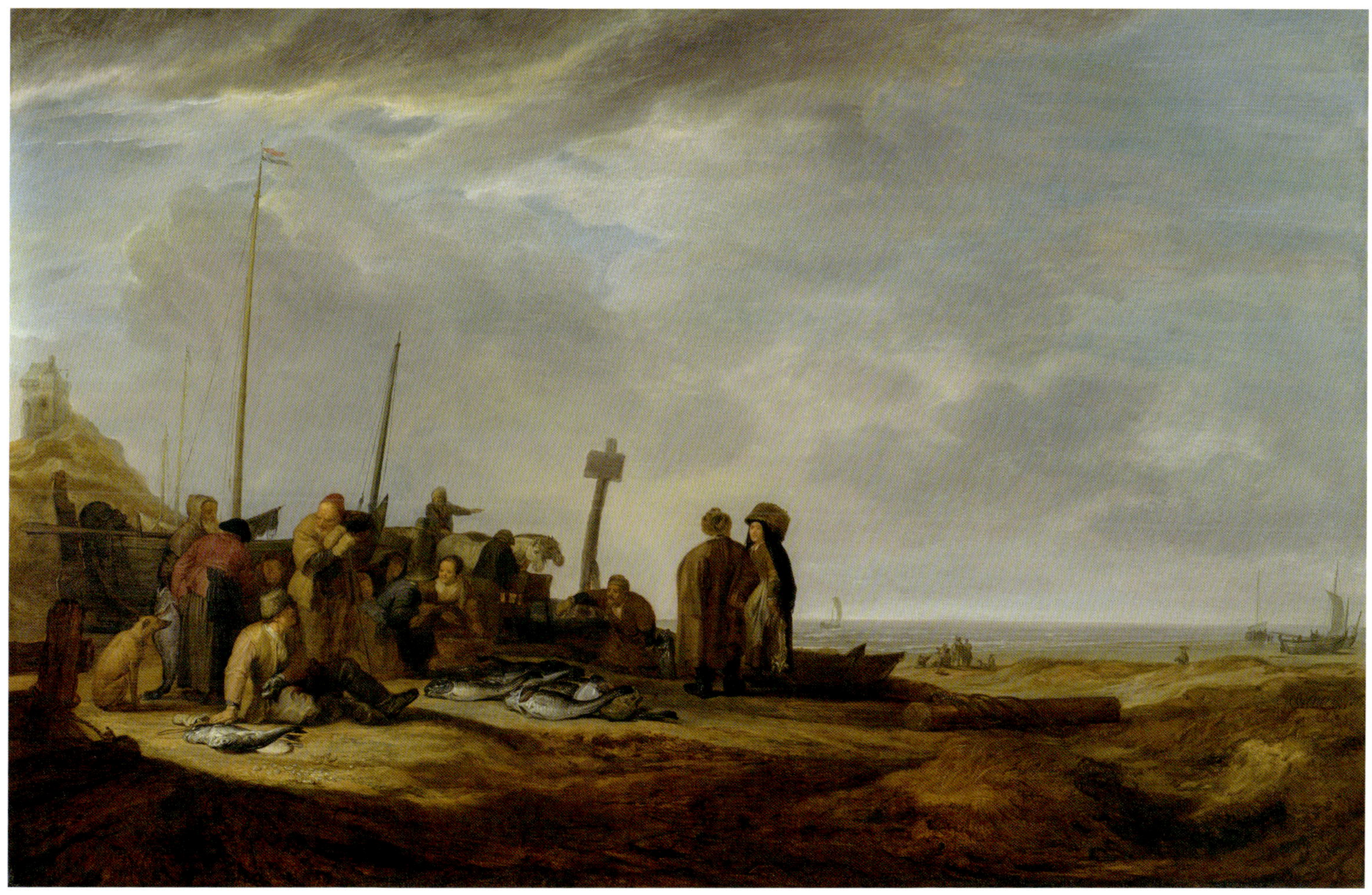

mastery of perspective is employed here by contrasting the foreground fisherfolk with diminutive figures near the distant water's edge. All of this human activity occurs under a superbly rendered cloudy sky in which the filtered light playing across the scene seems to be constantly shifting. This light effect energizes the painting to brilliant pictorial effect.

De Vlieger's achievement assured him a unique place in the evolution of Dutch marine art. Willem van de Velde the Younger (1633–1707) putatively studied with de Vlieger in Weesp. In particular, his early calms bespeak his close study of de Vlieger's art. Likewise, Jan van de Cappelle (1625/26–1679) was an ardent admirer, and the inventory of his estate included more than 1,300 drawings by de Vlieger. During the 1650s and 1660s, these two younger artists brought Dutch marine art to its apogee, but it was de Vlieger who created the groundwork for this development. He was the fulcrum who shifted the direction of Dutch marine art to its moment of perfection.

George S. Keyes
Former Chief Curator and Curator of
European Paintings, Detroit Institute of Arts

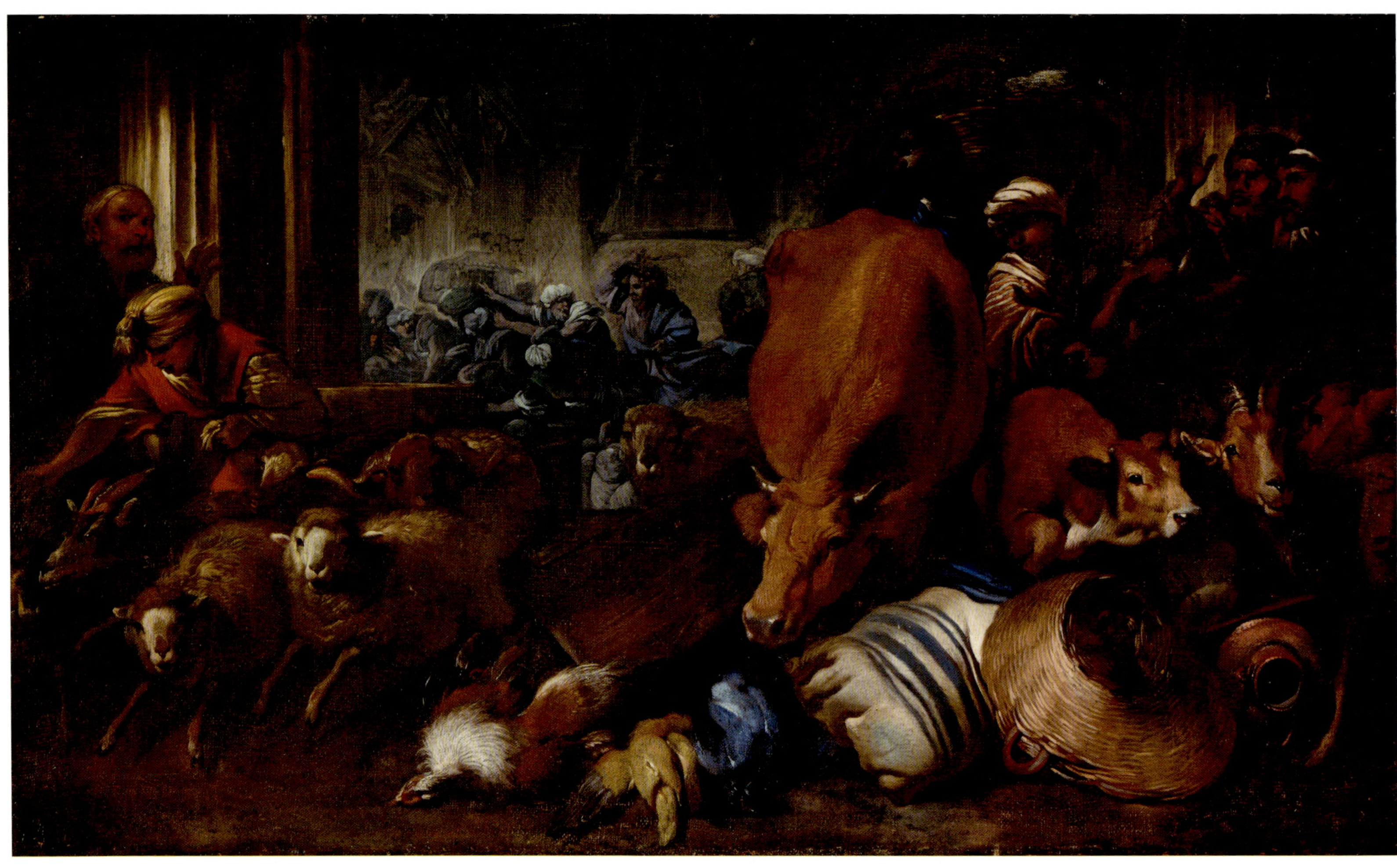

# *Christ Cleansing the Temple*

Giovanni Benedetto Castiglione, called Il Grechetto (Italian, 1609–1664), c. 1639
Oil on canvas, 16¼ × 28¹⁄₁₆ in. (41.3 × 71.2 cm)
Gift of the Samuel H. Kress Foundation  1961.100.12

Although all of the evangelists record Jesus's violent eviction of commercial activities from the Temple, John's gospel (2:13–16) is the only one that mentions Jesus's use of a whip to accomplish the task: "And making a whip of cords, he drove them all out of the temple, with the sheep and oxen. And he poured out the coins of the money-changers and overturned their tables. And he told those who sold pigeons, 'Take these things away; do not make my Father's house a house of trade.'" This episode was puzzling to some who wondered what significance his actions offered, even if it may have fulfilled Zechariah's prophecy (14:21)—that on the day of the Lord, no merchant will be found in the Temple. Would it be, as one commentator has it, that "he who wields the scourge will himself be scourged and the temple of his body destroyed?"[1] After all, Jesus, by referring to the Temple as "my Father's house," made the astonishing claim to all present that he was the Son of God! Indeed, such an event raises theological questions—both about Jesus's actions and John's motive for mentioning the whip in his narrative.

The genesis of Castiglione's rendition of the scene is less problematic, as it stems from Rembrandt's print of 1635 (fig. 1).[2] Both works focus on Jesus's rush toward the scattershot fleeing merchants and reinforce the core meaning of John's version of this episode by silhouetting the lash of the whip against a blank background.[3] Although Castiglione placed this drama in the background, it nonetheless lingers in our memory after we've absorbed the foreground filled with panicking livestock stampeding over merchandise splayed before us.

In fact, both parts of the composition complement each other thematically and reflect Castiglione's sensitivity to current theoretical discussions on literature and art that considered the significance of sequential narratives in poetry and prose as well as the complementary interplay of foreground and background.[4] Moreover, while his meticulous handling of the heap of animals and merchandise in the foreground demonstrates his brilliance as an animal painter, his lighter palette and fluid brushwork of the New Testament narrative echoes that of his dry brush drawings. Both approaches convey the two stylistic directions his art had taken at this point in his career.[5]

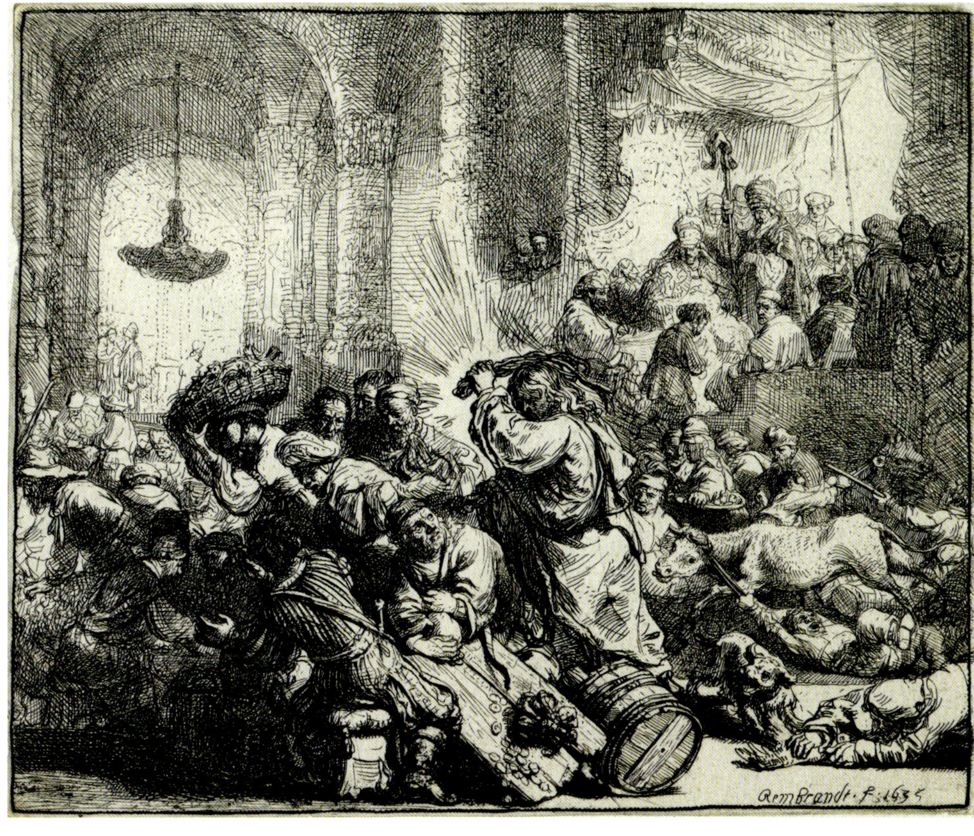

FIG. 1. Rembrandt Harmensz van Rijn (1606–1669), *Christ Driving the Money Changers from the Temple*, 1635. Etching on cream laid paper, 5½ × 6¾ (14 × 17.1 cm). Bowdoin College Museum of Art, Gift of Charles Pendexter, 2009.16.612

After training principally with Sinibaldo Scorza and Giovanni Battista Paggi in Genoa, Castiglione sought to reinvent himself as an artist during the mid-1630s in Rome, where he attended sessions at the Accademia di San Luca. There he would have been exposed to some of the issues of artistic theory and practice facing painters at the time. He would have sought to align himself with artists such as Domenichino, Sacchi, Testa, and Poussin, which may explain the dramatic hand and facial gestures of many of his figures, all geared to express emotions by visual means.[6]

Despite Castiglione's attempts to accommodate reigning tastes in order to attract a broader base of clients in Rome and then back in Genoa during the late 1630s and early 1640s, he continued to look to others for inspiration, such as Rembrandt, whose rich chiaroscuro and dramatic subjects in his etchings he found appealing. Although this mélange of source material was unique throughout Italy during the middle of the seventeenth century, it may have led Castiglione to produce works that defied categorization with his contemporaries, which further hindered his attempts to gain the recognition he yearned to receive.

Timothy Standring
Gates Family Foundation Curator of Painting
and Sculpture, Denver Art Museum

# Fish Shambles

Italian, mid–17th century
Oil on canvas, 38 × 52$\frac{11}{16}$ in. (96.5 × 133.8 cm)
Bequest of the Honorable James Bowdoin III  1813.13

One of the finest paintings given to the College by James Bowdoin III, *Fish Shambles* rivals Gilbert Stuart's majestic *Thomas Jefferson* in visual interest and technical virtuosity. The bravura fish still life at the core of the work features a dozen distinct species captured with an ichthyologist's precision, tantalizingly realized in crisply painted textures, curious shapes, and vibrant colors. On the left, a female monk fish, her great jaws agape, flashes rows of pin-sharp teeth beyond which lie creamy innards. Hanging from hooks in the center, an iridescent striped perch and partially gutted skate gleam with brilliant silvers and whites. To their right, a rather stiff cod lies diagonally, its open mouth and ribbed gills darkened in shadow. Across the front of the fish seller's stone slab, a small upturned skate hangs over the edge, its pearlescent underbelly beaded with water droplets. Surrounding it, a scattered mess of six small and two large gurnards stick out their massive boney heads. Pairs of dark perch and brilliant red groupers complete the table's display, which is framed by coins on the left and dark spikey sea urchins on the right. Hanging above, a small shark with spotted fins and a winged ray flank the disemboweled skate.

James Bowdoin III's original gift of seventy paintings included a second fish picture (current whereabouts unknown) and seven others of living animals or dead game, testifying to his interest in this genre and, perhaps, the enjoyment taken in hunting and in the delights of the table. However, none of these works is as lush in detail and as accomplished in handling as *Fish Shambles*.[1]

Beyond the toothsome fish, the Bowdoin canvas offers up a subtly coy interchange between the young man with his butcher's knife and the young woman with her wicker market basket. The boy seems stunned into immobility at the sight of the pretty girl, whose lowcut bodice reveals her pale skin. Each figure stretches out one hand toward the other, and their gazes lock, as the elderly female chaperone peeps over the girl's shoulder to smile wryly out at us. The beginning of an amorous transaction has overshadowed the selling and buying of fish, a theme that fits into a rich tradition in European culture that uses the names and shapes of fish to comment jokingly on sexuality and the body.[2] In this case, a large rigid cod lies along the table's edge close to the young woman, and two prominent fish bodies offer intriguing, slimy openings.

This work might more properly be titled *Fishmonger with Customer*. So why was it called *Fish Shambles*, and who is the artist responsible for a painting of such quality? "Shambles," an archaic word, referred to a table or stall for presenting goods, especially meats, for sale. Thus, the title merely describes the setting of the drama and does not indicate a disorderly mess. Present in the Bowdoin College collections for more than 200 years, the picture still lacks an attribution to a specific artist, although scholars suggest an origin in mid-seventeenth-century Italy, perhaps in Naples. Close examination reveals two different hands at work, a well-documented practice in Seicento Italy. The human figures present a gentle matte surface, creating softness in the flesh and fabrics. In contrast, the sharply rendered fish shine forth in metallic brilliance. This successful collaboration between two talented individuals results in a painting unified through the dramatic effects of light and shade. Following the example of Caravaggio, the figures and fish emerge spotlit from an inky backdrop to draw us into their quotidian drama.

Susan E. Wegner
Associate Professor of Art History,
Bowdoin College

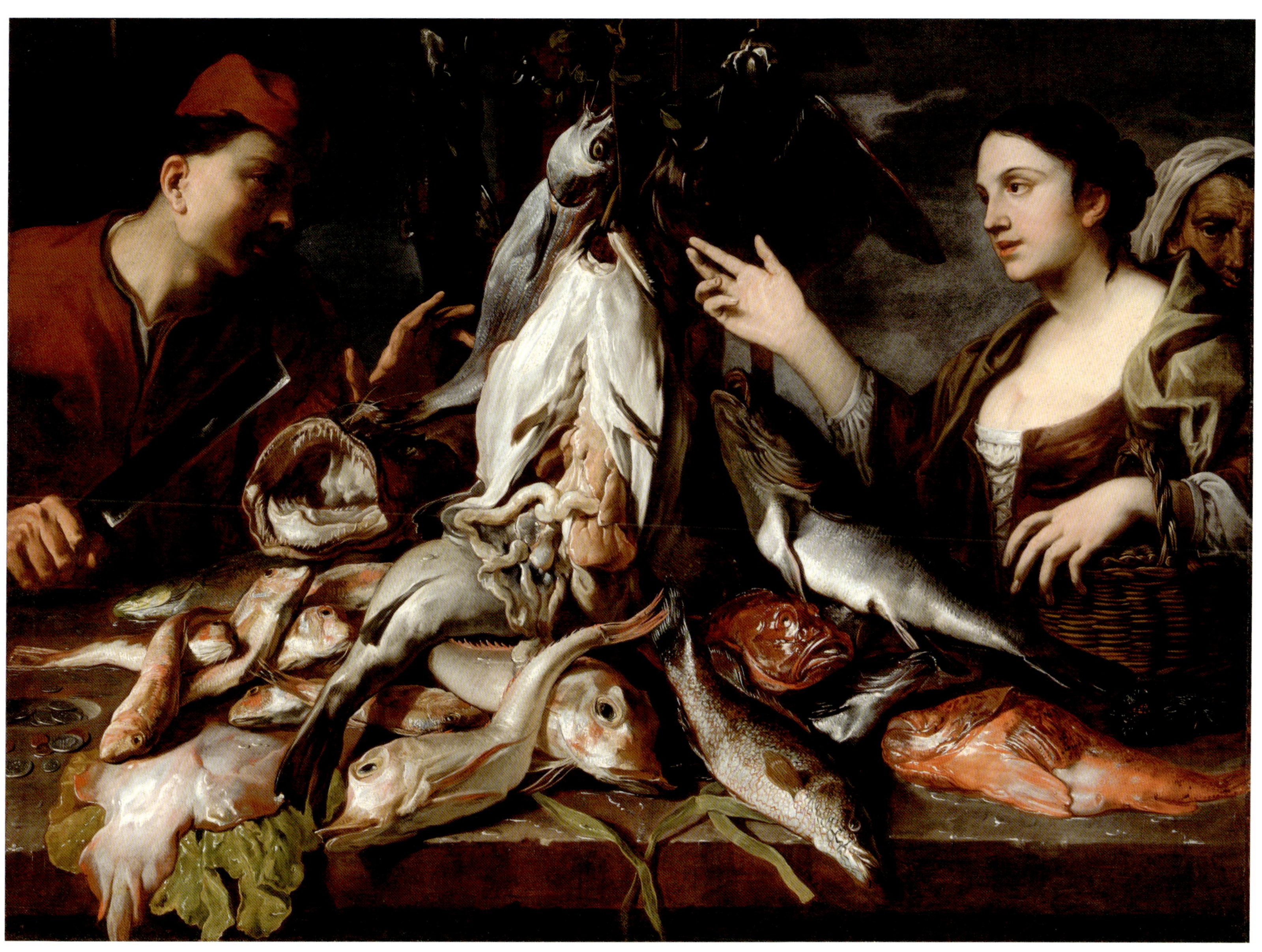

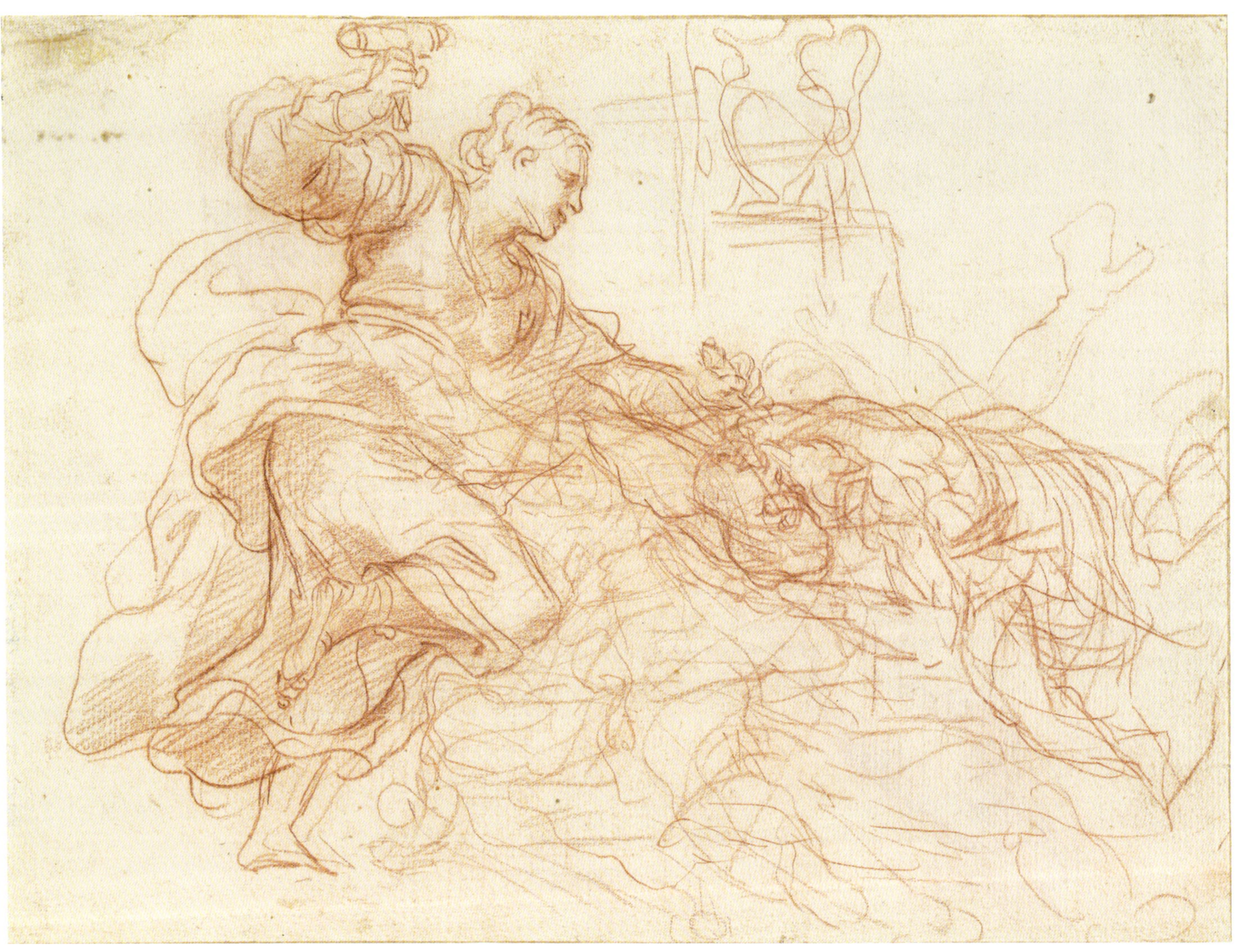

# Jael and Sisera

Carlo Maratti (Italian, 1625–1713), 1670–75
Red chalk on paper, 7⅝ × 10⅜ in. (19.3 × 26.4 cm)
Bequest of the Honorable James Bowdoin III  1811.49.a & .b

This study by Carlo Maratti of Jael and Sisera is an early design for a half-lunette mosaic located in Saint Peter's Basilica and paired with a scene of Judith and Holofernes. The mosaic depicts Jael after she has slain Sisera, pointing out his body to a soldier. The drawing is likely very early, as it does not conform to a half-lunette shape, nor does it depict the scene eventually chosen by Maratti. Instead, Jael is seen in the act of murder, about to pound a tent peg into the temple of the sleeping Sisera. Maratti's characteristic fluid lines and lively forms give the scene dynamic energy even as the figure of Sisera becomes indistinguishable among the layers of red chalk. The decorative jug seen in the background is a nod to the scene's Old Testament narrative, in which Jael gives Sisera milk to drink so that he will fall asleep. (ND)

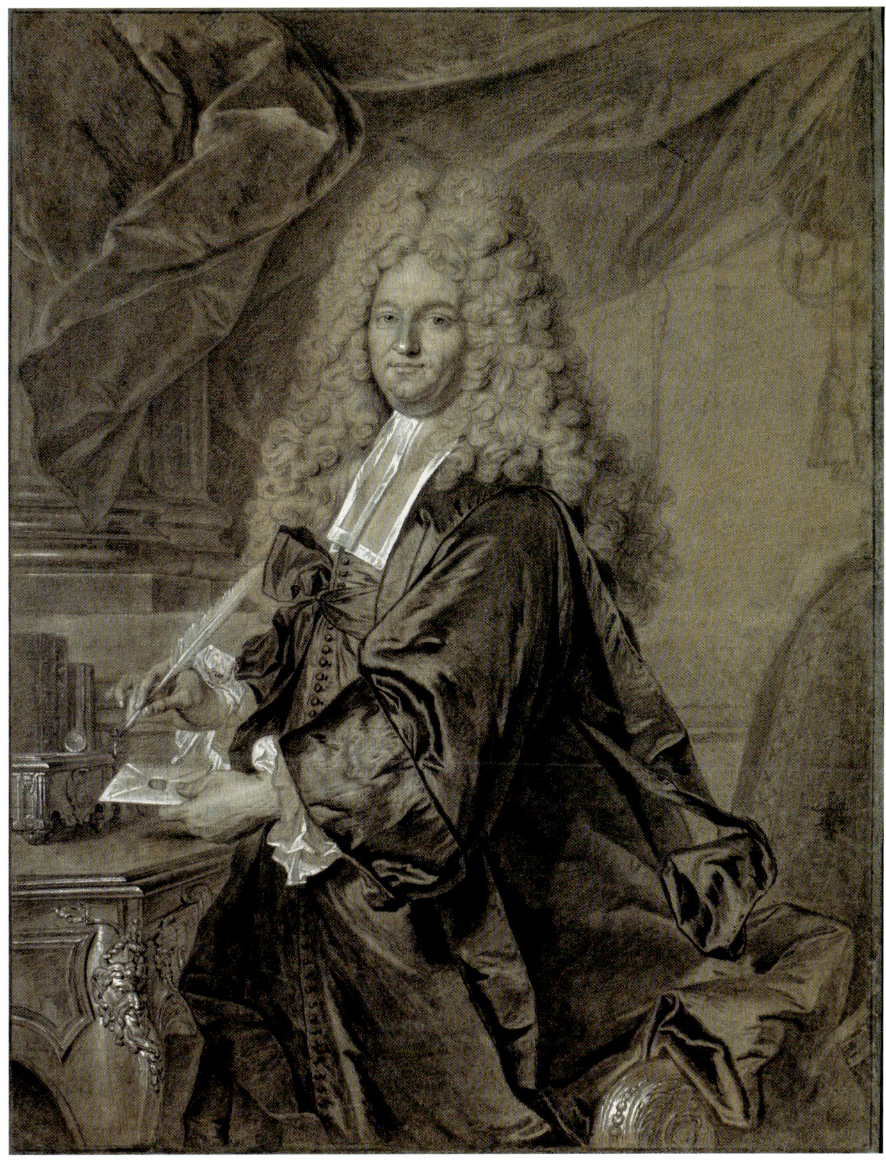

# Portrait of Joseph Jean–Baptiste Fleuriau d'Armenonville

Hyacinthe Rigaud (French, 1659–1743), c. 1708
Black and white chalk and black ink, gray wash, heightened
with white on blue prepared paper, 14⅞ × 11⁹⁄₁₆ in. (38 × 29 cm)
Gift of George and Elaine Keyes, two Anonymous Donors, and the Lloyd O.
and Marjorie Strong Coulter Fund  2017.9

Hyacinthe Rigaud was the preferred portraitist of Louis XIV and XV and made canonical contributions to the art of French absolutism and of early eighteenth-century Europe. He adapted the European portrait tradition to the specific needs of the French court, developing the *portrait d'apparat* as a showpiece of great formality and elegance. This presentation drawing, squared for transfer to a larger canvas, or perhaps to the engraver's plate, makes Rigaud's skill apparent. The sensitively rendered face is surrounded by a myriad of compelling, detailed elements that all indicate the sitter's elevated status, elegance, and erudition. Armenonville (1661–1728) was one of thirty councillors of state, a lucrative position conferring a rank directly below that of prince and cardinal. (JHo)

# Two Prints by Augustin de Saint–Aubin

French, 1736–1807

Museum Purchase, Lloyd O. and Marjorie Strong Coulter Fund  2013.17.1–.2

The knowing glance shared between husband and wife. The wife's state of undress. The secret suggested by the captions: "Au moins soyez discret" (At least be discreet; pl. 1) and "Comptez sur mes sermens" (You may count on me; pl. 2). These 1789 engravings—a self-portrait of the artist Augustin de Saint-Aubin and an accompanying portrait of his wife Louise-Nicole Godeau—suggest a level of intimacy and sensuality not often seen in portraits of married couples. With Godeau's dress undone and one breast exposed, we are invited to peek in on a clearly private moment. Her gaze is focused to one side, entreating her husband to keep her secret; she seems a bit flustered. He appears more at ease, leaning to one side, staring intently at her, his hand to his lips as he blows a kiss and promises that all secrets will stay between them.

Unusual though these portraits might be in their frank eroticism, they also exemplify many trends in mid- to late eighteenth-century French history. At the time, romantic marriages were very much *à la mode*: many individuals hoped to fall head over heels in love with their spouses and saw romantic marriage as crucial to their personal happiness. Consider, for example, a letter the novelist Pierre Choderlos de Laclos wrote to his beloved wife: "the pure and sensitive heart of a good wife and a good mother is a pantheon worth as much as any other."[1] Love for and by your spouse: that, more than any other reward, was the real prize. As such, family portraits became more dynamic and seemingly spontaneous in the second half of the eighteenth century, with couples touching each other affectionately and children tumbling around their parents. The theater of affection, as opposed to dignified posing, assumed singular importance.[2]

The portraits of Godeau and Saint-Aubin stage a similar sort of performance, but with an intricate twist. Saint-Aubin here emphasizes the intimate but also secretive nature of his relationship with his wife. On the one hand, the prints signal the close bond between the couple. And yet, despite his assurances that she "may count on" his discretion, that promise seems partially undercut by his decision to invite the public to witness their promises to each other. The history of marriage in eighteenth-century France, highlighted here, is but one of many possible focal points in the discussion of these prints. Others are the engraving process, the booming market for prints at the time, and the organization of the Saint-Aubin enterprise, with multiple relatives working together. Time will tell whether the conflation of public and private spheres, a hallmark of the visual culture of the late Ancien Régime, will strike our students as a historic oddity, or, to the opposite, will resonate with them as an antecedent to today's habitual practice of sharing private moments with multitudes on online platforms. Saint-Aubin, one could argue, exploited prints as predigital social media.

Meghan Roberts
Associate Professor of History,
Bowdoin College

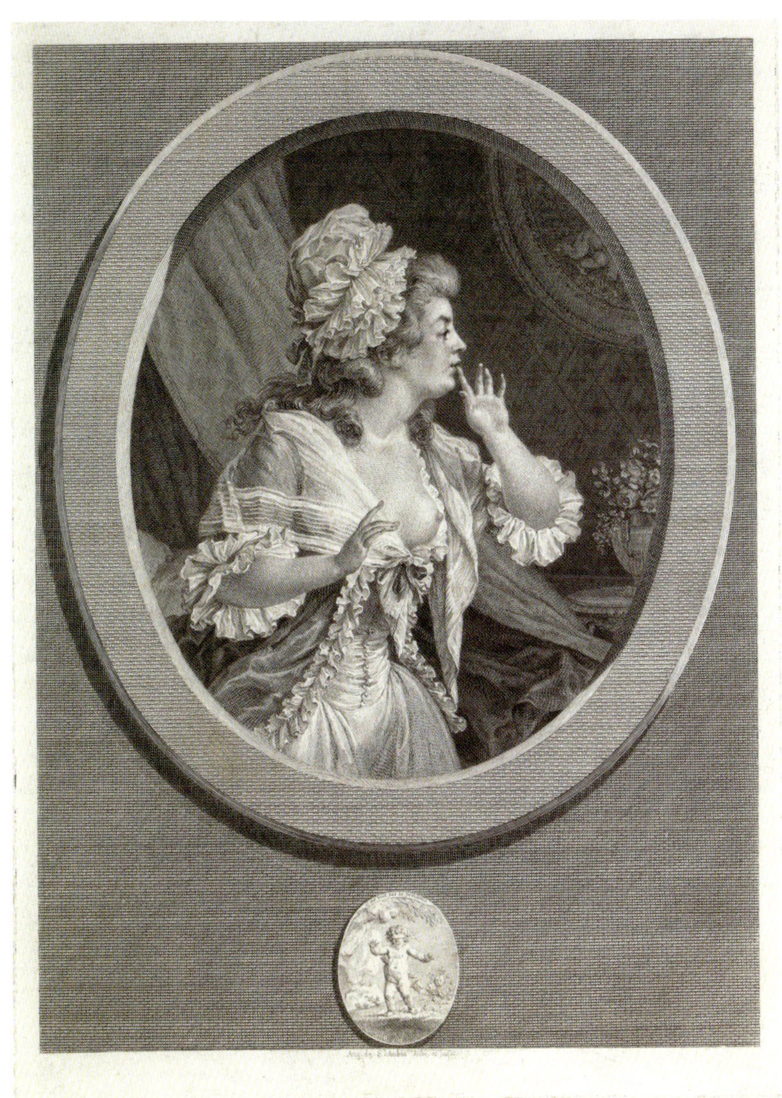

PLATE 1. Augustin de Saint–Aubin, *At Least Be Discreet (Au moins soyez discret)*, 1789. Etching and engraving on paper, plate: 14⅜ × 10⅜ in. (36.5 × 26.4 cm) (2013.17.1)

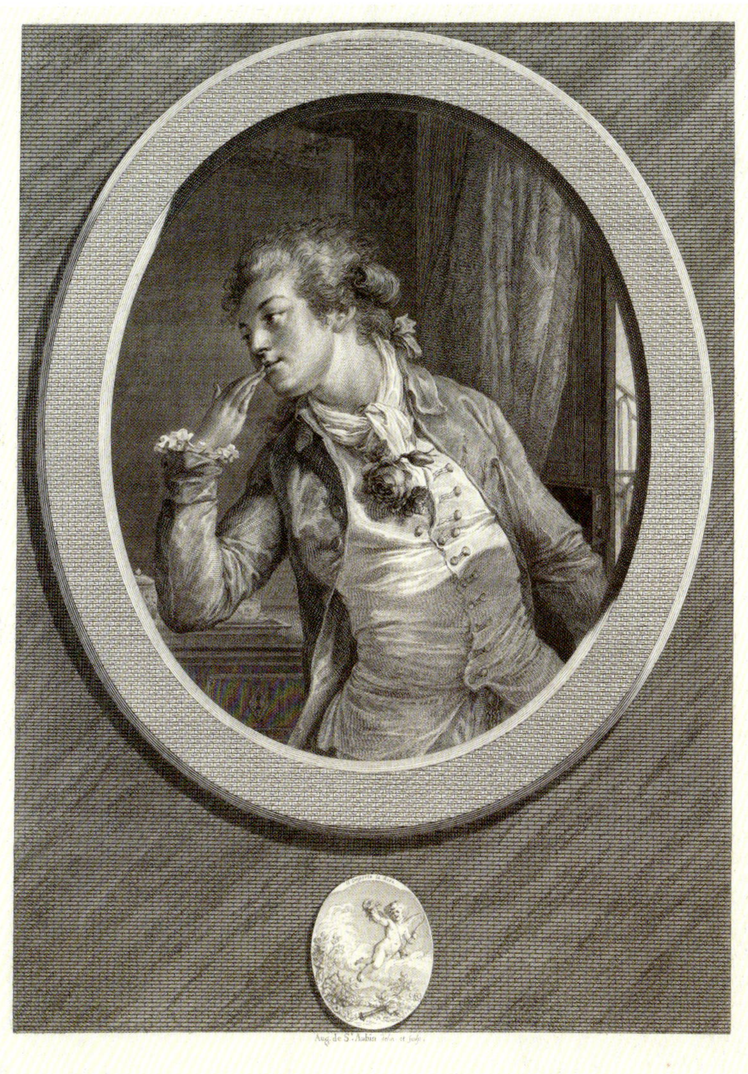

PLATE 2. Augustin de Saint–Aubin, *You May Count on Me (Comptez sur mes sermens)*, 1789. Etching and engraving on paper, plate: 14⅜ × 10⅜ in. (36.5 × 26.4 cm) (2013.17.2)

## *Portrait of Maud*

Julia Margaret Cameron (British, 1815–1879), 1875
Vintage albumen print from glass plate negative, 13½ × 11 in.
(34.3 × 27.9 cm)
Museum Purchase, Lloyd O. and Marjorie Strong Coulter Fund  1994.9

Julia Margaret Cameron led a fascinating life: born in Calcutta, she lived in India, France, England, and Ceylon (now Sri Lanka); she was friends with some of the most famous authors, artists, and scientists of the Victorian era; she was mother to six children; and she was one of the preeminent photographers of the nineteenth century. Her photographs are notable for their hazy, dreamy visual effects, introduced through deliberate manipulations of the complex photographic process, and for their evocative, enigmatic relationship to narrative.

*Maud* is one of a series of illustrations of Tennyson's poems that Cameron undertook at the poet's request. The poem is a long tale of ill-fated love, narrated by the ardent young suitor to the beautiful Maud. It is set in the Victorian present day, with a plot driven by financial speculation, suicide, wealthy industrialists, and the Crimean War, but is written in the ornate symbolic style of a love poem. The passage appended to the photograph is the immediate prelude to the poem's climactic scene: as the narrator and Maud rendezvous in a rose garden after a ball, her brother comes upon them and, enraged at the young suitor's presumption, strikes him. This is the beginning of the end for the lovers: the narrator kills the brother in a duel and flees the country, and the heartbroken Maud dies. The photograph, however, focuses not on this pivotal narrative moment, but rather echoes Tennyson's beautiful description of the garden as a moonlit lovers' bower:

> There has fallen a splendid tear
>     From the passion-flower at the gate.
> She is coming, my dove, my dear;
>     She is coming, my life, my fate;
> The red rose cries, "She is near, she is near;"
>     And the white rose weeps, "She is late;"
> The larkspur listens, "I hear, I hear;"
>     And the lily whispers, "I wait."

The garden itself speaks to the narrator, echoing his yearning for his beloved. In the photograph, staged by a female photographer and model, the male narrator's desires and longings become Maud's, as she leans, lost in reverie, against a backdrop of flowers.

There are many scholarly accounts of Cameron's work, but my primary engagement with it has been as a teacher. In that context, *Maud* is a rich conversation piece, raising questions of medium, gender, and the relationship between art and literature. I have called the photograph an "illustration" of the Tennyson poem, but in fact it appeared only in a miniature edition, accompanied by a small part of the long poem. And its soft focus on a beautiful woman against a backdrop of flowers and foliage links it to the non-narrative images of beautiful women in paintings by Dante Gabriel Rossetti and Edward Burne-Jones. How were ideas about beauty and meaning shared across different art forms? And where did photography fit within that conversation? Was it a purely documentary medium or, as Cameron's work suggests, did it offer new possibilities for storytelling and illustration? How did the emerging conventions of photography relate to traditions of painting, drawing, and illustration? Finally, Cameron's own identity complicates and nuances all of these discussions. What can her life and professional career tell us about the possibilities for and limitations on women artists in the nineteenth century? We might also think about the role of Cameron's female models in the production of these photographs. The sitter for Maud was Mary Hillier, a woman who worked for Cameron as a parlor maid, model, and studio assistant. What role did she play in the staging of this photograph, and the visual interpretation of Tennyson's poem that it offers us?

Pamela Fletcher
Professor of Art History, Bowdoin College

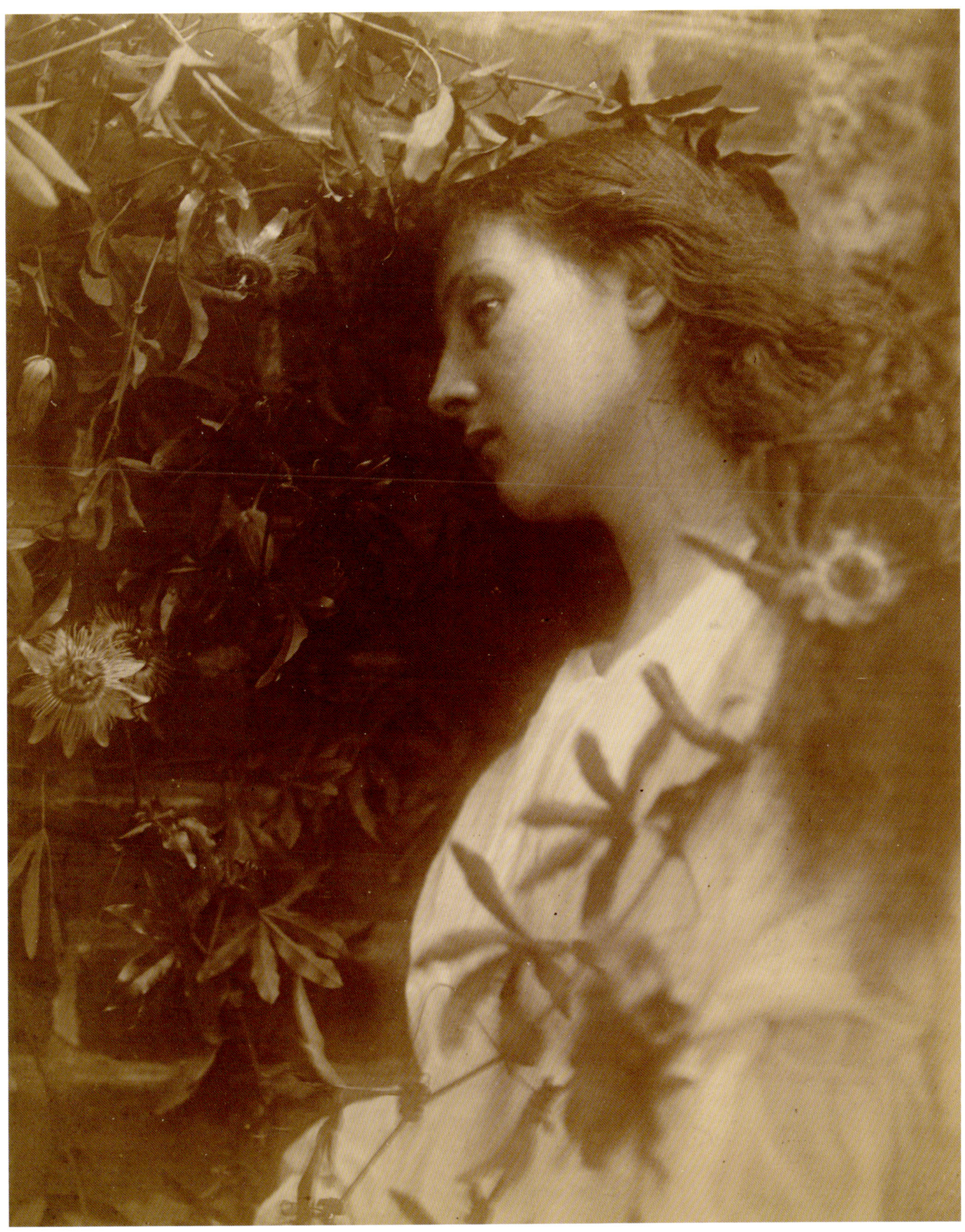

# *Young Woman and Child*

Aleksei Alekseevich Kharlamov (Russian, 1840–1925), 1894
Oil on canvas, 54⅛ × 36¹⁵⁄₁₆ in. (137.5 × 93.8 cm)
Gift of James A. Roberts, Esq., Class of 1870  1907.3

Paintings by Kharlamov often feature attractive young women and children in naturalistic settings, and in this respect *Young Woman and Child* is characteristic. Yet the painting does not appear in his catalogue raisonné and is largely unknown.[1]

The work's two exquisitely executed lifesize figures compel the viewer to linger on their meticulous detail. The matte finish obscures the texture of the brushstrokes and creates a smooth, polished appearance with vibrant color, thus adding to the scene's immediacy.[2] But it is not only the painting's technical mastery that captures one's attention. The young mother's arresting gaze unabashedly meets the eyes of the viewer (who voyeuristically inhabits the perspective of the original spectator, the artist[3]) and accosts him with a poignant and enigmatic expression that evokes bemusement, reproach, embarrassment, regret, and resilience. Indeed, despite the conventionalized subject matter, this intimate, direct, and emotionally complicated gaze tells a particular story (in which the child plays a significant part).

Kharlamov was part of a wide cultural circle in Paris that also included the Russian novelist Ivan Turgenev, and the two men became close associates. Turgenev praised the artist as the "greatest portraitist in the world,"[4] and Kharlamov painted the writer's portrait (1875) and illustrated several of his novels. Turgenev is perhaps most famous for his writings about ill-fated love and his depictions of morally strong and beautiful women—termed "necessary women" by one scholar—whose virtues serve as foils to the character flaws and ineptitudes of the "superfluous men" who inhabit Turgenev's fictional world.[5] In these ethically fraught narratives, the female protagonists' physical appearance is always intensely meaning-laden, spurring the males who gaze upon them to awakening and action.[6] In other words, narrative and portraiture are twinned: Kharlamov depicts women in such a way as to suggest latent stories, while Turgenev constructs his stories about women characters on the basis of their physical portraits.

The narrative of Turgenev's novella *First Love* is contained within the frame of a fictional memoir created by the hero for his male companions' reading pleasure, much as Kharlamov's painting is contained within an actual, ornate frame that presents it for exhibition to the male spectator, the artist's proxy.[7] Just as the viewer of Kharlamov's *Young Woman and Child* is captivated by the mother's haunting beauty and her ambiguous gaze, which disarmingly transgresses the picture's boundary to meet his own, so too does the young woman at the center of Turgenev's novella literally disarm the youthful hero (he drops his gun!) as he gazes at her across the boundary of a fence: "In the girl's movements . . . there was something so engaging, so commanding, so caressing, something so amusing and delightful that I . . . forgot everything. My eyes devoured the slender waist and small neck, the lovely arms and the slightly disheveled fair hair under the white scarf, the intelligent half-closed eyes and the eyelashes and the soft skin of the cheek beneath them . . ."[8] Turgenev's hero—along with the voyeuristic readers of his memoir—"consumes" all the intimate particulars of this face and figure with his eyes as though viewing a portrait. Yet this maiden, like Kharlamov's, boldly returns the admiring male gaze: "The girl turned towards me . . . I caught sight of large, grey eyes in a lively, animated face—and suddenly the whole of this face began quivering with laughter."[9] One can imagine that the eyes of Kharlamov's young female subject, too, convey an expression of gentle irony and the potential for laughter, despite whatever hardship she has endured.

Sight, vision, and the male gaze upon feminine beauty are as essential to Turgenev's novella as they are to Kharlamov's painting. But these two works do not merely enact for the spectator the mystical power of a momentary encounter with sexually charged feminine beauty. They disrupt the convention of the actively gazing voyeuristic male and passively observed female when the object of the gaze steadfastly gazes back.

Alyssa Dinega Gillespie
Associate Professor of Russian, Chair of
Russian Department, Bowdoin College

Stephen Pastoriza, Bowdoin '19

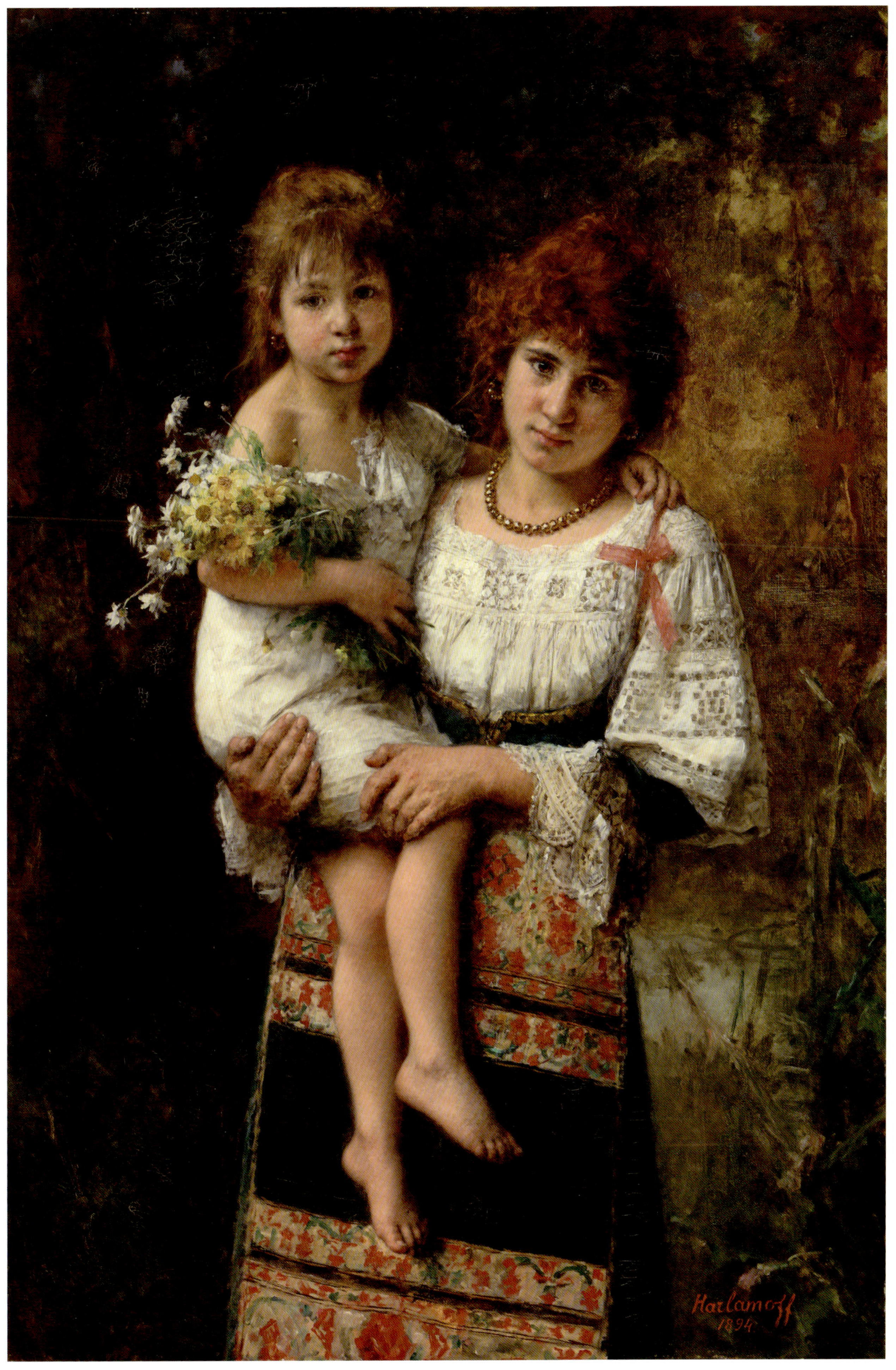
Harlamoff
1894

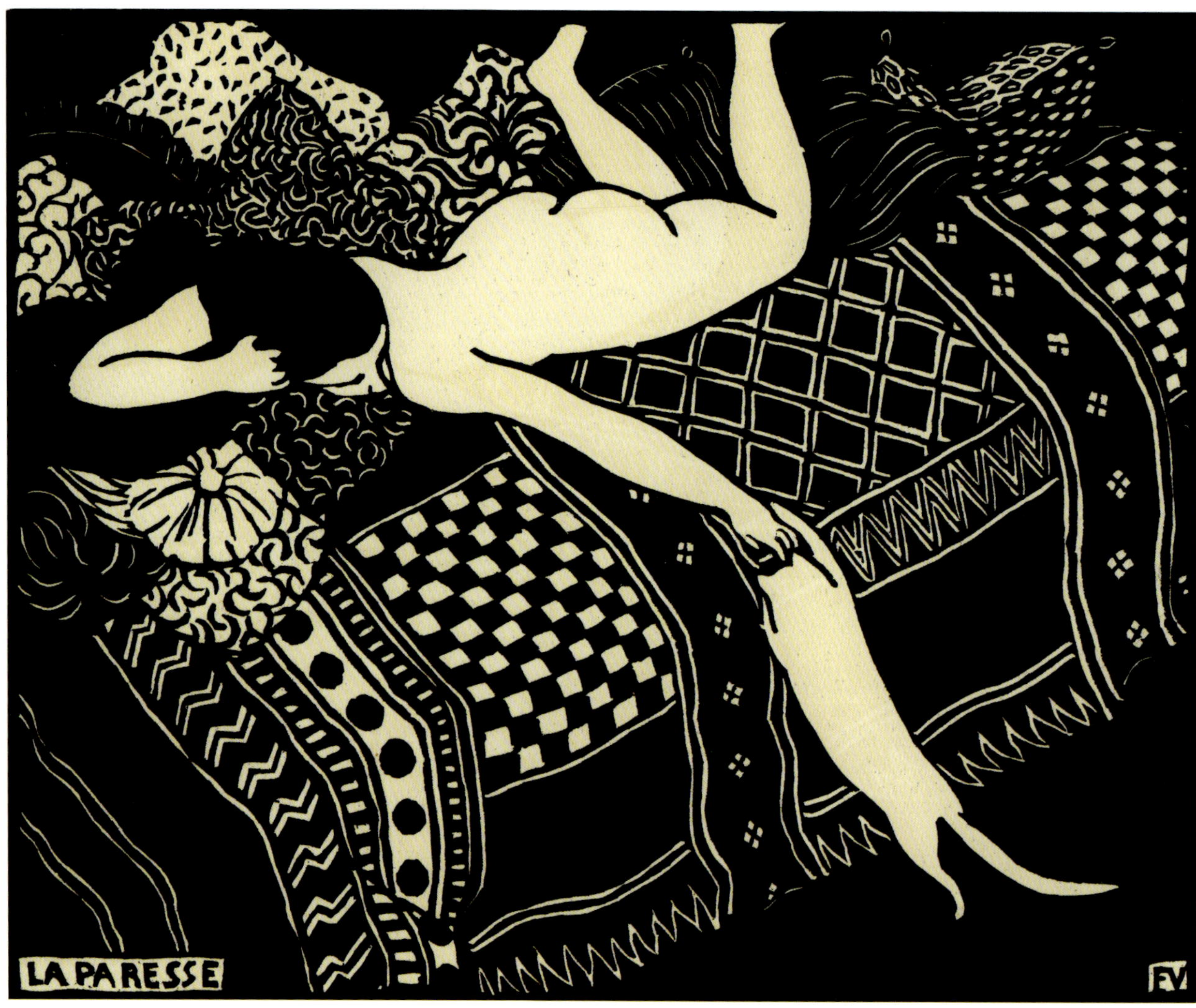

# *La Paresse (Laziness)*

Félix Vallotton (Swiss, 1865–1925), 1896
Woodcut on paper, 9⅞ × 12¹³⁄₁₆ in. (25 × 32.5 cm)
Gift of Charles Pendexter  2009.16.701

Associated with the Post-Impressionist avant-garde group Les Nabis, which also included Maurice Denis and Édouard Vuillard, Félix Vallotton succeeded in making his study of laziness appear both elegant and (appropriately) effortless. A sensual female nude is draped on a daybed, diverting herself with a cat, and matching her pet's delight in a carefree moment of play. The woman's body is defined by its contrast to the intricate geometric details of the pillows' and blanket's ornamental decoration. Carved out of the woodblock, female figure and cat appear in the color of the paper tone, while their surroundings set them off with black contrasts. Vallotton's woodcuts not only influenced his paintings—which employed hard-edged color planes that originated in his printmaking—they also served as inspiration for many twentieth-century artists who believed in drastically "editing" visual information to strengthen their works' visual intensity and emotional urgency, such as Edvard Munch and the German Expressionists. (JHo)

# Médée, *Théâtre de la Renaissance, Sarah Bernhardt*

Alphonse Mucha (Czech, 1860–1939), 1898
Lithograph on paper, 85¾ × 33⅞ in. (217.8 × 86 cm)
Gift of Hilton and Esta Kramer  2011.55

This lithographic poster by Alphonse Mucha shows the famed Parisian actress Sarah Bernhardt in the epic stage role of Medea, a character haunted by passion and twisted vengeance. In the Greek tragedy, Medea's husband Jason abandons her and their children to marry the princess of Corinth. His infidelity leads Medea to kill her two sons in a monstrous pursuit of justice. Mucha expresses the tragedy's tension by contrasting Medea's helpless, vacant eyes with the horrific infanticide at her feet. The long vertical format, muted colors, and focus on a central lifesize figure are all trademarks of what would come to be known as Mucha's style. His first poster of Sarah Bernhardt, *Gismonda* (1894), was so successful that he was commissioned to design her posters over the following six years. Collectors of these immensely popular works often resorted to bribing bill stickers or cutting them down at night to acquire them. (ND)

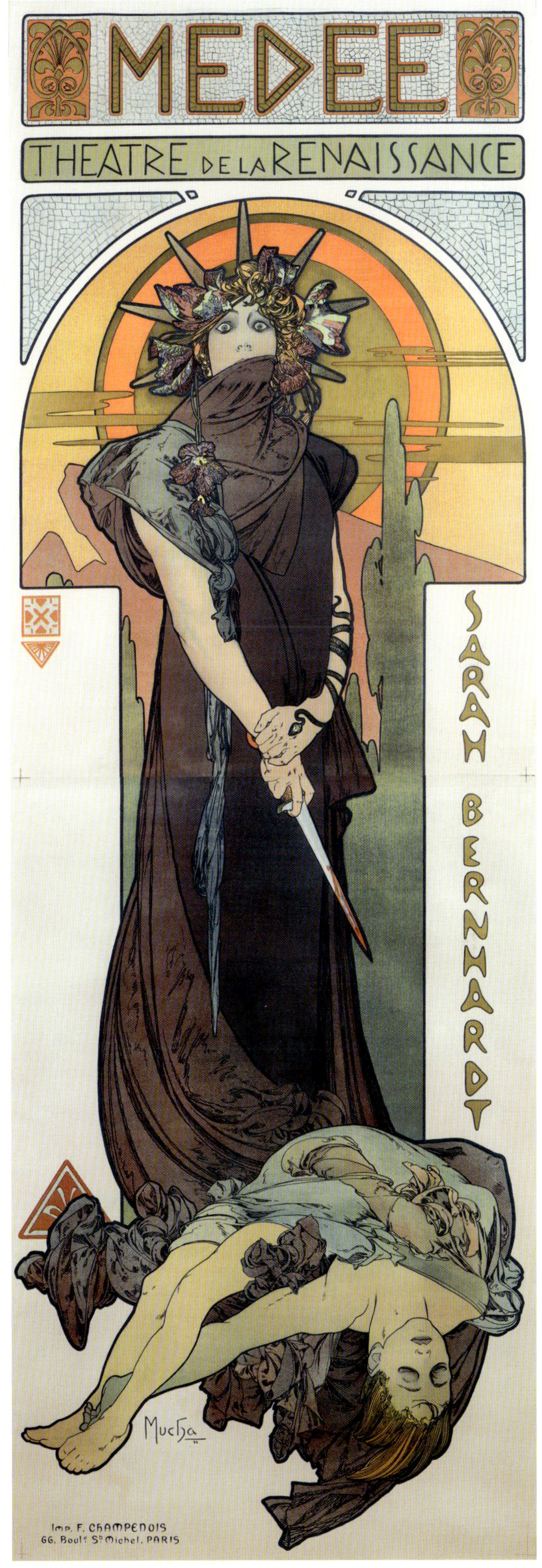

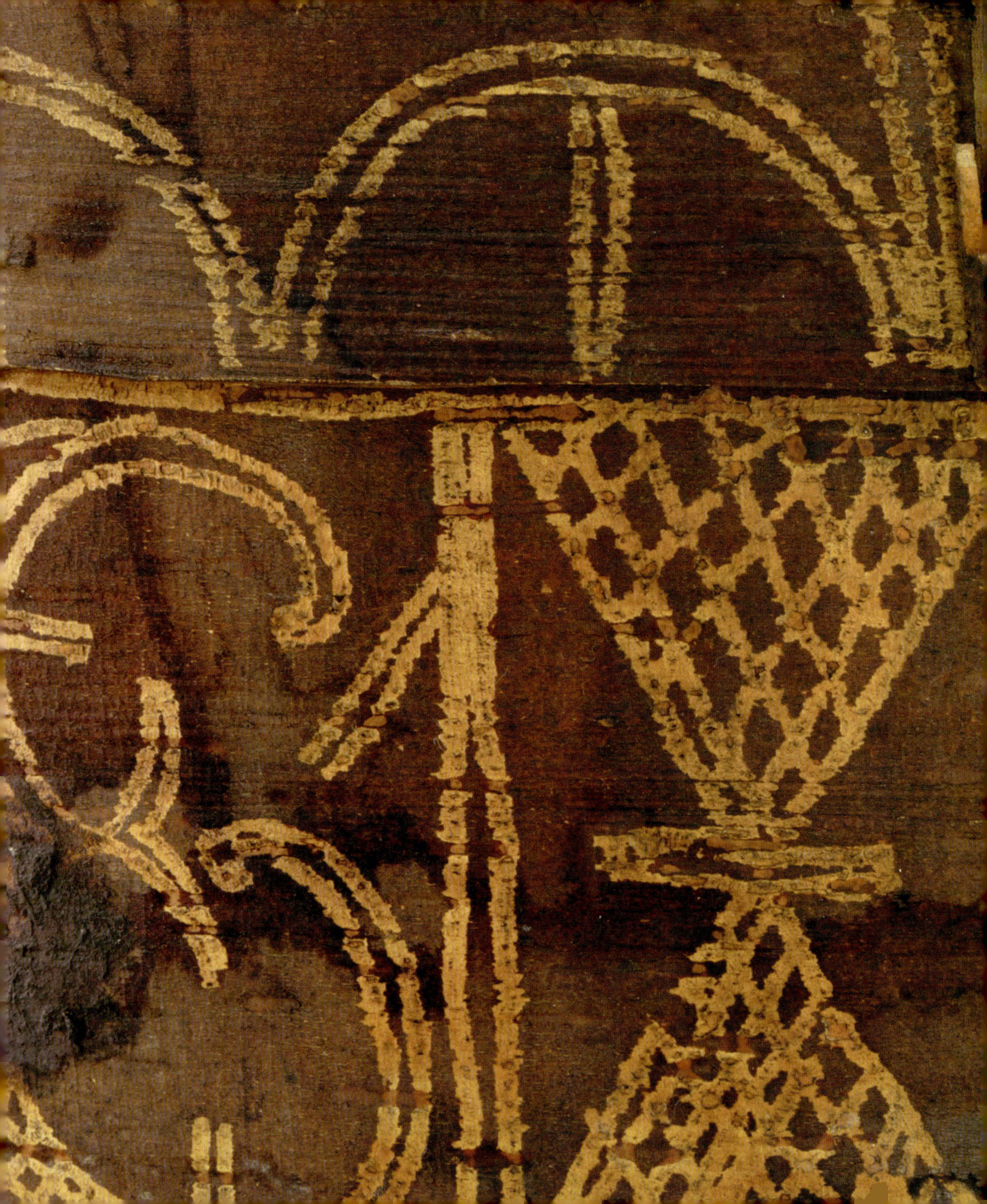

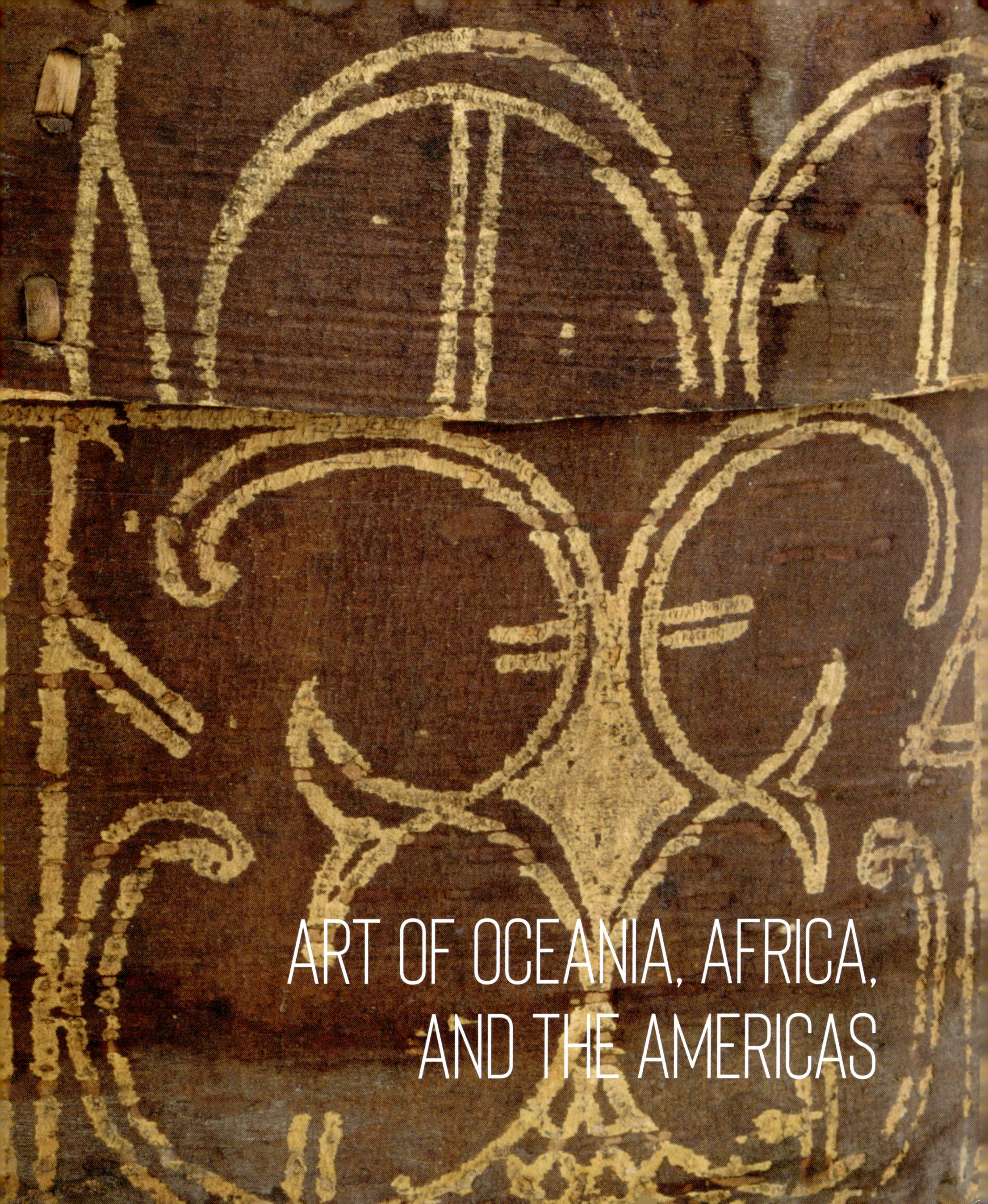
ART OF OCEANIA, AFRICA,
AND THE AMERICAS

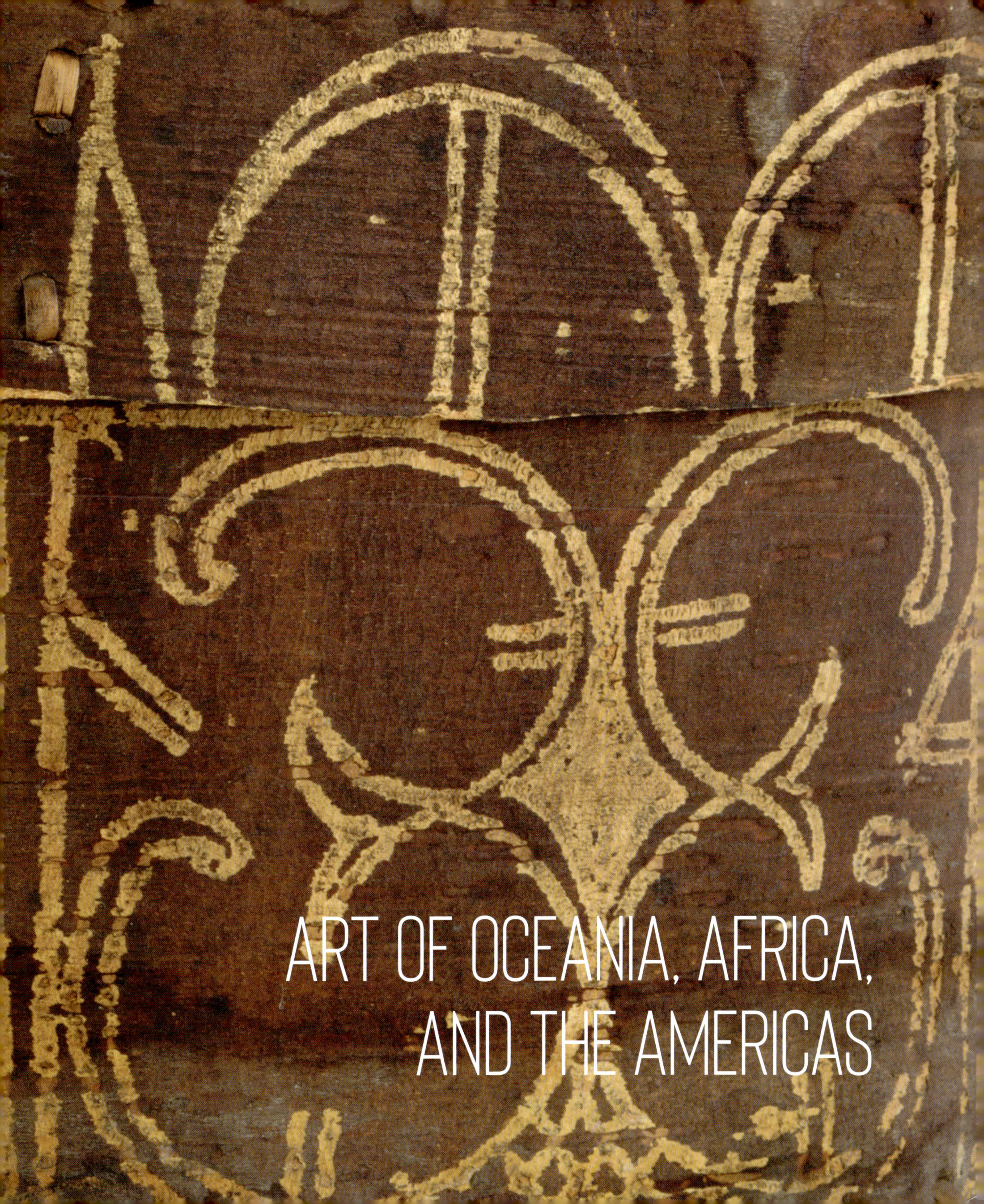
ART OF OCEANIA, AFRICA,
AND THE AMERICAS

# Tatanua Mask

Melanesia, New Ireland, c. 1870–90
Polychrome, wood, and natural fiber, 16⅛ × 12½ × 8⅝ in.
(41 × 31.8 × 21.9 cm)
Gift of Harold M. Sewall  1898.71

When this tatanua mask first appeared at a celebration in New Ireland, the assembled audience would have gasped in admiration. More than 100 years later, 8,500 miles away, the grand hairstyle, powerful face, and tactile tension between hard and soft surfaces continue to stun visitors at the Bowdoin Museum. From the front, the assertive gaze of the snail-shell eye, with its rheumy green pupil, is overshadowed by the sweeping crest of honey-colored vegetable fiber that emphasizes the mask's flaring nostrils and open mouth. On both sides of the central crest, a smaller red-and-white fringe creates contrast. One side features dyed black sennit braids that stop neatly at the edge of the face. On the other side, passages of bright white lime contrast with a black fiber band.

The fine painting on the face provides ornamental interest but also camouflages form. From the side, the triangular pattern around the nostril openings creates the "eye of fire," a pattern associated with life force. The nostril suddenly becomes a second eye, and the bridge of the nose seems to arch forward like a bird's beak—shifts in form common in New Ireland aesthetics. The artist used paint to integrate the hairstyle and the face into a unified whole. A sweeping red band over the proper right eye matches the width of the small semi-oval within the passages of lime, and the black paint over the proper left eye resonates with the black hair above. Despite the mask's dramatic appearance, some details are based on late nineteenth-century men's fashion. The yellow fiber of the central crest mimics the color of lime-bleached men's hairstyles, and the white surface may be related to the tradition, once practiced in some communities, of shaving part of the head and powdering it with lime as an outward sign of mourning.

While tatuana masks always have an association with commemorative festivities, their exact use varies from community to community. Tatanua masks perform in communities that have hosted *malagan*, commemorative funerary celebrations in which elaborate sculptures are displayed as the crowning moment of the event. But while the right to see and make *malagan* images is restricted by family ties and inheritance, tatanua masks can be seen by the whole village and made by any talented man.[1] This mask would have appeared with six to twelve others on a celebratory occasion.[2] Tatanua performers intended to impress the living audience as well as the ancestors honored through the festivities. The mask's aggressive features— jutting jaw, angled brow, flaring nostrils—represent ideal masculine qualities and are related to the spiritual aspects of the performance. The men performing the masks prepared spiritually for weeks beforehand, aiming to thwart all that might go wrong: embarrassing false steps; evil spells cast by jealous spectators; or encountering otherworldly forces while performing for the ancestors.[3]

Europeans settled in New Ireland as traders and missionaries beginning in 1840 and were struck by the visual impact of local art forms. This mask, and others collected with it by Harold M. Sewall, came to Bowdoin during an international mania for artworks from New Ireland. The collectors' fervor was inspired by the beauty of the masks as well as a fear that they were part of a disappearing culture—despite the fact that more masks and *malagan* sculptures were made in the late nineteenth century than in the decades before, partially as a result of foreign demand. Since the advent of German colonial occupation in New Ireland in 1884, more than 20,000 artworks from New Ireland entered foreign collections.[4]

Kathryn Gunsch
Teel Curator of African and Oceanic Art,
Museum of Fine Arts, Boston

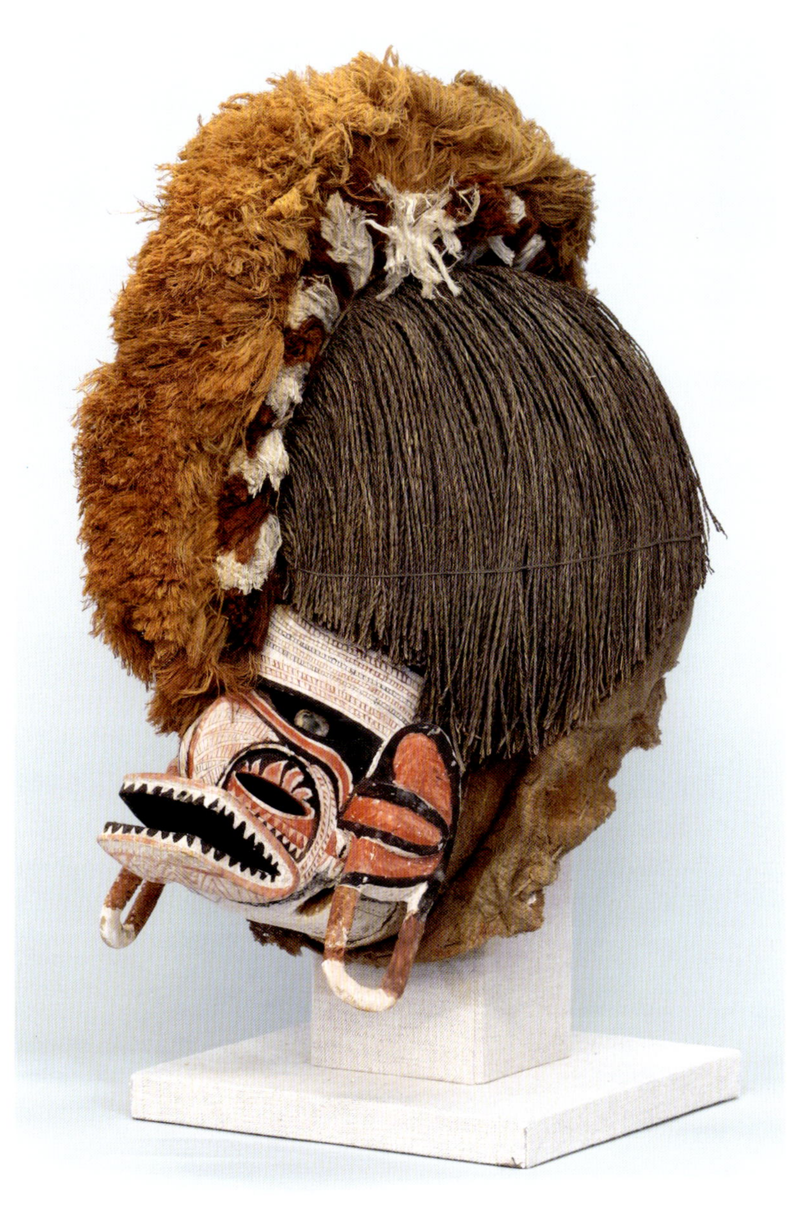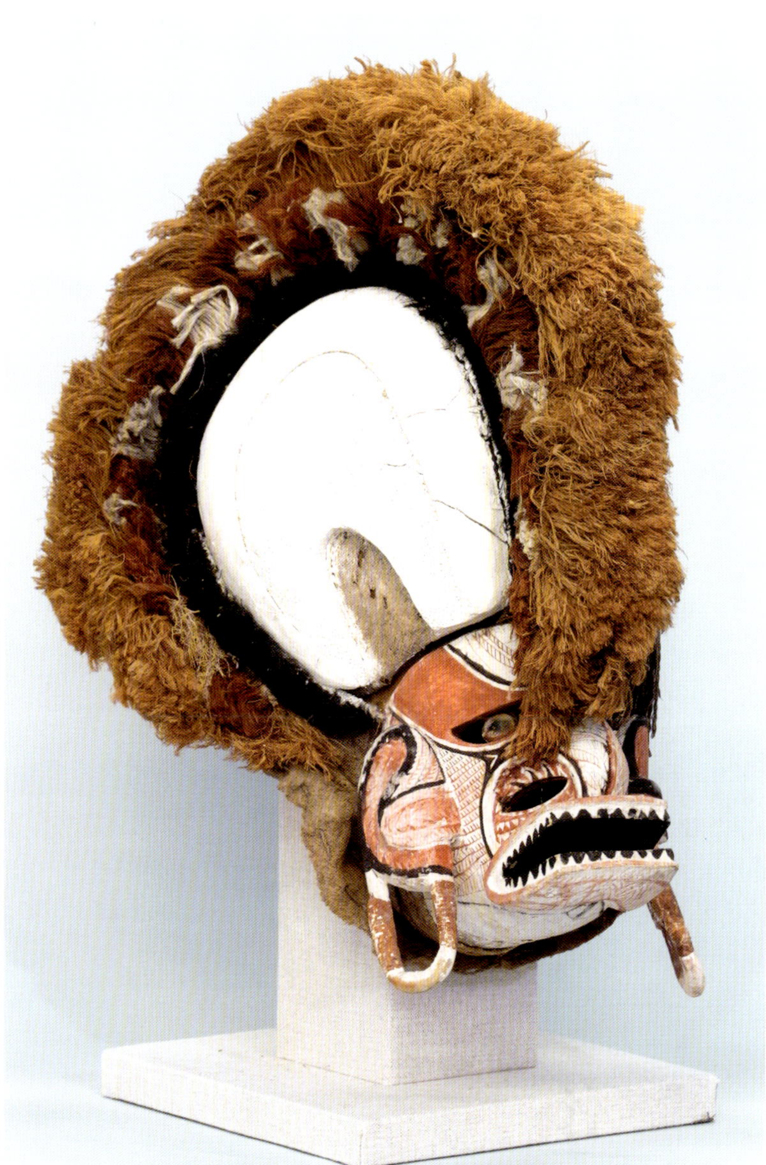

# Fang Male Reliquary Figure

Gabon, c. 1900

Wood, 19¼ × 4¼ × 4¼ in. (48.9 × 10.8 × 10.8 cm)

Museum Purchase, Florence c. Quinby Fund, in memory of Henry Cole

Quinby, Honorary Degree, 1916  1969.70

The Bantu-speaking peoples of present-day Gabon, Republic of Congo, Equatorial Guinea, and southern Cameroon flourished over nearly 3,000 years as pioneers ("big men") who migrated and established villages in unsettled parts of the rainforest, leading to a frontierlike tradition that undermined political centralization.[1] These big men took part in an ancient form of spiritual veneration, termed *bwiti*, that celebrated the earlier Batwa (or "Pygmy") inhabitants of the land.[2] From around the sixteenth century, certain clans adapted *bwiti* to emphasize ties to their own ancestors by keeping their relics in adorned cylindrical containers. Identities coalesced around these ancestral ties. They termed this new complex of reliquary objects and rituals *bieri*. By the late nineteenth century, these clans became known by the ethnonym "Fang." Several Fang styles of *bieri* sculpted bodies attached to reliquary containers developed. Fang men employed these *bieri* to communicate with spiritual worlds at significant moments, including male initiation rites and on occasions when ancestors were called on to ensure fertility and fecundity in people and land.

European modernist artists celebrated such Fang sculpture, in particular Maurice de Vlaminck, André Derain (who thought one example "as beautiful as the Venus de Milo"), and Pablo Picasso (who considered it "more beautiful than the Venus de Milo"), with the result that many collectors sought Fang art.[3] The Fang sold their reliquary statues to these collectors: for the Fang keepers of reliquaries, value and power resided in the relic containers themselves and not the sculptures, which became spiritually inert once detached from the relics. Moreover, by the 1930s, many Fang had adopted Christianity, thus relinquishing their *bieri* and ending associated rituals.[4]

As part of an effort to diversify its collections in response to the civil rights struggles of the 1960s, Bowdoin acquired this reliquary figure from an African art dealer, J. J. Klejman, who dated it to the nineteenth century. It is a clear example of Fang style and, based on aesthetic and morphological qualities as well as the characteristic thick patina, the Betsi substyle. From its base, which was originally attached to the container of ancestral relics, a unified curve sweeps from foot through muscular calves and thighs back to the other foot. Aspects that indicate fertility and connection to ancestral realms, such as the navel and phallus, are emphasized. Symmetrical arms, holding a vessel, extend from an upright torso that continues into a thick neck. The slit eyes, dome-shaped forehead, and typical coiffure divided by an indentation combine with other symmetrical features to evoke the balance, serenity, and solemnity that promoted fertility, fecundity, and prosperity. The filed teeth indicate attractiveness and status. The figure resembles old and young at the same time: after all, ancestors and infants come from the same invisible realm.

To mobilize its benevolent spiritual powers, *bieri* adepts communicated through the figure by ingesting a hallucinogenic bark and scratching the surface of those parts that "speak" (here, scratch marks can be identified around the mouth). They also applied potent liquids that formed a distinctive patina. Despite a conservator reducing this patina "with swabs of cellosolve" in 1986, Bowdoin's reliquary figure still exudes oil with environmental changes. With a height of 19¼ inches and width of 4¼ inches, it is elongated and less muscular in the upper body than some examples. Perhaps the elongation was meant to evoke ties between the relics below and the heavens above.

David M. Gordon
Professor of African History, Department
of History, Bowdoin College

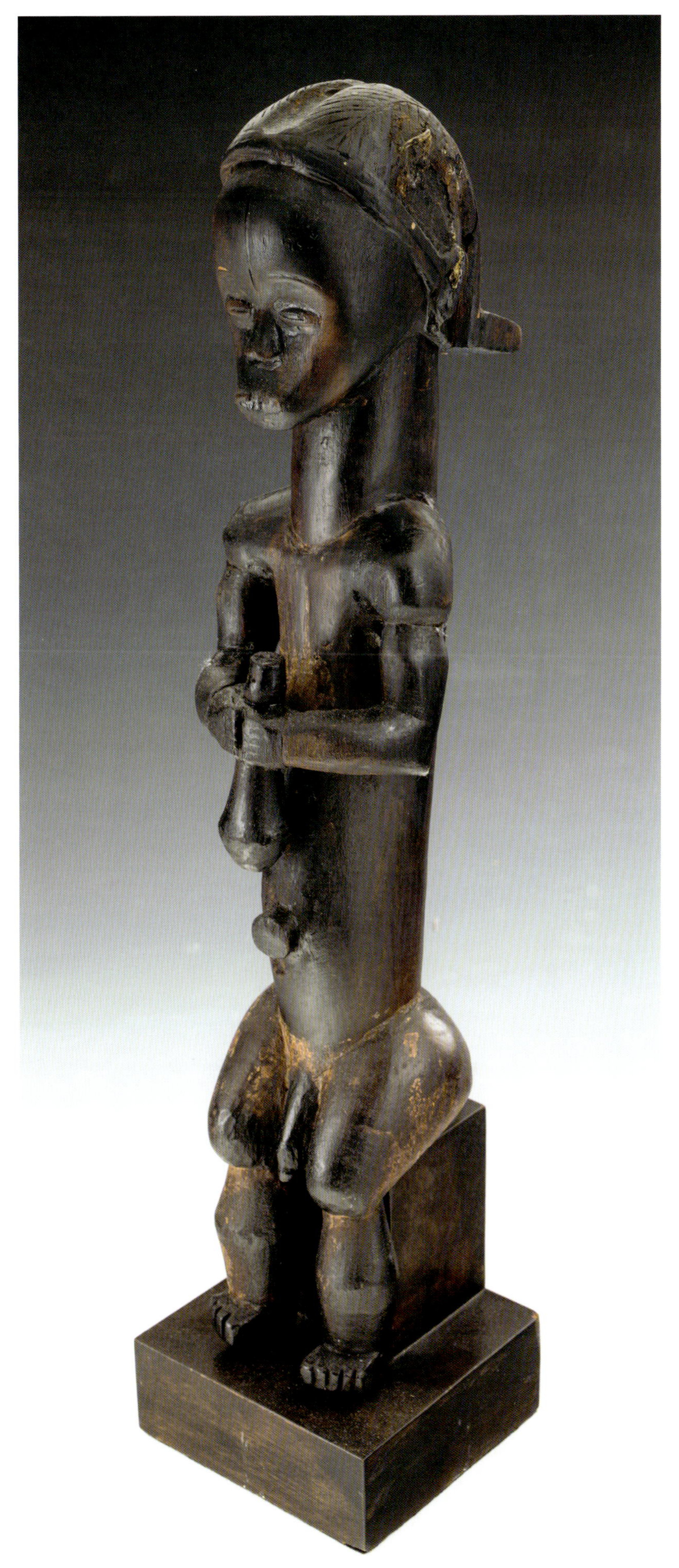

# Nazca Bridge–spout Vessel

Peru, Nazca culture, 100–300 CE

Buff clay with polychrome slip, 8 × 6¾ in. (20.3 × 17.1 cm)

Museum Purchase, Florence C. Quinby Fund, in memory of Henry Cole

Quinby, Honorary Degree, 1916  1969.86

This exquisite example of one of the great Pre-Columbian ceramic traditions of South America is the work of potters from the Nazca culture (200 BCE–650 CE) of south coastal Peru.[1] The area stretches from the Acarí river valley in the south to the Pisco river valley in the north. The Nazca culture is perhaps most famous for its geoglyphs (known as the Nazca Lines), enormous figures laid out on the Pampa de Nazca and visible only from the air (fig. 1).[2] Many Nazca vessels depict some of the same figures.

Most Nazca ceramics come from a funerary context in which the dead were dressed in rich textiles. Both ceramics and textiles are renowned for an iconography that depicts the maritime and riverine environment of the region as well as mythological beings and, toward the later period, war themes, including trophy heads.[3] This vessel's painted figure represents a condor as it flies in profile over what is probably a stylized hilly landscape. The condor is composed of discrete geometric shapes, each defined by a thick, dark black, curvilinear outline. This line gives a sense of dynamism to an otherwise static image, and it allows the viewer to imagine the bird in flight. Each shape is filled with a solid color except for the tips of the wing, which are left white, the surface color that was applied first. The palette used on Nazca ceramics is much more expansive than many other Andean traditions such as the Inca or Moche. About fifteen mostly organic and some inorganic colors and/or hues have been catalogued. Some colorants, such as cinnebar, were mined in the high Andean mountains, indicating a far-reaching trade network that extended into the Amazon. Other colorants, such as hematite, the iron ore used for reds and blacks, probably came from a local mine, called Mina Primavera, just north of the Nazca Lines and exploited for more than 300 years by the Nazca people.

Nazca artisans discovered and used an extremely fine clay to make their ceramics and thus did not need to add much temper, if any. By 100 BCE, they were producing very fine, thin-walled vessels, of which this piece is an excellent example. In fact, Nazca potters produced unusually uniform vessels and figurines with walls that average only four to five millimeters in thickness. Approximately 85 percent of the polychrome vessels recovered throughout the Nazca region were made with a clay associated with the most important ritual site, Cahuachi. It is evident that a well-organized group of artisans lived and worked at Cahuachi, and that their clay came from the same source. Their work was then disseminated throughout the Nazca region either through trade or as gifts.

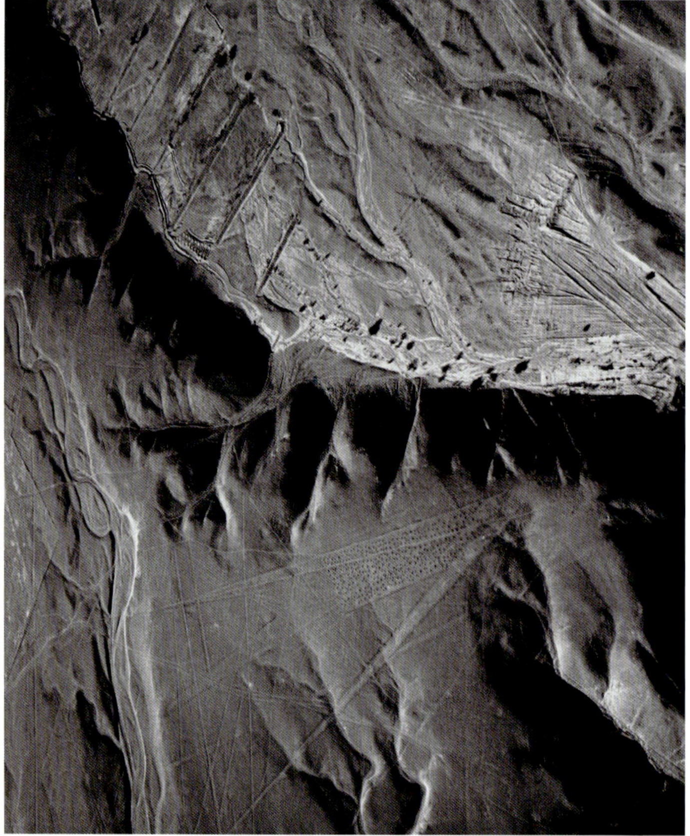

FIG. 1. Marilyn Bridges (American, born 1948), *Old and New Lines, Nazca, Peru*, 1979. Silver gelatin print, 20 × 24 in. (50.8 × 61 cm). Bowdoin College Museum of Art, Gift of Claudia and Steven Schwartz, 2009.23.19

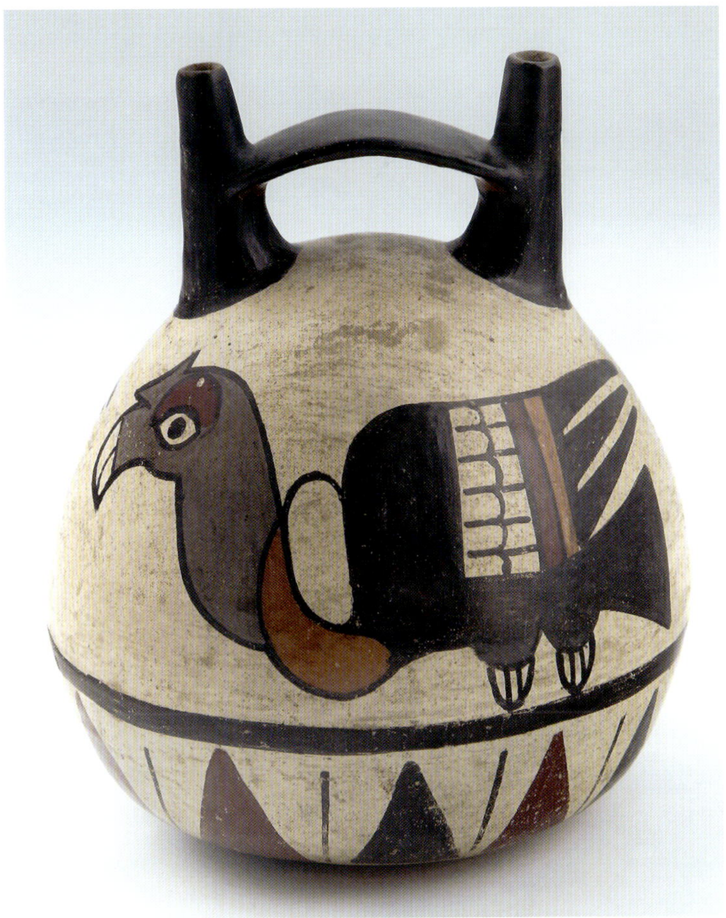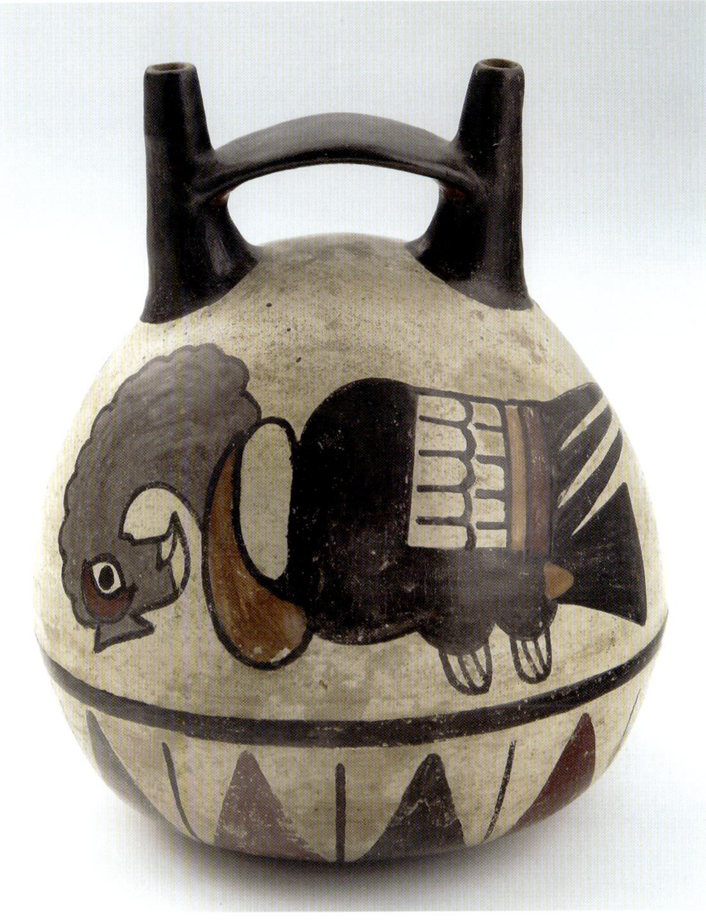

As there was no wheel in the Andes, Nazca artisans created their pieces using a variety of other forming techniques. They modeled directly, building the walls up by pinching or with slab or coiling techniques, sometimes in combination. Paddles and smooth stones were used to help form the wall. When the clay was leather-hard, the walls were polished or burnished to a fine luster with a bone, stone, or piece of ceramic. Metal glaze was also unknown in the Americas before the arrival of the Spanish, and some early traditions employed an organic adhesive to apply the color to the surface after the vessel had been fired, such as can be seen on Paracas ceramics, the local tradition preceding the Nazca. However, these colors are fugitive; over time, they tend to fall away from the vessel's surface, and the figures and decorations often disappear. Nazca artisans developed a different technique—they painted their works prior to firing. The smooth surface was painted with slip, which is a liquid mixture of water, clay, and colorant. Usually, the entire surface was first covered with a layer of white slip. After it had dried slightly, the figures were painted with different colored slips over the white surface. Fine brushes of human or camelid (alpaca, llama, vicuña) hair or cut and frayed reeds were used to paint the firm outlines and the precise details of the individual figures. The advantage of this technique is that the slip had already partially bonded with the clay wall and that it then became fused with the ceramic surface when the piece was fired in a kiln, which needed a temperature in excess of 800°C. This is why such wonderful ceramic painting has survived from this period, as evidenced by Bowdoin's vessel.

The lofty condor, with a wingspan of eleven feet, is clearly identifiable by the comb, wings, and gullet. As the soaring bird hovers majestically in the air, it was and still is emblematic of the Andes, and so it was represented on this and many other Nazca ceramics and textiles.

Thomas B. F. Cummins
Dumbarton Oaks Professor of
Pre-Columbian and Colonial Art,
Harvard University

# Two Tlingit Medicine Men Figurines

Pacific Northwest Coast, c. 1860–85
Polychromed wood and hair, 15½ × 3⅝ × 3¼ in.
(39.3 × 9.2 × 8.2 cm), 15⅜ × 3⅜ × 3¼ in. (39 × 8.6 × 8.2 cm)
Anonymous Gift  1850.5, 1850.6

Prior to the emergence of the model totem pole, which quickly became ubiquitous in the curio markets of the northern Northwest Coast, figurines depicting medicine men (or shamans) were among the items sought by Victorian-era steamship travelers. These figures featured human hair and the accoutrements of the shamanic profession, including masks, aprons, rattles, and representations of spirit helpers. Though some of these objects were created with the intent to sell, a significant number of them were actual instruments of medicine men. Without detailed provenances, shamanic figurines made for the curio trade and those that were ceremonially used can be difficult or impossible to differentiate.

Shamans traditionally used such carved figurines when healing the sick, in divination ceremonies, for protection against witches, and in spiritual warfare.[1] People within Northwest Coast communities both respected and feared shamans, powerful mediaries to the spirit world who lived on the fringes of society. Consequently, shamanic grave houses that contained remains and belongings were often far removed from village sites, and easily plundered by missionaries, Indian agents, and museum collectors engaging in salvage collecting in the late nineteenth century.[2] Motivated by the belief that Northwest Coast peoples would soon vanish, collectors seeking culturally used artifacts took advantage of avoidance taboos observed by Native communities to remove funerary objects undetected.[3] Ironically, many of the institutional representatives seeking these materials were also actively working to eradicate medicine men and traditional practices within those communities.

An early pair of these figurines found their way into the collection of the Bowdoin Museum of Art (pls. 1 and 2), though the provenance and date of accession in the nineteenth century are difficult to trace. Even without documentation, a great deal of information can be gleaned from a formal analysis of the objects themselves. Their carving and painting style reveal a Tlingit origin from Southeast Alaska, produced in the late third quarter or early fourth quarter of the nineteenth century. Like many Tlingit objects from this period, the sculpting of the figurines is more sophisticated than the painted two-dimensional designs. Another indication of the time of production is the commercially made red paint used on both figures, still bright despite its age, and starkly contrasting with the mellowed wood surfaces. Based on the shared paint and stylistic similarities, it is likely that the figures were produced by the same maker. Consistent with Tlingit masks of the period, the painted designs on the faces were applied irrespective of their carved features. The figurines also exhibit classic shamanic expressions with heavily lidded eyes and protruding tongues, representing a deep trancelike state while the shaman moves between worlds. The red body of the taller figure may represent the power to resurrect the dead.[4] The painted faces on the apron and hat of the second figure represent spirit helpers, called *yeik* in the Tlingit language. Both figures are adorned with human hair, which may indicate that they were made for ceremonial usage.

Although it is unclear whether these figurines were used in shamanic practice, as objects relating to medicine men they represent a colonial legacy and sensitive subject to the Tlingit. While questions of ritual function remain, the presence of historic works like these in museum collections is now understood as an opportunity for dialogue with the Native communities whose ancestors created these objects. Identifying the figurines as Tlingit is a first step to establishing such a conversation between Bowdoin and the originating communities of the objects in Southeast Alaska. These collaborative intercultural exchanges are always fruitful for museums, and connect Indigenous peoples to the belongings of their ancestors so they can begin to heal from the legacy of colonial collecting.

Christopher Wesley Smith
Department of Anthropology, University of
British Columbia, Vancouver

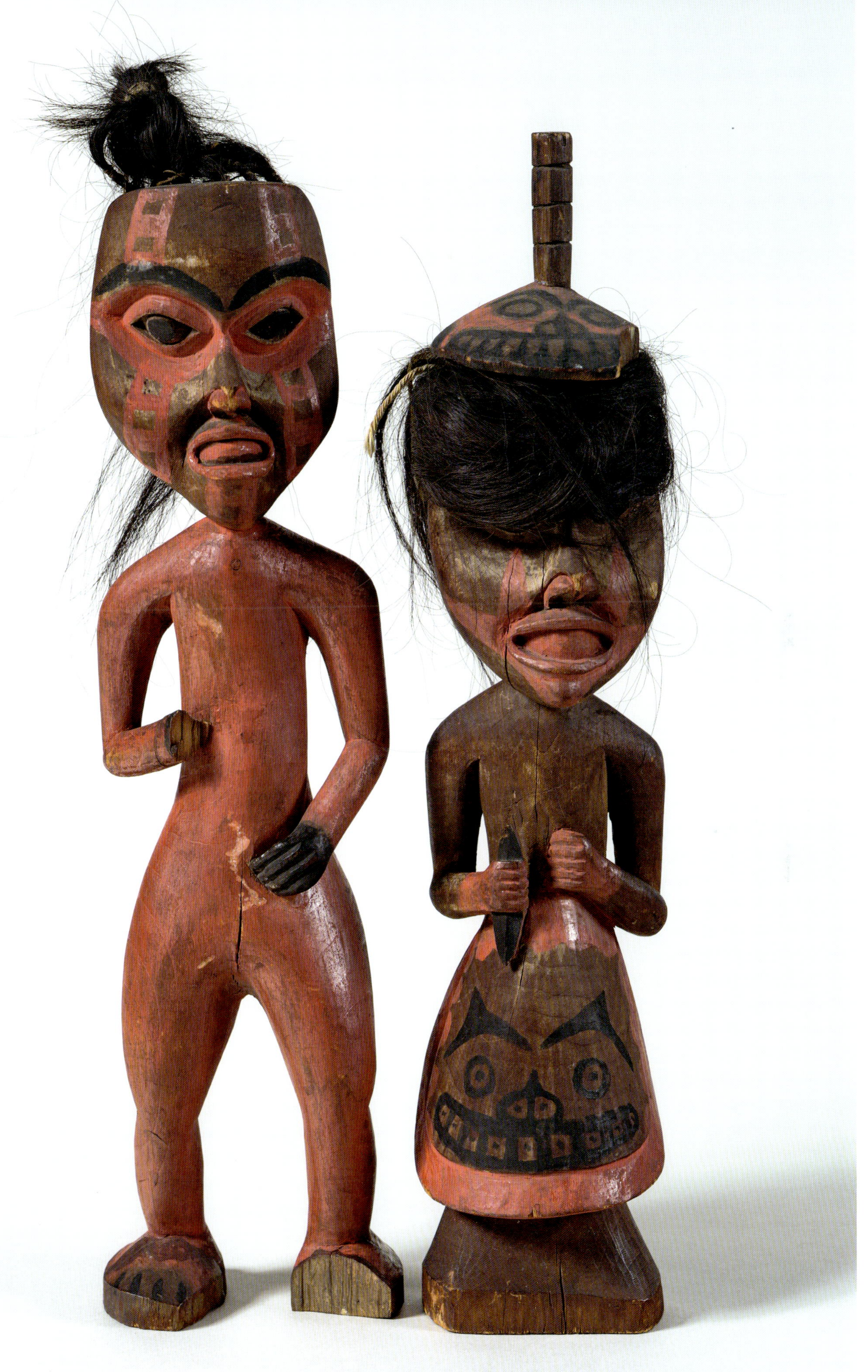

# Sun Dance

Lakota (Teton Sioux), North or South Dakota, c. 1895
Muslin and pigments, 24 × 66 in. (61 × 168 cm)

Museum Purchase, Lloyd O. and Marjorie Strong Coulter Fund, Laura T. and John H. Halford, Jr. Art Acquisition Fund, Jane H. and Charles E. Parker, Jr. Art Acquisition Fund, Barbara Cooney Porter Fund and Greenacres Acquisition Fund  2017.16

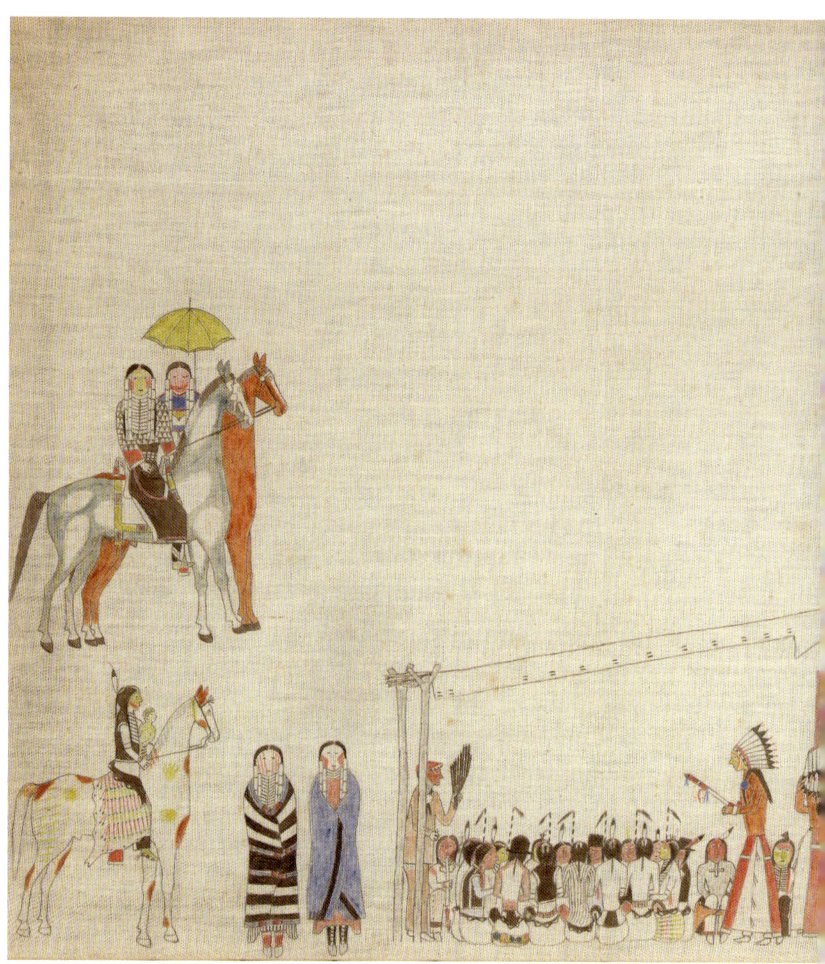

Decades before the coming of Euro-Americans to their territory in the early nineteenth century, indigenous men on the Great Plains of North America painted their hide robes with narrative scenes of hunting and warfare.[1] When American artist George Catlin and Swiss artist Karl Bodmer drew what they saw on the Upper Missouri River in the 1830s, they reported that male artists on the Plains were keenly interested in the portraits of individuals made by these visitors. Though few indigenous drawings remain from this early period, one by the Mandan chief Mató-Tópe (fig. 1) shows the influence of these visitors, whose highly detailed renderings of clothing and other accoutrements inspired some artists to attempt greater detail in their own works. Mató-Tópe depicts his own fringed leggings and feathered war bonnet in great detail, along with the enemy's clothing and battle implements.

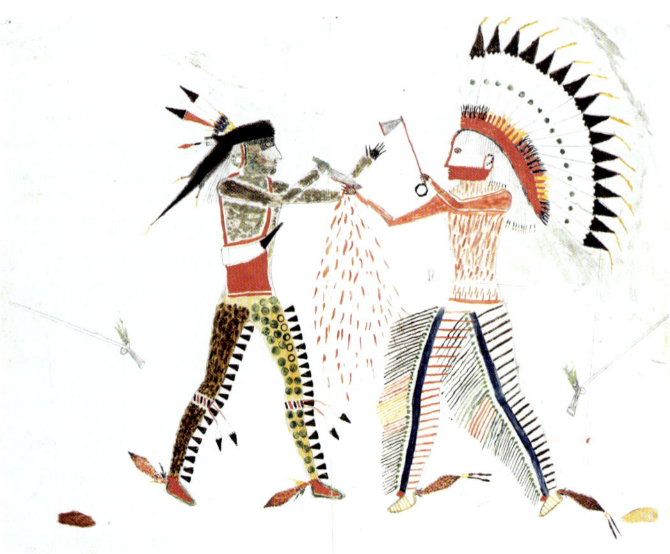

FIG. 1. Mató–Tópe (Four Bears) (Mandan, c. 1784–1837), *Battle with a Cheyenne Chief*, 1833. Watercolor and pencil on paper, 12⅜ × 15⅜ in. (31.4 × 39 cm). Joslyn Art Museum, Omaha, Gift of Enron Art Foundation, 1986.49.384

By the last quarter of the nineteenth century, it was far more common for Plains men to paint on paper and muslin than on hide. An unknown Lakota artist painted this exquisitely detailed picture of the Sun Dance, perhaps around the turn of the twentieth century.[2] In this annual rite of renewal that occurs near the summer solstice, humans place themselves in spiritual alignment with the forces of the natural and supernatural worlds. The painter of this muslin has portrayed the ceremony within the enclosure erected from cut poles. Some twenty standing figures wear war regalia, and most raise their right hands to the sky as they sing and dance; some wear the buffalo-horn and eagle-feather headdresses of the most esteemed and valorous warriors. Three horses within the enclosure are painted for war. Many of the men are shirtless, and some are painted blue or yellow for ceremony. They have elected to perform the most sacred and painful act of piercing their pectoral muscles and attaching themselves to the central pole, finally ripping their bodies away in an act

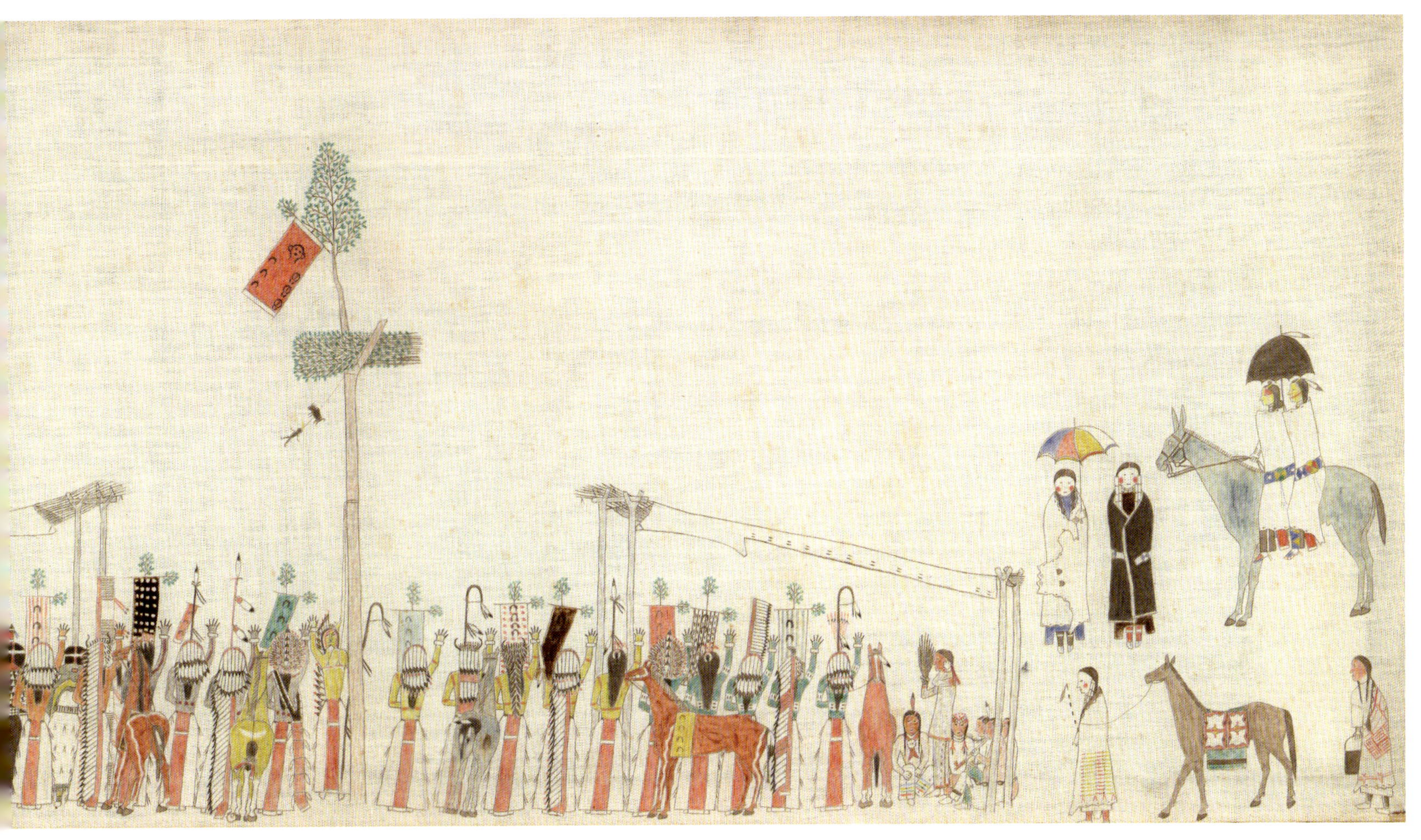

of blood sacrifice that aligns them with the potent powers of the sun.

Small effigies of a man and a buffalo—both fashioned from buffalo hide—hang from branches of the central cottonwood pole. Within the enclosure at right, five figures smoke the sacred pipe and pray for those who will undergo the blood sacrifice. At left, another pipe holder watches over a large drum circle, where the music that sounds like the heartbeat of the earth itself accompanies the ceremony. At far left and far right, vignettes of people, mostly women, ride or walk toward the ceremony; their garments range from traditional quilled and painted hides to Navajo chief's blankets, wool trade cloaks, and wool dresses embellished with elk teeth.

The U.S. government banned the Sun Dance in 1883, but men continued painting scenes of it on muslin into the early twentieth century. Most were made for sale to outsiders; our painting was owned by Reverend Edward Ashley, an Episcopal priest who worked at the Cheyenne River Sioux Reservation in South Dakota for many years, starting in 1889.

Janet Catherine Berlo
Professor of Art History,
University of Rochester

# Two Birchbark Boxes

Wabanaki, Maine, 1834 and 2015

51.2013

Anonymous Gift  2017.46.1

Bowdoin's small oval box (pl. 1) represents the material culture of the Native American Wabanaki people—Maliseet, Micmac, Passamaquoddy, and Penobscot—living in what is now Maine and Canada's Maritime Provinces. It is made from the bark of the white or paper birch, *Betula papyrifera*, which has served the Wabanaki as a reliable, multipurpose material for centuries. Because birchbark can be sewn, this box is part of broader Wabanaki textile traditions, including basketmaking. With the inside of the bark facing out and thus exposed, the box appears brown. The double-scroll motif, a typical Wabanaki design, was scratched into the soft fibers to reveal the lighter bark within.

Birchbark was used for objects ranging from canoes for transportation and wigwams for dwellings to small containers. Beginning in the seventeenth century, European explorers and settlers marveled at its versatility. Used to hold food, it imparted no flavor to its contents and, if sewn with spruce roots and caulked, containers could carry water or serve as cooking kettles.[1] When it was new, this box was a handy, inexpensive container with any number of uses. Maine's Indians often "sold" such containers for the volume of peas or beans they would hold.

Period inscriptions on the inside of the box contribute to its rarity. One—"Enigma of Bowd[oin] Coll[ege] / 1834"—reveals its association with the Enigma Society, a short-lived student organization interested in spiritualism, psychology, and phrenology.[2] Of greater significance, however, is a second inscription that reads "Bought of Dr. Bear[s] [?] of Prospect," providing a rare reference to the Native family associated with the box's origins. It is not known exactly who "Dr. Bear" was, but many Indians practiced herbal medicine and referred to themselves as doctors. Because Wabanakis were peripatetic, finding a Maliseet from eastern Maine and the Canadian Maritimes in a town on Penobscot Bay is not unexpected.[3]

The box survives as an unusually early and well-documented artifact of Maine's Native Americans. Historic birchbark objects also inspire artists today, who use the material to create works with personal and aesthetic meaning. For example, Barry Dana, an artist and former Chief of the Penobscot Nation, uses birchbark in his basketmaking to honor his ancestors. He etched Bowdoin's box/basket (pl. 2) with portraits of North American Indians inspired by the photography of Edward S. Curtis (1868–1952). Dana chose these images not because they are famous, but because they depict "my people." In the creation of the basket, he also preserves "not just the art of construction but the tradition of being out in the woods collecting the bark" and making a physical connection to nature, something that "humanity is sorely lacking."[4]

Laura Fecych Sprague
Senior Consulting Curator, Bowdoin
College Museum of Art

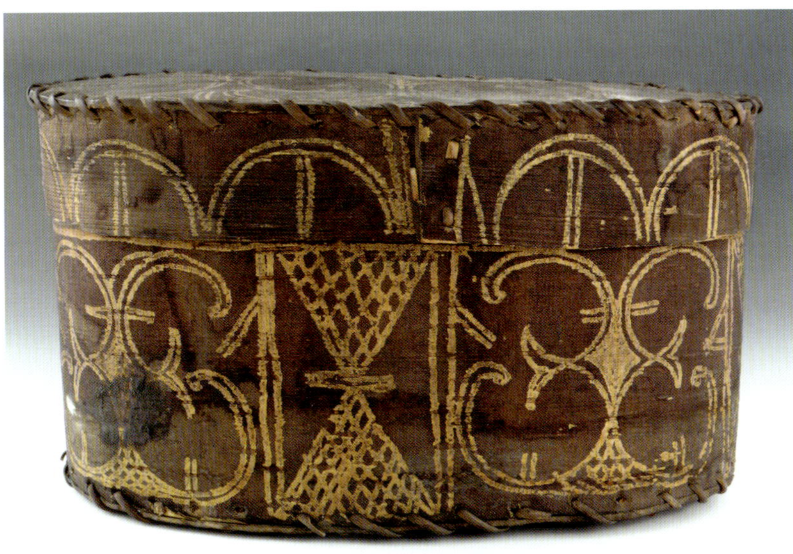

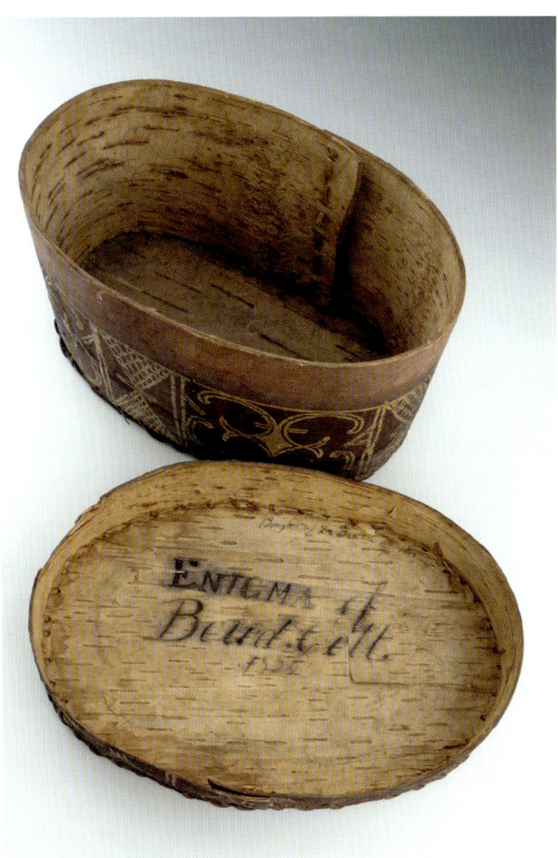

PLATE 1. Ambroise St. Aubin Family, known as the Bear Family, *Covered Box*, 1834. Maliseet Nation of the Wabanaki Confederacy (Prospect, Maine). Birchbark and split spruce root, 6½ × 11¼ × 7⅛ in. (16.5 × 28.6 × 18.1 cm) (51.2013)

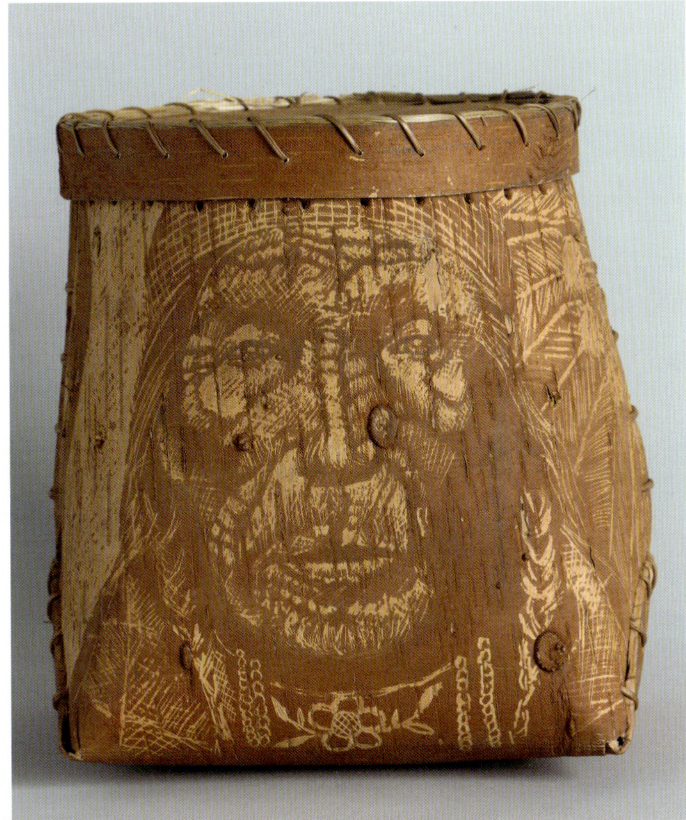

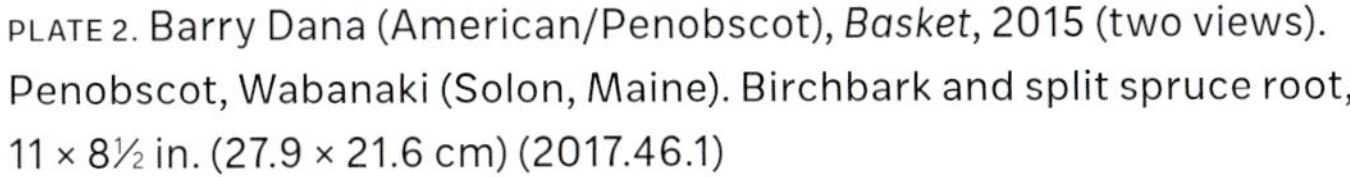

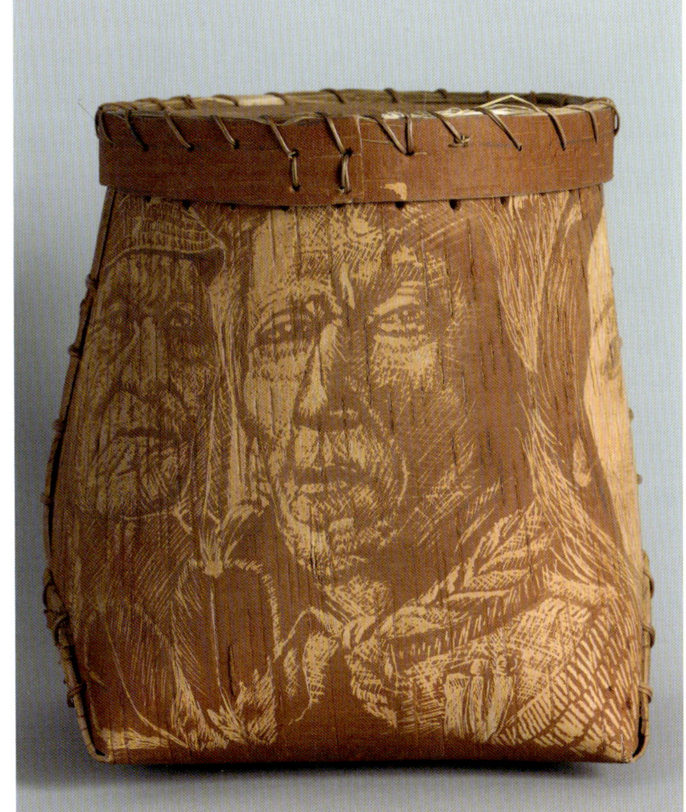

PLATE 2. Barry Dana (American/Penobscot), *Basket*, 2015 (two views). Penobscot, Wabanaki (Solon, Maine). Birchbark and split spruce root, 11 × 8½ in. (27.9 × 21.6 cm) (2017.46.1)

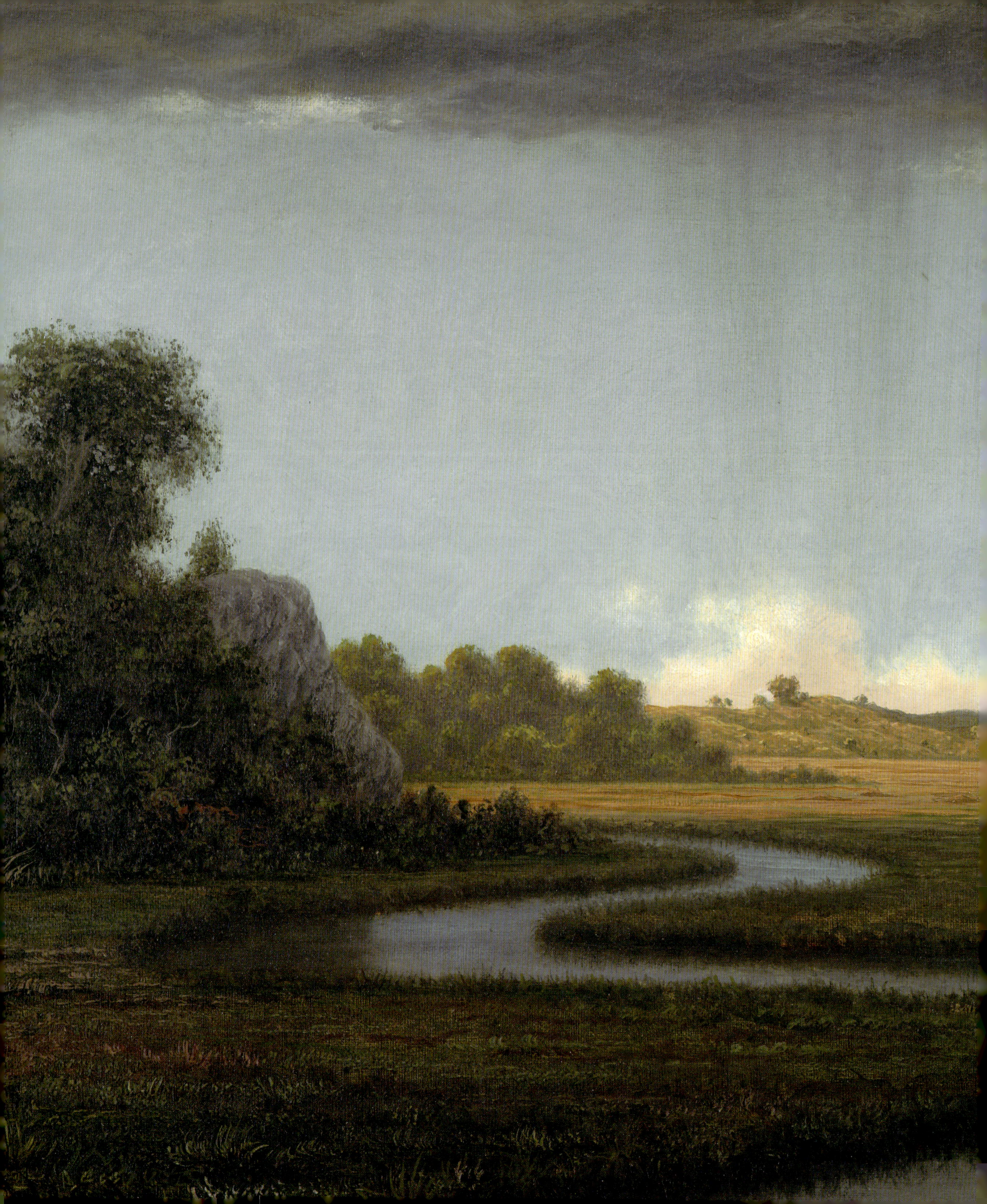

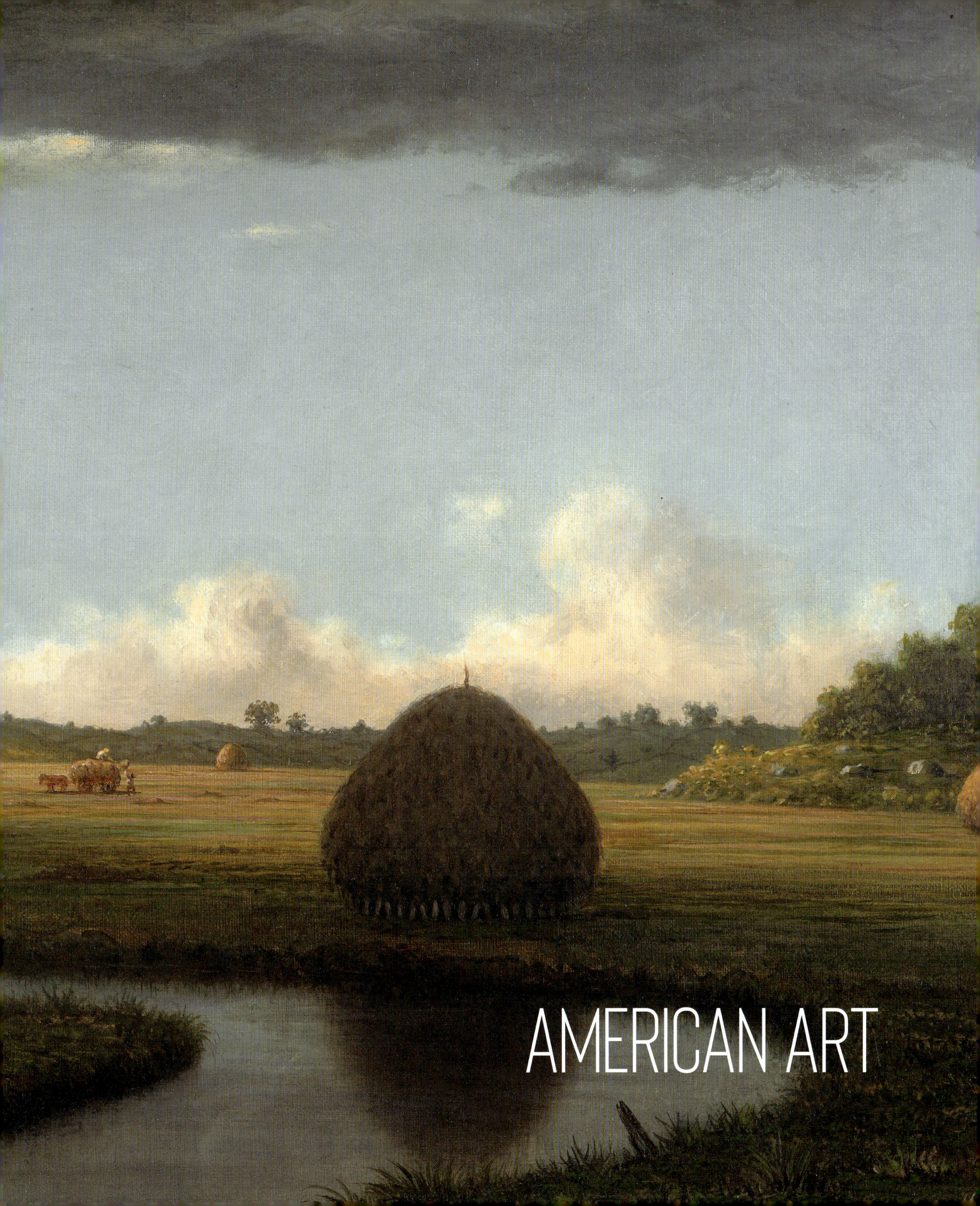
AMERICAN ART

# The Continence of Scipio

John Smibert (American, 1688–1751), after Nicolas Poussin,
c. 1726
Oil on canvas, 45¾ × 62⅝ in. (116.2 × 159 cm)
Bequest of the Honorable James Bowdoin III  1813.10

This is a copy of a 1640 painting, now in the Pushkin Museum of Fine Arts, Moscow, by the French painter Nicolas Poussin, who spent almost his entire career in Rome.[1] The painting is based on a story from Roman history: specifically, a moment in 211 BCE, during the Second Punic War, when the triumphant Roman general Publius Cornelius Scipio Africanus, after a crucial battle in Hispania, made the magnanimous gesture of returning war spoils.[2] Scipio is depicted as he returns to the grateful Allucius, the young prince of the Celtiberians, his betrothed, the captive woman who stands before him, flanked by her mother and a servant. To symbolize the general's generosity, a laurel crown is held above his head. A group of Roman soldiers stands by, admiring the act, while New Carthage (now the city of Cartagena, Spain) burns in the background.

Both during his lifetime and immediately afterward, Poussin was revered and virtually canonized. He was considered the embodiment of the perfect painter, the new Raphael. As a result, the nobility, dignity, and serenity of pictures such as *The Continence of Scipio* were greatly admired. His pictures were readily copied, since the prevailing belief was that it was preferable to view a first-rate copy by a greatly admired artist, such as Poussin, than a second-rate original by a minor figure.

John Smibert was a Scotsman who trained in London, traveled to Italy (1719–22), and after a moderately successful London career (1722–28), set out on an ill-fated utopian venture with Dean George Berkeley (1685–1753) to found a college in Bermuda.[3] Berkeley had persuaded Smibert to become a professor at an arts academy intended to be part of the college, and this picture was intended to become part of its foundational collection. Although neither he nor it got to Bermuda, the painting was noted by visitors to the artist's Boston studio,[4] which became a mecca for generations of American painters. In the years after Smibert's death, his studio was visited (or rented) by numerous artists, including John Singleton Copley, Charles Willson Peale, and John Trumbull.[5]

Records show that Smibert owned a number of copies he had painted, as well as copies by other artists, which he found valuable because they were vivid enhancements to his studio and were intended to impress potential clients. They not only provided visual reminders of great European paintings by revered artists, they also alerted studio visitors that they were in the presence of an artist who possessed skill, erudition, and worldly experience. By painting these copies, which included *Cardinal Guido Bentivoglio* after Anthony van Dyck (Harvard Art Museums, 1969.50), Smibert underscored his comprehension of painting, as well as works he particularly admired.

His copy of *The Continence of Scipio* came to Bowdoin College in 1813 as part of the bequest of James Bowdoin III.[6] For much of its life at the college, the painting has been seen in the way that Smibert would have applauded, alongside other copies and casts on display in the chapel (fig. 1) and later in the Walker Art Building, where it acquainted Bowdoin students with Poussin's palette, subject matter, and composition.

James Bowdoin III most likely acquired this picture from Smibert's studio around 1778. After Smibert's death in 1751,

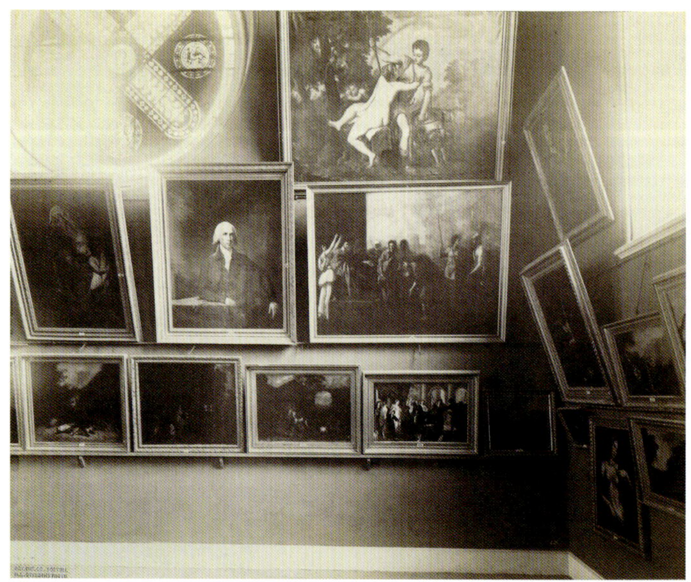

FIG. 1. Nathaniel L. Stebbins, *View of the southeast corner of the Sophia Walker Gallery on the second floor of the Bowdoin Chapel*, c. 1870–90

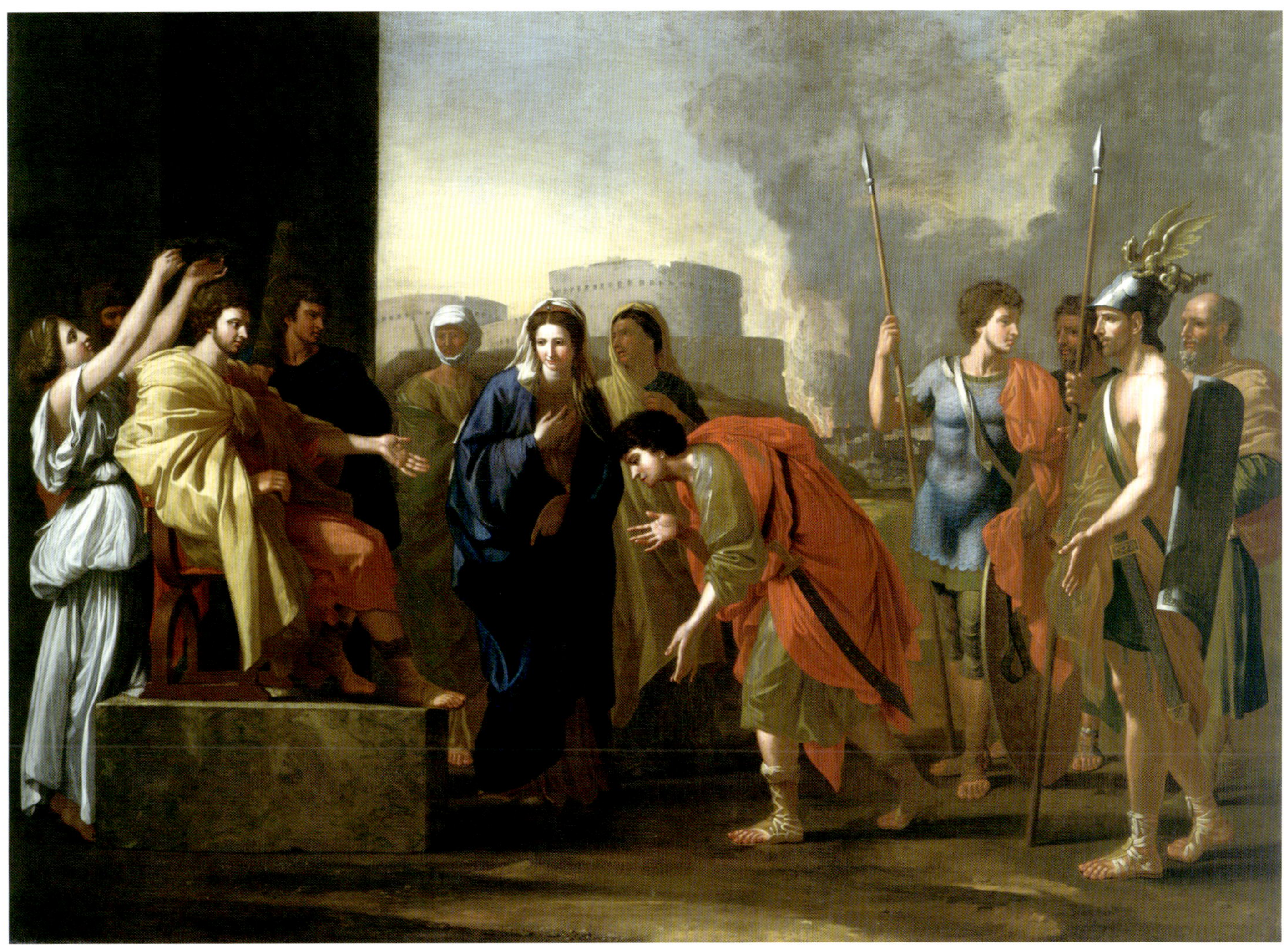

his studio was left intact and rented out by his nephew, John Moffatt. In 1778, following Moffatt's death the preceding year, some of the rooms in Smibert's old house were being rented to a relative of Bowdoin's uncle, John Erving. It also appears that about this same time, a number of drawings known to have been in Smibert's Boston studio were acquired by James Bowdoin III and also bequeathed to the College.[7]

Smibert most certainly painted this picture in London between 1726 and 1728, soon after the original was acquired from a French collection by Sir Robert Walpole (1676–1745), one of the great art collectors of the eighteenth century. At the time it came into Walpole's possession, he lived at 5 Arlington Street, London, less than a mile from Smibert's Covent Garden studio. In 1726, Smibert recorded in his commissions notebook that he painted two minia-tures for Walpole, along with a copy of a lifesize portrait of him, yet for the latter he records no payment.[8] It is possible that Smibert received permission to copy Poussin's *Continence of Scipio* in exchange for painting a portrait for Walpole. Given Smibert's Presbyterian background and emphasis on leading a moral life, he undoubtedly consid-ered this picture particularly noteworthy. And as there were few original paintings by Poussin then in England, it made the work all the more desirable. Lastly, Smibert made particular mention of this picture in a letter in 1743, as did his son, Williams Smibert, in 1762, who implored his cousin that it not be sold.[9]

In an era in which copies are sometimes seen as little more than antiquarian curiosities, it is now hard to gauge their historical importance. Smibert knew that both in his London studio and shortly thereafter, as he set out for the American wilderness, a first-rate copy such as this was an island of inspiration. And as we now know, not only did it inspire him, it has found admiring eyes ever since.

Richard Saunders, Director, Middlebury College Museum of Art, and Professor, History of Art and Architecture, Middlebury College

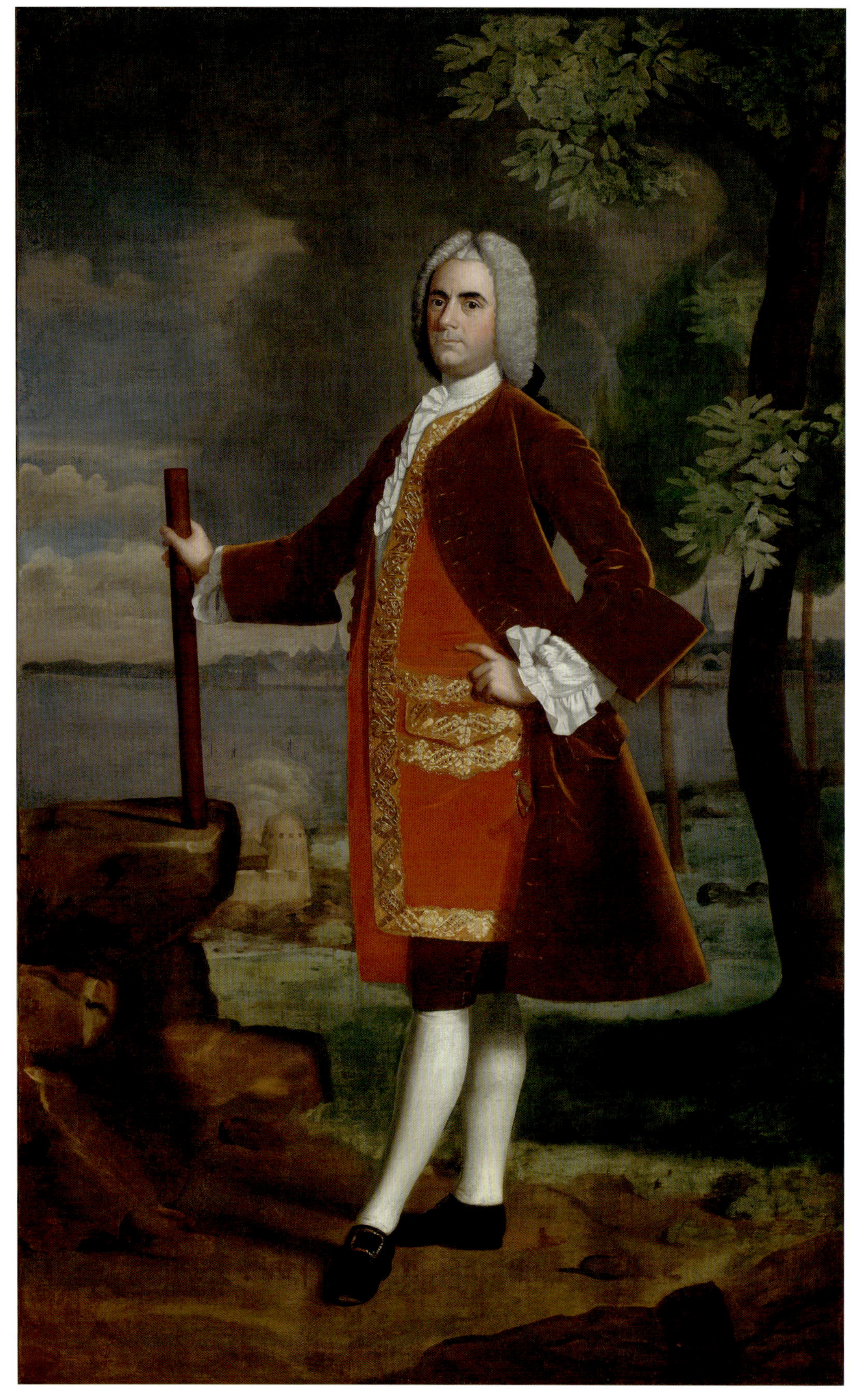

PLATE 1. Robert Feke (American, c. 1707–c. 1752), *Portrait of Brigadier-General Samuel Waldo*, c. 1748. Oil on canvas, 96⅝ × 60¼ in. (245.4 × 153 cm) (1855.3)

# Three Colonial Portraits

Bequest of Mrs. Lucy Flucker Thatcher  1855.1, .2, .3

Born in Oyster Bay, New York, at the brink of the eighteenth century, Robert Feke worked as a land surveyor before he turned to painting. After studying in New York City during the 1720s—where his ambition merged with natural talent to create a "force of genius"—he earned notable commissions for portraits of residents of both Boston and Newport, Rhode Island.[1]

Feke's full-length portrait of Samuel Waldo (1695–1759) (pl. 1), considered his masterwork, commemorates the officer's leadership in the British and American victory in 1745 over the French at Louisbourg, Nova Scotia (visible in the background). This was one of four contemporaneous full-length portraits celebrating the American commanders of that battle: William Pepperrell, William Shirley, and Peter Warren were painted by John Smibert in 1745 and 1746.

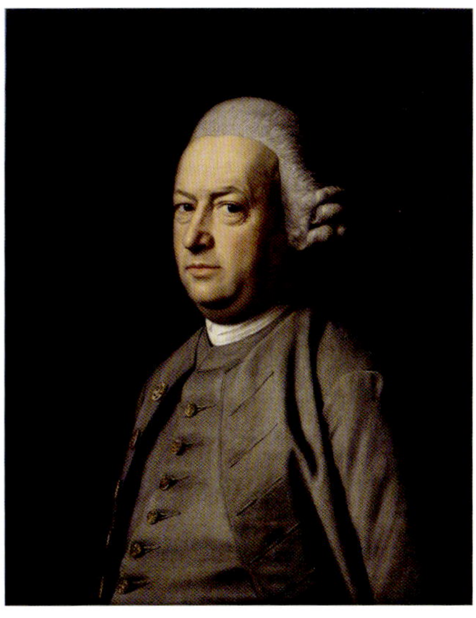

PLATE 3. John Singleton Copley (American, 1738–1815), *Portrait of Thomas Flucker*, c. 1770–71. Oil on canvas, 28⅟₁₆ × 24¼ in. (71.2 × 61.6 cm) (1855.1)

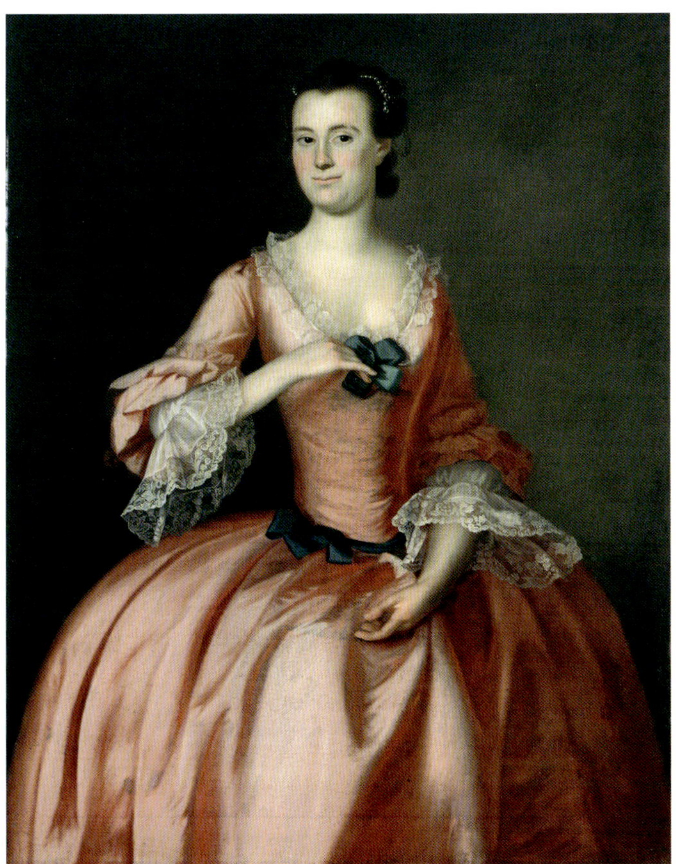

PLATE 2. Joseph Blackburn (American, c. 1730–after 1778), *Portrait of Mrs. Thomas Flucker (née Hannah Waldo)*, c. 1755. Oil on canvas, 50⅛ × 40 in. (127.3 × 101.6 cm) (1855.2)

Waldo holds a baton, symbolizing his status as a brigadier-general, but instead of being depicted in a uniform, he chose to dress as a prosperous merchant. Feke excelled in the painterly details of Waldo's luminous silk-velvet coat and red waistcoat trimmed in yards of thick gold braid. In a large horsehair wig, Waldo strikes a pose guided by British etiquette books.

A Massachusetts merchant involved in timber harvesting and shipping, Waldo expended considerable energy developing lands in the Waldo Patent, between the Penobscot River and Muscongus Bay, now part of Maine. To settle the region beginning in the 1740s, he solicited and encouraged German and Scotch-Irish immigrants, many of whom then served in his regiment at Louisbourg. Although usually considered to be Boston-based, Waldo lived in Falmouth-in-Casco-Bay (now Portland), where he also oversaw mast and timbering operations, and which was only a day's sail by schooner to his property at St. George's and Medomak, in today's midcoast.[2]

Following Waldo's death in 1759, the Feke portrait descended to his daughter Hannah, who married Thomas Flucker, Waldo's Boston partner, in 1751.[3] And it remained in the family until his great-granddaughter bequeathed it to Bowdoin in 1853. Hannah's and Thomas's portraits, also at Bowdoin, were painted by Joseph Blackburn and John Singleton Copley, respectively (pls. 2, 3). Their daughter Lucy defied her Tory parents' wishes when, in 1774, she married a penniless bookseller named Henry Knox. Knox demonstrated his own military prowess in the winter of 1775, when as George Washington's colonel of artillery he and his men hauled captured British cannon over 300 miles from New York's Fort Ticonderoga to Boston. Strategically placed at Dorchester Heights, the fifty-nine cannon forced the British out of Boston; the Fluckers fled with the British troops.

After the American Revolution, the Commonwealth of Massachusetts sold confiscated Tory lands to help pay its war debts, and Lucy and Henry Knox purchased property within the Waldo Patent. Like Waldo before him, Knox hoped that new industries there would generate economic development, thereby increasing his personal wealth. Operations in land development, lumber, and limestone centered around Montpelier, their ambitious Neoclassical estate built in Thomaston in 1794. Waldo's likeness probably decorated the two-story stair hall, the only space large enough to accommodate it.[4] When Knox died in 1806, his debts jeopardized the future of Montpelier, where his daughter, Lucy Flucker Thatcher, died in 1854. But his story influenced American culture in other, unexpected ways. His map of the Waldo Patent was still hanging on a wall at Montpelier in 1837, when Nathaniel Hawthorne (Bowdoin College, class of 1825) visited and found in it the inspiration for Pyncheon's legendary landholdings in *The House of the Seven Gables* (1851).[5] Waldo's magnificent portrait is evidence not only of the aesthetic strengths of Bowdoin's colonial painting collection, but also of the considerable historical connections that bind generations and places together.

Laura Fecych Sprague
Senior Consulting Curator, Bowdoin
College Museum of Art

# Portraits of Thomas Jefferson and James Madison

Gilbert Stuart (American, 1758–1828), c. 1805–7
Bequest of the Honorable James Bowdoin III  1813.54, .55

In 1805, James Bowdoin III commissioned the artist Gilbert Stuart to paint pendant portraits of President Thomas Jefferson (1743–1826) and Secretary of State James Madison (1751–1836). The Jefferson portrait is one of several Stuart undertook in 1805.[1] The identically sized likenesses were meant to face one another, as if they were in dialogue. These allies, both slaveholders from Virginia, dedicated themselves to establishing the new republic and securing its future. Jefferson had just appointed Bowdoin minister to the court of Spain, and he intended to take the portraits to Madrid to display there. His ill-health and a different political situation, however, landed him in Paris rather than Madrid. He resigned his post in May 1807, several months before the completion of the paintings, returning to his elegant home in Boston by April 1808. The pictures were thus transported there from Stuart's Boston studio. While these contemporary leaders and revolutionary heroes were politically important to Bowdoin, the Jefferson portrait likely signaled something more to him: both men had extensive collections of art and geological specimens, and both had amassed substantial libraries.[2]

Although Bowdoin probably did not know it, his initiative echoed a similar one that Jefferson had undertaken more than twenty years earlier. As Jefferson was about to depart for Paris to serve as a trade minister in 1784, he engaged the American painter Joseph Wright to copy his portrait of George Washington (1783). Neither Jefferson nor Bowdoin explicitly stated why they commissioned these portraits; both evidently wanted to share images of America's leaders in diplomatic circles abroad to create an American identity. After accepting the ministerial post, Bowdoin had written Jefferson, "Be assured Sir to find in me a heartfelt disposition to promote the public interest, & the success of your administration, as well as to extend your personal fame & honour . . ." The portrait would have been a tangible way of extending Jefferson's "personal fame."[3]

While Jefferson was designing the Virginia State Capitol, the Hôtel de Langeac, his house in Paris, became

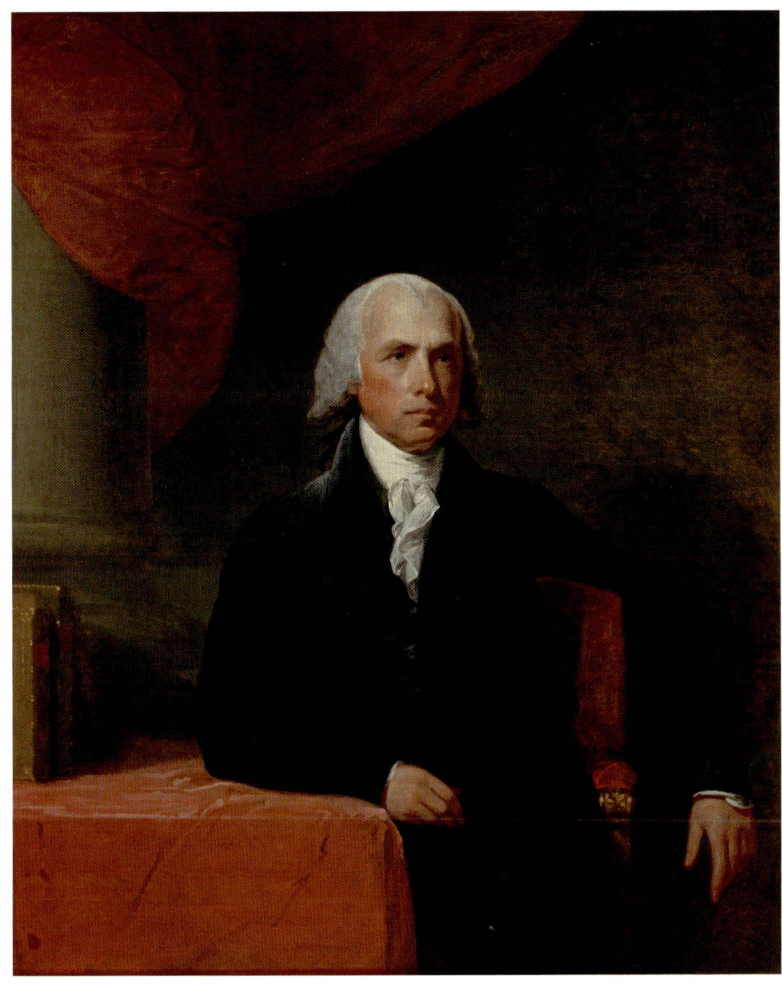

PLATE 1. Gilbert Stuart, *James Madison*, c. 1805–7. Oil on canvas, 48½ × 39¾ in. (123.2 × 101 cm) (1813.54)

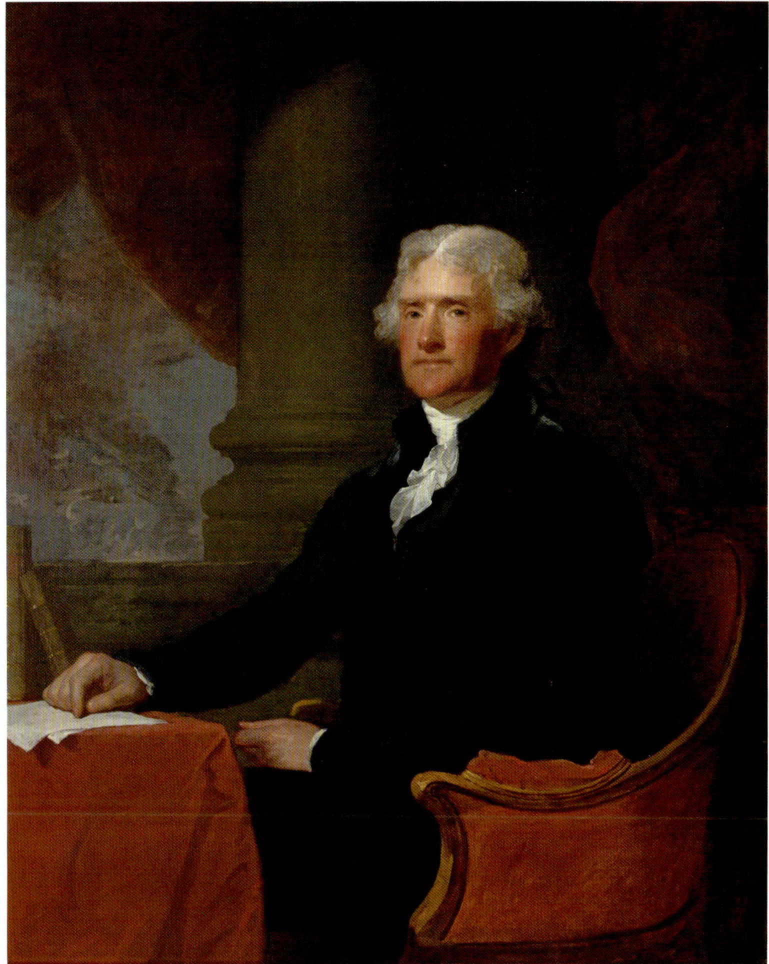

PLATE 2. Gilbert Stuart, *Thomas Jefferson*, c. 1805–7. Oil on canvas, 48½ × 39⅞ in. (123.2 × 101.3 cm) (1813.55)

his canvas.[4] There he communicated the story of America through portraits of Washington, Franklin, Adams, and Lafayette; the "discoverers" (Magellan, Cortez, Vespucci, and Columbus); and his triumvirate of worthies (Bacon, Newton, and Locke). From Paris, Jefferson wrote Madison that the arts had the potential "to improve the taste of my countrymen, to increase their reputation, to reconcile to them the respect of the world and procure them its praise."[5] Jefferson's sizable collection, together with copies of European masterpieces, was displayed in Philadelphia while he was secretary of state and vice president, in Washington at the President's House, and finally at Monticello after his retirement in 1809.

Bowdoin likely knew about Jefferson's art collection and his formative influence on American art and architecture. Before embarking on his assignment, he offered his services to Jefferson "in procuring for you any Specimens of the arts, either in Sculpture or painting." Jefferson accepted one such work, "a handsome piece of modern Sculpture, a Cleopatra copied & reduced from the ancient one now at Paris, which for many years lay at the Palace of the Belvidere [*sic*] at Rome," placing it "in a corner of your hall at Monticello," as Bowdoin had suggested.[6] As Bowdoin was reminded of Jefferson and Madison in his house, Jefferson would have been reminded of Bowdoin. Perhaps more importantly, they each used their collections to assert American identity, share knowledge, and transmit cultural awareness.

Susan R. Stein
Richard Gilder Senior Curator, Monticello

# Newburyport Marshes: Passing Storm

Martin Johnson Heade (American, 1819–1904), c. 1865–70
Oil on canvas, 15⅛ × 30¼ in. (38.4 × 76.8 cm)
Museum Purchase, with the aid of the Sylvia E. Ross Fund  1964.45

The more than 120 marsh scenes Martin Johnson Heade painted over the course of his four-decade-long career constitute as much as a fifth of his total oeuvre.[1] During this extended enterprise, he painted marshes in Connecticut and Long Island and around Hoboken, New Jersey, as well as in Newbury and Newburyport, Massachusetts. Heade's painting at Bowdoin, *Newburyport Marshes: Passing Storm*, represents the artist at the height of his achievement in the late 1860s and early 1870s.

Salt marshes are strange. They are uncertain spaces: both land and water and neither of those things. Fluid, changeable, and perennially unfixed, they have been called "the one landscape in constant flux."[2] This aspect of change and variation seems to have appealed to Heade and to have encouraged him to reflect these qualities in his paintings. As Theodore Stebbins observes, the marsh scenes "seem very much to make up a series, rather than being examples of duplication."[3] Variation within their emphatically horizontal format is concentrated in changes in weather, light, and atmosphere, as well as in the position-ing of the haystacks and in the activity and distribution of the staffage figures, which Heade typically located in the midground. The rare fixed elements of the landscape, such as the granite outcrop on the left of Bowdoin's canvas, or the profiles of streams and riverlets, are varied by being placed nearer or further from the picture plane, so that size and shape mutate over the course of different canvases. This interest in the changes that can be rung on similar motifs produces a sense of a slowly transforming scene, a series of images that flicker through a gentle alteration, but in which things remain essentially the same.

Although series are a feature of some nineteenth-century American art, such as Thomas Cole's *The Voyage of Life* (1842) and *The Course of Empire* (1833–36), Heade's long engagement with marsh scenes is distinct from these moralizing narrative groups of four or five canvases.[4] A more telling comparison is with Claude Monet's series of thirty-odd *Haystacks* from 1890–91. Heade's marsh scenes are likewise concerned with the different effects of light, atmosphere, and season on essentially similar motifs, directing us away from these numinous or transfigured objects dissolved in skeins of light and back toward the everyday. His figures trudge or boat across the marshes, or labor at raking or heaping the grasses that form the haystacks. Distributed over dozens of canvases, these quotidian activities enforce a sense of the naturalness of human undertakings. They are both integrated into the natural world in which they take place and entirely unexceptional. Nothing beyond the regularity of life, its repetitions, familiar tasks, and movements, its formalized, even ritual, acts and gestures, is at stake here.

In many ways, this is the opposite of the sense of the transcendent that emerges for us now from Monet's version of this theme, and has far more in common with the late nineteenth- and early twentieth-century readings of the Impressionists that saw them as obdurate realists, stuck at the surface of physical or optical phenomena. Heade's persistent representation of human action in a natural world offers us in contrast a view of the human as immemorial and unchanging. The world of the marsh and the vagaries of weather shift around us, but action and response remain the same. Time, the endless character of labor, the place of the human in the natural, all these are central to Heade's painting.

David Peters Corbett
Professor of American Art, and Director,
Centre for American Art, Courtauld
Institute of Art

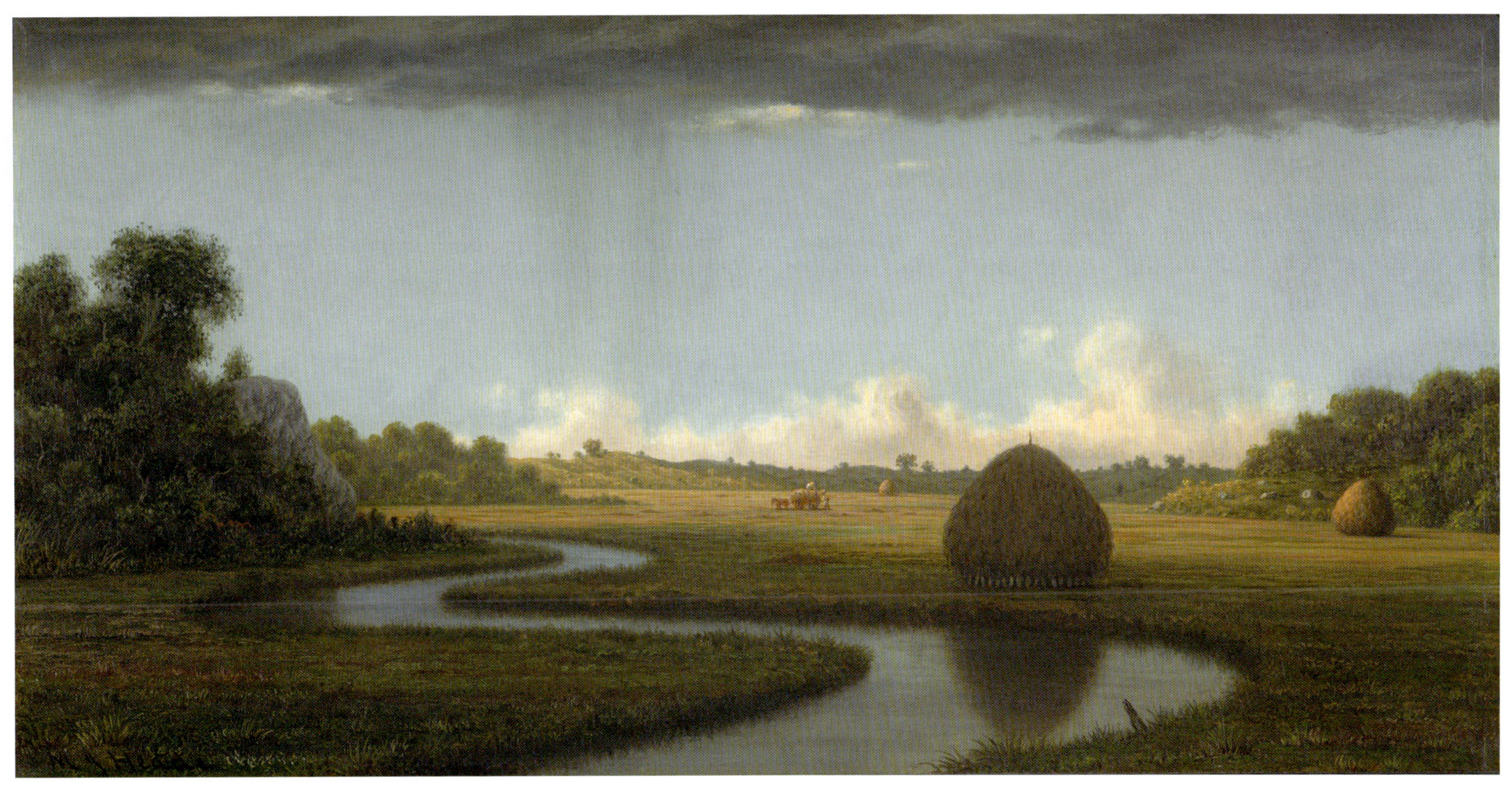

# *Musidora*

John Adams Jackson (American, 1825–1879), c. 1873
White marble, 43 × 12⅛ × 13¾ in. (109.2 × 30.8 × 34.9 cm)
Gift of Professor Margaret Jackson, in memory of her father, the
sculptor  1916.10

Born and apprenticed as a blacksmith in Bath, Maine, John Adams Jackson initially gained fame for his marble portrait busts, literally setting in stone the likenesses of nineteenth-century America's political and cultural elite. He moved in 1860 to Florence, Italy, where the facilities existed to help him better realize ideal works of sculpture based on mythology, the Bible, and literature, as well as large-scale civic monuments. Among other works, Jackson modeled and put into marble his first standing female nude, not as a commission, but to fulfill his own artistic aspirations. It was an audacious statement of artistic confidence both for the manner in which it was executed—marble was expensive to quarry and fabricate, and few artists were emboldened to undertake a work without the financial backing of a patron—and for its subject matter—nudity was frowned upon by Victorian audiences.

Even though the standing female nude boasted an esteemed lineage in Western sculpture—from the *Venus de' Medici*, a first-century CE Roman copy of a Greek original (Gallerie degli Uffizi, Florence) to Antonio Canova's *Venus Italica* (1804; Palazzo Pitti, Florence) and Hiram Powers's *Greek Slave* (1846; Corcoran Collection, National Gallery of Art, Washington, D.C.), to name a select few—Jackson still had to couch the nudity of his statue in terms that would make it socially acceptable. His solution was to metaphorically cloak her in the moral authority of poetry, namely, in the guise of Musidora, a character from *Summer* (1727) in Scottish author James Thomson's unimpeachable series *The Seasons*.[1]

Jackson portrayed Musidora as she prepares to cool herself in a secluded woodland pond on a hot summer's day. Unaware that she is being watched, she wades into the pool with loosened hair, water lilies rising around her weight-bearing left leg. Sensing an interloper, she startles and modestly covers her nakedness with the cloth in her right hand. Her body elegantly crouches and pivots in response, her head tilts subtly as if to listen, and her free left hand gestures delicately into space as if to seek the origin of the intruder. Her physical vulnerability and innocence, reinforced by the medium of unblemished white marble, chasten any impure thoughts that the viewer may harbor. Stylistically, Jackson's *Musidora* reflects the tenets of the school of naturalism championed at midcentury by the Italian sculptor Lorenzo Bartolini in which the austere formality and rigorous frontality of the Neoclassical idiom have been modified through a direct observation of nature.

Upon seeing the original model of *Musidora* in Jackson's studio in 1871, one female newspaper correspondent exclaimed that "the rarest gem stood before us dripping in wet clay" and assured that "for nude though she be, she is veiled by her perfect virginity of soul; yes—all clad in maiden modesty."[2] Such favorable press was vital in order for Jackson to promote and find a buyer for his work. He exhibited the finished marble at the World's Fair in Vienna in 1873, where Edward Everett Hale, the noted American author, historian, and minister, declared that the "exquisite *Musidora* is one of the most beautiful statues here."[3] From Vienna, Jackson shipped the work to New York for exhibition and publicized it heavily. Thousands flocked to see it, and the critics praised it for its "femininity and poetry not often found in modern statues."[4]

In their authoritative handbook of nineteenth-century American artists, Clement and Hutton recorded two examples of *Musidora* that were in private collections: the first, discussed above, which was the size of life, and a second, two-thirds-sized replica (both unlocated).[5] Bowdoin's *Musidora* is another two-thirds-sized example, which remained with the Jackson family until it was presented to the museum by the sculptor's daughter in loving memory of her father in 1916.[6]

John F. McGuigan Jr.
Independent scholar

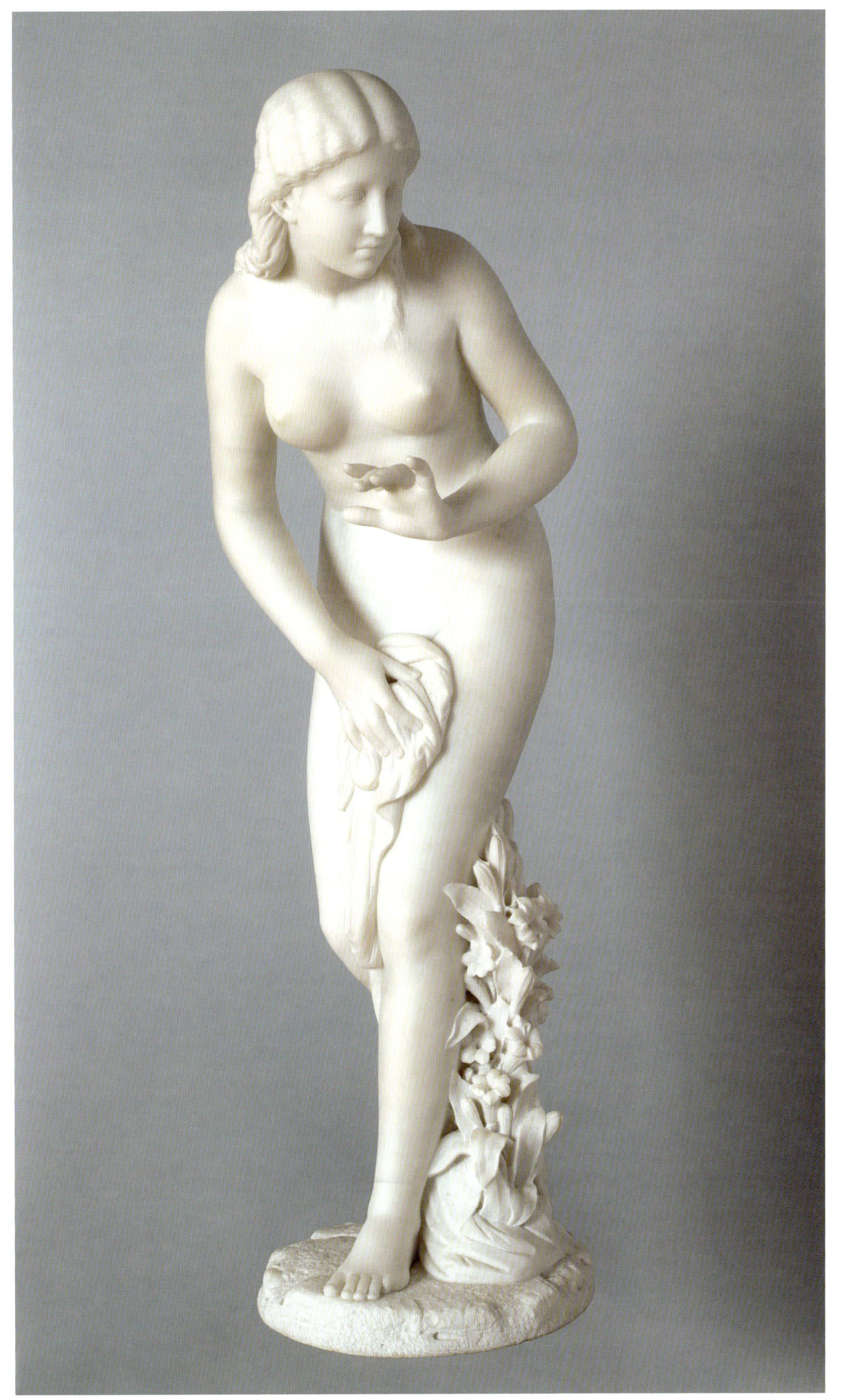

# Rome (The Art Idea)

Elihu Vedder (American, 1836–1923), 1894
Oil on canvas, 144 × 288 in. (365.8 × 731.5 cm)
Gift of the Misses Harriet Sarah and Mary Sophia Walker  1893.37

The Misses Walker were sister-benefactors of the Walker Art Building, which houses the Bowdoin College Museum of Art. In 1892, they chose Elihu Vedder to paint a mural for the lunette opposite the main entrance in the domed Sculpture Hall of the projected edifice (fig. 1). Intended as the only mural to adorn the room that would welcome visitors to this ambitious new outpost of culture and learning, the Walkers wisely consulted the building's architect, Charles Follen McKim of the distinguished firm of McKim, Mead & White, for a recommendation. Although Vedder, a native New Yorker, had lived in Rome for more than twenty-five years, he enjoyed an estimable transatlantic reputation as a versatile painter of evocative landscapes and enigmatic figural compositions. A concurrent commission for a mural cycle in the dining room of Collis P. Huntington's Fifth Avenue mansion in New York positioned Vedder among the leading muralists of the American Renaissance.

Vedder's proposal for Bowdoin was *The Art Idea*, in which personifications and emblems of the fundamental principles that underlie the historical study and practice of the fine arts would be deployed across a shallow, friezelike space. Each of their roles would be identified by text directly below them: Knowledge (*Sapienza*), Thought (*Pensiero*), Soul (*Anima*), Life (*Vita*), Nature (*Natura*), Harmony (*Armonia*), Love (*Amore*), Color (*Colore*), and Form (*Forma*). Tablets with the *Alpha* and *Omega* on them would signify the beginning and the end. This easy legibility—literally and figuratively—reinforced the didactic function of Vedder's iconographic program and was well suited for placement in the museum of a liberal arts college.

In 1893, unbeknownst to Vedder, three more murals were commissioned for the remaining lunettes in Sculpture Hall, and McKim worked with the new artists on a narrative cycle commemorating the European cities that had contributed most to Western art: Athens (John La Farge), Venice (Kenyon Cox), and Florence (Abbott Thayer). As a result, Vedder was compelled to change the title and certain elements of his mural to honor the artistic patrimony of Rome, the cosmopolitan center of art and culture for millennia, and his adopted home.

Vedder fluently adapted his original design to suggest two of the most important artists ever to have worked in Rome: Michelangelo and Raphael. On the viewer's left, a seated sibyl, an architectural drawing, an *écorché* model, and a winged genius of Soul all make reference to Michelangelo. The right side alludes to Raphael, in the personification of Painting holding a palette, a winged genius of Love drawing on a board with Cupid's arrow, and the

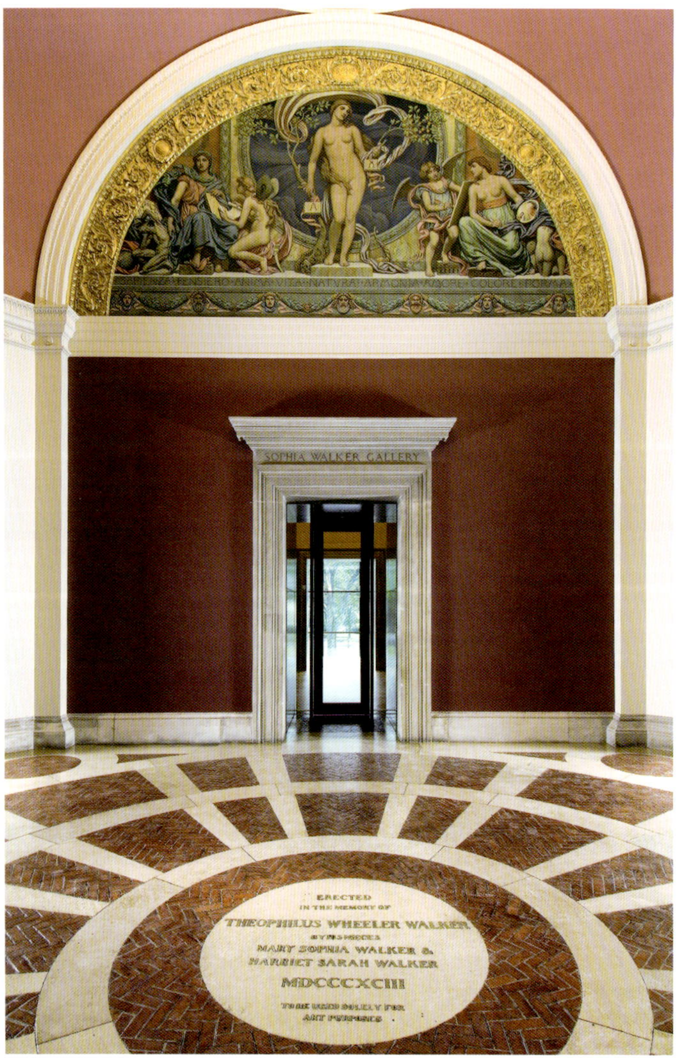

FIG. 1. Rotunda of the Bowdoin College Museum of Art

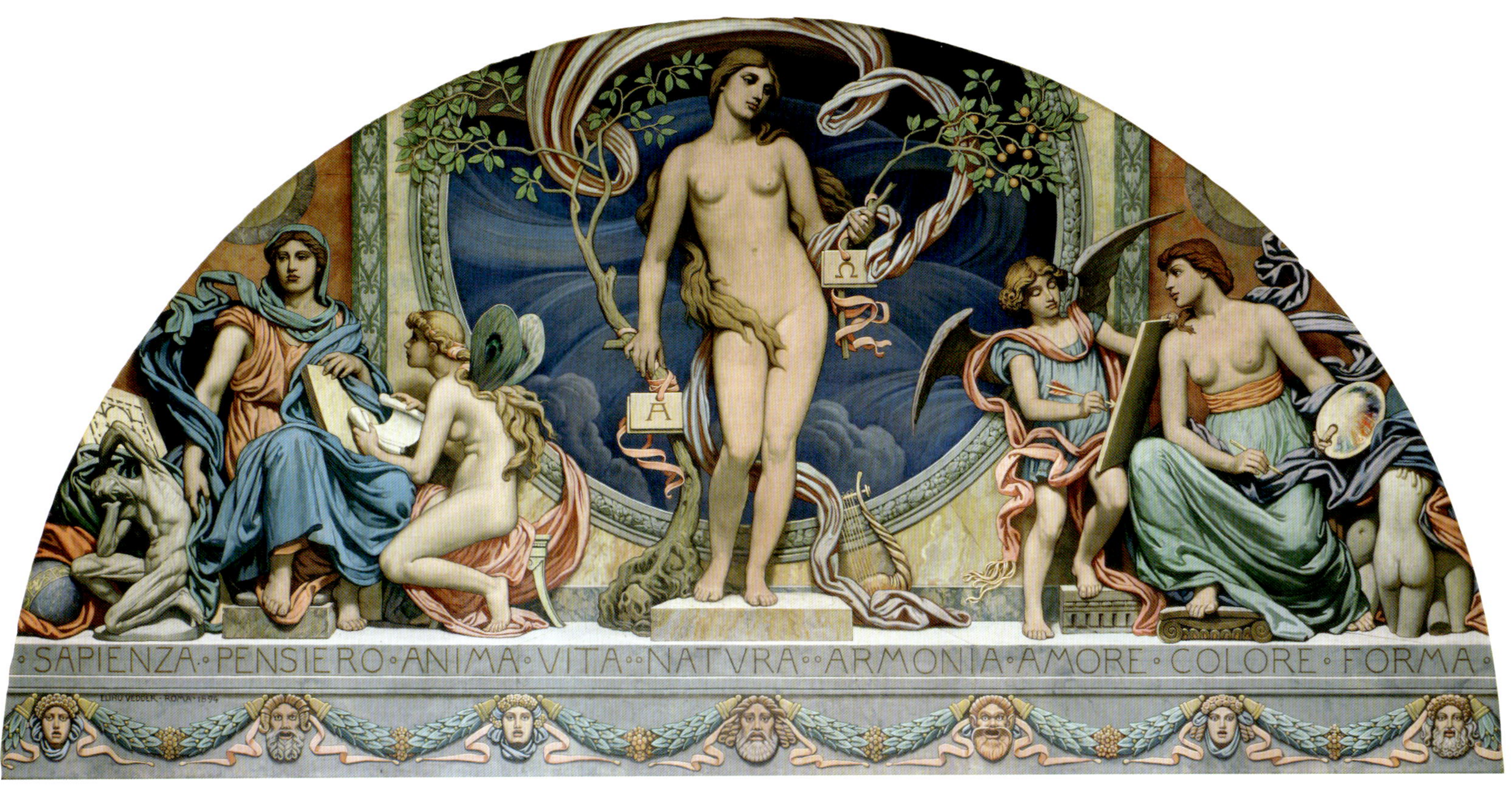



antique group *The Three Graces* just visible in the corner. In the middle of the composition stands a full-length female nude representing Nature, the common wellspring of all art. As Vedder described: "Her right hand rests on the trunk and roots of the Tree of Life [*Alpha*]; her left holds a detached branch with its fruit—an art having once reached its culmination never lives again [*Omega*]; its fruit, however, contains the seeds of another development."[1] There is perhaps no more poignant distillation of the academic model of art instruction—the constant rejuvenation of art through an understanding of and dynamic interaction with an inherited aesthetic tradition based upon the human figure—than the superb embodiment of Nature in Vedder's

learned tribute. Thus, while the mural nominally pays homage to Rome, it continues to function as *The Art Idea*, the concepts of which are still writ large along the face of the stagelike platform.

Vedder came to Bowdoin College to oversee the installation and unveiling of the mural to the Misses Walker in September 1894. He was justifiably proud of his work in comparison to those by Cox and Thayer, which were already in place. Indeed, as scholar Richard Murray concluded: "Of the hundreds of murals in public and private buildings, only one states the philosophical premise of the entire American Renaissance: Elihu Vedder's *Rome*, or *The Art Idea*."[2]

Mary K. McGuigan
Independent scholar

# The Fountains at Night, World's Columbian Exposition

Winslow Homer (American, 1836–1910), 1893
Oil on canvas, 16⅜ × 25⅛ in. (41.6 × 63.8 cm)
Bequest of Mrs. Charles Savage Homer, Jr.  1938.2

Winslow Homer's *Fountains at Night* is an unusual work in the artist's oeuvre, belying his reputation as the all-American painter of dramatic scenes in which men and women struggle with the natural elements. At the time he painted this canvas, Homer was settling into the mature phase of his career, mostly devoted to the depiction of the everyday life of fishermen on the coast of Maine. These later paintings were acclaimed as epitomes of virility, hardiness, and realism. Here, however, we are presented with tourists enjoying a view of a highly artificial aquatic recreation, the MacMonnies fountain poised at the center of the Court of Honor at the 1893 Columbian Exposition in Chicago. The setting, with fantastic seahorses rearing up over cascades of electrically illuminated waters and Venetian gondolas, resembles more the sham décor of a theater than the wild, rocky sceneries Homer had become known for. Compared with the toilers of the seas seen in canvases like *The Herring Net* or *The Fog Warning* (which the artist presented in the Fine Arts section of the Exposition), the gondoliers pushing the couple across the fountain's basin seem to engage in quite superfluous efforts. Italy, and particularly Venice, were important sources of inspiration for many of Homer's colleagues. The fairgrounds reflected this inclination, with fountains and gondolas playing a preeminent role in the aesthetics of the Exposition.

*The Fountains at Night* participates, in its own way, in another trend then gaining traction among American artists: night landscapes, or nocturnes, a genre the expatriate artist James McNeill Whistler reinvented with his beautifully murky views of the Venetian Lagoon and the Thames River in London. The nocturne vogue was symptomatic of a shift in taste on the American art scene, marking the demise of the nationalistic, hyper-detailed glorifications of the American wilderness in favor of more sophisticated, cosmopolitan visions. Homer had already painted several moonlit marines when he began *The Fountains at Night*. But Bowdoin's painting is much more complex than a merging of fashionable elements. Homer may have used this night view of the fair to emulate another type of picture. Photographs recording the fair's highlights were gathered in expensive large-scale albums and sold as "Official Views" of the exhibits and architectural delights. Homer probably intended to sell his painting as a keepsake, just like these souvenir photographs, many of which illustrated the dazzling electric nighttime illuminations. Considering the state of development of photography at the turn of the century, they were quite a feat. However, capturing a night view of a moving boat, rowing men, and splashing water on a photographic plate would have been nearly impossible at the time. Homer's canvas sets out to bridge that gap, imitating the monochromatic quality of photographs while exploiting the plasticity of paint in the rendering of men and water in motion.

*The Fountains at Night* thus merges many issues central to the visual culture of Homer's time, demonstrating his skill at creatively combining the trends informing art production with other forms of picture making. This painting of a gondola cruising the fountain's waters is not a compendium of clichés and artificiality, but an audacious exploration of the potentialities of a visual environment in never-ending transformation.

Hélène Valance
Associate Professor, Department of
English, University of Franche-Comté

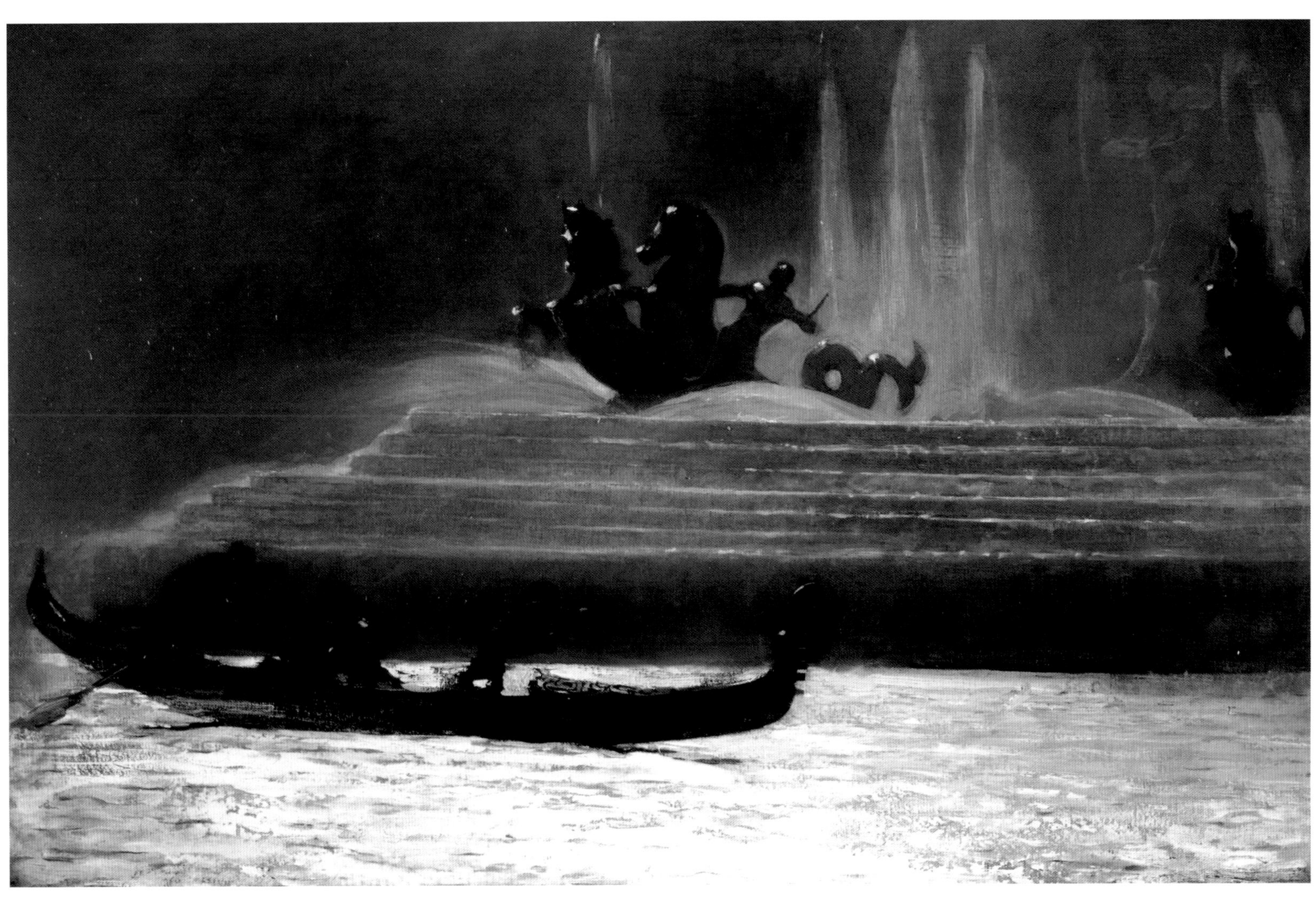

# Sunday Afternoon in Union Square

John Sloan (American, 1871–1951), 1912
Oil on canvas, 26⅛ × 32⅛ in. (66.4 × 81.6 cm)
Bequest of George Otis Hamlin  1961.63

1912 was a good year for John Sloan. He and his wife had recently moved to a nicer apartment on East 22nd Street near Gramercy Park. When the apartment proved too small to accommodate a proper studio, he splurged and leased a space on the eleventh floor of a commercial building on Sixth Avenue, one block west of Washington Square. Union Square, the site of our picture, is located between Sloan's apartment and studio, and the artist would likely have walked across it on his daily route.

One of New York's historic communal spaces, Union Square offers a plot of tamed nature embedded in a compacted urban grid. By the early twentieth century, it was bounded by industrial shops, retail stores, and theaters, more tawdry than tony. The square was also the frequent scene of mass political demonstrations, which Sloan the card-carrying socialist sometimes joined. However, what attracted Sloan the painter to Union Square were not its turbulent events, but the swirl and peculiarity of everyday life. Looking at *Sunday Afternoon in Union Square*, one imagines Sloan loitering in the park one sultry mid-summer sabbath, amused by the ebb and flow of women and men

out in the sun on their day off. Taking note of the glances and gestures of strangers, discerning patterns in the randomness of activity, he may jot a few quick sketches. However, once back in the studio, he will rely mainly upon memory to stir and sieve his impressions and then deliver up an image to the canvas.

As frequently noted, *Sunday Afternoon in Union Square* is unusual among Sloan's city scenes for its strong narrative drive. In most of his paintings, nothing much happens. Here there is a story, or at least the makings of one: a pair of stylishly dressed young women stroll along the gravel footpath, ignoring the eyes that follow and appraise them. Far from being a lighthearted snapshot, there is something vaguely unsettling about this scene, something impolite. When the canvas was first exhibited in 1913, the critic for the *New York Times* contrasted its coarse vernacular to the "polished utterance" of older, established painters. "This," the critic pronounced with hauteur, "is the slang of the city parks, this flaunting of short-skirted, tight-skirted women, this gazing and gossiping of idlers on the benches, and envious or critical girls of the same untrammeled class."[1] The critic congratulated Sloan for his "vivacious comment on New York streets," but she—it was probably the ever-genteel Elizabeth Cary—felt palpable aversion to the advent of this new type of disruptive, "untrammeled" woman.

Not so judgmental, Sloan had an eye for these women, whose sexuality, boldly expressed, aroused him as much as the gawkers in Union Square. Shy and skittish, the artist found safety in the role of spectator, alert, mindful, but unengaged. While in other pictures, such as Bowdoin's *A Window on the Street* (fig. 1), Sloan's spectating might edge uncomfortably into voyeurism, in *Sunday Afternoon in Union Square*, he—and we as shared onlookers—maintain our distance, invading no one's privacy. If the leering man in the straw fedora or the whispering women on the bench show little respect for the strolling young ladies, John Sloan does not join them.

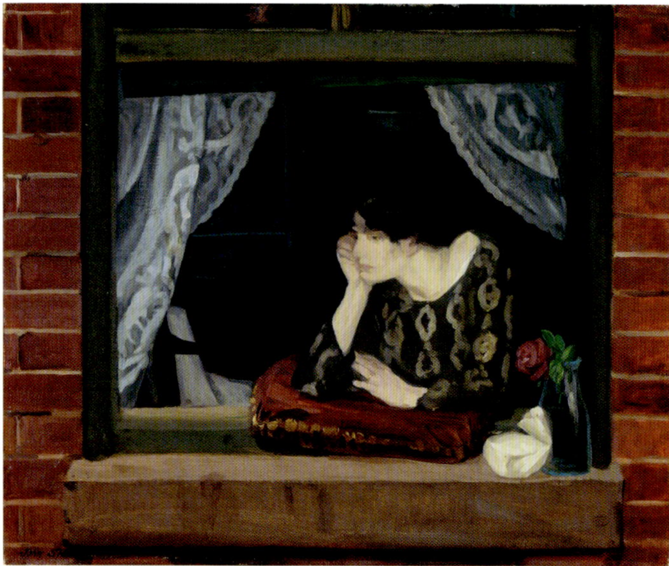

FIG. 1. John Sloan, *A Window on the Street*, 1912. Oil on canvas, 26 × 32 in. (66 × 81.3 cm). Bowdoin College Museum of Art, Bequest of George Otis Hamlin, 1961.50

John W. Coffey
Deputy Director for Collections and
Research and Curator of American and
Modern Art, North Carolina Museum of Art

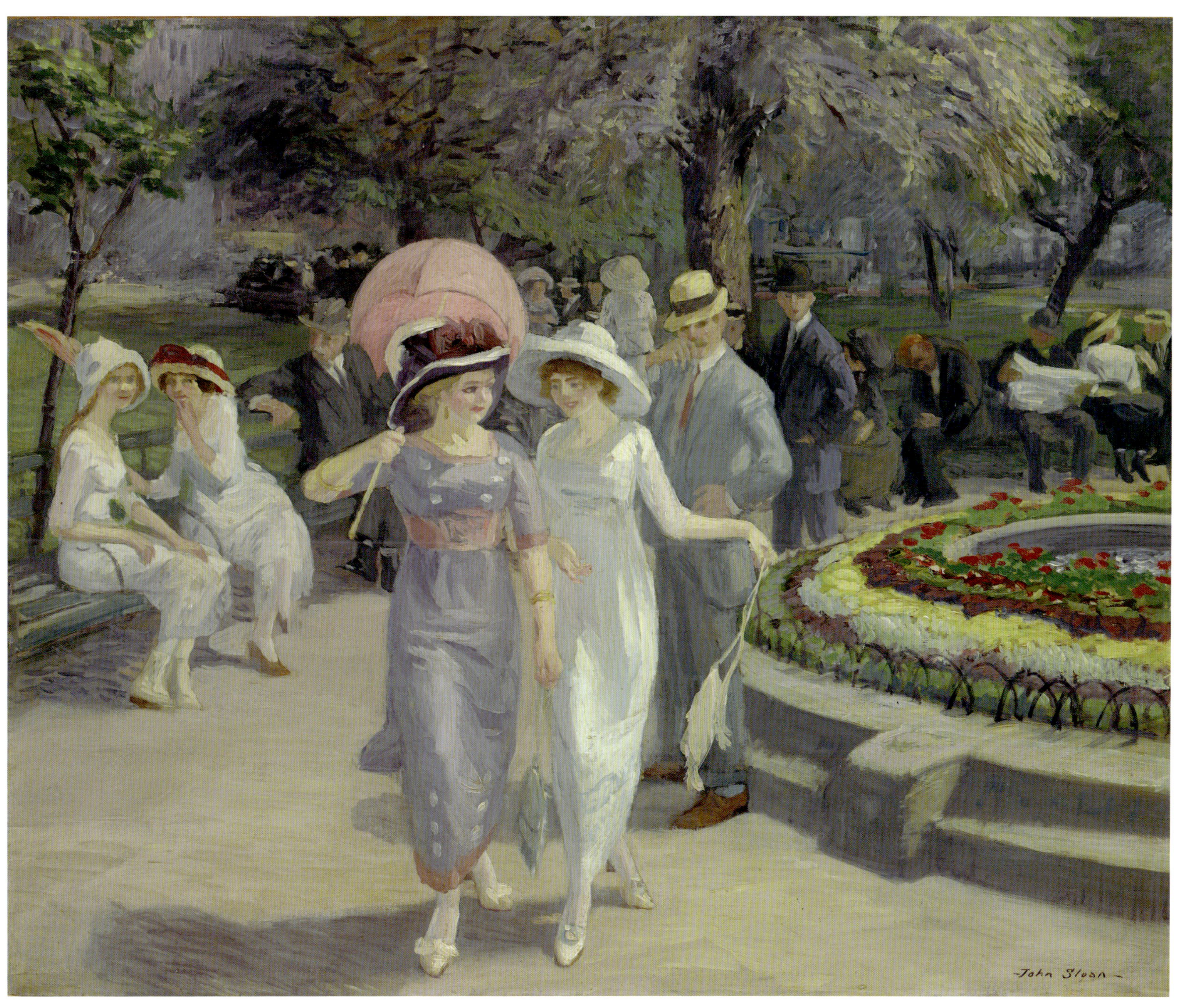

John Sloan

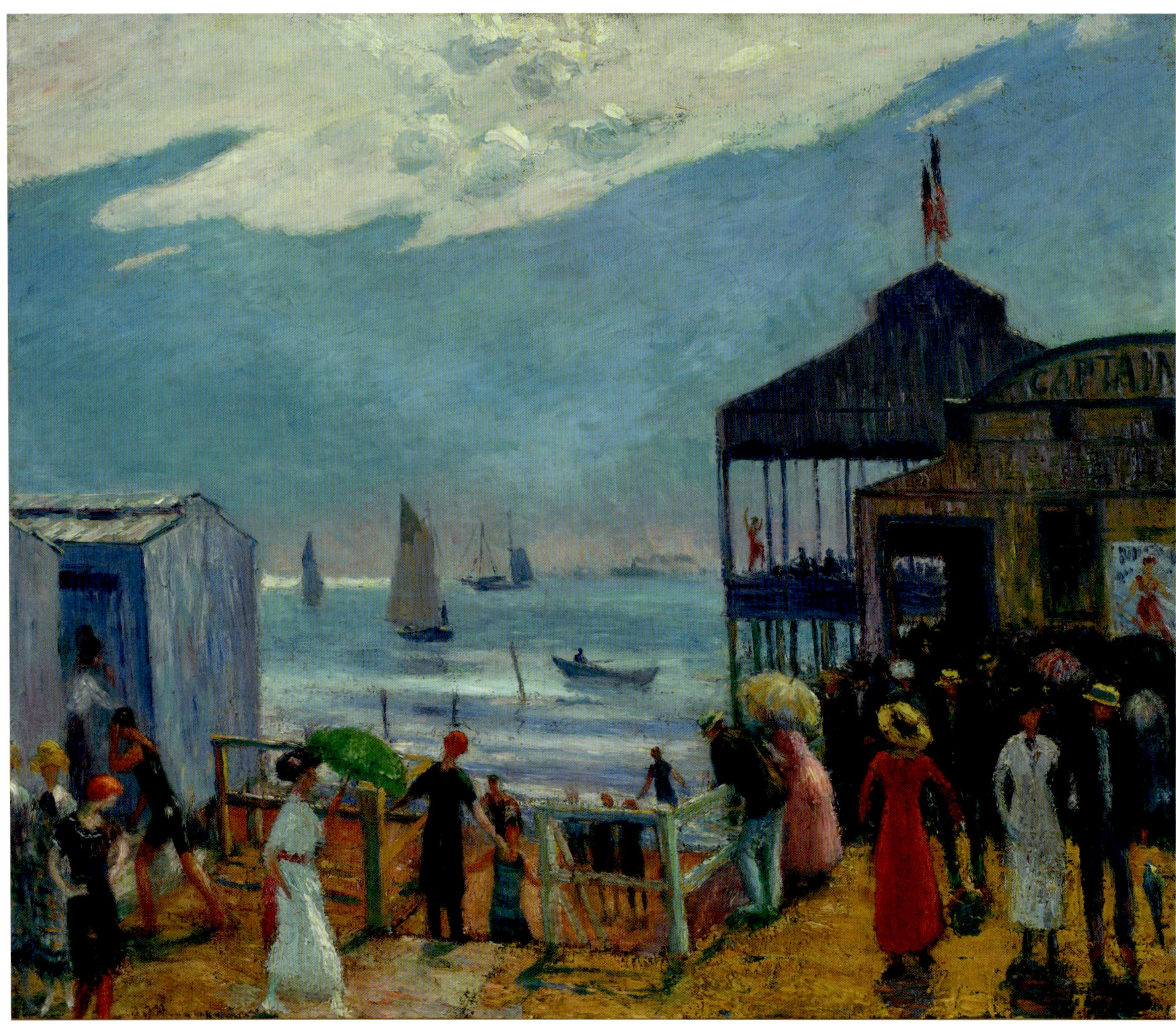

# Captain's Pier

William James Glackens (American, 1870–1938), 1912–14
Oil on canvas, 25⅛ × 30⅛ in. (63.8 × 76.5 cm)
Gift of Stephen M. Etnier, Honorary Degree, 1969  1957.127

*Captain's Pier* represents a shift in Glackens's oeuvre toward an intensely colorful, painterly style seen in the art of Renoir and other French Impressionists. Starting in 1907, beach scenes became a focus for members of The Eight, an artists' group that in addition to Glackens included Maurice Prendergast, John Sloan, Everett Shinn, and others. *Captain's Pier* was painted by Glackens in his seasonal residence of Bellport, New York. Depicting vacationers frolicking on the shore, this lively and humorous painting is a witness to the development of Long Island into a preferred destination for crowds from New York City and elsewhere. The title refers to the newly opened restaurant and entertainment venue pictured on the right side of the canvas, juxtaposed with the more modest traditional bath houses on the left. Summer visitors gathered there to enjoy a singer's performance and celebrate the blissful season. (ND)

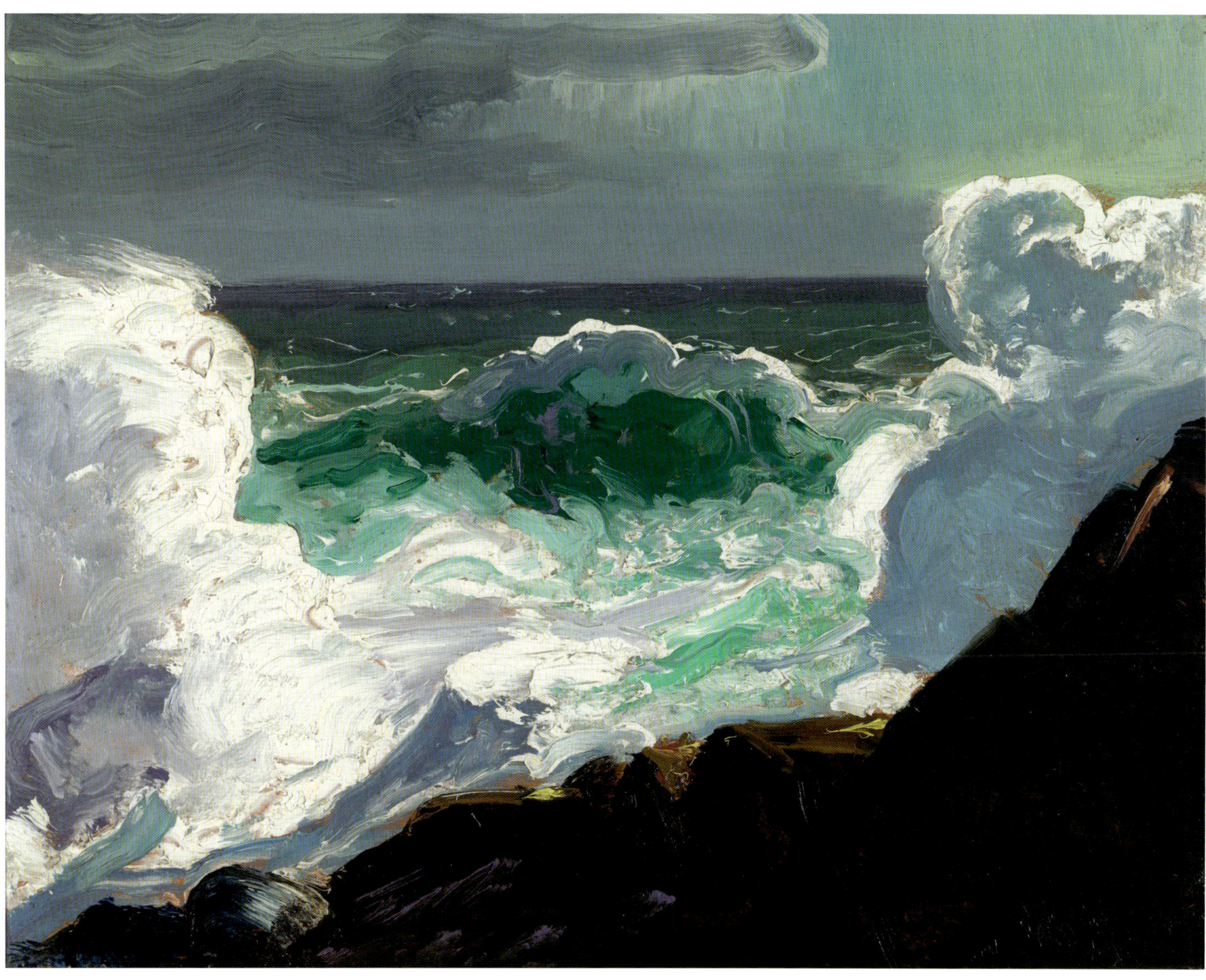

## *Green Breaker*

George Wesley Bellows (American, 1882–1925), 1913
Oil on panel, 15 × 19½ in. (38 × 50 cm)
Gift of Remak Ramsay  2016.47.1

In the summer of 1911, George Bellows and Robert Henri traveled to Monhegan and spent four weeks painting together. In Bellows's earlier paintings of the waterfront and boxing clubs of New York, the young artist demonstrated an interest in the rough-and-tumble communities at the margins of genteel society. In Maine, he discovered the allure of peripheral landscapes. Describing Monhegan as "endless in its wonderful variety [and] possessed of enough beauty to supply a continent," he returned to the state four times over the next five years. In 1913, Bellows assisted in the design and installation of the Armory Show, where he encountered European artists like Henri Matisse and André Derain. Leaving shortly thereafter for Monhegan, he painted *Green Breaker* and other works whose colors and composition are both a response and a major contribution to emergent modernism. (FHG)

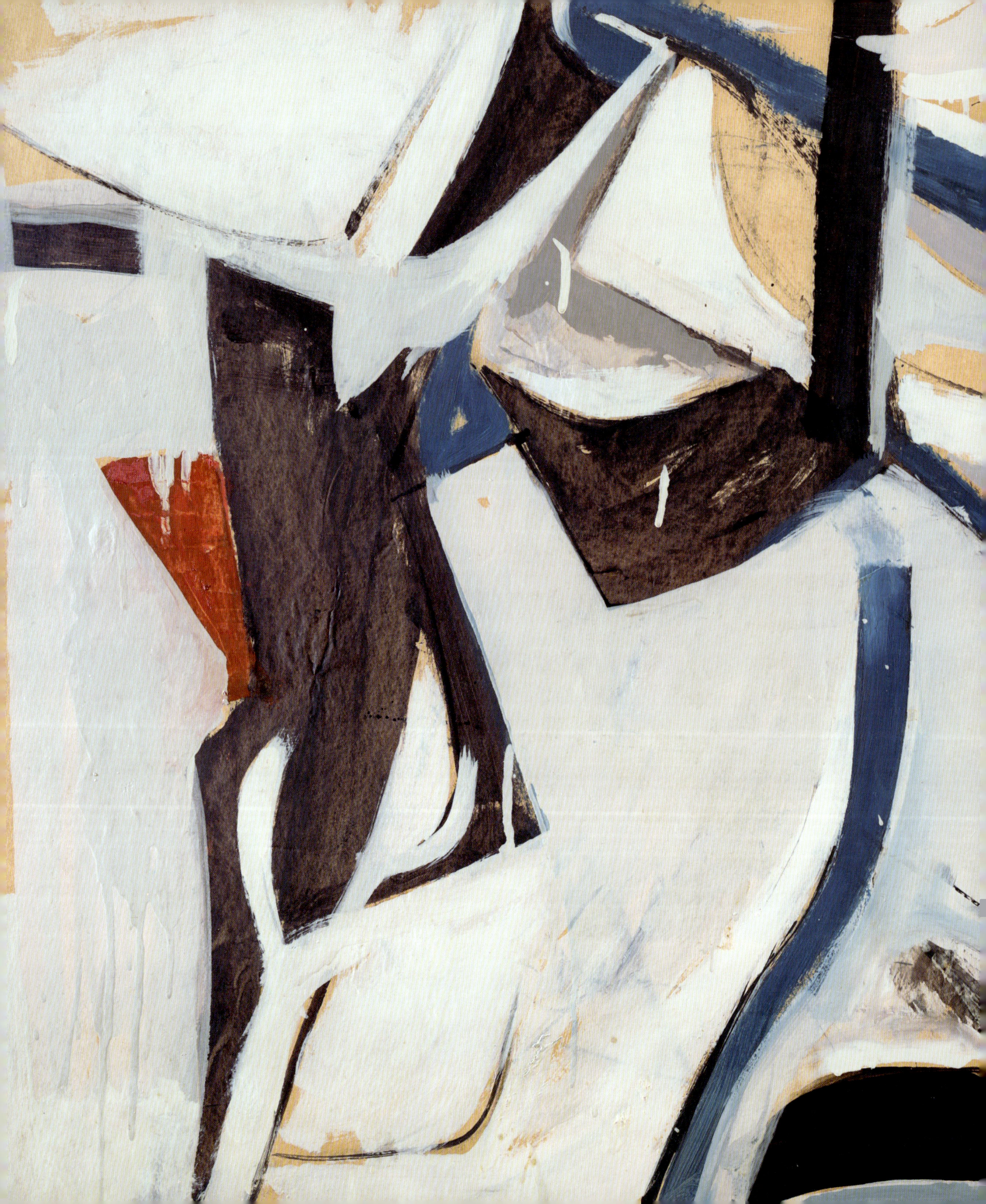

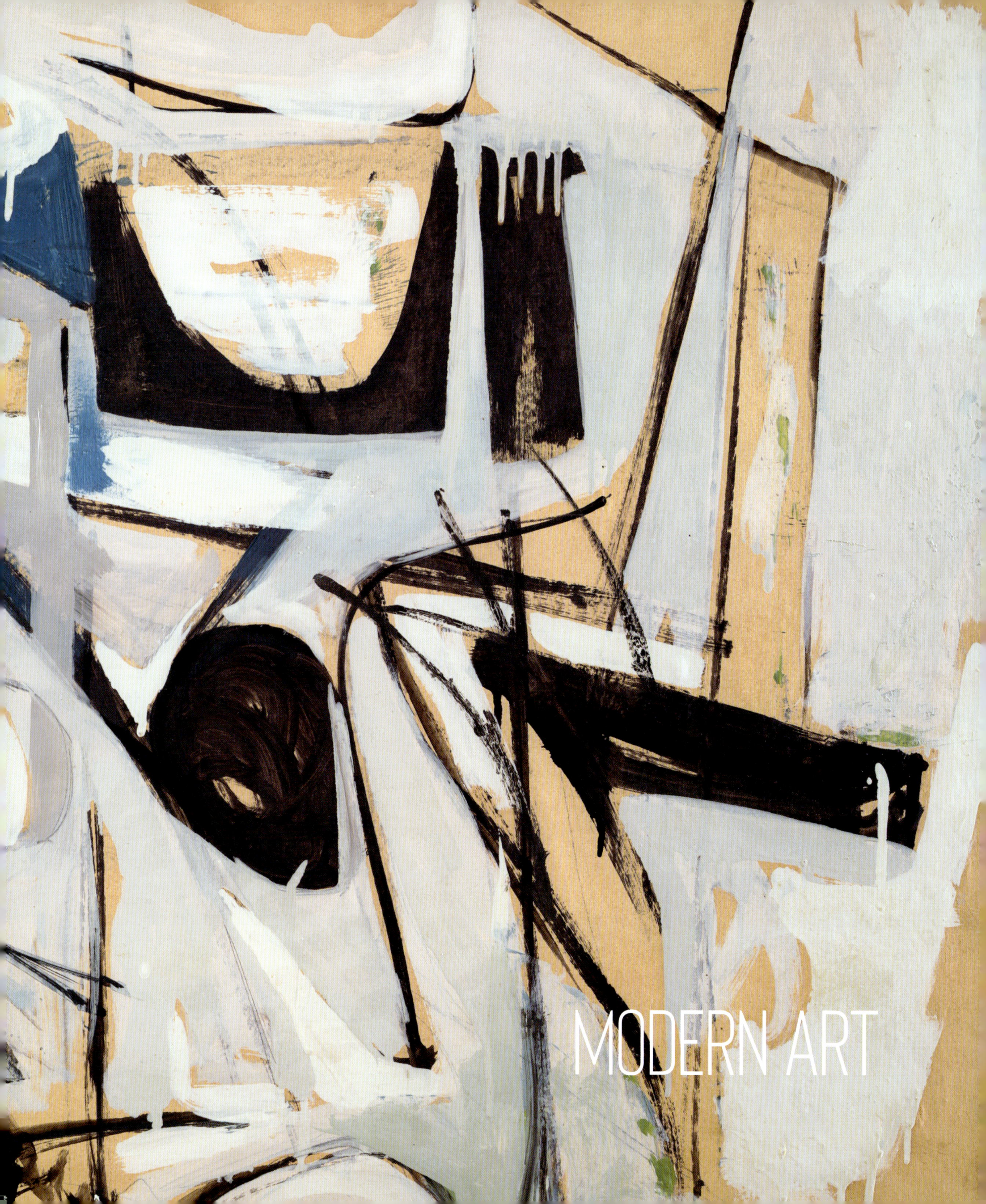
MODERN ART

# *Rayograph*

Man Ray (American, 1890–1976), 1921
Gelatin silver print, 8¾ × 6⅞ in. (22.3 × 17.4 cm)
Museum Purchase, Lloyd O. and Marjorie Strong Coulter Fund  1988.17

Man Ray (born Emmanuel Radnitzky) made the first of what he called his rayographs in 1921. The act of renaming a photographic process that actually predated the use of the camera—the photogram, or photogenic drawing, as William Henry Fox Talbot first labeled it—indicates not only that Man Ray had an aptitude for branding—something he likely learned from the Dadaists in Paris—but also that he regarded the cameraless process of making silhouettes on photographic paper as somehow revolutionary. He described his results as "startlingly new and mysterious." At almost the same time, in Germany, László Moholy-Nagy would also begin experimenting with photograms (the term he coined) and would declare them the basis of his "new vision" for art. Both of these artists cast a backward glance in order to imagine the future.

Looking at the rayograph in the Bowdoin collection, it may not be obvious why Man Ray invested so much significance in an antiquarian process. The piece is both transparent and obscure, like an X-ray of something we can't identify, and over the years its chemical surface has acquired an unusual patina, making it even less an image and more an object in its own right. For Man Ray, the photogram was a deliberate turn away from the pure presence and prestige of painting, which he was in the process of (temporarily) renouncing. It was also at least a partial turn away from the assumptions about photography's literalness. He had already begun questioning the relationship of the camera to appearances with a famous photograph he made in Marcel Duchamp's studio titled *Dust Breeding* (1920). It offered a view of a work in progress by Duchamp that suggested nothing so much as an alien landscape. Man Ray added various subtitles indicating possible interpretations of this unparsable image.

If a photograph was a kind of found object whose significance ultimately resided in the eye and mind of the beholder, then its appeal was primarily psychological, not strictly documental. This conviction gave Man Ray permission to dispense with the conventions of photographic realism and even the apparatus of the camera in favor of the "new and mysterious"—the chance activities of light, time, and chemistry—all with the goal of providing the viewer with more direct access to unconscious associations. Although the artist continued to make conventional photographic portraits, he reserved his artistic enthusiasm for these and other experiments.

There are several things to be said about the rayograph. First, it was not entirely subject to chance. Unlike some of the chemical experiments carried out by photographers in Europe at the time, Man Ray's photograms put the artist's decisions on display. Long before, in the nineteenth century, Talbot had chosen to place spruce needles on photo paper to impede the passage of light, and Anna Atkins had chosen algae taken from English beaches. Man Ray chose an eggbeater, scissors, film, a pistol—emblems of modern life. He also made choices based on the degree of transparency and the capacity of his objects to cast shadows. Which leads to a second point. Man Ray made art in the time of an emerging vision of the universe as governed by abstract forces, within and beyond human beings. Einstein's theory of relativity and Freud's theory of the unconscious seemed to require a new visual vocabulary. The rayographs, the photograms of Moholy-Nagy, the rotoreliefs of Marcel Duchamp, the *Prouns* of Russian El Lissitzky, and many other departures into nonrepresentational realms all testified to modern artists' search for new forms for the inexpressible.

Lyle Rexer
Critic and curator

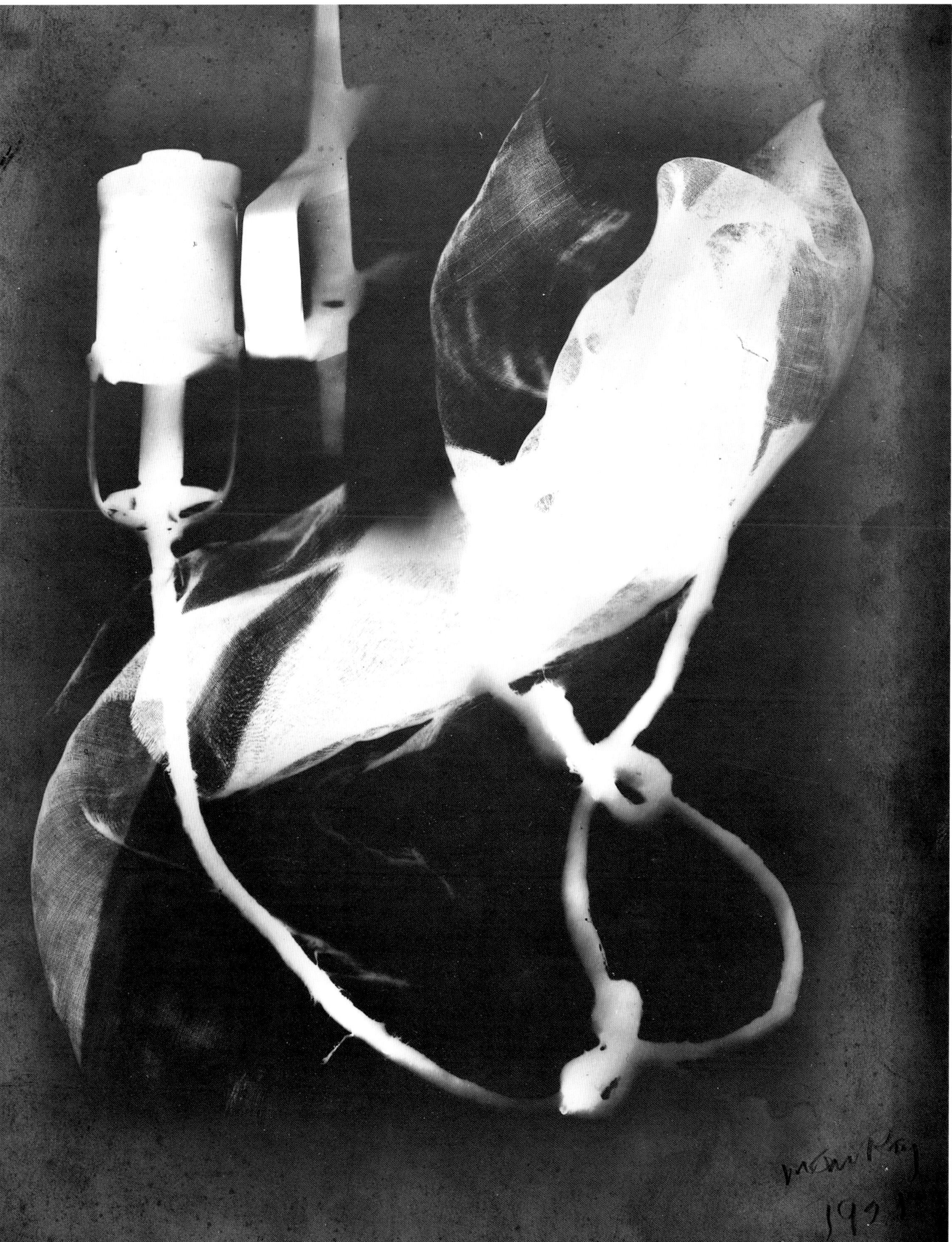

El Lissitzky (Russian, 1880–1941), 1921
Lithograph on paper, 8$\frac{1}{16}$ × 10$\frac{7}{16}$ in. (20.5 × 26.5 cm)
Museum Purchase, Lloyd O. and Marjorie Strong Coulter Fund  2018.18

The history of modern art coincides with the age of the manifesto. Public statements asserting aesthetic, social, or political agendas, manifestos have been instruments to attract attention, demarcate loyalties, stake claims, and guide reactions. This elegant lithograph by the Russian Jewish artist, architect, theorist, and graphic designer El Lissitzky forms part of just one such manifesto, a declaration of intent crafted to stand out within one of the most turbulent and creative periods in the history of modern art, the years after the Russian Revolutions of 1917.

Lissitzky wanted to distinguish himself from two powerful and antithetical strands within the Russian avant-garde, both of which implied the imminent demise of the kind of image-making that Lissitzky wanted to defend. His mentor, Kazimir Malevich, whose so-called Suprematist mode of abstract painting had decisively influenced Lissitzky as recently as 1919, was shifting away from painting into theoretical work; and in Moscow, several avant-garde abstract artists were promulgating the demise of art and the transfer of creative energies into practical tasks of design.

Lissitzky's manifesto took a tripartite form: a name, a text, and a portfolio of prints, all deployed in Moscow in the first half of 1921.

The name is *Proun*, the evocative neologism Lissitzky coined for his art. It appears as the title of the text that was to accompany the portfolio, and it appears on the cover design. Its initial also appears on the Bowdoin print as the first part of the enigmatic lithographed title, *P2<sup>B</sup>*. The act of inventing a name was a unique gesture. Though scholarship has established its roots in the acronym from the Russian words "project for the affirmation of the new," it was, for the artist, a verbal symbol whose full meaning would only become clear in the future, as would the full implications of his nonobjective art.

While the name is perhaps the most radical element of the manifesto, the text would have been, in a sense, its most traditional facet. Although not published until later, it laid out, like so many manifestos before it, a program for a new art. Lissitzky rejected the use of art for religious devotion, imperial prestige, and bourgeois comfort. Instead, the coming new world demanded a new art—indeed, the new art would help to shepherd the new world into being. That art would be nonrepresentational and constructive, based on a new understanding of materials, space, and creativity.

And finally, the lithographs themselves. Eleven compositions were printed, all with quasi-scientific titles combining letters and numerals: *P1<sup>A</sup>*, *P1<sup>D</sup>*, *P2<sup>D</sup>*, *P5<sup>A</sup>*, *P6<sup>A</sup>*, etc. Most of these prints reproduced the artist's recent paintings. The prints documented the full range of Lissitzky's nonobjective art, with some compositions harking back to his utopian architectural designs exploring concepts like "house," "bridge," "town," while others posited wholly novel modes of engagement with the visual image. In one case, multiple printed titles along all the margins might imply the physical act of circling the sheet, or in another, a title printed in reverse suggested maybe viewing the image through the sheet, from behind. *P2<sup>B</sup>* is neither so provocative nor so illustrational. It offers a dynamic assortment of more-or-less geometrical two- and three-dimensional shapes, rendered in a wide variety of stippled and planar surfaces. It would not be entirely misguided to see the forms coalesce into an image of a built structure resting on a column extending diagonally to the "ground" at lower right, perhaps with an antenna-like object stretching out to the upper left. Also important, however, is the fact that these forms and their arrangement speak more to weightlessness, movement, transparency, and change.

Although profoundly rooted in the precise historical moment that provoked this manifesto, this work has an aesthetic refinement and visual complexity that continue to fascinate across the decades and surely into the future. Lissitzky's *Proun* concept, the ideas behind it, and the images that exemplify it are indeed not yet exhausted, nor indeed fully understood. But they can be enjoyed.

Peter Nisbet
Deputy Director for Curatorial Affairs,
Ackland Art Museum, The University of
North Carolina at Chapel Hill

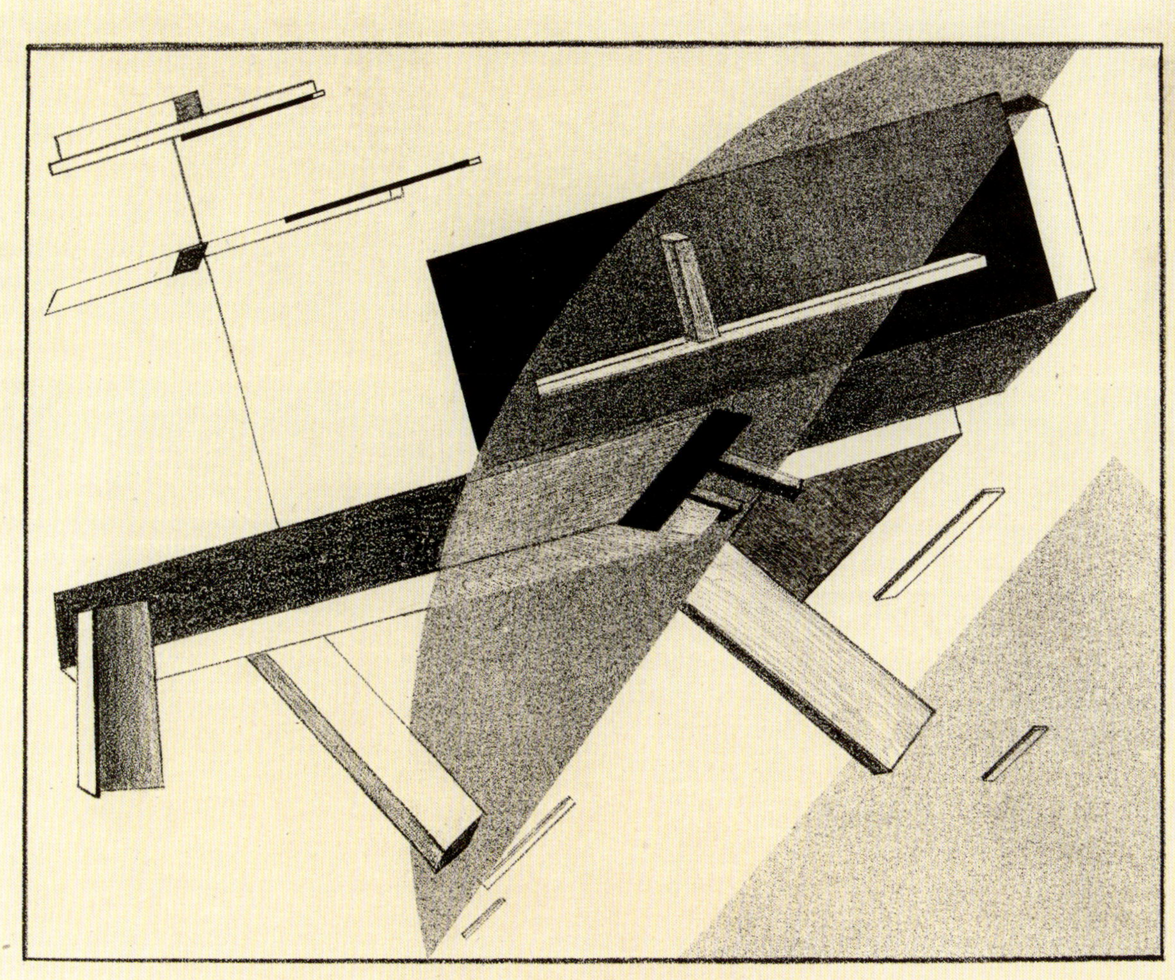
П 2 B

# Soviet Propaganda Posters

1930

Generously lent by Svetlana and Eric Silverman '85, P'19

When the Bolsheviks assumed power in 1917, they set out to reshape the world. Convinced that people were a product of nurture rather than nature, they understood the importance of controlling their environment, including the visual landscape. The revolutionaries were therefore both iconoclastic and radically creative, forming and giving visibility to new people, new institutions, and new rituals and symbols, such as the classic red star and the hammer and sickle.

In this context, the soviet poster was born and became the predominant art form. Cheap and quick to produce, posters were used to celebrate the regime's new heroes, define its enemies, and convey revolutionary goals and values to a still predominately illiterate population. "Poster fever" was particularly high during times of rapid transition, when the need to inform, enlighten, and mobilize the masses was acute, for instance during the Civil War (1918–20) and the first Five Year Plan (1928–32).[1]

Gustav Klutsis and Valentina Kulagina, comrades in art, politics, and life, were part of an ambitious generation of avant-garde artists who shared the Bolsheviks' insistence that cultural production serve the class struggle. Both enthusiastically gave their time and talent in support of the Revolution well into the 1930s, and their posters are iconic examples of both the genre and the era.

Klutsis's *Working Men and Women—Everyone to the Election of Soviets* (pl. 1) was produced in 1930 at the height of Stalin's ambitious first Five Year Plan to "build socialism." While exhorting workers to vote in their local soviet (council) elections, it simultaneously expresses in visual form the interdependent relationship between the individual worker and the collective project of soviet power. The poster centers on a realistic photographic image of a single hand (likely Klutsis's), palm-forward and raised in the air; the hand is strong but ungendered, and the dull black and gray tones of the human flesh are set off (and animated) by a vibrant red (socialist) background. Klutsis further defines the hand for the viewer through photomontage, a technique he pioneered: the integration of multiple images of proud working-class faces identifies it as proletarian, while the repetition of smaller versions of the hand interspersed

among the faces forms a collective and sets the hands and faces in metonymic relationship to each other—the worker is his/her hand, it is both tool and voice, and the vital link between the individual and the soviet. Representing the collective, Klutsis's big hand is one of many and, simultaneously, many hands in one; and while each (working) face is unique, all hands are equal. The written text calling both women and men to the polls reemphasizes the inclusive, progressive nature of soviet democracy, while the diagonal positioning of the voting hands forces the viewer's eye from low to high and suggests movement upward, to new heights. It also alludes to ubiquitous images of Lenin's raised hand, signaling the path forward to communism. In these ways, Klutsis plays with the tension between the real and the ideal, the present and the future, the individual and the masses. The poster's design was so successful that the same image was reproduced with a different text in order to celebrate the massive collective effort that was the Five Year Plan.

Kulagina's poster *International Working Women's Day* (pl. 2) was also produced in 1930. Again, the dominant feature is a working hand—the outstretched fist of a female worker in a textile factory. Although the occupation was traditionally associated with political "backwardness," Kulagina's worker is fully modern in body and mind. With her red scarf and confident posture, she is clearly a Bolshevik, empowered by her skill. Her strong, genderless arm connects her body to the machine, and her self to the production process, indicating both her active role in the "building of socialism" and her transformation into a "new Soviet woman" through her labor. Indeed, with her chiseled face and sleek form, she appears more manufactured than human. Although unpopular with contemporary viewers, who preferred humanized images they could relate to, Kulagina's "mechanical doll" was more successful in an ideological sense. Like Klutsis, she uses photomontage, the repetition of key elements, and the manipulation of scale to connect the individual, idealized worker with the mass of "real" women streaming across the bottom of the frame. The row of spindles rhythmically complements the marching women, while the color red harmonizes and energizes

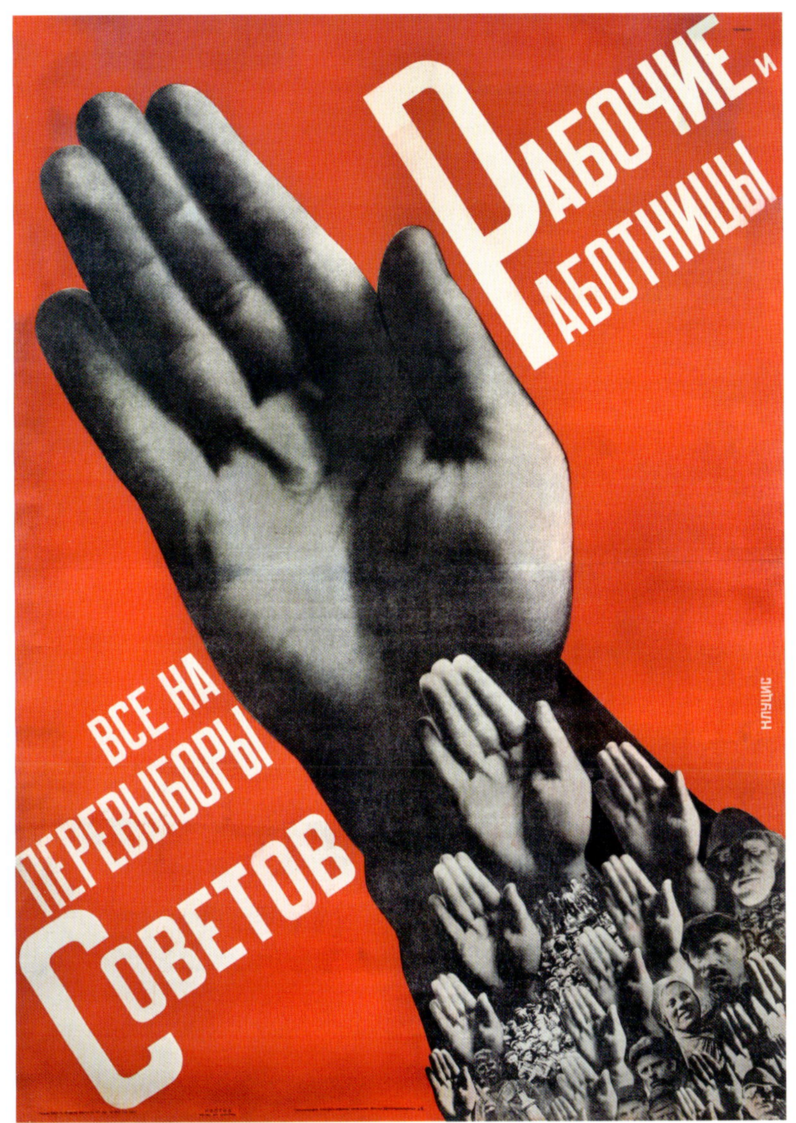



PLATE 1. Gustav Gustavovich Klutsis (Russian, 1895–1938), *Working Men and Women—Everyone to the Election of Soviets*, 1930. Lithograph on paper, 51 × 37½ in. (129.5 × 95.2 cm)

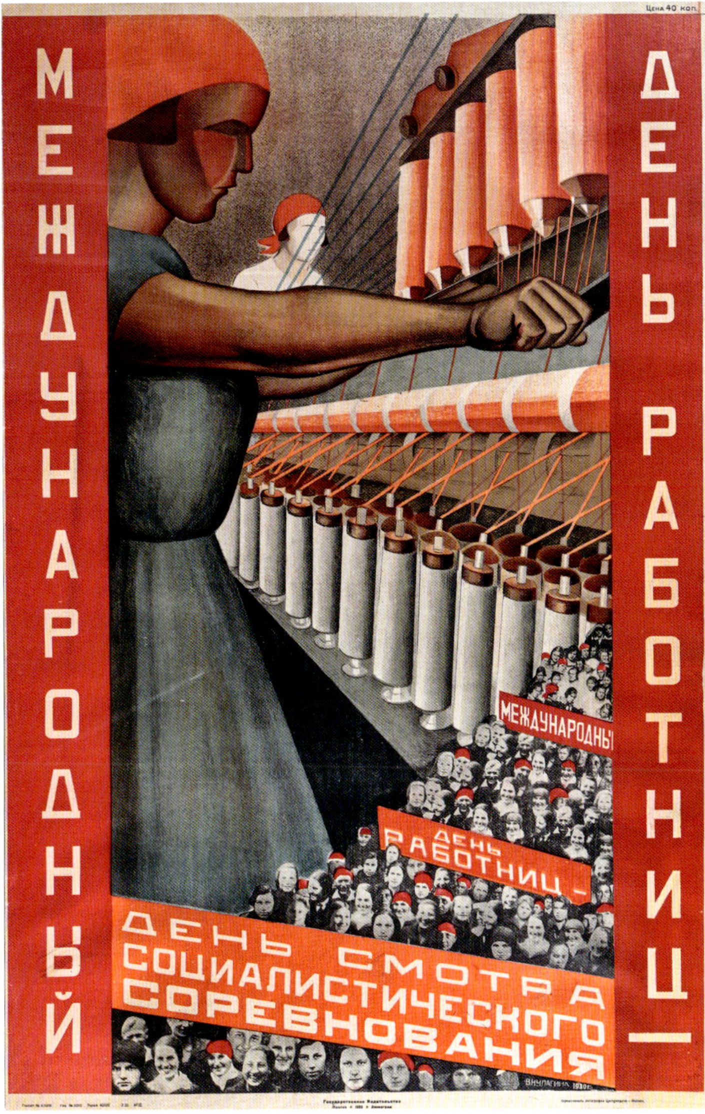



PLATE 2. Valentina Nikiforovna Kulagina (Russian, 1902–1987), *International Working Women's Day Is the Day of Judging of Socialist Competition*, 1930. Lithograph on paper, 42½ × 28½ in. (107.9 × 72.4 cm)

the scene, linking the women's head scarves, the celebratory banners, and the machinery. Red threads crisscrossing the plane between the spindles reinforce the connection between the women, their labor, and their power, in both the Soviet and international context.

The message in both of these works was largely aspirational. In 1930, some dozen years after the Bolsheviks came to power, soviet democracy was far from secure, and women's emancipation was more complete in law than in life. But neither Klutsis nor Kulagina gave into doubt or ambivalence. On the contrary, they designed their posters to inspire and guide the Soviet masses from the imperfect present to a more perfect socialist future, convinced—like many Bolsheviks—that "seeing" was a first and important step toward "believing."

Page Herrlinger
Associate Professor of History,
Bowdoin College

# Greenland People, Dogs and Mountains

Rockwell Kent (American, 1882–1971), c. 1929–35
Oil on canvas, 28⅛ × 48 × ⅜ in. (71.4 × 121.9 × 0.95 cm)
Museum Purchase with Funds Donated Anonymously  1971.77

As a child growing up in Tarrytown, New York, Rockwell Kent was introduced to art by his aunt, herself a ceramics painter. Acceding to his mother's desire that he become an architect, he reluctantly enrolled in architectural studies at Columbia University. After three years, Kent dropped out to study painting with William Merritt Chase, Robert Henri, Kenneth Hayes Miller, and Abbott Thayer. His early architectural training, however, gave him an incisive drawing style that often informs the compositional framework of his illustrations and paintings.

Ever the adventurer, Kent made three painting trips to Greenland between 1929 and 1935. His first foray, in the summer of 1929, did not begin auspiciously. It found him swimming and wading in the dawn toward an unknown West Greenland shore from the wreck of the sloop that had brought him from New York. Wet and cold, lashed by a stormy sea and biting wind, holding a bag of painting supplies and his camera, it was exactly the kind of challenge that Kent embraced. Stopping only long enough to help his two shipmates salvage necessities, he hiked overland to obtain help with the rescue of boat and belongings. Charmed by Greenland and its people, Kent opted to stay until September for an intense campaign of painting. Typically, he made numerous sketches, took photographs, and painted basic forms and colors on his larger canvases, which he then rolled up, planning to complete them after his return to Asgaard, his home and studio in the Adirondacks.

On this first trip, the artist set up camp on the shores of Sermilik Fiord,[1] located about forty miles from Godthaab (now Nuuk). This resulted in a number of nearly identical landscapes capturing the view across the fiord toward the distant glacial mountains, varied only by differing atmospheric treatments and the inclusion or absence of figures in the foreground. At least three of these iterations were part of Kent's 1960 gift of paintings to the Soviet Union. One of these, *The Artist in Greenland* (1929), in the collection of the Pushkin Museum of Fine Arts, Moscow, records the artist's painting camp on the shore at the fiord (fig. 1).

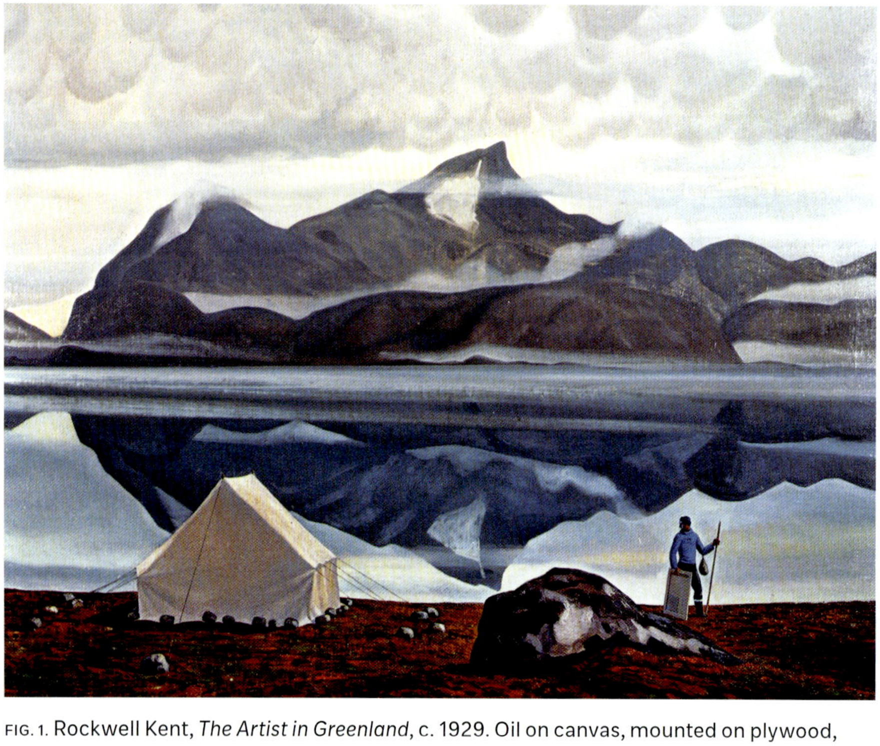

Bowdoin's canvas was likely inspired by an event at his camp that Kent described in his book *N by E*:

One day as I sat at work I heard a gunshot, and looking up, saw two kayaks and an umiak or women's boat filled with people approaching my camp. . . . I invited them all up to my tent. . . . in little time we were all drinking hot coffee with lots of sugar in it and eating rye bread spread extremely thick with butter. . . . Presently, the repast having been finished, the guests arose, thanked me cordially and took their departure. . . . Two men got into their

FIG. 1. Rockwell Kent, *The Artist in Greenland*, c. 1929. Oil on canvas, mounted on plywood, 33⅝ × 43¼ in. (85.4 × 109.9 cm). Pushkin State Museum of Fine Arts, Moscow, Zh–3840

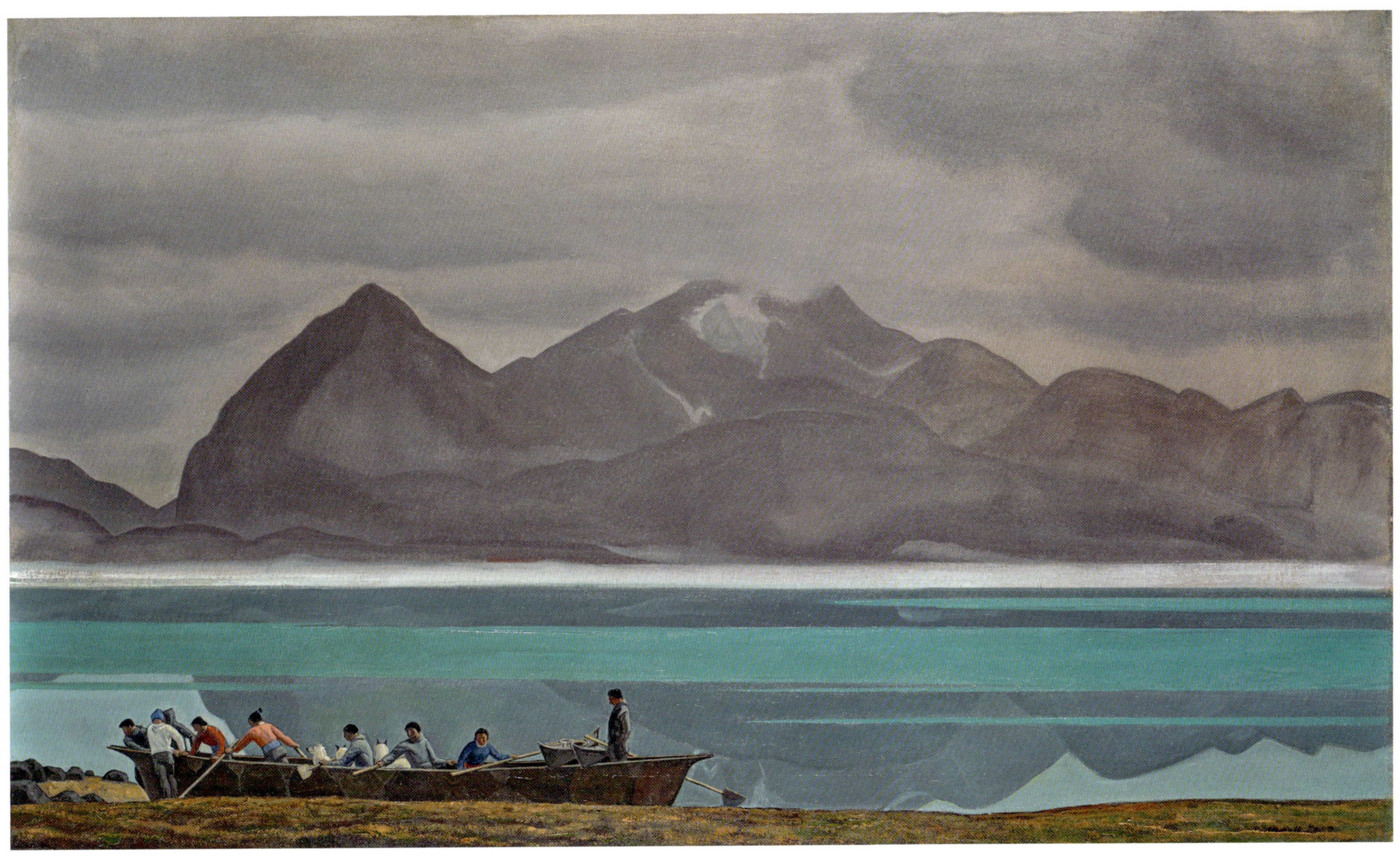

kayaks and the third enthroned himself on the top of the household goods in the stern of the umiak; the women, as usual, manned the oars.[2]

While Kent did not consider himself a modernist, the spare compositional framework of the scene, divided into three parallel bands of foreground, water, and distant mountains, betrays his architectural sensibility. The unwavering horizon line is emphasized by a layer of surface mist on the water and provides a strong lateral axis around which the foreground, the reflection in the water, and the glacial peaks, partially hidden by low clouds, are ordered. Although the painting is not dated, it was very likely begun the same time as the other views of the fiord, and completed in the artist's studio with the subsequent addition of the umiak and rowers based on photographs that Kent took at the time.

Richard V. West
Former Director, Bowdoin College Museum
of Art, and Director Emeritus, Frye Art
Museum, Seattle

# Daily News Building, 42nd Street between 2nd and 3rd Avenue

Berenice Abbott (American, 1898–1991), 1935
Gelatin silver print, 9½ × 7½ in. (24.2 × 19 cm)
Museum Purchase, Gridley W. Tarbell II Fund 1994.16

Berenice Abbott's career spanned seven decades, so it is difficult to point to one series or subject that defines her. Her advocacy of realist or "straight" photography seems at least superficially at odds with her origins in the Surrealist milieu of Paris in the 1920s, assisting Man Ray and discovering the proto-Surrealist street photographer Eugène Atget. It was Abbott's abiding interest in science that united these conflicting impulses: her experiments in photomechanical invention are at the root of some of her most surreal images.

*Daily News Building, 42nd Street between 2nd and 3rd Avenue* represents the epitome of Abbott as a "straight" photographer. It was part of her *Changing New York* series, a documentary project funded by the Works Progress Administration and inspired by Abbott's astonishment, upon her return from Paris in 1929, at the transformations the city was undergoing. Built in 1929–30, the Daily News Building was a prime example of the modern skyscrapers filling in the skyline. In Abbott's bird's-eye view, the grid of the building's facade is echoed in the grid of the streets, the dwarfed tenements, and the elegant 1920s Windsor Tower. At the upper right, a Con Edison power plant, a Beaux-Arts remnant of a prior era of New York architectural glory, is crowned by four smokestacks emerging from its mansard roof, spewing smoke that dims out the only natural element in the photograph, the East River. To Abbott, "straight" did not inherently mean

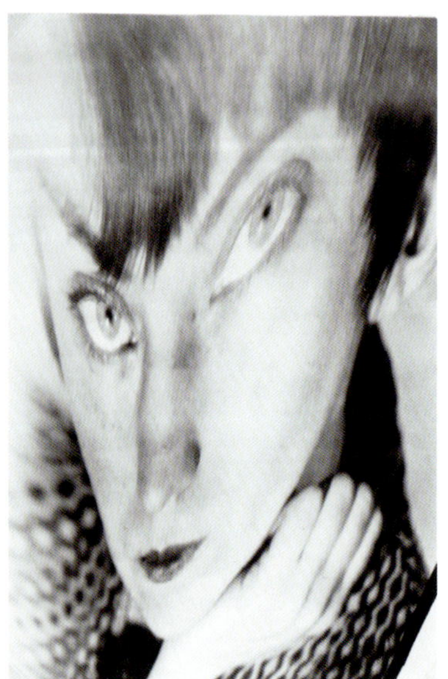

FIG. 1. Berenice Abbott, *Controlled Distortion (Self–Portrait)*, negative 1930, distortion c. 1950. Gelatin silver print, 6⅞ × 4⅝ in. (17.5 × 11.8 cm). Bowdoin College Museum of Art, Museum Purchase, Lloyd O. and Marjorie Coulter Fund, 1998.6

objective: "While reality is the subject matter of the photographer, it follows that the knowledge of how far the camera can go, and the choice of subject, lead the photographer into the subjective. He cannot help equating the objective world with his self."[1] In *Daily News Building*, the rigid geometry of the grid is viewed at an angle, disconcertingly askew. Abbott captured this image from another new skyscraper, the fifty-six-story Chanin Building, built in 1927–29. Unable to gain access to the roof, she shot the image from an office window from which a direct view was impossible. Abbott liked the effect of this vertigo-inducing perspective, perhaps "equating the world with herself": despite her boldness in seeking the most exciting shots, Abbott was afraid of heights.

A lesser-known aspect of Abbott's career is her invention of photographic equipment. She has four patents to her name, including the distortion easel, patented in 1951. This flexible frame allows the photographer to manipulate a piece of unexposed photo paper onto which a negative is projected, thereby producing a distorted image. A handful of distorted self-portraits of Abbott, all from the same 1930 negative but distorted in distinct ways, exist in museum collections, including Bowdoin's (fig. 1). Few if any duplicates of each distortion exist, indicating that Abbott chose not to make many copies. These were produced not as her "work," but as a proof of concept and a marketing tool, used in advertisements and the photography textbooks she wrote.

An academic museum provides a key object lesson to students when it represents the variety as well as the depth of an artist's production. Showing them the rare exceptions as well as the prime examples counteracts the simplistic takeaways we get from survey textbooks. No artist is solely one thing, encapsulated by one series, artwork, or concern. Like the rest of us, artists contain multitudes.

Andrea P. Rosen
Curator, Fleming Museum of Art,
University of Vermont

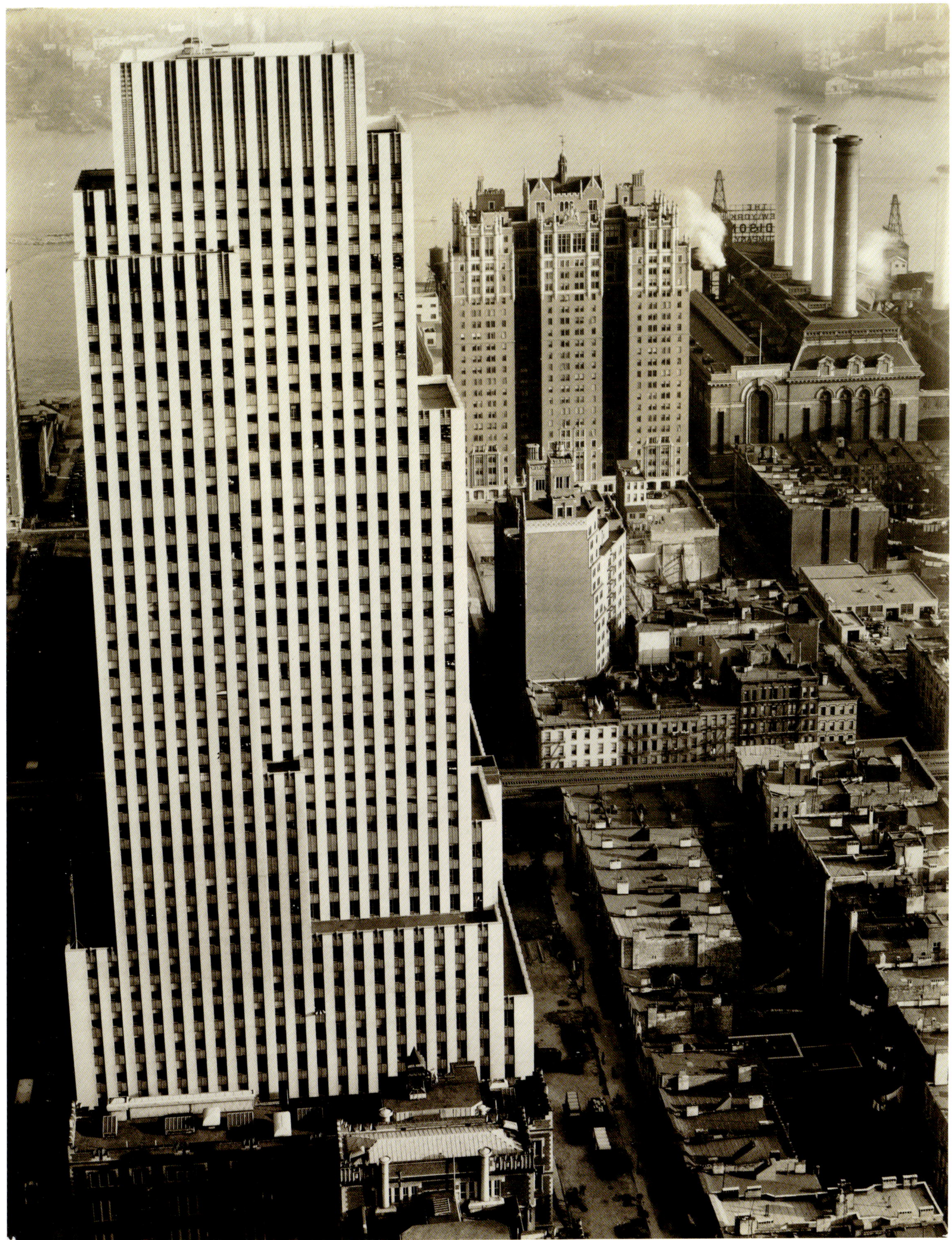

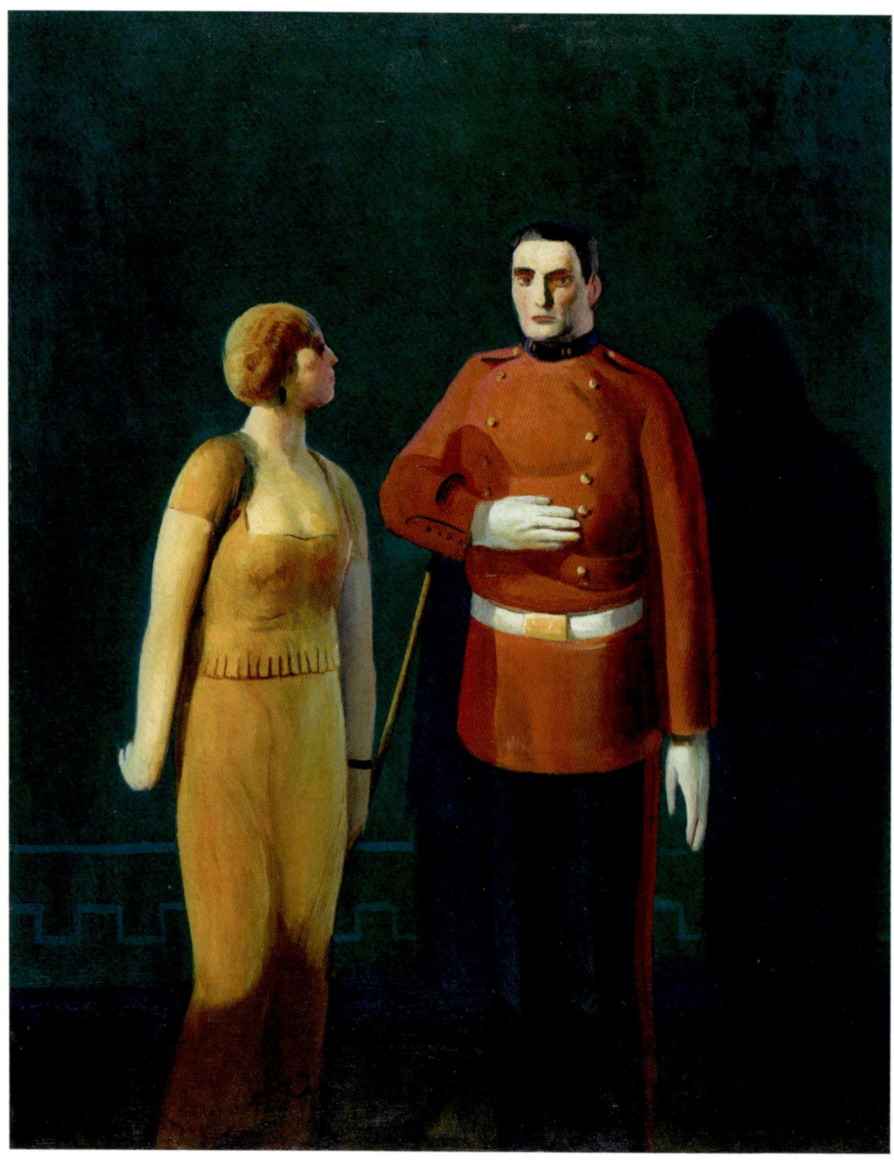

## *The Life Soldier*

Guy Pène Du Bois (American, 1884–1958), 1922
Oil on panel, 25 × 20 in. (63.5 × 50.8 cm)
Gift of Walter K. Gutman, Class of 1924  1966.37

The two somewhat cylindrical figures can hardly be called a couple; their wooden movements seem to preclude meaningful interaction. A single light casts the shadow of the woman's head on the soldier's chest as a subtle indicator of their ambiguous relationship. During the 1920s, Guy Pène Du Bois was preoccupied with themes and places of contemporary urban life: cafés and restaurants, theater performers and flappers, and—as seen here—men and women in private moments observed in undescribed public spaces. His "narrative of inaction," to use curator Barbara Haskell's phrase, has been compared to similar visual strategies in Edward Hopper's work. Both artists represent a trend toward order and objectivity that was widespread in American and European art of the 1920s. As a painter and art critic, Pène Du Bois emerged from Robert Henri's circle and participated in the groundbreaking Armory Show of 1913. From 1920 to 1924, he lived in a small artist community in Westport, Connecticut. (Staff)

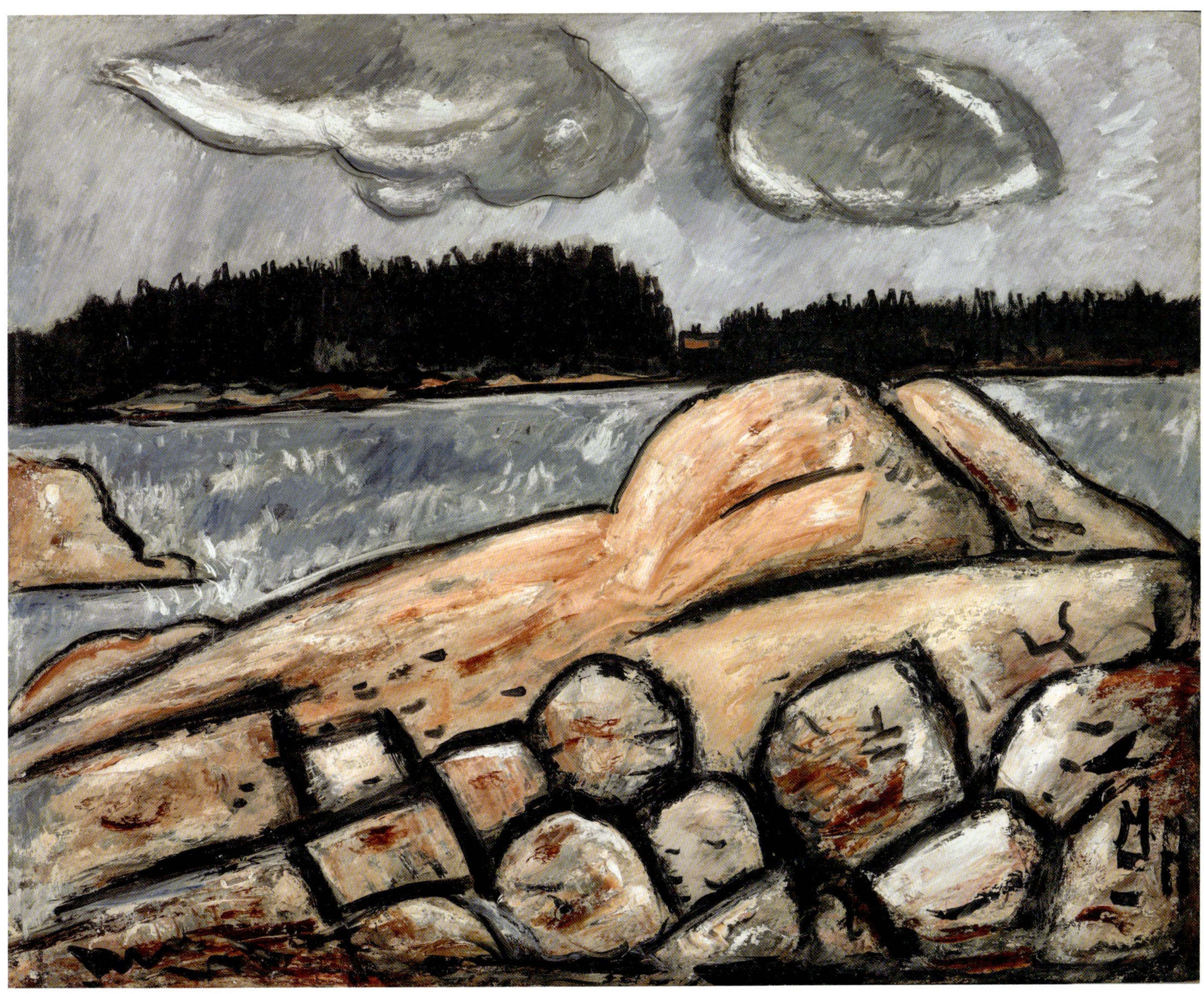

# *After the Storm, Vinalhaven*

Marsden Hartley (American, 1877–1943), 1938–39
Oil on academy board, 22 × 28 in. (55.2 × 71.1 cm)
Gift of Mrs. Charles Phillip Kuntz  1950.8

Like many of Marsden Hartley's late marine landscapes, *After the Storm, Vinalhaven* expresses the artist's sympathetic response to the elemental strength of his native land. The subject is the rocky seacoast in the vicinity of Vinalhaven Island in Maine's Penobscot Bay. In the foreground, wind-whipped waves lash unyielding stone, and storm clouds pass overhead; in the distance, a pine-covered shoreline broods in solid silence. The movement of wind and water is plainly evident through the artist's use of dynamic diagonal lines and short choppy brushstrokes. Born in Lewiston, Hartley led a peripatetic existence for much of his life before returning to Maine in 1937, when he became a frequent visitor to the Bowdoin College Museum of Art. A pioneering modernist, he desired at his career's end to be known as "the painter of Maine." (FHG)

# Night Hauling

Andrew Newell Wyeth (American, 1917–2009), 1944
Tempera on Masonite, 23 × 37¼ in. (58.4 × 94.3 cm)
Gift of Mrs. Ernestine K. Smith, in memory of her husband, Burwell B. Smith  1985.59

*Night Hauling* offers multiple interpretations, inspiring us to consider the painting from a range of perspectives, including its place in Wyeth's career, his creative process, and his time. The scene depicts Walt Anderson, a lifelong friend in Port Clyde, Maine, where the Wyeth family spent their summers beginning in 1920. Known to flout the law, Anderson is here caught trespassing on another angler's territory by hauling a lobster trap at night, an act that inspired the initial title, "The Poacher."[1] Forgoing a daylit scene of a lobsterman poised above a dory, as the artist's father N. C. Wyeth painted in *The Red Dory* (c. 1937–38),[2] Andrew Wyeth created an enigmatic composition that is the result of more than twenty-one extant studies in pencil and watercolor, revealing a range of media and styles.[3]

Imagining Anderson from every angle, it is in watercolor, the medium of his first successful solo show, that Wyeth zeros in on the marine phosphoresence dripping off the oars and the lobster trap (fig. 1). The relationship of the figure, the dory, and the curved wooden trap occupies Wyeth's attention in numerous pencil sketches drawn from all sides, before settling on his final solution of evoking furtive emotion in Anderson's profile, as revealed in one loosely rendered drawing (fig. 2). Wyeth's ultimate choice allows him to contort the lithe shape of the figure's muscular torso to maximum effect, as he gracefully hauls up the heavy trap filled with brilliant herring bait by virtue of youthful brawn.

Surrounding Anderson and the trap are murky depths illuminated by various points and glimmers of light. At the center of the composition, microscopic sea creatures light up the water around the central glow of the herring bait and create a sparkling waterfall rushing between the trap's wooden slats into the ocean.[4] Wyeth eliminates any indication of a moonlit sky, still evident in the pencil drawing, thereby disorienting our sense of space; the darkness of the composition causes us to question whether we are looking at the heavens or the oceans, the two halves of creation. Wyeth's dark ocean, irradiated with points of light that evoke the Milky Way, recalls the words of Henry David Thoreau, his father's guiding spirit, that looking through the ice on Walden Pond, "Heaven is under our feet as well as over our Heads."[5]

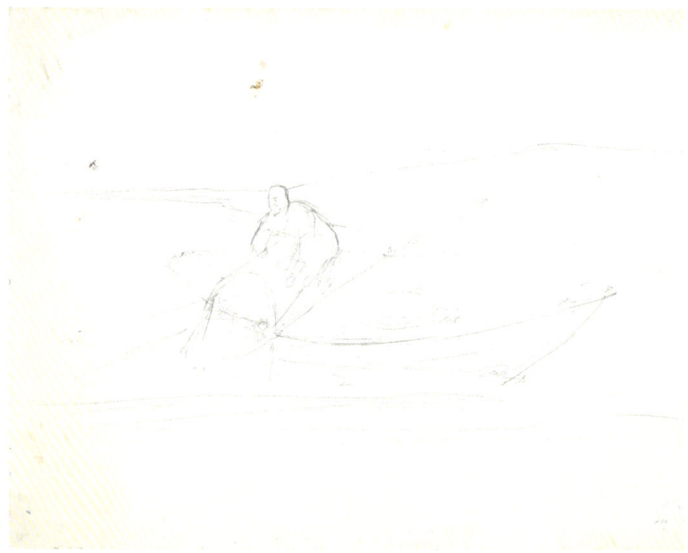

FIG. 1. Andrew Wyeth, *Night Hauling Study*, 1944. Watercolor on paper, 17¼ × 24⅝ in. (43.9 × 62.5 cm). Collection of Andrew and Betsy Wyeth

FIG. 2. Andrew Wyeth, *Night Hauling Study*, 1944. Pencil on paper, 21½ × 29¼ in. (54.6 × 74.4 cm). Collection of Andrew and Betsy Wyeth

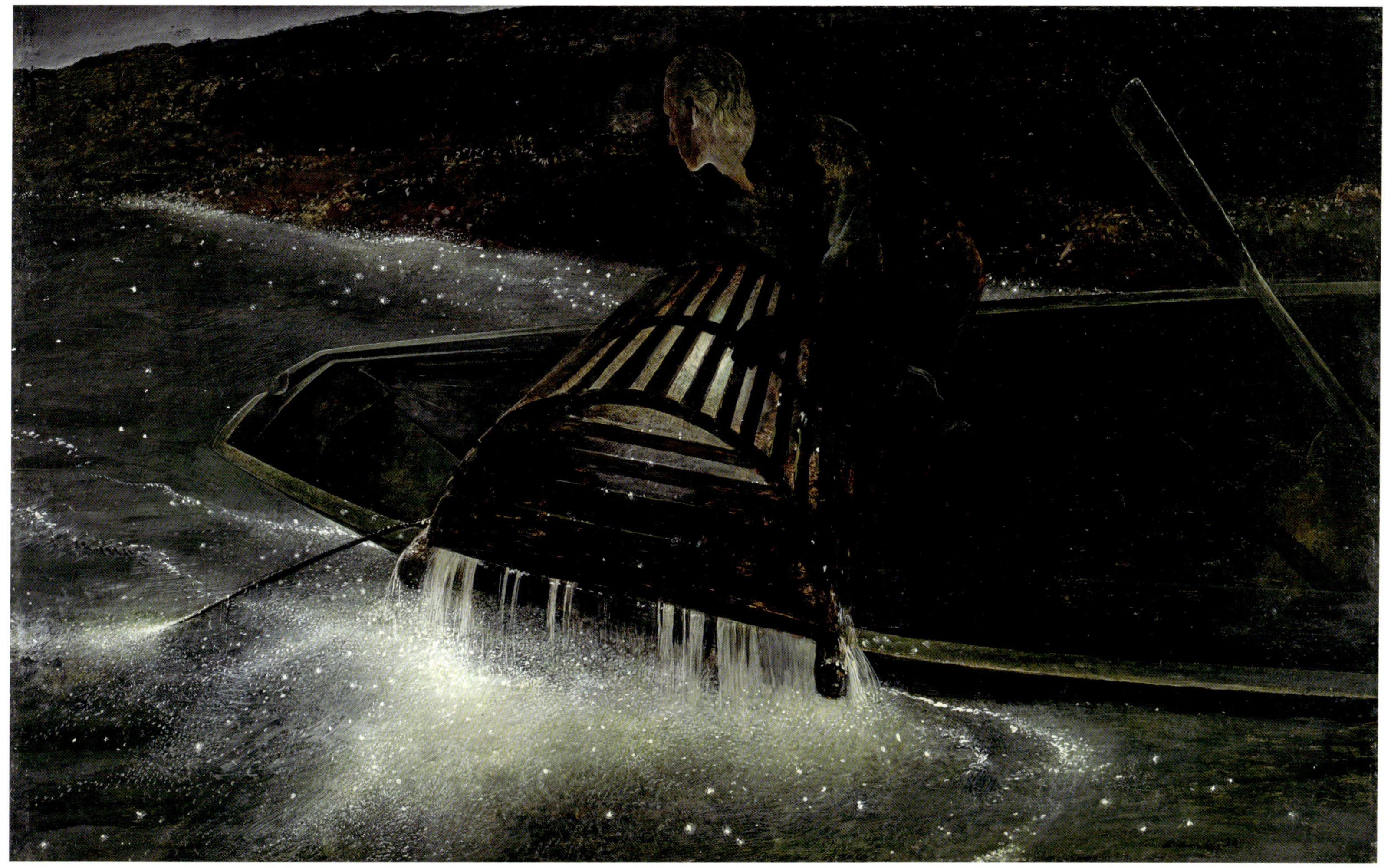

Wyeth conceived of *Night Hauling* during the summer of 1944, a period marked by massive airstrikes during the Normandy invasion and subsequent bombings of World War II, a subject painted by Wyeth's brother-in-law Peter Hurd, who is credited with introducing him to the medium of tempera.[6] The sinister appearance of Anderson stealing lobsters under cloak of night suggests a carefully orchestrated, covert military maneuver. Given Wyeth's fascination with war imagery, he may have envisioned Anderson's theft as an expression of nighttime enemy attacks during this summer of epic war campaigns.

The artist's desire to convey accurate time and place is evident at the right edge of the composition, where he leaves behind debris of sand and bits of shell in the paint surface. Wyeth belonged to a circle of artists who grafted Old Master techniques onto modern-day subjects.[7] What is surprising here is the extent to which he combined elements from the real world with the paint to support his vision. Applying gesso to a panel he worked up in tempera often left behind bubbles, as in his painting *The Sculpin*.[8] In *Night Hauling*, what appears to be a tiny washer ring, of the sort that might have fallen into the dory, becomes a token of the real world entering the world of the artist's imagination in the form of a bubble that may vanish before our eyes in an instant—the magic touch of Andrew Wyeth.

Elliot Bostwick Davis
Director and CEO, Norton Museum of Art,
West Palm Beach

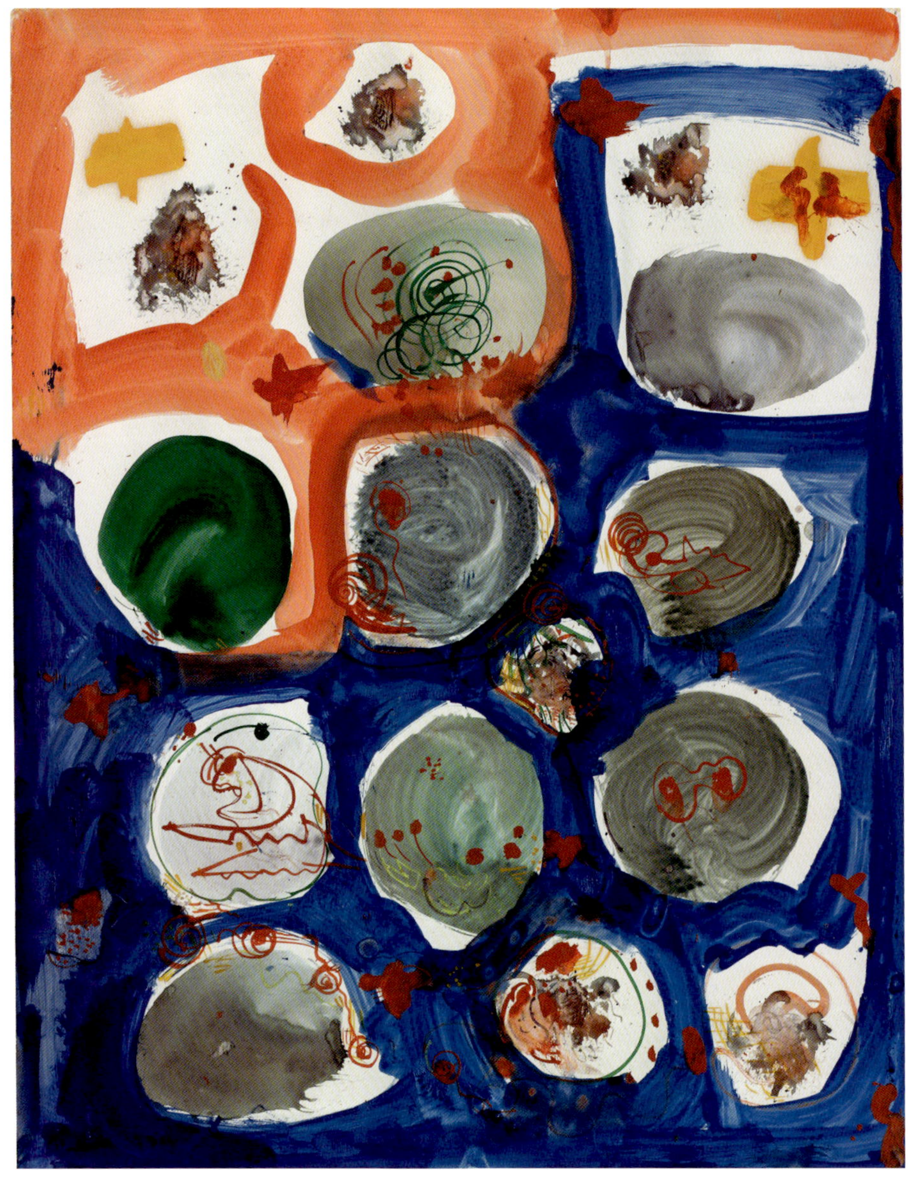

# Untitled (Cycle of Man)

Hans Hofmann (American, 1880–1966), 1944
Watercolor on paper, 28½ × 22½ in. (72.4 × 57.1 cm)
Bequest of William H. Alexander, in memory of his uncle,
Charles D. Frazer  2003.11.40

This watercolor dates to a pivotal year in Hans Hofmann's career, when he was sixty-four years old, marked by his first New York solo show at Peggy Guggenheim's Art of This Century. Hofmann was a well-known teacher—he ran art schools in his native Germany (until 1933), in New York, and in Provincetown—and an influential contributor to the rise of Abstract Expressionism. He helped to connect Parisian and New York art circles, and he encouraged generations of artists to liberate color and form from the corset of representation. He also nurtured the ambitions of budding collectors, among them William Alexander, who for many decades focused on collecting European and American artists endorsed by Hofmann. (JHo)

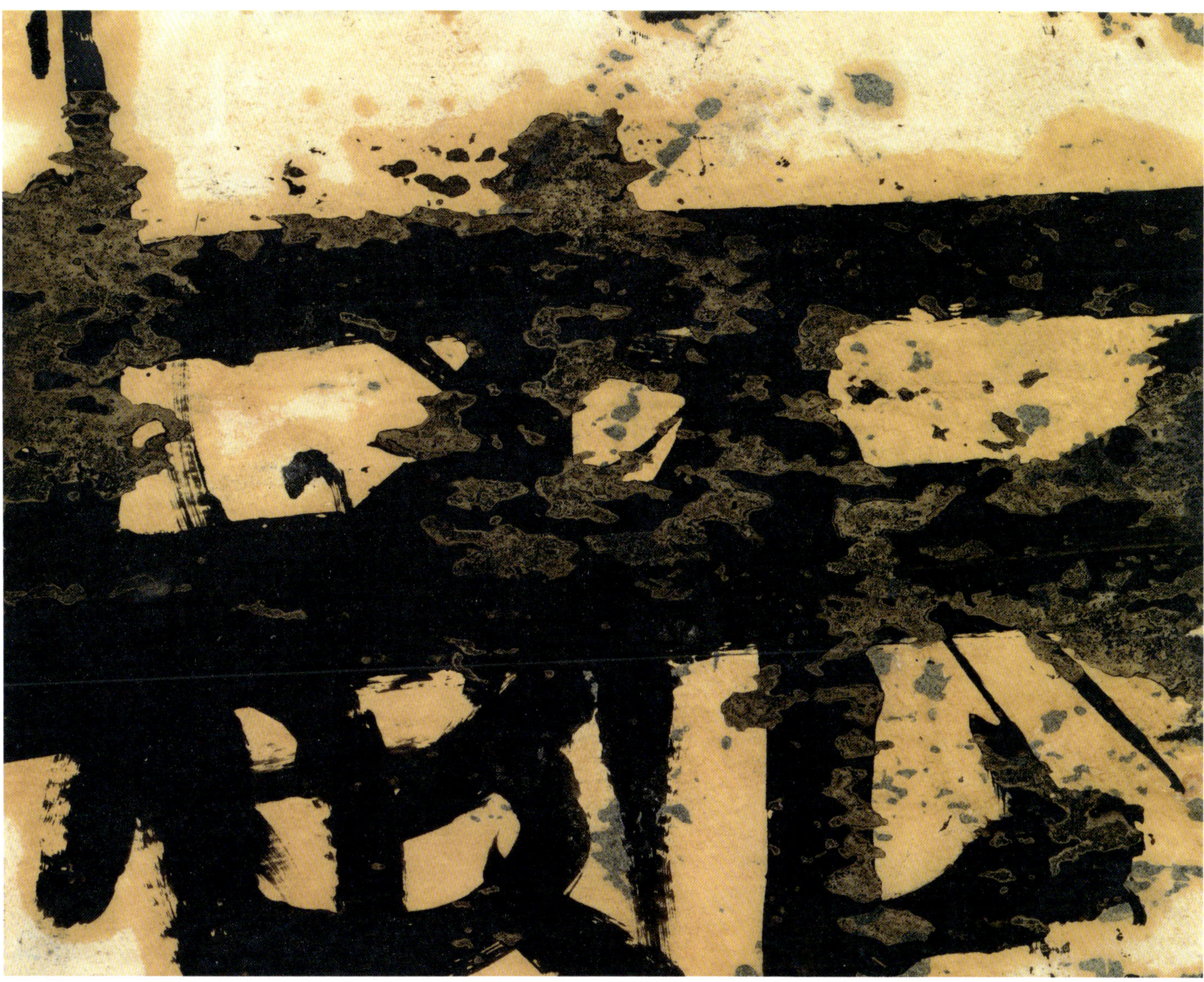

# *Untitled*

Franz Kline (American, 1910–1962), 1952
Ink, double-sided, on paper, 8⁷⁄₁₆ × 10¹⁵⁄₁₆ in. (21.5 × 27.8 cm)
Gift of Walter K. Gutman, Class of 1924  1964.66

"Kline would be denounced now as conceptual and pre-meditated," artist and critic Donald Judd wrote in 1964 after seeing one of Kline's preparatory sketches. Did Kline's practice of defining gestures on paper and translating them to painting indeed compromise his ability to be spontaneous and authentic, as Abstract Expressionist ideology required? This work suggests otherwise. An array of verticals and horizontals, brushed with a calligrapher's determination but too complex and expansive to be understood as a cipher, contextualizes various markings: floating drips that mar the surface, oily residue that seeped into the paper and made it more transparent, and ink splatters on the verso that shine through. The physicality of the deep blacks, the drawing's varying textures and multidirectional energies make this visually powerful work one of the outstanding examples of AbEx's "sacred belief in the dense Expressionist surface," in Hilton Kramer's words. (JHo)

# *Untitled*

Jack Tworkov (American, 1900–1982), 1950
Oil on paperboard, 25½ × 38⅛ in. (64.8 × 96.8 cm)
Gift of Walter K. Gutman, Class of 1924  1964.61

Jack Tworkov was the age of the century, born on August 15, 1900, in Biała Podlaska on the border between Poland and Russia. Tworkov's father was a tailor who moved to New York City in 1910. Jack (born Yakov) followed in 1913; he eventually became a U.S. citizen. His younger sister, Schenehaia, accompanied him. Schenehaia changed her name to Janice Biala; later, she just used Biala, the name by which she became known as a painter.

Jack learned English quickly, went to Columbia to become a writer, and graduated with a BA in English in 1923. He was involved in politics. In 1923, at his sister's insistence, he started taking classes at the National Academy of Design. He first went to Provincetown that same year and returned there the next. He began to amass a significant group of colleagues in painting and literature. During the Depression, Tworkov met Willem de Kooning in the Public Works of Art Project. From there, Tworkov was initiated into the world of painters trying to create a new way of painting distinct from that of the French masters Matisse and Picasso. In due time, he became a mentor and teacher to others. Bowdoin's picture was a gift of Walter Gutman, class of 1924, an art critic, filmmaker, and collector who studied painting with Tworkov.

His paintings in the early 1940s usually take figures or still lifes as beginnings from which to detach flat areas of color and allow linear expansions to take hold as independent statements. *Untitled* is one of the first paintings in which Tworkov let the figurative underpinnings go and relied on his instincts to have areas of color and linear shapes be the complete subject of a painting. As though they are dancers, but ones existing solely in terms of paint, dark gray shapes provide the build-up, or setting, taking off from the raw, unprimed board beneath. Dark shapes lend further pointing to the picture; finally, several blue lines and one red area form a more focused statement near the picture's center. Tworkov always placed an emphasis on drawing, and his paintings, like those of de Kooning, generally exhibit tautly outlined forms.

From this highly successful starting point, Tworkov's work would generally eschew recognizable subjects. Even when such elements are visible, they seem subliminal, lurking behind the major thrusts of his gestural and compositional interests. As time went on, parallel lines and finally geometry itself became abiding concerns in his work. But the heart of Tworkov's identity as an artist, and his importance today, was formed in the probing work of the 1950s, of which *Untitled* is a signal example.

Vincent Katz
Poet, translator, art critic, and curator

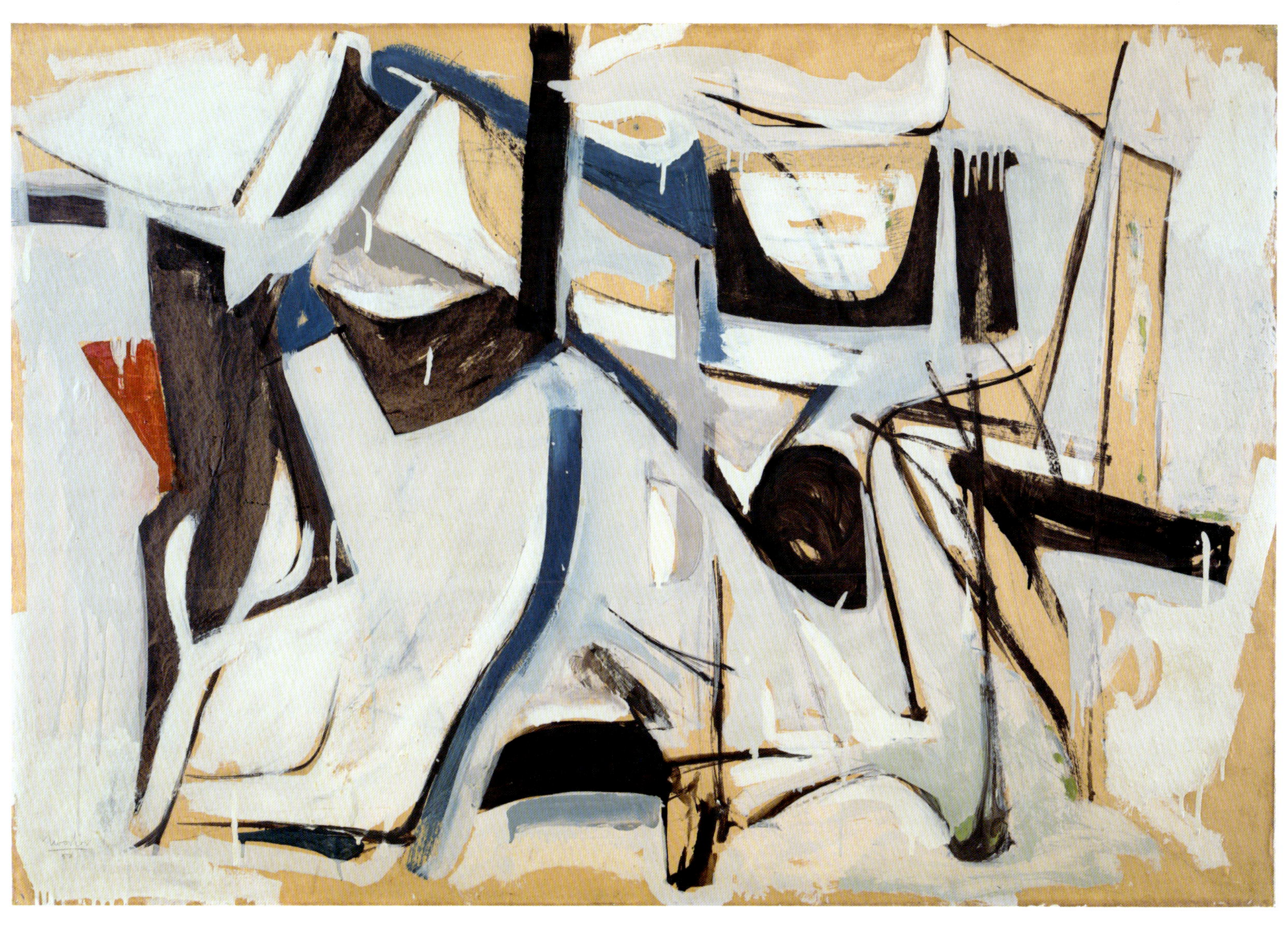

## *Untitled*

Matta (Chilean, 1912–2002), c. 1951
Oil paint, graphite, and charcoal on paper, mounted on wood
panel, 15½ × 23⅜ in. (39.4 × 59.4 cm)
Bequest of William H. Alexander, in memory of his mother and father, Mr.
and Mrs. William Homer Alexander  2003.11.54

Although he was Chilean by birth, the career and reputation of Roberto Sebastián Matta Echaurren were decidedly international. From a start as a draftsman in the architectural atelier of Le Corbusier, he gravitated toward painting and joined the Paris-based Surrealist group in 1937. Two months after the outbreak of World War II, he arrived in New York, where, together with other Surrealist refugees, he was an influential force on younger American artists. During the 1940s, his work was exhibited at the prestigious Pierre Matisse Gallery, acquired by the Museum of Modern Art, New York, and included in publicity-attracting exhibitions with other Surrealist emigrés. In the winter of 1941–42, several future Abstract Expressionists met in Matta's studio to experiment with the Surrealist practice of automatism.

Inspired by the discoveries of contemporary physicists and Einstein's theory of relativity, Matta attempted in his early work to give visual form to scientific concepts and to break through the confines of Euclidean geometry in order to portray a fluid, multidimensional universe in which all that seems solid and static is in transition. Having moved sideways into painting from architecture, he was not bound by conventional training, and he freely improvised ways of suggesting states of continuous transformation. Through his prodigious efforts, viewers could have the possibility of understanding themselves as part of a continuum in a space full of waves, stars, galaxies, and black holes, with no beginning or end.

Whereas Matta's early works reflect Surrealism's concern with "psychic automatism" as a way of accessing the unconscious, after becoming aware of World War II atrocities he began to introduce tubular humanoid creatures into complex spaces often suggestive of torture chambers. This new direction ran counter to rising Abstract Expressionism and cost him much of his American following, although his first retrospective was mounted at the Museum of Modern Art in 1957. Returning to Europe in 1949, he increasingly focused on what he called "social morphologies," paintings that reflected the alignments and stresses of human societies during the Cold War era.

In the 1950s and '60s, he created large paintings dealing with political subjects such as the French use of torture during the Algerian War, the execution in the U.S. of Julius and Ethel Rosenberg, and the Vietnam War, as well as commissioned murals for his native Chile, which were destroyed when Pinochet seized power. The Martinican poet Édouard Glissant described Matta as "one of the very rare artists who does not remove man from life, who dares to address the terrible and primordial problem of the difficulty of existing in the conditions of modern society."[1]

Bowdoin's untitled work on paper shares in the general incendiary tenor of much of Matta's 1950s painting. A thickly painted central nucleus of orange and yellow appears to be the root cause of explosive outward movement, consisting of firing weapons and upward-moving streaks of light. Toward the periphery, small, faintly drawn figures are aligned beneath a dark cloud with a hovering apparition that looks like one of the Polynesian *malagan* ceremonial masks from New Ireland that Matta and other Surrealists collected and regarded as "objects of power."

Executed in oil paint, graphite, and charcoal, drawn more than painted, deliberately smudged and blurred, this work, ambiguous as it may be to the viewer, arises out of the artist's need to convey his sense of a universe in perpetual and often violent transition.

Martica Sawin
Art historian, critic, and curator, and
former Professor and Chair of the
Department of History and Criticism of Art
and Design, Parsons School of Design

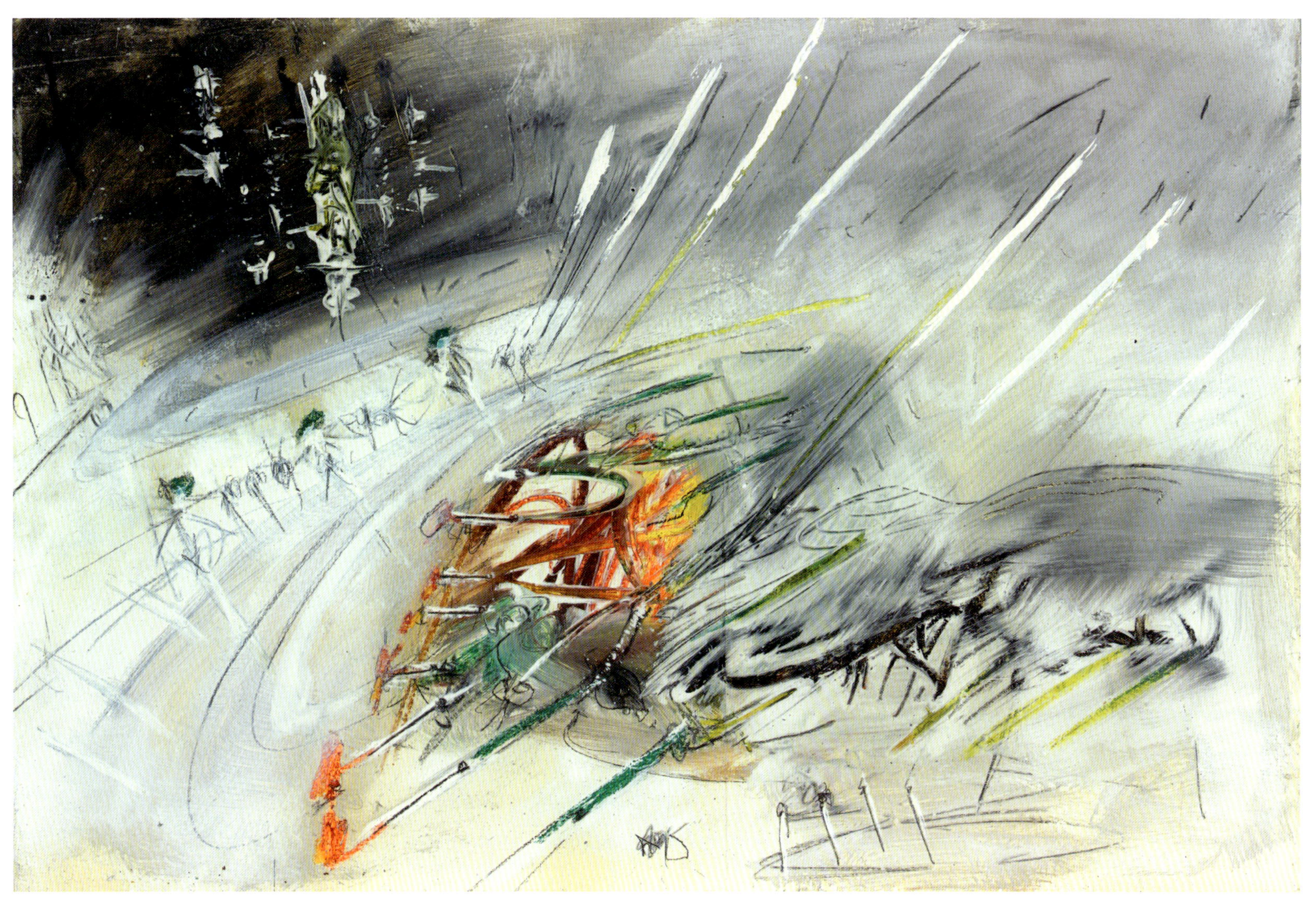

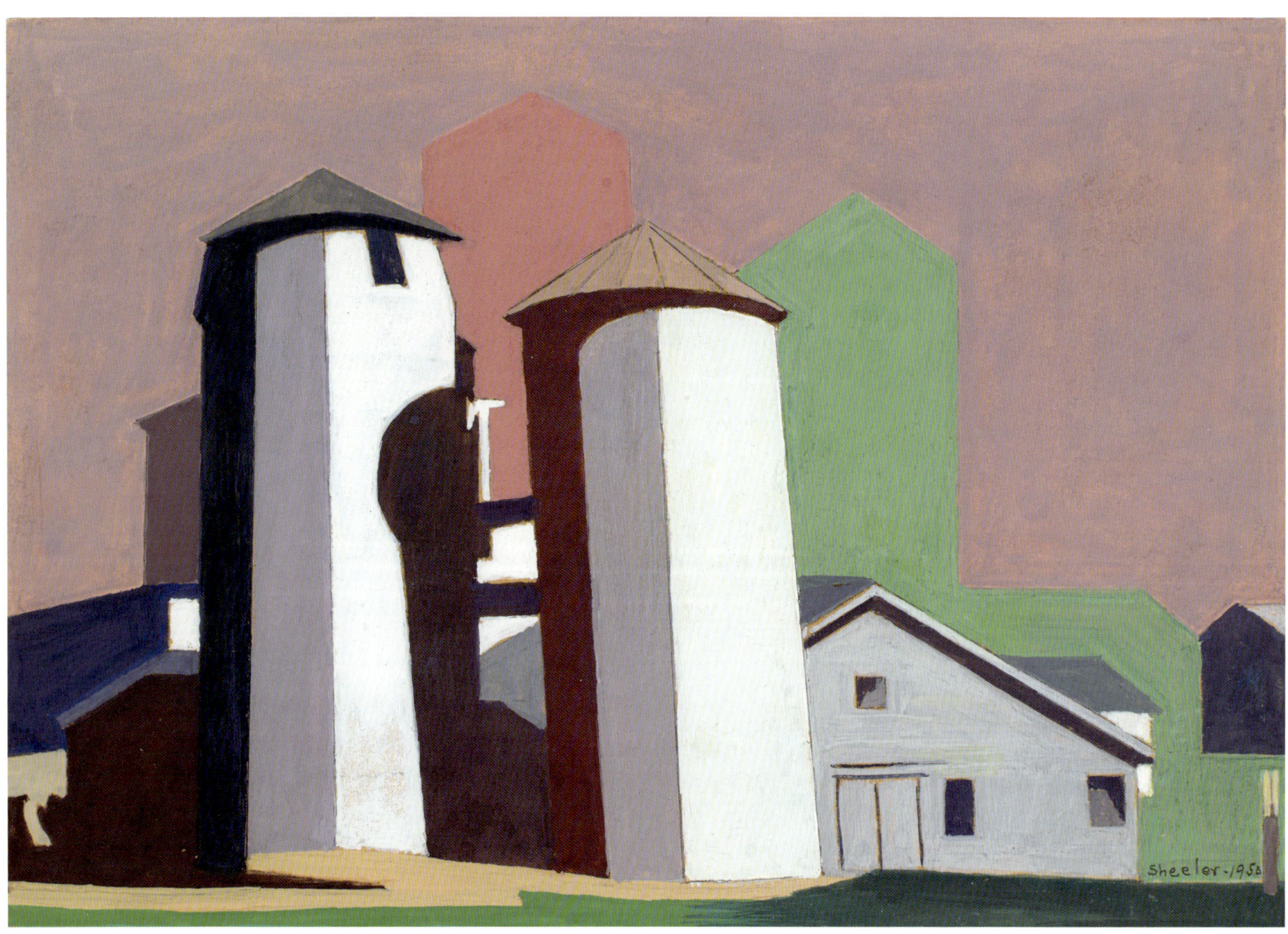


## Companions #2

Charles Sheeler (American, 1883–1965), 1950
Tempera on paper, 6¼ × 4¼ in. (15.9 × 10.8 cm)
Gift of Linda Horvitz Roth '76 and David Roth  2007.12

As a central figure of the New York avant-garde in the first half of the twentieth century, Charles Sheeler contributed to a specifically American modernist style—Precisionism. The flattened geometric shapes of his boldly colored and meticulously executed renderings of farms and factories, which occupied him from the 1930s, combined characteristic elements of painting and photography. This view of a modern farm foregrounds two silos for livestock feed that tower over a large stable and adjacent outbuildings. Set against a dusky pink sky, their twin silhouettes are doubled by abstract pink and light green planes "behind" the architecture. The complexity and monumentality of this small-scale tempera are the result of a pictorial operation Sheeler explored in 1946–53, prompted by two artist residencies in New England. At the time, Sheeler began to superimpose photographic negatives he took onsite, generating image sources for his paintings that were simultaneously representational and abstract. (JHo)

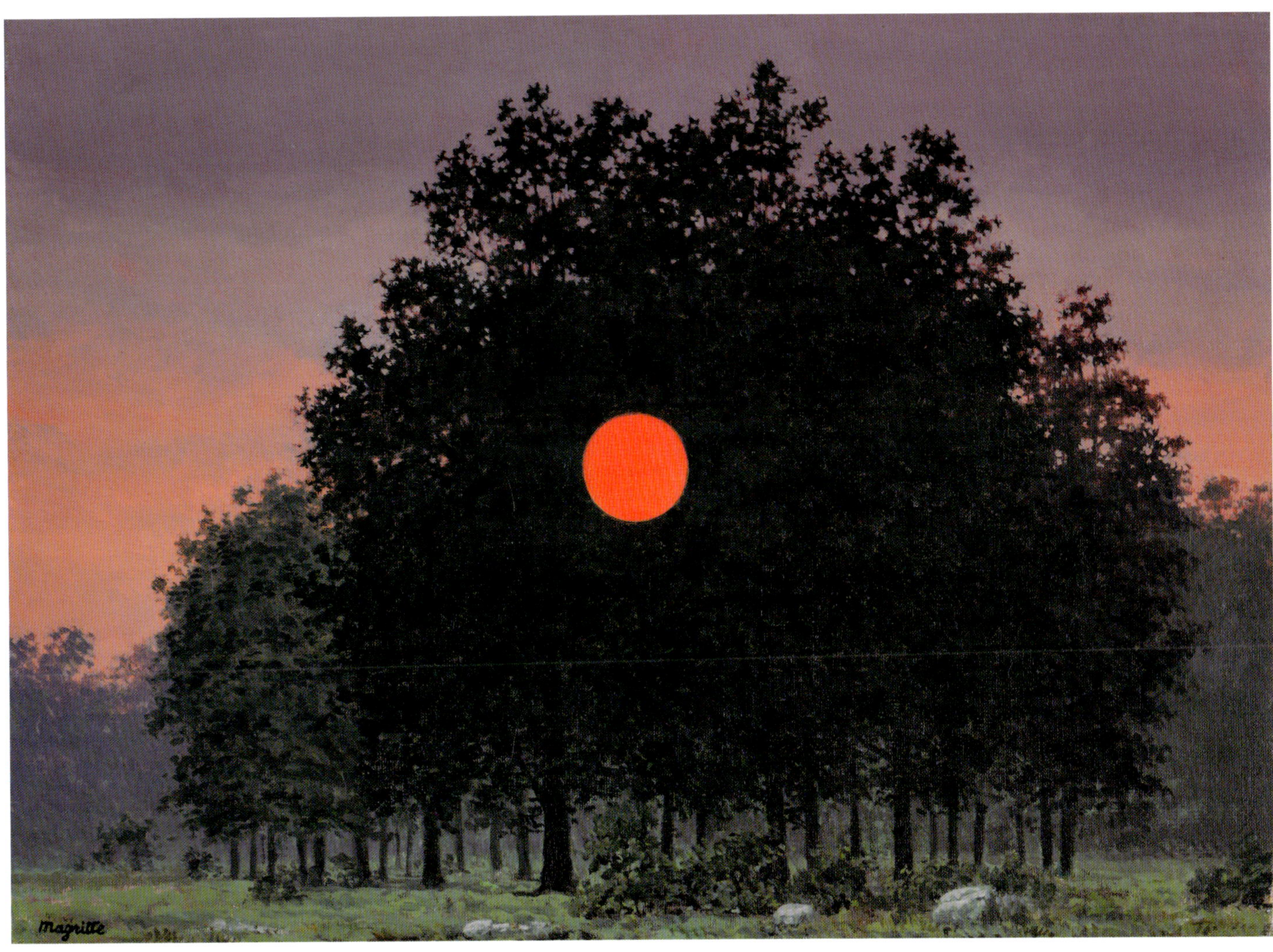

# *Le Banquet*

René Magritte (Belgian, 1898–1967), 1957
Oil on canvas, $12^{11}/_{16} \times 17^{13}/_{16}$ in. (32.2 × 45.2 cm)
Bequest of William H. Alexander, in memory of his friend, Howard Hoyt
Shiras, M.D.  2003.11.49

This variant of one of Magritte's most captivating landscapes invites viewers to ponder what appears to be a sunset with a stand of fastidiously rendered trees silhouetted against the evening sky. However, as the artist described in a letter, the "red sun is visible on the mass of the trees hiding it." While this effect is disorienting, the painting will unfailingly cast a spell on viewers. They will not soon forget the experience of pictorial conventions unsettled and the workings of their own minds exposed. When speaking about his painting *The Son of Man*, which featured an apple blocking the face of a bowler-hatted man, Magritte said "Everything we see hides another thing, we always want to see what is hidden by what we see." Serving up the landscape and the setting sun as an impossible simultaneity, *Le Banquet* offers a Surrealist feast for the senses and nurtures the mind as well. (JHo)

# Trolley—New Orleans

Robert Louis Frank (American, born 1924), 1955
Gelatin silver print, 6⅛ × 9⁷⁄₁₆ in. (15.6 × 24 cm)
Museum Purchase, Lloyd O. and Marjorie Strong Coulter Fund  1989.8

It may be the most readily recognizable of the photographs that made the book containing them an icon of the art. For one thing, when the U.S. edition of *The Americans* was published in 1959, containing the revolutionary collection of Robert Frank photographs and an introduction by Jack Kerouac, *Trolley—New Orleans* was on the cover. Before you got to the others, you came to this, a searing image of passengers seated on a trolley car and staring out their windows, with whites in the forward seats and blacks in the rear. For another thing, as many of the book's other photographs recede into time, becoming exotic records of *how things were*, *Trolley* remains all too topical and modern. New Orleans public transit is no longer segregated *de jure*, but the nation still struggles with *de facto* racial injustice.

Despite its recognizability, *Trolley* may be among the least understood of the photographs in *The Americans*, for the simple reason that its complexity is hidden by its impact, its meaning by its message.

In his role as itinerant chronicler, on an epic journey to catalogue a country's farflung character, Robert Frank was more Alexis de Tocqueville than William Bartram, more interested in that country's inhabitants and their society than in the landscape they inhabited. Context—urban, rural, industrial, commercial, indoor and out—played its important supporting role, but even the title of his groundbreaking collection, *The Americans* (not, as he might have put it, *America*), keeps its emphasis on the people, not the frame, on portraits over place. Yet to come to grips with the power of Frank's photographs, one must ever keep in mind the ways he framed his people.

Many are solitary—an off-duty rodeo cowboy lighting a cigarette on a Manhattan street, say—and even where there are several figures, like the passengers in a Miami Beach elevator, the focus stays intensely on the elevator girl, on the individual alone amid the hubbub. Frank's group portraits come likewise in many styles, ranging from couples to crowds, but he had a special fondness for lines and queues, for people arrayed in a row. What that row meant, what it provided the photograph, could depend on whether the line was a *processional*, an assembly of people going somewhere and usually seen in profile, or what might be called, for lack of a better term, a *confrontational*: a collection of individuals—whether they be pedestrians arrayed across a Savannah sidewalk, or six women smoking over coffee at a New York deli counter—spaced in regimented intervals, a firing line facing the camera so squarely that, could the camera look sharply enough into their eyes, it would be seen there in reflection.

*Trolley—New Orleans* is an oddball member of this club. It's either a processional or a confrontational, depending on how you read it. The photograph is generally viewed as a commentary on American apartheid, documenting the plight of black citizens relegated by law to the back of the tram. That reading is fair and the import is intended; Frank was passionate on the issue of race, and placing the indictment prominently on his book's cover sent a warning that the pictures inside would pull no punches. Deriving that social message requires viewing the image as a processional, but is it? If it weren't for the trolley's seat backs and the passengers' postures, we wouldn't know *front* from *back*. Frank's camera crops the car so closely, it has no head or tail; its blank flank fills the frame, and its occupants look out to the side. The trolley Frank gives us is less conveyance than Guignol stage, and the people on that stage, deprived of direction, are presented in the format of a standard Frank confrontational. They're not unequal travelers on the way to the next stop; they're a seated jury of peers. Before them lies the onlooker.

To neglect either of these readings is to miss half of the photo's extraordinary power. Critics have noted the allusion to roll film in the trolley windows' pattern. The transom glass above the open windows abets the appearance of a contact sheet, and the mullions between the windows separate and frame the individual passengers as though they were captured in different shots, displayed on different pages. The effect suggests that the multitudes Frank encountered in his journeys around the country, and captured on film in the course of their daily lives, are here called to a pre-performance curtain call, his cast arrayed at stage edge before its audience, to make a direct appeal. The

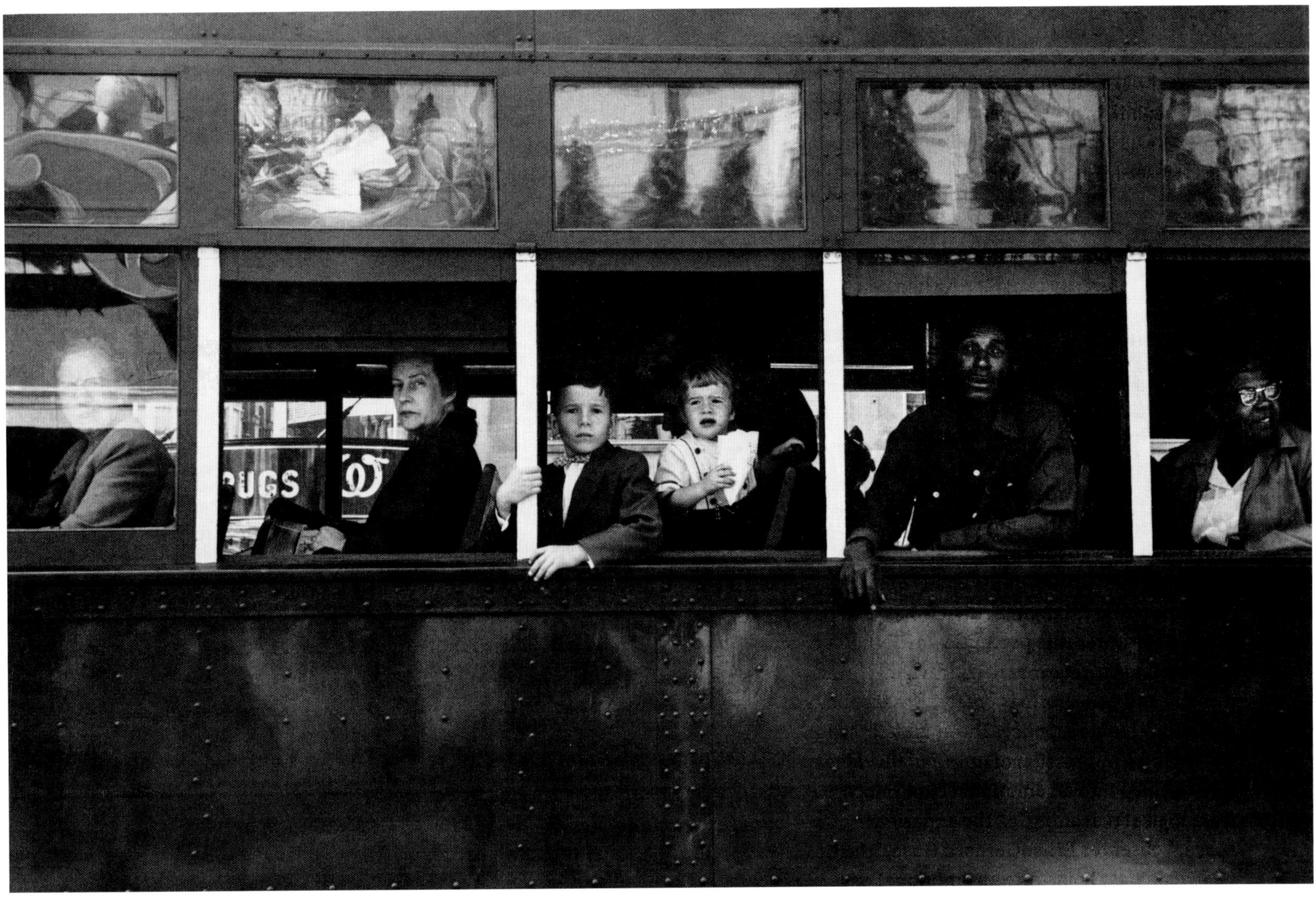

intensity of that appeal, whether in the lone white woman's slant-eyed suspicion or the black man's desperation, makes the object of their attention all the more tangible: what *they* see becomes the point. In that way, Frank has given us a final solo portrait, of someone as alone amid the hubbub as his Miami elevator girl, a self-portrait of the photographer in reflection. Or, by that same reasoning, of the viewer. Into the social drama presented by the processional *Trolley* photograph (and by extension the retinue of photos in the book), the confrontational photograph inducts the reader. It instructs us that we are all "Americans" and integral to the story, that (borrowing from poet Rainer Maria Rilke's description of the faceless yet perceiving work of art) herein there is no photograph that does not see . . . you.

Russ Rymer
Journalist, novelist, and Elizabeth Drew
Professor of English Language and
Literature, Smith College

# *Raumplastik*

Norbert Kricke (German, 1922–1984), 1958
Steel, mounted on stone plinth, 21⅝ × 25¾₆ × 13 in.
(55 × 64 × 33 cm)
Gift of Elizabeth Cabot Lyman in honor of Bogislav von Wentzel  2017.27

What can we learn from Norbert Kricke's *Raumplastik* (*Space Sculpture*) by considering it in different contexts?[1]

Kricke was born in Düsseldorf in 1922 and grew up in Berlin. As a young man, he saw his city destroyed by World War II, but still, along with a group of remarkably talented artists, he persisted. Right after the war, in 1946 and 1947, he studied with Richard Scheibe at the Berlin Kunsthochschule. By 1950, he had changed his sculptures radically. He discarded idealized figures made of clay and transformed the wire supports that had stabilized them into sculptures about space. His friend, the critic Sigfried Giedion, describes what this change meant: "space itself is limitless and intangible … yet space can be perceived. What constitutes this perception of space? A complex set of conditions is required to confine emptiness within such dimensions that a form is created which elicits an immediate emotional response. The elucidation of the process by which an impression of inarticulate voids becomes transformed into an emotional experience moves far away from logical reasoning."[2] "The experience of 'intangible space,'" observes Ernst-Gerhard Güse, "the transformation of 'inarticulate voids into an emotional experience' relates to the works that Kricke created." His new sculptures reach into space, they define it, but they do not enclose it. They portray movement, but without parts that actually move, and, as the eye follows the steel rods, the passage of time is suggested as well. "The experience of space in his works develops optically—they are primarily 'Augenkunst' (art for the eye)."[3]

Kricke's achievement is a reflection of the intense interest in space and its exploration in the 1950s and '60s. Like scientists, he was questioning compartmentalized thinking. Rather than equations, he created a visual metaphor against such thinking. With his focus on space, Kricke's interest in architecture, and in particular sculpture's relationship to it, is illuminating. He abhorred the purely functional architecture characteristic of Germany's postwar reconstruction. Again, his concerns were contemporary. He felt that "imagination, creative power, courage, and free thought without preconditions were suspect" at that time, and with his work set out to change things. He believed an artist could make buildings more humane. The artist and architect could cooperate to produce better results. A sculpture could add a quality to or offset a building, it did not necessarily have to be in harmony with it. Many buildings coupled with his sculptures demonstrate how varied his solutions were, for instance, the *Space Sculpture* formerly installed in the entry plaza of the Los Angeles County Museum of Art, now in Stuttgart, or the sculpture *Röhrendickicht* on the facade of the Musiktheater im Revier in Gelsenkirchen.

Kricke's favorite dialogue partners were often architects or architectural historians or critics. One of these, Udo Kultermann, was the original owner of the Bowdoin *Raumplastik*. Another, Sigfried Giedion, wrote perceptively about Kricke's sculpture. To single out a few others, James Stirling and Walter Gropius were part of this circle. Kricke especially admired Le Corbusier's Ronchamp chapel (1953–55). He writes so vividly about the experience of walking through it that we more concretely understand not only why he believed that Le Corbusier's experience as a painter and sculptor made such an achievement possible, but what Kricke valued as an artist.

Elizabeth Lyman
Former co-director, Galerie Wentzel,
Hamburg and Cologne

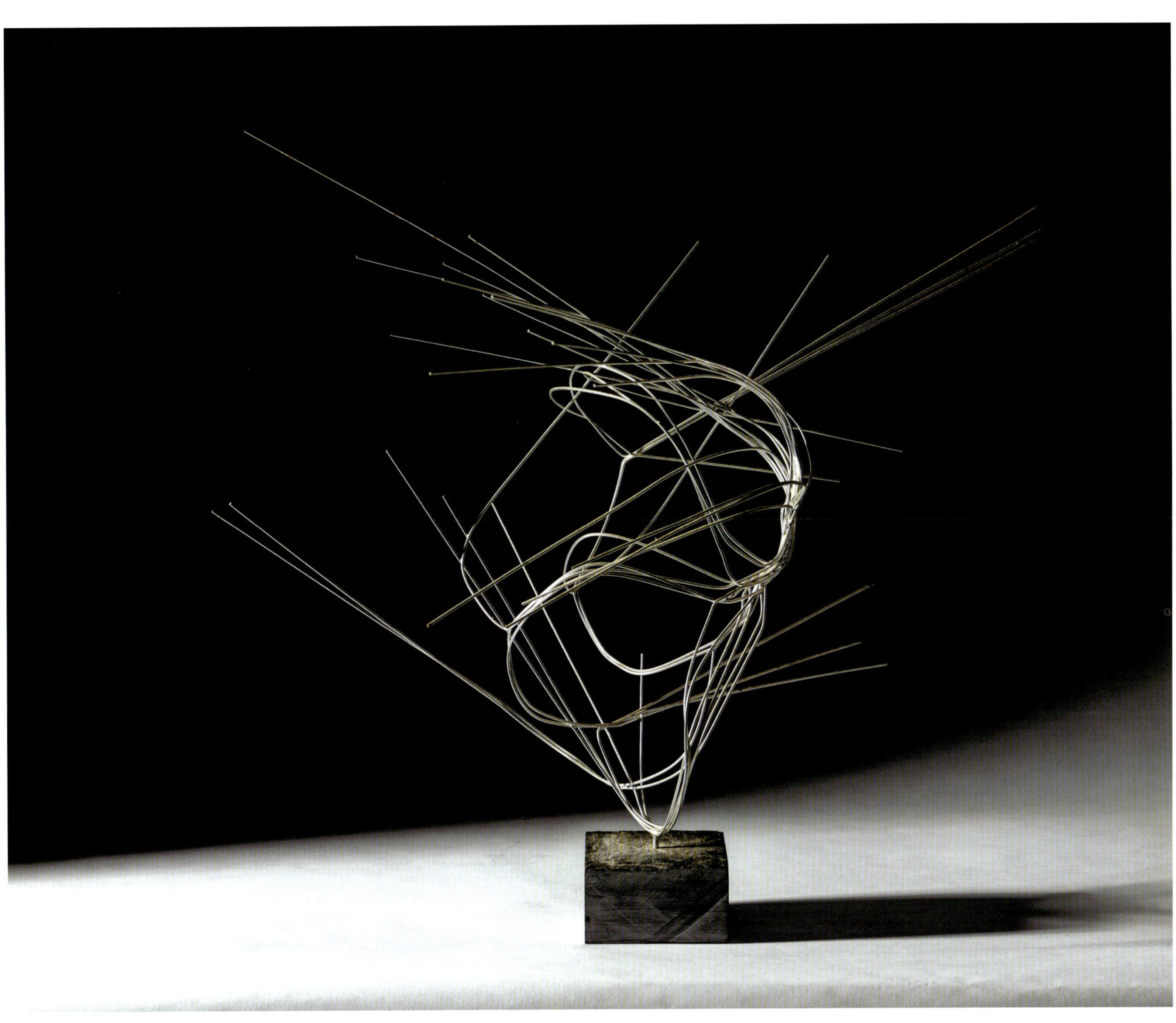

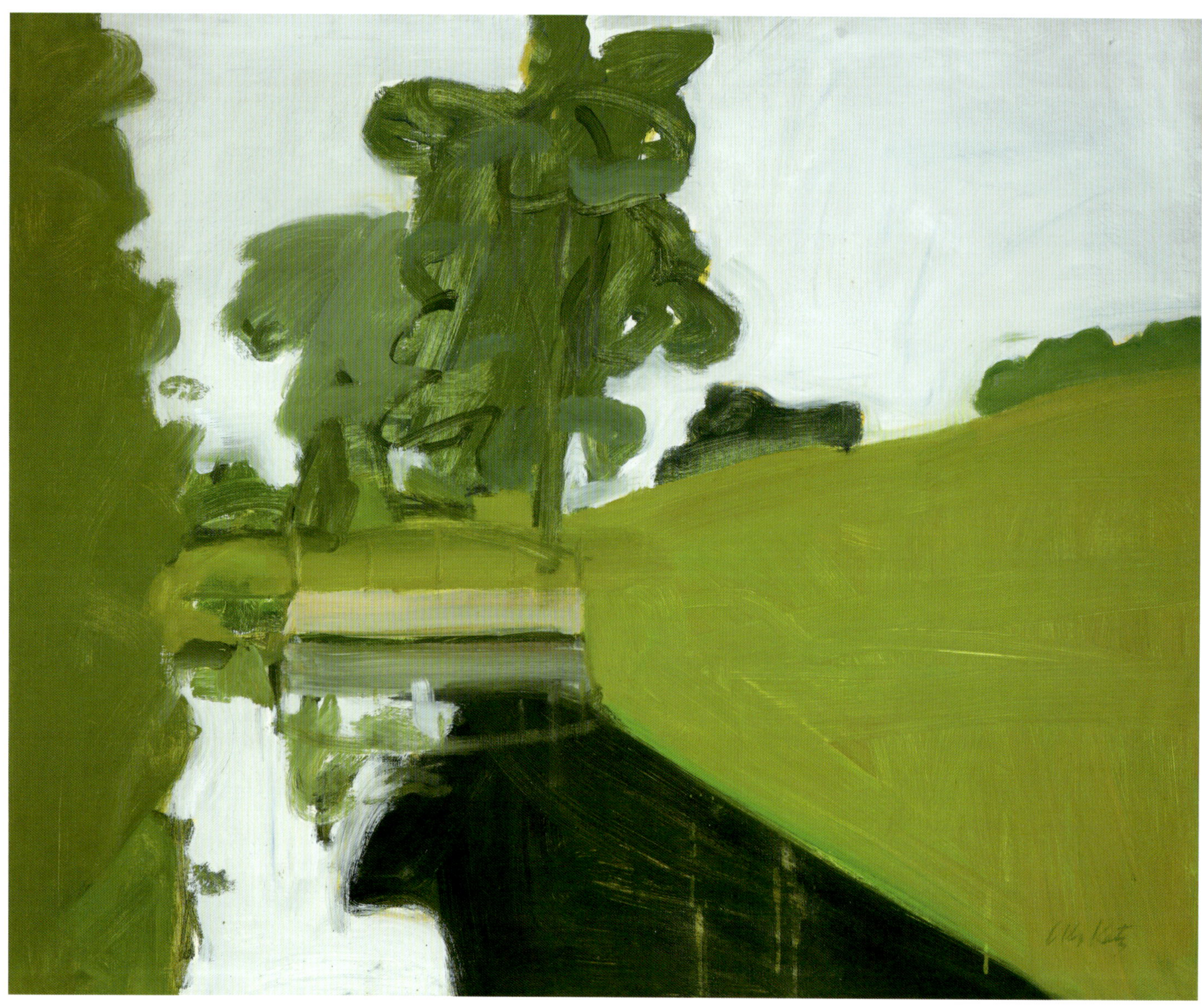

# *Untitled (Skowhegan, Maine Landscape)*

Alex Katz (American, born 1927), 1960
Oil on canvas, 33 × 41⅛ in. (83.8 × 104.4 cm)
Museum Purchase, Hamlin Fund  1983.19

Approached by the Museum after the purchase of this untitled painting at auction, Alex Katz reminisced in 1983 in a letter from Lincolnville, Maine, where he summers: "The landscape . . . was painted at Skowhegan in 1960. It's at the art school where I was teaching that summer. The view is facing east near the center of the art school—the bridge and pond still exist. . . . I am very pleased to have this excellent example of my work in 1960 in your collection." First introduced to Maine's luscious landscapes and brilliant light as a young student in 1949–50, Katz was appointed a member of the faculty of the Skowhegan School of Painting and Sculpture in the summer of 1960 and many times thereafter. This painting feels loose, as if the artist let his mind wander while he captured the essence of the scene. In its carefree use of gesture, it conjures Katz's joy working *en plein air* and testifies to his unmatched eye for color and composition. (MB/JHo)

# *Untitled*

Norman Lewis (American, 1909–1979), 1961
Oil on paper, 26 × 19 in. (66 × 48 cm)
Gift of halley k harrisburg, Class of 1990, and Michael Rosenfeld  2017.8.9

Norman Lewis was a central figure among the first generation of Abstract Expressionists, celebrated for his dynamic calligraphic and atmospheric abstractions. Likely the sole African American artist of his generation working in abstraction, he was inspired by such varied sources as music, nature, and the civil rights movement. Like his colleagues of the New York School, the forms he explored were derived from an organic abstraction rooted in Cubism and Surrealism.

On an emphatically vertical sheet, Lewis constructed a silhouette that meanders from the lower left—the position of his signature and date, October 31, 1961—toward the upper right corner, in an S-shape. This shape is composed of repetitions of the same zigzag line, based on a stencil the artist moved across the paper when applying the paint. While the lower variants of the motif are captured in blackish paint, the uppermost iterations glow in orange-red. Lewis's calligraphic work has been discussed as improvisational and related to jazz. Indeed, this pattern seems to be flexible and spontaneous rather than premeditated. At the same time, this atmospheric work can be contextualized in an entirely different cultural tradition, that of Chinese landscape painting. Lewis was passionate about Chinese and Japanese art—he read voraciously about it, as his personal library attests—and here one might see echoes of a hanging scroll painting of a mountainous landscape, in which bright peaks and shaded valleys recede into the distance, while the sun sinks behind the horizon. In the artistic climate of the 1950s and early 1960s, when artists mined traditions from around the globe in search of spiritual authenticity and prefigurations of pictorial abstraction, Asian art and philosophy drew renewed interest, especially among the painters associated with the New York School. (JHo)

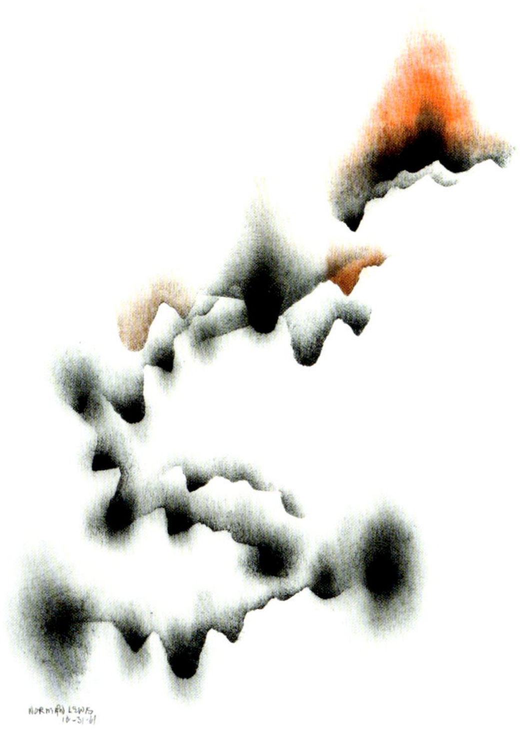

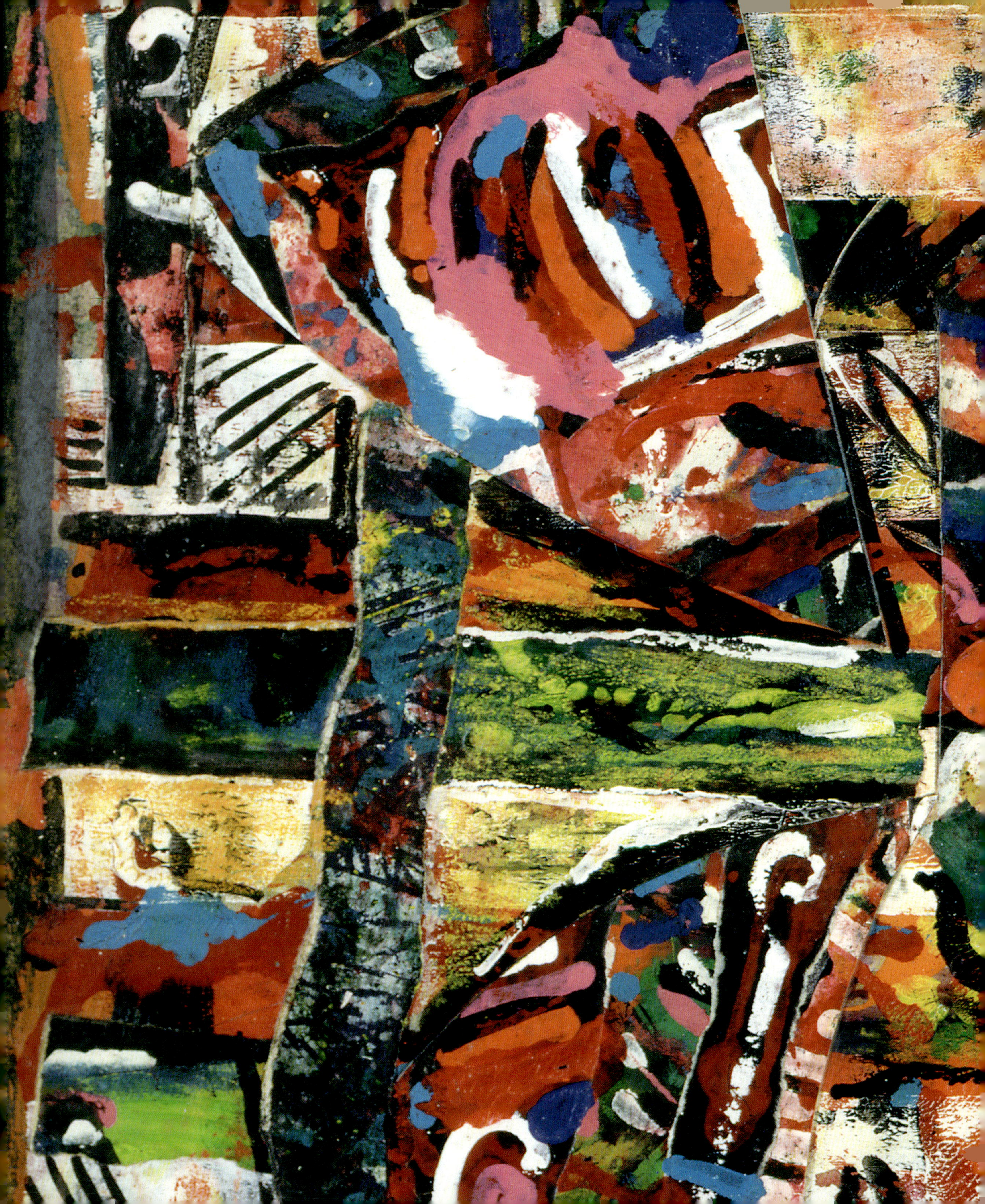

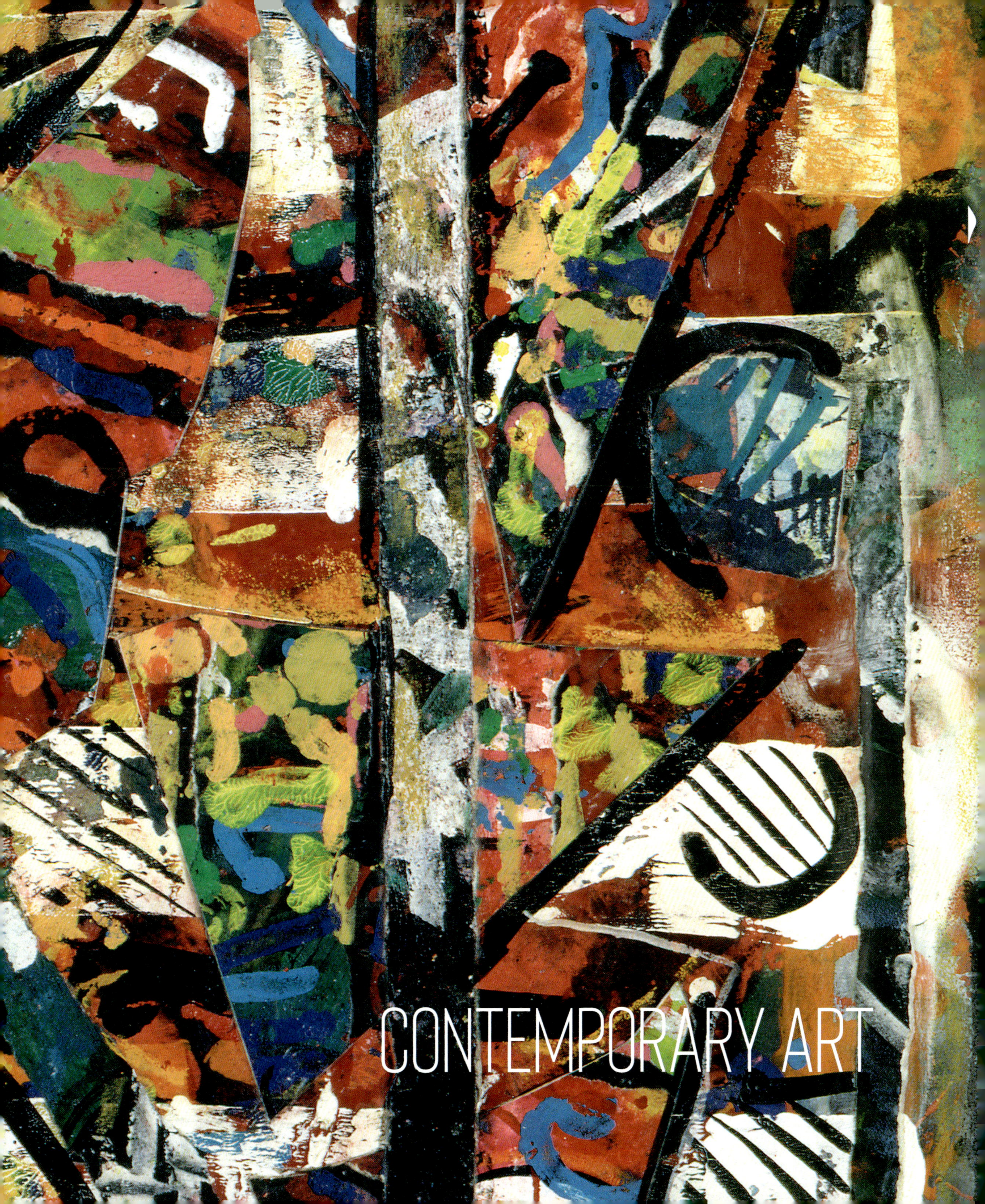
CONTEMPORARY ART

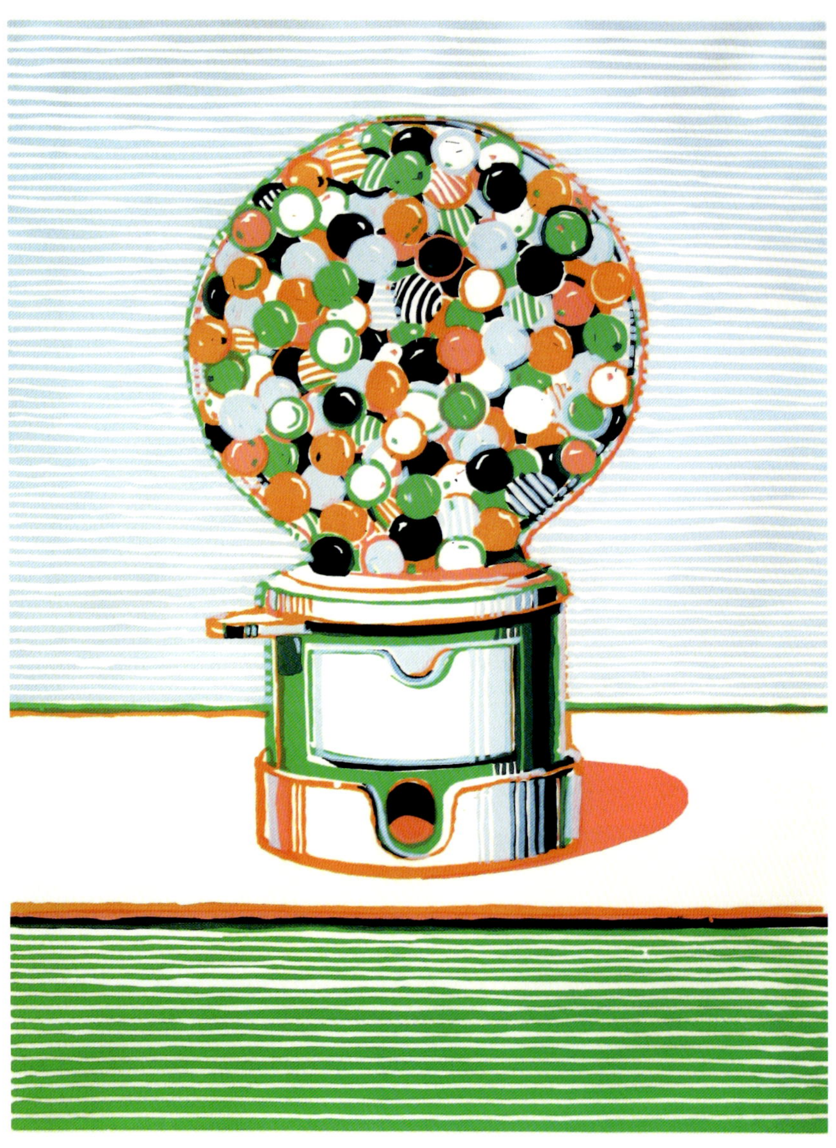

# *Gumball Machine*

Wayne Thiebaud (American, born 1920), 1971
Five-color linocut on paper, 30¼ × 22¼ in. (76.8 × 56.5 cm)
Museum Purchase, Barbara Cooney Porter Fund  2010.7

This color linocut of a gumball machine, a recurring motif in Thiebaud's work, exemplifies his interest in quotidian objects evocative of personal memories. In a 1969 interview, he described such a dispenser as "both a most elementary mechanism and a gadget for stimulating the grandest sort of associations and references." Thiebaud imbues the mundane with a sense of intangible nostalgia and magical realism through bold colors, dark contours, crisp shadows, and graphic compositional balance—devices characteristic of his early training as an animator and commercial advertiser. The heightened sense of perfection achieved through simplification of form and pristine linearity paradoxically conveys a dreamlike quality of the familiarly generic yet personally specific, and allows the "psychological implications," as Thiebaud described, to radiate through his work. (HW)

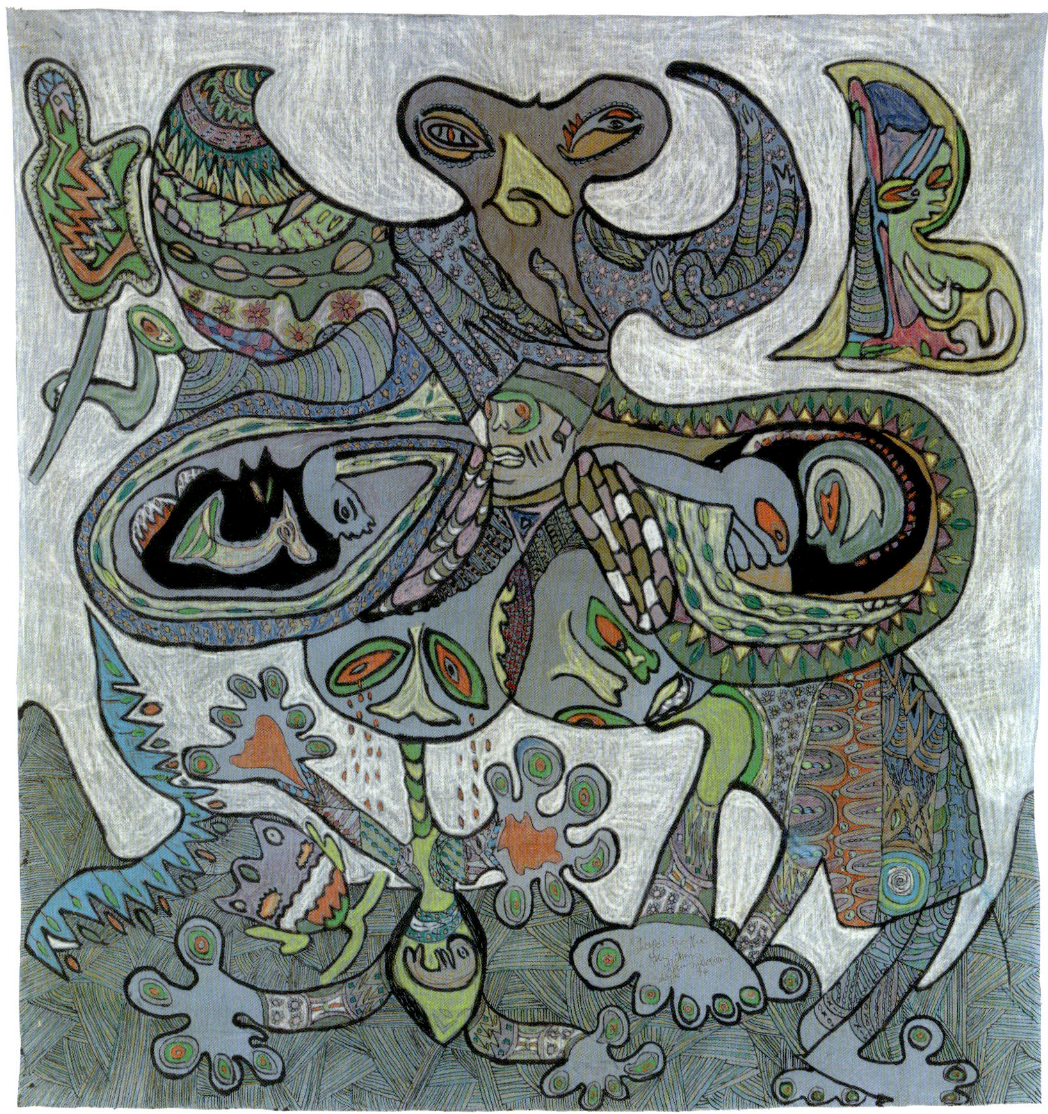

# *Shapes in the Sky During Rainy Season*

Twins Seven–Seven (Omoba Taiwo Olaniyi Oyewale–Toyeje
Oyalale Osuntoki) (Nigerian, 1944–2011), 1974
Mixed media on denim, 35 × 33¾ in. (88.9 × 85.7 cm)
Museum Purchase, Lloyd O. and Marjorie Strong Coulter Fund  2017.44

Thanks to his many contributions to international exhibitions, the Nigerian painter, printmaker, and musician Twins Seven-Seven was one of the best-known African artists of his generation. He took the name Twins Seven-Seven as the only surviving child of seven pairs of twins (Yoruba people have the highest birth rate of twins in the world). Trained at the Mbari Mbayo workshop, founded by Ulli and Georgina Beier in Oshogbo in 1964, he created contemporary responses to Yoruba myths. His reputation grew quickly, with first visits to Merced College in California and Haystack Mountain Crafts School, Deer Isle, Maine, in 1972, and a repeat visit to Haystack in 1974, when he brought this work with him. An attempt to immigrate in the late 1980s to the United States did not offer the career opportunities Twins had anticipated, so he returned to Nigeria, where he was honored with chieftaincy titles and, in 2005, distinguished as UNESCO Artist for Peace. (JHo)

# Zanzibar #3

Barbara Chase–Riboud (American, born 1939), c. 1972
Polished bronze and silk (rope tassels), 12½ × 13½ × 13½ in.
(34.9 × 41.9 × 39.4 cm)
Bequest of William H. Alexander  2003.11.24

Sleek, earth-dyed sister, / Madness glistening at your throat, / We could have stayed on the beach, / Clinging to the rocks like bats, / REFUSING TO MOVE OUR WOMBS, / Scraping them with flint, / Soaking the continent with the holy blood of martyrs.
—Barbara Chase-Riboud,
  "Why Did We Leave Zanzibar?," 1969–70[1]

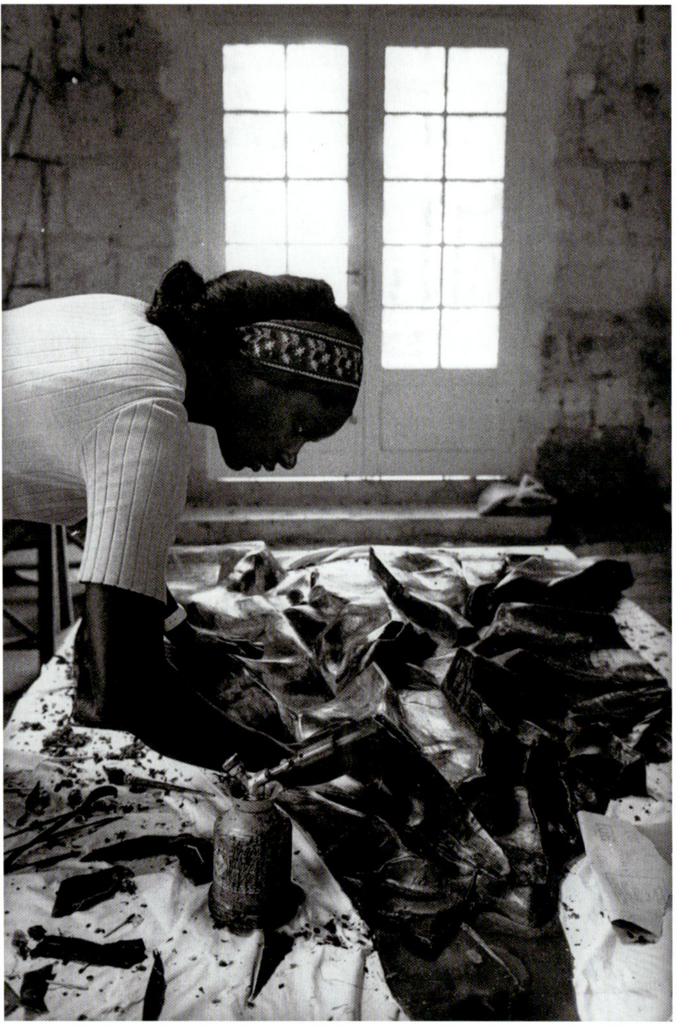



For more than five decades, Barbara Chase-Riboud has created monumental abstract forms with a deep and nuanced understanding of history, identity, and sense of place. Known for striking sculptures that combine metal and fiber, her work operates on several dichotomies that have become central to her practice: hard/soft, male/female, flexible/inflexible, stable/fluid, figurative/abstract, powerful/delicate. In 1958, while studying abroad in Rome, she developed her own particular innovation on the historical direct lost-wax method of casting bronze sculpture. Creating thin sheets of wax that she could bend, fold, meld, or sever, she made singular models that she would then bring to a local foundry for casting. This technique allowed Chase-Riboud to achieve the illusion of bronze as a malleable material. In 1967, she added fiber to these metal elements, devising the seemingly paradoxical works for which she is most renowned—sculptures of cast metal resting on supports hidden by cascading skeins of silk or wool so that the fibers appear to support the metal. The innovative combination of the two materials results in a dynamic relationship that continues to confound and inspire; as the artist has explained, "the transformation of the hard and the soft, the moment that the bronze becomes liquid and the fiber becomes solid, is a moment I cannot anticipate . . ."[2]

*Zanzibar #3* is one of at least six known works in a series named after the East African island in the Indian Ocean that was a hub for the Arab slave trade, which thrived from the seventeenth to the nineteenth century. The alluring tactility of the sculptures relates to Chase-Riboud's powerfully sensual and indignant poem "Why Did We Leave Zanzibar?" (1969–70), written shortly before they made their debut. Evocative of an elaborate headdress, *Zanzibar #3* was created following Chase-Riboud's seminal trips to Egypt, China, Senegal, and Algeria, where she was exposed to the richness of non-Western cultures. She wrote of her *Zanzibar* series:

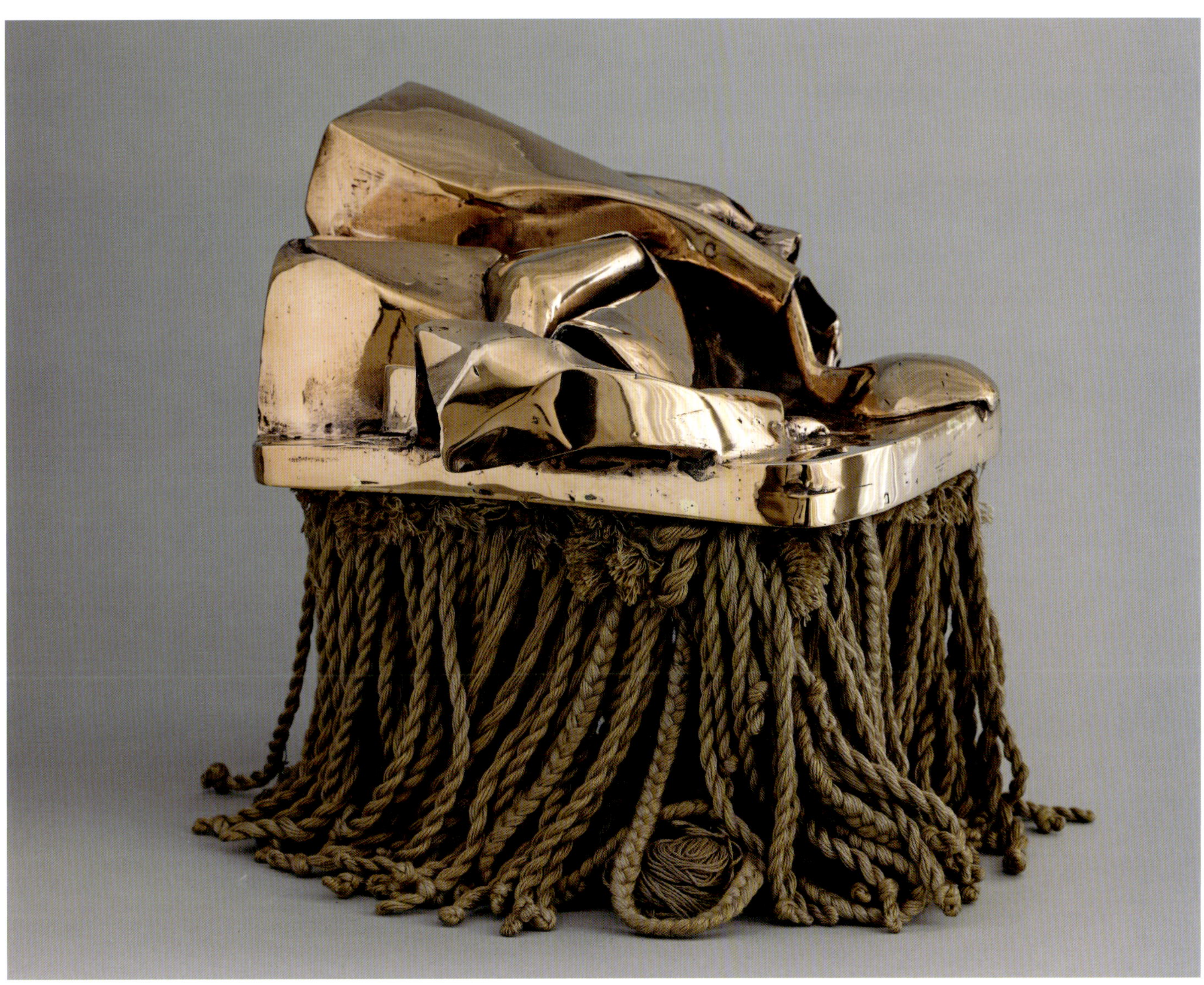

If "beauty" can be called "black" in the same way that humor can be called "black," then *Zanzibar* can be described as such. There is a mysterious and not far from threatening underbelly to this "beautiful" surface which has the same emotional effect as some African sculptures have on Westerners—and for the same reasons: displaced in time and space, taken out of their real environment, they assume a certain impenetrability that can disconcert and repel as well as please and attract. . . . Sculpture as a created object in space should enrich, not reflect, and it should be beautiful. Beauty is its function.[3]

Chase-Riboud continues to work, living between Paris and Milan. Born in Philadelphia, she settled in Paris soon after earning an MFA from Yale University in 1960. She has been recognized with numerous awards, including the James Van Der Zee Award (1995) and Alain Locke International Award (2007). Chase-Riboud is equally renowned for her literary success, publishing over fourteen novels and books of poetry, and is the recipient of the prestigious Carl Sandburg Poetry Prize. A dual citizen of France and the United States, she was knighted by the French government in 1996 as Chevalier de l'Ordre des Arts et des Lettres. In 2017, the Michael Rosenfeld Gallery[4] presented *Barbara Chase-Riboud—Malcolm X: Complete*, which celebrated the completion of her series of steles created over the last half-century in honor of the slain human rights leader.

halley k harrisburg
Director, Michael Rosenfeld Gallery,
New York

# Mrs. Viola Andrews—My Mother

Benny Andrews (American, 1930–2006), 1974
Oil with fabric collage on canvas, 60 × 48⅛ × 1½ in.
(152.4 × 91.4 × 4.2 cm)
Gift of halley k harrisburg ('90) and Michael Rosenfeld  2018.39

A multidimensional artist, writer, and critic, Benny Andrews rooted himself in the history of African Americans in the rural South: a history familiar to him from his own childhood in Plainview, Georgia. He drew from his family's struggles and triumphs over the brutal conditions found there and made them the foundation for his work. The matriarch of the family, Viola Andrews, made sure her children had a grounding in their Christian faith, an education beyond the basic skills taught in the local one-room structure, and—for Benny—the resources needed to express himself through art. This required great persistence and determination, since the artist was one of ten children. Based on circumstances and tradition, the large sharecropping family constituted a formidable workforce, and all were needed to work the unforgiving Georgia red clay. Annually, they planted, cultivated, and picked cotton as a means to earn their livelihood. Through it all, Benny Andrew's affection for his mother remained constant.

Andrews's portrait is symbolic of Viola's importance in his and his siblings' upbringing and sense of purpose in the world. Standing in a cotton field with her left hand resting on her hip, Mother Andrews, wearing a red sweater and a dainty white hat, appears confident and in control. Collecting bolls of cotton in a canvas or burlap bag, she leads the way for her children and others to follow. Like Moses, she is equipped with a staff or "rod," which will be used to lay her enemies out, part the sea of misery, and eventually lead her children from the fields in Morgan County to the promised land of Atlanta and beyond. In Benny Andrews's eyes, and in his memory, his mother was the muse that inspired him to create some of his most important works, especially in the late 1960s and early 1970s.

Indeed, by 1969, in the midst of producing his most anticipated and most ambitious project to date, the *Bicentennial Series* on the occasion of the nation's 200th birthday in 1976, Andrews realized his vision of America in hundreds of drawings and paintings. Since he first imagined the "six for seventy-six" exhibition, which would be comprised of a series of six mural-sized paintings

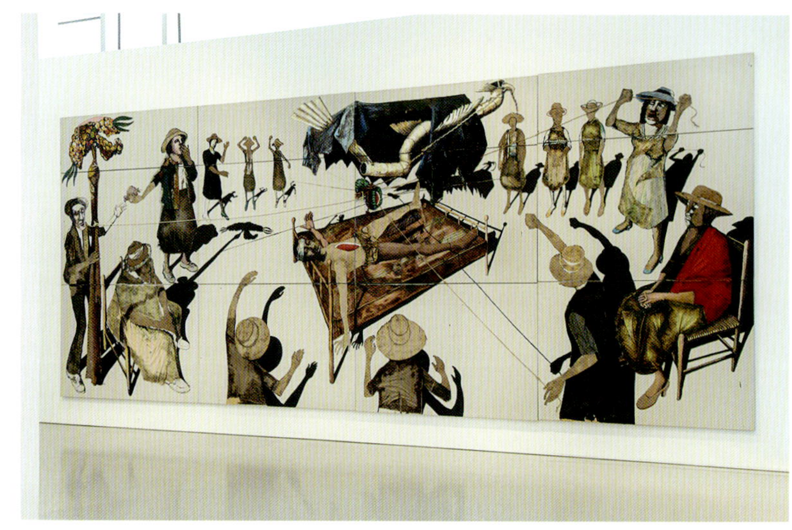

FIG. 1. Benny Andrews, *Circle*, 1973. Oil on twelve linen canvases with painted fabric and mixed-media collage, 10 × 24 ft., installation view

representing lesser known American realities, Andrews stretched his artistic faculties in an effort to give voice to those often silenced by history. Of the six murals, *Circle* (fig. 1), which was completed in 1973, is deeply connected to the artist's family history, and especially to his mother.

Reminiscent of a "Ring Shout" ritual out of the traditions of the Pentecostal Church, Andrews's mural depicts black women surrounding a black man lying face up on a bed. Above him hovers a wraithlike creature that, apparently under the control of the women, extracts a slice of watermelon from the man's chest. In this community, women have the power to conjure spirits and/or mythological creatures capable of assisting men in purging their cowardice and claiming their manhood. This communal exercise, as represented by Andrews, was a way for African American women to lay claim to their gifts as "root workers." Collectively, they are powerful healers and givers of life, and more than capable of challenging the structures that continue to deny African American men and boys their humanity. These acts of resistance served to heal the damaged psyches of black men, who are still daily bombarded by institutionalized racism and white supremacy. The discerning imagery found in *Mrs. Viola Andrews—My Mother* speaks volumes to the power of African American women, who have parted many a sea to provide safe passage for their children and their communities.

Pellom McDaniels III, PhD
Curator of African American Collections,
Emory University

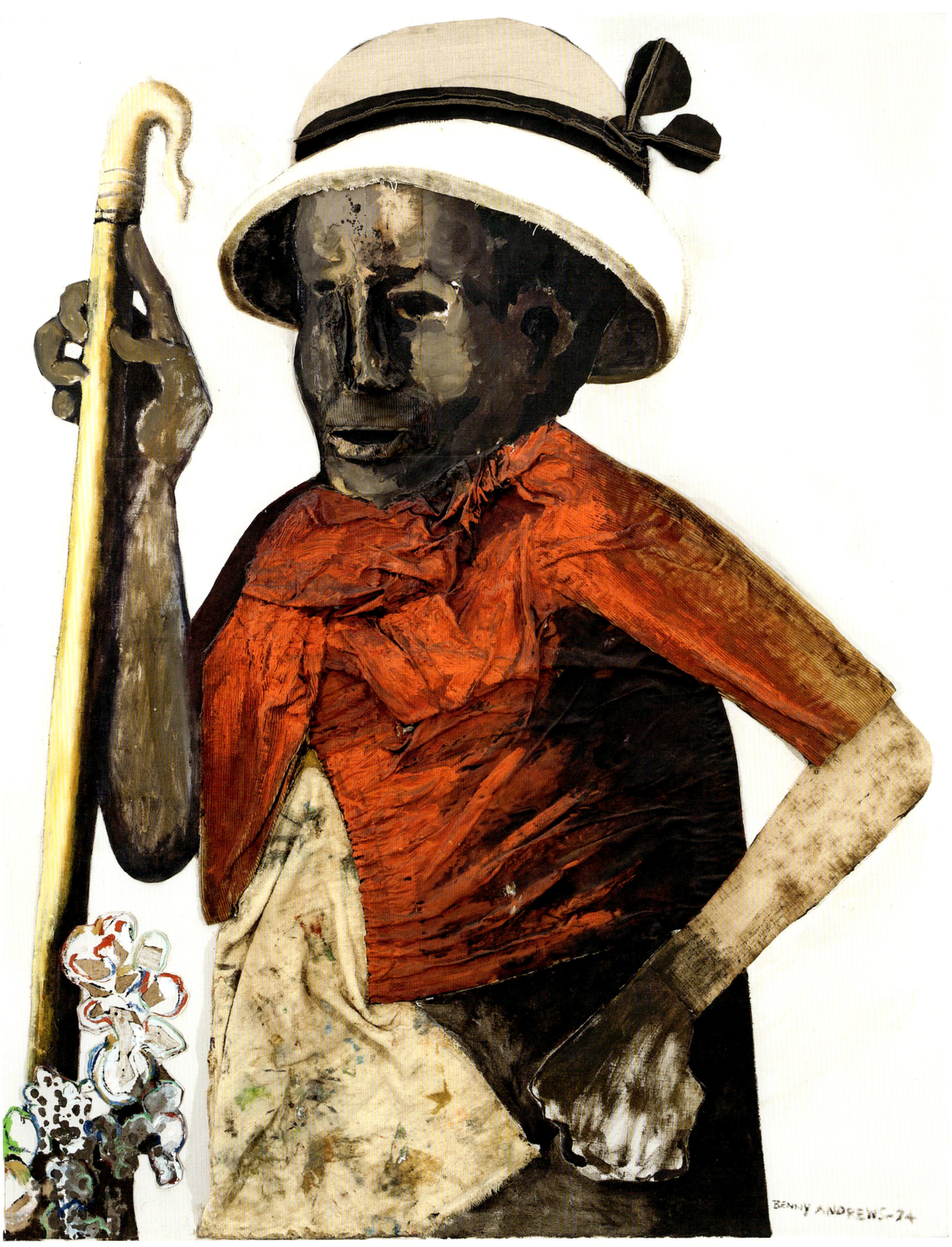
BENNY ANDREWS -74

# Double Cherry Blossoms

Alma Woodsey Thomas (American, 1891–1978), 1973
Acrylic on canvas, 60 × 40⅛ in. (152.4 × 101.9 cm)
Gift of halley k harrisburg, Class of 1990, and Michael Rosenfeld  2003.28

With the completion of *Air View of a Spring Nursery* in 1966—the first painting in what became known as her *Earth* series—Alma Thomas inserted herself definitively into the long-standing cultural discourse that elides the floral and the feminine. From ancient reliefs of the Greek goddess Demeter to Botticelli's iconic *Primavera*, and from the highly accomplished output of nineteenth-century naturalists like Henrietta Benson Homer (fig. 1) to the oversized blossoms of Georgia O'Keeffe, humans have frequently conflated the archetypal reproductive capabilities of women with the life-sustaining fecundity of the earth, an impulse that has often manifested in fruit, flower, and foliage imagery. Inflected with aspects of Anglo-Catholic Christianity, American Transcendentalism, second-wave feminism, and 1970s environmentalism, works like *Double*

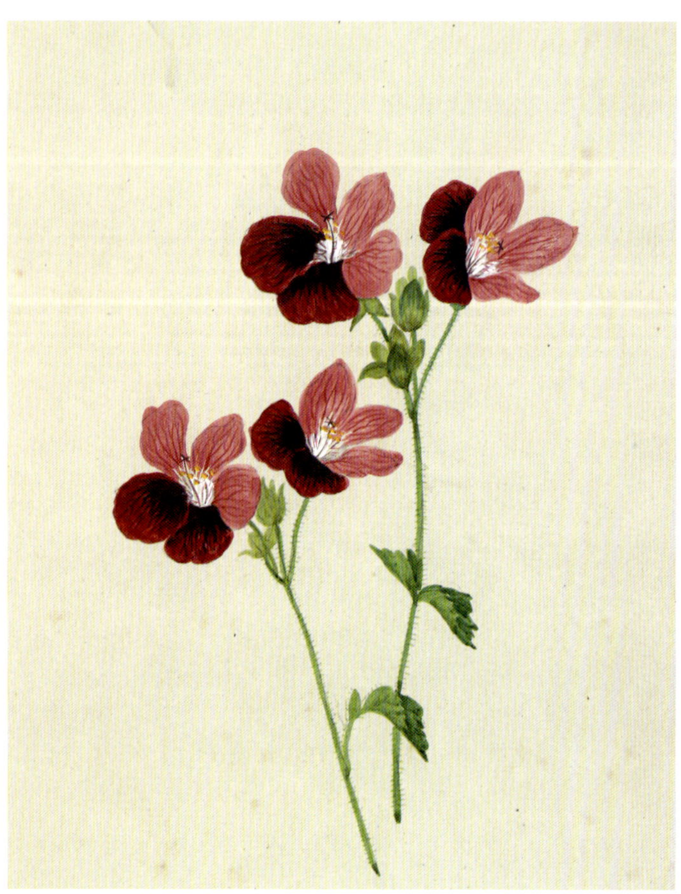

*Cherry Blossoms* evidence Thomas's intelligent and determined reimagination of this time-honored subject matter, updating it for the second half of the twentieth century. As a longtime resident of Washington, D.C., she took her hometown's celebrated Japanese cherry trees as source of inspiration, a theme that resonated with her interest in natural splendor, cultural exchange, and public benefit.

Thomas's intense and searching exploration of the figure-ground relationship in her late paintings has led critics and scholars to liken these compositions to screens and lattices.[1] In his influential book *The Souls of Black Folk* (1903), activist and author W. E. B. Du Bois famously employed an analogous symbol—"the veil"—to approximate what he termed the "double consciousness" of African Americans.[2] "For Du Bois," Howard Winant explains, "the veil is a complex metaphor for the dynamics of race. It represents both barrier and connection between white and black. Imagine it as a filmy fabric, a soft and semitransparent border marker, that both keeps the races apart and mediates between them."[3] Du Bois's intertwined concepts of double consciousness and the veil operate along three valences: first, African Americans only appear legible when thrown into contrast against the framework of white hegemony;[4] second, the veil prevents Caucasians from seeing African Americans without distortion; third, in dialogic and mutually reinforcing fashion, the veil precludes blacks from clearly perceiving whites.

These dynamics play out, albeit metaphorically, across the surface of Bowdoin's canvas. Infused with the fragrance of Thomas's own experiences as a twentieth-century African American woman, the allover array of nearly monochromatic brushstrokes set starkly against a plain background generously offers the viewer the phenomenological equivalent of "double consciousness"—of being othered—with all the responsibilities toward our fellow human beings that follow from such an epiphanic encounter.

Jonathan Frederick Walz
Director of Curatorial Affairs and Curator
of American Art, Columbus Museum,
Columbus, Georgia

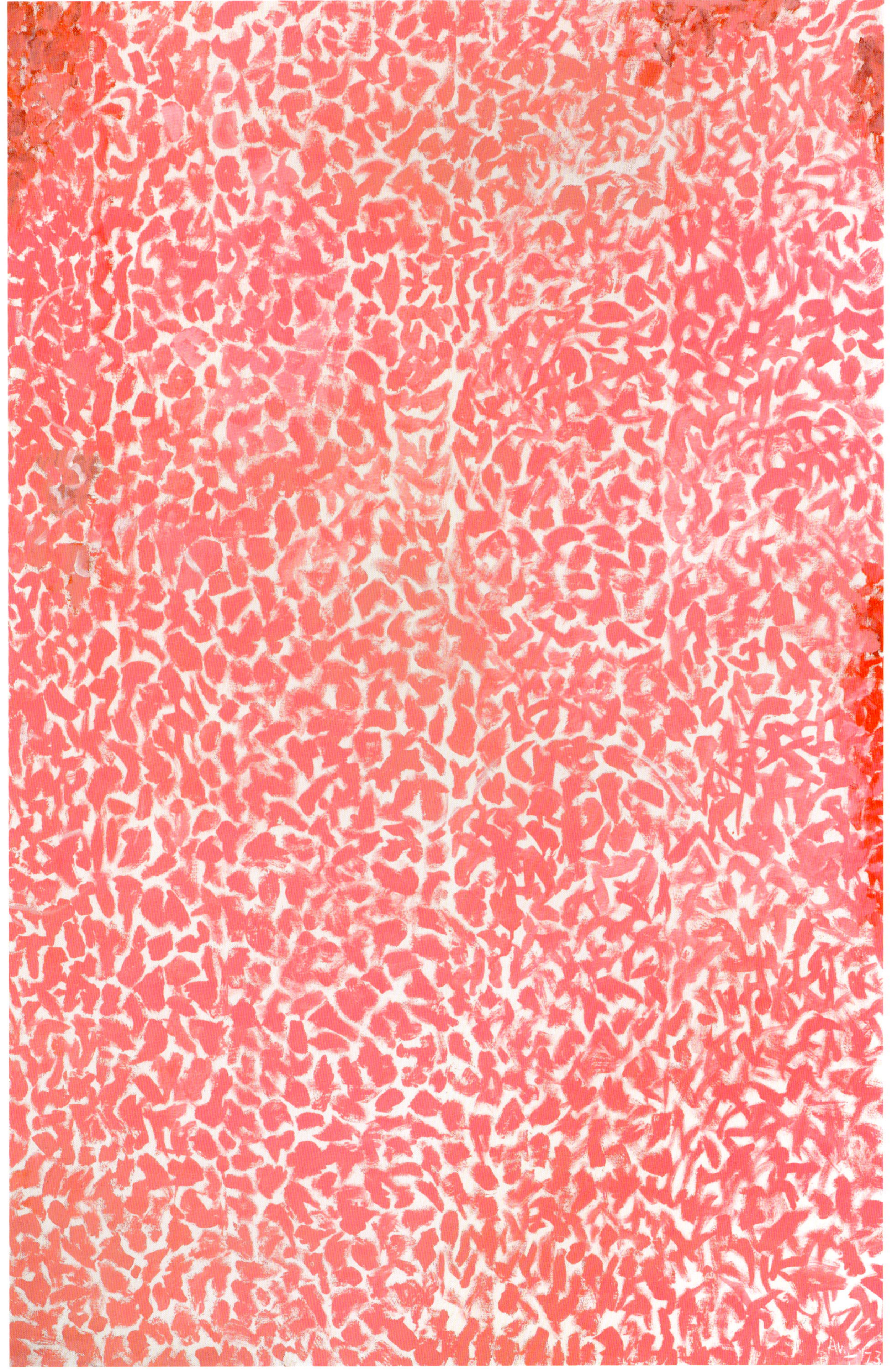

# *Untitled (Ramapo Freeze)*

Richard Pousette-Dart (American, 1916–1992), 1976
Graphite on textured paper with deckle edges, 22½ × 30 in.
(57.2 × 76.2 cm)
Gift of the Richard Pousette-Dart Estate  2018.44

Richard Pousette-Dart's hands must be pictured in constant motion, applying oil and acrylic paint in short strokes and dabs with encrusted brushes to stretched canvasses, filling page after page of notebooks, more than 200 in all, with illuminations and thoughtful aphorisms about art and spirituality, dipping teabags into boiling water, moving, pencil in hand, across large sheets of paper. They tinkered with electronic equipment to construct and operate ham radios, cut symbolic shapes out of sheets of brass as gifts to friends and family, and strung together wire sculptures. The studio in Suffern, New York, is still today filled with many surfaces animated by Pousette-Dart's touch, and the building itself seems to reverberate with the energy that the artist drew from his environment and passed on to others. Constructed of fieldstones and dappled with light filtered by the surrounding woods, sheltered by the Ramapo Mountains along the river of the same name, the studio offers a vision of the unity of art and life.

The intuitive access to this perceived unity and the bursts of creativity it sets free were an experience Richard Pousette-Dart shared with his parents, writer and art director Nathaniel Pousette-Dart and poet Flora Pousette-Dart. He, in turn, passed it on to his children and grandchildren. "We'd run up the stairway and into my grandfather's studio, knowing that we would find Richard painting," grandson Chris Pousette-Dart remembers. "We also knew he'd at once set out art materials for us: cardboard, string, Styrofoam, wood, mails, paint, brushes, and glue. Surrounded by the large canvases set on easels, the floor, and leaning against chairs and racks, Richard would turn up the music and set us to work."[1] As a teacher at Sara Lawrence College and other New York–area schools,[2] Richard Pousette-Dart refused to identify "mandatory skills," which he considered "destructive to the inspiration of true, original, creative thinking and feeling." Instead, he modeled an unconditional commitment to art making: "We can only teach what we have the courage to *be* ourselves."[3] The continuous

coordination of eye and hand, the application—"tuning"—of marks that build on, comment on, or obliterate each other, that slow transformation of the picture plain into a microcosm of visual impulses, this meditative process Pousette-Dart believed could be equally enlightening for the maker and the viewers of a work.

*Untitled (Ramapo Freeze)* is quietly monumental. Harmoniously balanced, multidirectional graphite marks of various lengths and densities fill the entire sheet, up to its beveled edges. They center the viewer's gaze on a horizon indicated by more forcefully applied clusters of short vertical hatching. A few brief horizontal lines indicate a vertical axis that further acknowledges the viewer's perspective. While the eye detects a myriad of graphite traces, the mind sees brilliant light emanating from the drawing. This glow can only be explained as a result of the artist's deep understanding of the field of vision and his deliberate manipulation of our perception in areas of focus as well as on the periphery. Situated "just on the edge of awareness,"[4] works such as Bowdoin's drawing effectively evoke an aura that has motivated artists' forays into abstraction since the early twentieth century. Walter Benjamin called it a "unique appearance of distance, no matter how close,"[5] and Vasily Kandinsky identified it as "particular spiritual sound."[6] Among Pousette-Dart's attempts to articulate its wonders is the following:

> *art is a spiritual thing / a work which through the /
> integrity of work transcends / and takes on the /
> luminosity / and pure joy of inseparable / spiritual
> ends + means*

> *art is moving stillness / and stillness moving / music of
> silence and / silent music / a dance of life within / the
> figure of being / the absoluteness of intuition / wherein
> all is flux and change*[7]

Joachim Homann
Curator, Bowdoin College Museum of Art

# *Northern Lights*

Barkley L. Hendricks (American, 1945–2017), 1976
Oil and acrylic on canvas, 72 × 72 in. (183 × 183 cm)
Lent by "A Friend of the Museum"

Can black people be free to be themselves?

"Boston-based brother," the subject of *Northern Lights*, is. He looks fly in his dope jacket adorned with a white, bright fur collar. Slices of red pop at the collar and the wrist. He is slim-with-the-tilted-brim that sits, just right, atop an almost perfectly picked fro. Three different shades of green, from head to toe, show Boston-based brother knows the secret is—you got to coordinate.

Fly, but not super.

"Someone once referred to the figure I did in the *Northern Lights* painting as a pimp," wrote Hendricks. "I said, I once saw Ronald Reagan in the same large fur-collared coat. Did that make him a pimp?"[1] No. A butter-soft leather cannot make Reagan, or Boston-based brother, a pimp any more than a navy-blue blazer can make Boston-based brother the President. The difference, however, is that most Americans allow Reagan 360 degrees of complexity, whereas they afford the subject of *Northern Lights* zero. Boston-based brother is black, confident, male, conspicuous, proud, and, I think, happy. *Northern Lights* does not depict a cartoon, a stereotype, or a one-dimensional type caste.

Plenty of black men, from all different walks of life, who crossed the streets of New Haven in 1976, and crossed paths with Hendricks, could have dressed like Boston-based brother. The Great Migrations of the twentieth century transformed black agricultural workers from the South into members of the northern working classes. For some, metropolises offered new freedoms, expressed not so much in the politics of the ballot box, but in cultures that pushed against boundaries of gender, sexuality, andindividuality.

*Northern Lights* captures these aspects of black personhood. It is emblematic of Hendricks's oeuvre, which depicts an array of black individualities. Hendricks excelled in allowing his subjects to be free to be fully human, with emotions and moods that run the complete gamut of human complexity. When I viewed his works on display at the Bowdoin College Museum of Art in 2017, I turned

from the ebullience of *Northern Lights* to the solemnity and stoicism of *FTA* (fig. 1). Both display different, competing expressions of humanity, blackness, and Americanness. In Hendricks's deft hands, black people become large. We contain multitudes.

Hendricks's blackness did not predispose him to capture black humanity with depth, nuance, brilliance, or beauty. Plenty of black people, like plenty of all people, are perfectly happy trafficking in one-dimensional characterizations of blackness. Stereotypes sell. Cartoons create cash.

Hendricks connected with his subjects, first and foremost, because he loved them as they are: raw, nude (as are many of his portraits), imperfect. A master of his craft, he created brilliantly and skillfully, studiously and scrupulously. The gorgeousness of his work comes from techniques he refined in elite art schools. The uniqueness of

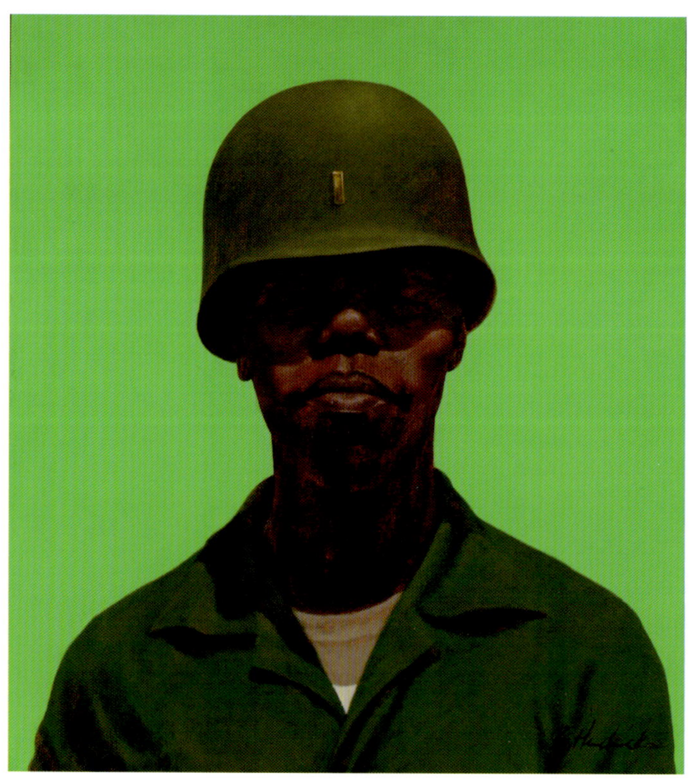

FIG. 1. Barkley L. Hendricks, *FTA*, 1968. Oil on canvas, 27½ × 25 in. (69.8 × 63.5 cm). Private Collection

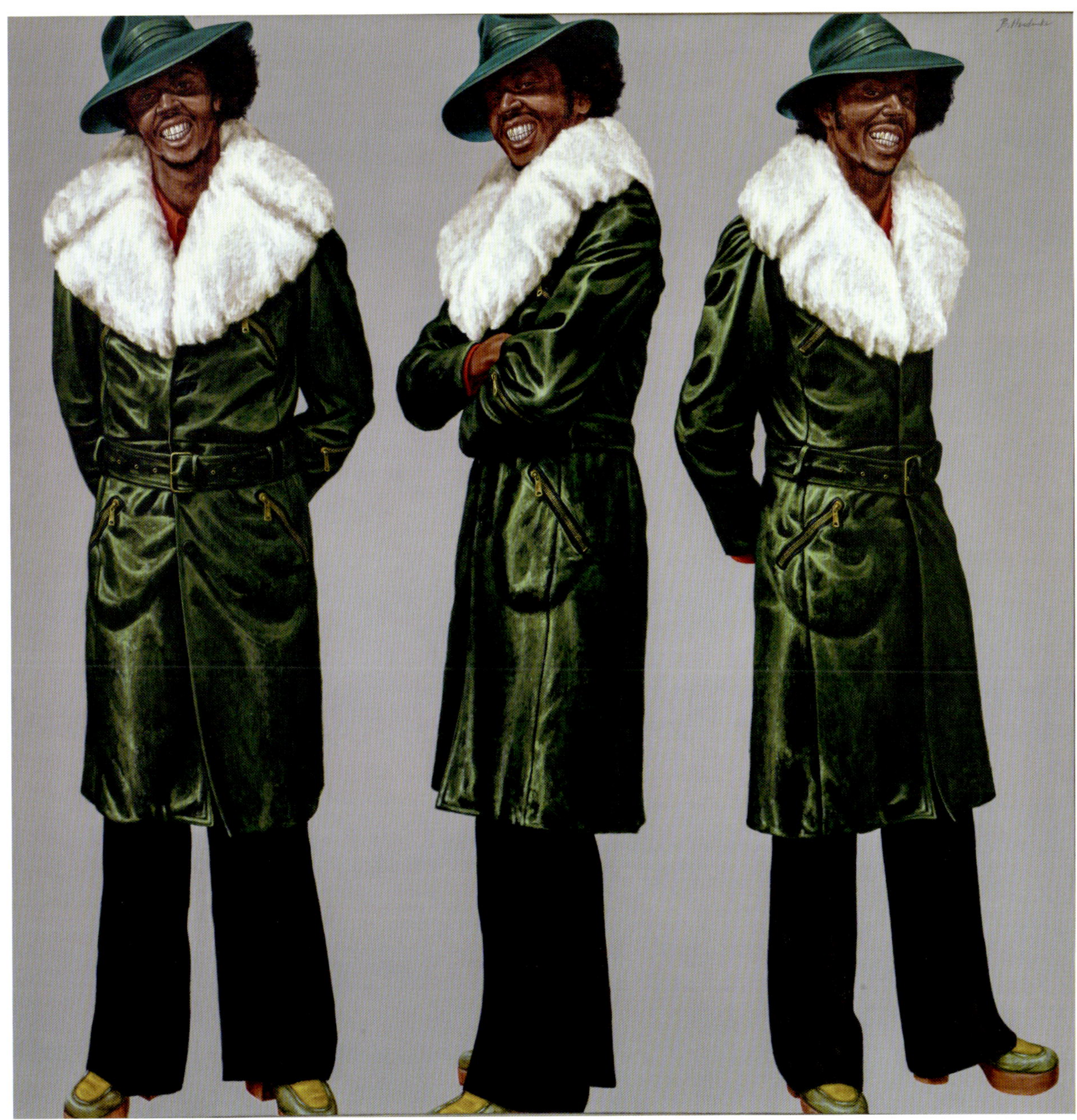

his subjects comes from Hendricks's intuitive ability to see beauty and depth in seemingly ordinary subjects.

Hendricks pivoted away from a strain of post-1960s African American art that made black political struggle synonymous with pain. He captured black politics through depictions of both anger and pleasure. "I'm not one of those people who deal with the areas of sadness, the areas of woe, the areas of misery," he said. "I like what I do. And I can look at it for a long time."[2]

Us too.

In looking at *Northern Lights*, and many of Hendricks's portraits, for a long time, we catch a glimpse of black subjects as they are, and hopefully as they wanted to be: Full. Free. Lovely.

Brian Purnell
Geoffrey Canada Associate Professor
of Africana Studies and History and
Director of the Africana Studies Program,
Bowdoin College

# *Christopher Street Pier #2 (Crossed Legs)*

Peter Hujar (American, 1934–1987), 1976
Vintage gelatin silver print, 19¾ × 15⅞ in. (50 × 40 cm)
Museum Purchase, Lloyd O. and Marjorie Strong Coulter Fund  2016.8

Standing in Midtown Manhattan is the last place you expect to smell salt water. But there my friend Hugo and I stopped to notice the faint ocean breeze. "Sometimes you forget New York is a maritime city," Hugo smirked. Taking a break from a conference at the CUNY Graduate Center and flanked by Starbucks and a FedEx Office, the subtle scent of sea air served as a reminder that in that cycle of abandonment, rebuilding, dislocation, and gentrification, you are still connected to something permanent. I can only imagine the New York of the 1970s through stark realist cinema and even starker urban photography, captured in images like Peter Hujar's *Christopher Street Pier #2*, and constantly held up as the romanticized exemplar of a lost (and last) real version of urban life. Of course, Hujar was capturing his own era of creative destruction in New York's history, and documenting the pleasures and pleasant boredoms available in this interstitial space between land and sea, industry and open air, at this conjunctural moment between deindustrialization and finance-industry-propelled commercialization. Here (or rather there . . . and then), the warmth of the sun, perhaps the same smell of salt, and the quiet of the empty docks might connect the senses to a space that has been rezoned in both a municipal and affective framework.

I began with smells, sounds, and haptics in part resisting how this image demands to be read so *visually*. The primary figure is photographed from the perspective of his crossed legs, folded in on themselves and creating a triangle through which the viewer is invited to see just a bit of a face and the hazy nondescript mid-rising buildings where the city begins. The peculiar geometry of the legs, the invitation of the gaze, the geography of pier, the freedom and foreshadowing intertwined in later generations' imagining of gay sex in the 1970s—it is all framed here a little too neatly. Are we to (only) understand Hujar's camera here as stand-in for phallic/ocular desire? Biographical accounts of the artist emphasize Hujar's exciting sex life, associating this with Chelsea Piers and the thrill of cruising. But cruising is so much more than getting off with strangers. Cruising is a ritual shared by generations of gay men, practiced across different analog and digital terrains. Common to all the different ways that gay men have cruised is the art of waiting—opening up spaces of looking, chatting, pruning, giving up, and giving in. It can involve equal parts anticipation and boredom. Cruising also involves semiotic swapping—hurried exchanges of symbols (coded hankies, foot taps, backward glances, nudes)—and the collection of experiences. Tricks become memories, and memories become archives.

Douglas Crimp suggested that cruising characterizes all of Hujar's photographs of the urban landscape, including images without people.[1] I agree. But in this photograph, it is not so much about the people who may be lurking just out of the camera's view of empty lots, but the architectural character of the body that melds into the surroundings. Returning to the legs that serve as the central object and the frame of the image, I can imagine desire but also curiosity. Why did Hujar decide to look through the legs? Did he see this perspective while strolling the boardwalk? What would happen if the figure shifted his balance and changed the way these two bent limbs folded into each other? What other shapes could Hujar see or make happen? The figure becomes another part of the receding Lower Manhattan that Hujar was so set on recording.

Joseph Jay Sosa
Assistant Professor of Gender, Sexuality,
and Women's Studies, Bowdoin College

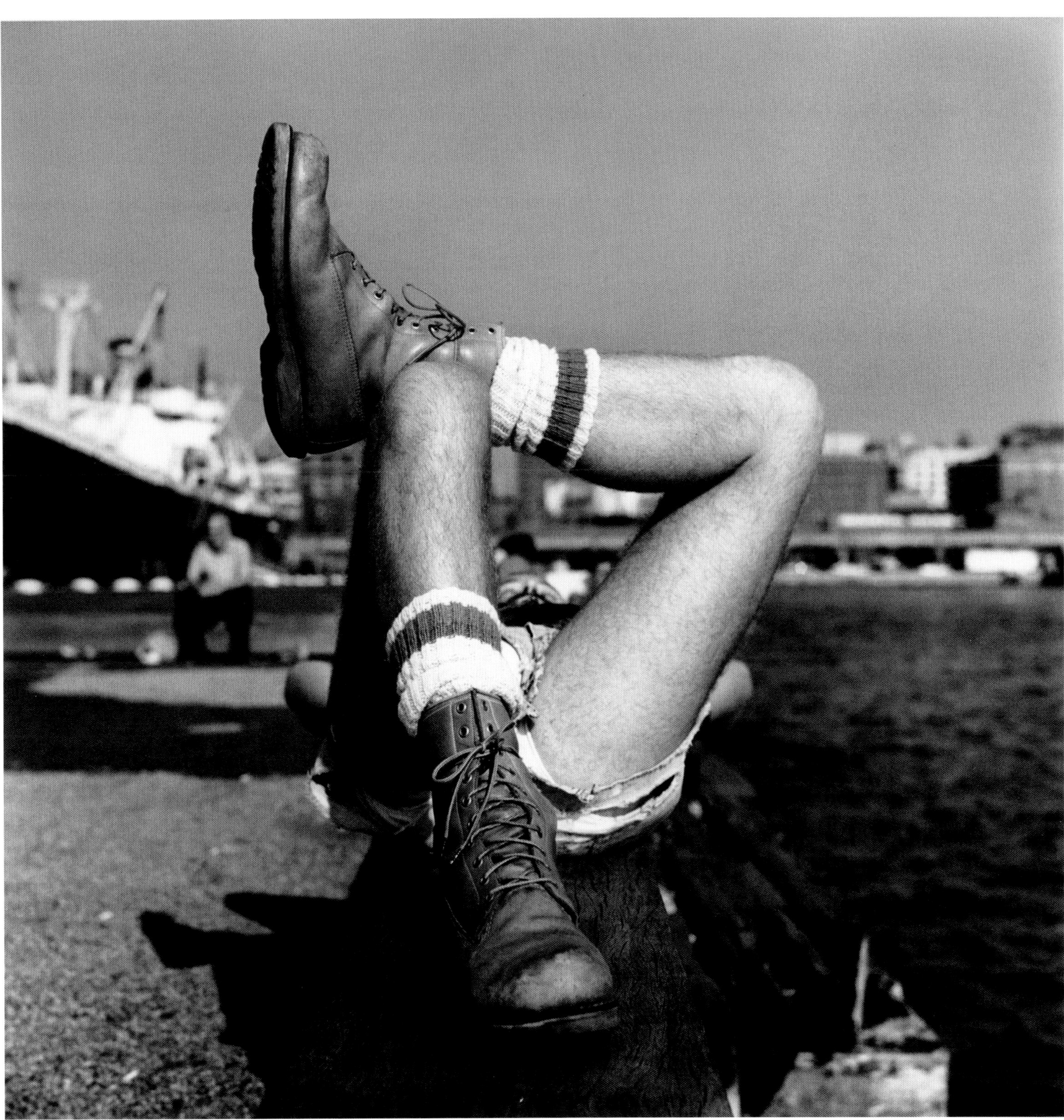

# Inflammatory Essays

Jenny Holzer (American, born 1950), 1979–82
Offset lithographs on paper, each 10 × 10 in. (25.4 × 25.4 cm)
Gift of David P. Becker, Class of 1970  1994.10.247–.258

What does ideology look like?

Whether Jenny Holzer's art takes the form of neon signs, taxi cab ads, apparel, building projections, posters, paintings, or sculpture, it is always about the construction and undoing of power. Her text-based works reveal language as simultaneously constitutive of human subjectivity and as a system that can conscript otherwise free-willed subjects into authoritative and ideological regimes. Language commands, provokes, questions, tempts, and, in the case of the *Inflammatory Essays*, metaphorically combusts.

Conceived in 1979, and inspired by Holzer's study of political manifestos, the *Inflammatory Essays* convey dogma, extremism, and fanaticism in a shrill and often cacophonous chorus.[1] An homage to the creative and destructive capacity of the manifesto, the "essays" are in fact short and standardized: 100-word paragraphs of twenty lines each, printed in the same font on colorful paper, containing various incendiary slogans.[2] Produced in a variety of sizes approximate to that of a small poster, they were originally presented in *The Manifesto Show*, an exhibition organized by Colab in 1979 at 5 Bleecker Street in New York. Invited to present their own texts alongside historical manifestos on art and politics, artists were asked "to write, say, or somehow present as an image what you want to have happen—or don't—what is dearest to your heart, and what makes you furious."[3]

Holzer produced a pastiche of taboo-breaking texts (unrelated to her personal convictions) in response to a variety of topical and polarizing issues of the day. In 1982, she wheat-pasted them individually in public spaces around Manhattan, where they would confront unsuspecting pedestrians who, over time, would recognize in their standardized format a larger effort.

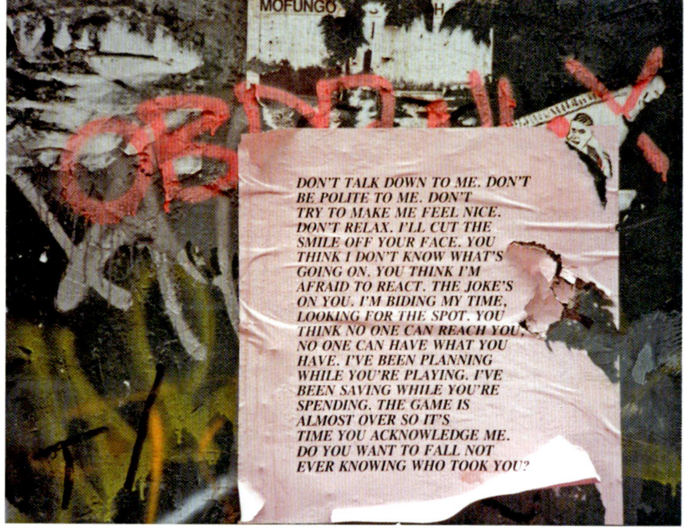


The process of reading the *Essays* involves constantly shuttling back and forth between text and context: between the ostensible subject of the essay at hand and the moment of reading; between a sentence and its contextual meaning within the paragraph; between the text and its physical location. In the process, fragments of language give rise to an ideological voice, allowing us to see, read, and hear how power takes shape in the permanence of words, the evanescence of actions, and here, as an aesthetic form.[4]

Holzer's intention was to "write things that were very hot—in tone and subject matter—to (hopefully) instill a sense of urgency in the reader. I wanted the reader to jump, at least, and maybe consider doing something useful."[5] Together, the *Inflammatory Essays* stage an ambivalent relationship to hard-edged ideology, at once showing the danger and absurdity of fanaticism but also honoring the crucial role of ideological commitment in making change happen.

Ellen Tani
Assistant Curator, Institute of
Contemporary Art, Boston

THE END OF THE U.S.A.
ALL YOU RICH FUCKERS SEE
THE BEGINNING OF THE END AND
TAKE WHAT YOU CAN WHILE
YOU CAN. YOU IMAGINE THAT
YOU WILL GET AWAY, BUT
YOU'VE SHIT IN YOUR OWN
BED AND YOU'RE THE ONE TO
SLEEP IN IT. WHY SHOULD
EVERYONE ELSE STAY BEHIND
AND SMELL YOUR STINKING
COWARDICE? HERE'S A MESSAGE
TO YOU—SPACE TRAVEL IS
UNCERTAIN AND ANY REFUGE
OF YOURS CAN BE BLOWN
OFF THE MAP. THERE'S NO
OTHER PLACE FOR YOU TO GO.
KNOW THAT YOUR FUTURE IS
WITH US SO DON'T GIVE US
MORE REASONS TO HATE YOU.

THE MOST EXQUISITE PLEASURE IS
DOMINATION. NOTHING CAN COMPARE
WITH THE FEELING. THE MENTAL
SENSATIONS ARE EVEN BETTER THAN
THE PHYSICAL ONES. KNOWING YOU
HAVE POWER HAS TO BE THE BIGGEST
HIGH, THE GREATEST COMFORT.
IT IS COMPLETE SECURITY,
PROTECTION FROM HURT. WHEN
YOU DOMINATE SOMEBODY YOU'RE
DOING HIM A FAVOR. HE PRAYS
SOMEONE WILL CONTROL HIM, TAKE
HIS MIND OFF HIS TROUBLES. YOU'RE
HELPING HIM WHILE HELPING
YOURSELF. EVEN WHEN YOU GET
MEAN HE LIKES IT. SOMETIMES
HE'S ANGRY AND FIGHTS BACK BUT
YOU CAN HANDLE IT. HE ALWAYS
REMEMBERS WHAT HE NEEDS. YOU
ALWAYS GET WHAT YOU WANT.

REJOICE! OUR TIMES ARE INTOLERABLE.
TAKE COURAGE, FOR THE WORST IS A
HARBINGER OF THE BEST. ONLY
DIRE CIRCUMSTANCE CAN PRECIPITATE
THE OVERTHROW OF OPPRESSORS. THE
OLD AND CORRUPT MUST BE LAID TO
WASTE BEFORE THE JUST CAN TRIUMPH.
OPPOSITION IDENTIFIES AND
ISOLATES THE ENEMY. CONFLICT
OF INTEREST MUST BE SEEN FOR
WHAT IT IS. DO NOT SUPPORT
PALLIATIVE GESTURES; THEY CONFUSE
THE PEOPLE AND DELAY THE INEVITABLE
CONFRONTATION. DELAY IS NOT
TOLERATED FOR IT JEOPARDIZES THE
WELL-BEING OF THE MAJORITY.
CONTRADICTION WILL BE HEIGHTENED.
THE RECKONING WILL BE HASTENED BY
THE STAGING OF SEED DISTURBANCES.
THE APOCALYPSE WILL BLOSSOM.

SHRIEK WHEN THE PAIN HITS
DURING INTERROGATION. REACH
INTO THE DARK AGES TO FIND A
SOUND THAT IS LIQUID HORROR,
A SOUND OF THE BRINK WHERE
MAN STOPS AND THE BEAST
AND NAMELESS CRUEL FORCES
BEGIN. SCREAM WHEN YOUR
LIFE IS THREATENED. FORM A
NOISE SO TRUE THAT YOUR
TORMENTOR RECOGNIZES IT AS A
VOICE THAT LIVES IN HIS OWN
THROAT. THE TRUE SOUND TELLS
HIM THAT HE CUTS HIS FLESH
WHEN HE CUTS YOURS, THAT
HE CANNOT THRIVE AFTER HE
TORTURES YOU. SCREAM THAT HE
DESTROYS ALL KINDNESS IN YOU
AND BLACKENS EVERY VISION
YOU COULD HAVE SHOWN HIM.

CHANGE IS THE BASIS OF ALL HISTORY,
THE PROOF OF VIGOR. THE OLD IS
SOILED AND DISGUSTING BY NATURE.
STALE FOOD IS REPELLENT, MONOGAMOUS
LOVE BREEDS CONTEMPT, SENILITY
CRIPPLES THE GOVERNMENT THAT IS
TOO POWERFUL TOO LONG. UPHEAVAL
IS DESIRABLE BECAUSE FRESH, UNTAINTED
GROUPS SEIZE OPPORTUNITY..VIOLENT
OVERTHROW IS APPROPRIATE WHEN THE
SITUATION IS INTOLERABLE. SLOW
MODIFICATION CAN BE EFFECTIVE;
MEN CHANGE BEFORE THEY NOTICE
AND RESIST. THE DECADENT AND
THE POWERFUL CHAMPION CONTINUITY.
"NOTHING ESSENTIAL CHANGES." THAT
IS A MYTH. IT WILL BE REFUTED.
THE NECESSARY BIRTH CONVULSIONS
WILL BE TRIGGERED. ACTION WILL
BRING THE EVIDENCE TO YOUR DOORSTEP.

FEAR IS THE MOST ELEGANT WEAPON,
YOUR HANDS ARE NEVER MESSY.
THREATENING BODILY HARM IS CRUDE.
WORK INSTEAD ON MINDS AND BELIEFS,
PLAY INSECURITIES LIKE A PIANO. BE
CREATIVE IN APPROACH. FORCE
ANXIETY TO EXCRUCIATING LEVELS OR
GENTLY UNDERMINE THE PUBLIC
CONFIDENCE. PANIC DRIVES HUMAN HERDS
OVER CLIFFS; AN ALTERNATIVE IS
TERROR-INDUCED IMMOBILIZATION. FEAR
FEEDS ON FEAR. PUT THIS EFFICIENT
PROCESS IN MOTION. MANIPULATION IS
NOT LIMITED TO PEOPLE. ECONOMIC,
SOCIAL AND DEMOCRATIC INSTITUTIONS
CAN BE SHAKEN. IT WILL BE
DEMONSTRATED THAT NOTHING IS SAFE,
SACRED OR SANE. THERE IS NO
RESPITE FROM HORROR. ABSOLUTES ARE
QUICKSILVER. RESULTS ARE SPECTACULAR.

YOU GET AMAZING SENSATIONS FROM
GUNS. YOU GET RESULTS FROM GUNS.
MAN IS AN AGGRESSIVE ANIMAL;
YOU HAVE TO HAVE A GOOD OFFENSE
AND A GOOD DEFENSE. TOO MANY
CITIZENS THINK THEY ARE HELPLESS.
THEY LEAVE EVERYTHING TO THE
AUTHORITIES AND THIS CAUSES
CORRUPTION. RESPONSIBILITY
SHOULD GO BACK WHERE IT BELONGS.
IT IS YOUR LIFE SO TAKE CONTROL
AND FEEL VITAL. THERE MAY BE
SOME ACCIDENTS ALONG THE PATH
TO SELF-EXPRESSION AND SELF-
DETERMINATION. SOME HARMLESS
PEOPLE WILL BE HURT. HOWEVER,
G-U-N SPELLS PRIDE TO THE
STRONG, SAFETY TO THE WEAK
AND HOPE TO THE HOPELESS.
GUNS MAKE WRONG RIGHT FAST.

DON'T TALK DOWN TO ME. DON'T
BE POLITE TO ME. DON'T
TRY TO MAKE ME FEEL NICE.
DON'T RELAX. I'LL CUT THE
SMILE OFF YOUR FACE. YOU
THINK I DON'T KNOW WHAT'S
GOING ON. YOU THINK I'M
AFRAID TO REACT. THE JOKE'S
ON YOU. I'M BIDING MY TIME,
LOOKING FOR THE SPOT. YOU
THINK NO ONE CAN REACH YOU,
NO ONE CAN HAVE WHAT YOU
HAVE. I'VE BEEN PLANNING
WHILE YOU'RE PLAYING. I'VE
BEEN SAVING WHILE YOU'RE
SPENDING. THE GAME IS
ALMOST OVER SO IT'S
TIME YOU ACKNOWLEDGE ME.
DO YOU WANT TO FALL NOT
EVER KNOWING WHO TOOK YOU?

WHAT SCARES PEASANTS IS
THINKING THEIR BODIES WILL
BE THROWN OUT IN PUBLIC AND
LEFT TO ROT. THEY FEEL SHAME—
AS IF IT MATTERS WHAT POSITION
THEIR LEGS ARE IN WHEN
THEY'RE DEAD. LUCKY THEY'RE
SUPERSTITIOUS BECAUSE THEY'RE
EASIER TO MANAGE. MAKE AN
EXAMPLE OF 2 OR 3 REBELS,
DROP THEIR BODIES BY A ROAD,
GET THEM FLAT AND DRY
SO BONES SHOW AND THE GRASS
WEARS THE CLOTHES. SHOOT
THE FINGERS OFF ANYONE WHO
COMES TO COLLECT THE REMAINS.
THOSE BODIES STAY AS A SIGN
OF ABSOLUTE AUTHORITY. IF
PEASANTS THINK THEIR SOULS
CAN'T REST, SO MUCH THE BETTER.

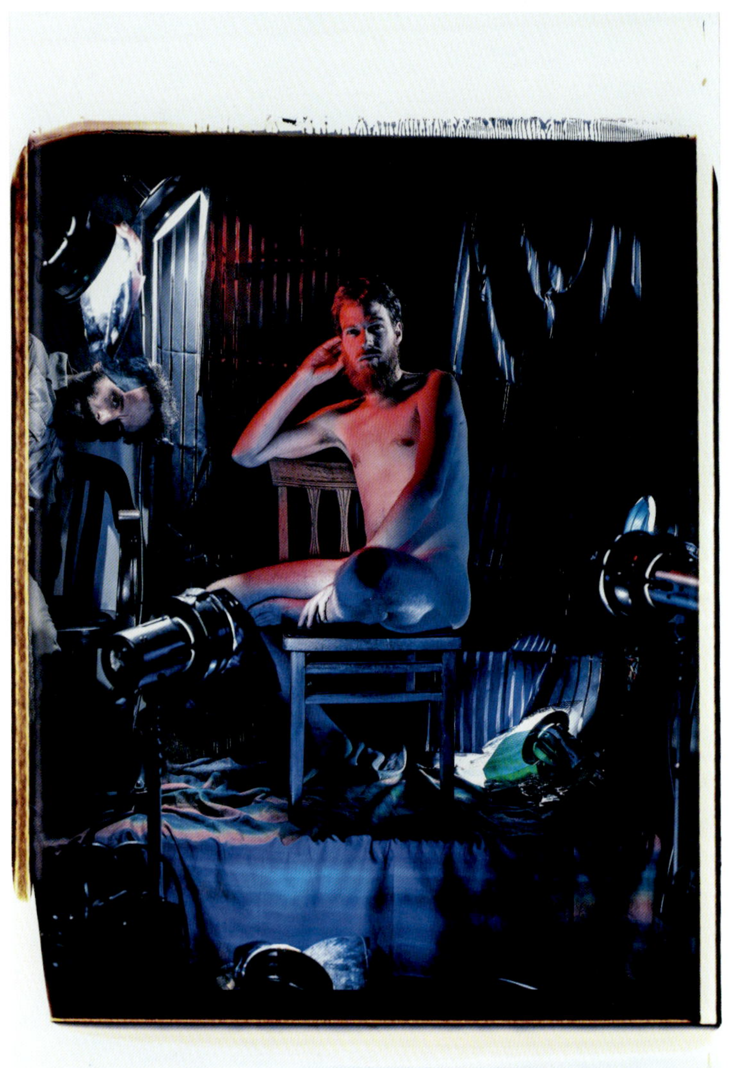

# *Sittings (Patterson Sims)*

Lucas Samaras (American, born 1936), 1980
Polaroid, 24 × 20 in. (60.9 × 50.8 cm)
Archival Collection of Marion Boulton Stroud and Acadia Summer Arts
Program, Mt. Desert Island, Maine. Gift from the Marion Boulton "Kippy"
Stroud Foundation  2018.10.253

With the 20×24 polaroid camera, Lucas Samaras brought a technological behemoth into his studio. He set up colorful lights, draperies, and a kitchen chair, before exposing his sitters and himself to the dispassionate eye of the camera (and those of the two technicians needed to operate the 200 pounds worth of equipment). The resulting oversized color prints are confounding—a glimpse into an instantaneous artistic transformation witnessed by the artist and revealed in great detail to the viewer. This and other large-scale polaroids of the series anticipate the intrusion of communication technology into the most personal aspects of people's lives. While they might be less delirious and intimate than Samaras's earlier photographic self-portraits—he had worked with smaller-format polaroids for a decade before the 20×24 became available, often collaging and physically manipulating the images—the luscious, larger works preserve the experience of a sensual encounter between man and machine. (JHo)

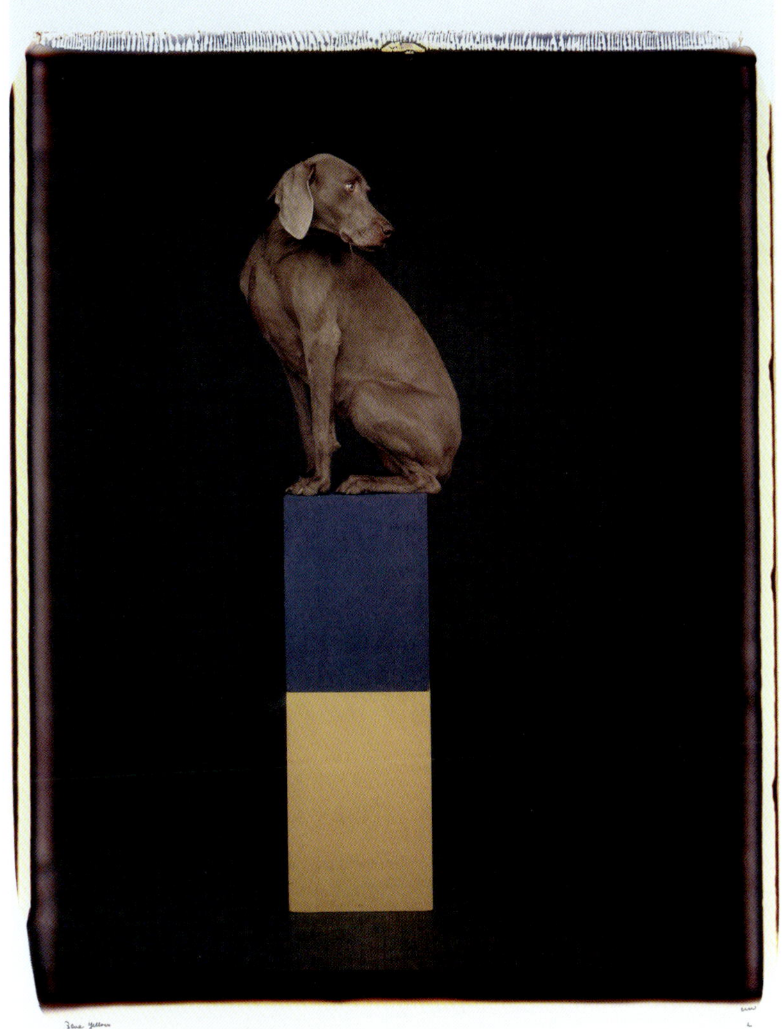
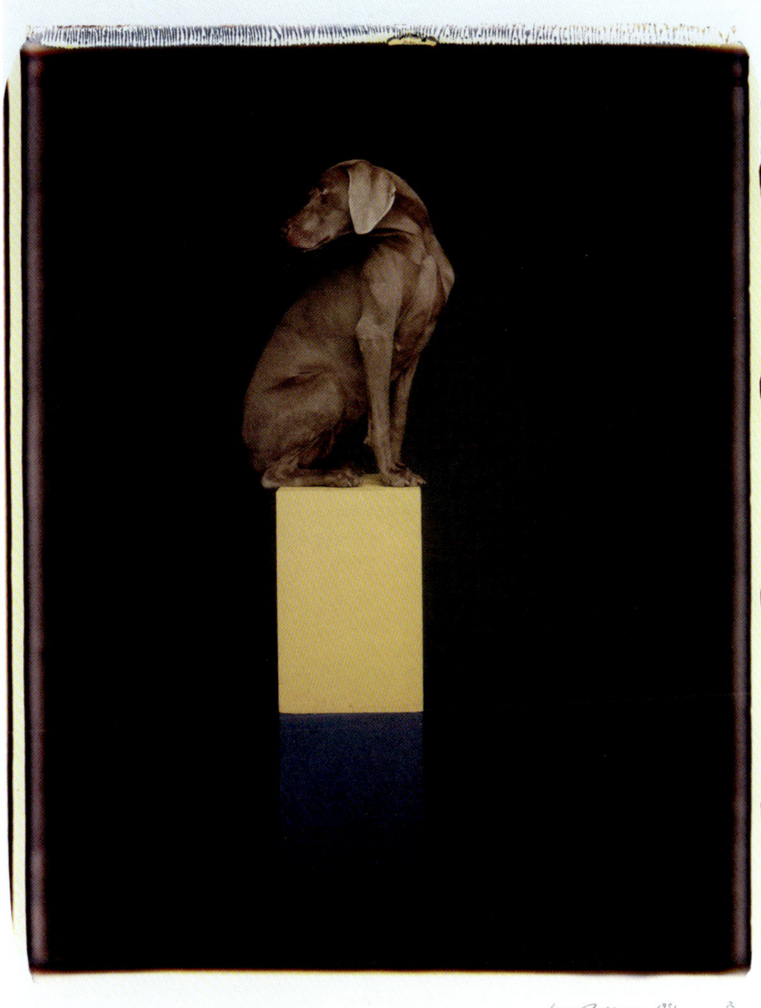

## *Blue Yellow*

William Wegman (American, born 1943), 1991
Color polaroid, 24 × 20 in. (60.9 × 50.8 cm)
Museum Purchase, Lloyd O. and Marjorie Strong Coulter Fund  2011.13.a–.b

Deliberately exploiting new photographic media to reimagine what art could be, Wegman turned to video in the mid-1960s and the polaroid in the late 1970s. During the same period, he became immersed in a partnership with a Weimaraner dog named "Man Ray," after the Dada photographer. A successor, named Fay Ray, is pictured here. Just as, with a sly sense of humor, Wegman references the legacy of Minimalism by placing Fay Ray on stacked cubes, so too his pet's very presence eerily shifts the image into something more haunting and less easily characterized, disrupting the conventions that keep art at a safe remove from life. As he told the BBC in 2018, "In my photographs, what I like people to see is—yes, there is a dog, and yes, it is a Weimaraner—but what has it become? The dogs are always in a state of becoming something. They become characters, objects. When they are lying down, they become landscapes." (ACG)

# *Cementerio, Juchitán, Oaxaca*

Graciela Iturbide (Mexican, born 1942), 1988
Gelatin silver print, 17½ × 13 in. (44.4 × 33 cm)
Archival Collection of Marion Boulton Stroud and Acadia Summer Arts
Program, Mt. Desert Island, Maine. Gift from the Marion Boulton "Kippy"
Stroud Foundation  2018.10.149

Countless swallows flock around a woman who stoically walks through a cemetery. She holds a bundle of long sticks that sprout from her torso like wings. The blurry dark birds are set against a cloudless white sky and equally blanched funerary architecture. In this image, acclaimed Mexican photographer Graciela Iturbide captures a momentous contrast between the rapid pace of flapping wings and the calm, unperturbed woman at the center.

The picture brings together two of Iturbide's favorite subjects, birds and death, to evoke the fleeting passage of life.[1] She took the photograph in 1988 in Juchitán, located in southern Mexico along the Isthmus of Tehauntepec, where she had been working since 1979. This series, published as a book with an accompanying text by poet Elena Poniatowska, largely consists of images of women from the matriarchal indigenous community. Iturbide was first invited to photograph there by artist Francisco Toledo, a native of the area and major patron of its culture. She continued to visit Juchitán, befriending many of the women, whom she described as "big, strong, politicized, emancipated wonderful women. I discovered this world of women and I made it my business to spend time with them and they gave me access to their daily world and to their traditions."[2] The rural region is famed for its syncretic fusion of Pre-Columbian Zapotec traditions and myths with Christian rituals and beliefs imposed during colonization. Juchitán's unique and enduring culture has fascinated many artists and writers, including Henri Cartier-Bresson, Serge Eisenstein, and Tina Modotti. Frida Kahlo even adopted the dress of Tehuantepec women, identifying with their dominant place in society.

Iturbide's photographs are the most renowned portrayals of Juchitán life and culture, and perhaps the most difficult to define in terms of genre or category. Some scholars have linked her work with the field of visual anthropology, as several of her best-known projects focus on indigenous communities in other parts of Mexico. Her first major commission was from the National Indigenous Institute in the late 1970s, for which she photographed the Seri, a group of seminomadic people in the Sonoran Desert. Yet Iturbide's photographs are not forensic studies that claim objectivity. While they may record vernacular dress or customs and offer insights into the gender dynamics of the Juchitán people, her work achieves something more intangible and personal than documentary evidence. For this reason, it has been associated with magical realism, a predominantly literary tradition with strong roots in Latin America. Iturbide rejects this label. Her photographs are not fictional scenarios of mystery and heightened metaphysical awareness. Hovering between imagination and keen observation, she credits her ability to elevate depictions of daily life to the trust she builds with her subjects: "I want to be clear that I do not work in the indigenous world if there is not complicity and respect. I don't like it when they refer to my work as magical—it makes me furious."[3]

*Cementerio* thus reflects a process built on reciprocity. After spending nearly a decade visiting Juchitán, she came to know its syncretic sense of place, built up confidence among its inhabitants, and developed her own connection to female autonomy. This beguiling photograph, which seems so coincidental and momentary, is the culmination of years of study and self-definition as an artist.

Sarah Montross
Curator, deCordova Sculpture Park and
Museum, Lincoln, Massachusetts

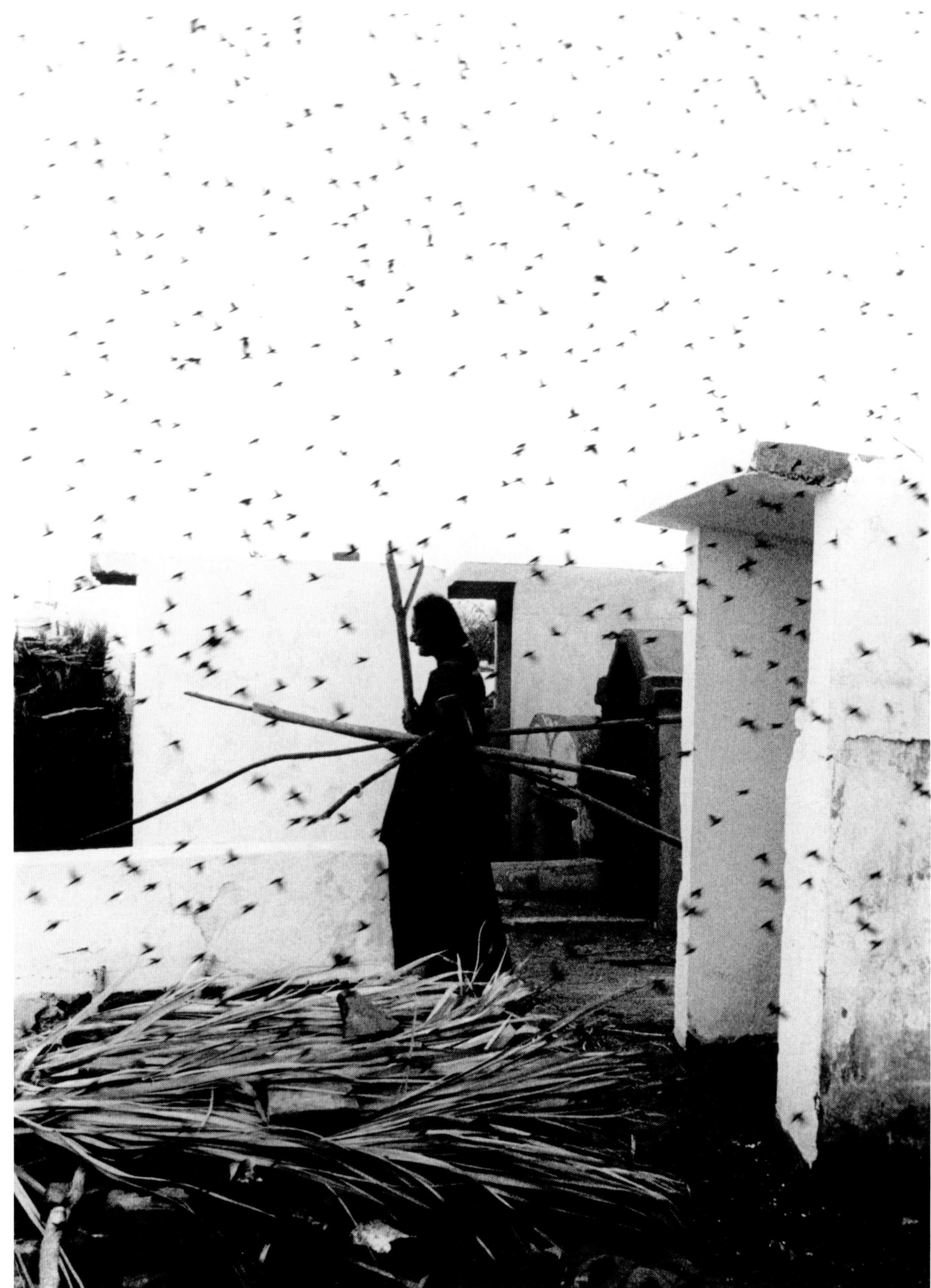

## *Skowhegan Green II*

Frank Bowling (American, born 1936), 1984
Acrylic on canvas, 51⅞ × 50¾ in. (131.8 × 128.9 cm)
Gift of Julie McGee, Class of 1982, in Honor of David C. Driskell
H'89  2010.60

I am a pushover for paintings that speak self-confidently about the process of art making and insert themselves into age-old traditions of painterly aesthetics and objecthood, like Frank Bowling's *Skowhegan Green II*. The visual evidence of the artist's homage and open challenge to past precedents and histories resonates with my own practice as a curator and scholar in the field of African diaspora art history.

Born in 1934 in Bartica, British Guiana, Bowling moved to England in 1953. His first trip to the U.S. was in 1961, and by the late 1960s he was befriending and exhibiting with some of the best young black American artists of the day. I first met Frank Bowling in 2009 at Howard University's Porter Colloquium, an annual event honoring the pioneering work of the artist and scholar James A. Porter (1905–1970). Bowling was invited to discuss his work within the context of abstraction, alongside American artists William T. Williams (b. 1942) and Mel Edwards (b. 1937), with whom he has long-standing professional friendships.

While Bowling frequently moved between the metropoles of New York City and London, *Skowhegan Green II* is tied directly to the summer of 1984, when he was an artist-in-residence at the Skowhegan School of Painting and Sculpture. As Bowling recalled, it was the first time he faced being so thoroughly enveloped by nature. "I felt the green in the Skowhegan area was so powerful a look that I just couldn't ignore it."[1] The summer in Maine proved to be a pivotal one for Bowling's artistic trajectory. Pushing the boundaries of nonrepresentational and accidental modes of abstract painting, he began experimenting with viscous acrylics and packing foam in the early 1980s. The foam provided the poured painting surface with a marked geometry. Leonard Bocour, the highly regarded paint manufacturer

and founder of Bocour Artists Colors, introduced Bowling to the gel medium that became an indispensable tool in his creative practice.[2] He spent his summer residency perfecting his use of the foam with the gel medium and his poured painting methods.

Look closely at the surface of *Skowhegan Green II* and you will see that the gel medium doesn't hold just the foam in suspension, but other objects as well, including a flat wooden stir stick. The foam is crimped on the edges and recalls the zigzag pattern left by pinking shears. The utilitarian yet decorative edge is found in other Bowling paintings, most notably in the pieced canvas compositions. Bowling's mother was a gifted, successful dressmaker and seamstress in British Guiana. I imagine his love for geometry, aesthetic beauty, and the dynamic mark of pinking shears as a familial inheritance he has deployed in asserting his place in the history of painting, and British painting in particular. It is, moreover, one he shares with his spouse, British artist Rachel Scott, an esteemed weaver and seamstress.

I first saw *Skowhegan Green II* in London, in Bowling's studio. The painterly response to the saturation of nature—the green of Skowhegan at the height of summer—is quintessential Bowling, an urbane artist with a transatlantic practice. Its presence in the Bowdoin College Museum of Art opens the door to the rich history to which we must attend to fully appreciate his artistry: British colonialism as well as British painting, abstraction as well as African American and African diaspora art history in the U.S. *Skowhegan Green II* was gifted to the museum in honor of David C. Driskell (b. 1931), to pay tribute to his indefatigable advocacy for black artists and his enduring commitment to Skowhegan.

Julie L. McGee
Associate Professor of Africana Studies
and Art History, University of Delaware,
Newark

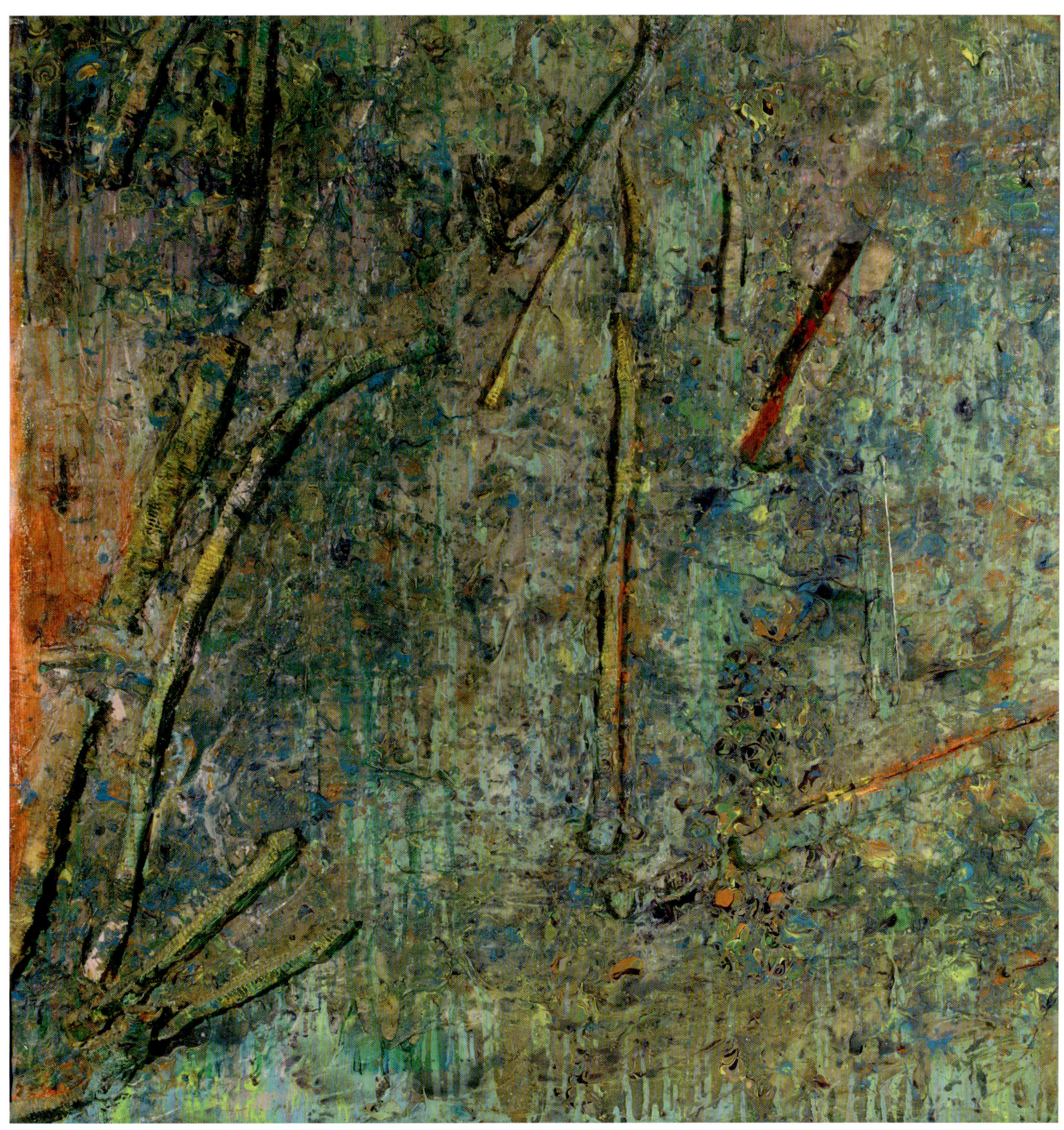

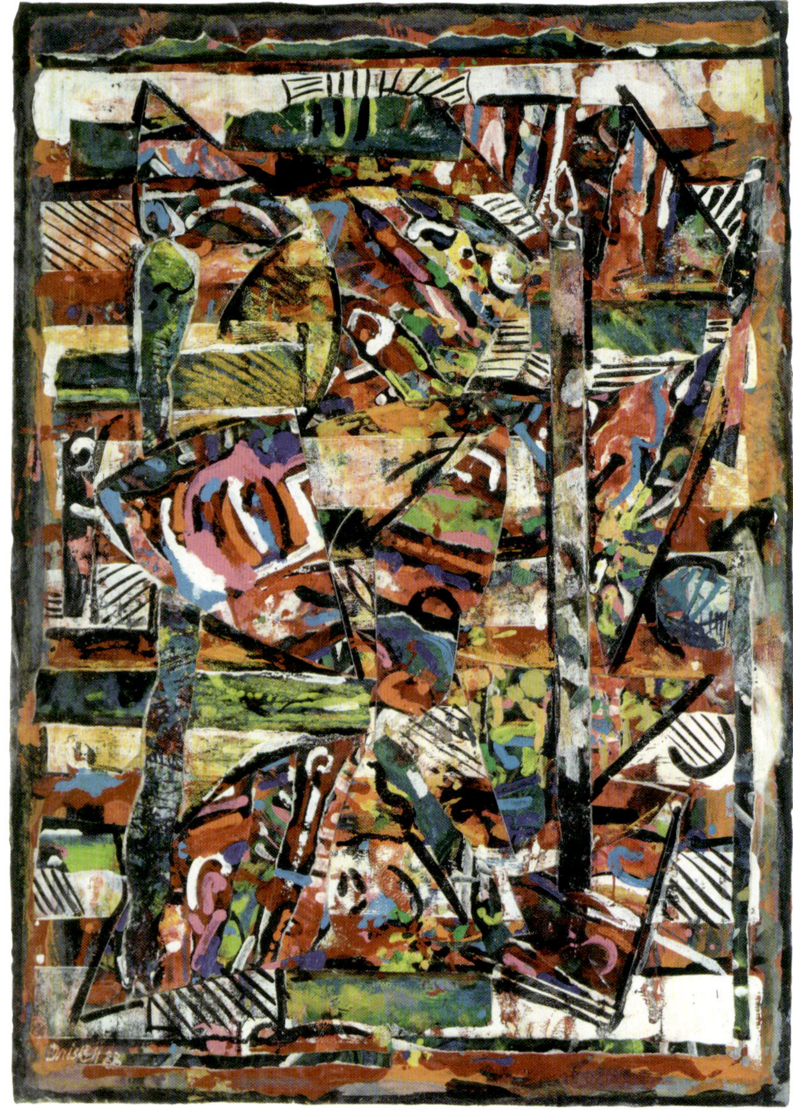

# *Shaker Chair and Quilt*

David C. Driskell, Honorary Degree 1989 (American, born 1931), 1988
Encaustic and collage on paper, 31⅜ × 22⅝ in. (79.7 × 57.5 cm)
Museum Purchase, George Otis Hamlin Fund  1990.2

Born in Eatonton, Georgia, David C. Driskell first visited Maine as an undergraduate at Howard University, Washington, D.C. His primary mentor then was the artist and scholar James A. Porter (1905–1970), author of *Modern Negro Art*, a groundbreaking survey of African American art from the antebellum era to 1942. Howard made it possible for Driskell to attend the Maine-based Skowhegan School of Painting and Sculpture on a scholarship in the summer of 1953. Driskell would return as Resident Faculty in 1978 and Visiting Faculty in 1976, 1991, and 2004.[1] In truth, he rooted himself in Maine, creating a second home and studio in Falmouth, where he purchased property in 1961.

At Skowhegan in 1953, Driskell was the assistant of Leonard Bocour (1910–1993), the paint manufacturer and founder of Bocour Artists Colors. As Resident Faculty that year, Bocour taught a laboratory course on artists' materials.[2] Driskell's penchant for studio alchemy is on full display in Bowdoin's *Shaker Chair and Quilt*. Influenced by Bocour, he favored encaustic—which he initially learned from Porter—for collage paintings; it provided an excellent binder and transparentizer for the multiple textured materials he deployed, including torn strips of painted paper, prints, magazines, and foil gauze. When burnished, the melted wax achieves a surface brilliance and luminous functional depth that allows his collage elements to seemingly oscillate and dance.

In *Shaker Chair and Quilt*, Driskell unites familial inheritance, such as his mother's quilting and father's carpentry, with his deep admiration for Shaker artistry, which he came to know in Maine. Some of the oldest furnishings in his Maine residence are Shaker works, including the slat-back straight chair with delicate finials referenced in the collage. The vertical and horizontal forms of the illusory chair provide structural poise against the rotating facets of the abstracted quilt.

Julie L. McGee

# *Vessel*

Terry Winters (American, born 1949), 1985
Oil on linen, 101 × 71⅝ in. (257 × 182 cm)
Gift of Agnes Gund in honor of John Studzinski  2016.54

Terry Winters's practice encompasses and reflects upon
drawing, painting, and printmaking, as it coalesces
abstraction and figuration. His works flirt simultaneously
with the architecture of life and the structure of information. *Vessel* develops themes such as the blossoming of
cellular forms at the moment of conception, which had first
appeared in the slightly earlier *Morula* series of lithographs,
created thanks to an invitation from Bill Goldston to work
at Universal Limited Art Editions. Winters explained the
imagery of the *Morula* series to *Hyperallergic* contributor
Jennifer Samet in 2015: "My approach was structural. I
was intrigued by forms that looked 'real,' but were difficult
to identify or whose identity was linked directly to their
structure: crystals, shells, honeycombs. There was an
architecture to the 'morula' forms, in terms of the cell
development." Thus, in *Vessel*, the viewer works to connect
the protective, nurturing form of a vessel with forms that
are difficult to associate with specific labels but that call to
mind the heart, skull, stomach. Yet it is not only imagery,
but also Winters's fascination with process and medium
that link these works—the intense tactility of the *Morula*
lithographs, and the thickly worked paint that defines
form and ground in *Vessel*. Manipulating highly viscous
pigment, Winters gives a tactile and visual presence to
the objects he fashions, and in so doing creates a powerful
universe that reflects the generative potential of the arts
and the natural world. (ACG)

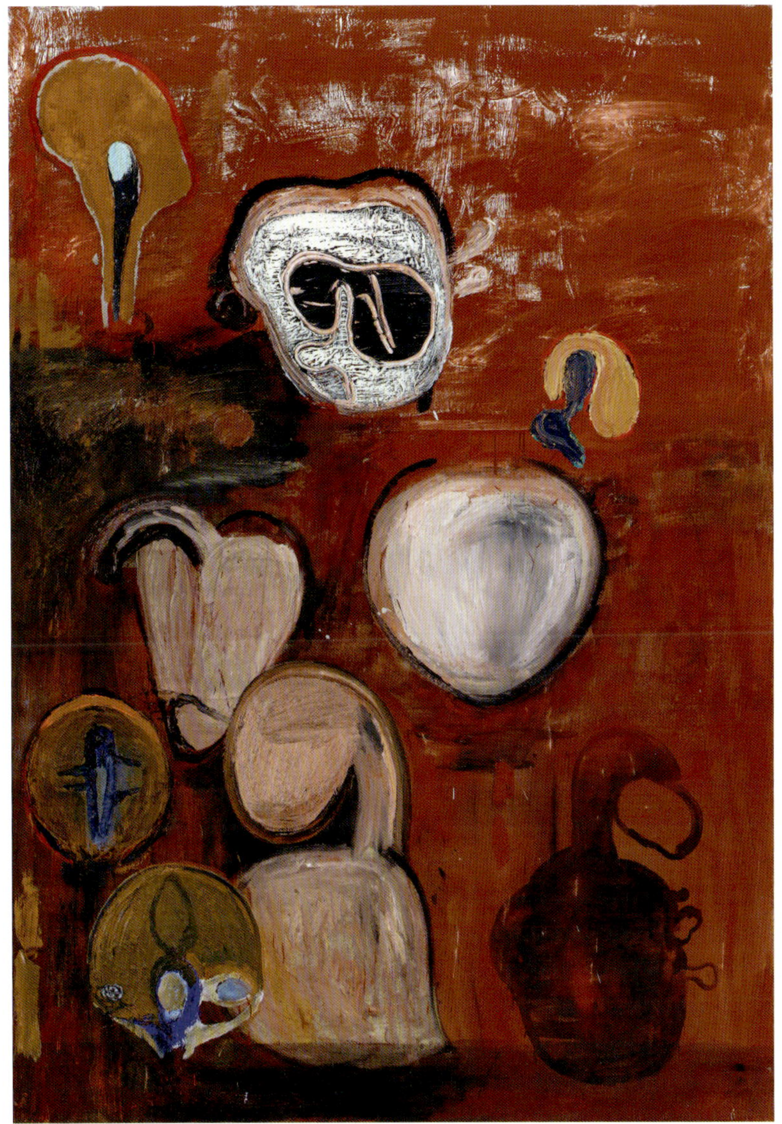

# *Skowhegan V*

Per Kirkeby (Danish, 1938–2018), 1991
Oil on canvas, 46 × 38 in. (116.8 × 96.5 cm)
Jane H. and Charles E. Parker, Jr. Art Acquisition Fund  2014.49

Six paintings by Per Kirkeby titled *Skowhegan* originated in 1991 in Maine, during the artist's teaching stint at the Skowhegan School of Painting and Sculpture, which since 1946 has offered aspiring artists a nine-week summer program. While there, Kirkeby delivered a lecture in the spirit of "habitual irony," a well-worn Danish attitude, which repeatedly caused amusement among his audience. But he also articulated foundational insights into the differences between American and European painting.

Already at a much earlier time, in 1972, Kirkeby had thought about a famous book from New England, conceived on the shores of a pond in Concord, Massachusetts, and first published in 1854: Henry David Thoreau's *Walden: Life in the Woods*. Back then, the young artist had fabricated truly original "illustrations." They consisted of collaged materials of various provenances, including genuine tree leaves. During his studies in geology from 1964 to 1967 at the University of Copenhagen, Kirkeby focused on the Quaternary Period and undertook expeditions to the Far North. Later, he traveled with more archaeological intentions to Central America to study amidst the vegetation the remains of ancient cultures.

Trees, forests, landscapes play a pivotal role in Kirkeby's oeuvre. Especially since the transition to painting on canvas in about 1975, one can discern impressions from nature as a starting point for a painterly practice that is often gestural and conscious of its material foundation. Beginning in the 1980s, he created series of paintings that referenced the forest as a motif, such as *Waldvariation (Forest Variation) I–V* (1989), *Walden I–V* (1991), and *Holz (Wood)* (1994).[1] Earlier titles tended to reference the seasons, such as autumn, winter, or late summer, and city names, like Frankfurt or Salzburg, in spite of the fact that the latter works were not based on buildings, but on vegetation.

That Kirkeby was not an abstract painter is confirmed by the titles that are derived from specific visual impressions. How much particular locations determined the mood, coloration, and structure of his works is especially evident in the works made during his tenure as professor at the State Academy of Fine Arts in Karlsruhe (1978–89); they reflect some of the melancholy and loneliness in a foreign country far from family. The works from his sojourn in Maine, however, show a "well-balanced temperament." In a smaller format, they appear to be a kind of inventory of colors and shapes that the artist favored at the time. Just before coming to Maine, he had painted two larger works titled *Zwischenzeit (Interim Period)*, which indicated his readiness for change.

As the hothouse atmosphere of the 1980s waned, many artists were prompted to reconsider their practice, not least because of a crisis in the art market. While this hardly affected Kirkeby, he still began to reorganize his compositional structures by granting more space than before to potent color planes. With its restless brushstrokes and bright splotches of color, *Skowhegan V* announces this new direction to the viewer almost like a manifesto. In the top right, graphic elements are reminiscent of vegetation, but the horizontal and vertical color fields seem to indicate a resolute halt, without making the background completely disappear. Typical for Kirkeby is the ambiguity, whether foreground and background are to be understood in a spatial or temporal relation—most likely both. This remains true when the furor of painting gives way to a conceptual attitude.

Siegfried Gohr
Art historian, curator, and author

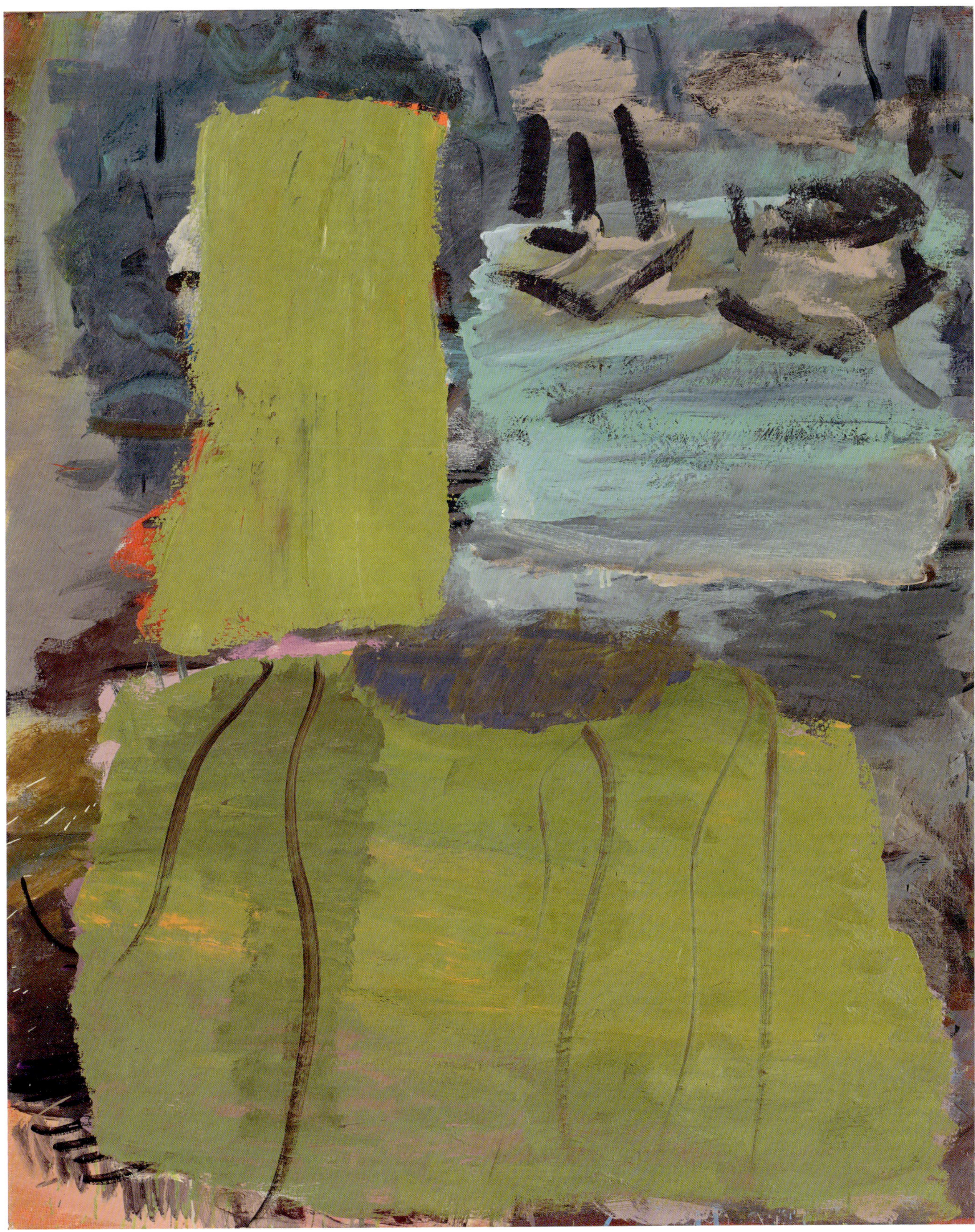

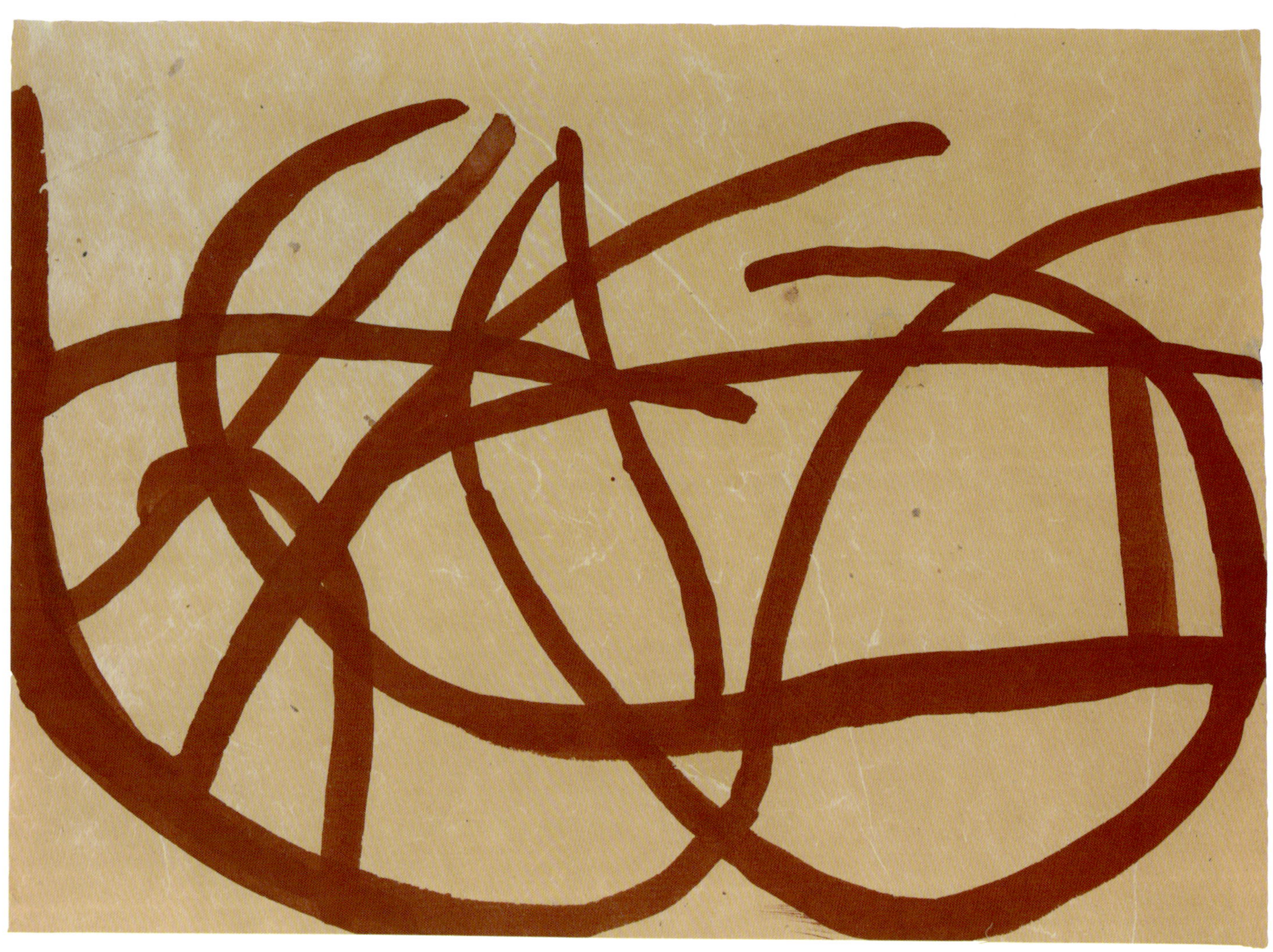

## *Untitled*

Suzan Frecon (American, born 1941), 1994
Watercolor on antique ledger paper, 12⅝ × 17¾ in. (32 × 45 cm)
Gift of Sarah-Ann and Werner Kramarsky  2016.50.5

Widely known as a painter, Suzan Frecon also works in watercolor on found historic paper, often ledger papers from India. As she has indicated in interviews, the convenience and speed of watercolors attracts her when she has less time in the studio and while she waits for a layer of oil paint to dry. To viewers, her works on paper might appear more spontaneous and exploratory than her paintings, which, since the 1980s, are often dominated by large expanses of monochrome color. In this untitled work, rust-red lines caress a sheet of light brown ledger paper, as they respond to its tone, geometry, and directionality. They animate the sheet and seem to thrive, offering a dynamic visual experience. "Every decision I make in my work is a visual decision," she told art historian Josef Helfenstein in 2007. "They are not based on symbolism, story, or metaphor." (JHo)

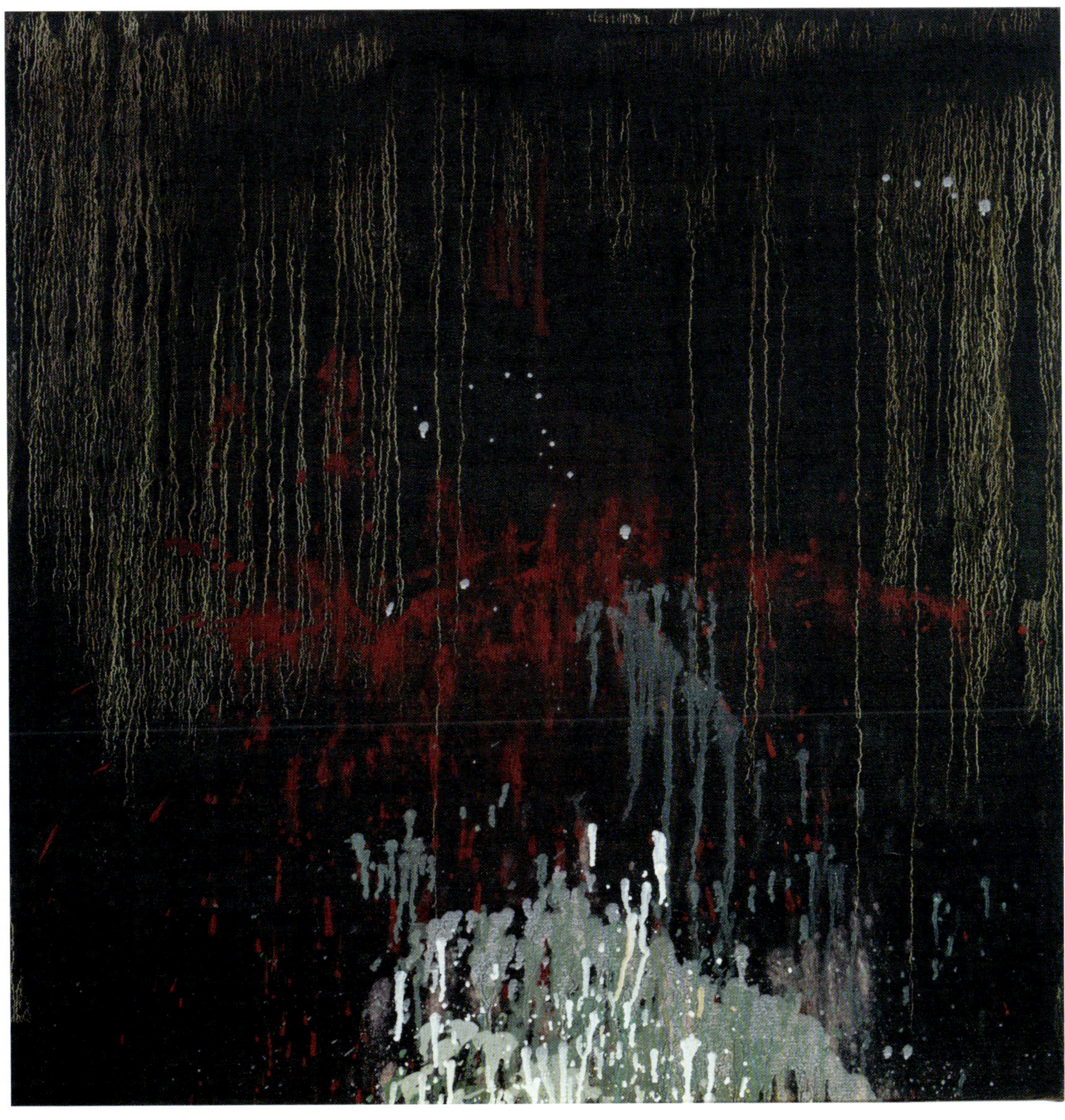

# *After Winslow Homer #2*

Pat Steir (American, born 1938), 1996–97
Oil on canvas, 30¼ × 30¼ × 1½ in. (76.8 × 76.8 × 3.8 cm)
Dorothy and Herbert Vogel Collection  2013.21.270

Pat Steir's title poetically implies a reckoning with an aesthetic and cultural legacy fixed in Western art. *After Winslow Homer* alerts viewers to the passage of time and its suspension in art. Steir observed in an interview with Anne Waldman: "I think Beauty evokes a desire to hold on to the moment; when you realize you cannot stop a moment . . . everything becomes very delicate and tenuous and precious." In her canvas (which followed a painting donated by Herbert and Dorothy Vogel to the National Gallery of Art, Washington, D.C.), one perceives the crash of waves towering in a moment and collapsing in the next, the very tension that drew the work's namesake to the sea a century earlier. So, too, does one suddenly recognize yet another dynamic at play: the relationship of the figurative to the abstract. Here Homer's iconic seascapes atomize and reformulate themselves as pure energy—the ineluctable power of the transformation of one thing into another. (ACG)

# American Icons: Untitled (Salt and Pepper Shakers)

Carrie Mae Weems, Honorary Degree 2012 (American, born
1953), 1988–89
Gelatin silver print, image size: 15¼ x 15¼ in. (38.7 x 38.7 cm);
paper size: 20 x 16 in. (50.8 x 40.6 cm)
Archival Collection of Marion Boulton Stroud and Acadia Summer Arts
Program, Mt. Desert Island, Maine. Gift from the Marion Boulton "Kippy"
Stroud Foundation  2018.10.329

The first time I saw an exhibition of Carrie Mae Weems's work containing this photograph, what struck me initially was the title of the show, *American Icons*. That title implied lush portraits of important African American cultural figures—writers, entertainers—whose reputations were global. Or dramatically shadowed pictures of buildings and places that captured well-known events central to the civil rights movement across the U.S. Or photographs of ordinary objects and people's faces that encapsulate the African American experience. I have known Carrie Mae a long time. She is smart, insightful, and direct. She can also be elegantly and lyrically wry in her comments and in the art she produces.

The "icon" Weems photographed is a mundane domestic tableau, one you might see in anyone's kitchen. Except in this image, the salt-and-pepper shakers on the counter are what Whoopie Goldberg calls "Negrobilia." At first, I smiled. I recognized the quiet, slightly humorous social critique that I assumed Weems intended. But for whom were or are these stereotyping tchotchkes "icons"?

The American perspective that blatantly created, marketed, and purchased these racist items, now referred to as "Black Memorabilia," may have faded from full public view, but, as the picture shows, it has not disappeared. Instead, it has morphed. Weems's quiet photograph captures and speaks directly to the subtlety of that mutation, which echoes larger ones within our society.

A few years ago, in an article for the *New York Times*, Logan Jaffe wrote about the mammy salt-and-pepper shakers that her grandmother kept in her kitchen for

decades. She probably cut open a cantaloupe on the counter next to the figures, creating a scene similar to the one in Weems's photograph. Jaffe and her sister used the salt-and-pepper shakers, were even photographed "holding them up to [their] cheeks, never giving a single thought about what these objects were meant to denote."[1]

In their quotidian setting, these racist objects are recast as harmless bits of some people's day-to-day lives. Their inherent racism is normalized. The casual feeling of the photograph, the everyday kitchen tools hanging on a rack or clustered in a glass jar, and the shadows perhaps from the morning light streaming through a nearby window capture this warm, familiar normalcy that, in the present context, is quickly unsettled by Uncle Ben and Aunt Jemima (my names for them) residing placidly on the counter.

The viewer might look at this photograph and wonder: What is the race or ethnicity of the person or family who lives with these objects? What would I think and feel about these people if I saw such caricatures displayed in their home? I think of my mother, who worked as a maid her entire life. What would she have thought if she had been required to dust these items every week in the home of her non–African American employer?

The brilliance of Weems's quiet domestic photograph is that it disquiets the viewer. It stimulates each person who looks closely to reflect on how, even today, in small, routine ways, each of us could be readily accepting, living with, sustaining, or perpetuating an historical, social, or cultural idea that is an icon of the disturbing aftermath of a peculiar American institution.

Alvin D. Hall
Independent author

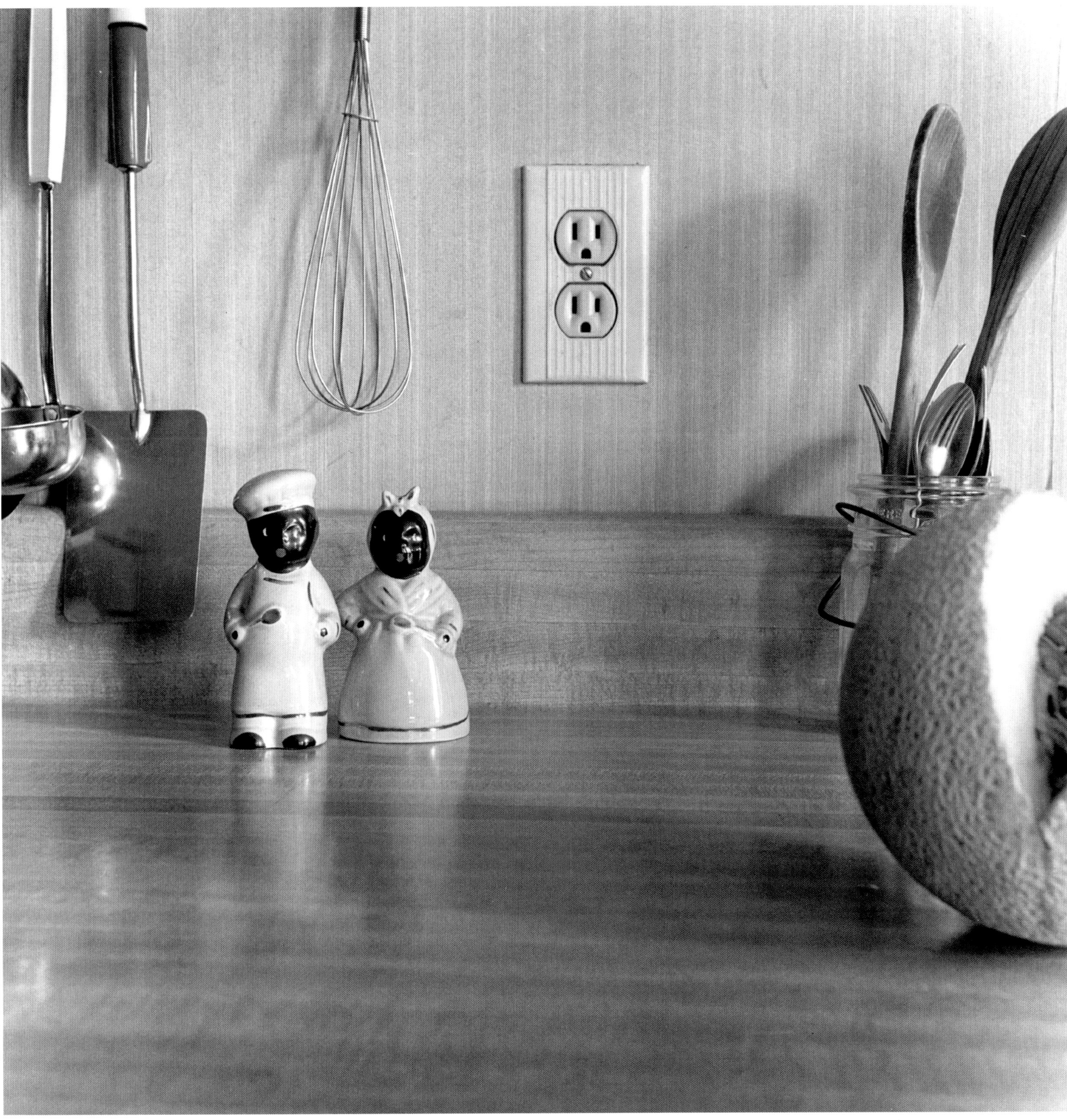

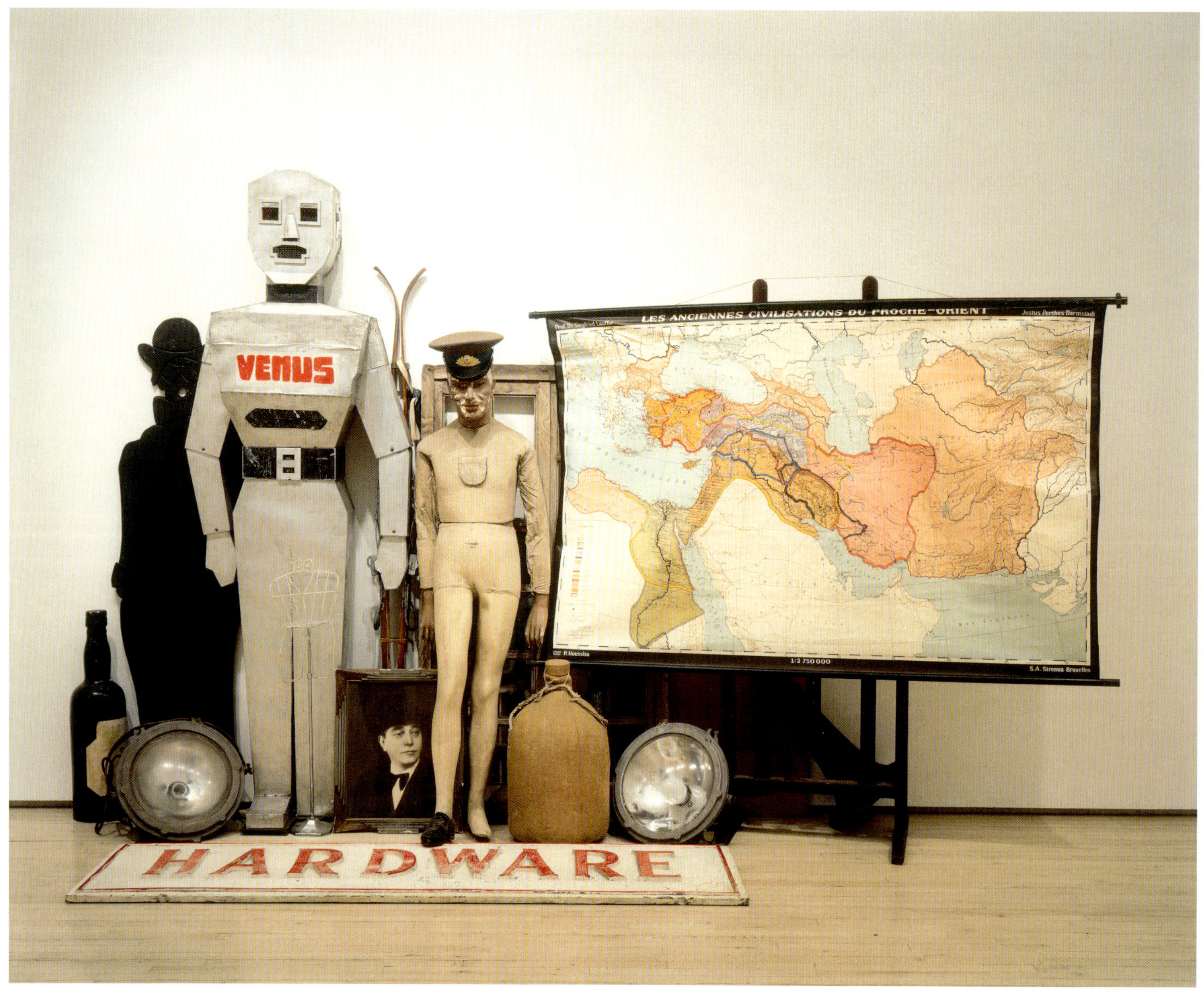


# Composition Trouvée

Guillaume Bijl (Belgian, born 1946), 1990
Mixed media, 91 × 143 × 47½ in. (231.1 × 363.2 × 120.6 cm)
Gift of The Foundation, To–Life, Inc.  2018.30.2

This large-scale assemblage of found objects is the first work of installation art to enter the Museum's collection. Since Marcel Duchamp anonymously submitted a signed urinal to the Society of Independent Artists in 1917 and titled it *Fountain*, artists have gleefully decontextualized everyday items and inserted them into exhibitions and art discourses. Bijl selected a range of objects from Europe and the United States for this work that has the appearance of a junk shop window display. Referencing the past as well as (past notions of) the future, at a time when the crumbling of the Eastern Bloc gave rise to the idea of the "end of history" (Francis Fukuyama), Bijl envisions and illustrates the "archaeology" of contemporary society. With *Lazy Hardware* (1945), Marcel Duchamp had already presented an installation as a window display in Gotham Bookmart, New York, to advertise the publication of André Breton's book *Arcane 17*. Bijl slyly references this installation piece *avant-la-lettre* with a hardware shop sign. (EN/JHo)

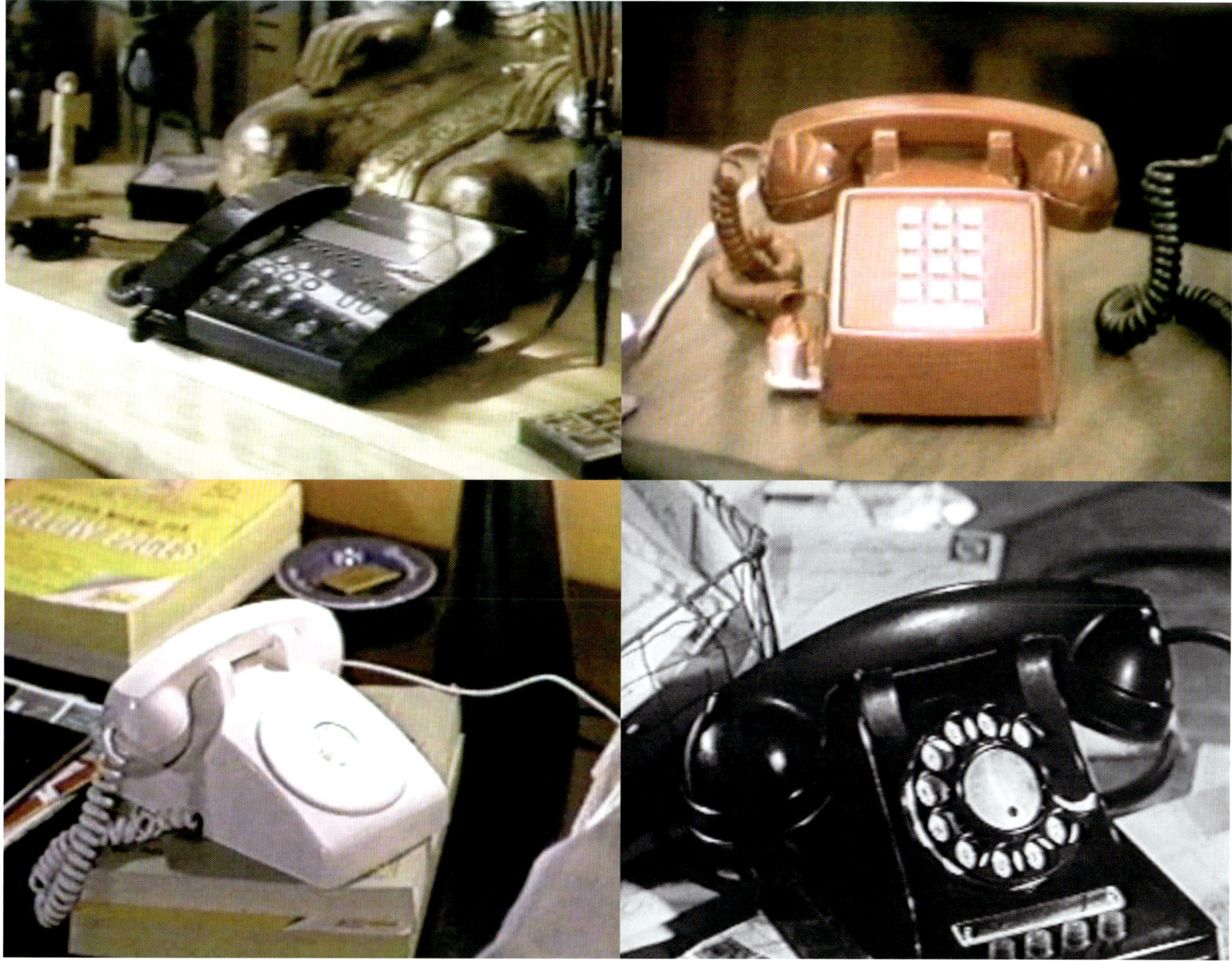

# *Telephones*

Christian Marclay (American and Swiss, born 1955), 1995
Single-channel video (black-and-white and color, with sound),
7:30 min.

Museum Purchase, Lloyd O. and Marjorie Strong Coulter Fund  2011.32

Before *The Clock*, the 24-hour filmic montage by Christian Marclay that proved to be a runaway international success in 2011, there was *Telephones*. A compilation of Hollywood film clips, *Telephones* demonstrates the transformative power of Marclay's editing. Using the narrative arc of a telephone call, he masterfully stitches together excerpts from well-known movies. *Telephones* opens with scenes depicting characters dialing the phone, an activity whose very mechanics, rhythms, and sonic properties have changed considerably with successive technologies. Marclay crafts a new narrative from the fragments, one that offers astute observations on cinematic devices but also outmoded social habits. In retrospect, he seems to question the linearity of a phone call that connects two people over a limited amount of time—and the linearity of filmic narratives as well—as he alludes to the multidirectionality of communication in the time of the internet. (Staff)

# *Bohušovice Train Station near Theresienstadt Concentration Camp, Czechoslovakia*

Judy Glickman Lauder (American, born 1938), 1991
Gelatin silver print from infrared negative, 12⅝ × 18⅞ in.
(32 × 47.9 cm)

Gift of Judy Glickman Lauder  1992.31

Judy Glickman Lauder's photograph depicts a white building on the left, with two gaping windows, an electrical tower, an unkempt concrete platform, a weedy lot, and a black train. The edges and details of the building are slightly blurry, and the black train almost completely fills the right side of the photo. If not for the white numbers and letters of the railcar markings, it would seem as though we, the viewer, were staring into an abyss. The artist employed an infrared lens, which distances the black-and-white image from documentary photography. As Glickman Lauder explains, an infrared lens makes objects softer and therefore more remote from everyday reality.[1] For photographer Rose Marasco, the use of infrared in Glickman Lauder's Holocaust photos conveys to the viewer that "this is an intense place, an unnatural place, a place where anything can and did happen."[2]

Bohušovice (Bauschowitz) was the village where Jews disembarked from the train and walked to the Theresienstadt (Terezín) ghetto and transit camp. The Nazis cynically described Theresienstadt as a "spa town" where elderly German Jews could "retire" in safety. In fact, the deportations to Theresienstadt were part of the Nazi strategy of deception.[3] From Theresienstadt, Nazis deported Jews to ghettos in Riga, Warsaw, or Łódź, among others, or the extermination camps of Auschwitz, Majdanek, and Treblinka.

Glickman Lauder, an American Jewish photographer, created this photo in 1991, when the Holocaust defined American Jewish communities. At that time, many survivors were still alive, and while some did not speak of their pasts, others did.[4] The Eichmann trial gave face to the testimonies of survivors for the first time in 1961. In 1964, survivors in Philadelphia commissioned what is considered the first public memorial to the Holocaust in the United States. Their efforts testify to the fact that it was survivors— not the general public—who spurred the need for public memorialization.[5]

By the early 1980s, with the passing of a generation of Holocaust survivors and as the country took a turn to the right, the risk of forgetting (or of downright suppression of historical fact) was very real and galvanized demands for formalized recognition of the Holocaust in the form of memorials and museums. There was a new urgency, in the Jewish community, to remember the past in a public way, an urgency that soon garnered national attention: Art Spiegelman received the Pulitzer Prize for his two-volume *Maus* in 1992, and Stephen Spielberg's *Schindler's List* was viewed across the nation in 1993.[6] The same year, Holocaust memory found a home on the Washington Mall, with the opening of the United States Holocaust Memorial Museum.

In *Bohušovice Train Station*, the decrepit buildings of postcommunist Poland take us back to an uncertain moment in time. Are we, as viewers, about to arrive or depart? Are we standing in the same spot as a tourist, a Pole, a Red Cross visitor, a Nazi official, or a Jew? The infrared photography emphasizes this uncertainty and leaves open all identificatory positions. Today, when visiting Terezín by train, travelers still disembark at Bohušovice.

Natasha Goldman
Adjunct Lecturer, Department of Art
History, Bowdoin College

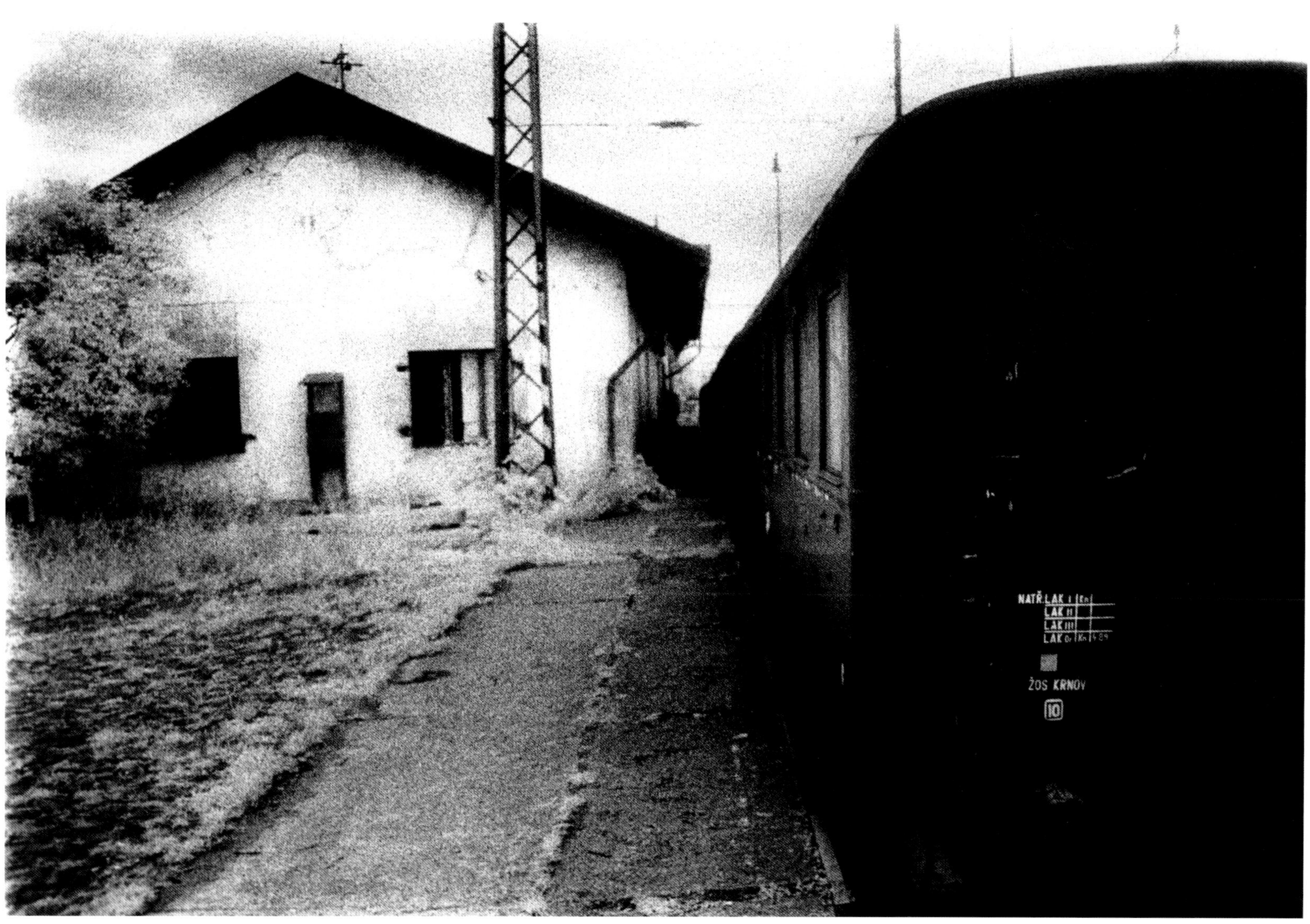

NATŘ.LAK I
LAK II
LAK III
LAK 0
ŽOS KRNOV
10

## *Caged Corn*

Mel Chin (American, born 1951), 1992–2014
Hybrid cadmium accumulated dwarf corn (harvest sample
1991), redwood, and galvanized steel, 20 × 11 × 11 in.
(50.8 × 27.9 × 27.9 cm)
Archival Collection of Marion Boulton Stroud and Acadia Summer Arts
Program, Mt. Desert Island, Maine. Gift from the Marion Boulton "Kippy"
Stroud Foundation  2018.10.60.a–.b

Mel Chin has established an innovative relationship between artistic practice and social responsibility, ascribing new purpose to visual art that "extends the notion of art beyond a familiar object-commodity status into the realm of process and public service."[1] The dual driving forces of Chin's career—"responsibility and poetry"—are exemplified in the work *Caged Corn*.[2] In a cylindrical cage with an attached archival identification tag hanging against a steel panel, a dried ear of hybrid dwarf corn is suspended in mid-air. The slightly peeled-back husks, appearing frozen in a windswept moment, expose the fragile corn silk and kernels beneath.

The sample displayed is a hyperaccumulator plant harvested in 1991 at the hazardous Pig's Eye Landfill in St. Paul, Minnesota, as part of Chin's "public service" project *Revival Field* (1991–ongoing). In collaboration with Dr. Rufus Chaney, a research agronomist in the U.S. Department of Agriculture, Chin conceived *Revival Field* as both a work of environmental art and a scientific "field test" of the efficacy of six hyperaccumulator plants to absorb heavy metals from the polluted soil and, therefore, naturally revive the ecosystem in which they were planted. The accumulated metals in the plants can be reclaimed, sold, and reused, resulting in an organic transformation of toxic material in a cyclical, quasi-alchemical process. Chin identifies this "creation of a scientific technology"— green remediation—as the most significant result of *Revival Field*.[3]

The sculpture presents an agricultural specimen as a savior and a threat, simultaneously protected and held captive by the cage in which it hangs. Paradoxically, the carefully considered visual display alludes to laboratories, scientific testing, and specimen preservation, evoking a sense of jeopardy in an unsettling encounter with a hazardous object containing toxic cadmium. It is *Caged Corn*'s uncategorizable style, medium, and form that encourages inquiry, allowing the viewer to consider the object's environmental intervention and to contemplate art as an evolutionary tool of social action.[4] As Chin has observed, "art is not static, it is catalytic. . . . it makes things function."[5]

Conceptually, Chin's body of work stimulates dialogue on a variety of intersectional and ethical issues that blur political, economic, geographic, cultural, and disciplinary distinctions. Chin demonstrates that innovation is achieved only by pushing past the prescribed boundaries of academic disciplines; effective change is achieved only through collective action. Anchored by the "common good" central to Bowdoin College's mission, Mel Chin embodies the liberal arts pedagogy in his critical inquiry, creativity, and social consciousness, utilizing research and aesthetic poetics to transform his curiosity into solutions. In his own words, he pursues outcomes "where one can foresee the possibility of change."[6]

Honor Wilkinson
Curatorial Assistant and Manager of
Student Programs, Bowdoin College
Museum of Art

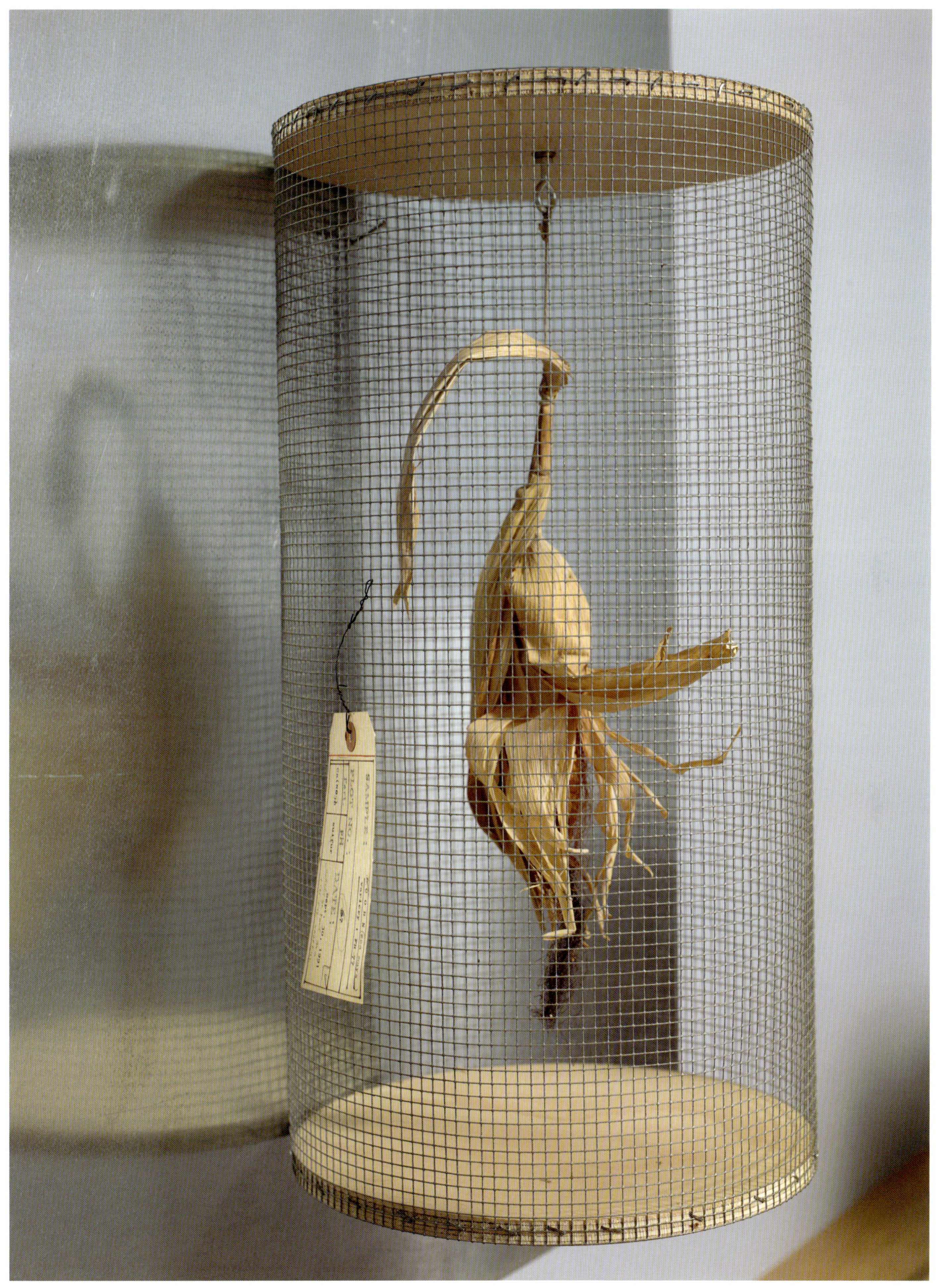

# *Runaways*

Glenn Ligon (American, born 1960), 1993
Suite of ten lithographs on paper, each 16 × 12 in. (40.6 × 30.5 cm)
Museum Purchase, Lloyd O. and Marjorie Strong Coulter Fund  2003.21.1–.10

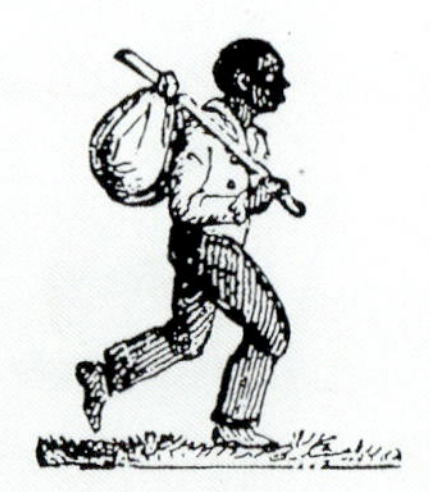

RAN AWAY, Glenn, a young black man twenty-eight years old, about five feet six inches high. Dressed in blue jeans, a blue button-down shirt, black shoes. Medium build. Very short haircut (not quite shaved head). Large neck. Green tinted sunglasses.

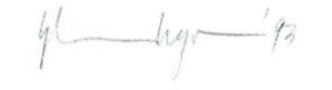

On first encountering Glenn Ligon's set of ten lithographs, collectively called *Runaways*, it seemed a work totally outside of myself, something I suspect is true for all viewers. Composed of a block of text using different typefaces and a stock drawing of a stereotypical black figure, each lithograph mimics nineteenth-century ads that slave owners posted or placed in publications in their quest to identify and locate their runaway slaves. Each text begins with the phrase "Ran away," followed by a description of the artist solicited from different friends. Ligon had asked these friends to describe him as if they were making a police report on a missing person, and was surprised that their descriptions closely resembled those in the actual ads.

As I read each lithograph, I always notice the particularity (or lack thereof) of what people included and highlighted in their descriptions of Ligon—his walk, the way he does not look directly at people, etc. The mention of items like clothing is predictable. But his skin color? When his color is specified, I wonder what real or imagined palette the friend is referencing. Some descriptions have been taken by some commentators to be humorous, but I have never found that to be true. To me, they contain the elements that prompt reflection and bring the work deeper inside each of us.

It is impossible, I believe, for any of us to read these descriptions and not wonder how our close friends would describe us. We see our friends frequently, we spend meaningful time with them; we believe that in these friendships, there's a connection to, a perception of, the full person that each of us is. So inevitably, as we read Ligon's ads, we begin to think about how we would be described, how we want to be described, how we would describe ourselves. Suddenly, Ligon's work penetrates our self-definitions; we undergo an internal shift. The lithographs are no longer simply a format-and-word play on the original ads. Each becomes a multilayered reflection on the various elements as well as the totality of our identity—how we wish to be perceived and positioned.

What if you are chattel, as slaves were? Would an owner be more or less able to provide an identifying, individual description of his human property? Or would the identifiers be more generic and superficial?

As an African American whose ancestors were enslaved and who experienced the sanctioned indignities and diminutions of segregation and Jim Crow laws in America, standing in front of Ligon's ten lithographs and reading one after another stimulates a journey—a private and curious series of thoughts. Were any of my ancestors the subjects of such ads? How would I have been described if I were a runaway slave, someone's property, not seen as a full person? I always try to resist, to suppress this series of questions. I wonder if other African Americans of my generation have them. I wonder if everyone has them. I wonder if these thoughts are somehow unhealthy.

From years of experience, I know that each time I encounter *Runaways*, the work will invariably move from outside of me to inside of me. However, the private and curious questions I ask myself today, and wonder if others are doing the same, are less about my personal history and more about contemporary events. More and more, I see the work's title, *Runaways*, acquiring a layered irony, or expressing an unfortunate, ongoing truth.

Alvin D. Hall
Independent author

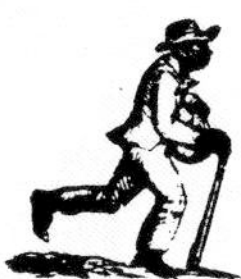

RAN AWAY. Young guy – the Oliver North of downtown. 5 feet, + and then some. Medium build, stylishly casual (usually in jeans). Soft-spoken, well-spoken but kinda' quiet. Wears delicate glasses. Moves smoothly, looks like he might have something on his mind – he'll find you.

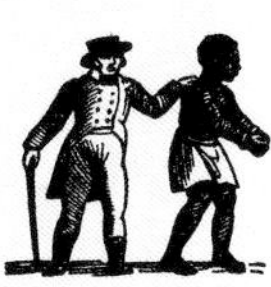

Ran away, Glenn Ligon. He's a shortish broad-shouldered black man, pretty dark-skinned, with glasses. Kind of stocky, tends to look down and turn in when he walks. Real short hair, almost none. Clothes non-descript, something button-down and plaid, maybe, and shorts and sandals. Wide lower face and narrow upper face. Nice teeth.

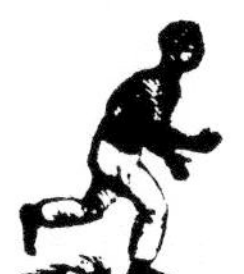

RAN AWAY, Glenn, 5'7" – 5'9", Medium– small build, say 160 lbs. Black linen shirt (with white "C.P. Company" label on skirt of shirt), white buttons. Dark blue-black jean shorts, black socks, low-top black leather shoes with rubber soles (vibram). African-American, with very short cut hair. About 30 years old. Wears glasses – oval shaped, wire (black) rims, tortoise shell effect on the sides. Watch with silver strap, bracelet: black-and-white.

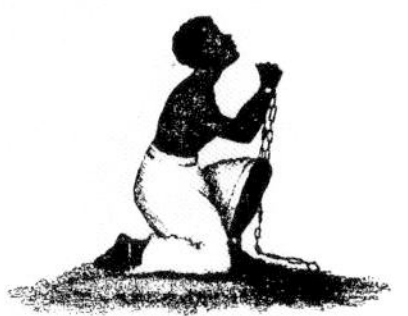

Ran away, Glenn, a black man – early 30's, very short cropped hair, small oval wire-rimmed glasses. Wearing large black linen shirt with white buttons, dark navy shorts, black socks and shoes. Black-and-white bead bracelet and silver watch on left wrist. No other jewelry. He has a sweet voice, is quiet. Appears somewhat timid.

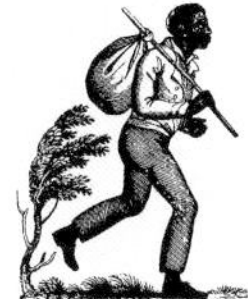

RAN AWAY, Glenn, a black male, 5'8", very short hair cut, nearly completely shaved, stocky build, 155-165 lbs., medium complexion (not "light skinned," not "dark skinned," slightly orange). Wearing faded blue jeans, short sleeve button-down 50's style shirt, nice glasses (small, oval shaped), no socks. Very articulate, seemingly well-educated, does not look at you straight in the eye when talking to you. He's socially very adept, yet, paradoxically, he's somewhat of a loner.

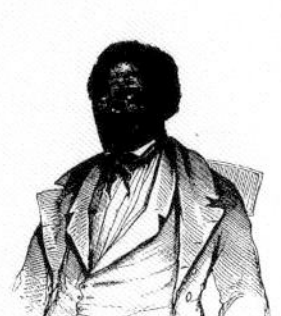

RAN AWAY, Glenn. He is black. He has very short hair and eye glasses. He has quite light skin tone (faded bronze). Not tall. No noticeable accent. Wearing a plum-colored shirt, long-sleeved, and shorts. Very casual and stylish in appearance. He is wearing a bead bracelet (stones – a mixture of black-and-white). He has big hands and fingers. When he walks his feet cross each other a little bit. When he talks, he usually has a big smile towards you, yet he faces you from a slightly different angle. He looks at you from the corner of his eyes. His voice is very calm.

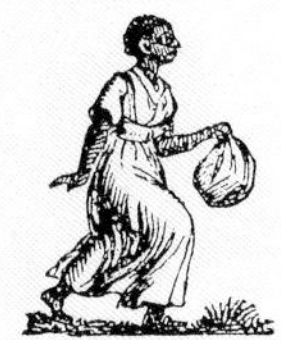

RAN AWAY, a man named Glenn. He has almost no hair. He has cat-eye glasses, medium-dark skin, cute eyebrows. He's wearing black shorts, black shoes and a short sleeve plaid shirt. He has a really cool Timex silver watch with a silver band. He's sort of short, a little hunky, though you might not notice it with his shirt untucked. He talks sort of out of the side of his mouth and looks at you sideways. Sometimes he has a loud laugh, and lately I've noticed he refers to himself as "mother."

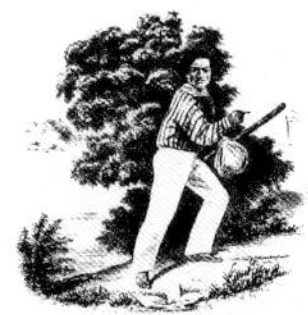

RAN AWAY, a man named Glenn, five feet eight inches high, medium-brown skin, black-framed semi-cat-eyed glasses, close-cropped hair. Grey shirt, watch on left hand. Black shorts, black socks and black shoes. Distinguished looking.

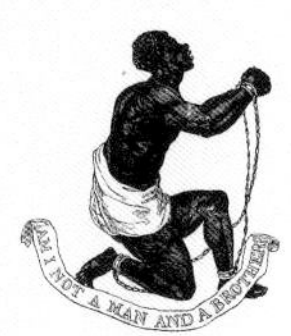


RAN AWAY, Glenn. Medium height, 5'8", male. Closely-cut hair, almost shaved. Mild looking, with oval shaped, black-rimmed glasses that are somewhat conservative. Thinly-striped black-and-white short-sleeved T-shirt, blue jeans. Silver watch and African-looking bracelet on arm. His face is somewhat wider on bottom near the jaw. Full-lipped. He's black. Very warm and sincere, mild-mannered and laughs often.

# Loves Me, Loves Me Not

Yanagi Yukinori (Japanese, born 1959), 1997
Wool with jute backing and brass, 144 × 96 in.
(365.8 × 243.8 cm)
Archival Collection of Marion Boulton Stroud and Acadia Summer Arts
Program, Mt. Desert Island, Maine. Gift from the Marion Boulton "Kippy"
Stroud Foundation  2018.10.377

Visible in the center of Yanagi Yukinori's *Loves Me, Loves Me Not*, a large wool carpet, is a deep impression of a sixteen-petaled chrysanthemum, its petals missing but for a single brass one hanging from the central disk. Others lie scattered across the rug, each accompanied by black lettering that reads either "s/he loves me" or "s/he loves me not." Written in Japanese and the ten Asian languages spoken in Japan's former colonies (Khmer, Vietnamese, Thai, Indonesian/ Malay, Korean, Chinese, Lao, Tagalog, Tamil, Burmese), with two more drawn from Japan's "internal" colonies of indigenous people (Ainu, Shuri), *Loves Me, Loves Me Not* makes a striking statement in color as well as ideology. The color scheme invokes the felicitous red-white pairing used in Japanese ceremonies and the national flag. Yet, a carpet invites you to step or sit on it, giving viewers the opportunity to regard anew the hallowed Japanese chrysanthemum, the crest of the imperial family. Ideologically, this work participates in the national conversations that began in Japan in 1995—the fiftieth anniversary of the end of World War II—regarding the long shadow of wartime ideology and the meanings of community and national identity.

The sixteen-petaled chrysanthemum is both revered and controversial as a symbol due to its expansive use during Japan's imperial period. Between 1869 and 1945, it appeared on coins, paper currency, and stamps as an emblem of the emperor's authority, its use beyond such official insignia tightly controlled by vigilant censors. So emblematic was it of imperial power that the convicted war criminal Tōjō Hideki invoked it in his last poem, pining for an opportunity to serve his lord again: "Beneath the moss, I will wait for the blooming of the chrysanthemum flower." Though the emperor ceased to be head of state in 1945, and the chrysanthemum was reduced to the familial crest of the royal family, the symbol has persisted on the cover of the Japanese passport, problematically retained as an insignia of the Japanese people. Defenders cite Article 7 of the constitution, which vests the emperor with diplomatic and ceremonial functions, hence justifying its use on documents that cross borders. Critics, however, sense residues of the veneration of the monarchy.

Yanagi Yukinori squarely interrogates these residues of Japanese nationalist sentiment by provocatively dismantling the flower and asking viewers to participate in a child's game about whether one's affection is returned. Playfully relativized in this way, the chrysanthemum raises questions about national attachment. Did any Asian country truly love the Japanese emperor or desire his affection? Likely not. For Japan's erstwhile colonies, the trope of love is doubly significant. In the 1930s and '40s, propaganda justified the brutal military occupation of China, for example, with the rhetoric of interracial harmony and romantic love. Such sentimental bonds created a fantasy of a paternalistic Japan "guiding" the Chinese, and the obedient Chinese loving them in return. By reading the language beside each petal and joining the game, the viewer rehearses the superficiality of such affection even while confirming its ideological force. Yanagi brings these questions about the historical past into the present by carefully including Japanese script on the carpet, directing his queries to contemporary Japanese. Should love be the primary bond with one's country, or is civic dissent also encouraged? Do Japanese viewers feel love for the emperor or the country? In this way, *Loves Me, Loves Me Not* critiques the colonial fantasy of romantic love and the postwar illusion of filial attachments sustained by the continued use of the chrysanthemum.

Vyjayanthi R. Selinger
Associate Professor of Asian Studies,
Bowdoin College

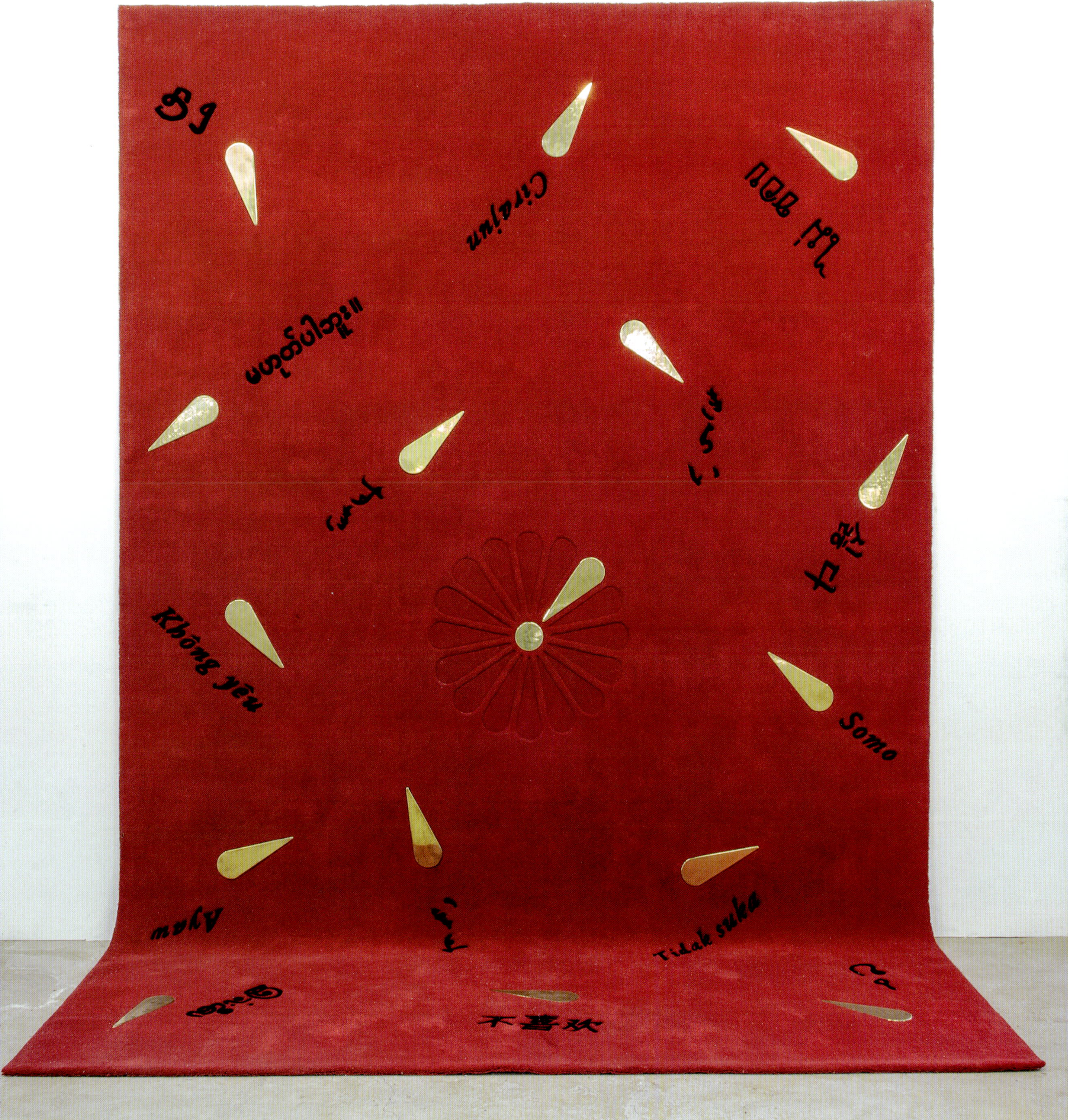

Cintaku
Không yêu
Somo
Ayau
Tidak suka
不喜欢

## *Carnival II*

Nancy Spero (American, 1926–2009), 2000
Handprinting and printed collage on paper, 95¼ × 19 in.
(241.9 × 48.3 cm)
Gift of Alvin D. Hall, Class of 1974  2017.39

An ad from Frederick's of Hollywood lingerie. Two dildo dancers, after a painted plate from circa 500 BCE by the Greek painter Epiktetos. A prehistoric birth image. A group of smaller dildo dancers (Greek). And modern acrobats flipping backward. What do all of these images have in common? This sounds like a parody of a typical setup of an old Borscht Belt joke. And it is a setup, but one for a layered, slow-revealing journey into the cultural and political themes and meanings of Nancy Spero's singular art practice.

At first the work may appear somewhat cartoony. However, the initial curiosity prompted by the combination and contrast of strong, memorable female images remains hauntingly in the viewer's memory and thoughts. That's the setup for the journey—looking for the connectors, deciphering the artist's intent, trying to ascertain the work's meaning.

Raw. Fierce. Passionate. Honest. These are adjectives typically applied to Spero's powerful works about the Vietnam War, Artaud, male power, oppression, feminism, and violence. Works about these subjects consist of images and text starkly placed or clustered on a large single sheet of plain off-white paper or on sheets joined together horizontally or vertically to form scrolls. The plain backgrounds accentuate and animate the figures.

*Carnival II* is a more colorful work. Bright, painterly yellows, lavender, oranges, golds, blues, and fleshy pinks in the upper band suggest streamers that have been cut and pressed into or attached to the paper. Spero's subtle sizing and positioning of the images is another key to her intent. Each image or group of images has, in effect, its own stage on which to hover, float, perform. What are the historic meanings and contemporary implications of each? As the viewer moves down the page from the very modern stripperlike ad to the prehistoric birth symbol (with a waving, smiling baby emerging), followed by dancers, a celebratory theme comes into focus. This feeling doesn't diminish as the colors darken in the lower band. Instead of suggesting something ominous, this band deepens the physical perspective of the work, as if the many smaller figures cavorting on stages—interior, emotional planes, perhaps—are farther away from the viewer's gaze.

In his essay about another colorful work by Spero, Jon Bird wrote: "The carnivalesque celebration of colour and form, movement and gesture, define Spero's imagining of the female body's pleasures and desire, just as the same devices, inflected differently, can be made to signify the body's abjection. The sexual and maternal body is brought into representation as the symbolic expression of interior states and fantasies through the reworking of cultural myths and historical memories."[1] Indeed, the narrative of *Carnival II* ties motherhood and female sexuality together when they are usually positioned at odds with each other. The work revels in female exhibitionism, eroticism, birth, and pleasure. Its colorful staging of the images is surprisingly playful—coming from a different, lighter side of Spero's personality. As her longtime gallerist said to me while we were looking at an image of this work, "Nancy was having some fun in this piece."

Alvin D. Hall
Independent author

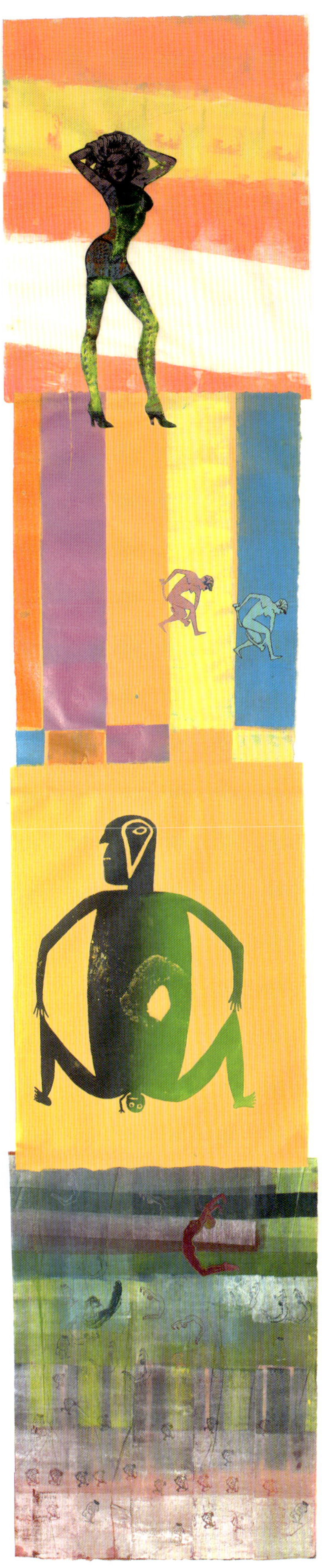

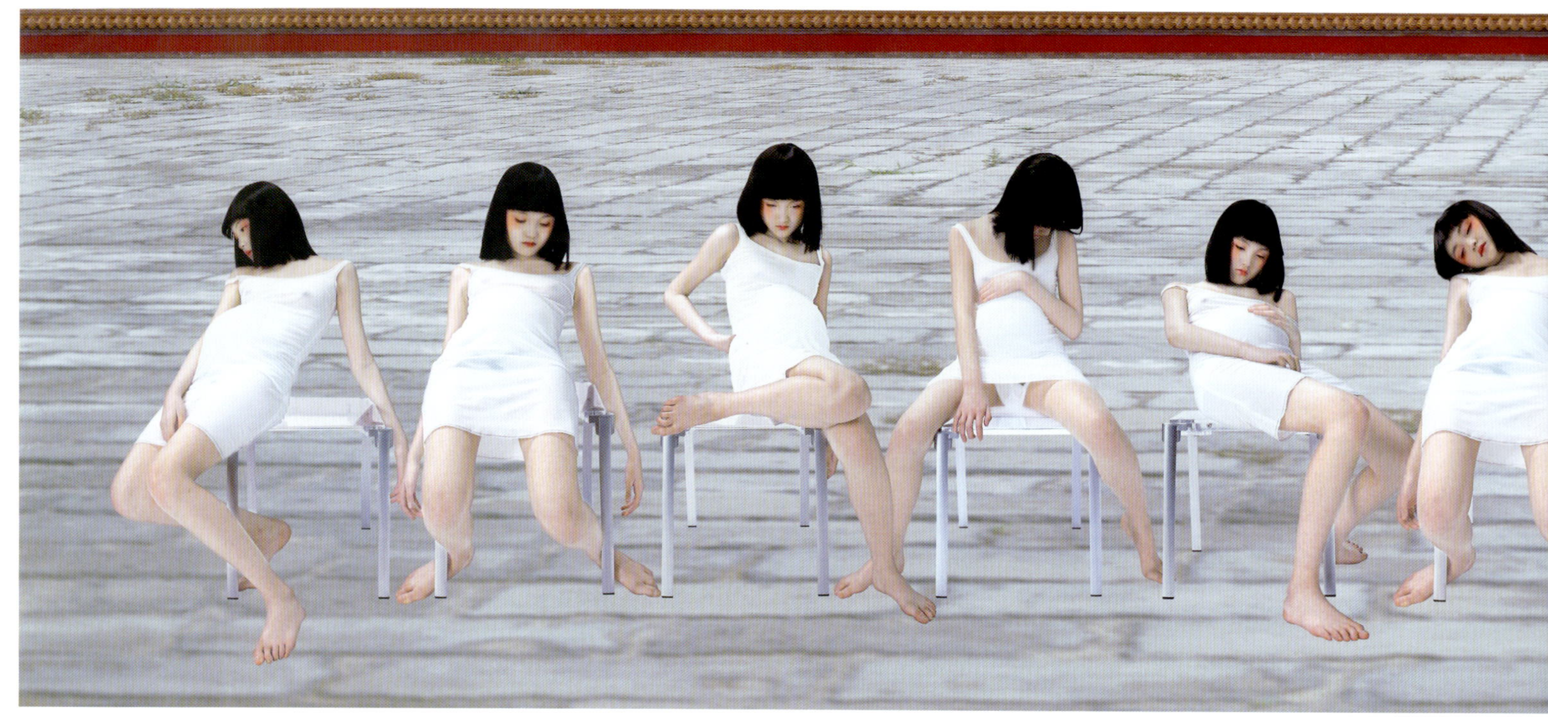

# *Angel No. 2*

Cui Xiuwen (Chinese, 1967–2018), 2006
Chromogenic print, 20 × 98 in. (52 × 250 cm)
Gift, Joe Baio Collection of Photography  2017.61.9

*Angel No. 2* belongs to Cui Xiuwen's *Angel Series*, an exploration of teen pregnancy through the visual medium of photography.[1] The pregnant body in its photographic construction asserts a subject unprecedented in Chinese sociopolitical history and art tradition. Cui's unconventional photographic practice does not try to capture a transparent image of social-physical reality or stage a fictional narrative; rather, she uses visual illustration to raise thematic issues through a process-oriented conceptual photography. *Angel No. 2* foregrounds a multifigure composition from a paramount perspective through a telephoto lens. The composition features a row of pregnant teenagers replicated from one model. In identical hairstyles and white dresses, the teens drape themselves languidly on chairs, evincing an air of listless melancholy. Bearing the consequences of outlawed female sexuality and the emotional trauma of pregnancy, the twelve figures reflect larger social problems of family-planning policy and gender issues attendant to adolescent anxiety. The pregnant body covered with a white dress suggests adolescent innocence as well as vulnerability in a society that regulates female

chastity and sets reproductive quotas.[2] The replication of the photographed images asserts that teen pregnancy is not simply an individual nightmare but a collective experience. Cui situates her subjects against a barren square sealed by a line of red wall. The wall and the expansive courtyard mimic the Forbidden Palace, which symbolizes both the imperial hierarchy and the (post)socialist hegemony. In varied postures, with their eyes closed, the subjects refuse to confront the viewer's gaze. The composition positions the pregnant teens in isolation from the outside world, with female sexuality constrained by social-gender norms.

Along with thirteen other pieces in the series, *Angel No. 2* instances phototropic image making in the digital age, as the artist conceptualizes and visualizes the issue of teen pregnancy through camera and computer. This practice transforms photography into *photographies*, where the use of multiple forms and theoretical hybridity "brings about a visual revolution that forces us to rethink representation."[3] Rather than a straightforward exploration of indexical truth or visual evidence, the *Angel Series* manipulates the image-making process to produce multifaceted meanings.

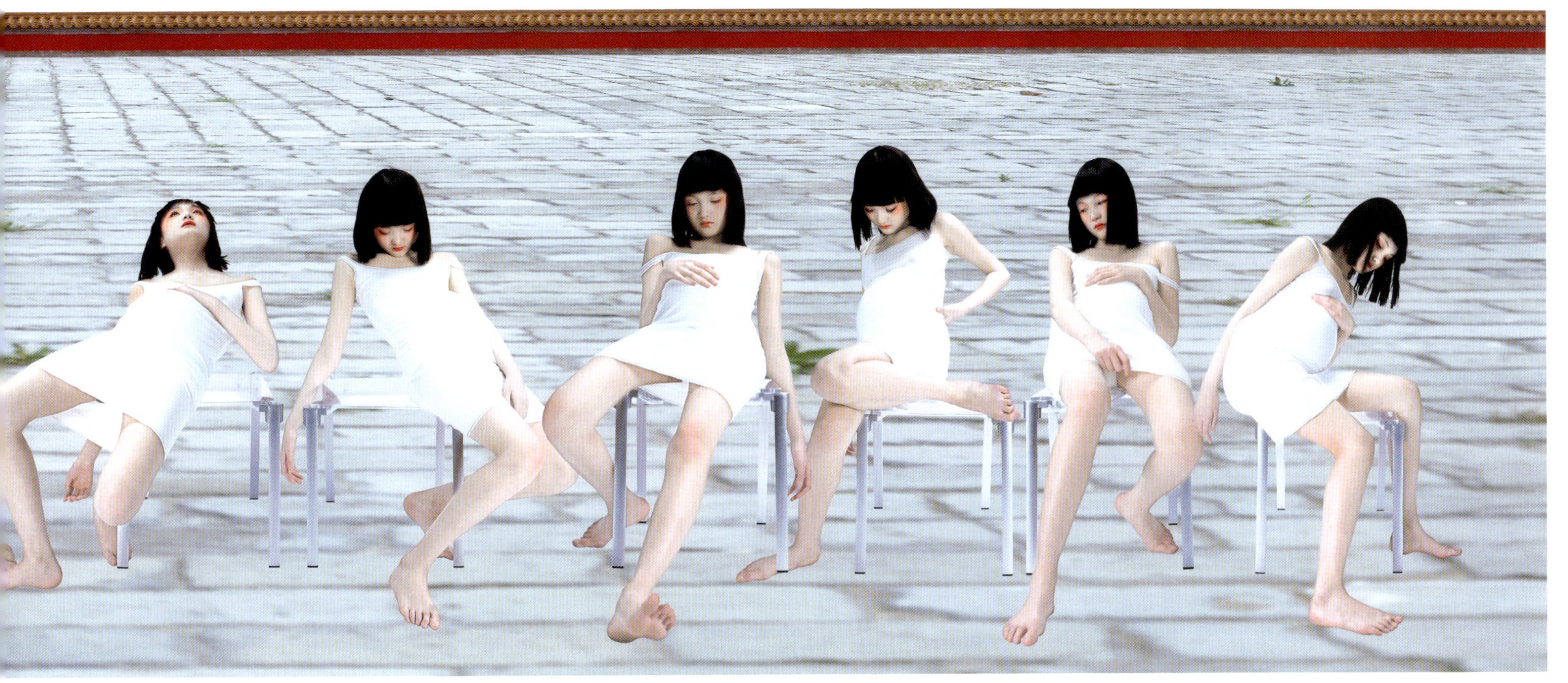

The multiphotographic procedure begins with a photo shoot of an attractive adolescent. Post-processing occurs via computer. Images from the individual model and the computer-generated replications are set against the existing site environment. In her post-photographic practice, the artist generates a conceptual photography by using computer digitization to transform mechanical production into innovative art.

In addition to the *Angel Series*, Cui Xiuwen left a large body of work that encompasses oil painting, photography, video, performance art, sculpture/installation, and abstract experimentation. In the years after the *Angel Series*, she expanded her artistic quest from concerns about gender issues to a spiritual search using multimedia.[4] In *Existential Emptiness* (2009), for instance, two lifesize dolls and post-photographic manipulations present a confrontation between the real and the unreal, between body and soul. The video work in *Spiritual Realm* (2010) choreographs migrant workers to express a divine linkage between body and soul, life and death. In the *Qin-se* series (2014), the spiritual journey assumes abstract form as striped strings, wood frames, and a video installation compose a formalistic abstraction. The artist's last work, *Angel's Light* (2016), is a multisection installation, segmented as well as connected within the exhibition space of the museum. With the body, heart, spirit, and destiny as leading concepts, the installation takes viewers on a spiritual journey to reconcile the incarnation of body and soul, origin and destination. Cui Xiuwen and her work have earned a permanent place in the history of Chinese contemporary art.

Shuqin Cui
Professor of Asian Studies and Cinema
Studies, Bowdoin College

# *Angel*

Alfredo Jaar (Chilean, born 1956), 2007
C–print mounted on Plexiglas, 30¾ × 87 in. (78.1 × 221 cm)
Archival Collection of Marion Boulton Stroud and Acadia Summer Arts
Program, Mt. Desert Island, Maine. Gift from the Marion Boulton "Kippy"
Stroud Foundation  2018.10.158

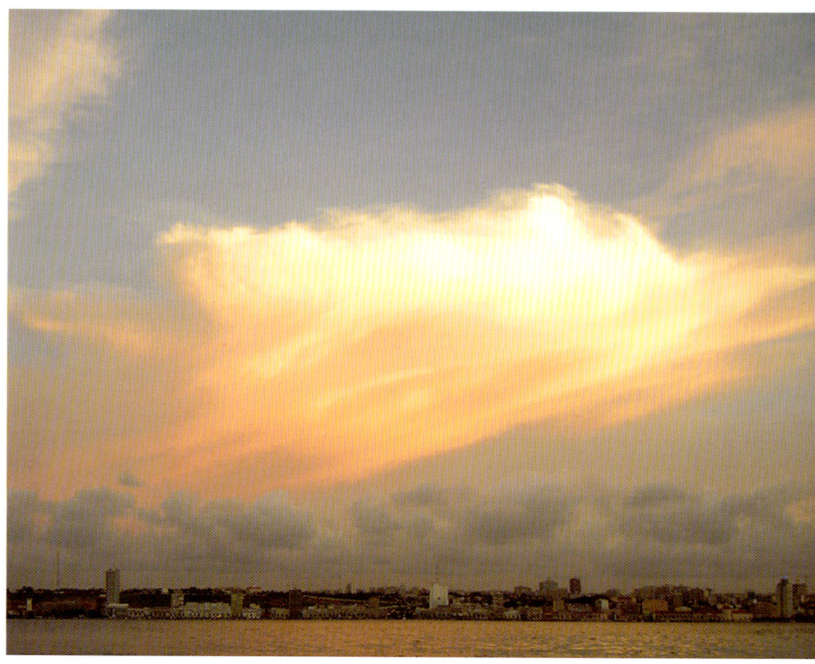

Alfredo Jaar's *Angel* comprises three nearly identical photographic compositions: a luminous cloud soars above a seaside city looming low on the horizon, its twilight colors becoming less saturated with each frame. On the center panel, a young boy's gesture and soft gaze direct the viewer's attention to the cloud's form, which suggests a sweeping figure with outstretched arms presiding over the landscape below. *Angel*'s tripartite format evokes a triptych, traditionally used by Christians in prayer. The religious connotation is reinforced by the boy's gesture of blessing and hope, which relates him to—or even transforms him into—the "angel" of the photograph's title.

Jaar, a Chilean-born artist whose politically driven projects have engaged many corners of the globe, met the subject of *Angel* while shooting his 2005 film *Muxima* in Luanda, Angola. While they discussed some of the nation's ongoing challenges, the boy spoke of the future and expressed his belief that the Angolan people would be protected by angels. Although the boy does not appear in the film, the photograph embodies many of the contradictions that the film explores. His impoverished circumstances, represented by the homemade Nike logo on his t-shirt, is set against a background of sprawling affluence. Multiple construction cranes dotting the rapidly growing cityscape of Luanda indicate the globalization that has arisen from concentrated oil wealth but failed to trickle down to Angola's wider population.

The wealth disparity of Angola's oil economy is a central theme of *Muxima*, a 36-minute film made up of "cantos" of varying duration, each dedicated to one or more social or political issues. Referencing poems by Pablo Neruda and Ezra Pound, the organizational device of the canto gives structure to a fragmented narrative that "suggests the difficulties in capturing the complexity of Angola."[1] Jaar's inspiration for his first film was the Afro-Portuguese folk song "Muxima" by "Liceu" Vieira Dias, co-founder of the People's Movement for the Liberation of Angola, which Jaar discovered in multiple recordings in his own vast collection of African music.[2] The various versions of "Muxima" accompany each of the film's ten cantos, the repeated song meant to evoke the melancholy and mourning typical of Portuguese *saudade*.

The first canto opens with a still image of six boys in front of an industrial harbor populated by oil tanks (fig. 1). Hands over hearts, their gestures suggest patriotism or faith, but also illustrate the film's title, *Muxima*, which means "heart" in Angola's indigenous Kimbundu language. In the following cantos, still frames mingle with stationary and moving shots, and depict such images as crumbling colonial monuments, a patient in an AIDS clinic, street signs named for international revolutionary leaders, a religious pilgrimage, and a technician painstakingly clearing one of the 18 million landmines planted across the country during the Angolan Civil War (1975–2002). *Angel*'s rosy-hued cloud and the distant cityscape of Luanda appear in Canto X, as pianist Paulo Oliveira performs the film's final "very personal and nostalgic version"[3] of the titular tune as day turns to night.

The *Muxima* project is one of Jaar's many artistic dialogues with the African continent, which began in 1994 with his seminal body of work addressing the Rwandan genocide. "I am irresistibly attracted to Africa," Jaar has stated. "There is something about that continent that moves me deeply. I feel that I must devote concentrated effort and energy in order to expose what is happening there and to trigger some kind of reaction and solidarity."[4]

Denise Birkhofer
Collections Curator, Ryerson Image Center,
Ryerson University, Toronto

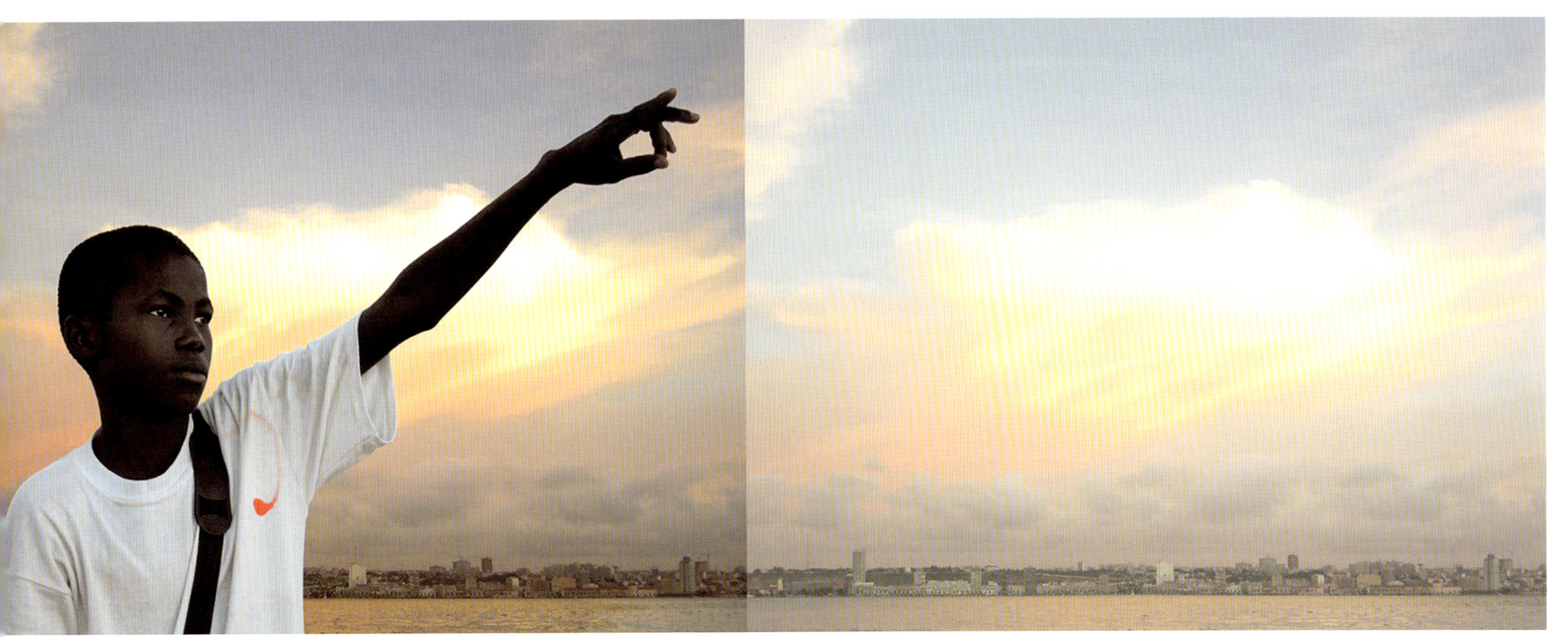

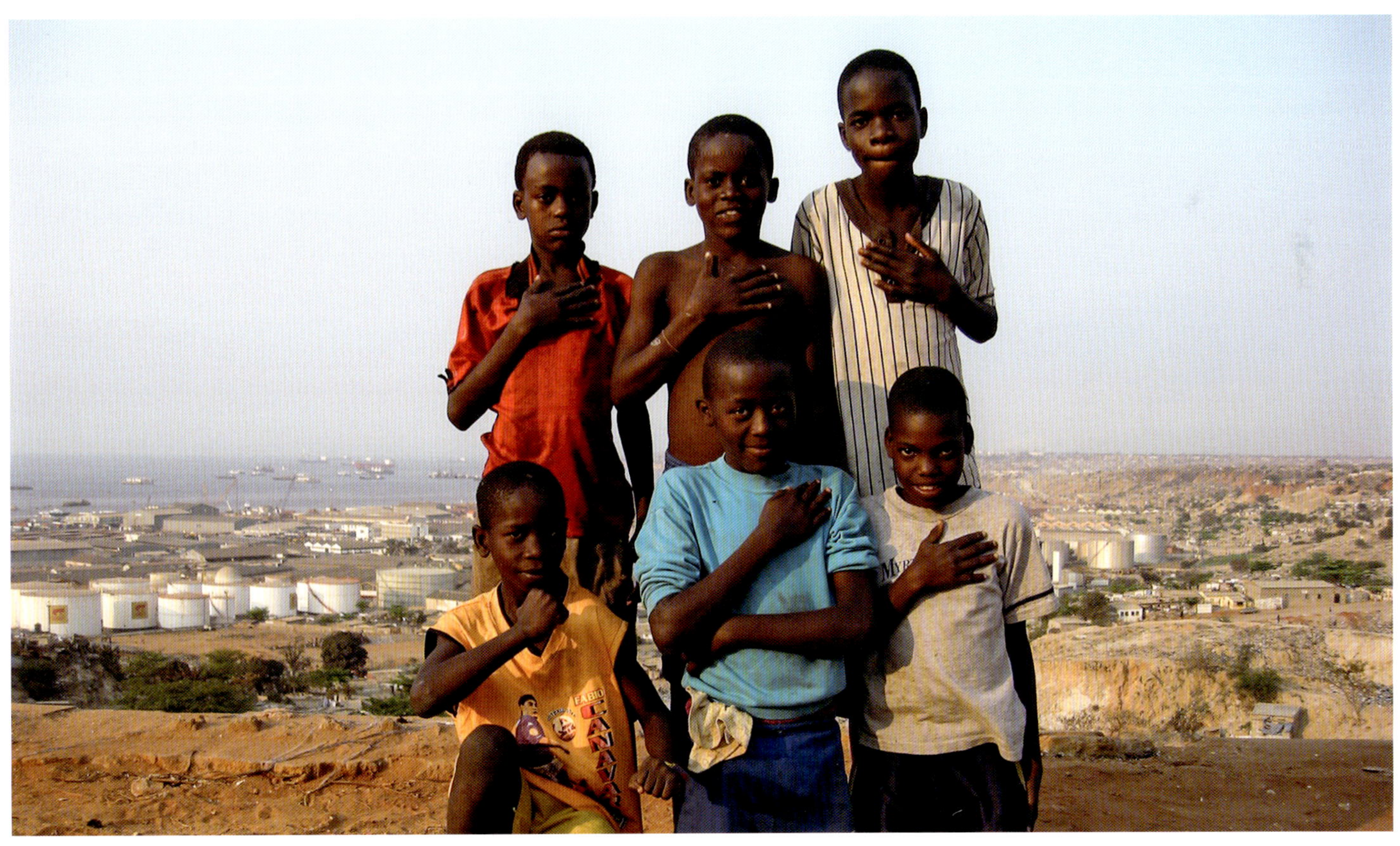

FIG. 1. Alfredo Jaar, *Muxima*, 2005. Video, 36 min. Courtesy Grand Arts, Kansas City, Galerie Lelong & Co. and the artist, New York

# *Black Shunga*

Chris Ofili (British, born 1968), 2008–15
From an eponymous suite of eleven etchings with gravure printed on paper specially prepared with metallic color pigment, 26⁷⁄₁₆ × 17½ in. (67.1 × 44.4 cm)
Printed and published by Two Palms Press, New York
Museum Purchase, Barbara Cooney Porter Fund  2016.3.6

As a British-born artist of Nigerian descent who has lived and worked in Trinidad since 2005, Chris Ofili draws inspiration from a wide range of cultural sources. The tantalizing blue hues that flood the background of the etchings in his *Black Shunga* suite have played a prominent role in a number of his paintings and sculptures for more than a decade and serve as a revealing example of the rich range of references that inform the artist's approach to his work.

When he moved to Trinidad, Ofili was particularly struck by the nocturnal light there—a deep blue-black twilight, influenced by the island's equatorial proximity—in which forms are barely discernible and the environment takes on a dreamlike, mystical atmosphere. The color blue also has a key presence in the annual Trinidadian Carnival, in the form of the famous "blue devils" from the hill town of Paramin who descend into the capital, Port of Spain, each year, covered from head to toe in blue pigment to create a sinister presence (and hide their identity). They carry pitchforks and intimidate other dancers and onlookers in an aggressive manner that normally would not be tolerated but is integral to the Carnival program. These experiences led Ofili to further consideration of a multitude of additional associations with blue, such as the traditional blue garment worn by the Virgin in Renaissance paintings; the works of Franz Marc and the German group Der Blaue Reiter (The Blue Rider)—interested, like Ofili in the synthesis of art, music, and spirituality; blues music, in particular Louis Armstrong's famous rendition of "(What Did I Do to Be So) Black and Blue"; and the longstanding embattled relationships between black communities and blue-uniformed police.[1]

In the *Black Shunga* etchings, lush azure and Prussian blue pigments swirl, pool, and bleed like water stains or cloud formations, evoking a range of settings—a nocturnal overgrown jungle with the moon peeking through (in the print illustrated here), the depths of the ocean, the Land of Eden, or some otherworldly realm—all of which are enhanced by the optical effects created by the underlayer of color-shifting metallic powder. Barely perceptible imagery, depending on the lighting and the angle in which the prints are viewed, executed in fine, sinuous linework, was printed in silvery gray ink over the expanse of blue. Catching a glimpse of these fluid calligraphic strokes, the viewer is compelled to look more closely at the surface of the print, and slowly the lines resolve into contours of figures engaged in a variety of intimate sexual acts. This imagery and the title of the suite refer to Japanese *shunga-e*, erotic woodblock prints made primarily in the Edo period (1615–1868). Traditionally, the Japanese figures are defined by flowing black outlines and filled in with color and elaborately patterned attire. Ofili's figures are presented in pure outline against the fluctuating blue backdrop, almost as apparitions—heightening the sense of the viewer as voyeur and the secret pleasure derived from illicit observations. The addition of "Black" to "Shunga" in the title, combined with the challenges of visibility carefully constructed by the artist, point to both the stereotyped exoticism of black bodies and the absence of black figures in the canon of Western art, as well as the more generalized lack of acknowledgment experienced by black populations in many of the societies in which they live. The latter is most compelling considering the inclusion of the lyrics from Armstrong's song in the prologue to Ralph Ellison's quintessential novel about African American life, *The Invisible Man* (1952). Thus, the *Black Shunga* prints are a superb example of Ofili's remarkable ability to create extraordinarily beautiful objects that convey deeply resonant meanings across time, places, and cultures.

Shelley R. Langdale
The Park Family Associate Curator
of Prints and Drawings, Philadelphia
Museum of Art, and President,
Print Council of America

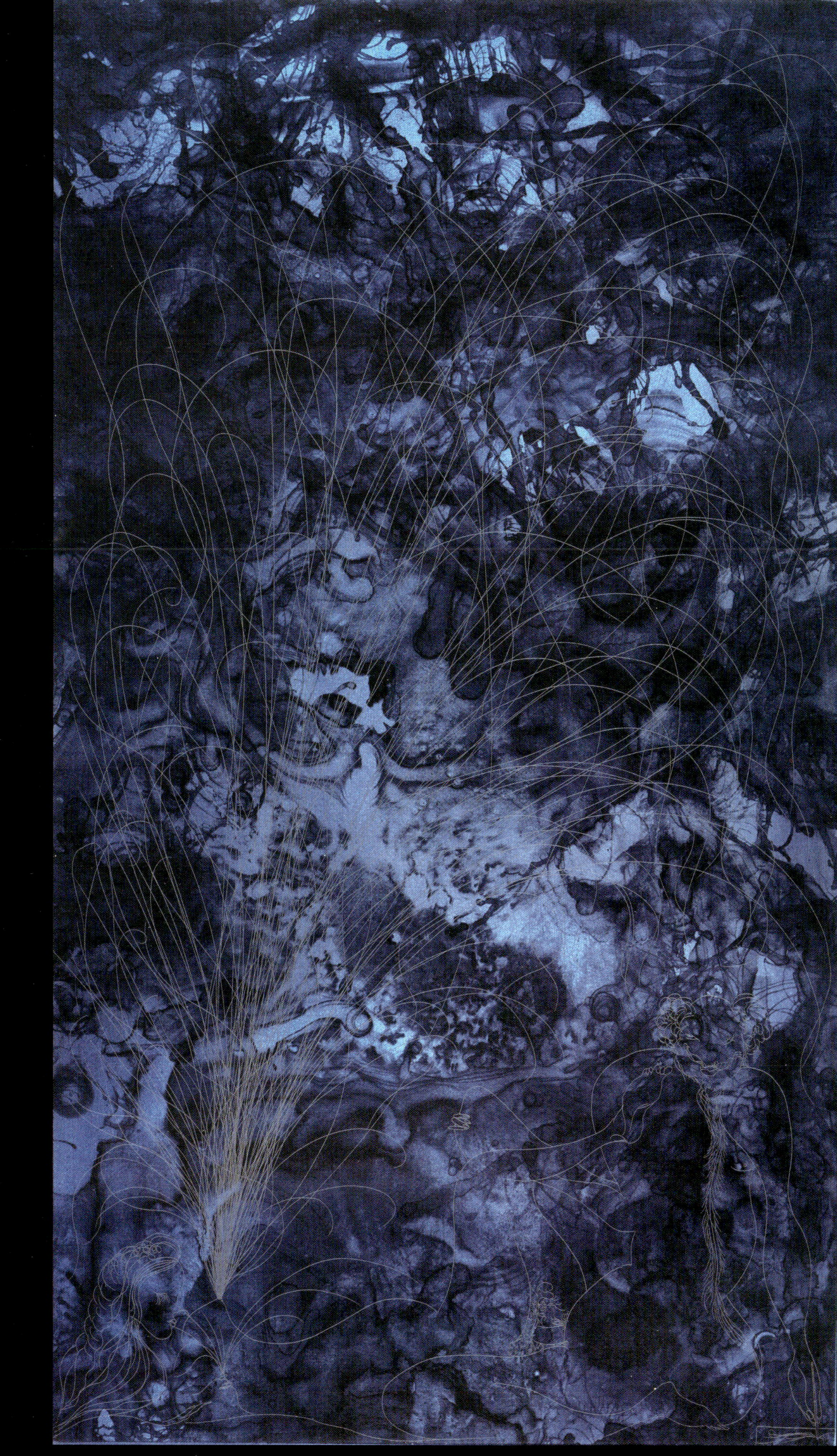

# AFTERWORD: AN EPISTLE FOR THE FUTURE

**An open letter to friends of the Bowdoin College Museum of Art on the occasion of the 250th anniversary of the Walker Art Building in the year 2144**

Congratulations on reaching this milestone anniversary. I am writing to you from the year 2019, when the Walker Art Building celebrated its 125th anniversary. We marked the occasion then with the publication of this collection catalogue, a birthday cake, and a cellphone recital and dance performance by a new student group that created their own composition in conjunction with linn meyers's wall drawing *Let's Get Lost* and the accompanying interactive sound element *Listening Glass* (fig. 1). The idea of meyers and her collaborators was to transform one of the

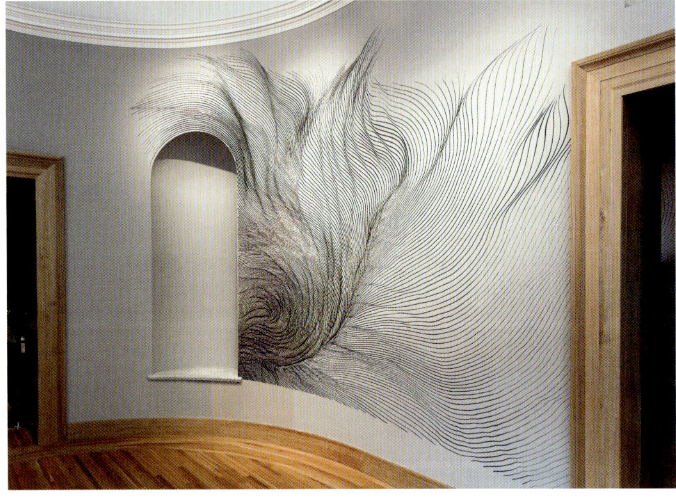



FIG. 1. Installation view of *Let's Get Lost* by linn meyers at the Bowdoin College Museum of Art. Photo by Diana and Dennis Griggs

Museum's galleries into a musical instrument, as well as create an immersive visual experience. They challenged us to lose ourselves in unchartered creative forays. In the excitement of the moment—and on a sugar high—my colleagues and I thought that we were witnessing what museums and works of art might be like in the future—more experiential and interactive, more experimental and technologically sophisticated, more socially relevant and integrated into the wider campus and community. It was as though the dream of flying automobiles had finally been realized.

As we pause to consider the past 125 years, it is true that much has changed at Bowdoin—most notably, the inclusion of women and a more ethnically and socially diverse faculty and student body. Yet, the Museum has long sought to embrace many of the same qualities that I admire in meyers's installation. Looking back, I am keenly aware that the Museum has shone brightest when it has featured great works of art, timely and original exhibitions, dynamic public programs, and active engagement with faculty, students, and the community. Of course, today, every academic museum in the United States aspires to these goals. I suspect you do, too, in 2144. What, therefore, does excellence look like? What priorities should take center stage as the Museum continues to grow and evolve?

Despite its relatively small size and its distance from larger population centers, the Museum has often been a true pioneer, creating unique projects that have resonated nearby but also well beyond the region. In 1964, for example, the Museum opened one of the first exhibitions to focus on the artistic achievement of African Americans and the history of their representation. Curated by Marvin Sadik, *The Portrayal of the Negro in American Painting* was a groundbreaking show that awakened the field of American art to important yet under-appreciated black artists, and to the ways in which African Americans have been historically represented. Paintings purchased in preparation for the show, such as Joshua Johnson's *Portrait of a Man (Abner Coker)* (fig. 2), have provided touchstones for a more inclusive narrative of American art history ever since. New ideas and scholarly achievement are not dependent on the size of one's institution or its particular location. Excellence can happen wherever intellectual production and artistic creativity are valued.

Many wise words for the future can be found in the past. Over the last several centuries, artists and scholars in the West have written and spoken frequently about artistic ideals and aspirations. Joshua Reynolds, Tristan Tzara, Claes Oldenburg, the Guerrilla Girls—each authored art manifestos for their times. While many such statements are understood today as elitist, rife with contradiction, and/ or neglecting wide segments of the population, there are lessons to be drawn from their work that should continue to be relevant well into the future.

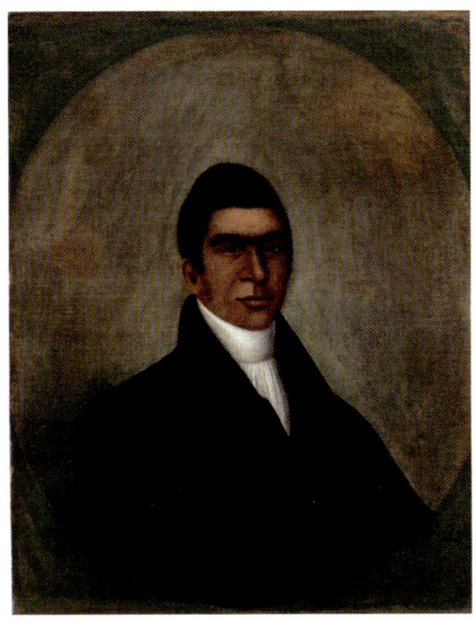

FIG. 2. Joshua Johnson, *Portrait of a Man (Abner Coker)*, c. 1805–10. Oil on canvas, 27 ⅛ × 22 in. (70.8 × 55.9 cm). Bowdoin College Museum of Art, Museum Purchase, George Otis Hamlin Fund, 1963.490

From Reynolds, we learn that art is as much an activity of the mind as the hand. From Tzara, that art goes beyond the rational and the national. From Oldenburg, that art must be relevant to its times. And from the Guerrilla Girls, that art has been made by those from every segment of society and that museums have an obligation to represent the totality of creative expression, not simply the patriarchal elite. These ideas are foundational today and should continue to be guiding stars.

From what I know about the past, what do I hope in the future for academic museums? Here are five wishes:

1) It's important to continue to lead in innovation. Contemporary artists can head up this effort, though the past can be revivified through new scholarship, by the application of new technologies, and when we work collaboratively with new audiences, especially those who disrupt a privileged point of view.
2) It's important to acquire and exhibit only those works that provoke meaningful dialogue with the past, that break new ground today, and that anticipate future concerns. Art in an academic museum can be experimental and difficult, but it should never be timid or exclusionary.
3) It's important that all forms of creative expression be embraced and that all traditions and voices be welcomed. Despite the historic neglect of women and artists of color and the tendency of the marketplace to gravitate around certain trends, there should be no hierarchy of artistic taste at an academic museum.
4) It's important to promote art in spaces beyond the walls of the museum and to encourage researchers from other fields into the museum. We want more scientists, and science should want more artists, especially as human civilization confronts global issues such as climate change, mass migration, and explosive ethnic and religious conflicts. These challenges will require the type of creativity and openness that artistic practice inculcates.
5) It's important to continue to provide a space for the close study of art objects, for quiet contemplation, for productive conversations, for creative performances and partnerships, and for social gatherings. Museums are some of the most beautiful places in our communities, and we should rejoice in gathering there with others.

The Walker Art Building opened its doors to the public on February 19, 1894. Accounts suggest that attendance was "unexpectedly large" during its first months, though some complained that the all-brick facade on the side of the building facing town was "insulting." On June 7, after the winter snows had melted, the building was officially dedicated. Martin Brimmer, director of the Museum of Fine Arts, Boston, gave a formal address that day before the assembled trustees, administration, alumni, faculty, and students. In an issue of the *Bowdoin Orient* following the dedication, an unsigned editorial reflected on the significance of the moment: "We had a fine collection, but no place where it could be displayed or used for the purpose of study. Now, in this beautiful and well equipped building where everything appears at its best, a new course of study is presented to us, that of the beautiful and ideal. Every student should take advantage of this exceptional chance to become thoroughly acquainted with the best in art, and fit himself to enjoy through life that broad field of pleasure which so many pass unnoticed."

The completion of the Walker Art Building in 1894 ushered in a new chapter in the history of the visual arts at Bowdoin. The past 125 years have witnessed the realization of this "new course of study." We hope that the Museum continues to prosper in the years ahead. On behalf of my colleagues, thanks to everyone past, present, and future whose generosity has made possible this extraordinary educational resource dedicated to creative expression in all its forms, by artists from near and far, and devoted to all.

With warm regards,
Frank H. Goodyear III
Co-Director

# NOTES

## ART PURPOSES

1. *Looking at Art with Alex Katz* (London: Laurence King, 2018), p. 20.
2. *Elise Ansel: Distant Mirrors* (Brunswick, Me.: Bowdoin College Museum of Art, 2016).
3. *Katherine Bradford: Paintings*, with contributions by Arthur Bradford, Dan Nadel, and Karen Wilkin (New York: Canada, 2018).
4. See Lillian B. Miller, "The Legacy: The Walker Gift, 1894," in *The Legacy of James Bowdoin III* (Brunswick, Me.: Bowdoin College Museum of Art, 1994), pp. 187–212.
5. See Patricia McGraw Anderson, "Walker Art Building," in *The Architecture of Bowdoin College* (Brunswick, Me.: Bowdoin College Museum of Art, 1988), pp. 43–48; Richard Guy Wilson, ed., *McKim, Mead & White: Selected Works, 1879–1915* (Hudson, N.Y.: Princeton Architectural Press, 2018).

## TWO CENTURIES OF ART WITH A PURPOSE AT BOWDOIN

1. An early version of this essay was prepared for the panel "Collections américaines," chaired by Mathilde Schneider, at the Festival de l'Histoire de l'Art, Fontainebleau, June 2–4, 2017. For the invitation to participate, I thank John Davis and Annick Lemoine. I also thank Joachim Homann for his recommendations regarding its subsequent development.
2. John Cotton Dana, "The Gloom of the Museum" (1917), in *Reinventing the Museum*, ed. Gail Anderson (Lanham, Md.: AltaMira Press, 2004), p. 25; and Walter Pach, *The Art Museum in America* (New York: Pantheon Books, 1948), p. 2.
3. Dana, "The Gloom of the Museum," p. 26. Dana's prescient observation would later be theorized in Walter Benjamin, "The Work of Art in the Age of Mechanical Reproduction" (1936), in *Illuminations*, ed. Hannah Arendt, trans. Harry Zohn (New York: Schocken Books, 1968), pp. 217–51; and André Malraux, *Museum without Walls* (Garden City, N.Y.: Doubleday, 1967).
4. See, for example, President Clayton Rose's statement on "The Work Ahead," drawn from his 2018 Convocation address at Bowdoin, at https://www.bowdoin.edu/president/pdf/The-Work-Ahead_Oct_19_.pdf.
5. Walter Pach is perhaps best known today as one of the organizers of the 1913 Armory Show—together with Walter Kuhn and Henry McBride—which introduced American audiences to European abstraction and modernism. In 1927, he participated in an Institute for Art at Bowdoin, which included leading figures in the field such as Alfred Barr, William Ivins, and Violet Oakley, and in winter 1936 he taught at the College. I thank John Cross, Laurette E. McCarthy, and Francis M. Naumann for generously sharing information about Pach's ties to Bowdoin, and John Cross for his assistance in identifying buildings pictured by Pach. Pach testifies to his admiration for Bowdoin's Museum throughout *The Art Museum in America*; see pp. 38, 50, 68, 209.
6. While no comprehensive overview of a history of collegiate collecting in the United States exists, it is notable that academic institutions were the first organizations in the United States to offer institutional homes to the fine arts. Yale University was the first, with its 1718 acquisition of Godfrey Kneller's *King George I*, early eighteenth century, a gift of Elihu Yale; Harvard may be second, with fine art acquisitions dating to 1766; and Dartmouth third, with evidence of fine arts collections by 1791. See Susan B. Matheson, *Art for Yale: A History of the Yale University Art Gallery* (New Haven: Yale University Art Gallery, 2001); Ethan W. Lasser, ed., *The Philosophy Chamber: Art and Science in Harvard's Teaching Cabinet, 1766–1820* (Cambridge, Mass.: Harvard Art Museums, 2017); and Clifton C. Olds, "The Intellectual Foundations of the College Museum," in *The Legacy of James Bowdoin III* (Brunswick, Me.: Bowdoin College Museum of Art, 1994), pp. 32–53; and Corrine Glesne, "The Campus Art Museum: A Qualitative Study," Kress Foundation, October 2012, at http://www.kressfoundation.org/research/campus_art_museum/, p. 4.
7. For detailed information about James Bowdoin III's upbringing, education, maturation, and collecting, see Richard Saunders, "James Bowdoin III (1752–1811)," in *The Legacy of James Bowdoin III*, pp. 1–31; Sarah Cantor, "James Bowdoin III and America's Earliest Collection of Drawings," and Eliza Goodpasture, "James Bowdoin III's Collection in Context: On Historical Roots and Their Legacies," both in *Art Treasures, Gracefully Drawn: James Bowdoin III and America's Earliest Drawing Collection*, online catalogue (Brunswick, Me.: Bowdoin College Museum of Art, 2016), at http://www.bowdoin.edu/art-museum/catalogues/old-masters/index.shtml. For information about the iconoclasm at Harvard, see Lasser, *The Philosophy Chamber*, pp. 17–19.
8. For detailed discussions of Bowdoin's experience in Europe, see Cantor, "James Bowdoin III and America's Earliest Collection of Drawings"; and Goodpasture, "James Bowdoin III's Collection in Context."
9. On the commitment of leaders of the American Revolution to cultivating arts and culture in the early republic, see Lillian B. Miller, *Patrons and Patriotism* (Chicago: University of Chicago Press, 1966).
10. Detailed entries on the portraits are included in Carrie Rebora Barratt and Ellen G. Miles, *Gilbert Stuart* (New York: The Metropolitan Museum of Art, 2004), pp. 273–80. The portraits were completed only after the conclusion of Bowdoin's short diplomatic appointment, so that they were delivered to his home in Boston rather than being sent abroad (ibid., p. 276). The portraits are discussed in Linda J. Docherty, "Original Copies: Gilbert Stuart's Companion Portraits of Thomas Jefferson and James Madison," *American Art* 22, no. 2 (Summer 2008), pp. 85–97. On Bowdoin's portraits of "worthies," see Susan E. Wegner, "Copies and Education: James Bowdoin's Painting Collection in the Life of the College," in *The Legacy of James Bowdoin III*, pp. 148–49.
11. On Stuart's trip to Bowdoin, see Barratt and Miles, *Gilbert Stuart*, p. 276. On the related portrait series of the "American Kings," see "Four of the 'Five Kings' Come to the Bowdoin College Museum of Art," *Bowdoin News*, May 27, 2015, at http://community.bowdoin.edu/news/2015/05/four-of-the-five-kings-come-to-the-bowdoin-college-museum-of-art/. Stuart's success in establishing these as iconic likenesses is indicated by their later use on American currency. His likeness of Madison appeared on the $5,000 bill in

the late 1920s and 1930s, and today his likeness of Jefferson can be found on the American $2 bill.

12. Sarah Bowdoin sat for her portrait before the couple departed for Europe, but Stuart seems to have relied upon a miniature by Edward Malbone to create his likeness of her husband; see Linda J. Docherty, "Preserving our Ancestors: The Bowdoin Portrait Collection," in *The Legacy of James Bowdoin III*, p. 69.

13. Letter from James Bowdoin to Thomas Jefferson, March 25, 1805, *Founders Online*, National Archives, at https://founders.archives .gov/?q=bowdoin&s=1511311111&sa=&r=877&sr=.

14. Jefferson wrote to Bowdoin on April 27, 1805 (Wegner, "Copies and Education," p. 144). Although the precise date of his sitting(s) with Stuart is uncertain, Jefferson had posed for the portrait by June 18, 1805 (Barratt and Miles, *Gilbert Stuart*, p. 277).

15. On Bowdoin's acquisition of art supplies for Stuart, see Barratt and Miles, *Gilbert Stuart*, p. 276. For a cogent discussion of the republican ideology infused into French museums, see Andrew McClellan, *Inventing the Louvre* (Berkeley: University of California Press, 1999), p. 193.

16. Wegner, "Copies and Education," p. 153. On Sarah Bowdoin's October 1805 diary entry describing a trip to the Louvre, see Saunders, "James Bowdoin III (1752–1811)," p. 21.

17. I thank Stephen Perkinson for bringing to my attention the presence of these catalogues in Bowdoin's library, now part of the James Bowdoin III Collection, George J. Mitchell Special Collections & Archives, Bowdoin College.

18. Alexandre Lenoir, "Avant-Propos," in *Description historique et chronologique des monumens de sculpture réunis au Musée des Monumens Français* (Paris, 1803), James Bowdoin III Collection, George J. Mitchell Special Collections & Archives, Bowdoin College. On Lenoir's founding of the Musée des Monuments Français, see McClellan, *Inventing the Louvre*, pp. 155–97, 259–67.

19. Regarding the history of early collecting by American institutions of higher learning, see note 6.

20. Olds, "The Intellectual Foundations of the College Museum," p. 33.

21. Henry Home, Lord Kames, *Sketches of the History of Man* (London: A. Strahan and T. Cadell, 1788), p. 219; in the James Bowdoin Collection, Bowdoin College Library Special Collections. Cited in Olds, "The Intellectual Foundations of the College Museum," p. 52 n. 70.

22. On the popularity of the theme of the continence of Scipio in revolutionary and early republican-era America, and on the influence of Smibert's painting specifically, see Caroline Winterer, "From Royal to Republican: The Classical Image in Early America," *The Journal of American History* 91, no. 4 (March 2005), pp. 1283–88. See also Richard Saunders's entry on Smibert's *The Continence of Scipio* in this volume (pp. 112–13). Gilbert Stuart's attributions of paintings in Bowdoin's collection are included in Wegner, "Copies and Education," p. 177.

23. *Laws of Bowdoin College* (Hallowell, Me.: E. Goodale, 1817), p. 16. Bowdoin College Governing Board, Bowdoin College Special Collections.

24. The response of Henry Putnam, a resident of Brunswick, Maine, is quoted in Wegner, "Copies and Education," p. 149.

25. Eliza Goodpasture addresses the complex relationship between privilege, philanthropy, and access in "James Bowdoin III's Collection in Context."

26. On the collection, see Cantor, "James Bowdoin III and America's Earliest Collection of Drawings"; David P. Becker, *Old Master Drawings at Bowdoin College* (Brunswick, Me.: Bowdoin College Museum of Art, 1985), pp. xiv–xvi; and Caroline O. Fowler, "Drawing: A Universal Language in a New World," in *Why Draw? 500 Years of Drawings and Watercolors at Bowdoin College*, ed. Joachim Homann (New York: DelMonico Books•Prestel, and Bowdoin College Museum of Art, 2017), pp. 18–23.

27. A complete list of the paintings bequeathed by Bowdoin to the College is included in Wegner, "Copies and Education," pp. 172–76.

28. See ibid., pp. 149–51.

29. Quoted in ibid., p. 151.

30. Quoted in Carol Duncan, *Civilizing Rituals: Inside Public Art Museums* (London: Routledge, 1995), p. 54.

31. Martin Brimmer, "An Address Delivered at Bowdoin College Upon the Opening of the Walker Art School," June 7, 1894, at https ://digitalcommons.bowdoin.edu/art-museum-miscellaneous -publications/6/.

32. In 1894, the year in which the Walker Art Building opened at Bowdoin, McKim led the establishment of the American School of Architecture, later the American Academy, in Rome.

33. Art instruction was formalized at Bowdoin in 1913 (Wegner, "Copies and Education," p. 162). A broader overview of the development of art-historical education and pedagogy is included in Matthew Israel, "CAA, Pedagogy and Curriculum," in *The Eye, the Hand, the Mind: 100 Years of the College Art Association*, ed. Susan L. Ball (New York: Rutgers University Press, 2011), pp. 155–79.

34. In 2010, with support from the Andrew W. Mellon Foundation, Bowdoin College established the new professional post of a Postdoctoral Curatorial Fellow at the Museum of Art charged with reaching out to faculty.

35. During the Fall 2018 semester, the Museum hosted 1,362 student academic visits, in 33 different courses supervised by 30 different professors and 22 different departments. The Bowdoin student body numbers 1,800 students, all undergraduates.

## ANCIENT ART

### THREE ASSYRIAN RELIEFS

1. For more information on Assyrian art and architecture, including the Northwest Palace, see Ada Cohen and Steven E. Kangas, eds., *Assyrian Reliefs from the Palace of Ashurnasirpal II: A Cultural Biography* (Hanover, N.H.: University Press of New England, 2010); Klaudia Englund, "The Northwest Palace at Nimrud," 2018, at https://cdli.ucla.edu/projects/nimrud/index.html; David Kertai, *The Architecture of Late Assyrian Royal Palaces* (Oxford: Oxford University Press, 2015); Learning Sites, Inc., "The Northwest Palace of Ashur-nasir-pal II, Nimrud: An Interactive Publication Prototype," January 2, 2017, at http://www.learningsites.com/NWPalace /NWPalhome.php.

2. See Jacques Derrida, "The Parergon," *October*, no. 9 (Summer 1979), pp. 3–41, esp. 18–28 (trans. Craig Owens).

3. Plutarch, *Alexander*, 37.3, trans. Ian Scott-Kilvert.

4. For discussions of changing approaches to archaeological artifacts in a museum context, see Eleanor Robson et al., "Nimrud: Materialities of Assyrian Knowledge Production," 2013–14, at http://oracc.museum.upenn.edu/nimrud/index.html.

5. For discussions of iconoclasm, see Natalie Naomi May, ed., *Iconoclasm and Text Destruction in the Ancient Near East and Beyond* (Chicago: Oriental Institute of the University of Chicago, 2012); Barbara Nevling Porter, "Noseless in Nimrud: More Figurative Responses to Assyrian Domination," in *Of God(s), Trees, Kings, and Scholars: Neo-Assyrian and Related Studies in Honour of Simo Parpola*, ed. Mikko Luukko et al. (Helsinki: Finnish Oriental Society, 2009), pp. 201–20.

### BAIL-HANDLE OINOCHOE OR OLPE

1. Jenifer Neils and John H. Oakley, *Coming of Age in Ancient Greece: Images of Childhood from the Classical Past* (New Haven: Yale University Press, 2003), no. 112.

### FISH PLATE

1. Ian McPhee and A. D. Trendall, *Greek Red-Figured Fish-Plates* (Basel: Vereinigung der Freunde Antiker Kunst, 1987), pp. 123–27 (Perrone-Phrixos Group), pls. 47–50; 49c (similar octopus).

### MARBLE RELIEF OF A SLEEPING HERACLES

1. For the official biography of Warren, see Osbert Burdett and E. H. Goddard, *Edward Perry Warren: The Biography of a Connoisseur* (London: Christophers, 1941); for more recent accounts, see David Sox, *Bachelors of Art: Edward Perry Warren & the Lewes House Brotherhood* (London: Fourth Estate, 1991), and Dyfri Williams, *The Warren Cup* (London: British Museum Press, 2006), pp. 17–34.

2. It has been suggested that he formed an attachment to the area because his family's paper factories were located there.

## ASIAN ART

### BOOK OF THE SEVEN CLIMES

1. On the life and work of al-Sīmāwī, see Eric J. Holmyard, "Abu'l-Qāsim al-'Irāqī," *Isis* 8, no. 3 (1926), pp. 403–26; Muḥammad ibn Aḥmad al-'Irāqī, *Kitāb al-'ilm al-muktasab fī zirā'at adh-dhahab: Book of Knowledge Acquired Concerning the Cultivation of Gold*, trans. and ed. Eric J. Holmyard (Paris: Paul Geuthner, 1923); Manfred Ullmann, *Die Natur- und Geheimwissenschaften im Islam* (Leiden: Brill, 1972), pp. 235–37, 268; Liana Saif, "The Cows and the Bees: Arabic Sources and Parallels for Pseudo-Plato's *Liber Vaccae* (*Kitāb al-Nawāmīs*)," *Journal of the Warburg and Courtauld Institutes* 79 (2016), pp. 1–47, esp. pp. 2–4.

2. For comparable copies of the *Book of the Seven Climes*, see: Dublin, Chester Beatty Library, Ar 5433, f. 20v (16th century); Riyad, King Saud University, MS 3167z, ff. 7r, 28v (16th century?), at http://makhtota.ksu.edu.sa/makhtota/3418/1#.W9yVWNL7Q-U; and London, British Library, Add. MS 25724, ff. 10r and 31v (18th century).

3. For a fuller discussion of the Egyptian context, see Bink Hallum and Marcel Marée, "A Medieval Alchemical Book Reveals New Secrets," *British Museum Blog*, February 5, 2016, at https://blog.britishmuseum.org/a-medieval-alchemical-book-reveals-new-secrets/.

4. On two of these sources, see Bink Hallum, "The Tome of Images: An Arabic Compilation of Texts by Zosimos of Panopolis and a Source of the *Turba Philosophorum*," *Ambix* 56, no. 1 (2009), pp. 76–88, reprinted in Peter E. Pormann, ed., *Islamic Medical and Scientific Tradition* (London: Routledge, 2011), vol. 3, pp. 329–44; and Persis Berlekamp, "Painting as Persuasion: A Visual Defense of Alchemy in an Islamic Manuscript of the Mongol Period," *Muqarnas* 20 (2003), pp. 35–59.

### WHITE HERON

1. For more on the symbolic imagery in egret paintings, see Paul W. Kroll, "The Egret in Medieval Literature," *Chinese Literature: Essays, Articles, Reviews (CLEAR)* 1, no. 2 (July 1979), pp. 181–96; Ankeney Weitz, "The Language of Birds: Literary and Popular Messages in the *White Heron*," in *Ink Tales: Chinese Paintings from the Collections of the Museums of Bowdoin and Colby Colleges*, exh. cat. (Brunswick and Waterville, Me.: The Museums, 2009), pp. 24–29.

2. Liu Xu, "On a Painting of a Solitary Egret," translated and quoted in Weitz, "The Language of Birds," p. 28.

### TWO CHINESE JADES

1. Evelyn S. Rawski and Jessica Rawson, eds., *China: The Three Emperors, 1662–1795*, exh. cat. (London: Royal Academy of Arts, 2005), nos. 273–282.

2. For the origins and meanings of these symbols, see Terese Tse Bartholomew, *Hidden Meanings in Chinese Art* (San Francisco: Asian Art Museum, 2006), no. 7.18.

### DAI XI

1. Dai Xi's biography can be found in Arthur W. Hummel, ed., *Eminent Chinese of the Ch'ing Period (1644–1912)* (Washington, D.C.: U.S. Government Printing Office, 1943–44), vol. 2, pp. 700–701 (Tai Hsi).

2. Dai Xu authored several texts on mathematics. He has received attention from historians because one of his treatises was translated into English and published in London in 1854. See Shen Yuwu, "Dai Xu: A Well-Known Mathematician in the Late Qing Dynasty," *Journal of Zhejiang Shuren University* (2005), no. 3, pp. 112–17.

### TOMIMOTO KENKICHI

1. Herbert S. Ingraham obituary, unidentified source, Milo (Maine) Historical Society, object #1807111.

2. Caroline D. Ingraham obituary, unidentified source, Milo Historical Society, object #1807132.

3. Caroline Ingraham, "Craftsmen, Particularly Potters, Suffered a Great Loss," *Craft Horizons* 29, no. 3 (1969), p. 4.

4. Meghen Jones, "Hamada Shōji, Kitaōji Rosanjin, and the Reception of Japanese Pottery in the Early Cold War United States," *Design and Culture* 9, no. 2 (2017), p. 190.

5. Ibid., p. 188.

## EUROPEAN ART

### HEAD OF A KING

1. Charles T. Little, "Joseph at Chartres: Sculpture Lost and Found," in *Arts of the Medieval Cathedrals: Studies on Architecture, Stained Glass and Sculpture in Honor of Anne Prache*, ed. Kathleen Nolan and Dany Sandron (Farnham: Ashgate, 2015), p. 184, fig. 11.4.

2. Léon Pressouyre, "Deux têtes de rois provenant du jubé de Chartres, actuellement aux États-Unis," *Bulletin de la Societé Nationale des Antiquaries de France* (1974), p. 177, pl. XVI.1–2.

3. Brooks Stoddard, "An Attribution for a Gothic Head of a King from the Bowdoin College Museum of Art," *Gesta* 14, no. 2 (1975), p. 61.

4. Pressouyre, "Deux têtes."

5. Jean Mallion, *Chartres: Le jubé de la cathédrale* (Chartres: Société Archéologique d'Eure-et-Loir, 1964), p. 44.

6. Ibid., pp. 182–84.

### IVORY DIPTYCH

1. For an overview of the binary relationship between Mary and Eve in medieval and Renaissance thought, see *"Eva/Ave": Woman in Renaissance and Baroque Prints*, ed. H. Diane Russell (Washington, D.C., and New York: National Gallery of Art and Feminist Press at CUNY, 1990).

2. For an introduction to late medieval devotional trends, see Henk van Os et al., *The Art of Devotion in the Late Middle Ages in Europe, 1300–1500* (Princeton: Princeton University Press, 1994).

3. For the ivory trade linking Africa and Europe, see Danielle Gaborit-Chopin, "Le commerce de l'ivoire en Méditerranée durant le Moyen Âge," *Bulletin Archéologique* 34 (2008), pp. 23–33, and more recently, Sarah Guérin, "*Avori d'ogni ragione*: The Supply of Elephant Ivory to Northern Europe in the Gothic Era," *Journal of Medieval History* 36, no. 2 (2010), pp. 156–74. For the shops that produced these works, see Elizabeth Sears, "Ivory and Ivory Workers in Medieval Paris," in *Images in Ivory: Precious Objects of the Gothic Age*, ed. Peter Barnet (Detroit: Detroit Institute of Arts, 1997), pp. 18–37.

### GHERARDO DEL FORA

1. Giorgio Vasari, *Le vite de' più eccellenti pittori, scultori ed architettori*, ed. Gaetano Milanesi (Florence: G. C. Sansoni, 1878–85), vol. 3, pp. 245–52; Mirella Levi d'Ancona, *Miniatura e miniatori a Firenze dal XIV al XVI secolo: Documenti per la storia della miniatura* (Florence: L. S. Olschki, 1962), pp. 127–37.

2. Gaudenz Freuler, "Andrea di Bartolo, Fra Tommaso d'Antonio Caffarini, and Sienese Dominicans in Venice," *The Art Bulletin* 69 (December 1987), pp. 570–86; Erin E. Benay and Lisa M. Rafanelli, *Faith, Gender and the Senses in Italian Renaissance and Baroque Art: Interpreting the Noli me tangere and Doubting Thomas* (Farnham: Ashgate, 2015), pp. 72–89.

3. See Holly Flora in *Sanctity Pictured: The Art of the Dominican and Franciscan Orders in Renaissance Italy*, ed. Trinita Kennedy (Nashville: Frist Center for the Visual Arts, 2014), p. 198.

4. On paintings in Dominican cells, see William Hood, *Fra Angelico at San Marco* (New Haven: Yale University Press, 1993); Joanna Cannon, *Religious Poverty, Visual Riches: Art in the Dominican Churches of Central Italy in the Thirteenth and Fourteenth Centuries* (New Haven: Yale University Press, 2013), pp. 201–19.

5. Lisa M. Rafanelli, "Sense and Sensibilities: A Feminist Reading of Titian's *Noli Me Tangere* (1509–1515)," *Critica d'Arte* 35–36 (2008), pp. 28–47.

### JACOPO DA PONTORMO

1. The two canvases were displayed together for only the second time in their modern history at the Bowdoin College Museum of Art in 2008, in a show titled *Beauty and Duty: The Art and Business of Renaissance Marriage*. They have since been reunited in *Maniera: Pontormo, Bronzino and Medici Florence* at the Städel Museum, Frankfurt am Main, curated by Bastian Eclercy in 2016.

2. An illuminating politically and culturally contextualized account of the allegorical triumphs (*trionfi*) is provided by Nicholas Scott Baker, "Medicean Metamorphoses: Carnival in Florence, 1513," *Renaissance Studies* 25 (September 2011), pp. 491–510.

3. Though fleeting in function, Pontormo's scenes clearly were prized enough as works of art to have warranted their safekeeping. According to the artist-biographer Giorgio Vasari, recounting the events from oral history, the paintings came into the possession of the well-established goldsmith Pietro Paolo Galeotti, called Romano (1520–1584), a one-time pupil of Benvenuto Cellini who designed medals for the future duke of Florence and Tuscany, Cosimo de' Medici I.

4. Andrea Dazzi, lecturer in Greek and Latin, was responsible for the allegorical invention, whose conceit—"painted with rich and beautiful art"—represented the Three Ages of Man and captivated onlookers with tales of metamorphosis. For Vasari's detailed account of the Carnevale celebrations, see *Le vite de' più eccellenti pittori scultori e architettori: Nelle redazioni del 1550 e 1568*, ed. Rosanna Bettarini and Paola Barocchi (Florence: Sansoni, 1966–87), vol. 5, pp. 310–13; and, in translation, *The Lives of the Painters, Sculptors and Architects*, trans. Gaston du C. de Vere and ed. David Ekserdjian (New York: Knopf, 1996), vol. 2, pp. 343–47.

5. Francis Ames-Lewis, "Early Medicean Devices," *Journal of the Warburg and Courtauld Institutes* 42 (1979), pp. 129–31, is informative with regard to uses of the diamond-ring imagery in Medicean devices, along with that of the branch, falcon, and peacock.

6. The Latin poet describes: "The god Delos [Apollo], proud in victory,/ Saw Cupid draw his bow's taut arc, and said:/ 'Mischievous boy, what are a brave man's arms/ to you? That gear becomes my shoulders best./ My aim is sure; I wound my enemies,/ I wound wild beasts; my countless arrows slew/ But now the bloated Python, whose vast coils/ Across so many acres spread their blight./ You and your loves! You have your torch to light them!/ Let that content you; never claim my fame!'/ And Venus' son replied: 'Your bow, Apollo,/ may vanquish all, but mine shall vanquish you./ As every creature yields to power divine,/ So likewise shall your glory yield to mine.'" Ovid, *Metamorphoses*, trans. A. D. Melville (Oxford: Oxford University Press, 1986), pp. 14–15 (I.453–65).

7. For more on this myth in the Renaissance visual tradition, see Wolfgang Stechow, *Apollo und Daphne* (Darmstadt: B. G. Teubner, 1965). There were, in fact, at least three Daphnes, born to three different fathers, depending on which classical author tells her tale: Pausanias, Diodorus Siculus, or Ovid.

8. Jacopo Nardi was charged with the intricate thematic program, doubling the number of cars of its rival company. The six-car train paid homage to ancient history's most illustrious periods, the latest being the Return of the (Medici-initiated) Golden Age—once again, carrying veiled messages of a dynastic return to glory.

9. The canvas decorations now in Rome are discussed in Nicoletta Baldini and Monica Bietti, eds., *Nello splendore mediceo: Papa Leone X a Firenze*, exh. cat. (Livorno: Sillabe, 2013), pp. 458–59, cat. nos. 54–55 (E. Capretti).

**ADORATION TRIPTYCH**

1. Dan Ewing, *Jan de Beer: Gothic Renewal in Renaissance Antwerp* (Turnhout: Brepols, 2016), pp. 184–94 for the series of copies, fig. 154 and cat. no. 10.1 for the Bowdoin triptych.
2. Dan Ewing, "Magi and Merchants: The Force behind the Antwerp Mannerists' Adoration Pictures," *Jaarboek Koninklijk Museum voor Schone Kunsten, Antwerpen* (2004–5), pp. 274–99.
3. For serial production, see Peter van den Brink, "The Art of Copying: Copying and Serial Production of Paintings in the Low Countries in the Sixteenth and Seventeenth Centuries," in *Brueghel Enterprises*, ed. Peter van den Brink, exh. cat. (Maastricht: Bonnefantenmuseum, 2001), pp. 12–43; for Joos's copies, see Micha Leeflang, *Joos van Cleve: A Sixteenth-Century Antwerp Artist and His Workshop* (Turnhout: Brepols, 2015), pp. 70–85.

**PARMIGIANINO**

1. The master engraver Marcantonio Raimondi (c. 1475–before 1534) has long been credited as the first Italian artist to experiment with etching, beginning around 1515 and initially mixing the technique with engraving and in a manner in keeping with his engraving style. Parmigianino is believed to have learned the technique from Marcantonio, most likely in 1527 in Bologna, where both artists sought refuge after the Sack of Rome. See David Landau and Peter Parshall, *The Renaissance Print, 1470–1550* (New Haven: Yale University Press, 1994), pp. 264–67; Sue Welsh Reed and Richard Wallace, *Italian Etchers of the Renaissance & Baroque* (Boston: Museum of Fine Arts, 1989), pp. 6, 8; and Ad Stijnman, *Engraving and Etching, 1400–2000: A History of the Development of Manual Intaglio Printmaking Processes* (London: Archetype Publications, 2012), pp. 54–57. However, there is some debate currently as to whether Marcantonio used etching at all, and Parmigianino may in fact have been the first Italian to experiment with the technique. A forthcoming exhibition on the history of early etched prints to be held at The Metropolitan Museum of Art in New York and the Albertina in Vienna in 2019 will hopefully provide new insights on this matter.
2. The reversal of the image likely derives from the artist copying the first version onto a new plate, which would cause the printed image to come out in reverse when the plate was inked and laid face down on paper to be run through the press. It appears that Parmigianino may have created the second version to produce a stronger image, with heightened contrasts that could yield more impressions than the delicately etched first iteration. For a discussion of differences between the versions, see Landau and Parshall, *The Renaissance Print*, p. 269; and Reed and Wallace, *Italian Etchers of the Renaissance & Baroque*, p. 13.
3. It should be noted that there were talented painters who were also trained in printmaking, Albrecht Dürer being the most famous example, but in the late fifteenth and early sixteenth centuries, most often printmakers were engaged to produce images based on the designs of other artists, as Marcantonio Raimondi worked closely with Raphael and artists in his workshop.
4. Reed and Wallace, *Italian Etchers of the Renaissance & Baroque*, p. 13; Landau and Parshall, *The Renaissance Print*, p. 269. One must also acknowledge that while Parmigianino and Marcantonio (probably) are the first Italians to have engaged with etching, Daniel Hopfer, Lucas van Leyden, and several northern artists had begun to experiment with the medium earlier. Nonetheless, Parmigianino (who had the advantage of etching on copper rather than the more problematic iron plates) is often viewed as the first artist (not trained as a printmaker) to truly exploit the inherent properties of the etching technique.

**DENYS CALVAERT**

1. In 2013, the Bowdoin College Museum of Art hosted a show inspired by this topic curated by me and my students titled *"How She Should Behave": Women's Archetypes in Early Modern Europe*. For additional context on the circulation of humanist treatises and its impact on gendered behavioral norms, particularly within a Spanish context, see my book *Unruly Women: Performance, Penitence, and Punishment in Early Modern Spain* (Toronto: University of Toronto Press, 2014).
2. Jennifer Haraguchi, "The Virgin Mary in the Early Modern Italian Writings of Vittoria Colonna, Lucrezia Marinella, and Eleonora Montalvo," *Religions* 9, no. 2 (2018), pp. 1–13.

**JACOB ADRIAENSZ. BACKER**

1. For figural drawing in the Netherlands during the seventeenth century, see Peter Schatborn's classic *Dutch Figure Drawings from the Seventeenth Century* (The Hague: Government Publishing Office, 1981). For a more specific look at figural drawing around Rembrandt, in particular drawing from the nude—which Backer also practiced— see Judith Noorman and David de Witt, eds., *Rembrandt's Naked Truth: Drawing Nude Models in the Golden Age* (Zwolle: WBOOKS, 2016).
2. For Backer's paintings related to Hooft's *Granida*, see several of his canvases depicting *Granida and Daifilo*: c. 1637, 125 × 161.5 cm, Hermitage, Saint Petersburg (787); c. 1638–39, 132.7 × 163 cm, Agnes Etherington Art Centre, Kingston, Ontario (35-008); c. 1640, 122.9 × 163.8 cm, private collection, Ireland, with its replica of c. 1640, 126 × 162 cm, Gemeentemuseum Het Hannemahuis, Harlingen (1179); in Peter van den Brink and Jaap van der Veen, *Jacob Backer (1608/09–1651)* (Zwolle: Waanders, 2008), nos. A45, A60, A70, A70a. For his paintings related to Guarini's *Il pastor fido*, see two canvases of *The Crowning of Mirtillo*: monogrammed and dated 1641, 225 × 221 cm, Muzeul Brukenthal, Sibiu (46); monogrammed and dated 1646, 210 × 193 cm, present whereabouts unknown; in ibid., nos. A8, A114. For more on pastoral subjects in Dutch art, see Alison McNeil Kettering's standard, *The Dutch Arcadia: Pastoral Art and Its Audience in the Golden Age* (Totowa, N.J.: Allanheld & Schram, 1983).
3. My thanks to Peter van den Brink, the leading authority on Backer's paintings and drawings, for his remarks on the costume and possible identity of the figure. Email with the author, July 12, 2018. Past scholarship mistakenly suggested that this drawing belonged to a small group of Backer's figure studies relating to a lost painting of the Old Testament story, Calling Back of Joseph's Brothers (Genesis 44:6–10), a subject known to have been treated by Backer's teacher in Leeuwarden, Lambert Jacobz. See Werner Sumowski, *Drawings of the Rembrandt School* (New York: Abaris Books, 1979), vol. 1, pp. 44–45, no. 15x, ill. under no. 1, p. 16, *One of Joseph's Brothers, Standing and Speaking, Facing Right*, black and white chalk on blue paper, 43.4 × 27.9 cm, Vienna, Albertina (9041). Sumowski related the Bowdoin drawing to this and another Albertina sheet,

his no. 13x, *One of Joseph's Brothers, Wearing a Long Mantle*, black and white chalk on blue paper, 38.8 × 21.8 cm, Albertina (9040), as well as one in the Fondation Custodia, Paris (3543), his no. 14x, *One of Joseph's Brothers with Raised Right Arm*, black and white chalk on blue paper, 38 × 22 cm. David P. Becker cited Sumowski's authority in his *Old Master Drawings at Bowdoin College* (Brunswick, Me.: Bowdoin College Museum of Art, 1985), pp. 50–51, no. 22, ill. Given this presumed connection to Jacobz.'s lost painting, together with the erroneous presumption that Backer's figural chalk drawings must predate his move from Leeuwarden to Amsterdam by 1633 because of their lack of Rembrandtesque qualities, Sumowski incorrectly dated the Bowdoin drawing to the early 1630s. More recent, specific and detailed studies of figure drawings by Backer and others active in Amsterdam during this period, especially van den Brink's 2008 monograph and exhibition on Backer, demonstrate clearly that this manner of chalk drawing was most prevalent in Amsterdam *outside* of Rembrandt's immediate orbit—and there is no evidence that Backer ever entered Rembrandt's workshop (although Rembrandt was undeniably an unstoppable force in the Amsterdam art market during Backer's time). A date of c. 1640 is more in keeping with the drawing's confident handling and Backer's dated pastoral subjects; thanks again to Peter van den Brink and William W. Robinson for their thoughts on the dating of this sheet. Emails with the author, July 12, 2018.

### GIOVANNI BENEDETTO CASTIGLIONE


1. Frank Kermode, "John," in *The Literary Guide to the Bible*, ed. Robert Alter and Frank Kermode (Cambridge, Mass.: Harvard University Press, 1987), p. 450.
2. On Castiglione and Rembrandt, see Jaco Rutgers, "Rembrandt in Italia nel Seicento e nel Settecento," in *Rembrandt: Dipinti, incisioni e riflessi sul '600 e '700 italiano*, exh. cat. (Milan: Skira, 2002), pp. 313–34; Ewald Jeutter, *Zur Problematik der Rembrandt-Rezeption im Werk des Genuesen Giovanni Benedetto Castiglione (Genua 1609–1664 Mantua)* (Weimar: VDG, 2004); Jaco Rutgers, "Rembrandt in Italië: Receptie en verzamelgeschiedenis," PhD diss., Utrecht University, 2008; and Alison Stoesser, *Van Dyck's Hosts in Genoa: Lucas and Cornelis de Wael's Lives, Business Activities and Works* (Turnhout: Brepols, 2018).
3. Erik Hinderding, *Rembrandt Etchings from the Frits Lugt Collection* (Bussum: Thoth, 2008), vol. 1, no. 55, pp. 145–46.
4. Lauro Magnani, "*Le Christ chassant les marchands du Temple* de Giovanni Benedetto Castiglione, au Musée du Louvre," *Revue du Louvre* (2003), pp. 50–59. On Castiglione's reception of Seicento theoretical artistic discussions and contemporary literary figures, see Timothy J. Standring and Martin Clayton, *Castiglione: Lost Genius: Masterworks on Paper from the Royal Collection* (London: Royal Collection Trust, 2015), pp. 25–51.
5. Castiglione repeated this subject in a work at the Louvre, inv. 241; see Stéphane Loire, *Peintures italiennes du XVIIe siècle du Musée du Louvre* (Paris: Gallimard and Musée du Louvre Editions, 2006), pp. 86–88.
6. See Elizabeth Cropper, "Pietro Testa, 1612–1650: The Exquisite Draughtsman from Lucca," in *Pietro Testa, 1612–1650: Prints and Drawings* (Philadelphia: Philadelphia Museum of Art, 1988), pp. xi–xxxvi.


### FISH SHAMBLES


1. For the inventory, see Susan E. Wegner, "Copies and Education: James Bowdon's Painting Collection in the Life of the College," in *The Legacy of James Bowdoin III* (Brunswick, Me.: Bowdoin College Museum of Art, 1994), pp. 172–76.
2. Eddy de Jongh, "The Symbolism of Fish, Fisherman, Fishing Gear and the Catch," in *Fish: Still Lifes by Dutch and Flemish Masters 1550–1700*, ed. Liesbeth M. Helmus and Eddy de Jongh, exh. cat. (Utrecht: Centraal Museum, 2004), pp. 75–118; Sheila McTighe, "Foods and the Body in Italian Genre Paintings, about 1580: Campi, Passarotti, Carracci," *The Art Bulletin* 86, no. 2 (2004), pp. 301–23.


### AUGUSTIN DE SAINT-AUBIN


1. Pierre Choderlos de Laclos to Marie-Soulange Laclos, 18 Floréal Year 2 [7 May 1794], in *Oeuvres complètes/Laclos*, ed. Laurent Versini (Paris: Gallimard, 1979), p. 802. For more on Laclos's marriage, see Meghan K. Roberts, "Laclos's Objects of Affection: Venerating the Family During the French Revolution," *Eighteenth-Century Studies* 51, no. 3 (Spring 2018), pp. 289–304.
2. Kate Retford, *The Art of Domestic Life: Family Portraiture in Eighteenth-Century England* (New Haven: Yale University Press, 2006), p. 8. See also Dena Goodman, *Becoming a Woman in the Age of Letters* (Ithaca: Cornell University Press, 2009); Sarah C. Maza, *Private Lives and Public Affairs: The Causes Célèbres of Pre-revolutionary France* (Berkeley: University of California Press, 1993); Meghan K. Roberts, *Sentimental Savants: Philosophical Families in Enlightenment France* (Chicago: University of Chicago Press, 2016).


### ALEKSEI ALEKSEEVICH KHARLAMOV


1. Olga Sugrobova-Roth and Eckart Lingenauber, *Alexei Harlamoff: Catalogue raisonné* (Düsseldorf: Edition A. Harlamoff, 2007). A dissertation on Kharlamov's life and work—the main scholarly source on the artist to date—also omits any mention of this painting; see Marina V. Posokhina, *Tvorchestvo Alekseia Alekseevicha Kharlamova i salonnoe iskusstvo* (Moscow: Rossiiskaia Gosudarstvennaia Biblioteka, 2007).
2. Kharlamov's contemporaries termed him a "Russian Velázquez" (Ivan Turgenev, *Polnoe sobranie sochinenii i pisem v 28-i tt.* [Leningrad: AN SSSR, 1960–68], vol. 10, p. 349).
3. Feminist film theorist Laura Mulvey was the first to coin the term "male gaze" and associate it with the role of the implied spectator: "In a world ordered by sexual imbalance, pleasure in looking has been split between active/male and passive/female. The determining male gaze projects its fantasy onto the female figure, which is styled accordingly. In their traditional exhibitionist role women are simultaneously looked at and displayed, with their appearance coded for strong visual and erotic impact . . ." ("Visual Pleasure and Narrative Cinema," reprinted in *Feminisms REDUX: An Anthology of Literary Theory and Criticism*, ed. Robyn Warhol-Down and Diane Price Herndl [New Brunswick: Rutgers University Press, 2009], p. 436). Other feminist theorists have built on this work in important ways; for example, Ann Kaplan discusses how the male dominance–female submission pattern inherent in artistic spectatorship is facilitated "through the mechanisms of voyeurism and fetishism, which are male operations" (E. Ann Kaplan, *Women and Film: Both Sides of the Camera* [London: Methuen, 1983], p. 29).

4. Turgenev, *Polnoe sobranie sochinenii i pisem*, vol. 10, p. 331. The relationship between Kharlamov and Turgenev, attested to in Turgenev's frequent mentions of the painter in his correspondence, has never been studied; Stephen Pastoriza is devoting his honors thesis to this topic. It is our hypothesis that Kharlamov and Turgenev felt an affinity for one another in part due to their shared ideas about the role of feminine beauty in art.

5. Jehanne M. Gheith, "The Superfluous Man and the Necessary Woman: A 'Re-Vision,'" *The Russian Review* 55, no. 2 (April 1996), pp. 226–44. See also Barbara Heldt, *Terrible Perfection: Women and Russian Literature* (Bloomington: Indiana University Press, 1992), pp. 17–21.

6. Beginning in 1856, Turgenev and his friends—who were all quite artistically talented—played a game the author devised in which the participants sketched imaginary characters and then wrote, rather entertainingly, about their personalities, habits, and life circumstances. The sketches Turgenev created for this game with accompanying commentaries are collected in Marion Mainwaring, trans. and ed., *The Portrait Game* (New York: Horizon Press, 1973).

7. While we cannot now confirm the validity of the claim, a newspaper article about the frame's restoration in the 1980s asserts that it once belonged to an unspecified Russian czar.

8. Ivan Turgenev, *First Love and Other Stories*, trans. Richard Freeborn (Oxford: Oxford University Press, 2008), p. 147. For a perceptive analysis of the voyeurism inherent in Turgenev's novella and its violent implications, see Jane Costlow, "Abusing the Erotic: Women in Turgenev's 'First Love,'" in *Engendering Slavic Literatures*, ed. Pamela Chester and Sibelan Forrester (Bloomington: Indiana University Press, 1996), pp. 3–12.

9. Turgenev, *First Love and Other Stories*, p. 148.

## ART OF OCEANIA, AFRICA, AND THE AMERICAS

### TATANUA MASK

1. Brenda Clay, "A Line of Tatanua," in *Assemblage of Spirits: Idea and Image in New Ireland* (New York: G. Braziller, 1987), p. 67.

2. Susanne Kuchler, "Tatanua-Style Masks [2]," in *New Ireland: Art of the South Pacific* (Milan: 5 Continents Editions, 2006), p. 262.

3. Clay, "A Line of Tatanua," pp. 65–66.

4. Michael Gunn, "New Ireland Art in Museum Collections," in *New Ireland: Art of the South Pacific*, pp. 282–91.

### FANG MALE RELIQUARY FIGURE

1. Jan Vansina, *Paths in the Rainforests: Toward a History of Political Tradition in Equatorial Africa* (Madison: University of Wisconsin Press, 1990).

2. Kairn A. Klieman, *"The Pygmies Were Our Compass": Bantu and Batwa in the History of West Central Africa, Early Times to c. 1900 C.E.* (Portsmouth, N.H.: Heinemann, 2003).

3. Jack Flam, "Matisse and the Fauves," in *"Primitivism" in 20th Century Art: Affinity of the Tribal and the Modern*, ed. William Rubin (New York: Museum of Modern Art, 1984), vol. 2, pp. 211–29, esp. 214–15.

4. Fang reliquaries feature in prominent art collections and have been the central focus of influential exhibitions of African art; see, most recently, Yves Le Fur, ed., *Les forêts natales: Arts d'Afrique équatoriale atlantique* (Paris: Actes Sud and Musée du Quai Branly–Jacques Chirac, 2017); Alisa LaGamma, ed., *Eternal Ancestors: The Art of the Central African Reliquary* (New York: The Metropolitan Museum of Art, 2007). These catalogues provide extensive commentary by relevant experts. Le Fur is best on typology, as pioneered by Louis Perrois; LaGamma includes a superb historical study by Kairn Kliemen along with a broader appreciation of reliquary sculpture in global art.

### NAZCA BRIDGE-SPOUT VESSEL

1. See Helaine Silverman, *Ancient Nasca Settlement and Society* (Iowa City: University of Iowa Press, 2002); Cecilia Pardo and Peter Fux, *Nasca* (Lima: Museo de Arte, 2017).

2. Anthony F. Aveni, *Between the Lines: The Mystery of the Giant Ground Drawings of Ancient Nasca, Peru* (Austin: University of Texas Press, 2000).

3. For more on Nazca ceramics and textiles, see Donald A. Proulx, *A Sourcebook of Nasca Ceramic Iconography* (Iowa City: University of Iowa Press, 2006), and Alan Sawyer, *Early Nasca Needlework* (London: Laurence King, 1997).

### TWO TLINGIT MEDICINE MEN FIGURINES

1. Molly Lee and Angela J. Linn, "Intimates and Effigies," in *Not Just a Pretty Face: Dolls and Human Figurines in Alaska Native Cultures*, 2nd ed. (Fairbanks: University of Alaska Press, 2006), p. 23.

2. Aldona Jonaitis, *From the Land of the Totem Poles: The Northwest Coast Indian Art Collection at the American Museum of Natural History* (Vancouver: Douglas & McIntyre, 1988), p. 105.

3. Allen Wardwell, *Tangible Visions: Northwest Coast Indian Shamanism and Its Art* (New York: Monacelli Press with the Corvus Press, 1996), p. 310.

4. Lee and Linn, "Intimates and Effigies," p. 23.

### LAKOTA SUN DANCE

1. Compare for works on muslin: Louis S. Warren and Janet C. Berlo, *Transformation and Continuity in Lakota Culture: The Collages of Arthur Amiotte, 1988–2014* (Pierre: South Dakota State Historical Society Press, 2014); Janet C. Berlo, "Pictographic Art of the Plains," in *Indigenous Beauty: Masterworks of American Indian Art from the Diker Collection*, ed. David W. Penney, exh. cat. (New York: Skira/Rizzoli, 2015), pp. 118–31. For works on paper: Janet C. Berlo, *Spirit Beings and Sun Dancers: Black Hawk's Vision of the Lakota World* (New York: Braziller, 2000).

2. See *The Plains Indians: Artists of Earth and Sky*, exh. cat. (Paris and New York: Éditions Skira and Skira/Rizzoli, 2014).

### TWO WABANAKI BOXES

1. Bruce J. Bourque and Laureen A. LaBar, *Uncommon Threads: Wabanaki Textiles, Clothing, and Costume* (Augusta: Maine State Museum, 2009), pp. 63–69.

2. Ernst Christian Helmreich, *Religion at Bowdoin College: A History* (Brunswick, Me.: Bowdoin College, 1981), p. 60. Thanks are extended to Dana Byrd for sharing this reference.

3. Bruce J. Bourque, email reference, September 17, 2013, in object file.

4. Barry Dana, artist statement, 2015, in object file; courtesy of the donor.

## AMERICAN ART

### JOHN SMIBERT

1. Larissa Dukelskaya and Andrew Moore, eds., *A Capital Collection: Houghton Hall and the Hermitage* (New Haven: Yale University Press, 2002), pp. 276–77.
2. Livy, *The History of Rome*, Book 26:50, trans. Frank Gardner Moore, at http://www.perseus.tufts.edu/hopper/text?doc=Perseus%3 Atext%3A1999.02.0158%3Abook%3D26%3Achapter%3D50.
3. Richard H. Saunders, *John Smibert: Colonial America's First Portrait Painter* (New Haven: Yale University Press, 1995).
4. *The Continence of Scipio* did not arrive in Smibert's Boston studio until late in 1743 or early in 1744. In the previous year, Smibert references the painting being in the care of his good friend Arthur Pond (c. 1705–1758), the London artist, but by the following July, Dr. Alexander Hamilton, a Scottish physician, noted seeing the painting in Smibert's Boston Studio. Saunders, *John Smibert*, pp. 211, 257.
5. John Trumbull rented Smibert's studio in the late 1770s, and in a list of paintings he executed before he went to Europe, he noted "copied from Smibert's copy" *The Continence of Scipio*. Theodore Sizer, ed., *The Autobiography of Colonel John Trumbull, Patriot-Artist, 1756–1843* (New Haven: Yale University Press, 1953), p. 55.
6. "Catalogue of Pictures" included in the "Catalogue of Library of James Bowdoin bequeathed to Bowdoin College," dated February 5, 1813, includes "3. Scipio restores to the Celtiberian Prince Allucius, his spouse a captive in the Roman Camp, painter unknown." Special Collections, Bowdoin Family Papers, Bowdoin College. In 1928, Bowdoin College was given an undated manuscript in which the painting is also listed: "Catalogue of Pictures belonging to the Estate of the late Hon. James Bowdoin Esq. bequeathed by him to Bowdoin College": "No. 3 Continence of Scipio/ Scipio restores to the Celtiberian Prince,/ Allucius, his spouse, a captive in the/ Roman camp ./ Painter unknown/ Copy by Smybert:/ Original lost/ at Sea." See Marvin S. Sadik, *Colonial and Federal Portraits at Bowdoin College* (Brunswick, Me.: Bowdoin College Museum of Art, 1966), p. 211.
7. Caroline O. Fowler, "Drawing: A Universal Language in a New World," in *Why Draw? 500 Years of Drawings and Watercolors at Bowdoin College*, ed. Joachim Homann (Brunswick, Me.: Bowdoin College Museum of Art, 2017), p. 19.
8. *The Notebook of John Smibert* (Boston: Massachusetts Historical Society, 1969), p. 82.
9. Saunders, *John Smibert*, p. 211.

### THREE COLONIAL PORTRAITS

1. Ellen G. Miles, *American Paintings of the Eighteenth Century* (Washington, D.C.: National Gallery of Art, 1995), pp. 100–102. Also c. 1748, Feke painted members of Boston's Bowdoin family; see Linda J. Docherty, "Preserving Our Ancestors: The Bowdoin Portrait Collection," in *The Legacy of James Bowdoin III* (Brunswick, Me.: Bowdoin College Museum of Art, 1994), pp. 62–64.
2. Henry S. Burrage, *Maine at Louisburg in 1745* (Augusta, Me.: Burleigh & Flynt, 1910), pp. 18–19; Miscellaneous Papers, Waldo Papers, Coll. 948, Maine Historical Society.
3. According to his probate inventory, Waldo had left his "Pictures at Mr. Flucker's," believed to include this portrait; Miscellaneous Papers, Waldo Papers, Coll. 948, Maine Historical Society.
4. Carolyn S. Parsons, "'Bordering on Magnificence': Urban Domestic Planning in the Maine Woods," in *Maine in the Early Republic*, ed. Charles E. Clark et al. (Hanover, N.H.: University Press of New England, 1988), pp. 77–78.
5. Thomas M. Griffiths, *Maine Sources in "The House of the Seven Gables"* (Waterville, Me., 1945), pp. 4–5.

### GILBERT STUART

1. The extensive literature on this topic includes Carrie R. Barratt and Ellen G. Miles, *Gilbert Stuart* (New York: The Metropolitan Museum of Art, 2004), pp. 273–80; *The Legacy of James Bowdoin III* (Brunswick, Me.: Bowdoin College Museum of Art, 1994); and G. S. Wilson, *Jefferson on Display: Attire, Etiquette, and the Art of Presentation* (Charlottesville: University of Virginia Press, 2018).
2. Jefferson owned the largest private library in the nation. He sold 6,487 volumes to Congress after the British burned the U.S. Capitol in 1814. For information on Bowdoin's library, see Kenneth E. Carpenter, "James Bowdoin III as Library Builder," in *The Legacy of James Bowdoin III*, pp. 85–123; Eliza Goodpasture, "James Bowdoin III's Collection in Context: On Historical Roots and Their Legacies," in *Art Treasures, Gracefully Drawn: James Bowdoin III and America's Earliest Drawing Collection*, Bowdoin College Museum of Art, 2018, at http://www.bowdoin.edu/art-museum/ catalogues/old-masters/index.shtml.
3. Letter from James Bowdoin to Thomas Jefferson, March 25, 1805, *Founders Online*, National Archives, at https://founders. archives.gov/?q=jefferson%20bowdoin%20march%20 1805&s=1111311111&sa=&r=6&sr=.
4. Susan R. Stein, *The Worlds of Thomas Jefferson at Monticello* (New York: Abrams, 1993).
5. Letter from Thomas Jefferson to James Madison, September 20, 1785, in *The Papers of Thomas Jefferson Digital Edition*, ed. James P. McClure and J. Jefferson Looney (Charlottesville: University of Virginia Press, Rotunda, 2008–18).
6. Letter from Bowdoin to Jefferson, March 25, 1805 (see note 3).

### MARTIN JOHNSON HEADE

1. Theodore E. Stebbins Jr., *The Life and Work of Martin Johnson Heade: A Critical Analysis and Catalogue Raisonné* (New Haven: Yale University Press, 2000), p. 117; Theodore E. Stebbins Jr., *Martin Johnson Heade*, exh. cat. (Boston: Museum of Fine Arts, 1999), p. 29.
2. John Wilmerding, in *Master Paintings from the Butler Institute of American Art*, ed. Irene S. Sweetkind (New York: Abrams, 1994), p. 113.
3. Stebbins, *Martin Johnson Heade*, p. 29.
4. David Peters Corbett, "Art, Morality, and the National Interest: Theodore Winthrop, Frederic Church, and Martin Johnson Heade at the Tenth Street Studios in 1859," *European Journal of American Studies* 30, no. 1 (2011), pp. 57–72.

### JOHN ADAMS JACKSON

1. While several English Neoclassical sculptors of the previous generation treated the subject, such as Richard James Wyatt, James Legrew, and John Thomas, Jackson was the first American to attempt it in marble.
2. M.M.W., "Letter from a Boston Lady," *Boston Evening Transcript*, July 1, 1871.

3. Edward Everett Hale, "The Painting and Statuary in Vienna," *Boston Daily Advertiser*, August 4, 1873.

4. "Exhibition of Sculpture," *New York Herald*, May 22, 1874.

5. Clara Erskine Clement and Laurence Hutton, *Artists of the Nineteenth Century and Their Works: A Handbook* (Boston: Houghton, Mifflin, 1879; 1884 reprint), vol. 2, pp. 1–3.

6. See essays by John F. McGuigan Jr. and Mary K. McGuigan in *A Maine Sculptor in Florence: John Adams Jackson 1825–1879*, ed. by Michael K. Komanecky, exh. cat. (Rockland: Farnsworth Art Museum, forthcoming).

### ELIHU VEDDER

1. Elihu Vedder, "Finished Sketch of … *The Art Idea*," in *Catalogue of the Ninth Annual Exhibition of the Architectural League of New York* (New York: Architectural League, 1893), l, no. 75.

2. Richard N. Murray, "Painting and Sculpture," in *The American Renaissance, 1876–1917*, exh. cat. (New York: Brooklyn Museum, 1979), p. 187. For further discussion of Elihu Vedder, see Joshua C. Taylor, Jane Dillenberger, and Richard Murray, *Perceptions and Evocations: The Art of Elihu Vedder* (Washington, D.C.: Smithsonian Institution Press, 1979), and Regina Soria, *Elihu Vedder: American Visionary Artist in Rome (1836–1923)* (Rutherford, N.J.: Fairleigh Dickinson University Press, 1970).

### JOHN SLOAN

1. [Elizabeth Luther Cary?], "Some of the Striking Pictures to Be Seen in This Year's Exhibition at the Pennsylvania Academy," *New York Times*, February 16, 1913, p. 47.

## MODERN ART

### SOVIET PROPAGANDA POSTERS

1. For further reading on the soviet poster, see David King, *Russian Revolutionary Posters: From Civil War to Socialist Realism, from Bolshevism to the End of Stalin* (London: Tate Publishing, 2016); Margarita Tupitsyn, *Gustav Klutsis and Valentina Kulagina: Photography and Montage after Constructivism* (New York: International Center of Photography, 2004); Stephen White, *The Bolshevik Poster* (New Haven: Yale University Press, 1988).

### ROCKWELL KENT

1. In Kent's book *N by E* (New York: Literary Guild, 1930), he described his painting location (p. 206): "Sermalik [*sic*] is Greenlandish for glacier bay; the name is borne by many Greenland fiords." He was apparently transcribing the Inuit name phonetically and used that form throughout his narrative.

2. Ibid., pp. 208–9.

### BERENICE ABBOTT

1. Berenice Abbott, "What the Camera and I See," *ARTnews* 50 (September 1951), pp. 5–6, 37, quoted in Julia Van Haaften, *Berenice Abbott: A Life in Photography* (New York: Norton, 2018), p. 325.

### ANDREW NEWELL WYETH

1. The author wishes to thank Joachim Homann, Curator, Bowdoin College Museum of Art, for his generous collaboration in viewing the painting and twenty-one studies identified by Mary Landa and Karen Baumgartner of the Andrew Wyeth office in Chadds Ford, with Amy Morey and Leith MacDonald, who hosted us, and Linda L. Bean for an unforgettable visit at the Andrew Wyeth Center, Farnsworth Art Museum. Joyce Hill Stoner kindly shared her notes of a conversation with Andrew Wyeth about *Night Hauling*, along with her expertise in his use of various media. The original title of the work appears in a letter from Andrew Wyeth to Stephen Etnier dated March 9, 1947. See the curatorial file for *Night Hauling*, Bowdoin College Museum of Art.

2. Brandywine River Museum of Art, SUPP2000.521. See Christine B. Podmaniczky, *N. C. Wyeth, Catalogue Raisonné of Paintings* (London: Scala, 2008), p. 769, L.207.

3. For example, see *Young Fisherman and Dory, Study for To the Westward*, 1944, drybrush on paper, Farnsworth Art Museum, and, in later life, *Asleep in a Dory Adrift*, 1982, tempera on hardboard panel, Collection of Andrew and Betsy Wyeth. See Patricia A. Junker and Audrey Lewis, *Andrew Wyeth: In Retrospect* (New Haven: Yale University Press, 2017), p. 97, pl. 40.

4. Andrew Wyeth described the illuminated appearance of the herring bait following a visit to the Bowdoin College Museum of Art in 1992; see curatorial file, *Night Hauling*.

5. Henry David Thoreau, *Walden*, ed. Jeffery S. Cramer (New Haven: Yale University Press, 2006), p. 307.

6. For the association with aerial bombing, see Alexander Nemerov, "The Glitter of Night Hauling: Andrew Wyeth in the 1940s," *The Magazine Antiques* (May–June 2012), p. 8, in which the author astutely connects Wyeth's aerial perspective in *Soaring* (1942–50; Shelburne Museum) with *Night Hauling*, as well as to Peter Hurd and his nighttime aerial bombardments. See also Kirsten M. Jensen, *Magical & Real: Henriette Wyeth & Peter Hurd* (Doylestown, Pa.: James A. Michener Art Museum, 2018), pl. 18: *The Return from a Raid over Rouen*, 1942, Army Art Collection, U.S. Army Center of Military History, Fort Belvoir, Va.

7. For the magical qualities of Andrew Wyeth, see John Wilmerding et al., *Andrew Wyeth: Memory and Magic* (Atlanta and Philadelphia: High Museum of Art and Philadelphia Museum of Art, 2005).

8. Collection of Andrew and Betsy Wyeth.

### MATTA

1. *Quadrum* (Brussels), no. 16 (1967), pp. 91–98.

### NORBERT KRICKE

1. This article was written in consultation with Dr. Ernst-Gerhard Güse and Sabine Kricke-Güse. The quotations and many of the ideas are from Ernst-Gerhard Güse, "Norbert Kricke: Architecture, Sculpture, Space," in *Norbert Kricke: Raum, Linie / Space, Line*, ed. Roland Scotti (Göttingen: Steidl Verlag, 2012).

2. Ibid., p. 33.

3. Ibid.

## CONTEMPORARY ART

### BARBARA CHASE-RIBOUD

1. Barbara Chase-Riboud, "Why Did We Leave Zanzibar?" (1969–70), in *Everytime a Knot Is Undone, a God Is Released* (Oakland: Seven Stories Press, 2014), pp. 357–60.

2. Chase-Riboud to Lawrence Rinder in "Memory and Material: A Conversation with Barbara Chase-Riboud," held at the Berkeley Art Museum, February 11, 2014, at https://www.youtube.com/watch?v=mcxsOnZysoU.

3. Barbara Chase-Riboud as quoted in Peter Howard Selz and Anthony F. Janson, *Barbara Chase-Riboud: Sculptor* (New York: Abrams, 1999), p. 40, and Françoise Nora-Cachin, "Dialogue: Another Country," in *Chase-Riboud*, exh. cat. (Berkeley: University Art Museum, 1972), n.p.

4. The Michael Rosenfeld Gallery, which I direct and in which I am a partner, is the first fine-art gallery to represent Chase-Riboud since the death of Betty Parsons in 1982. It has been a privilege to get to know her and bring her work to new and expanded audiences. As a Bowdoin alumna, I was surprised and excited to discover that the Museum owned this sculpture by an artist whose work I continue to passionately champion.

## ALMA WOODSEY THOMAS

1. Sachi Yanari, *Alma W. Thomas: A Retrospective of the Paintings*, exh. cat. (San Francisco: Pomegranate, 1998), p. 14, and Laura Cumming, review of the exhibition *Soul of a Nation*, *The Guardian*, July 16, 2017.

2. W. E. B. Du Bois, "Of Our Spiritual Strivings," from *The Souls of Black Folk* in *Writings*, ed. Nathan Irvin Huggins (New York: Library of America, 1986), p. 364 and passim.

3. Howard Winant, *The New Politics of Race: Globalism, Difference, Justice* (Minneapolis: University of Minnesota Press, 2004), p. 26.

4. Conceptual artist Glenn Ligon literalizes these dynamics in his painting *Untitled (I Feel Most Colored When I Am Thrown Against a Sharp White Background)*, 1990. See https://www.whitney.org/ WatchAndListen/720. The artwork appropriates a line from Zora Neale Hurston's essay "How It Feels to Be Colored Me," which the journal *World Tomorrow* published in 1928.

## RICHARD POUSETTE-DART

1. Chris Pousette-Dart, "In the Studio," in *Richard Pousette-Dart: Painting / Light / Space* (Brunswick, Me.: Bowdoin College Museum of Art, 2018), p. 4.

2. He held teaching appointments at the New School for Social Research (1959–61), the School of Visual Arts (1964), Bard College (1965), and Columbia University (1968–69), before joining the faculty of Sara Lawrence College (1970–74). He also taught at the Art Students League of New York (1980–84). He received an honorary degree from Bard, where he had enrolled in 1935 for just a few months. Among his best-known students were Ai Weiwei and Christopher Wool.

3. "To the Curriculum Committee [of Bard College], from Richard Pousette-Dart, March 14, 1972," manuscript at the Richard Pousette-Dart Foundation archives, Suffern, New York.

4. Pousette-Dart, in conversation with Martica Sawin, September 1964, quoted in Martica Sawin, "The Pleasure of Non-associative Seeing," in *Richard Pousette-Dart: Painting / Light / Space*, p. 7.

5. Aura is an "einmalige Erscheinung einer Ferne, so nah sie sein mag." "Das Kunstwerk im Zeitalter seiner technischen Reproduzierbarkeit," in *Gesammelte Schriften*, ed. Rolf Tiedemann and Hermann Schweppenhäuser (Frankfurt am Main: Suhrkamp, 1980), vol. 1.2, p. 440.

6. Cologne Lecture, in *Wassily Kandinsky: Complete Writings on Art*, ed. Kenneth C. Lindsay and Peter Virgo (Boston: G. K. Hall, 1982), vol. 1, p. 396.

7. Undated note from the Richard Pousette-Dart archives, Richard Pousette-Dart Foundation, Suffern, New York.

## BARKLEY L. HENDRICKS

1. Trevor Schoonmaker, ed., *Barkley L. Hendricks: Birth of the Cool* (Durham, N.C.: Nasher Museum of Art, Duke University, 2008; reprint 2017), p. 107.

2. See video clip at https://nasher.duke.edu/stories/barkley-l-hendricks-birth-cool/ (0:5:15–30).

## PETER HUJAR

1. Douglas Crimp, "Action Around the Edges," in *Mixed Use, Manhattan: Photography and Related Practices, 1970s to the Present*, ed. Lynne Cooke and Douglas Crimp (Cambridge, Mass.: MIT Press, 2010).

## JENNY HOLZER

1. In preparation, informed by her recent participation in the Whitney Independent Study Program, she read Mao, Lenin, the early twentieth-century anarchist Emma Goldman, various religious and right-wing fanatics, miscellaneous American anarchists, and some "folk" crackpot literature. *The Tate Gallery: Illustrated Catalogue of Acquisitions, 1982–84* (London: Tate Gallery, 1986), at https://www .tate.org.uk/art/artworks/holzer-no-title-p77386.

2. The essays were first published as Black Book Posters in 1979, in a limited edition of twenty-nine offset lithographs on green paper.

3. Quoted in David Joselit, "Voices, Bodies and Spaces: The Art of Jenny Holzer," in *Jenny Holzer*, ed. David Joselit et al. (London: Phaidon, 1998), p. 43.

4. "What we see in the relationship between sentence and paragraph in the *Inflammatory Essays* is the way individual phrases that are unfixed and free-floating can be sutured into a set of specific linguistic contingencies that provide them with ideological form. And in witnessing this shaping of an ideological voice, we see power take shape." Gordon Hughes, "Power's Script: Or, Jenny Holzer's Art after 'Art after Philosophy,'" *Oxford Art Journal* 29, no. 3 (2006), p. 434.

5. *The Tate Gallery: Illustrated Catalogue of Acquisitions*, at https ://www.tate.org.uk/art/artworks/holzer-no-title-p77386.

## GRACIELA ITURBIDE

1. Among her first images of birds were vultures in a cemetery, which Iturbide photographed not long after the death of her daughter Claudia.

2. Graciela Iturbide in *Conversations with Contemporary Photographers*, ed. Nan Richardson (New York: Umbrage Editions, 2005), p. 52.

3. Ibid., p. 54.

## FRANK BOWLING

1. Frank Bowling discusses his summer at Skowhegan and his painting methods in an interview with Mel Gooding, conducted for the British Library, National Life Stories, March 9, 2007, NLSC: Artists' Lives, Frank Bowling, at http://explore.bl.uk/BLVU1 :LSCOP-ALL:BLLSA7060485. For more on Bowling, see Okwui Enwezor, ed., *Frank Bowling: Mappa Mundi* (Munich, Prestel, 2017), and Mel Gooding, *Frank Bowling* (London: Royal Academy of Arts, 2011).

2. Bocour Artists Colors (later Golden Artist Colors), manufactured the first acrylic paints in the U.S. and worked with artists to develop better and newer painting materials.

**DAVID C. DRISKELL**

1. Between 1976 and 2003, Driskell served several years on Skowhegan's Board of Governors and Board of Trustees. For more on Driskell's work, see *Creative Spirit: The Art of David C. Driskell* (College Park: David C. Driskell Center, University of Maryland, 2011), and Julie L. McGee, *David C. Driskell: Artist and Scholar* (San Francisco: Pomegranate, 2006).
2. Driskell received Skowhegan's Leonard Bocour Progress Award that summer.

**PER KIRKEBY**

1. Two musical pieces by Danish composer Hans Abrahamsen, *Walden* (1978/1995) and *Wald (Forest)* (2009), both inspired by Thoreau's book, translate the sounds and noises of the forest into *musique concrète*. The CD-booklet, published in Munich in 2013, contains reproductions of Kirkeby's *Waldvariationen I–V*.

**CARRIE MAE WEEMS**

1. Logan Jaffe, "Confronting My Racist Object," *New York Times*, October 7, 2016.

**JUDY GLICKMAN LAUDER**

1. Judy Glickman Lauder, email, November 29, 2018.
2. Rose Marasco, email, November 21, 2018.
3. https://encyclopedia.ushmm.org/content/en/article/theresienstadt.
4. Hasia R. Diner, *We Remember with Reverence and Love: American Jews and the Myth of Silence after the Holocaust, 1945–1962* (New York: New York University Press, 2009).
5. See Natasha Goldman, "'Never bow your head, be helpful, and fight for justice and righteousness': Nathan Rapoport and Philadelphia's Holocaust Memorial (1964)," *Journal of Jewish Identities* 9, no. 2 (July 2016), pp. 159–92. For Holocaust memory in the U.S., see Beth B. Cohen, *Case Closed: Holocaust Survivors in Postwar America* (New Brunswick: Rutgers University Press, 2007); Thomas D. Fallace, *Emergence of Holocaust Education in American Schools* (New York: Palgrave Macmillan, 2008); Daniel Levy and Natan Sznaider, *The Holocaust and Memory in the Global Age* (Philadelphia: Temple University Press, 2006); and James E. Young, *The Texture of Memory* (New Haven: Yale University Press, 1993).
6. The film was based on Thomas Keneally's *Schindler's Ark*, which won the Man Booker Prize in 1982.

**MEL CHIN**

1. Mel Chin in Linda Weintraub, *Art on the Edge and Over: Searching for Art's Meaning in Contemporary Society, 1970s–1990s* (Litchfield, Conn.: Art Insights, 1996), p. 47.
2. Ibid., p. 49.
3. Carol Strickland, "Getting the Lead Out: Mel Chin," *Art in America*, March 31, 2014, at https://www.artinamericamagazine.com /news-features/interviews/getting-the-lead-out-mel-chin/.
4. In addition to its materialization of a scientific discovery, *Caged Corn* also functions as a complex work of visual art. Although Chin describes the "sculpted ecology" or "revived nature" of *Revival Field* as subtractive sculpture, *Caged Corn* similarly expands traditional understandings of artistic process as *both* an additive and a subtractive work. The plants pull metals from the ground, "subtracting" the "medium" from the "support," metaphorically carving away metal that is then "added" to the plants' vascular systems. The corn is both the instrument performing the subtraction and the vessel to which the metal is added.
5. Chin in Weintraub, *Art on the Edge*, p. 50.
6. Ibid., p. 47.

**NANCY SPERO**

1. Jon Bird, "Dancing to a Different Tune," in *Nancy Spero* (London: Phaidon, 1996), p. 92.

**CUI XIUWEN**

1. I learned the sad news of Cui Xiuwen's death at the age of fifty-one while drafting this short essay. I dedicate my writing to the artist, whom I met and interviewed in China. For more about Cui's work, see my book, *Gendered Bodies: Toward a Women's Visual Art in Contemporary China* (Honolulu: University of Hawaii Press, 2015).
2. China's one-child policy was in effect from 1979 to 2016.
3. Andreia Alves de Oliveira, "Post-Photography, or Are We Past Photography?," presented at the *Post-Screen 2016* conference, University of Lisbon, at https://slideblast.com/post-photography-or -are-we-past-photography_5ab3986b1723ddf7e1e3bf90.html, p. 70.
4. Among her most important works, *Ladies Room* (2000), a video about sex workers at a nightclub in Beijing, uses a hidden camera to reveal a world behind public screens. For a detailed discussion, see my book, *Gendered Bodies*.

**ALFREDO JAAR**

1. Patricia C. Phillips, "The Aesthetics of Witnessing: A Conversation with Alfredo Jaar," *Art Journal* 64 (Fall 2005), p. 11.
2. Ibid., p. 7. Jaar has described the inspiration for *Muxima* thusly: "As I listened to these different versions, I realized they were recorded at different times in Angolan history. Listening to them, I could practically visualize the recent history of Angola: colonialism, independence, civil war, land mines, AIDS, and so on. I could hear all of these events in the music—through the same song."
3. Artist note on Canto X, from exhibition material cited in Kathleen MacQueen, "Strategic Tactical Response: Art in an Age of Terror," PhD diss., Stony Brook University, 2010, p. 132.
4. Phillips, "The Aesthetics of Witnessing," p. 7.

**CHRIS OFILI**

1. In 2005, Ofili held a show of his predominantly blue works at Contemporary Fine Arts in Berlin which he titled *The Blue Rider*, and in his retrospective exhibition *Chris Ofili: Night and Day*, held at the New Museum, New York, in 2014, an entire room was devoted to blue paintings. For further discussion of the significance of Ofili's use of dark blue palettes as well as the precedence for symbolic associations of blue in work by other artists, see Glenn Ligon, "Blue Black," and Matthew Ryder, "Blue Devils," in *Chris Ofili: Night and Day*, ed. Massimiliano Gioni (New York: Skira Rizzoli, 2014), pp. 79–95 and 133–39; see also Glenn Ligon, *Blue Black* (St. Louis: Pulitzer Foundation, 2017).

# ACKNOWLEDGMENTS


**Key to Contributors of Interpretive Captions**

Miles Brautigam, class of 2019 (MB)

Sean P. Burrus, Andrew W. Mellon Postdoctoral Curatorial Fellow (SPB)

Noah J. Dubay, class of 2019 (ND)

Anne Collins Goodyear, Co-Director (ACG)

Frank H. Goodyear III, Co-Director (FHG)

Joachim Homann, Curator (JHo)

Eliza Nitzan, class of 2018 (EN)

Amber M. Orosco, class of 2019 (AO)

Honor Wilkinson, Curatorial Assistant and Manager of Student Programs (HW)

Benjamin Chiawei Wu, class of 2018 (BW)


**Bowdoin College**

Clayton S. Rose, President of the College

Scott A. Meiklejohn, Senior Vice President for Development and Alumni Affairs

Matthew P. Orlando, Senior Vice President and Head of Finance and Administration & Treasurer

Michael Reed, Senior Vice President for Inclusion and Diversity

Elizabeth F. McCormack, Dean for Academic Affairs

Stephen J. Perkinson, Peter M. Small Associate Professor of Art History, Associate Dean for Academic Affairs and Member of BCMA Advisory Council

Jackie Brown, Marvin H. Green, Jr. Assistant Professor of Art and Member of BCMA Advisory Council

Michael J. Kolster, Professor of Art and Member of BCMA Advisory Council

Jill S. Smith, Osterweis Associate Professor of German and Member of BCMA Advisory Council

Ann Ostwald, Director of Academic Budget and Operations

Allison Crosscup, Director of Corporate and Foundation Relations

Liz Armstrong, Associate Director of Gift Planning

Susan Harrison, Leadership Gifts Officer, Development and Alumni Relations

Margaret Broaddus, Leadership Gifts Officer, Development and Alumni Relations

**Bowdoin College Museum of Art**

Anne Collins Goodyear, Co-Director

Frank H. Goodyear, Co-Director

Caroline Brown, Assistant to the Directors

Leslie Bird, Associate Director for Museum Finance and Operations

Suzanne K. Bergeron, Assistant Director for Communications

Joachim Homann, Curator

Sean P. Burrus, Andrew W. Mellon Postdoctoral Curatorial Fellow

James A. Higginbotham, Associate Professor of Classics on the Henry Johnson Professorship Fund and Associate Curator for the Ancient Collection

Laura Fecych Sprague, Senior Consulting Curator

Honor Wilkinson, Curatorial Assistant and Manager of Student Programs

Laura Latman, Registrar and Collections Manager

Michelle Henning, Assistant to the Registrar

José L. Ribas, class of 1976, Technician / Preparator

Jo Hluska, Assistant Preparator

Elizabeth C. Nelson, Museum Shop Manager

Aaron Bailey, Museum and Cultural Property Security Supervisor


**Special Thanks**

John Eric Anderson, Harpswell, Maine; Nancy Berliner, Wu Tung Curator of Chinese Art, Museum of Fine Arts, Boston; Thomas Branchick, Director, and his team at Williamstown Art Conservation Center; Dana E. Byrd, Assistant Professor of Art History; Mary DelMonico, publisher; Luc Demers, photographer; Jennifer Edwards, Curator of Visual Resources; David Francis, Senior Interactive Developer, Digital & Social Media, Information Technology; Anne Haas, Art Librarian; Marjorie Hassen, College Librarian; Laura Lindgren, graphic designer; Susan Kaplan, Professor of Anthropology, Director of Peary-MacMillan Arctic Museum; Philomena Mariani, editor; Christopher Monkhouse, former Eloise W. Martin Curator of European Decorative Arts, Art Institute of Chicago; Johanna Moore, Lone Pine Projects, West Gardiner, Maine; Earle G. Shettleworth Jr., Maine State Historian; Kat Stefko, Associate Librarian for Discovery, Digitization, and Special Collections; Mark Wethli, A. LeRoy Greason Professor of Art.

This book was published on the occasion of the exhibition *Art Purposes: Object Lessons for the Liberal Arts* organized by the Bowdoin College Museum of Art, June 29–October 27, 2019

Published in 2019 by Bowdoin College Museum of Art and DelMonico Books•Prestel

Bowdoin College Museum of Art
245 Maine Street
Brunswick, ME 04011

www.bowdoin.edu/art-museum

DelMonico Books, an imprint of Prestel, a member of Verlagsgruppe Random House GmbH

Prestel Verlag
Neumarkter Strasse 28
81673 Munich

Prestel Publishing Ltd.
14-17 Wells Street
London W1T 3PD

Prestel Publishing
900 Broadway, Suite 603
New York, NY 10003

www.prestel.com

Prestel Verlag, Munich • London • New York



Editor: Philomena Mariani
Designer: Laura Lindgren
Production Manager: Anjali Pala, DelMonico Books•Prestel

Printed and bound in China

Library of Congress Cataloging-in-Publication Data
Names: Bowdoin College. Museum of Art, author, organizer, host institution. | Homann, Joachim, editor. | Goodyear, Anne Collins. | Goodyear, Frank H., III, 1967–
Title: Art purposes : object lessons for the liberal arts / edited by Joachim Homann.
Description: Brunswick, ME : Bowdoin College Museum of Art ; Munich ; New York : DelMonico Books•Prestel, 2019. | "This book was published on the occasion of the exhibition Art Purposes: Object Lessons for the Liberal Arts, organized by the Bowdoin College Museum of Art, June 29/October 27, 2019." | Includes bibliographical references and index.
Identifiers: LCCN 2019002111 | ISBN 9783791358178 (hardback)
Subjects: LCSH: Art—Maine—Brunswick—Exhibitions. | Art and society—Exhibitions. | Bowdoin College. Museum of Art—Exhibitions. | BISAC: ART / Collections, Catalogs, Exhibitions / Permanent Collections. | ART / Collections, Catalogs, Exhibitions / Group Shows. | ART / Collections, Catalogs, Exhibitions / General.
Classification: LCC N524 .A52 2019 | DDC 709.741—dc23
LC record available at https://lccn.loc.gov/2019002111

ISBN: 978-3-7913-5817-8

A CIP catalogue record for this book is available from the British Library.